Esoteric Pure Land Buddhism

PURE LAND BUDDHIST STUDIES

Esoteric Pure Land Buddhism

Aaron P. Proffitt

University of Hawai‘i Press / Honolulu

Paperback edition 2024
Printed in the United States of America

First printed, 2023

Library of Congress Cataloging-in-Publication Data

Names: Proffitt, Aaron P., author, translator, annotator. | Dōhan, 1179–1252. Himitsu nenbutsu shō. English.
Title: Esoteric Pure Land Buddhism / Aaron P. Proffitt.
Other titles: Pure Land Buddhist studies.
Description: Honolulu : University of Hawaiʻi Press, 2023. | Series: Pure Land Buddhist studies | Includes bibliographical references and index.
Identifiers: LCCN 2022043559 (print) | LCCN 2022043560 (ebook) | ISBN 9780824893613 (hardback) | ISBN 9780824893804 (pdf) | ISBN 9780824893811 (epub) | ISBN 9780824893828 (kindle edition)
Subjects: LCSH: Dōhan, 1179–1252. | Dōhan, 1179–1252. Himitsu nenbutsu shō. | Pure Land Buddhism—Japan—History. | Tantric Buddhism—Japan—History.
Classification: LCC BQ8512.9.J3 P76 2023 (print) | LCC BQ8512.9.J3 (ebook) | DDC 294.3/926—dc23/eng/20221012
LC record available at https://lccn.loc.gov/2022043559
LC ebook record available at https://lccn.loc.gov/2022043560

ISBN 9780824893712 (paperback)

The Pure Land Buddhist Studies series publishes scholarly works on all aspects of the Pure Land Buddhist tradition. Historically, this includes studies of the origins of the tradition in India, its transmission into a variety of religious cultures, and its continuity into the present. Methodologically, the series is committed to providing a venue for a diversity of approaches, including, but not limited to, anthropological, sociological, historical, textual, biographical, philosophical, and interpretive, as well as translations of primary and secondary works. The series will also seek to reprint important works so that they may continue to be available to the scholarly and lay communities. The series is made possible through the generosity of the Buddhist Churches of America's Fraternal Benefit Association. We wish to express our deep appreciation for its support to the Institute of Buddhist Studies.

University of Hawaiʻi Press books are printed on acid-free paper and meet the guidelines for permanence and durability of the Council on Library Resources.

Cover art: *Red Amida,* 1300s. Japan, Kamakura period (1185–1333). Hanging scroll; ink, color, and gold on silk. The Cleveland Museum of Art. Leonard C. Hanna Jr. Fund 1971.164.

Contents

Series Editor's Preface

How broad is the stream of Pure Land Buddhism? In Aaron P. Proffitt's study of the monk Dōhan (1179–1252), we encounter what Proffitt engagingly identifies as "Esoteric Pure Land Buddhism." Conventionally, many scholars and practitioners have treated Amitābha's Sukhāvatī as *the* Pure Land. Correlatively, the "three Pure Land sutras" have been considered the primary textual sources for the study of the origins of Pure Land Buddhist thought and practice.[1]

A tightly focused examination of the line of development from the cult of Amitābha in India, through its transmission to China, then to Japan, and from there to Europe and the Americas, indicates one style of scholarly undertaking—a style that along with other characteristics has a diachronic orientation. Another style might be characterized as having a synchronic orientation, or one that looks to context as necessary for understanding. Certainly the religious milieu that contextualizes the three Pure Land sutras in India includes more than the various strains of Mahāyāna, but also the roughly contemporaneous incipient tantric strains being integrated into Buddhist practice. Similarly, contextualized study of Pure Land Buddhism in China might well take into account the symbolic similarities between Amitābha's Sukhāvatī and the land of the Daoist Queen Mother of the West. Perhaps more important for the context of ongoing formulations of Pure Land doctrine in China would be the Chan arguments regarding an imminent interpretation of the Pure Land. Contributing to our increasingly complex understanding of Pure Land Buddhism is scholarship on the importance of the Buddha Amitābha in Tibet and the role of pure realms in the thought and practice of esoteric Buddhists there.

Proffitt's formulation of the category of Esoteric Pure Land grows out of his examination of the work of Dōhan, who lived during Japan's

1 Fujita Kōtatsu, "Pure Land Buddhism in India," in James Foard, Michael Solomon, and Richard K. Payne, eds., *The Pure Land Tradition: History and Development* (Berkeley: Center for South and Southeast Asian Studies, University of California, Berkeley, and the Institute of Buddhist Studies, 1996), p. 6.

Kamakura era (1185–1333)—a period during which the forms of Japanese Buddhism that are most prominent today have their origins. Modern scholarship on the era has long focused on the founders and early history of these forms of Buddhism, in many cases employing the kind of diachronic emphasis on a single line of thought and practice. Many important works developed in this way, although maintaining an understanding of Kamakura Buddhism as defined by a limited set of traditions. In the last quarter of the twentieth century, however, critiques of this basic framework were increasingly in evidence. In what might be considered a natural development of scholarly inquiry, three additional areas of study began to work across these established representations. First, key figures besides the founders were studied, calling into question the Romantic image of them as religious geniuses working *sui generis* to unfold their own experiences as new revelations. The second area that contributed to the increasing complexity was the reexamination of the established Buddhist traditions of the time. Creative developments within these traditions were uncovered, ones that challenged the prevailing view of the establishment as corrupt and ossified. And, third, socio-economic analyses revealed the engagement of Buddhist institutions, both established and newly formed, with the era's political system.

Proffitt's study of Dōhan successfully integrates this variety of approaches, giving us a deep and rich understanding of a key figure of Kamakura Buddhism, demonstrating his creativity at a time of complex religious and social change. The goal of birth in a buddha field like Amitābha's Sukhāvatī was not only widely shared, but several religious technologies were brought to bear to attain that goal. In the case of Dōhan and the Shingon tradition, this meant the esoteric practices Kūkai brought to Japan from China four centuries earlier. Dōhan's *Himitsu nenbutsu shō*, the first Western-language translation of which is included here as *Compendium on the Contemplation of Buddha*, is a key work for understanding esoteric versions of Pure Land thought and practice. Proffitt's translation alone makes his book one of the most important contributions to Pure Land Buddhist studies, to studies of Kamakura Buddhism, and to a better understanding of esoteric Buddhism.

More applicable for Buddhist studies generally is how Proffitt's work undermines conceptions of purity, authenticity, and authority, which are set in opposition to conceptions of impure syncretism, necessarily cast as inauthentic and lacking authority. (As shown by Charles Orzech, these conceptions grew out of nineteenth-century ideas about race purity versus miscegenation.) Proffitt points out that such ideas, characterized by some scholars as "overlap" between traditions, reflect an unexamined presumption of separation, which informs not only scholarship on Japanese Buddhism, but many other areas of specialized study.

Preface

"A Monk and His Text"

Sukhāvatī 極樂淨土, the Land of Bliss, is arguably the most sought-after postmortem soteriological goal in Mahayana Buddhism in general and East Asian Buddhism in particular. The Buddha Amida 阿彌陀佛, lord of Sukhāvatī, also known as Amitābha 無量光 (Infinite Light) and Amitāyus 無量壽 (Infinite Life), is perhaps the most common object of devotion in East Asian Buddhist culture. The form of Buddhist practice known as *buddhānusmṛti* 念佛 (buddha mindfulness) is one of the most widespread in the world and indicates the contemplation of and meditation on Amitābha Buddha, as well as the recitation of the holy name of this buddha (J. *Namo Amida Butsu* 南無阿彌陀佛; Skt. Namo'mitābhāya Buddhāya; Ch. Namo Amituo Fo). Taken together, this soteriological goal, object of reverence, and form of practice are often said to constitute something called Pure Land Buddhism 淨土教, one of the most widely practiced forms of Buddhism. Though early scholars of Buddhism outside of East Asia have long ignored and dismissed this important dimension of Buddhist culture, due in part to greater cross-cultural dialogue, more scholars are exploring the depth and diversity of Mahayana Buddhist Pure Land thought and practice.

The largest school of Japanese Buddhism and possibly the largest (and nearly the oldest) form of Buddhism in the Americas is Jōdo Shinshū 淨土真宗, founded by the monk Shinran 親鸞 (1173–1263). Due to its popularity and international reach, Shin Buddhism has played a significant role in shaping how we study Japanese and East Asian Buddhism in general and Pure Land Buddhism in particular.

My own interests in Pure Land Buddhism began while living in Japan and working as an English teacher after I graduated from college in 2005. Virtually all of my students, friends, neighbors, and colleagues were affiliated with Jōdo Shinshū temples, and once they learned that I was interested in Buddhism, they regularly took me with them to visit their temples and chat with their priests. I would often travel around the countryside on my bicycle, visiting temples and pestering patient priests with questions in my poor Japanese.

I first became interested in Buddhism as a teenager; in college I studied Japanese and majored in religious studies with an emphasis on Buddhism. Yet I somehow completely missed the Jōdo Shinshū tradition in my studies. When I encountered Shin Buddhism as a living tradition, I became interested in why Anglophone scholars seem to have had such antipathy toward Pure Land Buddhism. Galen Amstutz's *Interpreting Amida: History and Orientalism in the Study of Pure Land Buddhism* sparked my interest in pursuing Pure Land Buddhist studies, and I began learning more about the role that Orientalism and colonialism had played in the establishment of Buddhist studies as a field. At the same time, I began to see that Pure Land Buddhism functioned in a complex environment, drawing upon and influencing the great philosophical and ritual traditions found throughout the Mahayana world. I understood that it is in this context that the study of the diversity of Pure Land Buddhism, including Shin Buddhism, is best conducted.

As my Japanese-language skills improved, I began to investigate the origins of Shin Buddhism in the twelfth- and thirteenth-century early medieval Japanese environment. Time and again I searched for books that would help fill in the context in which Shinran's thought had developed, only to find the author circling back around to Shinran, the person. In 2012, while attending a talk at Ryūkoku University, in which the Nishi Honganji 西本願寺 Shin Buddhist seminary is housed, I heard one scholar explain that he had recently spoken with some young seminarians about their interest in Shin Buddhist studies. When these students proudly declared that they had already read everything Shinran had written, he asked if they had read the *Lotus Sutra,* one of the most important texts in all of East Asian Mahayana Buddhism and especially important in the Tendai school 天台宗 of Japanese Buddhism, the lineage in which Shinran trained as a young man. They admitted that they had not read this seminal text. Chiding them, he replied that if you want to understand Shinran, you need to read what Shinran wrote, yes—but you must also read what Shinran *read.*

This scholar had encapsulated exactly what I found frustrating about the founder-centric historiography I encountered in some of the scholarship on Japanese Buddhism. In other words, I wanted to understand the broader systems at play in the early medieval Japanese environment within which the Japanese Pure Land lineages had developed, but I found an interesting lacuna in both the Japanese and Anglophone scholarship. Japanese scholars had studied every aspect of Shinran's thought, and Japanese and Western scholars had broadly studied the early medieval

Japanese religious institutions. Yet it seemed to me then that few had examined contemporaneous early medieval Pure Land culture, or what I refer to as "Esoteric Pure Land Buddhism."

In early medieval Japan, what scholars have come to refer to as Esoteric Buddhism 密教 dominated Japanese ritual culture. Esoteric Buddhism in East Asia is often defined in relation to the practices and teachings found in the tantras. The tantras are a loosely defined genre of Indian ritual texts that promise rapid attainment of Buddhahood through practices such as the orchestrated recitation of mantra 真言, the performance of coded hand-and-finger configurations known as mudra 印, and the conceptualization and visualization of mandalas 曼陀羅 and geometrically arranged depictions of deities and Sanskrit seed syllables, or *bīja* 種子. Even as East Asian Esoteric Buddhist studies as an area of academic inquiry has grown dramatically year by year since I first conceived of this project (around 2009), very few scholars in Japan or the United States have considered the role that this dominant ritual culture (Esoteric Buddhism) might have played in the pursuit of the dominant soteriological goal (rebirth in Sukhāvatī) in early medieval Japan.

Around this time I discovered the work of a contemporary of Shinran, Dōhan 道範 (1179–1252), an Esoteric Pure Land Buddhist thinker and ritual master. Taking Dōhan's *Himitsu nenbutsu shō* 秘密念佛抄 (Compendium on the Secret Contemplation of Buddha) as a starting point, I then widened the focus to sketch the contours of Pure Land Buddhism and Esoteric Buddhism as areas of study. In the process I discovered so many areas of "overlap" that I ultimately came to question whether it was productive to think of these areas of Mahayana concern as distinct at all. At the same time, I also noticed a pervasive ambivalence toward Pure Land Buddhism within scholarship on Esoteric Buddhism, and vice versa. The assumption in popular and much academic writing is that Esoteric Buddhism is fundamentally monistic and "this-worldly," while Pure Land Buddhism is supposedly dualistic and "otherworldly." Yet numerous ritual manuals, records of ritual performances, doctrinal treatises, and commentaries written throughout the history of the East Asian Mahayana Buddhist tradition tell a very different story.

In fact, modern European and American Buddhist studies scholarship has generally exhibited ambivalence toward so-called devotionalism and ritualism, and these terms have served at times as derogatory descriptors for Buddhist traditions and practices deemed inauthentic. Scholarship influenced by Japanese sectarianism also tends to emphasize a taxonomic/phylogenic approach to Buddhism, portraying distinct kinds of Buddhism comprising unique teachings, practices, founders, and so on. Because devotionalism and ritualism both serve as sites for fluid engagement across traditions, they are often either left out completely as a topic worthy of study or explained away, by both camps. Taking up the study of Esoteric Pure Land Buddhism thus reveals new ways to conceive of the role that devotionalism and ritual play in Mahayana Buddhism in general.

The *Himitsu nenbutsu shō* (a fully annotated translation appears in the appendix to this book) may at first glance appear to be a brief and relatively minor text, by a seemingly obscure scholar-monk, and yet, upon closer investigation, this text and its author provide an important vantage point from which to view medieval Japanese Buddhism. Moreover, in placing this text and its author in regional, historical, and religious contexts, this book on Dōhan and Esoteric Pure Land Buddhism serves to illuminate important and previously unnoticed aspects of East Asian Buddhism. Research for this book was made possible thanks to generous funding from the Fulbright Foundation that allowed me to study in Japan at Ōtani University, Kōyasan University, and Ryūkoku University.

Across East Asia in the twelfth and thirteenth centuries, major sociocultural changes and upheaval occurred. As centralized governments experienced periods of instability, local cultures flourished, and new trade routes and channels of exchange and communication developed. Paying attention to the economy of texts—who was reading whom—further clarifies the interconnected environment beyond the sectarian and nation-state frameworks currently employed in the field. Scholars of Pure Land Buddhism and Esoteric Buddhism may find Dōhan's approach at times either alien or familiar. In confronting these scholarly reactions, the aim of this book is to open a new area of inquiry within the broader academic conversation on premodern East Asian religion.

The fact that the contemporary academic study of East Asian Buddhism remains closely tied to particular sectarian institutional interests is not necessarily a bad thing. Through affiliation with orthodox schools of Buddhism, students and researchers are often granted access to scholars who freely share invaluable insights into the historical, doctrinal, and methodological tricks of the trade, often in the course of a late-night *nomikai* 飲み会 (postconference dinner and drinks). Through working closely with scholars affiliated with particular Buddhist schools, we may be initiated into the secret teachings of the field. The more time we spend in such environments, the more the obvious truth of the depth of our interconnection with and dependence upon others emerges. Still, "orthodoxy" can be a tricky thing, whether it is "religious" or "academic" or somewhere in between. Orthodox approaches to an object of study may prevent the researcher from seeing important developments or interconnections; some topics come into sharper focus, while the rest of the scene remains blurry in comparison. Inconsistencies and contradictions may be straightened out, ruptures and wrinkles smoothed out, as coherence is imposed upon a messy, tangled web of causes and conditions. Yet as these coherent narratives form in the field, much gets left on the cutting-room floor.

Dōhan and the *Himitsu nenbutsu shō* are just one of many areas of inquiry potentially lost to this kind of academic tunnel vision. Many more exciting texts and historical figures are certainly hiding in plain sight, just outside the received view. Dōhan did not found a new religion, and later generations of his disciples did not deify him. His views, though normative for his time, do not neatly fit into the orthodoxies of the dominant Esoteric or Pure Land traditions today. Yet this is precisely why the study of Dōhan, and those like him, has so much value for the field.

In writing this book, I feel as if I am walking a tightrope. The general format, "a monk and his text," is well established, even conservative and normative, in Buddhist studies, and to a degree I have followed this model.

Usually, such studies draw clear lines connecting the Buddha to a founder and the teachings within to a text. In an effort to engage this popular format more critically and perhaps subvert it to some extent, I have considered the ways in which Pure Land Buddhism and Esoteric Buddhism have been constructed as objects of inquiry within Buddhist studies, pointing to problems inherent in both Western and Japanese scholarship. In the end I hope that with this work I make a case for a new approach to this genre and these topics. I would like to thank my generous teachers, advisors, mentors, colleagues, friends, and the staff at the institutions that have supported my work leading up to this project. In particular I would like to thank Terry and Faye Kleeman, George Keyworth, Rodney Taylor, Kyoko Saegusa, Holly Gayley, Mark Toole, Keller Kimbrough, Micah Auerback, Don Lopez, Ben Brose, Juhn Ahn, Kevin Carr, Tomoko Masuzawa, Hitomi Tonomura, Ken Ito, Yoshihiro Mochizuki, Esperanza Ramirez-Christensen, Orion Klautau, Kameyama Takahiko, Satō Mona, Nasu Eisho, Robert Rhodes, Michael Conway, Inoue Takami, Kazune Uchimoto, Azuma Shingyo, Thomas Dreitlein, Nakamura Honnen, Paul Swanson, Matthew McMullen, Ryuichi Abé, Richard Payne, Scott Mitchell, Natalie Quli, David Matsumoto, Harry Bridge, Galen

Amstutz, James Dobbins, Brian Ruppert, Paul Groner, Dominick Scarangello, Jacqueline Stone, Levi McLaughlin, Steve Covell, Bryan Lowe, Mark Rowe, Xiao Yue, Eric Swanson, Elizabeth Tinsley, Anna Andreeva, Matt and Pam Mitchell, Dylan Luers Toda, Natasha Mikles, Daniel Friedrich, Jason Protass, Caleb Carter, Paula Curtis, Ori Porath, Jessica Main, Mikael Bauer, Chris Callahan, Melissa Curley, Jessica Starling, the Inter-University Center for Japanese Studies, and the Fulbright Foundation. I dedicate this book to my wife, Claire, and my children, Maya and Julian, who sustain me along this academic path.

Abbreviations

BKD	*Bussho kaisetsu daijiten* 佛書解說大辭典. Ono Gemmyō 小野玄妙, ed. Tokyo: Daitō shuppansha, 1999.
DDB	*Digital Dictionary of Buddhism*. Charles A. Muller, ed. http://buddhism-dict.net/ddb. December 31, 2014, ed.
DNBZ	*Dai Nihon Bukkyō zensho* 大日本佛教全書, 100 vols. Suzuki Gakujutsu Zaidan 鈴木學術財團, ed. Tokyo: Kōdansha, 1970–1973.
DNK	*Dai Nihon komonjo* 大日本古文書. Tōkyō Daigaku Shiryō Hensanjo 東京大學史料編纂所, ed. Tokyo: Tōkyō Teikoku Daigaku, 1901.
EBTEA	*Esoteric Buddhism and the Tantras in East Asia*. Charles D. Orzech, Henrik H. Sørensen, and Richard K. Payne, eds. Leiden: Brill, 2011.
GR	*Gunsho ruijū* 群書類従, 19 vols. Hanawa Hokiichi 塙保己一, ed. Tokyo: Keizai zasshisha, 1898–1902.
KD	*Kokushi daijiten* 國史大辭典, 17 vols. Kokushi Daijiten Henshū Iinkai 国史大辞典編集委員会, ed. Tokyo: Yoshikawa kōbunkan, 1986.
KDCZ	*Kōbō Daishi chosaku zenshū* 弘法大師著作全集, 3 vols. Katsuma Shunkyō 勝又俊教, ed. Tokyo: Sankibō busshorin, 1997.
KDS	*Kōgyō Daishi senjutsushū* 興教大師撰述集, 2 vols. Miyasaka Yūshō, ed. Tokyo: Sankibo busshorin, 1977.
KDZ	*Kōbō Daishi zenshū* 弘法大師全集, 6 vols. Hase Hōshū 長谷寶秀, ed. Ōsaka: Mikkyō bunka kenkyūjo, 1909–1911 (Repr. 1966).
KS	*Shinkō Kōya shunju hennen shūroku* 新校高野春秋編年輯録. Hinonishi Shinjō 日野西眞定, ed. Tokyo: Micho shuppan, 1982 (rev. 2nd ed., 1998).
KT	Kokushi Taikei 國史大系, 60 vols. Kuroita Katsumi 黑板勝美, ed. Tokyo: Yoshikawa kōbunkan, 1929–1967.
MBDJ	*Mochizuki Bukkyō daijiten* 望月佛教大辭典, 10 vols. Mochizuki Shinkō et al., eds. Tokyo: Sekai seiten kankō kyōkai, 1974.
MD	*Mikkyō daijiten* 密教大辭典 (rev. ed. 縮刷版, 改訂增補). Mikkyō Jiten Hensankai 密教辞典編纂会, ed. Kyoto: Hōzōkan, 1983.

NDZ	*Nihon daizōkyō* 日本大蔵経, 51 vols. Matsumoto Bunzaburō 松本文三郎, Nakano Tetsue 中野達慧, eds. Tokyo: Nihon daizōkyō hensankai, 1914–1921.
	Nihon daizōkyō, 100 vols. Suzuki Gakujutsu Zaidan 鈴木学術財団, ed. Tokyo: Suzuki Gakujutsu zaidan, 1973–1978.
NKBD	(Nakamura) *Kōsetsu Bukkyō daijiten* 中村広説佛教語大辞典. Nakamura Hajime 中村元, ed. Tokyo: Tokyō shoseki, 2001 (rev. ed. 2010).
NKBT	*Nihon koten bungaku taikei* 日本古典文學大系, 102 vols. Iwanami Shoten, ed. Tokyo: Iwanami shoten, 1968–1978.
SAZ	*Shingonshū anjin zensho* 眞言宗安心全書, 2 vols. Hase Hōshū 長谷寶秀, ed. Kyoto: Rokudai shinpōsha, 1913–1914.
SEJ	Satō Tetsuei 佐藤哲英. *Eizan jōdokyō no kenkyū* 叡山浄土教の研究, 2 vols. Kyoto: Hyakkaen, 1989.
SZ	*Shingonshū zensho* 眞言宗全書, 44 vols. Kōyasan Daigaku Mikkyō Bunka Kenkyūjo 高野山大学密教文化研究所, ed. Wakayama: Kōyasan Daigaku, 1977.
T.	*Taishō shinshū daizōkyō* 大正新修大藏經, 100 vols. Takakusu Junjirō 高楠順次郎 et al., eds. Tokyo: Taishō issaikyō kankōkai, 1924–1935.
TKDZ	*Teihon Kōbō Daishi zenshū* 定本弘法大師全集, 10 vols. Mikkyō Bunka Kenkyūjo, ed. Wakayama-ken Kōyasan: Mikkyō bunka kenkyūjo, 1991–1997.
ZJZ	*Zoku Jōdoshū zenshō* 續淨土宗全書, 15 vols. Tokyo: Shusho hozonkai, 1974.
ZSZ	*Zoku Shingonshū zensho* 續眞言宗全書, 42 vols. Zoku Shingonshū Zensho Kankōkai 續眞言宗全書刊行會, Nakagawa Zenkyō 中川善教, eds. Wakayama: Zoku shingonshū zensho kankōkai, 1975–1988.

Esoteric Pure Land Buddhism

Chapter 1

An Introduction to Esoteric Pure Land Buddhism

Since Buddhist studies first emerged as a modern academic discipline, scholars have often noted (sometimes in exasperation) the vast diversity of the Buddhist tradition. Among the corpora of Buddhist literature, scripture, ritual manuals, manga, pamphlets, and so on, it is sometimes challenging to account for how this diversity coheres if we are to speak of "Buddhism" at all. Many scholars propose definitions for what Buddhism is, or is not, and seek to account for this heterogeneity by employing organizational heuristics with varying degrees of abstraction, such as nation-states (Indian Buddhism, Chinese Buddhism, Japanese Buddhism), schools or sects (Zen Buddhism, Tiantai Buddhism, Pure Land Buddhism), regions (Indo-Tibetan Buddhism, East Asian Buddhism, Southeast Asian Buddhism), or objects of devotion (lineage patriarchs, sect founders, buddhas, bodhisattvas), and more.[1]

Recently, some scholars have suggested that rather than a singular Buddhism, we are rather studying "Buddhisms," while other scholars have rejected the act of definition altogether in favor of a more subtle approach that seeks to allow the diversity of the Buddhist world to stand without subsuming that diversity within a single organizing rubric. After all, the word "Buddhism" is a nonnative term, a modern construct like the word "religion," which J. Z. Smith notes was "created by scholars for their intellectual purposes. . . . It is a second-order, generic concept that plays the same role in establishing a disciplinary horizon that a concept such as 'language' plays in linguistics or 'culture' plays in anthropology."[2] In coming to terms with Buddhism, we are not only simply trying to understand something out there in the world; we are simultaneously engaging with the history of a field of academic inquiry that has not only mediated our access to this thing we call Buddhism but has also, in some sense, created it. In other words, the object of our inquiry is built not only on the constructs we employ in our study but also on the scholars' works upon which we draw. As Richard Payne notes:

> The "objects" of our study are not natural entities, not things that can be pointed to, but rather social entities, constructions. This means that we cannot use ostensive definitions that simply point out an exemplary instance of a category. We need rather to recognize that the terms and categories employed are in large part our own creation, and avoid reifying them by turning them into objects existing independently of our use. As such, we are responsible for the terms we use and for using them with adequate reflection on the presuppositions they bring—often covertly—into the field.[3]

The way we view the past is conditioned by the present, and our theological or methodological biases, agendas, and blind spots influence our understanding of Buddhism and its historical development. Indeed, as Christian Wedemeyer notes, long before students in Buddhist studies have acquired the linguistic skills necessary to actually read primary materials with any degree of fluency, they have likely already spent years being socialized into particular ways of thinking about Buddhism.[4] This is true for those we might label Buddhist academics and theologians alike, as well as those who fall somewhere in between. It is therefore essential to read both primary and secondary materials critically and against the grain in order to discover modes of thinking about Buddhism that either "the tradition" or "the academy" has ignored or misunderstood.

In this book I examine one such blind spot within Buddhist studies and identify a new area of academic inquiry: "Esoteric Pure Land Buddhism" 密教淨土教.[5] This term is defined as approaches to rebirth in a "pure land" through the use of various "esoteric" ritual techniques and doctrinal interpretations derived from the tantras.

The English term "pure land" derives from a literal reading of the Chinese *jingtu* 淨土, one of many translations of the Sanskrit term *buddha-kṣetra* 佛國土 (buddha sphere). A *buddha-kṣetra* is a paradisiacal realm or a world-sphere beyond our own, presided over by a living buddha. Texts and teachings associated with *buddha-kṣetra,* and a kind of Buddhist multiverse cosmology, came to be associated with Mahayana Buddhist canonical literature. Following this path may take many incalculable eons, and according to Mahayana literature, it may course through this world or in the infinite *buddha-kṣetra* in the ten directions of the multiverse. The Mahayana path promotes rebirth in a *buddha-kṣetra* as the means to gain access to more advanced teachings along the bodhisattva path, and it also serves as a fundamental soteriological theory.

According to the grand mythic narrative found in the *Sukhāvatī-vyūha-sūtra* 無量壽經 (T. 360–363), to the west of our world lies a perfect *buddha-kṣetra* called Sukhāvatī 極樂淨土, the Pure Land of Bliss. Sukhāvatī is the most popular *buddha-kṣetra* in Mahayana literature; indeed, in some contexts it is virtually synonymous with Mahayana conceptions of a favorable future rebirth or afterlife, or even nirvana itself, the ultimate goal of Buddhism. The lord of Sukhāvatī is a buddha referred to as either Amitābha, "Infinite Light" 無量光, or Amitāyus, "Infinite Life" 無量壽. This Buddha of Infinite Light and Life is commonly referred to as Amitābha Buddha in English and Amituo Fo and Amida Butsu 阿彌陀佛 in Chinese and Japanese, respectively. The single most effective practice for achieving rebirth in Sukhāvatī is known as *buddhānusmṛti* 念佛, which may refer to the contemplation of the Buddha's attributes as well as to the vocal recitation of the formula "I take refuge in the Buddha of Infinite Light and Life" (Ch. *Namo Amituo Fo* 南無阿彌陀佛, J. *Namo Amida Butsu*). The soteriological path to rebirth in Sukhāvatī through devotion to Amitābha Buddha and the recitation of the holy name of this buddha is often referred to as Pure Land Buddhism 淨土教. The study of Pure Land Buddhism within Buddhist studies scholarship has largely been defined by two Japanese Pure Land schools, the Jōdo-shū 淨土宗 tradition established by Hōnen 法然 (1133–1212) and the Jōdo Shinshū 淨土真宗 tradition established by Shinran 親鸞 (1173–1262).

Esoteric Buddhism, on the other hand, has often been understood as an East Asian descendant of Tantric Buddhism. The study of Esoteric Buddhism has often been defined by reference to the teachings of Kūkai 空海 (774–835), regarded as the founder of the Japanese Shingon school 真言宗. In particular, Esoteric Buddhism is often defined as an approach to the attainment of Buddhahood "in this very body" 即身成佛—that is, in one's present lifetime. This goal is achieved suddenly through the orchestrated practice of the three mysteries 三密: the performance of mudra 印, the chanting of mantra 真言 (from which Shingon takes its name), and the contemplation and visualization of mandala 曼荼羅 or other visualization exercises. Through the practice of the three mysteries, practitioners realize their inherent union in body, speech, and mind with Mahāvairocana Tathāgata 大日如來, an anthropomorphic symbol for the dharmakāya 法身 (ultimate reality). Though this has often been presented as the fundamental doctrinal and ritual innovation of Esoteric Buddhism, here I examine the sectarian agendas and disciplinary tunnel vision, rooted in the colonial era, that have inspired this narrow view and propose other ways of thinking about and defining Esoteric Buddhism.[6]

These esoteric techniques are often employed not only to attain rebirth in Sukhāvatī and other *buddha-kṣetra;* in some instances rebirth in Sukhāvatī is recognized as a path to acquire even more rarefied and sublime esoteric practices. However, in order to understand this abstract heuristic construct, Esoteric Pure Land Buddhism, we must first reconsider how Pure Land Buddhism and Esoteric Buddhism have come to be defined as mutually exclusive areas of inquiry within Buddhist studies—and as diametrically opposed approaches to liberation. The various traditions, texts, and historical and "mythistorical" figures commonly subsumed under these two heuristic constructs of Pure Land Buddhism and Esoteric Buddhism in actuality functioned in much more complex, interconnected, and contested environments. I do not contend that there was no such thing as Pure Land Buddhism or Esoteric Buddhism in premodern East Asia; rather, I argue that throughout much of East Asian Buddhist history, and within the early Japanese Buddhist environment, neither Pure Land Buddhism nor Esoteric Buddhism necessarily operated as distinct schools or sects but functioned as heterogeneous and mutually informative spheres of inquiry and specialization and at times as polemical discursive positions employed by Buddhists in specific contexts.

This book ultimately focuses on the Esoteric Pure Land thought of Dōhan 道範 (1179–1252) and includes the first fully annotated translation of the *Himitsu nenbutsu shō* 秘密念佛鈔 (Compendium on the Secret Contemplation of Buddha) into a modern language.[7] Dōhan was a prolific and influential scholar-monk who resided on Kōyasan 高野山, the mountain monastic complex surrounding the tomb of Kūkai. During Dōhan's lifetime, and for perhaps a century and a half before, Kūkai came to be known as a bodhisattva-like savior figure. Kōyasan was seen as a *buddha-kṣetra* in this world, a place of pilgrimage for aristocrats, emperors, samurai, and renunciants in search of salvation from the world of death and rebirth. Dōhan took this image of Kūkai as savior and of Kōyasan as a *buddha-kṣetra* as his devotional and scholastic center of gravity. He primarily focused on the interpretation of scriptures and ritual manuals now associated with the East Asian Esoteric and Japanese Shingon Buddhist traditions but also regularly drew upon the whole range of East

Asian Buddhist scholarship. Furthermore, Dōhan's scholarly output was significant and influenced several areas of later Shingon Buddhist thought, and dozens of his works are still extant.

In Dōhan's time there was nothing really novel about Esoteric Pure Land Buddhism. It is only due to modern Japanese Buddhist sectarianism (which tends to overemphasize the distinctions between traditions), along with the influence of modernist Buddhist studies scholarship (which tends to de-emphasize soteriology, devotionalism, and ritual), that this kind of "simultaneous study" 兼学 appears strange to us now. Dōhan and thinkers like him have been generally neglected in the study of medieval Japanese religion in favor of institutional histories or studies into the lives and thoughts of the well-known founders of the schools that dominate Japanese Buddhism today. Precisely because Dōhan's Esoteric Pure Land writing does not easily fit into the frameworks currently employed by scholars of Esoteric Buddhism or Pure Land Buddhism, the study of such a figure may provide an alternative framework for thinking about both.

Next I consider how Mahayana Buddhism, Pure Land Buddhism, and Esoteric Buddhism have been imagined as fields of inquiry within Buddhist studies more broadly and how the heuristic Esoteric Pure Land helps open up new ways of understanding each. A brief overview of the chapters that compose the book follows.

Rethinking the Study of Mahayana Buddhism

By the first century CE, some five hundred years after the death of Śākyamuni Buddha 釋迦牟尼佛, a diverse range of texts and traditions began to flow into East Asia. As Buddhists in East Asia worked to account for the diversity of the Buddhisms they were encountering, a variety of specialties and areas of study proliferated, each focusing on a particular set of texts and practices. This seems to have given rise to a catholic engagement with Buddhist diversity, and East Asian Buddhist culture developed into a competitive yet interconnected environment, as lineages associated with major temple complexes endeavored to procure patronage and influence through the mastery of multiple areas of study. For example, a member of the Chan lineage 禪宗 in China (or its offshoots, Korean Seon or Japanese Zen) was not restricted to the practice of a particular form of meditation. Rather, in addition to participating in the mythic lineage of the "Buddha Mind school" 佛心宗 (Chan/Seon/Zen), a practitioner was empowered to help beings attain rebirth in

Sukhāvatī, master mystical incantations called dhāraṇī, receive initiation into an Esoteric Buddhist ritual lineage, or focus on the study of the *Lotus Sutra* 妙法蓮華経 (T. 262, 263) in accordance with the doctrinal and meditative systems associated with the Tiantai lineage 天台宗 or on the *Avataṃsaka-sūtra* 華嚴経 (T. 278, 279, 293) in accordance with the Huayan lineage's 華嚴宗 system of exegesis.

Before the early seventeenth century, Japanese Buddhism was, for the most part, in step with this diverse, cosmopolitan, and fluid pan–East Asian Mahayana Buddhist culture. Japanese monks often specialized in multiple disciplines or areas of study simultaneously. However, with the establishment of the Tokugawa 徳川 regime (1600–1868), an important paradigm shift occurred in Japan. Still fresh in people's minds were the disruption and upheaval of the Warring States period 戦国時代 (1467–1603), when temples had often functioned as armed fortresses. In the interest of peace, the government instituted a general prohibition against inter- and intra-sectarian rivalry and competition. By government decree, officially recognized sectarian institutions were created, and all Japanese Buddhist temples were required to affiliate with a specific head temple. These head temples were tasked with the establishment of set sectarian orthodoxies, identities, lineages, and so on, effectively bringing an end to the dynamic and fluid (and at times violent and contentious) competition between rival factions, lineages, and sublineages within and between different institutions. The education of monks came to focus on the teachings of sect founders and the official representatives of these newly established orthodox positions. Ritual training was aimed at preserving and passing down the specific lineages associated with newly created sectarian institutions. The emergence of sectarian studies, and the exclusive study of a single body of doctrinal literature that resulted, led to the early modern compartmentalization of Japanese Buddhist cultural knowledge.[8]

Our tendency to study Buddhism as if it were composed of discrete "schools" or "kinds" or "species" emerged from complex machinations rooted in the blending of Japanese and Western academic environments. In the late nineteenth and early twentieth centuries, when Western-style universities were first established in Japan, traditional Buddhist seminaries were recast as modern universities that combined Tokugawa-era sectarian institutional models with the European university model. Meanwhile, for some time European scholars, missionaries, and colonial administrators had slowly begun to identify the diverse forms of "idolatry" in Siam, China, and Japan as modern-day descendants, or species, of an ancient Indian religion soon to be named Buddhism.[9]

The foundation of the discipline we know today as Buddhist studies was in some sense established by the French philologist and Orientalist Eugène Burnouf (1801–1852). Donald Lopez notes that Burnouf's foray into the textual world of Buddhism began in 1827, when Brian Hodgson (1800–1894) sent a cache of Sanskrit manuscripts to Europe. Burnouf's research into these texts, published in 1844 under the title *Introduction à l'histoire du Buddhisme indien,* was the first Western-language monograph on the history of Indian Buddhism.[10] According to Lopez, "we must acknowledge with the utmost respect the remarkable achievements of Eugène Burnouf. However, that feeling of respect carries with it a certain sense of disquiet, that something has gone wrong. . . . We might then regard 1844 as the year when everything changed, dividing time, as the Christians do, into two periods, before and after a fateful year. In this case, the period after the epoch-making date is not simply a period of redemption. It is also a period of loss."[11]

Burnouf worked tirelessly to uncover what he believed to be the earliest layers of the Buddha's teachings, attempting to extract from the "mass of words so empty" (i.e., Mahayana sutras and tantras) the simple moral teachings of the human buddha,[12] a figure that in some sense was crafted in Burnouf's own image.[13] The Buddha he discovered in his box of texts appeared to mirror the rational sciences of modern Europe and the philosophy of the Greeks and shared Burnouf's disdain for ritualism and metaphysics. Burnouf made little effort to hide his contempt for the so-called developed sutras and tantras now associated with Mahayana Buddhism, and this way of thinking about Buddhist literature greatly influenced and was adopted by early generations of Buddhist studies scholars, who did not recognize Mahayana Buddhism or Buddhism outside of India as authentic.[14] Burnouf's version of the Buddha, a figure "born from the brow of a European scholar who never set foot in Asia,"[15] was quickly employed by Orientalist scholars as a standard against which contemporary living Buddhist cultures were found lacking.

Following Burnouf, many early scholars of Buddhism regarded the texts we now identify with the Pāli canon, the so-called simple *suttas,* as constituting the original teachings of the Buddha himself, and they saw the "developed" Mahayana texts simply as spurious later additions.[16] However, recent scholarship in Pāli and Theravāda Buddhist studies has significantly undermined this foundational assumption, as scholars of "early" Mahayana have investigated the many areas of overlap between the so-called simple and developed textual lineages. It is possible that the Pāli canon was compiled around the end of the first century BCE.[17] However, the Pāli canon to which we actually have historical access was finally edited in the fifth century CE by Buddhaghoṣa. Furthermore, though indeed the Pāli *suttas* at first glance appear to be simpler than the often extremely ornate and lengthy Mahayana sutras, scholars such as Burnouf and others must have had to read very selectively to extrapolate a rational "human" Buddha from the Pāli canon. Pāli specialists are now critical of the notion that the Pāli canon and Theravāda Buddhism somehow represent a pristine early Buddhism.[18] Because early scholars of Buddhism assumed that the Mahayana was necessarily a later addition, they tended to look at the features of Mahayana literature that differentiate it from the simple *suttas*, such as the bodhisattva path, the *buddha-kṣetra* and "celestial" buddhas, and certain genres of philosophical and ritual literature, and then to seek out explanations for the origins of those elements.[19]

Recent scholarship has, however, significantly complicated this "quest for origins" approach and forces us to reconceive what we might mean by the term "Mahayana Buddhism." For example, Jan Nattier has demonstrated that the bodhisattva path was but one of many early mainstream Buddhist "vocations."[20] Practitioners of the bodhisattva path memorized sutras that promoted the bodhisattva path while simultaneously participating in mainstream Buddhist monastic culture.[21] Bodhisattvas were not members of a different kind of Buddhism; rather, they were practitioners who pursued an approved, though perhaps distinct, vocation within the broader context of mainstream early Buddhism.[22] Gregory Schopen notes that "the history of Mahayana literature and the history of the religious movement that bears the same name are not necessarily the same thing."[23] In other words, we have evidence for sutras that we now label as Mahayana long before Mahayana Buddhism as such emerged as a sociologically distinct tradition.

Archaeological evidence suggests that Mahayana Buddhism did not emerge as a separate and distinct tradition until the sixth century, but there is textual evidence suggesting that some layers of Mahayana literature were in a relatively developed form by the first century BCE.[24] The intellectual currents we now label Mahayana, therefore, evolved gradually over a long period of development,[25] across various traditions and locations,[26] stretching back into the prehistorical Buddhist tradition.

Gregory Schopen has critically examined an inscription found in Govindnagar in Mathura, dating perhaps from the second to third century, that some scholars suggest is the earliest mention of the Buddha Amitābha, a "Mahayana" buddha, in a non-Mahayana context.[27] Luis Gomez has noted a high degree of continuity between the *Suttanipāta*, a non-Mahayana text, and the Mahayana philosophical traditions associated with the Madhyamaka and Prajñāpāramitā 般若波羅蜜, or Perfection of Wisdom traditions. In particular he argues that Madhyamaka and Prajñāpāramitā literature may have represented conservative rejections of what were perceived as innovations in Abhidharma, a philosophical tradition associated with non-Mahayana canonical literature.[28] In other words, how to differentiate Mahayana from non-Mahayana Buddhism in the earliest layers of the Buddhist literature to which we have historical access is not always clear-cut.

The key problem confronted by Burnouf in 1844, and other scholars for the subsequent hundred years, was how to make sense of the radical diversity of Buddhist texts without any knowledge of the historical context of their development. As more of the contextual framework has come to light, the seemingly clear division between Mahayana and non-Mahayana traditions has become blurred, and perhaps even in the early tradition those lines had yet to be clearly defined. According to Paul Mus (1902–1969),

> the currents whence the Mahāyāna derived seem to have influenced from the start the whole of the church: the tradition began by developing entirely in this direction and it is only later, by a reaction against a categorical re-ordering of the new theories, already introduced stealthily, that a Hīnayānists Buddhism detached itself from the common movement, leaving the Mahāyāna to continue and accentuate the latter, and attempting to rejoin the initial orthodoxy; it partially succeeded and to this extent its claims to authenticity are justified; but perhaps it overshot the target, as did the Great Vehicle, in the previous interpretation.[29]

Furthermore, as Jonathan Silk writes:

> Literature commonly cited in discussions of Mahāyāna Buddhism as that of 'Sectarian Buddhism,' and surely not rarely implied to represent some pre-Mahāyāna ideas, in fact dates from a period after the rise of the Mahāyāna Buddhist movement. . . . The materials to which we are comparing our extant Mahāyāna Buddhist literature may well have been written or revised in light of that very Mahāyāna Buddhist material itself, and vice versa ad infinitum.[30]

In other words, ideas, teachings, and practices that we have come to regard as inherently Mahayana in orientation may have already been present within a heterogeneous early Buddhist environment. As Mahayana Buddhists began to differentiate themselves from others, some communities that identified as Mahayana formed, while other communities identified as non-Mahayana. Gradual schisms led different groups to define and redefine their texts and teachings against those they perceived as opponents, or heretics.

In order to excavate a "pure" Buddhism more in line with modernist religious and philosophical points of view, early Orientalist scholars of Buddhism relied on essentialist modes of defining Mahayana Buddhism, divorcing it from its development within mainstream Buddhism. Mahayana soteriologies, as well as the tantric ritual texts so scandalous to Victorian readers, were the first to go. Japanese Buddhist thinkers, reacting to this dominant international academic milieu, set about clarifying the finer points of their particular lineages and formulated new ways to present their traditions on an international stage in order to counter the critique that Mahayana Buddhism in general and East Asian Buddhism in particular were inauthentically Buddhist.

It is not simply a case of Western scholars creating a narrow view of the Buddha; Asian intellectuals responded to, adapted, appropriated, and in turn influenced Western scholarship as well. In 1879, Kasawara Kenjū 笠原研寿 (1852–1893) and Nanjō Bun'yū 南条文雄 (1849–1927), both priests in the Jōdo Shinshū school of Japanese Pure Land Buddhism, arrived in England to study Sanskrit under the famous Orientalist Max Muller (1823–1900). Like many early European Buddhologists, Muller did not regard Mahayana Buddhism or East Asian Buddhism as authentic and condescendingly hoped that by training his Asian students they would in turn help their countrymen to return to the original, true teachings of the Buddha.[31] When Japanese scholars who first studied Sanskrit, Pāli, and Buddhist studies in Europe encountered the idea that Mahayana Buddhism was not the teaching of the Buddha, it became imperative for them to determine how to adapt to the new European Buddhist studies framework.

Some Pure Land Buddhists and Western interpreters alike defined Shin Buddhism as a religion of Pure Faith established by a great founder akin to a figure such as Martin Luther.[32] Esoteric Buddhist thinkers clarified that their reception of the tantras predated the practices so offensive to Burnouf and others.[33] As these apologias emerged in response to the Orientalist criticism of Mahayana Buddhism, they ultimately accommodated and supported the framework established by the Orientalists.

Just as essentialist readings of the origins of the various elements of Mahayana Buddhism may be called into question by recent research, so, too, can we critically examine how these traditions were contorted in the modern period to fit within the parameters of the Orientalist study of Buddhism. Scholars of Mahayana Buddhism and the Pāli Canon have come to evaluate how these heuristic constructs must be reconceived in light of recent research; scholars of Pure Land Buddhism and Esoteric Buddhism must also evaluate how modernist agendas in Europe and Japan led to the creation of overly reified objects of inquiry that are divorced from the complex networks of overlap and interaction within which those objects of inquiry actually functioned.

Rethinking Pure Land Buddhism

While scholars have commonly defined Pure Land Buddhism as a "kind" or "species" of Buddhism peculiar to the East Asian cultural sphere, rebirth in Sukhāvatī is a pervasive aspect of the Mahayana soteriological path to Buddhahood.[34] Because modern Japanese Pure Land scholar-priests made significant connections within the early European Buddhist studies environment, most scholarship and popular writing on Mahayana culture tends to rely on the modern Japanese Pure Land school's own self-presentation as the default perspective on Pure Land Buddhism. This streamlined version of the history of Pure Land Buddhism often simplifies the diverse forms of Mahayana practices and teachings related to *buddha-kṣetra* to fit this particular template, in which the teachings of Hōnen and Shinran often serve as the principle points of reference, or even the natural evolutionary goal (*telos*) of Pure Land thought and practice (if not of the Mahayana Buddhist tradition itself).

In his groundbreaking and highly controversial doctrinal writings, Hōnen argued for the establishment of a Pure Land *shū* 宗. The term *shū*, pronounced *zong* in Chinese, today means something close to the English terms "sect" or "school." However, in premodern East Asia it did not necessarily carry this connotation and often indicated something closer to "area of focus," "disciplinary specialty," or the "essence" of a given teaching or lineage.[35] Hōnen trained in the Tendai tradition (the Japanese descendant of the Chinese Tiantai lineage) on Hieizan 比叡山. Tendai was composed of four *shū:*

1. The Perfect 圓, or perhaps "well rounded," teachings of the Chinese Tiantai lineage. Tiantai constitutes a comprehensive Mahayana system that focuses on the universalistic teachings of the *Lotus Sutra,* on devotion to Amitābha Buddha, on Madhyamaka

philosophy, and on a comprehensive meditative system known as *śamatha-vipaśyanā* 止觀, among other things.
2. Meditation practices in the Chan lineage.
3. Monastic precepts 戒.
4. Esoteric ritual.

Seen in this context, Hōnen received a comprehensive elite education, studying across various disciplines. However, he ultimately argued that the instability of his contemporary social and political context was a result of the world having entered the age of the end of the Dharma 末法, in which traditional practices were no longer effective for attaining salvation. In Japan during Hōnen's lifetime, it appears that some, though not all, Buddhists believed that the end times were upon them. Traditional Buddhist historians believed that after the death of the Buddha the world and humanity's ability to practice the Dharma would decline gradually, in stages. According to Hōnen, the only recourse for salvation from the realm of death and rebirth was to rely upon the Pure Land path to rebirth in Sukhāvatī where progress along the bodhisattva path would be easier to achieve.

Mahayana Buddhists like Hōnen engaged the mythic reality presented in the *Sukhāvatī-vyūha-sūtra* from multiple perspectives. While some Buddhists sought postmortem rebirth in Sukhāvatī though meditative contemplation and visionary experiences, others conceived of Sukhāvatī as abiding in a nondual relationship with this world, with the Buddha Amitābha understood to be a symbol for one's own true nature. Often, these conceptions of the Sukhāvatī mythos functioned concurrently. Based on this Mahayana worldview, Hōnen argued that even the simple practice of the vocal recitation of the name of Amitābha Buddha, *Namo Amida Butsu,* was itself sufficient to achieve rebirth in Sukhāvatī, in part because it was the most universal and practical method for all beings and thus more in line with the all-encompassing nature of the compassionate activity of awakened reality.

Hōnen's approach to Buddhism was perceived as radical for two reasons. First, his teachings emphasized a conception of Buddhist practice as inherently, necessarily simple: just say *Namo Amida Butsu.* His teachings thus gave greater authority to the "common" practice of Buddhism—common in the sense that elites and peasants alike recited the name of Amitābha. Second, by imploring devotees to rely exclusively upon the Buddha's transcendent "other power" 他力, Hōnen and other proponents of the Pure Land path essentially negated the diverse range of mainstream Buddhist practices and undermined the government's role in the salvation (and pacification) of the people. Both the government and the powerful monks of Enryakuji 延暦寺 (the administrative center of Hieizan) eventually fabricated justification for persecuting, and prosecuting, Hōnen and his popular movement.

Shinran, one of Hōnen's disciples, came to be regarded as the founder of an offshoot tradition known as Jōdo Shinshū (often referred to as Shin Buddhism in English). Like Hōnen, Shinran argued that reliance on Amitābha Buddha was the only path to liberation in the decadent age of early medieval Japan. Shinran understood Amitābha Buddha as an expression of the compassionate activity of ultimate reality guiding beings to awakening. Shinran also differed from Hōnen in his views on the precepts. Hōnen maintained the precepts and may have engaged in other forms of meditative practices until his death. Shinran, on the other hand, took a wife and lived as "neither monk nor layman" 非僧非俗, and he purportedly ceased engaging in all other forms of Buddhist practice. The lay priesthood that followed Shinran's example eventually emerged as the dominant tradition in Japan and remains so today.

Because of its lay priesthood, the fact that it remained the largest sect throughout the Tokugawa era, and its key political connections during the Meiji Restoration of 1868, Shin Buddhism was well positioned to succeed during the modern period, while other traditions, such as Tendai and Shingon, were more negatively affected by new Meiji policies that targeted temples. Moreover, as mentioned above, some of the important early Japanese students of European-style Buddhist studies were Shin Buddhist priests. Modernist scholarship influenced Shin Buddhism in particular, and the Shin Buddhist view of Buddhist history was also influential in Japan and beyond. The Shin Buddhist view of the Pure Land and its place in the broader context of Mahayana Buddhism thus came to define how Pure Land Buddhism has been conceived as an area of study.

Early Western scholars were highly dismissive of Pure Land Buddhism in general and Shin Buddhism in particular; they saw it as a deviant, otherworldly East Asian tradition. Indeed, Shin Buddhism is an East Asian Mahayana tradition focused on the transhistorical Amitābha Buddha, not the historical Śākyamuni Buddha, and it does not valorize meditation or secret gnosis. Galen Amstutz has examined the role that Orientalism has played in the dismissal of Shin Buddhism in Western scholarship.[36] Though Shin Buddhism in particular, and Pure Land Buddhism in general, has generally been a less popular area of research outside Japan, Shin Buddhists were some of the first to adapt their approach to Buddhism to the Orientalist framework. As a result, when European American Buddhologists mentioned Pure Land, they would often reference the Shin point of view, seemingly assuming it to be universal. In some cases scholars even uncritically exactly repeated the sectarian historiography of Shin Buddhism as it if were a comprehensive historical account of the development of Pure Land thought and practice.[37]

Shin apologists could only go so far, however, as it was likely impossible to fully break down the Orientalist framework of the late nineteenth to early twentieth centuries. In defending Shin Buddhism as the standard against which to evaluate the place of *buddha-kṣetra* in Mahayana literature, the diverse way that *buddha-kṣetra* may have functioned in Mahayana Buddhism has been somewhat downgraded from a ubiquitous dimension of Mahayana Buddhism to the exclusive property of one sect of Japanese Buddhism.

In this book I lay the groundwork for a perspective on Pure Land Buddhism that is not teleologically oriented toward this particular normative sectarian historiography. In addition to presenting a new cast of Mahayana Pure Land thinkers, I hope that this work may in fact serve the interests of scholars associated with or working on the histories of the dominant Pure Land schools. It may well reveal a relatively unexamined side of the context for the development of Pure Land Buddhism.

Fujita Kōtatsu notes that references to Amitābha Buddha may be found in over one-third of the texts in the Chinese Buddhist canon,[38] and jātaka tales recounting the past lives of Amitābha Buddha are found in many Mahayana sutras.[39] Moreover, aspiration for rebirth in Sukhāvatī may have been a common goal for some early Buddhists.[40] Schopen notes that the goal of rebirth in Sukhāvatī is found throughout Mahayana sutra and tantra literature,[41] and it was likely "fully established" as one of the common tropes in this literature at least by the second century.[42] Schopen argues that evidence drawn from the third-century *Samādhirāja-sūtra* 月燈三昧經 (T. 639–641), the second-century *Aṣṭasāhasrika-prajñāpāramitā-sūtra* 道行般若經 (T. 224), and many other sutras suggests that rebirth in Sukhāvatī had already emerged as a generalized soteriological goal in the environment within which Mahayana sutras were first written down.[43] Moreover, some early versions of the *Sukhāvatī-vyūha-sūtra,* as well as the **Akṣobhyavyūha-sūtra* 阿閦佛經 (T. 313) and the *Ajitasena-vyākaraṇa-nirdeśana-mahāyāna-sūtra,*[44] include arhats among the beings (re)born in Sukhāvatī. This suggests that when it comes to Sukhāvatī devotion, there may be no clear line between Mahayana and non-Mahayana.

Reference to the infinite *buddha-kṣetra* of the ten directions is a major feature of the Mahayana textual world that remains, to some extent, undertheorized. Since the early twentieth century, scholars working on Pure Land Buddhism have observed this, including Teresina Rowell in her 1933 Yale PhD dissertation, published as a series of articles in the *Eastern Buddhist Journal* in 1934, 1935, and 1939.[45] Rowell notes, "In view of the great importance of the concept for an understanding of Mahāyāna literature, it is strange how universally the Buddha-kṣetra has been neglected by writers on the Mahāyāna."[46] She also argues that sustained study of the *buddha-kṣetra* concept across Mahayana and non-Mahayana literature illuminates "far-reaching ethical and philosophical implications."[47] More recently, Georgios Halkias has also noted that "the obscure origins of Buddha fields and their insignificant presence in Śrāvakayāna Buddhism have led a number of scholars and proponents of a European construction of 'pure and original Buddhism' to adapt a condescending or dismissive attitude toward the soteriology of pure lands, which is often disparaged as the wishful thinking of simpletons grasping for a better life in heavenly realms after death."[48]

Furthermore, Rupert Gethin has noted a general disinterest in the study of cosmology more broadly in Buddhist studies scholarship: "The overall paucity of scholarly materials dealing with Buddhist cosmology would seem to reflect a reluctance on the part of modern scholarship to treat this dimension of Buddhist thought as having any serious bearing on those fundamental Buddhist teachings with which we are so familiar: the four noble truths, the eightfold path, no-self, dependent arising, and so on. The effect of this is to divorce the bare doctrinal formulations of Buddhist thought from a traditional mythic context."[49]

Calling for renewed interest in *buddha-kṣetra*, Randy Kloetzli argues that "doctrine" and "cosmology" are inherently intertwined since cosmology may be taken as a concretization of doctrinal concepts.[50]

Origin Theories of *Buddha-kṣetra*

Because *buddha-kṣetra* were, according to the early Orientalists, at odds with the original teachings of the historical Buddha (again, something to which scholars actually have no historical access), scholars have tried to figure out where this teaching came from.[51] Explanations for the origins of the *buddha-kṣetra* concept have generally fallen into two categories: First, some scholars looked to non-Buddhist sources in the traditions of Greece, Persia, Iran, Christianity, or Hindu bhakti thought. Second, because early scholars believed the Pāli canon represented the earliest layers of Buddhist literature, many looked to it for precursors to the *buddha-kṣetra* concept, often seeking cognate concepts to those emphasized in the modern Pure Land schools. However, when we forget about "Burnouf's Buddha" (the Buddha created by and for white European imperialists),[52] acknowledge that both the non-Mahayana and Mahayana literature to which we have access actually emerged from a more complex and dynamic shared environment of myths and symbols, and read these texts against the grain of received knowledge, the need to assign foreign origins to this concept in the early Buddhist environment simply vanishes.

During the Kuṣān dynasty (30–375 CE), northwestern Indian culture had contact with Near Eastern, Greek, and central Asian cultures,[53] so scholars looking beyond India for the genesis of the Sukhāvatī ideal investigated potential ties to Eden or Elysium.[54] Others who focused on central Asian influence looked to the Zoroastrian paradises of Ecbatana and Uttarāpatha.[55] The Buddha Amitābha/Amitāyus was said to be an adaptation of the Zoroastrian god of light, Ahura Mazda, or the god Zrvanakarana, whose name means "Universal Time."[56] Such simplistic theories of influence, however, fail to take into account the generic nature of afterlife imagery, the ubiquity of light deities across cultures, and the fluidity of cultural boundaries across central Asia.

In response to the argument that the *buddha-kṣetra* concept originated outside of India, both Gomez and Halkias assert that there is no need to look beyond India for its roots. Indigenous South Asian religious culture provides just as much, if not more, material, such as light imagery and paradisiacal realms, upon which early Buddhists may have drawn.[57] With this in mind, some scholars have argued that the *buddha-kṣetra* teaching comes from non-Buddhist Indian religious influence. Fujita has examined different arguments that propose origins in "Viṣṇu mythology, Amitaujas ('immeasurable power') of Brahmaloka Heaven and the deity Varuṇa of [the] western quarter,"[58] as well as other imagery associated with utopian and paradisiacal realms and god kings: "(1) the mythology of the universal monarch (cacravartin), especially the description of King Mahāsudarśana's royal city Kuśāvatī, (2) the mythology of the Northern Kurus (Uttarakuru), (3) the mythology of the heavens of various deities, such as Brahmā, Paranirmitavaṣavartin, and others, and (4) the model of the ideals and glorified Buddhist stupa and its environs."[59]

Additionally, influence from various solar deities or other Vedic sources has been noted. For example, the word *aṃṛta* (ambrosia), possibly the root word for the names Amitābha/Amitāyus, was synonymous with the mythic psychotropic substance soma, which is said to enlighten the one who drinks it.[60] In this case *aṃṛta* is soma, which also carries the connotation of light and is thus connected with solar deities.[61]

Furthermore, some have looked to Kṛṣṇa bhakti devotionalism and references to deathbed practices in the *Bhagavad-Gītā,* in which Kṛṣṇa says, "Whoever at the time of death, when he casts aside his body, bears me in mind (*smaran*) and departs, comes to my mode of being: there is no doubt about this."[62] However, it is well known that bhakti-like forms of devotionalism were pan-Indian, not exclusive to Kṛṣṇa worship, so influence is hard to prove here as well.[63] The motif of being born from a lotus blossom, described in the *Sukhāvatī-vyūha-sūtra,* is well attested across South Asian religious traditions: gods such as Brahmā and Lakṣmī are described as emerging from lotuses along with other beings born into the Trāyastriṃśa Heaven 三十三天.[64]

In all of these cases, the different elements of the Sukhāvatī mythos, Amitābha devotion, and literary imagery found in descriptions of *buddha-kṣetra* can be seen not necessarily as influences from outside Buddhism but as signs that simply mark Buddhist authors and thinkers as participants in a broader South Asian cultural environment. According to Fujita, "The most sensible approach is to regard Amida as the necessary consequence of the evolving concept of Buddhahood."[65] The concept of buddhas purifying their spheres of influence or abiding in divine realms appears to be common across a variety of textual traditions, Mahayana and otherwise.[66] Many scholars now recognize, as Halkias notes, that "the cult of Amitābha and his Pure Land can be adequately explained doctrinally as an endemic evolution of Indian Buddhism."[67]

Rowell and others have examined the diversity of the *buddha-kṣetra* concept and its role in diverse early Buddhist literature. Rowell looks to Buddhaghoṣa's *Visuddhimagga,* which lists three definitions for *buddha-khetta* (the Pāli pronunciation of *buddha-kṣetra*):

1. *Jāti-khetta,* "birth field," or the ten thousand *cakravāḷas* (worlds) that shake when a buddha is born;
2. *Āṇā-khetta,* or field of authority, including 100,000 *koṭī;*
3. *Visaya-khetta,* or field of knowledge, which is infinite.[68] Buddhaghoṣa also describes *buddha-khetta* as being pure, impure, and mixed.[69]

Furthermore, the *Kathāvatthu,* a Theravādin text, reveals that some Mahāsaṃghikas believed that "buddhas pervade all directions of the universe."[70] The *Mahāvastu* of the Lokottaravādins also discusses the existence of multiple buddhas and mentions that some world systems do not have buddhas in them,[71] as buddhas are rare indeed.[72] John S. Strong's examination of *Avadāna* literature, collections of past life stories, reveals that preparations made for the arrival of a buddha closely mirror the descriptions found in Mahayana sutras of the array of *buddha-kṣetra* and mandalas (which are technically also a kind of *buddha-kṣetra*).[73]

Dwijendralal Barau's analysis of the *Buddhāpadāna* reveals a non-Mahayana text that contains ways of thinking about *buddha-khetta* quite similar to what we now associate with *buddha-kṣetra.*[74] He notes that there are references to numerous buddhas throughout the ten directions—"as many as are there the numerous jewels, both in the heaven above and on the earth below."[75] This Buddhist multiverse is described in ways reminiscent of a mandala-like palace.[76]

Kenneth Norman's examination of the *Buddhāpadāna* builds upon Barau, who writes, "The Buddha himself tells of the *Buddhakhettas,* ideal lands of beauty where the Buddhas live. A picture is painted of Buddhas questioning each other, and there is mention of disciples questioning the Buddhas and vice versa."[77] Norman notes that some scholars have dismissed this evidence, which seems to point to a more complex relationship between Mahayana and non-Mahayana conceptions of cosmology and Buddhology, as merely Mahayana influence. However, he contends that "many ideas in Buddhism follow from the dynamics of early Buddhist thought, which lead to the existence of one and the same idea in two forms in two different traditions."[78] In other words, buddhas of the present abiding in worlds accessible to us may have been a feature of the early Buddhist environment and is not necessarily a later Mahayana concept.

Wedemeyer suggests that the exclusive focus on Śākyamuni commonly associated with non-Mahayana literature today may have emerged as a reaction against Buddhist traditions that had a more diverse "Buddhology," suggesting that, historically speaking, focusing on one buddha may be a minority position in the broader history of Buddhism.[79]

> All the Buddhist communities of which we know allowed for the existence of a number of buddhas other than Gautama. In fact, in the view of many

> early Buddhist schools (with the notable exception of the Mahaviharavasin branch that came to dominate later Theravāda), buddhas were considered "infinite in both space and time"—a view that became normative for the later Mahayana movements. However, even among contemporary Theravāda communities—who only admit to one buddha of the present—the following verse appears in widely recited liturgies: "The buddhas of the past, and those yet to come, Those (pl.) of the present, too—[to these] I pay homage always!" *All of which suggests that throughout the course of history, by far the majority of Buddhist communities considered themselves to inhabit a world in which there were multiple buddhas not only in the past and future, but also in the present.*[80]

Instead of viewing Pure Land Buddhism as distinct from Mahayana Buddhism, or even Mahayana Buddhism as clearly differentiated from "early" Buddhism, by looking to specific textual and cultural contexts we may productively reconsider how the diversity of the early Buddhist environment gave rise to multiple, potentially overlapping, visions of the Buddhist universe. Reading across genres, scholars have productively critiqued the often very narrow perspective from which Pure Land Buddhism has been approached as merely a kind of Mahayana Buddhism. We discover that concepts related to *buddha-kṣetra* have been fundamental to how Buddhists in many traditions have articulated their understanding of the Buddhist universe, transcending even the purported division between Mahayana and non-Mahayana. These insights help broaden our understanding both of the early prehistorical context for the development of Buddhism and the later Mahayana expressions of Sukhāvatī and Amitābha devotion.

Rethinking Tantric and Esoteric Buddhism

As with the terms "Mahayana Buddhism" and "Pure Land Buddhism," scholars have recently called for a critical reevaluation of the terms "Tantric Buddhism" and "Esoteric Buddhism."[81] In the same way that Pure Land Buddhist scholarship has (intentionally and unintentionally) defined Pure Land in reference to the medieval Japanese monks Hōnen and Shinran, Esoteric Buddhism has often narrowly been defined in relation to the life and thought of Kūkai, commonly regarded as the founder of the Shingon school and the transmitter of Tantric Buddhism to Japan. However, the breadth of traditions commonly subsumed under the label Esoteric Buddhism are not reducible to Kūkai's or the Shingon school's vision of the mantra path. The term "Esoteric Buddhism" has been used interchangeably and inconsistently (if not incoherently) with other terms, such as "Yoga," "Vajrayāna," and "Tantric Buddhism." In order to understand how Esoteric Buddhism has functioned as an area of study, we must look to the ways in which Tantric Buddhism was first defined and how that term was used in the early academic study of Buddhism.[82]

Just as with the so-called developed sutras, replete with *buddha-kṣetra* and the buddhas of the present, the tantras were another genre of Indian Buddhist literature maligned by Burnouf and Orientalist scholars of Buddhism. Burnouf writes:

> The *tantras* are indeed treatises with a very special character, where the cult of bizarre or terrible gods and goddesses is combined with a monotheist system and other developments of Northern Buddhism, that is to say, with the theory of a supreme buddha and superhuman buddhas and bodhisattvas. In the *tantras,* all these personages are the object of a cult for which their books minutely delineate rules; several of these treatises are merely collections of instructions directing devotees in the art of drawing and arranging circles and other magical figures (maṇḍala) intended to receive the images of these deities. Offering sacrifices addressed to them in order that they be favorable to oneself, wish as prayers and hymns sung in their honor, also occupy a considerable place in these books. Last, they contain magical formulas, or dhāraṇīs, veritable spells supposed to have been composed by these very divinities, which usually bear their name and which have the virtue of saving from the greatest perils one who is fortunate enough to possess and repeat them.[83]

Burnouf further describes the tantras as "the most disgusting relics that human superstition has invented,"[84] "long and tiresome,"[85] and "strange and terrible,"[86] as well as texts "whose importance for the history of human superstitions does not compensate for its mediocrity and vapidity."[87] Indeed, he questions whether or not one can truly call a tradition that traffics in the tantras Buddhist at all because "nothing would remind one of Buddhism if one did not see the name of the Buddha appear at rare intervals."[88]

Tantric Buddhism—as a heuristic construct, a category, a kind, a species of Buddhism—played a very important role in the early development of Buddhist studies as an academic discipline. Serving as a kind of catchall category, Tantric Buddhism helped the early Victorian-era interpreters of Buddhism deal with all the practices and traditions that seemed incompatible with the scientific clarity of Burnouf's Buddha. Lopez suggests that the category of Tantra was actually first constructed by scholars in order to resolve contradictions in the academic study of

Buddhism, though these contradictions are not found in the source material.[89]

In other words, because these scholars approached the material with certain presumptions, biases, and agendas, when they encountered outliers, such as a soteriology (Pure Land Buddhism) or ritualism (Tantric Buddhism), they had to find ways to explain them away. The elaborate cosmology of the developed sutras and the occasionally violent and sexual imagery of the tantras had to be accounted for and dismissed to protect the Buddha of modernist Orientalism, a rational Aryan human philosopher. Thus, the category of Tantric Buddhism was created for all the varieties of Buddhist practice and thought that did not fit into the narrative of a rationalist religion. As Wedemeyer notes, our tendency to separate Tantric Buddhism from the broader Mahayana tradition is derived from "ideology, not sociology."[90]

Tantra and Influence

As discussed above with Pure Land Buddhist elements, later generations of scholars worked to explain where the tantras came from. Lopez has examined the work of Rajendralala Mitra (1882),[91] Laurence Waddell (1895),[92] Benoytosh Bhattacharyya (1931),[93] and others, noting the remarkable consistency with which these scholars derided Tantric Buddhism as they were simultaneously, in some sense, creating it. As Wedemeyer suggests, we must interrogate "the very discourses used to represent Tantric Buddhism in order to demonstrate that the models taken for granted in modern academic research are themselves not only contingent and historical but reflect rather more of the constitutive imagination of the modern interpreter than the object they purport to explain."[94] Wedemeyer identifies three dominant theories Western scholars used to make sense of the rise of tantra: the decadent monk theory, the tribal origin theory, and the Śaivism origin theory. Proponents of the decadent monk theory argue that Tantric Buddhism served as a vehicle for renegade monks who sought to excuse their aberrant behavior. He ultimately rejects this purely speculative explanation, noting that there are more culturally appropriate ways to explain the "transgressive" elements found in the tantras, and ultimately argues that the tantras actually assume normative Mahayana Buddhist standards of conduct.[95]

Other scholars, such as Giuseppe Tucci, George Elder, and Edward Conze, appealed to a substratum or tribal origin theory, arguing that the elements we might identify as tantric came from the cultural practices of marginal tribes or that tantra represents the primal origin of Indian religion, serving as the substratum from which South Asian religious creativity emerged.[96] This view suggests that peripheral elements were integrated either due to degradation (Hindu influence on Buddhism) or as a means to reform Buddhism through contact with tribal communities. Wedemeyer argues that this theory has arisen primarily through overly literal readings of ambiguous textual references. Payne notes that appeals to tribal or substratum origins have also been articulated in such a way as to project a kind of Protestant reformer model, which was popular among some scholars of the origin of Mahayana Buddhism as well. This constitutes a kind of reversal in which the decadent monks are seen as the elitist mainstream monks, while the peripheral tantric practitioners are radical reformers.[97]

Finally, because early Orientalist scholars viewed the tantras as inherently inconsistent with the early teachings of the historical Buddha, and because later Buddhist tantras were often produced within a shared cultural environment with Śaivite (devotees of Śiva) competitors, some scholars argue that Buddhist tantrism actually came about as a result of borrowing from Śaivism. This view overlooks the fact that Buddhism and Śaivism functioned in a shared cultural context in which their boundaries were fluid, and both traditions borrowed extensively from the other.[98] "Blaming" Buddhist tantrism on Śaivistic influence entails, according to Payne, a "wrong-headed grammatical prejudice about who is the agent and who is the patient."[99] Ultimately, these attempts to explain the origin of Tantric Buddhism emerged from Western scholars' simplistic approach to the diversity of the Buddhist textual world, instead of paying closer attention to how that diversity functioned in particular contexts.

Tantra and Time

Tantric Buddhism has also often served as the foil for proposing various periodization schemes in Buddhist history, with tantrism variously constituting the beginning, middle, or late periods of Buddhism's development. How the "tantrism" phase fits into this history varies significantly from scholar to scholar. In some cases—for example, the substratum theory—tantrism is presented as the origin. In other cases, tantra is presented as emerging from a violent and decadent "medieval" Indian society, though it appears that few seem to agree on what constitutes the medieval period in Indian history. In this view, tantra is the by-product of a turbulent political environment that, as with the Śaivism or tribal origin theory, infiltrated Buddhist communities. Finally, tantra is in some cases presented as the end of Buddhism, a fatal development that ultimately destroyed the Buddhist faith in India. All these theories are ultimately problematic and unsatisfactory.

As noted, according to Lopez some scholars have used the term "tantra" as an empty signifier to make sense of aspects of Buddhism that do not tally with their expectations: "As the undifferentiated substratum of Indian culture, underlying all forms of Indian religiosity and manifesting itself overtly at certain key junctures in the development of the Hindu and Buddhist traditions . . . tantra is the substratum of authentic Indian religiosity, rendering the 'great tradition' epiphenomenal, the substratum that erupts into history at key moments, the corrective. It is the subversive origin that can only be temporarily repressed, the forever primitive."[100]

The substratum theory, while working perfectly to account for any element that seems out of place, ultimately leads to methodological laziness.[101] Wedemeyer notes that a fairly standard hierarchical binary has often been employed to define the features of tantra said to have originated in the substratum: esoteric/exoteric, pre-Vedic/Vedic, lay/monastic, magic/religion, and so on. These rigid binaries have been used throughout the years to paint tantra in an unflattering light, but since the recent reevaluation of tantra as "good," they have sometimes been reversed. Wedemeyer notes that even here, however, the underlying Orientalist evaluative structure remains unchallenged.[102] Whether or not a scholar found tantra to be a "good" or "bad" thing for Buddhism, appeals to a substratum are generally not based in documentable evidence and are therefore easily dismissed.

Tantrism has also been seen as a defining feature of medieval Indian religion, and Buddhist tantrism arose as a reaction to that environment through the incorporation of violent and sexual imagery. Yet, as Wedemeyer notes, the term "medieval" is variously and inconsistently defined, from Monier Monier-Williams in 1885, who deemed tantra to be the very worst part of Indian religion; to David L. Snellgrove in 1987, who defines tantra as medieval by comparing the use of "magic" in India to medieval Europe; to Ronald M. Davidson in 2002, who argues that tantra was an apotheosis of medieval Indian society. In all these cases, tantra is defined as medieval, and medieval is defined as tantric, but the dates for when this medieval period took place vary considerably within the scholarship. Wedemeyer notes that while the dates for medieval range anywhere from 0–600 CE to 100–1400 CE, the association of tantra with such terms as "medieval," "sexuality," or "violence" was consistent in its circularity.[103] Since the medieval period in India cannot be definitively fixed, it is inappropriate to deem tantrism a feature of a medieval, or middle period, of Indian Buddhist history.

Finally, tantra has also been used as a foil to explain the decline and disappearance of Buddhism in India. Lopez suggests that "Victorian scholars viewed tantra as a parasite that destroyed its host."[104] Wedemeyer and Payne have identified a progressive Hegelian theory of historical development,[105] or even Indian conceptions of time and cosmology (Kṛta, Duāpana, Tretā, Kali), as the source of this explanatory device, blaming the final phase in the development of an entity for its demise.[106] A common complaint among Orientalist scholars of Buddhism has been that even though the simple teachings of the Buddha seem to provide the antidote to idolatry, eventually, even Buddhism succumbed to the pervasive magical thinking of the Orient.

Rather than constituting a significant rupture in Buddhist literary history, it is more likely that the tantras, like Mahayana sutras, emerged and functioned within mainstream Buddhist culture, as Wedemeyer and others have noted.[107] One of the earliest scholars to observe this was Louis de la Vallée Poussin (1869–1937), who made the case that many of the elements in Buddhist literature that his contemporaries had identified as tantric had likely permeated the early Buddhist environment.[108] Lopez suggests that de la Vallée Poussin was perhaps the most "antiessentialist" Buddhologist of his day because he regarded the early Buddhist community as largely contiguous with Indian yogic traditions.[109] In other words, de la Vallée Poussin saw Buddhism as part of its environment, while many of his contemporaries labored under the notion that the historical founder of Buddhism stood apart from and above his contemporaries. Apparently, the idea that tantrism may to some extent be found in so-called early Buddhism was so roundly rejected that de la Vallée Poussin chose to pursue other avenues of research and did not write about Tantric Buddhism again.[110]

De la Vallée Poussin has been vindicated by recent scholarship significantly adding nuance to or critiquing the notion that tantrism is an inherently late development. John C. Huntington identifies the *Suvarṇaprabhāsa-sūtra* 金光明經 (T. 663) and other demonstrably early Mahayana texts as containing tantric characteristics, such as descriptions of mentally constructing a palace or mandala or paying homage to the buddhas of the four directions.[111] Alex Wayman's analysis of the *Guhyasamāja-tantra* led him to argue that tantra itself may have developed from the third century, if not earlier.[112] These examples provide ample reason to reconsider how Tantric Buddhism has been defined and how it might be reimagined as an area of academic inquiry.

Defining Tantra

So, then, what *is* Tantric Buddhism? Most scholarship employs either monothetic or polythetic strategies for arriving at a definition for this vexing term. Monothetic approaches seek to define a particular characteristic as essentially tantric: "Mantras, mudrās, and maṇḍalas . . . guru, abhiṣekha (empowerment), *vajra* (diamond or thunderbolt), *sukha* (bliss), *sahaja* ('together-born' [or natural]), and siddhis (powers) . . . practice that is secret, easy and rapid in its effect, based upon the premise that reality resides in the mundane . . . highly ritualistic, antinomian, and nonspeculative, evincing nonduality . . . esoteric physiology of cakras and *nāḍīs* that give special importance to the genitals."[113]

Rejecting the essentialist monothetic approach, other scholars choose to establish polythetic parameters whereby the "intersection . . . of a large number of family resemblances," when taken together, define Tantric Buddhism.[114] However, according to more recent scholarship by Lopez, Payne, and Wedemeyer, both monothetic and polythetic approaches are insufficient.

First, virtually all the criteria used in monothetic definitions may be found to greater or lesser degrees in purportedly "non-tantric" systems, and not all tantric systems contain all of these elements.[115] Furthermore, the "family resemblance" approach encompasses so many different variables that the term "tantra" becomes "overdetermined toward the point of meaninglessness."[116] The diversity of tantric literature—both the texts that bear the name "tantra" and related genres of ritual manuals and the texts that comment upon or draw upon that body of literature—is reduced to that of a single practitioner's point of view, the point of view of a single tradition, and thus is insufficient to represent the diversity of tantra.[117]

In any case, as with the terms examined above, whether we are talking about Mahayana Buddhism, Pure Land Buddhism, or others, the use of the term "tantra" must be rooted in a specific context understood relationally and not merely as "a free-floating category."[118] Etymologically, "[sūtra] comes from the root *siv*, 'to sew' and means most basically a thread that runs through, providing continuity and connection. Tantra is the woof or crossing thread in a fabric, providing the texture."[119] In Vedic contexts, it is "the primary part of the sacrifice, the *pradhāna,* which was made up of the main offerings and which varied according to deity and oblational material, and the tantra, the auxiliary acts that remained largely interchangeable among different sacrifices."[120] In the Tibetan context, tantra is defined in relation to sutras "as the member (usually the second member) of a dyad."[121] Sutras were the exoteric teachings defined as *pāramitā-yāna* (vehicle of the perfections, the gradual path), while the tantras were the esoteric teachings, the *vajra-yāna* (lightning-bolt vehicle, the rapid path).[122]

In order to understand how the tantras functioned in East Asia, we must first consider a fundamental feature of a Buddhist hermeneutic—namely, that all texts and teachings may be categorized either as *neyārtha* 不了義 (statements that require interpretation) or *nītārtha* 了義 (statements that may be taken at face value).[123] In East Asia there developed various bimodal strategies for dividing/integrating the diversity of Mahayana traditions, in some sense replicating the division between Mahayana and Hinayana 大乘/小乘: sudden/gradual 頓/漸, initial enlightenment/original enlightenment 始覺/本覺, self-power/other power 自力/他力, easy/difficult 難/易, and exoteric/esoteric 顯/密. In all cases these are not divisions between different kinds of Buddhism but rather dialogic binaries articulated in specific polemical and taxonomic contexts.

In situating Esoteric Buddhism in this broader context, we should first recognize that so-called esoteric discourse is not necessarily indicative of a kind of Buddhism; instead, it may be thought of as but one example of a pan-Mahayana "hierarchical universalism," an extension of the claim to Mahayana superiority over non-Mahayana Buddhisms, as well as a strategy for identifying the supposedly highest vehicles 最上乘 *within* the Mahayana. In certain contexts, the term "Esoteric Buddhism" can be taken as a synonym for Mahayana Buddhism itself. The term "esoteric" then becomes polemical, not necessarily descriptive.

Indeed, esotericism is one of the many strategies employed by Mahayana Buddhists to jockey for position against real or perceived rivals. For example, in the formation of the Chan tradition, by claiming the term *chan* (meditation), Chan Buddhists were essentially claiming privileged access or control over the practice of meditation and thus, access to awakening. Chan Buddhists also often claimed the label Buddha Mind school. Claiming to have access to the "mind of the Buddha" is fundamentally similar to claiming to have access to the esoteric teachings of the Buddha. In fact, as Richard McBride and Robert Sharf demonstrate, the concept of a "secret teaching" is found throughout Chinese Mahayana Buddhist texts, and only after the Song 宋 (960–1279) period was it conceived as a distinct bibliographic category, which is not to say that it inherently then constituted a distinct kind of Buddhism.[124] This polemical strategy, which we might label "Mahayana esotericism," is but one layer or dimension of the Mahayana Buddhist tradition broadly conceived, upon which various scholiasts throughout East Asian Buddhist history have drawn in different ways, and therefore is not exclusive to the so-called Esoteric Buddhist tradition.

Second, the vast and diverse Buddhist ritual culture includes a number of ritual technologies that might be deemed "spellcraft" 呪術, or esoterica. In broad terms this may include verbal or talismanic invocation of mantras, dhāraṇī, spells, and other powerful words employed for both this-worldly apotropaic and otherworldly soteriological goals. Many varieties of powerful words that could be defined as Buddhist esoterica are found across Mahayana and non-Mahayana literature. Indeed, incantations of this variety are common to most Buddhist traditions.[125] In some cases scholars have uncritically assumed that the inclusion of spells or certain rituals clearly denotes a distinct kind of Buddhism called Esoteric Buddhism, when in fact such practices are simply one of many features of Buddhism, broadly conceived.

Third, while it is common for scholars to speak of Tantric Buddhism as if it were a wholly distinct kind of Buddhism, recent research reveals that the discourse and material culture associated with the ritual genre known as the tantras not only functioned within normative Buddhist contexts but also presupposed a high degree of fluency in normative texts, literature, and practices.[126] Later Indian and then Tibetan scholiasts developed a vast commentarial literature for dealing with the tantras, very little of which made its way to East Asia, yet even in that highly developed context, the tantras were studied alongside both Mahayana and non-Mahayana texts.

In East Asian and Indo-Tibetan traditions, practices associated with the tantras required initiation and were (in theory) closely guarded and kept secret. In this sense these tantric Buddhist lineages were esoteric in nature. Esoteric tantric lineages built upon the foundations laid by various genres of normative Mahayana dhāraṇī and spell literature (Mahayana esoterica) and the pervasive esotericism inherent in Mahayana literature more broadly. Divisions between Mahayana esotericism,

Mahayana esoterica, and the tantric lineages we now associate with Esoteric Buddhism were not always so clearly defined, and each of these influenced the whole of the Sinitic Mahayana sphere. The rigid application of the heuristic Esoteric Buddhism, deployed in order to clearly distinguish between these three, negatively affects our ability to perceive their diversity and fluidity, as well as the various ways in which East Asian Buddhist scholastics employed this ambiguity in their own use of tantric lineages, spells and incantations, and Mahayana esotericism.

Sharf and McBride suggest that many of the practices often subsumed under the labels Tantric or Esoteric Buddhism can be understood simply as diverse elements of Mahayana ritual culture or polemical discourse—the concretization, or ritual enactment (and immediate attainment), of the grand Mahayana cosmic vision of reality and the immediacy of awakening.[127] Perhaps, in some cases, in "making sense" of Tantric or Esoteric Buddhism we instead miss something important about Buddhism's diversity. If, however, these dimensions of Buddhist literature are recognized as contiguous threads in a tapestry, aspects of a singular diversity in a state of continuous evolution and contestation, then the quest for the origins or exact boundaries of a particular kind of Buddhism may be recognized as an effort rooted in the misrecognition of the map as the territory it seeks to chart.

The heuristic constructs of Pure Land Buddhism or Esoteric Buddhism may have some utility when used conscientiously and in relation to specific contexts. Indeed, for some Buddhists an aspiration for rebirth in Sukhāvatī constituted a major area of concern, while some Buddhists' primary spiritual vocation was the acquisition of a higher initiation into esoteric tantra lineages. When these two are defined rigidly, however, whether as areas of scholarly inquiry, as Buddhist concerns, or both, their many areas of overlap and interrelation are obscured.

Esoteric Pure Land Buddhism

Like the heuristic construct Mahayana Buddhism, the terms "Pure Land Buddhism" and "Esoteric Buddhism" serve as fluid signifiers, temporary placeholders for forms of practice and groups with porous boundaries. As a kind of academic *upāya* 方便 (skill in means), such heuristic constructs are used with varying degrees of abstraction or function on multiple registers with varying degrees of precision as the religious studies scholar crafts a study in dialogue with other scholars, as well as within the scholastic traditions of the source material. When these fluid terms remain untethered to a specific historical context, however, or when wielded in an uncritical way in scholars' evaluations of source materials or by those who are unconscious of their own blind spots and biases, problems arise.

This investigation into Esoteric Pure Land Buddhism employs a new heuristic construct intended to reveal the diversity and fluidity of both Esoteric Buddhism and Pure Land Buddhism as areas of concern in premodern East Asian Mahayana Buddhist culture. My hope is that this will open up dialogue on new topics of academic inquiry. Practices and traditions that seem to include both terms and the forms of religious endeavor they describe have been ignored or suppressed both historically and in modern scholarship. From the persecution of unorthodox *buddhānusmṛti* practitioners by Shingon school scholiasts on Kōyasan to the Honganji's 本願寺 persecution of the *hiji bōmon* 秘事法門 (secret dharma gate) and *kakure nenbutsu* 隠れ念佛 (hidden *nenbutsu*) traditions, Esoteric Pure Land thought and practice have often been subject to oppression and exclusion.[128]

The scholars who have examined this area of overlap, or "dual cultivation," generally fall into two categories. First, some scholars interpret Esoteric Pure Land as the by-product of a late syncretism in which the Japanese Pure Land movement associated with Hōnen influenced the Shingon school of Esoteric Buddhism. Kushida Ryōkō 櫛田良洪 and James Sanford exemplify this first approach, as both scholars seem to regard Pure Land Buddhism and Esoteric Buddhism as inherently distinct and autonomous entities.[129]

Sharf's critique of the purported syncretism of Chan Buddhism and Pure Land Buddhism is instructive here: he demonstrates that whatever else Chan Buddhism may be, it certainly evolved within a diverse East Asian Mahayana environment in which the aspiration for rebirth in Sukhāvatī and the idea of *buddha-kṣetra* as a generic feature of the Mahayana worldview were simply taken for granted. There is thus no need to work to bring together Chan Buddhism and Pure Land Buddhism. Furthermore, Sharf explains that many of the most important Chan systematizers wrote on Sukhāvatī and Amitābha from various perspectives, and today Pure Land Buddhist praxis is a major component of Chan Buddhist communities in the broader East Asian cultural sphere of China, Korea, Taiwan, Vietnam, and beyond. He also notes that the assumption that Chan Buddhism and Pure Land Buddhism constitute two distinct and fundamentally opposing approaches to Buddhism may be due to influence from Japanese sectarian scholarship.[130] Sharf's observations about the place of *buddha-kṣetra* and Amitābha devotion within Chan are helpful for thinking about the place of these features of Mahayana Buddhist culture in Esoteric Buddhist contexts as well.

The second approach, found in the scholarship of H. van der Veere,[131] Satō Mona 佐藤もな,[132] and others, offers a counterpoint to the syncretism model. These scholars have recognized the importance of aspiration for rebirth in Sukhāvatī in Esoteric Buddhist texts and generally regard Esoteric Pure Land Buddhism as the orthodox Shingon Buddhist perspective on rebirth in Sukhāvatī (which may or may not be synonymous with the attainment of Buddhahood "in this body"). While this perspective is helpful in reorienting the conversation, it also runs the risk of taking for granted the continuity of the Shingon tradition as a single, unified entity with a defined doctrinal position.

Premodern Japanese Buddhism (as in the rest of East Asia) was largely nonsectarian in orientation before the seventeenth century, while the Shingon school evolved gradually through the early to late medieval period. Matthew McMullen writes:

> Until the late eleventh century, the term "Shingon" simply denoted mantra practice and theories concerning the efficacy of such practice. Of course, Kūkai was a proponent of such practice, and as Abé points out, he managed to convince the Nara schools of the legitimacy of mantra. "Shingon" did not refer to a particular institution. Although monastic centers such as Tōji, Kongōbuji, Daigoji, and Ninnaji gradually became united under the sectarian banner of a Shingon school, this institution developed over the course of centuries. There is no evidence that an independent school of mantra existed outside of the Tendai and Nara establishment during the ninth century. In terms of doctrine, the Tendai school was also the Shingon school in that Tendai scholiasts promoted the cultivation of mantra and theorized as to its soteriological significance. . . . From the eleventh century onward, scholastic monks at Ninnaji and other ritual centers began to differentiate Kūkai's Shingon school from the Tendai-Shingon school.[133]

In other words, not until the eleventh century, and in specific institutional and polemical contexts, do we begin to see the development of the distinctions through which a "Shingon school" would eventually be recognized.

Ryūichi Abé notes that as late as the fourteenth century, the Shingon school with Kūkai as its founder constituted a diverse body of lineages found across a number of institutions in the ancient capital in Nara 奈良 (Tōdaiji 東大寺, Kōfukuji 興福寺, etc.) and Kyoto (Tōji 東寺, Daigoji 醍醐寺,

Ninnaji 仁和寺, etc.) In some sense the Shingon school as we think of it today did not exist until the early modern period, and a considerable degree of lineage autonomy remains to this day.[134]

As an example, a brief personal anecdote: in 2014, while I was working on a project at Kōyasan University with my advisor, a Shingon priest and academic, he noticed a phrase I had written that gave him pause: *chūsei Kōyasan Shingon-shū* 中世高野山真言宗 (medieval Kōyasan Shingon school). He commented, "But, Aaron, there was no medieval Kōyasan Shingon school. There were diverse lineages and institutions, some independent, some connected with institutions in Nara and Hieizan, some with only two or three people. These lineages competed with one another and practiced a variety of traditions—" A light went on—I finally understood that the term "Shingon" points to a much more fluid Buddhist cultural context where different doctrinal and ritual traditions proliferated.

So in considering the place of Sukhāvatī, Amitābha, and *buddhānusmṛti* in the Shingon school, or in Esoteric Buddhism more generally, it is important to note both the fluidity of the institutional context within which many Shingon schools functioned, the heterogeneity of the Shingon school (i.e., the lineage of Kūkai), and the fact that Shingon as we think of it today did not historically have a monopoly on the practice of mantra or Esoteric Buddhist discourse.

If Esoteric Pure Land is not adequately explained by the syncretism of the Shingon school and Pure Land Buddhism, and if we accept that it is not simply the Shingon school's own orthodox interpretation of the path to Sukhāvatī, then how should we understand it? Some scholars have laid the groundwork for this study into the contours of Esoteric Pure Land Buddhism and the thought of Dōhan. My former advisor at Kōyasan University 高野山大学, Nakamura Honnen 中村本然, a scholar-priest and former director of the Mikkyō Bunka Kenkyūjo 密教文化研究所, is the leading scholar of Dōhan's thought. Nakamura's views on Dōhan's perspective on Esoteric Pure Land have influenced my approach to this material.[135]

Mona Satō has also been an important partner in dialogue; as she continues to pursue the study of Dōhan, it is likely that her meticulous work will emerge as the go-to source on Dōhan's thought.[136] Tomabechi Seiichi's 苫米地誠一 work on Esoteric Pure Land Buddhism in the late Heian period 平安時代 (794–1195) has helped illuminate key connections between Dōhan's thought and the broader Japanese Buddhist cultural context.[137] Several of Ryūichi Abé's Japanese publications have also guided my thinking in this study.[138] Furthermore, in English the scholarship of Richard Payne,[139] George Tanabe,[140] Jacqueline Stone,[141] Robert Sharf, and others who have focused their attention on the history of Shingon and Pure Land Buddhism has helped lay the foundation upon which this study aspires to build.[142]

For example, Payne's studies on the *Aparamitāyus Dhāraṇī* (T. 370, 936, 937) and the *Amida keiai goma* 阿彌陀敬愛護摩 led me to this area of inquiry.[143] He notes, for example, that the *Aparamitāyus Dhāraṇī* was very popular throughout Mahayana Buddhist cultures. Yet because scholars have generally ignored soteriology and spell craft, preferring instead to focus on philosophy and meditation, this Esoteric Pure Land text has been virtually ignored despite the fact that its popularity may reveal what Mahayana Buddhists were actually interested in.[144] Describing his initial encounter with this text, Payne writes:

> Initially I was attracted to this text because it appeared to be simultaneously a Pure Land and a Vajrayāna text, offering longevity and birth in Sukhāvatī through the recitation of a dhāraṇī. This struck me, those many years ago, as delightfully transgressive—it confounded the neat categories so familiar in the Buddhist studies of the 1970s, categories whose boundaries are overly-sharp, ahistorical, and either sectarian or ethnically defined. Since these boundaries continue to plague the field, the text continues to be a useful means of confounding these categories.[145]

He continues:

> Bibliographic classifications—including "Pure Land" and "tantra"—are themselves historically conditioned. Such conditioning extends beyond bibliographic concerns to include the very formation of these two categories and the common presumption that they are somehow mutually exclusive.[146]

From the groundwork laid by previous scholarship, this study considers an Esoteric Pure Land thinker, a specific text, and a specific context that have for the most part received little attention until now.

Dōhan and the *Himitsu nenbutsu*

The centerpiece of this book is the *Himitsu nenbutsu shō,* Dōhan's most influential Esoteric Pure Land text.[147] The *Himitsu nenbutsu shō* begins with an inquiry into the popularity of *buddhānusmṛti,* asking why this practice and the aspiration for rebirth in Sukhāvatī have become so ubiquitous among monastic and lay practitioners of various traditions.

As mentioned, interpreters of Dōhan and other Esoteric Pure Land thinkers have generally read Dōhan in one of two ways. He has been seen as attempting to figure out how Pure Land Buddhism fits within Shingon, "syncretizing" the two, or as using Shingon thought to respond to the Pure Land movement (Kōyasan, where Dōhan spent much of his life, was a major pilgrimage site for Amitābha Buddha devotees).

Based on my close reading and translation of the *Himitsu nenbutsu shō*, I argue here that Dōhan's approach to the idea of rebirth and the various practices connected to this concept represents not simply the Esoteric Buddhist approach to Pure Land Buddhism. Dōhan in fact draws upon and examines the diversity of approaches to rebirth in Sukhāvatī, a dialogic exo-esoteric 顯密 view in which the diversity of Buddhist thought and practice is engaged dynamically and fluidly, allowing for the diversity of medieval Japanese religion to stand while also positioning the mantra practitioner as especially capable of mastering the path to awakening via *buddhānusmṛti*.

Throughout this study I employ the term "Esoteric Pure Land"; however, the intended meaning of this term is not limited to so-called Esoteric Buddhism as representative of a single autonomous perspective. The term "Esoteric Pure Land," and, I would argue, the term "Esoteric Buddhism" as well, necessarily implies and constitutes its opposite, the exoteric. Esoteric Pure Land may thus be synonymous with diverse exo-esoteric conceptions of the relationship between Sukhāvatī, Amitābha Buddha, and *buddhānusmṛti*.[148] Because the term "esoteric" necessarily implies its opposite, the exoteric (and in practice the esoteric is often said to subsume or be revealed as the truth within the exoteric), my use of the term "esoteric" in this sense is a kind of shorthand that ultimately derives from Dōhan's own use of the term *himitsu nenbutsu*, or esoteric *buddhānusmṛti*.

The term "exo-esoteric" became popular in Anglophone and Japanese scholarship through studies of the social and political thought of Kuroda Toshio 黒田俊雄 (1926–1993).[149] Kuroda coined a number of influential terms, such as *kenmitsu taisei* 顯密体制 (exo-esoteric system), in order to account for the interconnected political and religious orthodoxy of medieval Buddhist practitioners who acquired mastery of esoteric tantric (*mitsu*) ritual as well as exoteric doctrine (*ken*). I have chosen to retain the term precisely because it seems to accurately characterize Dōhan's thought and speaks broadly to the diversity of medieval Japanese approaches to rebirth in Sukhāvatī.

Just as with the terms "esoteric" and "exoteric" in general, Esoteric Buddhism, like Mahayana Buddhism, is a polemical construct implying its opposite, Exoteric Buddhism or Hinayana Buddhism, respectively. Early medieval Japanese Buddhists employed both esoteric tantric ritual lineages and more generalized Mahayana esotericism and esoterica to jockey for position in a very diverse environment where lineages competed for patronage and power, often through acquiring lineage affiliations and mastery of numerous areas of study. In this way Esoteric Buddhism was not a kind of Japanese Buddhism; the teachings and practices now associated with Esoteric Buddhism were part of a pervasive discursive strategy used in elite circles within Japan and beyond.

Ultimately, it can be argued that the term "exo-esoteric" may be productively used to engage the fluid (and at times ambiguous) role that the tantras, Mahayana esotericism, and Mahayana esoterica played in East Asia. Kamikawa Michio 上川通夫 and others have argued for the study of Japanese Buddhism and exo-esotericism as one node in a much broader East Asian Mahayana cultural network.[150] Just as some scholars of Indian, Tibetan, and Chinese Buddhism have already made the case that Tantric Buddhism should not be thought of as somehow standing apart from Mahayana Buddhism, my use of the exo-esoteric concept simply seeks to make the case that the role of Japanese Esoteric Buddhism may as well be productively reimagined along similar lines.

Summary of Chapters

Chapter 2 examines the prominent role of *buddha-kṣetra* and aspiration for rebirth in Sukhāvatī across various genres of Chinese Mahayana literature (diverse genres of dhāraṇī literature, spell texts, and mantra texts, as well as sutras and tantras) and interrogates the modern academic distinction between dhāraṇī literature and Esoteric Buddhism. Through examining early dhāraṇī literature and the works attributed to the Tang monks commonly regarded as the founders of Chinese Esoteric Buddhism, Śubhakarasiṃha 善無畏 (637–735), Vajrabodhi 金剛智 (671–741), and Amoghavajra 不空金剛 (705–774), I argue that the prevalence of Sukhāvatī aspiration throughout reveals a clear link between these seemingly disparate areas of Mahayana literature.

The focal point of this chapter is the *Dhāraṇīsaṃgraha-sūta* 陀羅尼集經 (T. 901) by Atikūṭa 阿地瞿多 (mid-seventh century). Recent scholarship by Koichi Shinohara, Charles D. Orzech, and Ronald M. Davidson suggests that this text represents a transitional stage between the somewhat disparate and diverse genres of dhāraṇī literature and spell texts and the highly developed and systematized traditions of the elite Tang masters.[151] Atikūṭa's text contains a significant section on Amitābha and Sukhāvatī wherein the practitioner is encouraged to seek rebirth in Sukhāvatī for the purpose of studying advanced tantric techniques, some of which may be used in this world to aid the devotee in achieving rebirth more quickly. By situating this text in its larger historical and ritual context, I establish that before Esoteric Buddhism was systematized in Japan, Sukhāvatī-oriented soteriology was an important dimension of all phases of the development of Chinese Buddhist texts and traditions that eventually led to the category we now call East Asian Esoteric Buddhism.

The study of Esoteric Buddhism in Japanese and Anglophone scholarship tends to establish as the default perspective the life and teachings of Kūkai and his major interpreters. In chapter 3 I first demonstrate that the history of Japanese Esoteric Buddhism does not necessarily hinge solely on Kūkai's career, as the use of images and rituals in Japan were to a significant degree contiguous with developments on the Continent. The dhāraṇī culture of pre-ninth-century Japan also presupposed the power of ritualized speech acts as efficacious practices resulting in this-worldly and otherworldly benefits, including rebirth in Sukhāvatī.

Second, with the systematization and wide dissemination of ritual lineages first introduced by Kūkai to the major temples in Nara, Kyoto, Hieizan, and Kōyasan, the earlier interest in rebirth in Sukhāvatī did not disappear but was instead supplemented by this new ritual culture. This is demonstrated through an investigation into texts attributed to Kūkai and later systematizers of Japanese Esoteric Buddhism who also maintained an interest in Sukhāvatī, including Eikan 永觀 (1033–1111) and Chingai 珍海 (1091–1152).

The career of Kakuban 覺鑁 (1095–1143), arguably the most famous Esoteric Pure Land thinker and one of the most important interpreters of Kūkai's works, is examined in the context of the localized Esoteric Pure Land culture of early medieval Kōyasan. Sukhāvatī aspiration was an important driving force behind the revival of Kōyasan from the eleventh to the thirteenth century and a dominant focus of the ritual environment in which Dōhan lived and studied. In this section I demonstrate that the revival of Kōyasan and the propagation of the cult of Kūkai as a bodhisattva-like savior figure were both built upon a firm foundation of Sukhāvatī aspiration and Amitābha devotionalism.

Chapter 4 presents Dōhan's biography, focusing on his early education and training on Kōyasan and in Kyoto, his exile from Kōyasan, and his ultimate return. Thinking of scholars like Dōhan as having syncretized something called Esoteric Buddhism and something called Pure Land Buddhism is incorrect since during his lifetime these two categories did not function as mutually exclusive areas of interest or concern. Devotion and meditation upon the Buddha Amitābha were major features at every stage of Dōhan's education. It is no surprise, then, that Dōhan's Esoteric Buddhist thought focused intently on Amitābha Buddha, the nature of Sukhāvatī rebirth, and the diversity of approaches to *buddhānusmṛti.*

In chapter 5 I offer a summary and contextual introduction to Dōhan's major extant works. Part 1 examines the foundational scholarship that has redefined the contemporary study of "Kamakura Buddhism," in particular drawing from the work of David Quinter, Jacqueline Stone, Sueki Fumihiko 末木文美士, Tanaka Hisao 田中久夫, Richard Payne, James Dobbins, and Brian Ruppert. Part 2 introduces Dōhan's major works, and I argue that many of Stone's observations about Tendai in the early medieval period may also account for major features of Dōhan's thought, revealing the dominant role that Tendai thought played in the early medieval world within which Dōhan's Shingon identity was constructed.

This chapter also serves as an introductory study on early medieval Shingon scholarship as well as an introduction to the breadth of Dōhan's scholarship. Shingon at this time was not a single thing but rather a contested and widely sought-after area of specialty. Dōhan's scholarship on Shingon can be seen as a starting point, or perhaps a center of gravity, from which to engage the breadth of Mahayana Buddhist thought and encourage scholars to reconceive of the parameters of Shingon Buddhism during the Kamakura period. Even though Dōhan lived on a remote mountaintop, his scholarship was highly regarded and sought after during his time, and it had a lasting impact on Tendai, Shingon, Zen, and Pure Land Buddhist thought. I suggest that further study of Dōhan's major works may lead to new areas for dialogue and comparative study across contemporary sectarian divisions.

Chapter 6 provides a summary of the content of all three fascicles of the *Himitsu nenbutsu shō.* This text begins with a question: Why is it that practitioners of diverse traditions often also rely upon the *buddhānusmṛti* samādhi 念佛三昧? Is it because *buddhānusmṛti* is easy, or is it something more nuanced than that? Dōhan establishes a taxonomy for dealing with diverse approaches to the Buddha Amitābha in which the mantra practitioner may discover that the fundamental unity of buddhas and ordinary beings can be found even within the seemingly exoteric interpretation of the Sukhāvatī mythos and the attainment of postmortem rebirth. Dōhan suggests that his approach to *buddhānusmṛti,* the so-called *himitsu nenbutsu,* may reveal the multiple levels of meaning inherent in Buddha Amitābha as an object of devotion, Sukhāvatī as a soteriological goal, and *buddhānusmṛti* as a form of practice.

Chapter 7 focuses on Dōhan's synthesis of a diverse range of views presented in Mahayana literature on the relationship between ordinary sentient beings and extraordinary enlightened beings such as buddhas and bodhisattvas. Dōhan asks, "What is Amitābha Buddha?" As he lays out in the introduction, from one perspective Amitābha Buddha began as a bodhisattva named Dharmākara who originally set out on the path to Buddhahood under the direction of the Buddha Lokeśvararāja. From another perspective, Amitābha Buddha is merely an emanation of Mahāvairocana Tathāgata, ultimate reality. From another perspective, Amitābha Buddha is but one object of devotion found within the dual-mandala system of the Esoteric Buddhist tradition. From yet another perspective, Amitābha Buddha is the true nature of the body-mind of all sentient beings, an awakened reality coursing through and in some sense constituting all beings.

For some Buddhists the proximity of the Buddha is emphasized. For other Buddhists, however, such as the many pilgrims who traveled to Kōyasan during the Kamakura period, the remoteness of the Buddha Amitābha, a buddha in a faraway *buddha-kṣetra,* a bodhisattva who pursued the path successfully and created a refuge from this world, seemed more approachable or relevant. For such seekers this view was just as important as some of the more esoteric interpretations. I argue that Dōhan's views on the Buddha Amitābha exemplify a synthesis of the Mahayana teachings he encountered on Kōyasan—views of the Buddha as immanent and as transcendent, with both functioning together. In essence, that the Buddha is "within" does not mean that the Buddha is not in some sense also "out there" as well. For Dōhan, both views of awakened reality stood together as part of a unified whole.

As chapter 8 illustrates, ultimately, for Dōhan, there is nothing that is not *buddhānusmṛti.* All Buddhist practice could be interpreted as a variety of *buddhānusmṛti,* or "mindfulness of buddha," which Dōhan extends to include all human activity. Because buddhas are not separate from ordinary beings and our world is not separate from Sukhāvatī, the Buddha Amitābha as the compassionate activity of ultimate reality is able to perform speech acts through ordinary beings and move beings beyond the conditioned realm into the realm of the unconditioned. This dichotomous way of thinking is useful to a certain extent, but it is ultimately an illusion. Throughout the *Himitsu nenbutsu shō,* Dōhan draws out and then subverts the reader's expectations in a consistent play with established dichotomies. For those who understand the *himitsu nenbutsu,* even the simple act of reciting the name of the Buddha encompasses all the power within the Buddhist universe. The Buddha's words are not apart from our words, as the Buddha is present within the breath that animates beings, the organs of speech that render the vocal act possible, and the act of speech represented by the *himitsu nenbutsu.* Dōhan suggests that through this "mystery of speech and breath" the true potency of even the simple act of reciting the name of Buddha is found.

In chapter 9 I examine Dōhan's view of the relationship between this defiled realm and the otherworldly, purified realm of Sukhāvatī. Just as with his view of the Buddha, Dōhan's ideas about Sukhāvatī can be characterized by several seemingly contradictory views functioning together. He not only draws upon the Japanese Tendai and Kegon traditions of his day but also quotes past Chinese Tiantai and Huayan masters as well to explain the interdependent (though functionally independent) relationship between this world, the defiled realm of death and rebirth, and the *buddha-kṣetra* of Amitābha.

Following the conclusion, which consists of a list of desiderata, reflections, and suggestions for future investigation into Dōhan's thought and the study of Esoteric Pure Land Buddhism, the appendix presents a fully annotated English-language translation of all three fascicles of the *Himitsu nenbutsu shō.*

It is my sincere hope that this book, with its exploration of this overlooked text and a preliminary attempt at a translation, may bring Dōhan's long-forgotten voice into the conversation and open up space for a richer dialogue on both the study and practice of East Asian Mahayana Buddhism.

Notes

Chapter 1: An Introduction to Esoteric Pure Land Buddhism

1 Richard K. Payne and Kenneth K. Tanaka, "Introduction," in *Approaching the Land of Bliss: Religious Praxis in the Cult of Amitābha,* ed. Richard K. Payne and Kenneth K. Tanaka (Honolulu: University of Hawai'i Press, 2003), pp. 1–3.

2 Jonathan Z. Smith, *Relating Religion: Essays in the Study of Religion* (Chicago: University of Chicago Press, 2004), pp. 193–194.

3 Richard K. Payne, "Introduction," in *Tantric Buddhism in East Asia,* ed. Richard K. Payne (Somerville, MA: Wisdom, 2006), p. 3.

4 Christian Wedemeyer, *Making Sense of Tantric Buddhism: History, Semiology, and Transgression in the Indian Traditions* (New York: Columbia University Press, 2012), p. 4.

5 Tomabechi Seiichi 苫米地誠一, *Heianki shingonmikkyō no kenkyū: Heianki no shingonmikkyō to mikkyōjōdokyō* 平安期真言密教の研究: 平安期の真言教学と密教浄土教, vol. 2 (Tokyo: Nonburu sha, 2008); Satō Tetsuei 佐藤哲英, *Eizan jōdokyō no kenkyū* 叡山浄土教の研究 (Kyoto: Hyakkaen, 1979).

6 Robert Sharf, *Coming to Terms with Chinese Buddhism: A Reading of the Treasure Store Treatise* (Honolulu: University of Hawai'i Press, 2002), pp. 263–278; Sharf, "On Pure Land Buddhism and Ch'an/Pure Land Syncretism in Medieval China," *T'oung Pao* 33, no. 4/5 (2002): 282–331; Richard D. McBride II, "Is There Really 'Esoteric' Buddhism?," *Journal of the International Association of Buddhist Studies* 27 (2004): 329–356; Richard D. McBride II, "Dhāraṇī and Spells in Medieval Sinitic Buddhism," *Journal of the International Association of Buddhist Studies* 28 (2005): 85–114; Richard D. McBride II, "The Mysteries of Body, Speech, and Mind: The Three Esoterica (*sanmi*) in Medieval Sinitic Buddhism," *Journal of the International Association of Buddhist Studies* 29 (2006): 305–355.

7 DNBZ 70:51–82; SAZ 2:225–266; ZJZ 15:79–110.

8 Jimmy Yu, "Revisiting the Notion of *Zong:* Contextualizing the Dharma Drum Lineage of Modern Chan Buddhism," *Chung-Hwa Buddhist Journal* 26 (2013): 113–151; Carl Bielefeldt, "Filling the Zen-shū: Notes on the 'Jisshū yōdō ki,'" *Cahiers d'Extrême-Asie* 7 (1993–1994): 221–248; William Bodiford, "When Secrecy Ends: The Tokugawa Reformation of Tendai Buddhism and Its Implications," in *The Culture of Secrecy in Japanese Religion*, ed. Bernhard Scheid and Mark Teeuwen (London: Routledge, 2006), pp. 309–330; Duncan Williams, *The Other Side of Zen: A Social History of Sōtō Zen Buddhism in Tokugawa Japan* (Princeton, NJ: Princeton University Press, 2005); Ryūichi Abé, *The Weaving of Mantra: Kūkai and the Construction of Esoteric Buddhist Discourse* (New York: Columbia University Press, 1999), pp. 399–415.

9 Tomoko Masuzawa, *The Invention of World Religions, or How European Universalism Was Preserved in the Language of Pluralism* (Chicago: University of Chicago Press, 2005), pp. 44–68, 121–146.

10 Donald S. Lopez Jr., "Introduction to the Translation," in *Introduction to the History of Indian Buddhism,* ed. Eugene Burnouf (Chicago: University of Chicago Press, 2010), p. 10; Donald S. Lopez Jr., "Burnouf and the Birth of Buddhist Studies," *Eastern Buddhist* 43, no. 1–2 (2012): 25–34.

11 Lopez, "Burnouf and the Birth of Buddhist Studies," p. 34.

12 Burnouf, *Introduction to the History of Indian Buddhism,* p. 424.

13 Ibid., p. 328:

> Indeed, there are few beliefs that rest on so small a number of dogmas, and that also impose fewer sacrifices to common sense. I speak here in particular of the Buddhism that appears to me to be the most ancient, the human Buddhism, if I care to call it so, which consists almost entirely in very simple rules of morality, and where it is enough to believe that the Buddha was a man who reached a degree of intelligence and of virtue that each must take as the exemplar for his life. I distinguish it intentionally for this other Buddhas of buddhas and bodhisattvas of contemplation, and above all from that of the Ādibuddha, where theological inventions rival the most complicated that modern Brahmanism has conceived. In this second age of Buddhism dogma develops, and morality, without disappearing entirely, is no longer the principal object of the religion. The discipline loses a part of its strength at the same time, as in Nepal, to mention only one example, where a new class of married monks formed, an institution that was impossible at the time of Śākya and of his first disciples.

14 Christian K. Wedemeyer, "Tropes, Typologies, and Turnarounds: A Brief Genealogy of the Historiography of Tantric Buddhism," *History of Religions* 40, no. 3 (2001): 223–259.

15 Donald S. Lopez Jr., *From Stone to Flesh: A Short History of the Buddha* (Chicago: University of Chicago Press, 2013), p. 3.

16 Burnouf, *Introduction to the History of Indian Buddhism,* p. 243:

> That there are two kinds of *sūtras* that differ from each other in form as well as in content, namely: the *sūtras* that I call simple and the *sūtras* that the Nepalese themselves in accord with our manuscripts, call developed. That this difference, marked by important modifications in doctrine, announces that these two kinds of *sūtras* were written at different periods; That the simple sutras are more ancient than the developed *sūtras,* also sometimes called *sūtras* used as a great vehicle; that is to say, they are closer to the preaching of Śākyamuni; That among the simple sutras, there is also necessary to distinguish those that recall events contemporary with Śākyamuni, and those that recount fact or mention personages manifestly subsequent to the epoch of the founder of Buddhism; Finally, that all the works that bear the title sūtra must not, by that alone, be ranked rightfully in one of the three preceding categories, namely in the two categories of the simple *sūtras,* and the category of the developed *sūtras;* but that there are *sūtras* even more modern, notably *sūtras* in verse, which are only a kind of amplification of other more or less ancient prose *sūtras.*

17 Paul Williams, *Mahāyāna Buddhism: The Doctrinal Foundations* (London: Routledge, 2008), pp. 33, 277n4.

18 Peter Skilling, Jason A. Carbine, Claudio Cicuzza, and Santi Pakdeekham, eds., *How Theravada Is Theravada? Exploring Buddhist Identities* (Chiang Mai, Thailand: Silkworm Books, 2012); Peter Skilling, "Mahāyāna and Bodhisattva: An Essay Towards Historical Understanding," in *Phothisatawa barami kap sangkom thais nai sahatsawat mai,* ed. P. Limpanusorn (Bangkok: Thammasat University Press, 2004), pp. 139–156; Johnathan S. Walters, "Mahāyāna Theravāda and the Origins of the Mahāvihāra," *Sri Lanka Journal of the Humanities* 23, no. 1–2 (1997): 100–119.

19 Jan Nattier, "The Realm of Akṣobhya: A Missing Piece in the History of Pure Land Buddhism," *Journal of the International Association of Buddhist Studies* 23, no. 1 (2000): 71–102; Georgios Halkias, *Luminous Bliss: A Religious History of Pure Land Literature in Tibet* (Honolulu: University of Hawai'i Press, 2013), pp. 4–5.

20 Jan Nattier, *A Few Good Men: The Bodhisattva Path according to the Inquiry of Ugra (Ugraparipṛcchā)* (Honolulu: University of Hawai'i Press, 2003), pp. 73, 93, 191; Paul Williams, *Mahāyāna Buddhism,* p. 22.

21 Nattier, *Few Good Men,* p. 102.

22 Ibid., pp. 84–85, 195.

23 Gregory Schopen, "Kuṣān Image of Amitābha and the Character of the Early Mahāyāna in India," in *Figments and Fragments of Mahāyāna Buddhism in India, More Collected Papers* (Honolulu: University of Hawai'i Press, 2005), p. 269.

24 Williams, *Mahāyāna Buddhism,* p. 28.

25 Nattier, *Few Good Men,* p. 193; Schopen, "Kuṣān Image of Amitābha," pp. 267–268; A. K. Warder, *Indian Buddhism* (1970; repr., Delhi: Motilal Banarsidass, 2008), pp. 335–336; Williams, *Mahāyāna Buddhism,* pp. 4, 7–8; Hajime Nakamura, *Indian Buddhism: A Survey with Bibliographical Notes* (Delhi: Motilal Banarsidass, 1987), p. 152.

26 Akira Hirakawa, *A History of Indian Buddhism: From Śākyamuni to Early Mahāyāna,* trans. and ed. Paul Groner (Honolulu: University of Hawai'i Press, 1990), p. 262.

27 Schopen, "Kuṣān Image of Amitābha and the Character of the Early Mahāyāna in India," pp. 267–268. See also Halkias, *Luminous Bliss,* p. 18, 225n88–95; Fujita Kōtatsu, "Pure Land Buddhism in India," in *The Pure Land Tradition: History and Development,* ed. James Foard, Michael Solomon, and Richard K. Payne (1996; repr., Berkeley: University of California Press, 2006), p. 9n10.

28 Williams, *Mahāyāna Buddhism,* pp. 29–30.

29 Paul Mus, *Barabuḍur: Sketch of a History of Buddhism Based on Archaeological Criticism of the Texts,* trans. Alexander W. Macdonald (New Delhi: Indira Gandhi National Centre for the Arts: Sterling, 1998), p. 46.

30 Jonathan Silk, "What, If Anything, Is Mahāyāna Buddhism? Problems of Definitions and Classifications," *Numen* 49, no. 4 (2002): 397.

31 Judith Snodgrass, *Presenting Japanese Buddhism to the West: Orientalism, Occidentalism, and the Columbian Exposition* (Chapel Hill: University of North Carolina Press, 2003), p. 110.

32 Paul O. Ingram, "Faith as Knowledge in the Teaching of Shinran Shonin and Martin Luther," *Buddhist-Christian Studies* 8 (1988): 23–35; Richard K. Payne, "How Not to Talk about Pure Land Buddhism: A Critique of Huston Smith's (Mis)Representations," in *Path of No Path: Contemporary Studies in Pure Land Buddhism Honoring Roger Corless*, ed. Richard K. Payne (Berkeley, CA: Institute of Buddhist Studies and Numata Center for Buddhist Translation and Research, 2009), pp. 147–172.

33 Toki Hōryū, "History of Buddhism and Its Sects in Japan," in *Neely's History of the Parliament of Religions*, ed. W. R. Houghton (Chicago: F. Tennyson Neely, 1894), pp. 222–226; Haruki Shizuka 静春樹, "Kongōjō to Indo Bukkyōshi" 金剛乗とインド仏教史, *Mikkyō kenkyū* 密教文化 216 (2006): 163.

34 Halkias, *Luminous Bliss*, p. xvii.

35 Christopher Callahan, "Kakunyo and the Making of Shinran and Jōdo Shinshū" (PhD diss., Harvard University, 2011), pp. 2–3n5.

36 Galen Amstutz, *Interpreting Amida: History and Orientalism in the Study of Pure Land Buddhism* (Albany: State University of New York Press, 1997).

37 See, for example, Paul Williams's highly problematic description of Pure Land history, which is essentially little more than an uncritical recitation of the Shin Buddhist "Seven Patriarchs" lineage; *Mahāyāna Buddhism*, pp. 256–276.

38 Hirakawa, *History of Indian Buddhism*, p. 290; Fujita, "Pure Land Buddhism in India," pp. 35, 41n53. Refer to the list of Sanskrit texts in Fujita Kotatsu, *Genshi Jōdo shisō no kenkyū* 原始浄土思想の研究 (Tokyo: Iwanami shoten, 1970), pp. 141–161; the list of Chinese texts is on pp. 161–164.

39 Halkias, *Luminous Bliss*, pp. 23–24, 227–228n115, n118.

40 Gregory Schopen, "Sukhāvatī as a Generalized Religious Goal in Sanskrit Mahāyāna Sūtra Literature," in *Figments and Fragments of Mahāyāna Buddhism in India: More Collected Papers* (Honolulu: University of Hawai'i Press, 2005), p. 155. Schopen lists a number of texts and activities that may lead to rebirth in Sukhāvatī: *The Medicine Buddha Sūtra* mentions Sukhāvatī as a destination for rebirth (p. 154); hearing the name of Śākyamuni can lead to rebirth in Sukhāvatī or Abhirati (pp. 157–158); practicing *dāna* and devotion to sutras in the form of copying, reciting, praising, and so on can lead to rebirth in Sukhāvatī (p. 159); other texts include the *Ajitasena-sūtra* (pp. 155–156), the *Lotus Sutra* (p. 159), the *Kāruṇḍavyūha* (p. 160), the *Bhadracaripraṇidhāna* (pp. 160–161), the *Sarvatathāgatādhiṣṭhīna-sattvāvalokana-buddhakṣetra-sandarśana-vyūha-sūtra*

(pp.162, 165), and the *Samādhirāja-sūtra* (pp. 162–165), among others. He also mentions that one takes rebirth in Sukhāvatī as a mature bodhisattva, and thereafter, one becomes a buddha (pp. 167–170). Moreover, Sukhāvatī is often regarded as a destination for advanced bodhisattvas (p. 171).

41 Schopen, "Sukhāvatī as a Generalized Religious Goal," pp. 155–156, 165–167; G. Fussman and J. Silk, "The Virtues of Amitābha: A Tibetan Poem from Dunhuang," *Bukkyō bunka kenkyūjo kiyo* 32 (1993): 11–12; Halkias, *Luminous Bliss*, p. 15; Fujita, "Pure Land Buddhism in India," p. 23.

42 Schopen, "Sukhāvatī as a Generalized Religious Goal," pp. 180–182.

43 Ibid., p. 178.

44 Nalinaksha Dutt, *Gilgit Manuscripts*, vol. 1 (Srinagar: Calcutta Oriental Press, 1939); William Brian Rasmussen, "An Annotated Transcription and Translation of the Gilgit Manuscript of the Ajitasena-vyākaraṇa-nirdeśana-mahāyāna-sūtra" (MA thesis, University of Texas, 1995).

45 Teresina Rowell, "The Background and Early Use of the Buddha-kṣetra Concept. Introduction and Chapter One," *Eastern Buddhist* 6, no. 3 (1932–1935): 199–246; "The Background and Early Use of the Buddha-kṣetra Concept. Chapters Two and Three," *Eastern Buddhist* 6, no. 4 (1932–1935): 379–431; "The Background and Early Use of the Buddha-kṣetra Concept. Chapter IV, with Appendices and Bibliography. (Concluded)," *Eastern Buddhist* 7 (1936–1939): 132–176.

46 See Rowell, "Background and Early Use of the Buddha-kṣetra Concept," 6:199–200. For the full list of texts examined, see pp. 202–203nn1,2.

47 Rowell, "Background and Early Use of the Buddha-kṣetra Concept," 6:200.

48 Halkias, *Luminous Bliss*, p. xxv.

49 Rupert Gethin, "Cosmology and Meditation: From the Aggañña-Sutta to the Mahāyāna," *History of Religions* 36, no. 3 (1997): 183–217.

50 Randy Kloetzli, *Buddhist Cosmology: From Single World System to Pure Land* (Delhi: Motilal Banarsidass, 1983), pp. 13, 145–171. See also the quote on pp. 136–137:

> If the mathematical cosmologies are in fact the two basic strands containing all the complexities of the Buddhist cosmological materials, we may speculate that the cakravāla cosmology and the Pure Land cosmologies actually constitute the shorthands or simplifications of the two great traditions. The cakravāla or single world system is an abbreviation of the "sāhasra-cosmology" for the benefit of the monastic vocation. The Pure Land cosmologies, on the other hand, are simplifications of the "asaṅkhyeya-cosmology" for the benefit of the devotional traditions of the Mahāyāna. Thus, the three phases . . . can best be resolved into two discrete strands, each with a simplified version.

See also Rowell, "Background and Early Use of the Buddha-kṣetra Concept," 6:241; Gethin, "Cosmology and Meditation," p. 188.

51 Fujita, *Genshi Jōdo shisō no kenkyū*, pp. 8, 286–291, 273–278. Fujita notes several scholars who promoted this view: "P. Carus, S. Beal, L. A. Waddel, S. Levi, P. Pelliot, J. Przyluski, A. Bareau, H. de Luback, L. de La Vallée Poussin, E. Lamotte, A. Grüwedel, A. B. Keith." See also Julian Pas, *Visions of Sukhāvatī, Shan-Tao's Commentary on the Kuan Wu-Liang-Shou-Fo Ching* (Albany: State University of New York Press, 1995), pp. 5–32. Pas notes that there are three basic positions in the "origins" theory: first, the Iranian/Persian theory promoted by L. A. Waddell, J. Edkins, S. Beal, P. Pelliot, S. Lévi, and J. Edkins; second, the Hindu/Vedic or Vaishnavite/bhakti theory; and finally, the "internal Buddhist theory," which is promoted over the others in Fujita, *Genshi Jōdo shisō no kenkyū*, pp. 466–468, 471–473 (cited in Kenneth K. Tanaka, *The Dawn of Chinese Pure Land Buddhist Doctrine: Chin-ying Huiyuan's Commentary on the Visualization Sūtra* [Albany: State University of New York Press, 1990], pp. 8, 208n42).

52 Donald S. Lopez Jr., *The Lotus Sutra: A Biography* (Princeton, NJ: Princeton University Press, 2016), p. 215.

53 Halkias, *Luminous Bliss*, pp. 20–24.

54 Fujita, *Genshi Jōdo shisō no kenkyū*, pp. 464–474 (cited in Fujita, "Pure Land Buddhism in India," pp. 23, 40n330).

55 Halkias, *Luminous Bliss*, pp. 23, 25, 227n113.

56 Fujita, "Pure Land Buddhism in India," p. 13.

57 Halkias, *Luminous Bliss*, pp. 23, 227n113.

58 Fujita, *Genshi Jōdo shisō no kenkyū*, pp. 280–282 (cited in Tanaka, *Dawn of Chinese Pure Land*, pp. 8, 208n37).

59 Fujita, "Pure Land Buddhism in India," pp. 23–24.

60 Halkias, *Luminous Bliss*, pp. 23, 227n113.

61 Ibid., pp. 22, 227n114; Fujita, "Pure Land Buddhism in India," p. 13.

62 Halkias, *Luminous Bliss*, pp. 18, 22, 225n86, 227n114; *Bhagavad Gītā* 8:5–14; Fujita, "Pure Land Buddhism in India," pp. 9, 39n12.

63 David Ruegg, "Aspects of the Study of the (Earlier) Indian Mahāyāna," *Journal of the International Association of Buddhist Studies* 27, no. 1 (2004): 31 (cited in Halkias, *Luminous Bliss*, pp. 22, 227n114). Fujita, "Pure Land Buddhism in India," p. 30, notes that the term *bhakti* is not found in Pure Land sutras.

64 Halkias, *Luminous Bliss*, p. 26.

65 Fujita, "Pure Land Buddhism in India," pp. 13–14; *Genshi Jōdo shisō no kenkyū*, pp. 261–286.

66 Heinz Bechert, "Buddha-Field and Transfer of Merit in a Theravāda Source," *Indo-Iranian Journal* 35 (1992): 95–108; Kotatsu Fujita, "An Aspect of the Buddhas, Found in the Early Buddhist Scriptures, with Reference to the Present-Other Worlds Buddhas," *Indogaku Bukkyōgaku Kenkyū* 6, no. 2 (1958): 70; F. K. Lehman, "On the Vocabulary and Semantics of 'Field' in Theravāda Buddhist Society," *Contributions to Asian Studies* 16 (1981): 101–111; Louis de la Vallée Poussin, "Cosmology and Cosmogony (Buddhist)," in *Encyclopedia of Religion and Ethics,* ed. James Hastings, vol. 2 (Edinburgh: T & T Clark, 1908–1927), pp. 129–138, especially p. 137b; Donald K. Swearer, *Becoming the Buddha: The Ritual of Image Consecration in Thailand* (Princeton, NJ: Princeton University Press, 2004), pp. 20, 40; Kenneth Roy Norman, *Pali Literature: Including the Canonical Literature in Prakrit and Sanskrit of All the Hinayana Schools of Buddhism,* in vol. 7, pt. 2 of *A History of Indian Literature: Buddhist and Jaina Literature,* ed. Jan Gonda (Wiesbaden: O. Harrassowitz, 1983), pp. 90–91; T. W. Rhys Davids and William B. Stede, eds., *The Pali Texts Society's Pali-English Dictionary* (1925; repr., London: Luzac, 1966), p. 238. Guang Xing, *The Concept of the Buddha: Its Evolution from Early Buddhism to the Trikaya Theory* (London: RoutledgeCurzon, 2004), cites the Chinese editions of the *Dīrghāgama* (*Chang ahan jing* 長阿含經, T. 1:76c, 163b, 255b), the *Saṃyuktāgama* (*Za ahan jing* 雜阿含經, T. 99:131a, 322a, 410a), and the *Ekottarāgama* (*Zengyi ahan jing* 增一阿含經, T. 125:708c–710a, 773a).

Schopen, "Sukhāvatī as a Generalized Religious Goal," p. 183n1, cites several important key texts on the concept of the *buddhakṣetra:* Paul Demiéville, "Butsudo," in *Hōbōgirin, troisie'me fascicule* (Paris: Librairie d'Amérique et d'Orient, Adrien Maisonneuve, 1937), pp. 198–203; Dwijendralal Barua, "'Buddha-khetta' in the Apadāna," in *B.C. Law Volume* (Poona: Bhandarkar Oriental Research Institute 1946), pt. 2, pp. 183–190; Étienne Lamotte, *L'enseignement de Vimalakīrti,* Bibliotheque du muséon 51 (Louvain: Publications universitaires, 1962), pp. 395–404, appendix nI, nJ; Jean Eracle, *La doctrine Bouddhique de la terre pure* (Paris: Dervy, 1973). See also Fujita, *Genshi Jōdo shisō no kenkyū,* pp. 356–360 (cited in "Pure Land Buddhism in India," pp. 15, 39n24).

67 Halkias, *Luminous Bliss,* p. 23.

68 Rowell, "Background and Early Use of the Buddha-kṣetra Concept," 6:216; Paul Williams, *Mahāyāna Buddhism,* p. 224, citing Rowell, "Background and Early Use of the Buddha-kṣetra Concept," 6:379–381; Halkias, *Luminous Bliss,* p. 6.

69 On the *Visuddhimagga,* see Halkias, *Luminous Bliss,* p. 7, 218n19.

70 Rowell, "Background and Early Use of the Buddha-kṣetra Concept," 6:426–431 (cited in Tanaka, *Dawn of Chinese Pure Land Buddhist Doctrine,* p. 3, 207n20). See also Fujita, *Genshi Jōdo shisō no kenkyū,* pp. 361–376; Kloetzli, *Buddhist Cosmology,* pp. 91–111; S. Z. Aung and C. A. F. Rhys Davids, *Points of Controversy: Kathāvatthu* (London: Pali Text Society, 1915), p. 355.

71 Fujita, *Genshi Jōdo shisō no kenkyū,* p. 366, cites *Mahāvastu* 1:123–124, 3:342 (cited in Tanaka, *Dawn of Chinese Pure Land Buddhist Doctrine,* pp. 3, 207n21).

72 Paul Williams, *Mahāyāna Buddhism,* p. 224; Halkias, *Luminous Bliss,* pp. 5, 216–217n7; John James Jones, *The Mahāvastu-Avadāna* (London: Luzac, 1949), 2:9, 276, 283, 298, 299, 302, 304, 318, 326, 342; Jones, *Mahāvastu-Avadāna,* 3:135, 262, 265, 337, 340; Bechert, "Buddha-field and Transfer of Merit in a Theravāda Source," pp. 95–108.

73 John S. Strong, "'Gandhakuṭī': The Perfumed Chamber of the Buddha," *History of Religions* 16, no. 4 (1977): 390–406, especially p. 401.

74 The term *apadāna* (*avadāna*), for one of many traditional Buddhist genres of literature, can be rendered in English as "parables" or "legends." This particular *apadāna* is remarkable for its extensive coverage of the *buddhakhetta* concept, purportedly a "Mahāyāna" concept. Barau notes that Buddhaghosa defines the *buddhakhetta* as synonymous with the *buddhabhūmi* (*Buddhavaṁsa,* chap. 2, v. 175). Barau paraphrases Buddhaghosa's definition of *buddhakhetta* as nativity (*jātikhettaṁ*) and ministry (*āṇākkhettaṁ*); *Visuddhimagga,* vol. 2, p. 414. The *buddhakhetta* was also thought of as a perfect learning institution, which led to later imagery of the Pure Land as the ideal monastery; Barau, "Buddha-khetta in the Apadana," pp. 183–190, especially p. 184.

75 Barau, "Buddha-khetta in the Apadana," pp. 186, 190.

76 Ibid., p. 187.

77 Ibid., pp. 183–190 (cited in Norman, *Pali Literature,* p. 90).

78 Norman, *Pali Literature,* p. 91.

79 Wedemeyer, *Making Sense of Tantric Buddhism,* pp. 72, 225n20.

80 Ibid., p. 74.

81 Donald S. Lopez Jr., *Elaborations on Emptiness: Uses of the Heart Sūtra* (Princeton, NJ: Princeton University Press, 1996), pp. 78–104; Payne, "Introduction," pp. 1–31; Charles D. Orzech, "The 'Great Teaching of Yoga': The Chinese Appropriation of the Tantras, and the Question of Esoteric Buddhism," *Journal of Chinese Religions* 34 (2006): 29–78; Charles D. Orzech, "The Trouble with Tantra in China: Reflections on Method and History," in *Religion and Society: Transformations and Transfer of Tantra in Asia and Beyond,* ed. István Keul (Hawthorne, NY: Walter de Gruyter, 2012), pp. 303–328.

82 The use of the word "tantra" in English language sources dates to 1799; Herbert V. Guenther, *The Tantric View of Life* (Berkeley, CA: Shambhala, 1972), p. 1 (cited in Payne, "Introduction," pp. 5, 228n12, and Lopez, *Elaborations on Emptiness,* p. 103). The earliest text (to which we have access) to contain the term "tantra" is likely the *Guhyasamāja-tantra,* which may date from as late as the third century CE. Hugh B. Urban, *Tantra: Sex, Secrecy, Politics, and Power in the Study of Religion* (Berkeley: University of California Press, 2003),

p. 29 (cited in Payne, "Introduction," pp. 4, 228n14). Lopez notes the danger inherent in allowing the term "tantra" (as a bibliographic category) to float free as an "abstract noun" in the form of "tantra" as such or "tantric"; *Elaborations on Emptiness,* p. 85 (cited in Payne, "Introduction," pp. 5, 228n15).

83 Burnouf, *Introduction to the History of Indian Buddhism,* p. 479.

84 Ibid., p. 344.

85 Ibid., p. 487.

86 Ibid., p. 490.

87 Ibid., p. 483.

88 Ibid., p. 491.

89 Lopez, *Elaborations on Emptiness,* pp. 103–104.

90 Wedemeyer, *Making Sense of Tantric Buddhism,* p. 202.

91 Rajendralala Mitra, *The Sanskrit Buddhist Literature of Nepal* (1888; repr., New Delhi: Cosmo, 1981), pp. 261, 264, writes: "We can only deplore the weakness of human understanding which yields to such delusion in the name of religion, and the villainy of the priesthood which so successfully inculcates them" (quoted in Lopez, *Elaborations on Emptiness,* p. 93n27).

92 Laurence A. Waddell, *The Buddhism of Tibet, or Lamaism: With Its Mystic Cults, Symbolism and Mythology, and in Its Relation to Indian Buddhism* (1895; repr., London: W. H. Allen, 1972).

93 Benoytosh Bhattacharyya, in *An Introduction to Buddhist Esotericism* (Delhi: Motilal Banarsidass, 1980), p. vii, writes: "If at any time in the history of India the mind of the nation as a whole has been diseased, it was in the Tāntric Age. . . . Someone should therefore take up the study comprising the diagnosis, aetiology, pathology, and prognosis of the disease, so that more capable men may take up its treatment and eradication in the future" (quoted in Lopez, *Elaborations on Emptiness,* p. 94n28). Many scholars have cited Bhattacharyya's introductory diatribes against "Tantra," but when this introductory essay is read in the context of the work as a whole, especially the conclusion, a very different picture emerges. He was clearly trying to find an explanation for how it was possible for India to be so humiliated by the British and how Indians might imagine a way forward. Bhattacharyya's criticism of tantra basically served as a foil for his theorization of a purified tantra-yoga as Indian culture's primordial and true esoteric religious contribution to the world; see, especially, *Introduction to Buddhist Esotericism,* pp. 165–174.

94 Wedemeyer, *Making Sense of Tantric Buddhism,* p. 68.

95 Ibid., pp. 11, 23, 43–45; for an evaluation of the "semiology" of transgression in Tantric Buddhism, see, especially, pp. 170–199. See also Payne, "Introduction," p. 22.

96 Wedemeyer, *Making Sense of Tantric Buddhism,* 51.

97 Payne, "Introduction," p. 13. Regarding the ways in which substratum and Vedic/pre-Vedic attribution may be read, see pp. 22–24.

98 Wedemeyer, *Making Sense of Tantric Buddhism,* pp. 11, 17, 22, 30–32. On the various problems involving discourses of "influence," see Michael Baxandallan, *Patterns of Intention: On the Historical Explanation of Pictures* (New Haven, CT: Yale University Press, 1985), pp. 58–59 (cited at length in Payne, "Introduction," p. 31).

99 Payne, "Introduction," p. 31.

100 Lopez, *Elaborations on Emptiness,* pp. 85–86.

101 Regarding the problems inherent in the "substratum" theorization, see Jan Gonda, "Introduction: Some Critical Remarks apropos of Substratum Theories," in *Charge and Continuity in Indian Religion* (The Hague: Mouton, 1965), pp. 7–37 (cited in Lopez, *Elaborations on Emptiness,* p. 86n12).

102 Wedemeyer, *Making Sense of Tantric Buddhism,* pp. 56–57; Payne, "Introduction," p. 13.

103 Wedemeyer, *Making Sense of Tantric Buddhism,* p. 60.

104 Lopez, *Elaborations on Emptiness,* p. 99.

105 For more on the Hegelian view of history and its influence on the study of tantra, see Wedemeyer, "Tropes, Typologies, and Turnarounds," p. 229 (cited in Payne, "Introduction," pp. 1, 227n1).

106 A. L. Basham, "Tantrism and the Decline of Buddhism in India," in *The Buddhist Tradition in India, China and Japan,* ed. William Theodore DeBary (New York: Modern Library, 1969), pp. 110–124 (cited in Wedemeyer, *Making Sense of Tantric Buddhism,* pp. 43–45).

107 Wedemeyer, "Tropes, Typologies, and Turnarounds," *Making Sense of Tantric Buddhism,* etc. See also John C. Huntington, "Note on a Chinese Text Demonstrating the Earliness of Tantra," *Journal of the International Association of Buddhist Studies* 10, no. 2 (1987): 88–98.

108 Louis de la Vallée Poussin, *Bouddhisme: Opinions sur l'histoire de la dogmatique* (Paris: Gabriel Beauchesne et Cie., 1908), pp. 342–412; Louis de la Vallée Poussin, *Bouddhisme: Études et Matériaux* (London: Luzac, 1989), pp. 72–81, 118–176 (cited in Lopez, *Elaborations on Emptiness,* p. 96n39). In "Tāntrism (Buddhist)," in *The Encyclopedia of Religion and Ethics*, vol. 12, ed. James Hastings (New York: C. Scribner's Sons, 1922), p. 194, de la Vallée Poussin writes: "The Old Buddhism, as preserved in the Pāli canon and in the Sanskrit Hīnayāna literature, has a number of features which are not specifically Buddhist, which are alien to the noble eightfold path, which, to put it otherwise, are more or less Tāntrik or open the way to Tantrism properly so called" (quoted in Lopez, *Elaborations on Emptiness,* p. 96n40).

109 De la Vallée Poussin, *Bouddhism: Etudes et Materiaux,* p. 43 (cited in Lopez, *Elaborations on Emptiness,* p. 98n47). Lopez notes, however, that de la Vallée Poussin regarded tantra as "alien" in some sense; *Elaborations on Emptiness,* p. 98.

110 Wedemeyer, "Tropes and Typologies," pp. 243–248.

111 John C. Huntington, "Notes on a Chinese Text Demonstrating the Earliness of Tantra," pp. 88–98.

112 Alex Wayman, *Introduction to the Buddhist Tantric Systems* (1978; repr., Delhi: Motilal Bandarsidass, 1998), and *Yoga of the Guhyasamājatantra, the Arcane Lore of Forty Verses, a Buddhist Tantra Commentary* (Delhi: Motilal Banarsidass, 1977). Warder, *Indian Buddhism,* p. 462, however, agrees that the *Guhyasamāja* may be the earliest Mantrayana text and suggests the sixth century for its date of composition. Warder also notes that the *Mahāsaṃnipāta-Ratnaketudhāraṇī* 寶星陀羅尼經 (T. 402), translated during the fourth to fifth centuries, depicts Śākyamuni drawing upon the power of all buddhas to deliver a dhāraṇī to our world that will aid in the dissemination of Buddhism; *Indian Buddhism,* p. 459; see also pp. 459–476. See also Hirakawa, *A History of Indian Buddhism,* pp. 296–298; Nakamura, *Indian Buddhism,* p. 170n39.

113 Lopez, *Elaborations on Emptiness,* p. 86.

114 Ibid., p. 86.

115 Stephen Hodge, "Considerations on the Dating and Geographical Origins of the Mahāvairocanābhisaṃbodhi-sūtra," in *The Buddhist Forum III,* ed. Tadeusz Skorupski and Ulrich Pagels (London: School of Oriental and African Studies, University of London, 1994), p. 59:

> 1. Tantric Buddhism offers an alternative path to Enlightenment in addition to the standard Mahāyāna one. 2. Its teachings are aimed at lay practitioners in particular, rather than monks and nuns. 3. As a consequence of this, it recognizes mundane aims and attainments, and often deals with practices which are more magical in character than spiritual. 4. It teaches special types of meditation (sādhana) as the path to realization, aimed at transforming the individual into an embodiment of the divine in this lifetime or after a short span of time. 5. Such kinds of meditation make extensive use of various kinds of maṇḍalas, mudrās, mantras, and dhāraṇīs as concrete expressions of the nature of reality. 6. The formation of images of the various deities during meditation by means of creative imagination plays a key role in the process of realization. These images may be viewed as being present externally or internally. 7. There is an exuberant proliferation in the number and types of Buddhas and other deities. 8. Great stress is laid upon the importance of the guru and the necessity of receiving the instructions and appropriate

initiations of the sādhanas from him. 9. Speculations on the nature and power of speech are prominent, especially with regard to the letters of the Sanskrit alphabet. 10. Various customs and rituals, often of non-Buddhist origins, such as the homa rituals, are incorporated and adapted to Buddhist ends. 11. A spiritual physiology is taught as part of the process of transformation. 12. It stresses the importance of the feminine and utilizes various forms of sexual yoga. (Quoted in Lopez, *Elaborations on Emptiness,* p. 87n14)

See also Stephen Hodge, *The Mahā-Vairocana-Abhisaṃbhodhi Tantra with Buddhaguhya's Commentary* (London: RoutledgeCurzon, 2003), p. 4 (cited in Payne, *Tantric Buddhism in East Asia,* pp. 10–11). Payne notes that Hodge's list resembles that in Teun Goudriaan, "Part One: Introduction, History and Philosophy," in *Hindu Tantrism, Handbuch der Orientalistik,* ed. Sanjukta Gupta, Dirk Jan Hoens, and Teun Goudriaan, vol. 2.4.2 (Leiden: Brill, 1979), pp. 7–93 (cited in Payne, *Tantric Buddhism in East Asia,* p. 229n34).

116 Lopez, *Elaborations on Emptiness,* p. 88. For additional considerations of the polythetic approach and potential pitfalls, see Rodney Needham, "Polythetic Classification," *Man* 10, no. 3 (1975): 349–369 (cited in Lopez, *Elaborations on Emptiness,* p. 86n13).

117 Payne, "Introduction," p. 12; Wedemeyer, *Making Sense of Tantric Buddhism,* pp. 200–206, drawing on Skilling's ten points in "Mahāyāna and Bodhisattva," pp. 141, 145–147.

118 Lopez, *Elaborations on Emptiness,* p. 90.

119 Ibid., pp. 90–91.

120 Ibid., p. 88.

121 Ibid., p. 88.

122 Ibid., p. 88.

123 Williams, *Mahāyāna Buddhism,* p. 79.

124 McBride, "Is there Really 'Esoteric' Buddhism?," pp. 351–352n71, citing Sharf, *Coming to Terms with Chinese Buddhism,* pp. 269–270.

125 Payne, "Introduction," p. 14. See also Richard K. Payne, *Language Conducive to Awakening: Categories of Language Use in East Asian Buddhism, with Particular Attention to the Vajrayāna Tradition* (Düsseldorf: Hauses der Japanischen Kulter, 1998).

126 Wedemeyer, *Making Sense of Tantric Buddhism,* p. 90; Payne, "Introduction," p. 14; Halkias, *Luminous Bliss,* p. 139; Warder, *Indian Buddhism,* p. 468.

127 DNBZ 70:51–82; SAZ 2:225–266; ZJZ 15:79–110.

128 Gorai Shigeru 五来重, *Kōya hijiri* 高野聖 (1975; repr., Tokyo: Kadokawa bunko 角川文庫, 2011), pp. 23–24, 83–84; Takuya Hino, "Creating Heresy: (Mis)representation, Fabrication, and the Tachikawa-ryu" (PhD diss.,

Columbia University, 2012); Chiba Jōryu, "Orthodoxy and Heterodoxy in Early Modern Shinshū: *Kakushi Nembutsu* and *Kakure Nembutsu*," in *The Pure Land Tradition: History and Development*, ed. James Foard, Michael Solomon, and Richard K. Payne (1996; repr., Berkeley: University of California Press, 2006), pp. 463–496.

129 Kushida Ryōkō 櫛田 良洪, "Himitsu nenbutsu shisō no bokkō" 秘密念仏思想の勃興, *Taishō daigaku kenkyū kiyō tsūgō* 大正大学研究紀要 48 (1963): 43–80. This essay is an earlier draft of *Shingon mikkyō seiritsu katei no kenkyū* 真言密教成立過程の研究 (Tokyo: Sankibō busshorin 山喜房佛書林, 1965), pp. 181–232; James Sanford, "Breath of Life: The Esoteric Nembutsu," in Payne, *Tantric Buddhism in East Asia*, pp. 161–190; James Sanford, "Amida's Secret Life: Kakuban's Amida hishaku," in Payne and Tanaka, *Approaching the Land of Bliss*, pp. 120–138. Though I have some disagreements with Kushida and Sanford's methodology (Sanford draws from Kushida), I fully recognize my debt to their scholarship in this area of inquiry.

130 Sharf, "On Pure Land Buddhism and Ch'an/Pure Land Syncretism," pp. 282–331.

131 Hendrik van der Veere, *A Study into the Thought of Kōgyo Daishi Kakuban with a Translation of His Gorin kuji myō himitsushaku* (Leiden: Hotei, 2000).

132 Mona Satō 佐藤もな, "Chūsei Shingonshū niokeru jōdo shisō kaishaku: Dōhan Himitsu *nenbutsu* shō wo megutte" 中世真言宗における浄土思想解釈道範『秘密念仏抄』をめぐって, *Indo tetsugaku Bukkyōgaku kenkyū* インド哲学仏教学研究 9 (2002): 80–92.

133 Matthew McMullen, "The Development of Esoteric Buddhist Scholasticism in Early Medieval Japan" (PhD diss., University of California, Berkeley, 2016), pp. 8–9.

134 For more on this issue, see Abé, *Weaving of Mantra*, pp. 375–376. For more information on the consolidation of the Shingon tradition around Mount Kōya, the teachings of Kūkai, and Kūkai as an object of worship, see Ryūichi Abe, "From Kūkai to Kakuban: A Study of Shingon Dharma Transmission" (PhD diss., Columbia University, 1991).

135 Nakamura Honnen 中村本然, "Dōhan no Jōdo kan" 道範の浄土観, *Kōyasan daigaku ronsō* 高野山大学論叢 29 (1994): 149–202.

136 Mona Satō 佐藤もな, "Chūsei Shingonshū niokeru jōdo shisō kaishaku: Dōhan Himitsu *nenbutsu* shō wo megutte" 中世真言宗における浄土思想解釈道範『秘密念仏抄』をめぐって, *Indo tetsugaku Bukkyōgaku kenkyū* インド哲学仏教学研究 9 (2002): 80–92.

137 Tomabechi Seiichi 苫米地誠一, *Heianki shingonmikkyō no kenkyū: Heianki no shingonmikkyō to mikkyōjōdokyō* 平安期真言密教の研究: 平安期の真言教学と密教浄土教, vol. 2 (Tokyo: Nonburu sha, 2008); Satō Tetsuei 佐藤哲英, *Eizan jōdokyō no kenkyū* 叡山浄土教の研究 (Kyoto: Hyakkaen, 1979).

138 Ryūichi Abe, "Gorinkujimyō himitusyaku" 五輪九字明秘密釈, in *Nihon no Bukkyō: Tēma Nihon Bukkyō no bunken gaido* 日本の仏教: テーマ 日本仏教の文献ガイド"日本仏教研究会, ed. Nihon Bukkyō kenkyūkai (Kyoto: Hōzōkan, 2001), pp. 80–83; "Mikkyō girei to kenmitsu bukkyō: Myōe Kōben no nyūmetsu girei wo megutte" 密教儀礼と顕密仏教: 明恵房高弁の入滅儀礼をめぐって, in *Chūsei Bukkyō no tenkai to sono kiban* 中世仏教の展開とその基盤, ed. Imai Masaharu 今井雅晴 (Tokyō: Daizō shuppan, 2002), pp. 38–57.

139 Richard K. Payne, "The Cult of Arya Aparamitayus: Proto-Pure Land Buddhism in the Context of Indian Mahayana," *Pure Land* 13, no. 14 (1997b): 19–36; Richard K. Payne, "The Shingon Subordinating Fire Offering for Amitābha: Amida Kei Ai Goma," *Pacific World,* 3rd ser., 8 (2006): 191–236; Richard K. Payne, "Aparamitāyus: 'Tantra' and 'Pure Land' in Late Medieval Indian Buddhism?," *Pacific World,* 3rd ser., 9 (2007): 273–308.

140 George Tanabe, "Kōyasan in the Countryside: The Rise of Shingon in the Kamakura Period," in *Revisioning "Kamakura" Buddhism,* ed. Richard K. Payne (Honolulu: University of Hawai'i Press, 1998), pp. 43–54.

141 Jacqueline I. Stone, "The Secret Art of Dying: Esoteric Deathbed Practices in Heian Japan," in *The Buddhist Dead: Practices, Discourses, Representations,* ed. Bryan J. Cuevas and Jacqueline I. Stone (Honolulu: University of Hawai'i Press, 2007), pp. 134–174; Stone, *Original Enlightenment,* pp. 134, 191–199; Jacqueline I. Stone, *Right Thoughts at the Last Moment: Buddhism and Deathbed Practices in Early Medieval Japan* (Honolulu: University of Hawai'i Press, 2016).

142 These issues are discussed as well in Aaron P. Proffitt, "Taking the Vajrayāna to Sukhāvatī," in *Methods in Buddhist Studies: Essays in Honor of Richard Payne,* ed. Scott A. Mitchell and Natalie E. F. Quli (New York: Bloomsbury Academic, 2019), pp. 54–64.

143 Payne, "Shingon Subordinating Fire Offering for Amitābha," pp. 191–236; Payne, "Cult of Arya Aparamitayus," pp. 19–36. This text was translated into Chinese beginning in 502 and 557. T. 936 was translated in the ninth century by a Tibetan monk in Dunhuang; T. 937 was translated in the late tenth century by a monk from Nalanda. See also Richard K. Payne, "The Tantric Transformation of Pūjā: Interpretation and Structure in the Study of Ritual," in *India and Beyond: Aspects of Literature, Meaning, Ritual and Thought—Essays in Honour of Frits Staal,* ed. Dick van der Meij (Leiden: International Institute for Asian Studies, 1997), p. 24 (cited in Halkias, *Luminous Bliss,* p. 141n11).

144 Payne, "Aparamitāyus: 'Tantra' and 'Pure Land' in Late Medieval Indian Buddhism?," p. 278.

145 Ibid., p. 273.

146 Ibid., p. 276.

147 Nakamura Honnen, *Shingon mikkyō ni okeru anjinron* 真言密教における安心論 (Kōyasan, Japan: Kōyasan University, 2003).

148 Regarding the term *kenmitsu nenbutsu,* see the colophon to the SAZ edition of the *Compendium on the Secret Contemplation of Buddha,* SAZ 266.

149 Kuroda Toshio 黒田俊雄, *Nihon chūsei no kokka to shūkyō* 日本中世の国家と宗教 (1975; repr., Tokyo: Iwanami shōten, 2007); *Nihon chūsei shakai to shūkyō* 日本中世社会と宗教 (Tokyo: Iwanami shōten, 1990); and *Kenmitsu taisei ron* 顕密体制論 (Kyoto: Hōzōkan, 1994); James C. Dobbins, ed., "Kuroda Toshio and His Scholarship," special issue, *Japanese Journal of Religious Studies* 23, no. 3–4 (1996); Richard K. Payne, ed., *Re-visioning "Kamakura" Buddhism* (Honolulu: University of Hawai'i Press, 1998).

150 Kamikawa Michio 上川通夫, *Nihon chūsei Bukkyō to Higashi Ajia sekai* 日本中世仏教と東アジア世界 (Tokyo: Hanawa shobō塙書房, 2012).

151 Ronald M. Davidson, "Some Observations on the Usṇīsa Abhiṣeka Rites in Atikūṭa's Dhāraṇīsaṃgraha," in *Transformations and Transfer of Tantra: Tantrism in Asia and Beyond,* ed. István Keul (Berlin: Walter de Gruyter, 2012), pp. 77–98; Charles D. Orzech, "Esoteric Buddhism in the Tang: From Atikūṭa to Amoghavajra (651–780)," in *Esoteric Buddhism and the Tantras in East Asia,* ed. Charles D. Orzech, Henrik H. Sørensen, and Richard K. Payne (Leiden: Brill, 2011), pp. 263–285; Koichi Shinohara, *Spells, Images and Maṇḍalas: Tracing the Evolution of Esoteric Buddhist Rituals* (New York: Columbia University Press, 2014).

Chapter 2

Sukhāvatī in the Secret *Piṭaka*

Amino Yoshihiko 網野善彦 (1928–2004) argued that the waters surrounding the Japanese Archipelago should not be considered a barrier but instead a highway that connects the archipelago to the continent.[1] In the past, some scholars of Japanese Buddhism, influenced by nationalist and nativist tendencies to view Japan in isolation, at times implicitly or explicitly posited Japanese Buddhism as the telos for the development of Mahayana Buddhism. In fact, the traditions we now refer to as "Japanese" Buddhism developed in the context of regular dialogue with contemporaneous developments on the Continent. Furthermore, current Buddhist studies scholarship commonly argues that Buddhists on the archipelago now called Japan did not necessarily think of themselves as "Japanese" Buddhists but as participants in a broader, cosmopolitan, East Asian Mahayana Buddhist culture. Before turning to the Japanese milieu for Dōhan's Esoteric Pure Land thought, a brief sketch of the contours of the broader East Asian Mahayana context for the development of the systems of thought and practice commonly labeled Esoteric Buddhism and Pure Land Buddhism, and their many areas of "overlap," is needed.

In this chapter I weave together the historiographies of Esoteric Buddhist studies and Pure Land Buddhist studies as found in their standard treatments, identifying texts and historical figures often presented by scholars as representative of the basis of either Pure Land Buddhism or Esoteric Buddhism in China. It is interesting to note that in many cases both groups of scholars, who generally do not interact with one another, refer to the very same text or person as playing an instrumental role in the development of their own particular school. In addition to these areas of overlap, I also examine the esoteric quality of some Pure Land texts and the Pure Land dimensions of some esoteric texts. I thus hope to identify problematic issues in essentialist readings of both avenues of scholarship and create a space for engaging Esoteric Pure Land traditions as a dynamic dimension of the greater East Asian Mahayana Buddhist cultural sphere.

Heuristic Approaches

As with such broad terms as "religion" or "Buddhism," Pure Land Buddhism and Esoteric Buddhism are not "things unto themselves," sui generis entities in the world, free of context. To borrow from Buddhist terminology, these labels, as well as the practices and ideas associated with them, do not possess *svabhāva* (inherent independent existence); they are better understood as "empty" of independent existence (śūnyatā) and dependently arisen. "Esoteric Pure Land Buddhism" is a heuristic device that shines light on how Sukhāvatī-oriented devotional/soteriological stances functioned to promote rebirth in Sukhāvatī as the superlative, essential, or "secret" path to Buddhahood. Moreover, the label also reveals the ubiquity of Sukhāvatī aspiration within all three "spheres" of what has commonly defined Esoteric Buddhism: Mahayana esotericism, Mahayana esoterica, and esoteric tantric ritual lineages. Ultimately, much of what I will examine as Esoteric Pure Land is simply Mahayana Buddhism seen from a new perspective. By illuminating how these various discursive positions and forms of practice actually overlap, however, we learn a great deal about some previously unexplored areas of Buddhist history, as well as gain a new perspective on familiar forms of practice and belief.

Central, South, and East Asian masters transmitted or developed a variety of texts and disciplines, including spell and dhāraṇī texts and new genres of Mahayana philosophical literature as well as various mainstream Mahayana sutras. The early missionaries and thinkers who promoted Pure Land Buddhism or Esoteric Buddhism as paths to awakening are in no way cut off from the broader cosmopolitan Mahayana milieu. Nevertheless, many of the texts examined below have been described by scholars as "proto-Pure Land" or "proto-Esoteric." In some cases, scholars of Pure Land Buddhism or Esoteric Buddhism designate the same text as somehow representative of a "proto-" phase of their particular area of study. I make no argument that these texts or practices instead represent some proto-Esoteric Pure Land lineage or teleological trajectory; rather, by showing that these discourses often occupy the same space (even if Esoteric Buddhism or Pure Land Buddhism scholars rarely do), I seek to reveal important areas of concern within early East Asian Buddhist culture that have often been occluded by anachronistic approaches in the study of Buddhism and how Mahayana soteriological cosmology, esotericism, and esoterica functioned together in early Chinese Buddhism.

In the second part, I discuss a variety of dhāraṇī texts, especially those texts associated with so-called esoteric emanations of Avalokiteśvara, the Bodhisattva of Compassion. Some of the most popular genres of dhāraṇī literature promote devotion to Avalokiteśvara and promise, among other benefits, to deliver practitioners to Sukhāvatī at the end of their lives.

In the chapter's third part, I consider the Buddhist masters of the Tang dynasty most closely associated with the Esoteric Buddhist tradition, in particular highlighting concern for rebirth in Sukhāvatī and devotion to Amitābha in works attributed to them. There is a great deal of continuity between early dhāraṇī literature and the elite Esoteric Buddhist lineages. Certainly, even if we grant that the ritual systems commonly designated as "Pure Esotericism" were new to China during the Tang, they were not wholly without precedent in India or China. Tantric Buddhism as a heuristic construct is problematic in some ways; the esoteric tantric systems in India developed within and assume a high degree of fluency in mainstream Mahayana Buddhism, often designated as exoteric within esoteric polemical contexts. By looking to the teachings on Sukhāvatī as a postmortem goal, alongside other soteriological goals such as the attainment of Buddhahood in one's present lifetime, my discussion seeks a nuanced approach to the problematic overreification of Esoteric Buddhism as a wholly distinct tradition.

Defining Esoteric Buddhism

In *Esoteric Buddhism and the Tantras in East Asia,* Charles D. Orzech, Henrik H. Sørensen, and Richard K. Payne outline four basic approaches to the study of Esoteric Buddhism in East Asia.[2]

First, some scholars contend that Esoteric Buddhism is equivalent to Tantrism in India and Tibet. I suggest that this is something of a default view among many popular and academic writers.

Second, some scholars contend that Esoteric Mahayana is distinct from Tantrism, which developed around the eighth century in India. Esotericism evolved along with the Mahayana as "ritualism and magic" and laid the groundwork for more "mature" or developed tantra.[3] This approach is most clearly exemplified by Sørensen's work.[4]

Third, Esoteric Buddhism is equivalent to Tantrism, emerging in the sixth century with the development of tantric systems that employed mantra and other incantations, mandala and other objects of contemplation and visualization, and ancient Indo-Iranian *homa* 護摩 fire rituals, among others. These systems coalesced around the ritualization and apotheosis of divine kingship as realized through the practice of abhiṣeka 灌頂 (consecration). Ronald Davidson is the most obvious proponent of this approach, and his scholarship has clearly influenced both Sørensen and Orzech.[5]

Fourth, while tantra as such may have functioned as a clearly defined bibliographic category within later Indian and Tibetan contexts, this was not necessarily the case for most of East Asia. Esoteric Buddhism in East Asia is better seen as "a new technological extension of the Mahāyāna," not a distinct kind of Buddhism.[6] Robert Sharf and Richard McBride's works on East Asian Esoteric Buddhism are representative of this position.

In addition to the diversity of perspectives among contemporary academics, the ritual masters and scholar-monks who compiled or composed the texts we tend to examine under the rubric of Esoteric Buddhism were not univocal.

Orzech considers key terms commonly used by both premodern scholiasts and modern scholars of Buddhism to define Esoteric Buddhism:[7]

1. Though popular today as the name of the Shingon School, the term Mantra school 真言宗 is relatively uncommon across Chinese sources and rarely found even in the works of Kūkai, with whom this term is most commonly associated.[8]
2. Mantra vehicle 真言乘 (Skt. **mantra-yāna*) is an uncommon term in premodern Buddhist sources, though it is popular in some contemporary Buddhist literature.
3. Mantra teachings 真言教, a fairly generic term found in various lineages and textual traditions, appears alongside such terms as "gate" 門, (i.e., "mantra gate") or "dharma" 法, which may also signify "mantra ritual manuals." I suggest that this term gives the impression of a teaching among teachings, an area of specialty practiced along with other practices and teachings.
4. Mantra storehouse 真言藏, which appears frequently in the works of Śubhakasiṃha and Yixing 一行 (684–727), seems to have the

connotation of Sanskrit terms like *mantra-nāya,* "mantra path," or *mantra-piṭaka,* "mantra repository."

5. The term *vajrayāna* 金剛乘 is found throughout the works of Vajrabodhi and the *Vajraśekhara* 金剛頂經 (T. 866) cycle,[9] in Yixing's *Dapiluzhenachengfo jingshu* 大毘盧遮那成佛經疏 (T. 1796; hereafter *Commentary on the Mahāvairocana-sūtra*), and in the works of Amoghavajra, Dānapāla 施護 (fl. 970s), and Dharmabhadra 法賢 (d. 1001). It is now common practice for scholars of Indo-Tibetan Buddhism to employ the term Vajrayāna, while scholars of East Asian Buddhism seem to prefer Esoteric Buddhism when discussing the East Asian reception of the tantras and related material and doctrinal culture.
6. Yoga 瑜伽, which can be translated as "the yoga" (or "the practice"), is commonly used along with the term Vajrayāna, especially in the works of Amoghavajra and Vajrabodhi.

This diverse terminology demonstrates that the label "Esoteric Buddhism" may occlude the multivocal, perhaps cacophonous, nature of the source material. Indeed, given the variety of terms subsumed under the label "Esoteric Buddhism" historically, how can scholars "make sense" of Esoteric Buddhism as an object of inquiry? Orzech notes: "Were we only to discuss phenomena in the language of the time or in terms that have indisputable equivalents in modern parlance (this is never the case) our investigations would be limited to listing native terms and categories and spurning all analysis. Although it is tempting to fall back on description, vocabulary, and taxonomies found only in the historical data, such an approach is naïve."[10]

A central point of contention has to do with how and to what degree these scholars recognize Esoteric Buddhism as a distinct or identifiable entity in East Asia. In his recent study of Amoghavajra, Geoffrey Goble reveals that while Amoghavajra may have promoted Esoteric Buddhism as a distinct tradition, he also played on the ambiguities inherent in the diversity of dhāraṇī literature and its connection to the tantras.[11]

Similar debates have been carried out in the study of early Indian and Tibetan Tantric Buddhism as well. The crux of the issue is how, and whether or not, Esoteric Buddhism is distinguishable from mainstream Mahayana Buddhism. On the one hand, Mahayana Buddhism contains esotericism, ritualism, spells, dhāraṇī texts, secret initiations, complex visualizations, and tales of visionary mind-bending encounters with buddhas that are simultaneously understood as beings outside of oneself but also as aspects of one's own mind. On the other hand, it would seem that the tantras are an identifiable distinct genre of Indian Buddhism ritual texts and the various lineages and systems that derive from them. How are we to understand the relationship between these two spheres of Buddhist activity?

Miscellaneous and Pure Esoteric Buddhism

Scholars have often relied on a two-tiered approach to describing the development of Esoteric Buddhism, clearly distinguishing between so-called miscellaneous esotericism雑密 and pure esotericism 純密. Robert Sharf, Ryūichi Abé, and others, drawing on the scholarship of Misaki Ryōshū 三崎良周, have examined the history of this approach. They note that it is an anachronistic polemical strategy developed in the late medieval period in Japan, and as such, it has little relevance to either early Japanese or Chinese Buddhist traditions.[12] Tomabechi Seiichi, on the other hand, while acknowledging the relatively late and polemical context for the origin of this distinction, argues for its utility in understanding the foundational nature of diverse dhāraṇī texts ("miscellaneous" esotericism) for the tantric systems of the Tang ācārya 阿闍梨 (esoteric masters).[13]

Similar problems have been identified in the study of Pure Land Buddhism in China. Pure Land Buddhism has become a clearly defined area of study in Buddhist studies principally because of the influence of contemporary Pure Land Buddhist schools in Japan. Without this influence, it stands to reason, much of what we identify as Pure Land elements, practices, and thoughts would simply be regarded as aspects of Mahayana Buddhism broadly conceived. This is arguably how Sukhāvatī devotion is treated by scholars of Tibetan Buddhism. As areas of academic inquiry, Pure Land Buddhism and Esoteric Buddhism already share some similarities. Sørensen notes: "A comparison between Esoteric Buddhism and the Jingtu is especially poignant, since both share similarities in their historical development, their largely non-institutional character, and the ways in which they both related to the canonical Mahāyāna literature. They were similarly integrated and absorbed into other forms of Chinese Buddhism while influencing each other."[14]

In order to lay the groundwork for a more engaged understanding of the place of Pure Land thought and practice in the Esoteric textual corpora, the "secret *piṭaka*," this chapter will look at the role of *buddha-kṣetra* and aspiration for rebirth in Sukhāvatī across the purported divide between "miscellaneous esotericism" and "pure esotericism."

From Dhāraṇī to Esoteric Buddhism: Development and Systematization

Ōtsuka Nobuo's 大塚伸夫 rubric for charting the development of early Esoteric Buddhist texts in China is especially useful for understanding the relationship between dhāraṇī literature (Mahayana esoterica) and the later esoteric tantric systems. First, he draws extensively from Sanskrit and Tibetan texts while emphasizing the importance of classical Chinese texts because often the Chinese translations of Indian texts represent the earliest datable versions.[15] Though many scholars have essentialized tantra as an inherently late phenomenon, if not the final or "terminal" phase in the development of Mahayana Buddhism,[16] Ōtsuka demonstrates that the roots of tantras as a distinguishable genre of Buddhist writing are in fact present from the very beginning of the dissemination of Buddhist texts in China.[17] Jinhua Chen as well notes that "the origin of Esoteric Buddhism is traceable to the third century or even earlier through textual evidence, at least that [which is] accessible through Chinese translations."[18]

Ōtsuka suggests that *shoki mikkyō* 初期密教 (early tantric/esoteric literature) may be divided into three periods:

1. Third to fifth century CE: This period corresponds roughly with the Kushana dynasty to the early Gupta.[19] Ōtsuka suggests that this phase demonstrates the prevalent "esotericization" of early Buddhism.[20] He notes the presence of practices such as image construction and *buddhānusmṛti* in the texts associated with this period. Dhāraṇī texts and protection spells were also especially important.[21]
2. Fifth to sixth century CE: Corresponding to the late Gupta period, texts from this period are characterized by spells and dhāraṇī for protection as well as mudra-, mantra-, and mandala-based systems. These texts present buddha image visualization employing mandalic configurations as well as incorporating mudras, abhiṣeka consecration, *homa* fire rituals, and rituals for the construction of images with many arms and heads. Ōtsuka asserts that while many elements of these texts may strike some scholars as "Hindu," such rituals are rooted in Mahayana conceptions of the bodhisattva path and broadly permeated South Asian religious traditions.[22]

3. Late sixth to early seventh centuries CE: From the end of the Gupta and afterward, texts begin to appear that emphasize the cultivation of *siddhi,* both spiritual and mundane, such as the rapid attainment of Buddhahood, the performance of abhiṣeka, and more elaborate instructions for the construction of mandalas and ritual images.[23]

   Important texts from this period include the following subgenres: *hṛdaya,* spell texts that purport to distill the power of a text or deity; new protection spells that place special emphasis on militaristic imagery and the *vajra;* Avalokiteśvara texts, some of which promote systematic mudra-mantra-mandalic practices; dhāraṇī texts associated with the *uṣṇīṣa* 佛頂 (the protuberance on the top of the Buddha's head); precepts; and abhiṣeka.

In addition to Ōtsuka's overview, Yoritomi Motohiro 頼富本宏, one of the leading scholars of Chinese Esoteric Buddhism in Japan, proposes a five-phase scheme for the development of Chinese Esoteric Buddhist history:

1. Spells and dhāraṇī. As noted above, spells and dhāraṇī are important features of the earliest layers of Mahayana literature to which we have access. Yoritomi contends that spellcraft was perhaps a predominant feature of central Asian religion and thus may have served as an important point of commonality with the evolving Chinese Buddhist culture, which also drew upon indigenous Chinese interest in spellcraft.[24]
2. Avalokiteśvara *nirmāṇa* 變化, spells believed to deliver the power of various emanations (*nirmāṇa*) of Avalokiteśvara Bodhisattva, constitute a major subgenre of dhāraṇī literature.[25]
3. The "middle period" 中期 (Tang 唐, 618–906). Often regarded as the "golden age" of Esoteric Buddhism, this period is associated with the careers of Vajrabodhi, Śubhakarasiṃha, Yixing, and Amoghavajra. Yoritomi notes the importance of abhiṣeka alongside the systematic incorporation of the "three mysteries" as well as ritualized consecration and construction of mandalas.
4. The later period 後期 (Song 宋, 960–1279). During this period the material, ritual, and meditative culture associated with Esoteric Buddhism became widely disseminated throughout Chinese culture and religion.[26]
5. The "Tibetan" period. From the Mongol Yuan 元 dynasty (1271–1368), the Han Chinese Ming 明 dynasty (1368–1644), and the Manchu

> Qing 清 dynasty (1644–1911), Tibetan Buddhist lamas were held in great esteem by the rulers of China.[27]

Ōtsuka's and Yoritomi's respective rubrics overlap, and they provide different yet complementary perspectives on the complexities of the cumulative development and systematization of the various textual and ritual traditions commonly lumped under Esoteric Buddhism.

Proto-Esoteric? Proto-Pure Land? Both? Neither?

Scholars of both Pure Land Buddhism and Esoteric Buddhism have looked to the **Pratyutpanna-samādhi-sūtra* 般舟三昧經 (T. 418) as representative of a "proto-" phase in the development of their respective traditions. Scholars of East Asian Esoteric Buddhism and Indo-Tibetan Tantric Buddhism have noted this text's emphasis on śūnyatā, the attainment of secret dhāraṇī, and the practice of visualizations that ultimately lead to an encounter with a particular deity.[28] This text also presupposes rebirth in the *buddha-kṣetra* of manifold buddhas and focuses in particular on Amitābha.[29] Indeed, in selecting Amitābha Buddha as its central object of contemplation, the *Pratyutpanna-samādhi-sūtra* laid the groundwork for later Amitābha-centered practices in East Asia. For example, Tiantai Zhiyi 天台智顗 (538–597) employed the *Pratyutpanna-samādhi-sūtra* as the template for his "constant walking samādhi."

The *Pratyutpanna-samādhi-sūtra* was translated by the prolific Western Indian monk Lokakṣema 支婁迦讖 (fl. second century CE), who also translated an early version of the *Sukhāvatī-vyūha-sūtra* 無量清淨平等覺經 (T. 361) and the *Akṣobhya-vyūha-sūtra*. In addition to these texts dedicated to Amitābha and Akṣobhya, respectively, Lokakṣema also transmitted the *Aṣṭasāhasrikā-prajñāpāramitā-sūtra* 道行般若經 (T. 224), an important early Prajñāpāramitā (Perfection of Wisdom) text. Paul Harrison suggests that the *Pratyutpanna-samādhi-sūtra* may be thought of as an approach to Mahayana Buddhism that synthesizes Pure Land Buddhism and Prajñāpāramitā philosophical literature.[30] This view, however, presupposes that aspiration for rebirth in Sukhāvatī or *buddha-kṣetra* cosmological soteriology is somehow incompatible with Prajñāpāramitā teachings. The fact that Sukhāvatī and Prajñāpāramitā philosophy function together in a text translated by a monk who transmitted diverse texts certainly suggests that these two perspectives may well have already functioned together as coextensive dimensions of Mahayana Buddhism in their original Indian context.

It may be more appropriate to follow the example of A. K. Warder, who employs the *Sukhāvatī-vyūha-sūtra* to explain concepts like śūnyatā and esotericism in Mahayana literature:[31] "The [*Sukhāvatī-vyūha-sūtra*] may seem puzzling at first sight. . . . Is this whole *sūtra* at the 'concealing' level of knowledge, its meaning requiring to be 'drawn out'? . . . The description of Sukhāvatī must be a kind of meditation at the concealing level, contrasting with the sordid experience of human society and in a way encouraging the cultivation of the roots of good and confidence in the doctrine, though empty."[32]

In other words, Mahayana texts often shift between the concealed (Skt. *saṃvṛti*) level and the ultimate (Skt. *paramārtha*). Warder presents the mythopoeic structure of the Sukhāvatī narrative as a way of exploring śūnyatā, thus demonstrating the dynamic intertextuality of Mahayana texts and genres.[33]

The *Pratyutpanna-samādhi-sūtra* presents a form of *buddhānusmṛti* said to bring about a vision of a buddha. When these two worlds collide, the inherent śūnyatā of the seemingly "imaginary" Sukhāvatī and the seemingly "real" world is rendered explicit. The "emptiness" of the vision does not mean that both are unreal, however, because the perceived vision is a sign of future rebirth in Amitābha's land:[34]

> 所聞西方阿彌陀佛刹。當念彼方佛不得缺戒。一心念若一晝夜。若七日七夜。過七日以後。見阿彌陀佛。於覺不見。於夢中見之。譬如人夢中所見。不知晝不知夜。亦不知內不知外。不用在冥中故不見。不用有所弊礙故不見。如是[颰友]陀和。菩薩 画像心當作是念。時諸佛國界名大山須彌山。其有幽冥之處悉爲開闢。目亦不弊。心亦不礙。是菩薩摩訶薩。不持天眼徹視。不持天耳徹聽。不持神足到其佛刹。不於是間終。生彼間佛刹乃見。便於是間坐。見阿彌陀佛。聞所說經悉受得。從三昧中悉能具足。爲人說之。

> Having learned of the buddha field of Amitābha in the western quarter, [one] should call to mind the buddha in that quarter. They should not break the precepts, and call him to mind single-mindedly, either for one day and one night, or for seven days and seven nights. After seven days they will see Amitābha Buddha. If they do not see him in the waking state, then they will see him in a dream. It is like the things a person sees in a dream—he is not conscious of day or night, nor is he conscious of inside or outside; he does not fail to see because he is in darkness, nor does he fail to see because there are obstructions. It is the same, Bhadrapala, for the minds of the bodhisattvas: when they perform this calling to mind, the famous great mountains and the Mount Sumerus in all the buddha realms, and all the places of darkness between them, are laid open to them, so that their vision is not obscured, and their minds are not obstructed. These bodhisattva

> mahāsattvas do not see through [the obstructions] with the divine eye, nor hear through them with the divine ear, nor travel to that buddha field by means of the supernormal power of motion, nor do they die here to be reborn in that buddha field there, and only then see; rather, while sitting here they see Amitābha Buddha, hear the sutras that he preaches, and receive them all. Rising from meditation, they are able to preach them to others in full.[35]

As Halkias notes, Sukhāvatī is not necessarily conceived as a self-existent place disconnected or autonomous from one's own mind or perception. In other words, the *buddha-kṣetra* in many Mahayana contexts is neither merely a postmortem destination nor simply a mirage conjured in deep states of meditation.[36] The broader Mahayana view instead holds both perspectives at once. This productive tension may in fact be a defining feature of Mahayana Buddhism in general, and it is certainly one of the defining features of Esoteric Pure Land thought.

Dhāraṇī and Sukhāvatī

Buddhism spread rapidly during the turbulent period between the Han and Tang dynasties. During this time many central and South Asian monks who were prolific transmitters of Mahayana sutras and spells and dhāraṇī texts came to China. Zhi Qian, a central Asian Yuezhi (Tocharian) layman, is regarded as the first transmitter of dhāraṇī texts into China.[37] As a result, some scholars have characterized him as a transmitter of "proto-tantric" dhāraṇī texts, including the **Anantamukha-dhāraṇī* 無量門微密持經 (T. 1011) and the *Puṣpakūṭa-dhāraṇī* 華積陀羅尼神呪經 (T. 1356),[38] both of which present *buddhānusmṛti* practice along with dhāraṇī practice and the goal of rebirth in Sukhāvatī.[39] Zhi Qian also translated another early version of the *Sukhāvatī-vyūha-sūtra* 阿彌陀三耶三佛薩樓佛檀過度人道經 (T. 362).[40] Some scholars therefore also regard him as an early transmitter of Pure Land Buddhism. Zhi Qian is also credited with having transmitted the *Vimalakīrtinirdeśa-sūtra* 維摩詰經 (T. 474) and the *Śūraṃgama-samādhi-sūtra* 首楞嚴三昧經 (T. 642). Here again is an example of one monk transmitting diverse genres of texts that reveal the complementarity of the philosophy of śūnyatā, dhāraṇī practice, and *buddha-kṣetra* cosmological soteriology.

The *Vimalakīrti* begins with a famous episode in which Śākyamuni Buddha reveals that our own world is in fact his own purified *buddha-kṣetra*, and when the minds of beings are sufficiently purified, they, too, may perceive this inherent purity. In this text multiple realities are superimposed, abiding in the same space. The concept of śūnyatā is also prevalent throughout the tale of the layman-bodhisattva Vimalakīrti, who seems to be an ordinary being but is in fact a great bodhisattva.

Dharmakṣema, active during the Northern Liang 北涼 (397–439), was from central India, where the first Buddhist cave temples were constructed. These cave temples constituted an immersive *buddha-kṣetra*-like environment, concretely reproducing the visions described in the Mahayana sutras. Dharmakṣema transmitted the *Karuṇā-puṇḍarīka-sūtra* 悲華經 (T. 157), which describes the past life tales of Amitābha and Śākyamuni. The text also includes dhāraṇī that are said to possess the same power as the text itself.[41] Dharmakṣema also translated the *Mahāparinirvāṇa-sūtra* 大般涅槃經 (T. 374), which, as Richard D. McBride notes, explicitly describes the true Mahayana as "esoteric" in nature.[42]

The central Asian monk Kālayaśas was active during the Liu Song 劉宋 (420–479) in the southern capital in Nanjing around 424. He "translated" the *Guanwuliangshuo jing* 觀無量壽經 (Contemplation Sutra; T. 365), a text that most scholars now recognize to be of central Asian origin. Like the *Pratyutpanna-samādhi-sūtra,* the *Contemplation Sutra* is sometimes noted for its "proto-tantric" qualities; the visualizations described in it have drawn comparisons to *sādhana* visualization practices.[43]

Kālayaśas also translated the *Guanyaowang yaoshang erpusa jing* 觀藥王藥上二菩薩經 (T. 1161). In this text, Bhaiṣajyarāja Bodhisattva 藥王菩薩 and Bhaiṣajyasamudgata Bodhisattva 藥上菩薩 are said to aid beings in the attainment of dhāraṇī and rebirth in Sukhāvatī. In particular, the "dhāraṇī gate" (a term later Buddhist thinkers employ as synonymous with Esoteric Buddhism) is promoted as efficacious for the attainment of rebirth in Sukhāvatī, and the text says that those who are born in the *buddha-kṣetra* abide in the dhāraṇī gate.[44]

Buddhabhadra, an extremely prolific translator, is known as the translator of the *Mahāparinirvāṇa-sūtra* 大般泥洹經 (T. 376), the *Sukhāvatīvyūha-sūtra* 無量壽經 (T. 360), the *Avataṃsaka-sūtra* 華嚴經 (T. 278), and many others. The *Avataṃsaka* in particular has at times been labeled proto-tantric due to its vivid and complex imagery and its descriptions of palaces associated with different deities, drawing comparisons to the later mandalas.[45] Buddhabhadra also produced an important "samādhi sutra," the *Guanfo sanmei hai jing* 觀佛三昧海經 (T. 643). Sharf notes that while samādhi sutras are commonly described as having proto-tantric attributes in their description of Buddhist visions and visionary encounters, such texts were quite important in early Chinese Buddhism.[46]

Pure Land Masters and the Esoteric Arts

In some cases texts regarded as either proto-tantric or proto-Pure Land are sometimes the very same texts, and many of the early transmitters and translators of Mahayana texts seem to have promoted not only so-called mainstream Mahayana literature but also Mahayana esoterica, such as dhāraṇī and spell texts that promise this-worldly and other-worldly benefits, up to and including rebirth in Sukhāvatī and Buddhahood. I now turn to consider the monks commonly associated with Pure Land Buddhism to show that they also engaged in or promoted Mahayana esoterica, such as dhāraṇī practice, and drew upon Mahayana esotericism.

Lushan Huiyuan 廬山慧遠 (334–416) was an influential *buddhānusmṛti* practitioner and Amitābha devotee. Huiyuan studied alongside Daoan 道安 (312 or 314–385), who promoted Maitreya devotionalism. Both Huiyuan and Daoan studied under the famous spell master Fotudeng 佛圖澄 (d. 348). While Fotudeng was associated with the north, the Kuchean monk Śrīmitra 帛尸梨蜜多羅 was active in Luoyang 洛陽 in 307.[47] Śrīmitra translated the *Guanding qiwan erqian shenwang hubiqiu zhoujing* 灌頂七萬二千神王護比丘呪經 (T. 1331),[48] a dhāraṇī text that promotes different paths to rebirth in the *buddha-kṣetra* of the ten directions, often focusing in particular on rebirth in Sukhāvatī.[49] Of particular interest is the section "Buddha Preaches the *Abhiṣekha* That Leads Immediately to Rebirth in the *Buddha-kṣetra* of the Ten Directions" 佛説灌頂隨願往生十方淨土經.[50]

In 402, Huiyuan led 123 fellow practitioners in the practice of the *buddhānusmṛti* samādhi. Some scholars highlight this event as the inception of Pure Land Buddhism in China. Erik Zürcher notes, however, that the first recorded communal devotional service focused on Amitābha was actually performed by Zhi Dun 支遁 (314–366), a *Zhuangzi* 莊子 specialist, in the Eastern Jin 東晉 (317–420). Early Sukhāvatī aspirants thus may have built upon an earlier Daoist orientation concerned with longevity and immortality.[51] Huiyuan's community included many lay members, and given his background in the classics, the influence of the cult of the *xian* 仙, commonly translated as "immortals," was not insignificant.[52] The *Lushanji* 廬山記 (T. 2095) records Huiyuan's vision of an immortal with "one thousand eyes." Yan Yaozhong 严耀中 speculates that this could have been a reference to one of the "esoteric" emanations of Avalokiteśvara Bodhisattva.[53]

Huiyuan's interests in Buddhist esoterica also included dhāraṇī practice, such as that found in the *Bayiqie yezhang genben desheng jingtu shenzhou* 拔一切業障根本得生淨土神呪 (T. 368), which contains an early version of the Amitābha dhāraṇī, also referred to as the *wangsheng zhou* 往生呪 (rebirth spell).[54] This dhāraṇī circulated widely and was later popularized at the Tang court by Amoghavajra.[55]

Tanluan 曇鸞 (467–543) is considered to be the first Chinese patriarch of the Shin Buddhist tradition, though he did not regard himself as the founder or recipient of a distinct Pure Land school of Mahayana Buddhism. The Shin Buddhist patriarchs Tanluan, Daochuo 道綽 (562-645), Shandao 善導 (613-681), and others certainly endeavored to forge an approach to Mahayana Buddhism that emphasized rebirth in Sukhāvatī as the superlative path, the secret way to achieve Buddhahood quickly and easily.

Kenneth Tanaka, Stanley Weinstein, Roger Corless, and others have examined the basic contours of Tanluan's life.[56] Active in the Eastern Wei 東魏 (534–550), Tanluan experienced a period of prolonged illness that inspired him to study immortality techniques under the direction of Tao Hongjing 陶弘景 (456–536). However, after he encountered Bodhiruci 菩提留支 (d. 527), Tanluan devoted himself to Amitābha Buddha and aspiration for rebirth in Sukhāvatī. Purportedly, Bodhiruci explained that even if one achieves immortality, one will still remain stuck in samsara and eventually die anyway. Mahayana long-life rituals often focus on Amitābha (whose other name, Amitāyus, literally means "limitless life"). Apparently, rebirth in Sukhāvatī was regarded by some in India and China, and later in Tibet, as a form of life extension. Rebirth in Sukhāvatī could therefore be seen as somewhat contiguous with Tanluan's earlier self-cultivation practices. Drawing from his knowledge of Chinese spellcraft, he explains "the efficacy of reciting the name of Amitābha by citing a spell from the [*Baopuzi*], a [Daoist] text, for curing edema and an incantation for protecting soldiers on the battlefield." Also, after noting the common use of quince moxibustion to cure sprains, he remarks that everyone is aware that a sprain can also be cured simply by reciting the word "quince."[57]

Tanluan adopted a common Mahayana Buddhist rhetorical strategy in his advocacy for rebirth in Sukhāvatī as a superlative path to Buddhahood, an "easy path" as opposed to the "difficult path" of rigorous and long-term meditative practice and study. In other words, the whole of the Mahayana tradition could be divided into two approaches—the easy and the difficult, the superlative and the inferior, the effective and the circuitous, the fast and the slow. The Pure Land path, or the Pure Land dharma gate 淨土法門, as the most effective way to attain Buddhahood can therefore be seen as one expression of Mahayana esotericism.

Jingying Huiyuan 淨影慧遠 (523–592) was an important Buddhist scholar active around the time of Tanluan, and like Tanluan, he promoted rebirth in Sukhāvatī as the superlative path. In his commentary on the *Contemplation Sutra* (*Guan wuliangshou jing yishu* 觀無量壽經義疏; T. 1749),[58] he presents the *Contemplation Sutra* as a "sudden teaching" alongside the *Sukhāvatī-vyūha-sūtra,* the *Śrīmālādevī-sūtra* 勝鬘經 (T. 353), the *Vimalakīrtinirdeśa-sūtra,* and others.[59] Huiyuan was also interested in dhāraṇī and mantra, viewing mantra as a kind of dhāraṇī and both as essential to progress on the bodhisattva path. He discusses the possibility of practicing higher dhāraṇī in Sukhāvatī, a common motif in dhāraṇī literature.[60] McBride notes that Huiyuan employed the exoteric-esoteric polemic in his scholarship, perhaps seeing it as "a useful heuristic device . . . to evaluate the respective merit of the competing systems of Buddhism."[61]

Daochuo follows Tanluan in the Shin Buddhist lineage of patriarchs. He promoted the idea of the end of the Dharma, the concept of three periods of the Dharma's gradual decline after the Buddha's lifetime. In this scheme, our world is in an advanced state of decline, and people's ability to succeed in traditional Buddhist practice is waning, so it is essential to rely on the power of Amitābha Buddha to achieve salvation.[62] Daochuo was also keenly interested in dhāraṇī and spells, and some scholars speculate that he regarded recitative *buddhānusmṛti* as another form of spellcraft. However, through a close reading of Daochuo's writings, Michael Conway demonstrates that he regarded recitative *buddhānusmṛti* as a distinct class of vocal ritual technology, over and above ordinary spells and dhāraṇī.[63]

In the *Anleji* 安樂集 (T. 1958), citing the *Guanfo sanmei jing* 觀佛三昧海經 (T. 643), Daochuo describes how Mañjuśrī Bodhisattva 文殊菩薩 entered the bodhisattva path through rebirth in Sukhāvatī. The text recounts how in Mañjuśrī's past life as a child he met a buddha, achieved rebirth in the Pure Land, and practiced dhāraṇī and the *buddhānusmṛti* samādhi.[64] Daochuo uses this story to illustrate that rebirth in Sukhāvatī is the most effective and "easiest" path to Buddhahood for foolish ordinary beings 凡夫.[65] Daochuo also cites the *Aparimitāyur-jñānahṛdaya-dhāraṇī* 阿彌陀鼓音聲王陀羅尼經 (T. 370), an important dhāraṇī text dedicated to Amitābha that is widely practiced throughout the Mahayana world.

Shandao, an important Pure Land thinker during the Tang, built on the contributions of Tanluan, Daochuo, and others. Shandao's writing in particular influenced the thought of Hōnen, the founder of the Japanese

Pure Land tradition. Charles Jones suggests that with Shandao we begin to see Pure Land Buddhism emerge as a distinct tradition within Chinese Mahayana Buddhism.[66] In the *Yi guanjing deng ming banzhousanmei xingdao wangsheng chu* 依觀經等明般舟三昧行道往生讃 (T. 1981), Shandao defines samādhi as the realization of *yue* 悦, a translation of the Sanskrit term *sukha* (bliss) within one's own body and mind.[67] In this way the external Buddha and the Buddha within are not inherently distinct.

Traces of both Mahayana esoterica and esotericism can be seen in Shandao's work. First, throughout his many works he uses terms such as *miyi* 密意, the Buddha's "secret intention," with some regularity. He also discusses the importance of dhāraṇī practice; for example, his commentary on the *Contemplation Sutra* (*Guan wuliangshou fo jing shu* 觀無量壽佛經疏; T. 1753), mentions that in Sukhāvatī one is able to study the dhāraṇī gate directly from the Buddha.[68] The *Yi guanjing deng ming banzhousanmei xingdao wangsheng chu* says that after rebirth in Sukhāvatī one will attain the awakening of limitless dhāraṇī.[69] The idea that Sukhāvatī is a place where more advanced esoterica can be learned and practiced is a consistent theme throughout dhāraṇī literature and in later tantra systems as well.

Tiantai Zhiyi

Tiantai Zhiyi is not traditionally regarded as a devout aspirant for rebirth in Sukhāvatī, and his career predated the tantra lineages we typically understand as constituting Esoteric Buddhism. Yet his thought had a profound impact on the course of East Asian Buddhist history as a whole because he was one of the first East Asian Buddhist thinkers to successfully systematize the diverse and complex Buddhist traditions that had flowed into China into a comprehensive doctrinal and meditative system. Zhiyi worked to account for the diversity of Buddhism, employing the *Lotus Sutra* and the *Nirvana Sutra* together as the highest teachings of the Buddha. The *Lotus* teaches that all Buddhist paths ultimately converge on the bodhisattva path to full Buddhahood, and the *Nirvana Sutra* teaches that all beings possess the fundamental Buddha-nature. Using these teachings as his foundation, Zhiyi was able to incorporate the whole range of Buddhist teachings.

Zhiyi employed Mahayana esotericism in some of his works. McBride, citing Leon Hurvitz, notes that Zhiyi employed the exoteric-esoteric heuristic in his ranking of Buddhist scriptures in the *Miaofa lianhua jing wenju* 妙法蓮華經文句 (T. 1718) and the *Weimojing xuanshu* 維摩經玄疏

(T. 1777), commentaries on the *Lotus* and *Vimalakirti* sutras, respectively.[70] According to McBride, "Zhiyi's explanation of 'esoteric teaching' is inextricably tied to his understanding of the chronological classification of sūtras, and yet it still refers directly to the advanced teachings of the Mahāyāna."[71] The *Lotus Sutra*'s narrative structure, as a "secret" teaching preserved only for those disciples wise enough to wait for the true teachings, is of primary importance here. As noted previously, the *Lotus Sutra* also expresses the "exoteric-esoteric" framework of the Mahayana tradition.

Dhāraṇī texts purport to lead to visions of *buddha-kṣetra,* if not to actual rebirth there at the end of one's life. In Zhiyi's magnum opus, the *Mohezhiguan* 摩訶止観 (T. 1911), he mentions that dhāraṇī may produce visions of *buddha-kṣetra* and also asserts that samādhi and dhāraṇī practice could purify the senses and grant entry into the secret *piṭaka*.[72] Later scholiasts in East Asia who promoted the traditions we now associate with Pure Land Buddhism and Esoteric Buddhism often labored to establish a connection between Zhiyi's engagement with *buddhānusmṛti* practice, dhāraṇī, and Mahayana esotericism. However, Zhiyi's career took place before the introduction of the tantras as lineage systems, and there is little evidence he was a devout aspirant for rebirth in Sukhāvatī as a postmortem goal. His own perspective was likely more in line with the Madhyamaka thought of Nāgārjuna 龍樹 (second to third century), who came to be regarded as a patriarch in the Tiantai system. In fact, Nāgārjuna is a patriarch in most, if not all, Mahayana lineages, including the Japanese Shingon and Jōdo Shinshū schools. Furthermore, Buddhists in East Asia and Tibet generally regarded Nāgārjuna as a Sukhāvatī aspirant. Here again, as with the *Pratyutpanna-samādhi-sūtra,* we see Sukhāvatī and śūnyatā perspectives functioning together.

Transforming Avalokiteśvara: The Dhāraṇī of the Bodhisattva of Compassion

The dhāraṇī texts associated with various "esoteric" emanation bodies of Avalokiteśvara Bodhisattva constitute one of the most important subgenres of Mahayana dhāraṇī literature.[73] Yoritomi Motohiro suggests that the emergence of this phase of Chinese Buddhist Esoteric literature had a profound impact on Chinese Buddhist culture, leading to the widespread popularity of this bodhisattva and, by association, the *Lotus Sutra* as well.[74]

Avalokiteśvara Bodhisattva is often depicted as female in East Asia, and as an important assistant to Amitābha Buddha in Sukhāvatī, many images of this bodhisattva include an image of Amitābha in her crown. As a result, many of the dhāraṇī texts in this subgenre emphasize that one of the benefits they may bestow is the attainment of rebirth in Sukhāvatī. Yan proposes that perhaps the plethora of spells and esoteric techniques that may deliver one to Sukhāvatī led to the widespread worship of this bodhisattva.[75]

The Qing Guanshiyin pusa xiaofu duhai tuoluonizhou jing 請觀世音菩薩消伏毒害陀羅尼呪經 (T. 1043) was translated by *Nandi, active during the Eastern Jin around 419. The well-known *Ṣaḍakṣara-vidyā-mantra,* or "six-syllable" mantra, *oṃ maṇi padme hūṃ,* appears in this text, and recitation of this mantra is said to deliver one to Sukhāvatī.[76]

The *Bukong juansuo zhou jing* 不空羂索呪經 (T. 1093), attributed to Jñānagupta, a prolific Gandhāran monk, contains the *Amoghapāśakalpa-hṛdaya-dhāraṇī* and promises rebirth in Sukhāvatī through the powers of Amoghapāśa,[77] a popular emanation of Avalokiteśvara. Yan notes the importance of *buddhānusmṛti* in the versions of the *Amoghapāśa* transmitted by Jñānagupta, as well as the translations done by Bodhiruci and Amoghavajra (see below).[78]

The *Dafa ju tuoluonijing* 大法炬陀羅尼經 (T. 1340), also attributed to Jñānagupta 闍那崛多 (523–600), promises the ability to attain rebirth into any of the *buddha-kṣetra* of the ten directions through the practice of the *Dharmolka-dhāraṇī.*[79]

The *Shiyimian Guanshiyin shenzhou jing* 十一面觀世音神咒經 (T. 1070), is attributed to Yaśogupta 耶舍崛多 (late sixth century), active in Chang'an from 561–578, and an associate of Jñānagupta. This text transmits the *Ekādaśamukha-dhāraṇī,* and is dedicated to the eleven-faced emanation of the Avalokiteśvara and states that through the practice of this spell, one may attain rebirth in Sukhāvatī.[80]

The *Qianshou qianyan Guanshiyin pusa guang dayuanman wuai dabeixin tuoluonijing* 千手千眼觀世音菩薩廣大圓滿無礙大悲心陀羅尼經 (T. 1060) contains the famous *Nīlakaṇṭha-dhāraṇī,* popularly known as the Great Compassion Dhāraṇī associated with the emanation of Avalokiteśvara with a thousand hands and a thousand eyes. This version is attributed to Bhagavaddharma 伽梵達摩, a Western Indian monk active during the Yonghui 永徽 era (650–656) of the Tang. In addition to the practice of this dhāraṇī, the text extols *buddhānusmṛti* and promises rebirth in Sukhāvatī in a lotus blossom, unsullied by birth through a womb.[81] Paul F. Copp notes that this dhāraṇī is claimed to be useful for enchanting the waters of a river so those who come in contact with the water will be purified of sins and attain rebirth in Sukhāvatī.[82]

The *Qianshou qianyan Guanshiyin Pusa zhibing heyao jing* 千手千眼觀世音菩薩治病合藥經 (T. 1059), also attributed to Bhagavaddharma, states that through the power of Avalokiteśvara one will travel to Sukhāvatī on a bejeweled cloud chariot, be reborn in a lotus, and attain Buddhahood.[83]

The *Qianyanqianbi Guanshiyin Pusaa tuoluoni shenzhoujing* 千眼千臂觀世音菩薩陀羅尼神呪經 (T. 1057A, T. 1057B),[84] another version of the "Great Compassion Dhāraṇī," is attributed to Zhitong 智通 (d.u.-653) and promises deliverance from the three evil realms of rebirth (the three lower realms of animals, hungry ghosts, and the hells) and rebirth in Sukhāvatī,[85] as well as the capacity to be reborn in any of the *buddha-kṣetra* of the ten directions.[86]

The *Qianzhuan tuoluoni Guanshiyin pusa zhou* 千轉陀羅尼觀世音菩薩呪 (T. 1035), attributed to Zhitong, contains the *Sahasrāvartā-dhāraṇī* and states that through the power of this dhāraṇī one will attain rebirth in whatever *buddha-kṣetra* one desires.[87] Toganoo Shōun 栂尾祥雲 notes that this text became popular because it promises rebirth in Sukhāvatī, the fulfillment of wishes, the purification of karma, and so on, and it was circulated widely.[88]

The *Qingjing Guanshiyin Puxian tuoluonijing* 清淨觀世音普賢陀羅尼經 (T. 1038) is also attributed to Zhitong and promises attainment of the capacity to be reborn in the *buddha-kṣetra* of the ten directions, where one may study the Dharma from the buddhas residing there.[89]

The *Guanzizai pusa suixinzhoujing* 觀自在菩薩隨心呪經 (T. 1103), also attributed to Zhitong, contains a somewhat more "systematic" approach to dhāraṇī practice through coordinated mudra and mantra. Some of the practices contained in this text are specifically geared toward the attainment of postmortem rebirth in Sukhāvatī.[90] Upon rebirth in Sukhāvatī, the practitioner will meet Avalokiteśvara face-to-face and learn dhāraṇī practices that will benefit all beings.[91]

The *Shiyimian shenzhou jing* 十一面神呪心經 (T. 1071) contains the *Ekādaśamukha-dhāraṇī* and is attributed to Xuanzang 玄奘 (602–664).[92] This text is dedicated to the eleven-faced Avalokiteśvara Bodhisattva and promises the attainment of rebirth in Sukhāvatī.[93]

The *Bukong juansuo zhouxin jing* 不空羂索神呪心經 (T. 1094), also attributed to Xuanzang, contains the *Amoghapāśa-dhāraṇī* and promises postmortem rebirth in the *buddha-kṣetra* of any buddha in accordance with one's vows.[94]

The *Da tuoluoni mofa zhong yizi xinzhō jing* 大陀羅尼末法中一字心呪經 (T. 956), attributed to *Maṇicinta 寶思惟, describes the "casting off of the body" and the attainment of rebirth in Sukhāvatī.[95]

The *Guanshiyin pusa ruyi moni tuoluoni jing* 觀世音菩薩如意摩尼陀羅尼經 (T. 1083), also attributed to *Maṇicinta, is dedicated to the *cintāmaṇi* 如意珠 (wish-granting jewel)—that is, Avalokiteśvara. This text describes visions of the bodhisattvas in the assemblies in Sukhāvatī and promises that one will go to Sukhāvatī and meet Amitāyus and then meet Avalokiteśvara in her *buddha-kṣetra*, Potala 補陀.[96]

The *Qianshouqianyan Guanshiyin Pusa laotuoluonishen jing* 千手千眼觀世音菩薩姥陀羅尼身經 (T. 1058) is another version of the "Great Compassion Dhāraṇī" attributed to Bodhiruci 菩提流志 (d. 727; sometimes referred to as Bodhiruci II), an Indian monk invited to the Chinese court by the Tang emperor Gaozong in 663. He arrived in 693 and served under Wu Zetian 則天武后 (628–705, r. 684–704). Bodhiruci is especially well known for his translation of the *Ratnakūṭa-sūtra* 大寶積經 (T. 310),[97] the *Adhyardhaśatikā prajñāpāramitā-sūtra* 實相般若波羅蜜經 (T. 240), and his work with Śikṣānanda in the translation of the *Avataṃsaka-sūtra*. His version of the "Great Compassion Dhāraṇī" discusses the ability to travel to the *buddha-kṣetra* of the ten directions and states that when one attains rebirth in Sukhāvatī, one will not be born in female form.[98] The *Ruyilun tuoluoni jing* 如意輪陀羅尼經 (T. 1080), attributed to Bodhiruci, is also dedicated to the "wish-granting jewel" Avalokiteśvara. This text discusses benefits such as postmortem rebirth in a lotus in Sukhāvatī.[99]

The *Bukong juansuo shenbian zhenyan jing* 不空羂索神變真言經 (T. 1092) is also attributed to Bodhiruci and contains the *Amoghapaśa-dhāraṇī*. This text extols visions of the *buddha-kṣetra* and the buddhas teaching there,[100] the promise of life extension and visions of the bodhisattva assemblies gathered around Amitābha,[101] the "casting off of one's womb-born body,"[102] the attainment of the stage of nonretrogression,[103] birth in a lotus in the *buddha-kṣetra* of various buddhas,[104] and the attainment of Buddhahood.[105]

Another *Amoghapaśa-dhāraṇī* text attributed to Bodhiruci, *Bukong juansuo zhouxin jing* 不空羂索呪心經 (T. 1095), extols the efficacy of *buddhānusmṛti* practice and promises not only rebirth in Sukhāvatī in the next life but also the ability to be reborn in whatever *buddha-kṣetra* one may wish.[106]

Pure Land Rebirth and the *Uṣṇīsavijayā-dhāraṇī*

The *Uṣṇīsavijayā-dhāraṇī* texts, which flourished in China in the seventh century alongside the Avalokiteśvara dhāraṇī texts described above, constitute another important subgenre of dhāraṇī literature. Yoritomi suggests that these texts may have been popular in India perhaps a century earlier.[107] Yan notes that the *Uṣṇīsavijayā-dhāraṇī* texts are notable for their emphasis on Sukhāvatī imagery and rebirth.[108]

The *Foding zunsheng tuoluoni jing* 佛頂尊勝陀羅尼經 (T. 967), translated by Buddhapāla 佛陀波利 (late seventh century), a central Asian Madhyamaka scholar who arrived in China in 676, promises that upon the attainment of rebirth in Sukhāvatī one will have the ability to course through the *buddha-kṣetra* of all buddhas and that one will be born in a lotus blossom and not through a womb.[109] Toganoo notes that according to traditional accounts, Buddhapāla was inspired to travel to India to seek out this text at the behest of an immortal he encountered while meditating on Wutaishan 五台山.[110]

The *Foding zuisheng tuoluoni jing* 佛頂最勝陀羅尼經 (T. 969) and the *Zuisheng foding tuoluoni jingchuyezhang zhoujing* 最勝佛頂陀羅尼淨除業障呪經 (T. 970) were translated by the central Indian monk Divākara 地婆訶羅 during the late seventh century. The former mentions rebirth in a lotus blossom in Sukhāvatī;[111] the latter claims that the dhāraṇī gives one the power to attain rebirth in the *buddha-kṣetra* of myriad buddhas and ultimately attain Buddhahood.[112] According to Copp, the *Zuisheng foding tuoluoni jingchuyezhang zhoujing* possesses other more substantial and immediate benefits. For example, if one blesses a stupa with this dhāraṇī, the wind that makes contact with that stupa will be similarly empowered, bestowing myriad benefits to those that it subsequently touches, up to and including rebirth in the heavens or in the *buddha-kṣetra*.[113]

The *Foding zunsheng duoluoni jing* 佛頂尊勝陀羅尼經 (T. 967, 968), translated by Du Xingkai 杜行顗 (late seventh century), active during the reign of the Tang emperor Gaozong 唐高宗 (Yifeng era 儀鳳, 676–679), promises the attainment of rebirth in Sukhāvatī at the end of one's life and the ability to travel to the *buddha-kṣetra* of myriad buddhas.[114]

The *Foding zunsheng tuoluoni jing* 佛頂尊勝陀羅尼經 (T. 971) is attributed to Yijing 義淨 (635–713), the famous Chinese pilgrim who traveled to India in 671 and returned in 695 with many important Buddhist texts. Yijing's journey is recorded in the *Nanhai jigui neifa zhuan* 南海寄歸內法傳 (T. 2125) and the *Datang xiyu qiufa gaoseng zhuan* 大唐西域求法高僧傳 (T. 2066). The *Foding zunsheng tuoluoni jing* was particularly important and discusses rebirth in Sukhāvatī throughout, stating that through this dhāraṇī one may course through the myriad heavens and *buddha-kṣetra* and meet the buddhas there.[115] In particular, it mentions Abhirati 妙喜世界, the *buddha-kṣetra* of Akṣobhya Buddha, and, as in other texts, it describes the shedding of one's mortal form and rebirth in a lotus blossom and not from a womb.[116] The text also discusses Sukhāvatī and the extension of one's life span, a feature of Sukhāvatī devotion that was attractive to Chinese seekers at this time.[117]

The *Yiqie gonde zhuangyanwang jing* 一切功德莊嚴王經 (T. 1374), also attributed to Yijing, promises rebirth in Sukhāvatī; the rapid attainment of enlightenment;[118] the ability to extend one's life span, be reborn in various *buddha-kṣetra,* and see all buddhas;[119] and the ability to course through the *buddha-kṣetra* of the ten directions.[120]

The *Sarvatathāgata-adhiṣṭhānasattva avalokanabuddha-kṣetra-sandarśana-vyūharāja-dhāraṇī-sūtra* 莊嚴王陀羅尼呪經 (T. 1375), also attributed to Yijing, promotes dhāraṇī practice as a means for attaining rebirth in Sukhāvatī.[121]

The *Dhāraṇīsaṃgraha-sūtra*

The *Dhāraṇīsaṃgraha-sūtra,* translated by the central Asian monk Atikūṭa after he arrived in Chang'an around 652, is composed of many smaller texts.[122] This text shares some features found in what scholars refer to as earlier and later tantric literature and thus fits somewhere between the miscellaneous spell and dhāraṇī texts mentioned above and the tantric systems of the Tang dynasty.[123] Orzech notes the appearance of "*abhiṣeka, homa,* mantra, and so on in the creation of a mandala/altar and the investiture of a disciple with royal symbols. In contrast to typical *dhāraṇī* texts, the disciple is enjoined here to utmost secrecy (T. 901:795a2–14)."[124]

Recent scholarship by Koichi Shinohara draws upon the *Dhāraṇīsaṃgraha-sūtra* to explore the relationship between earlier dhāraṇī culture and later tantric "systems," breaking down the division between "miscellaneous" and "pure" esotericism.[125]

The *Dhāraṇīsaṃgraha-sūtra* mentions Amitābha Buddha several times and also contains a lengthy section dealing with rebirth in Sukhāvatī and a variety of esoteric techniques associated with Amitābha.[126] The sutra begins:

> 阿彌陀佛大思惟經說序分第一　如是我聞。一時佛在補陀落伽山中(此云海島也)與大阿羅漢衆一千五百人俱。觀世音菩薩。大勢至菩薩摩訶薩等五千人俱。及諸天龍夜义阿素羅迦魯羅緊那羅摩睺羅伽人非人等。前後圍繞。來詣佛所到佛所已。五體投地頂禮佛足。禮佛足已繞佛三匝。却坐一面爾時觀世音菩薩白佛言。世尊若四部衆。及苾芻苾芻尼優婆塞優婆夷一切衆生。修行善法。得生阿彌陀佛國。并見彼佛云何而得。佛告觀世音菩薩言。若四部衆欲生彼國者。應當受持阿彌陀佛印并陀羅尼。及作壇法供養禮拜。方得往生彼佛國土。若四部衆。以衆華散阿彌陀佛。發願誦呪者。得十種功德。何者爲

十。一者自發善心。二者令他發善心。三者諸天歡喜。四者自身端正。六根具足無有損壞。五者死生變成寶地。六者生生世世生於中國。及貴姓中生。值佛聞法。不生邊地及下姓中。七者成轉輪王王四天下。八者生生世世常得男身。九者得生彌陀佛國七寶華上。結加趺坐成阿毘跋致。十者成阿耨多羅三藐三菩提。坐於七寶師子座上。放大光明。與阿彌陀佛等無有異也。是名十種散華功德。

The Great Contemplation of Amitābha Sutra. Introduction: Chapter One Thus have I heard. At one time the Buddha was in Mt. Potalaka (This is called an ocean island.) together with a multitude of five hundred great arhats, as well the many *devas, nāgas, yakṣas, asuras, garuḍas, kiṃnaras, mahoragas,* humans and non-humans and so on, who encircled the Buddha, and each came to the place where the Buddha was and bowed to the Buddha's feet, touching their heads to the ground, and circumambulated the Buddha three times, then stepped back and sat down.

At that time Avalokiteśvara spoke to the Buddha, saying, "World-honored One, for the fourfold sangha, monks, nuns, laymen, and laywomen, and all sentient beings, cultivating wholesome practices, how may they come to be born in the *buddha-kṣetra* of Amitābha Buddha and see him [face-to-face]?"

The Buddha replied to Avalokiteśvara Bodhisattva, saying, "If those in the fourfold sangha wish to be born in his land, they should uphold the Amitābha mudra together with his dhāraṇī, construct an altar, and worship him. Then they will attain rebirth in Sukhāvatī. If those in the fourfold sangha scatter flowers in offering to Amitābha Buddha, make vows [to him], and chant spells, they will achieve the tenfold virtues.

"What are these? One, they will give rise to a good mind. Two, they will cause others to give rise to a good mind. Three, they will [be aided by] the various gods, including Gaṇeśa. Four, one's body will become upright and beautiful, and the six sense faculties (eye, ear, nose, tongue, body, mind) will be completely eliminated. Five, samsara will be transformed into a jewel land. Six, you will always be born in a central kingdom in a family with a revered name, and you will directly hear the Dharma. You will not be born in a borderland with a low name. Seven, you will become a wheel-turning king, lord over the four continents. Eight, you will always be born in a man's body. Nine, you will attain birth in Sukhāvatī atop a seven-jeweled lotus in the lotus posture in the state of nonretrogression. Ten, you will attain *anuttara samyaksaṃbodhi* (highest, perfect enlightenment). Sitting atop the seven-jeweled lion throne, you will emit a great and brilliant light indistinguishable from Amitābha himself. These are called the tenfold virtues of scattering flowers [in offering to Amitābha].[127]

Throughout the rest of the introduction, Śākyamuni Buddha explains the various virtues that arise from worshipping Amitābha. In the next section, Śākyamuni then lists a number of mudras and dhāraṇī that deliver beings from samsara, purify negative karma, cure physical ailments, and help them attain rebirth in Sukhāvatī and the *buddha-kṣetra* of the ten directions. For example:

> The great heart of Amitābha Buddha mudra 阿彌陀佛大心印 leads to, among other things, rebirth in Sukhāvatī at will, and extinguishes the negative karma of the four grave sins of monks and nuns and the five unnatural sins.[128]
>
> The extinguishing afflictions Amitābha Buddha mudra 阿彌陀佛滅罪印 helps one to purify their karma and past sins through meditation.[129]
>
> The Amitābha seated meditation mudra 阿彌陀坐禪印 helps one recover from illness.[130]
>
> The *uṣṇīṣa* of Amitābha Buddha mudra 阿彌陀佛頂印, when paired with *buddhānusmṛti,* will cure illness.[131]
>
> The Amitābha Buddha *cakra* mudra 阿彌陀佛輪印, employed in conjunction with *buddhānusmṛti,* spells, and the use of a *mālā* 數珠, or rosary, made with beads of gold, silver, copper, or crystal, purifies one of their sins and cures illness.[132]
>
> The Amitābha Buddha Curing Illness Ritual mudra 阿彌陀佛療病法印 will both protect the practitioner from illness and malevolent demonic spirits.[133]

The *Dhāraṇīsaṃgraha-sūtra* explains as well that there are eighty-four thousand dharma gates to Amitābha Buddha, and these dhāraṇīs, spells, and mudras are abbreviated methods that will lead to infinite merits.[134]

In addition to the practices for Amitābha Buddha, the text emphasizes rebirth in the *buddha-kṣetra* of other buddhas and bodhisattvas, including various emanations of Avalokiteśvara, such as the eleven-headed Avalokiteśvara Bodhisattva,[135] as well as Mañjuśrī Bodhisattva,[136] Mahāsthāmaprāpta Bodhisattva,[137] and so on. As above, the practitioner is instructed in the particular techniques and practices associated with each bodhisattva that will lead to this-worldly benefits, rebirth in Sukhāvatī,[138] and rebirth in the *buddha-kṣetra* of the ten directions at will.[139] Through cultivating practices associated with Acalanātha Vidyārāja 不動明王, for example, one may purify all sins, even the five unforgivable sins 五逆,[140] and ultimately attain rebirth in Sukhāvatī.[141]

Throughout the *Dhāraṇīsaṃgraha-sūtra,* as with the dhāraṇī texts, references to rebirth in Sukhāvatī are ubiquitous.[142] Seeking rebirth in Sukhāvatī is found in texts such as this not because a kind of Buddhism called Pure Land Buddhism was combined with another kind of Buddhism called Esoteric Buddhism. Aspiration for rebirth in Sukhāvatī and opportunities to interact with and learn from the buddhas and bodhisattvas of the ten directions is fundamental to Mahayana Buddhism in general. In the *Dhāraṇīsaṃgraha-sūtra,* as in the tantric hermeneutics of Tibetan Buddhism, Mahayana Buddhism is conceived of as divisible into the *parāmitā-yāna* and the mantra teachings. Among the benefits promised by both paths, whether practiced together or separately, rebirth in Sukhāvatī is an important stage along the path.

> 爾時世尊正在大會。說般若波羅蜜。及說是真言法利益方便。能令一切人非人等。聞此陀羅尼者。悉發無上菩提之心。迴向十方諸佛國土。當得阿耨多羅三藐三菩提.
>
> At that time, the World-honored One, in the great assembly, preached teachings such as the Perfection of Wisdom, up to and including the *upāya* and benefits of the mantra-dharma, which is able to cause all humans and nonhumans to hear this dhāraṇī, to attain completely the unsurpassed bodhi mind, and to come and go to all the *buddha-kṣetra* of the ten directions and attain perfect and complete enlightenment.[143]

In addition to the general importance of this text, Buddhists in the Tang and later periods referenced the section on Amitābha and Sukhāvatī in particular. Zhisheng 智昇 (699–740) mentions the Amitābha section of the *Dhāraṇīsaṃgraha-sūtra* in his *Kaiyuan shijiao lu* 開元釋教錄 (T. 2154:599b1–2), a very important Tang catalog of Buddhist texts. He emphasizes the practice of the rosary with mudras, spells, and other incantations for the attainment of rebirth in Sukhāvatī.[144] Yuanzhao 圓照 (n.d.), a disciple of Amoghavajra, also mentions this section and quotes Zhisheng's reference in the *Zhenyuan xinding shijiao mulu* 貞元新定釋教目錄 (T. 2157:929b21–22), compiled around 800 CE. These examples demonstrate that rebirth in Sukhāvatī remained an area of concern for those working to promote the later tantric systems. As will be shown, Amoghavajra's major works, and the many works attributed to him, in fact consistently deal directly with such themes.

Śubhakarasiṃha and the "Mantra-*nāya*"

Śubhakarasiṃha is commonly regarded as the first great Tang ācārya and a pioneering Esoteric Buddhist patriarch. According to the classic hagiography, he was born a prince in central India. Later, during a period of great political unrest, he was forced to take up arms against his brothers in a succession dispute. Though victorious, he abdicated and became a monk. Under the tutelage of a monk named Dharmagupta, he is said to have studied dhāraṇī, yoga, and the three mysteries.[145] He later met Avalokiteśvara Bodhisattva and Mahākāśyapa face-to-face.

Śubhakarasiṃha arrived in Chang'an in 716, whereupon he translated a great number of texts and ritual manuals previously unseen in China. Upon his death he was entombed at Longmen 龍門, and his grave became a popular pilgrimage site.[146] Highly prolific, he is best remembered for his work on the *Mahāvairocana-sūtra,* a text in which Mahāvairocana Tathāgata preaches the Dharma in Akaniṣṭhāḥ Heaven 色究竟天. This sutra presents the "sudden path" by which beings may attain awakening in a single lifetime. It is noteworthy that in the Chinese context the *Mahāvairocana-sūtra* was labeled a *jing* 經, like all other sutras, while in Indian and Tibetan contexts it was labeled as a tantra text. Tantras functioned as a distinct bibliographic category in later Indian and Tibetan Buddhism, but this was not the case in China until much later.

Following the more philosophical and doctrinal orientation of the first chapter of the *Mahāvairocana-sūtra,* the text reads more like a tantra. In other words, it is organized around the coordinated ritual practice of mudra, mantra, and mandalic visualizations. Orzech suggests that it was precisely the systemic organizational structure of this text that let to its greater popularity over more amorphous popular collections such as the *Dhāraṇīsaṃgraha-sūtra.*[147]

Śubhakarasiṃha's most famous disciple was Yixing, the cotranslator of the *Mahāvairocana-sūtra.* Something of a renaissance man, Yixing was an important scholar in his own right and had some proficiency in engineering, astronomy, and mathematics as well as Daoism, Chan, Tiantai, and, under Śubhakarasiṃha, the mantra path. He also wrote the *Commentary on the Mahāvairocana-sūtra,* which is particularly focused on the concept of attaining Buddhahood in one's lifetime and establishes a precedent for the dual cultivation of the *Mahāvairocana* and *Vajraśekhara* cycle, which later flourished in Japan.[148]

The attainment of Buddhahood "in this very body," commonly regarded as the essential goal of Esoteric Buddhism, does not preclude devotional practice or other soteriological goals, such as aspiration for postmortem rebirth in Sukhāvatī or encounters with buddhas in *buddha-kṣetra.* Amitābha Buddha is one of the five central buddhas in the mandalas associated with the *Mahāvairocana* and *Vajraśekhara* systems, and he is mentioned consistently throughout these texts. Yixing's commentary also contains many references to *buddha-kṣetra* and rebirth in Sukhāvatī, a discussion about the bodhisattva's vow to cultivate the adornments of *buddha-kṣetra,*[149] and an often cited passage about Śākyamuni's eternal life span and his cultivation of this world as a *buddha-kṣetra.*[150] Yixing discusses the esoteric *buddhānusmṛti* samādhi and,[151] as in the *Mahāvairocana-sūtra,* he regards the bodhisattva's ability to visit the various *buddha-kṣetra* of the ten directions as one of the many attainments made possible through "this Mahayana secret teaching 此大乘祕教."[152]

Because of Śubhakarasiṃha's importance in the history of Chinese and Japanese Buddhism and his prolific output as an author/translator, numerous texts, apocryphal or otherwise, have been attributed to him. In many of these texts, the practice of the mantra path as an effective means for the achievement of rebirth in Sukhāvatī, or the notion that rebirth in Sukhāvatī is one way to gain access to higher tantric teachings, is promoted. Here is a brief list of some pertinent examples:

- The *Susiddhikara-sūtra* 蘇悉地羯囉經 (T. 893) and a ritual text, the *Suxidijieluo gongyangfa* 蘇悉地羯羅供養法 (T. 894), both describe mantras for purification of the body and the attainment of *buddha-kṣetra.*[153]
- The *Supohutongzhiqingwen jing* 蘇婆呼童子請經 (T. 895) makes numerous references to *buddha-kṣetra.*
- The *Foding zunshengxin podizhuan yezhang chusanjie mimisanshen fogou sanzhong xidi zhenyan yigui* 佛頂尊勝心破地獄轉業障出三界祕密三身佛果三種悉地真言儀軌 (T. 906) contains numerous references to Amitābha, *buddha-kṣetra,* and rebirth in Sukhāvatī, as well as postmortem rebirth, and discusses the attainments of beings in those lands.[154]
- The *Zunshengfoding xiuyu jiafa yigui* 尊勝佛頂脩瑜伽法儀軌 (T. 973) includes mantras for deliverance from unfortunate realms of rebirth, purification of sins, and the attainment of rebirth in *buddha-kṣetra.*[155]
- The *Qijuzhidubufa* 七俱胝獨部法 (T. 1079) describes practices said to result in rebirth in the *buddha-kṣetra* of the four directions.[156]

  The *Cishipusa lüexiuyu'e niansong fa* 慈氏菩薩略修愈誐念誦法 (T. 1141), a text devoted to Maitreya Bodhisattva, contains many references to rebirth in the *buddha-kṣetra* of the ten directions and freedom from unfortunate rebirth.[157]
- The *Dizangpusa yigui* 地藏菩薩儀軌 (T. 1158), dedicated to Kṣitigarbha Bodhisattva 地藏菩薩, commonly regarded as the bodhisattva of the netherworld, presents rituals for purifying the sins of the deceased and attaining rebirth in Sukhāvatī.[158]

Vajrabodhi and the "Vajrayāna"

Following Śubhakarasiṃha, Vajrabodhi, who arrived in southern China in 719, is traditionally regarded as the next great Tang ācārya. Originally from South India, he was born into the Brahmin caste but converted to Buddhism at a young age and subsequently entered Nālandā, one of the greatest universities in the world at the time. Vajrabodhi studied the three mysteries and dhāraṇī, and on hearing of Buddhism's success in China, he boarded a boat to continue his mission there. He traveled to various temples throughout China, building mandala altars and initiating monks through abhiṣekha rituals. After his death the emperor granted him the title Great Tripiṭaka Master and Expounder of the Teachings 大弘教三蔵.[159]

Vajrabodhi is known as the translator of the *Vajraśekhara* cycle of texts, which he purportedly learned from Nāgabodhi, an eight-hundred-year-old disciple of Nāgārjuna.[160] In the *Vajraśekhara* texts, the bodhisattva's ability to attain rebirth in the *buddha-kṣetra* of the ten directions is not so much presented as a major soteriological goal in itself; rather, as with the *Mahāvairocana-sūtra,* these texts assume *buddha-kṣetra* to be a generic dimension of Mahayana Buddhist cosmology and soteriology and focus on the rapid attainment of the prowess of a powerful bodhisattva via tantric practice. In other words, the ability to freely travel throughout the *buddha-kṣetra* of the ten directions is taken for granted, even if that travel takes place within one's own body. Some examples from this cycle of texts follow.

The *Yaoshirulai guanxing yigui fa* 藥師如來觀行儀軌法 (T. 923), a ritual text dedicated to Bhaiṣajyaguru Tathāgata 藥師如來 (hereafter referred to as Medicine Buddha) describes the attainment of rebirth in *buddha-kṣetra.*[161]

The *Jin'gang ding jing yuqie Guanzizaiwang rulai xiuxing fa* 金剛頂經瑜伽觀自在王如來修行法 (T. 932) is a relatively short deity yoga text dedicated to Lokeśvararāja Tathāgata 觀自在王如來, an alternate name for Amitābha associated with the *Vajraśekhara* cycle. Through the practice of various mudras, mantras, and visualizations, one is ultimately instructed to identify with the Buddha and recognize one's own inherent purity. This practice is said to ultimately lead to attainment of the first stage of the bodhisattva path, presumably in Sukhāvatī.

The *Qianshou qianyan Guanshiyin pusa dashen zhouben* 千手千眼觀世音菩薩大身呪本 (T. 1062a) is another text promoting the practice of the *Nīlakaṇṭha*-dhāraṇī. As with other Avalokiteśvara dhāraṇī texts, this particular dhāraṇī has been especially popular among monks and laypeople throughout the history of Chinese Buddhism because deliverance to Sukhāvatī is one of the many benefits it is said to bestow.

The *Qijuzhifomu zhuntidaming tuoluoni jing* 七俱胝佛母准提大明陀羅尼經 (T. 1075) is dedicated to Saptakoṭibuddhamātṛkā (Mother of Seven *Koṭis* of Buddhas), an epithet for Cundī-Avalokiteśvara Bodhisattva 准胝觀音, a popular "transformation body" of the Bodhisattva of Compassion. As with other dhāraṇī texts, this text promotes rebirth in Sukhāvatī.[162]

The *Wuda xukongzangpusa suji dashenyan mimi shijing* 五大虛空藏菩薩速疾大神驗祕密式經 (T. 1149), dedicated to Ākāśagarbha Bodhisattva 虛空藏菩薩, promises the liberation of all sentient beings from the hells and deliverance to Sukhāvatī.[163]

Amoghavajra

Amoghavajra is arguably one of the most significant figures in the historiography of East Asian Esoteric Buddhism. Descended from Indo-Sogdian immigrants to China, he became a monk under Vajrabodhi and studied the *Vajraśekhara* cycle of ritual texts. After Vajrabodhi's death, Amoghavajra purportedly traveled to the Malay peninsula and Sri Lanka, where he received initiation into a tantra lineage. He returned to the Tang capital in 756 and performed abhiṣeka and *homa* for the emperor. Through imperial sponsorship he established a hall dedicated to Mañjuśrī on Mount Wutai. He was revered for having conquered/converted a great snake that lived in the mountains and for his successful prayers for rain on numerous occasions.

During the An Lushan 安祿山 Rebellion (755–763), Amoghavajra was called to the front lines to help defeat the Tibetan armies. According to tradition, he employed the *Renwan huguo bore boluomiduo jing* 仁王護國般若波羅蜜多經 (T. 246; hereafter *Renwang jing*) to dispatch a "spiritual" army to aid in the battle.[164] Amoghavajra's *Renwang jing* elaborates on the *Renwang bore boluomi jing* 仁王般若波羅蜜經 (T. 245) attributed to Kumārajīva 鳩摩羅什 (344–413), with the addition of tantric rituals, mandalas, and more.[165] Scholars often assert that Esoteric Buddhism is markedly militaristic in its imagery and deployment, but it should be noted that state protection and sponsorship have long been important to the monastic sangha since the early days of the Buddhist tradition in China—and in India as well.

According to Yoritomi Motohiro, Amoghavajra's bicultural engagement with Chinese and Indian religion marks a turning point in the history of Chinese Buddhism, and this pluralism may have directly and positively affected his level of access to political power. When compared to Yixing, for example, for whom Esoteric technologies were just another area of specialty, Amoghavajra had studied under Vajrabodhi as a child.[166] Several of the texts he translated or composed, as well as those attributed to him posthumously, deal extensively with rebirth in Sukhāvatī; he is also said to have aided the emperor in the attainment of rebirth.[167]

Amoghavajra's *Wuliangshou rulai guanxing gongyang yigui* 無量壽如來觀行供養儀軌 (T. 930) is arguably one of the most influential Esoteric Pure Land texts in East Asia.[168] The centerpiece of this text is the widely practiced fundamental dhāraṇī of Amitāyus Tathāgata 無量壽如來根本陀羅尼:[169]

Ārya Amitābha nāma dhāraṇī
Namo ratna-trayāya,
Namaḥ āryāmitābhāyā,
Tathāgatāyārhate samyak-saṃbuddhāya, tad yathā,
Oṃ amṛte amṛtodbhave amṛta-saṃbhave amṛta-garbhe,
Amṛta-siddhe amṛta-teje amṛta-vikrānte,
Amṛta-vikrānta-gāmine amṛta-gagana-kīrti-kare,
Amṛta-dundubhi-svare sarvārtha-sādhane,
Sarva-karma-kleśa-kṣayaṃ-kare svāhā.[170]

Chanting this dhāraṇī one thousand times is said to purify all past karma, bestow rebirth in the highest level of Sukhāvatī,[171] and produce visions of Sukhāvatī, Amitāyus Buddha, and assemblies of bodhisattvas. From these honored ones, the practitioner will hear all of the sutras and, at the moment of death, attain rebirth in Sukhāvatī, emerging from a lotus blossom at the rank of a bodhisattva.[172] At the end of life, one will certainly attain rebirth in Sukhāvatī, see the Buddha, hear the Dharma, and quickly attain the highest level of bodhi.[173] As in some of the other texts discussed previously, this dhāraṇī text describes a seven-jeweled chariot that transports one to Sukhāvatī.[174]

The Sanskrit term *amṛta* appears several times in this dhāraṇī and others. In the *Ṛg Veda* this term refers to the elixir of eternal life. The iconography of and texts associated with Amitābha/Amitāyus often describe this buddha as one whose Dharma serves as the ambrosia that grants eternal life. This is also connected to great bliss (*mahāsukha*), which may refer in particular to the ultimate bliss attained through the practices found in the tantras.[175]

The fundamental dhāraṇī of Amitāyus Tathāgata appears in many different texts, and there are numerous variants in Chinese, Japanese, and Tibetan sources.[176] Several versions of this dhāraṇī circulated in China (T. 366, 368, and 1185A, in which it is noticeably shorter), and some of these versions remain in use in Chan and Zen lineages today, as well as in Japanese Shingon and Tendai and other Esoteric lineages as well. This text also contains the heart mantra of Amitāyus 無量壽如來心真言: *Oṃ amṛta teje hara hūṃ* (T. 930:72b7).

The following list presents texts written, translated, or attributed to Amoghavajra that deal in some significant way with rebirth in Sukhāvatī:

- The *Jin'gang ding jing Guanzizaiwang rulai xiuxing fa* 金剛頂經觀自在王如來修行法 (T. 931) is based on the text attributed to Vajrabodhi (T. 932), mentioned above, and assumes knowledge of the dhāraṇī dedicated to Amitābha Buddha.
- The *Jiupin wangsheng amituosanmodiji tuoluonijing* 九品往生阿彌陀三摩地集陀羅尼經 (T. 933) provides a dhāraṇī for rebirth in the nine levels of Sukhāvatī.
- The *Putichang suoshuo yizi dinglun wangjing* 菩提場所說一字頂輪王經 (T. 950) contains mantras and *adhiṣṭhāna* (empowerments) for rebirth in Sukhāvatī.[177]
- The *Uṣṇīṣa-cakravartī-tantra* 一字奇特佛頂 (T. 953) promises rebirth in Sukhāvatī and the opportunity to see Amitāyus Buddha.[178]
- The *Ruyibaozhu zhuanlun mimixianshenchengfo jinglun zhouwangjing* 如意寶珠轉輪祕密現身成佛金輪呪王經 (T. 961) lists various benefits, including rebirth in Sukhāvatī,[179] the casting off of the body, rebirth in the highest level of Sukhāvatī atop a lotus dais, traveling through the ten directions, worship at the feet of Mahāvairocana Tathāgata, and so on.[180]
- The *Baoxidi chengfo tuoluonijing* 寶悉地成佛陀羅尼經 (T. 962) is a dhāraṇī text dedicated to the worship of buddha relics, a practice that may lead one to postmortem rebirth in Sukhāvatī and attainment of dharmakāya,[181] as well as the ability to travel to any and all *buddha-kṣetra* of the ten directions and hear the buddhas preach in accordance with one's vows.[182]
- The **Āryatārā-dhāraṇī-arolika* 阿唎多羅陀羅尼阿嚕力經 (T. 1039) contains numerous references to practices leading to rebirth in Sukhāvatī and to casting off the body to attain rebirth in Sukhāvatī and rapidly attain Buddhahood.[183]
- The *Jin'gang kongbu jihui fangguang guiyi Guanzizai pusa sanshi zuisheng xinmingwangjing* 金剛恐怖集會方廣儀軌觀自在菩薩三世最勝心明王經 (T. 1033) mentions postmortem rebirth in Sukhāvatī.[184]

- The *Guanzizai pusa shuo puxian tuoluonijing* 觀自在菩薩説普賢陀羅尼經 (T. 1037) asserts that through the power of this dhāraṇī one will certainly achieve rebirth in Sukhāvatī at the end of this life.[185]
- The *Guanzizai pusa xinzhenyan yiyin niansong fa* 觀自在菩薩心真言一印念誦法 (T. 1041) describes the bodhisattva's ability to travel to the *buddha-kṣetra* of the ten directions and the rapid attainment of the highest level of bodhi.[186]
- The *Guanzizai pusa dabeizhiyin zhoubian fajie liyi zhongshengxunzhenrufa* 觀自在菩薩大悲智印周遍法界利益衆生薫真如法 (T. 1042) gives instructions whereby the "yoga practitioner" who aspires to postmortem rebirth in Sukhāvatī may attain rebirth in the highest grade of Sukhāvatī.[187]
- The *Jin'gangding yujia qianshou qianyan Guanzizai pusa xiuxing yiguijing* 金剛頂瑜伽千手千眼觀自在菩薩修行儀軌經 (T. 1056) contains numerous references to Amitāyus and Sukhāvatī and says that at the end of one's life the Buddha will appear and guide one to Sukhāvatī, where one will be born in the womb of a lotus as a bodhisattva of the highest grade and then rapidly attain the highest awakening.[188]
- The *Qianshou qianyan Guanshiyin pusa dabeixin tuoluoni* 千手千眼觀世音菩薩大悲心陀羅尼 (T. 1064) is another example of the Great Compassion Dhāraṇī. In this text, vows similar to those given in the *Sukhāvatīvyūha-sūtra* promise that beings who practice this dhāraṇī will not fall into the three evil realms and will attain rebirth in any *buddha-kṣetra* they desire lest Dharmākara Bodhisattva will not attain awakening.[189]
- The *Shiyimian Guanzizai pusa xinmiyan niansong yiguijing* 十一面觀自在菩薩心密言念誦儀軌經 (T. 1069), dedicated to the eleven-headed manifestation of Avalokiteśvara, describes mantras for postmortem rebirth in Sukhāvatī and a visualization practice in which one imagines riding to Sukhāvatī in a seven-jeweled chariot accompanied by Mahāsthāmaprāpta Bodhisattva, Amitāyus Buddha, and Avalokiteśvara Bodhisattva.[190]
- The *Shenheyehelifu daweinuwang lichen dashen yangongyang niansong yigui fapin* 聖賀野紇哩縛大威怒王立成大神驗供養念誦儀軌法品 (T. 1072A) is dedicated to Hayagrīva Avalokiteśvara馬頭觀音, a wrathful "horse-headed" manifestation of this bodhisattva. It promotes taking vows for rebirth in Sukhāvatī and promises salvation from the three evil realms and certain rebirth in Sukhāvatī.[191]
- The *Ekajatā-dhāraṇī* 一髻尊陀羅尼經 (T. 1110) discusses postmortem rebirth in Sukhāvatī.[192]

- The *Mahāpratisarā-vidyārājñī* 普遍光明清淨熾盛如意寶印心無能勝大明王大隨求陀羅尼經 (T. 1153) contains numerous references to Sukhāvatī, *buddhānusmṛti*.[193]
- The *Jin'gangding yujia zuisheng mimi chengfo suiqiujide shenbian jiachi chengjiu tuoluoni yigui* 金剛頂瑜伽最勝祕密成佛隨求即得神變加持成就陀羅尼儀軌 (T. 1155) describes postmortem birth in the highest level of Sukhāvatī via the *buddhānusmṛti* samādhi and the cultivation of the three mysteries and the transformation of hell into a *buddha-kṣetra*,[194] stating that upon attaining birth in the land of tranquility one will be born in a lotus blossom, not from a womb.[195]
- The *Dacheng yujia jin'gangxinghai manshushili qianbiqianbo dajiaowangjing* 大乘瑜伽金剛性海曼殊室利千臂千鉢大教王經 (T. 1177A) includes numerous references to the Pure Land dharma gate and rebirth in Sukhāvatī.[196] The Pure Land gate is listed as one gate among five, as outlined by Śākyamuni Buddha,[197] and is described as step four of five stages of progression through the mandala.
- The *Jiuba yankou egui tuoluoni jing* 救拔燄口餓鬼陀羅尼經 (T. 1313) is a ritual text said to liberate hungry ghosts. Śikṣānanda first translated the text (*Jiumianran egui tuoluoni shenzhoujing* 救面然餓鬼陀羅尼神咒經, T. 1314), but Amoghavajra's version was popularized by later Tiantai ritual specialists.[198]

This list of works suggests that Amoghavajra, and his later interpreters who attributed many of these texts to the famous patriarch, saw rebirth in Sukhāvatī and devotion to Amitābha Buddha as assumed features of the Mahayana path to Buddhahood and the mantra path as possessing superlative techniques for achieving that goal. Drawing on South and central Asian precedents, Amoghavajra produced a wide array of ritual texts that addressed the breadth and diversity of his Mahayana Buddhist audience. From rainmaking to victory on the battlefield, from rebirth in Sukhāvatī to the attainment of Buddhahood in one's lifetime, for a time Esoteric Buddhism emerged as a dominant repertoire among elite Chinese Buddhists.

After Amoghavajra: The Esotericization of Chinese Buddhism

Following Amoghavajra's career and the fall of the Tang, clearly defined and state-subsidized Esoteric Buddhist lineages, so-called High Esotericism, gradually disappeared. Nevertheless, building on the well-established foundation of Mahayana esotericism and esoterica, the various tantric rituals, ritual theory, images, and texts associated with the lineages of the great Tang ācārya came to pervade Chinese Buddhism. To some extent this can be seen as a generalized "esotericization" of Chinese Buddhism.[199] Zanning 贊寧 (920-1001) notes that there was initially a lineage of three people—Vajrabodhi, Amoghavajra, and Huilang 慧朗—but after that other lineages proliferated (and thus, implicitly, degraded), which, despite being widely practiced, produced no other great masters.[200]

From the Song dynasty to the present day, Chan meditation, Amitābha devotion, and apotropaic rituals (what some may label "Esoteric") are the defining characteristics of Buddhist practice in China and beyond.[201] One of the most salient differences between Tibetan Buddhism and Chinese Buddhism is the place of the tantras in the broader culture. While the Tibetan Buddhist cultural sphere continued to draw from later Indian śastra literature and tantras, this Indian commentarial and tantric literature played a less pronounced role in the Sinitic cultural sphere. This does not mean, however, that the tantras simply stopped being imported into China or that their influence completely disappeared.

For example, in 982 Emperor Taizong 太宗 (r. 976–997) of the Northern Song established a new translation bureau that produced many new texts, including tantras.[202] The *Dazhong Xiangfu fabao lu* 大中祥符法寶錄 catalogue of texts (produced in 1013) included Esoteric texts in a new bibliographic category: the "Secret Division of the Mahayana *Piṭaka*" 大乘経藏秘密部.[203] Later Indian Buddhist masters also continued to transmit some of the most famous tantras, including Dharmarakṣa 法護 (d. 1058), who translated the *Hevajra-tantra* 大悲空智金剛大教王儀軌經 (T. 892), and Dānapāla, who produced a new edition of the *Sarvatathāgata-tattvasaṃgrahaṃ nāmamahāyāna-sūtra* 一切如來真實攝大乘現證三昧大教王經 (T. 882) and the *Guhyasamāja-tantra* 一切如來金剛三業最上祕密大教王經 (T. 0885).

Within the context of these later transmissions of Indian tantric texts into China, some of the most prominent examples, unsurprisingly, continued to demonstrate interest in rebirth in Sukhāvatī. The Kashmiri Tianxizai 天息災 (d. 1000) translated the *Mañjuśrīmulakalpa* 大方廣菩薩藏文殊師利根本儀軌經 (T. 1191), a text that circulated widely and was sometimes divided into individual chapters that were independently circulated. This text contains numerous references to Sukhāvatī in particular, as well as such concepts as *buddhānusmṛti* and postmortem rebirth.[204] Tianxizai also translated the *Kāraṇḍavyūha* 大乘莊嚴寶王經 (T. 1050), produced through collaboration with Dānapāla and Fatian. This text suggests that once in Sukhāvatī, one will witness the preaching of the Buddha and quickly attain Buddhahood.[205]

Dharmabhadra of Nālandā translated the *Advayasamatāvijaya-nāma-kalpa-rāja* 瑜伽大教王經 (T. 890), which discusses Amitāyus Buddha and the delights of Sukhāvatī,[206] and the *Aparimitaguṇānuśāṃsā-dhāraṇī* 無量功德陀羅尼經 (T. 934), which states that practicing this dhāraṇī will lead to visions of Amitāyus Buddha.[207]

Dharmadeva 法天, originally from Nālandā, was active in China from 973 to 981. He translated the *Aparimitāyur-mahāyānasūtra* 大乘聖無量壽決定光明王如來陀羅尼經 (T. 937), an alternate version of T. 934 attributed to Dharmabhadra, and the *Samāyoga-tantra* 一切佛攝相應大教王經聖觀自在菩薩念誦儀軌 (T. 1051),[208] and postmortem rebirth in Sukhāvatī.[209]

It is evident that from roots to branches, aspiration for rebirth in Sukhāvatī has been an important soteriological goal throughout the various phases of the development of what scholars have come to define as Chinese Esoteric Buddhism. The degree to which dhāraṇī and spell texts are included under this rubric and the degree to which Esoteric Buddhism is regarded as a distinct form of Buddhism in the Chinese context continue to be debated by scholars in the field. Premodern East Asian scholiasts and ritual masters at times strategically conflated the more amorphous dhāraṇī-*piṭaka* and the tantras under the label "secret *piṭaka*." In this space, Mahayana esotericism, esoterica, and the tantra lineage discourse converged. By demonstrating that *buddha-kṣetra* and aspiration for rebirth in Sukhāvatī is well represented throughout the evolution of the secret *piṭaka*, I propose a perspective that reflects the diversity and complexity of this corner of the premodern East Asian environment.

Notes

Chapter 2: Sukhāvatī in the Secret *Piṭaka*

1 Yoshihiko Amino, *Rethinking Japanese History* (Ann Arbor: Center for Japanese Studies, University of Michigan, 2012), p. xxiii.

2 Charles D. Orzech et al., "Introduction: Esoteric Buddhism and the Tantras in East Asia: Some Methodological Considerations," in Orzech, Sørensen, and Payne, *Esoteric Buddhism and the Tantras in East Asia*, pp. 3–6.

3 Henrik H. Sørensen, "On Esoteric Buddhism in China: A Working Definition," in Orzech, Sørensen, and Payne, *Esoteric Buddhism and the Tantras in East Asia*, pp. 156, 157, 166–172.

4 Ibid., pp. 155–175.

5 Ronald M. Davidson, *Indian Esoteric Buddhism: A Social History of the Tantric Movement* (New York: Columbia University Press, 2002).

6 McBride, "Is there Really 'Esoteric' Buddhism?," p. 330n4.

7 Orzech, "Great Teaching of Yoga," pp. 47–52.

8 Abé, *Weaving of Mantra*, pp. 199–200.

9 *Vajraśekhara-sūtra* is a common abbreviation, or "back translation," of the abbreviated Japanese title *Kongōchōkyō* 金剛頂経 for the *Sarva-tathāgata-tattva-saṃgrahaṃ-nāma-mahāyāna-sūtra*, an abbreviated form of which was translated into Chinese by Vajrabodhi as the *Jingangding yujia zhong luechu niansong jing* 金剛頂瑜伽中略出念誦經 (T. 866) and by Amoghavajra, his student, as the *Jingangding yiqierulai zhenshishe dacheng xianzheng dajiaowangjing* 金剛頂一切如來真實攝大乘現證大教王經 (T. 865). A longer, more "complete" version, the *Yiqierulai zhenshishe dasheng xianzheng sanmei dajiaowang jing* 一切如來真實攝大乘現證三昧大教王經, is attributed to Dānapāla 施護 (T. 822). The *Vajraśekhara* cycle eventually surpassed the *Mahāvairocana-sūtra* in popularity and exerted a profound influence on Japanese ritual practice.

10 Orzech, "'Great Teaching of Yoga,'" p. 33.

11 Geoffrey C. Goble, *Chinese Esoteric Buddhism: Amoghavajra, the Ruling Elite, and the Emergence of a Tradition* (New York: Columbia University Press, 2019).

12 On this issue, see Sharf, *Coming to Terms with Chinese Buddhism*, pp. 266–267, 339n16, citing Abé, *Weaving of Mantra*, pp. 152–154, 177, who in turn cites Misaki Ryōshū 三﨑良周, "Nara jidai no mikkyō ni okeru shomondai" 奈良時代の密教における諸問題, *Nanto bukkyō* 南都仏教 22 (1968): 62–63. See also Misaki, "Junmitsu to zōmitsu ni tsuite" 純密と雑密について, *Indogaku bukkyōgaku kenkyū* 印度學佛教學研究 15 (1967): 535–540.

13 Tomabechi Seiichi 苫米地 誠一, "Nara jidai no mikkyō kyōten" 奈良時代の密教経典, in *Shoki mikkyō: Shisō, shinkō, bunka* 初期密教：思想・信仰・文化, ed. Takahashi Hisao 高橋尚夫 et al. (Tokyo: Shunjusha, 2013), pp. 293–296.

14 Sørensen, "On Esoteric Buddhism in China," p. 175.

15 Ōtsuka Nobuo 大塚伸夫, "Shoki mikkyō no zentaizō: Shoki mikkyō no hōga kara tenkai, kakuritsu he" 初期密教経典の全体像：初期密教の萌芽から展開・確立へ, in Takahashi Hisao, *Shoki mikkyō*, 5–21; Yoritomi Motohiro, "Chūgoku mikkyō no nagare 中国密教の流れ," in *Chūgoku mikkyō* 中国密教, ed. Yoritomi Motohiro 頼富本宏 and Tachikawa Musashi 立川武蔵 (1999; repr., Tokyo: Shunjusha, 2005), p. 23.

16 See Wedemeyer, "Tropes, Typologies, and Turnarounds."

17 The Ōtsuka article cited in this section is a summary of his massive tome, *Indo shoki mikkyō seiritsu katei no kenkyū* インド初期密教成立過程の研究 (Tokyo: Shunjusha, 2013).

18 Jinhua Chen, "The Formation of Early Esoteric Buddhism in Japan: A Study of the Three Japanese Esoteric Apocrypha" (PhD diss., McMaster University, 1997), p. 8.

19 Ōtsuka, "Shoki mikkyō no zentaizō," pp. 6–11

20 Ibid., p. 8.

21 Ibid., pp. 9–10.

22 Ibid., pp. 11–13.

23 Ibid., pp. 13–20.

24 Yoritomi, "Chūgoku mikkyo no nagare," p. 18.

25 Ibid., pp. 19–21; Yoritomi lists all of the major *henge Kannon* texts, most of which I will examine later.

26 Charles D. Orzech, "Seeing Chenyen Buddhism: Traditional Scholarship and the Vajrayāna in China," *History of Religions* 29 (1989): 101–109.

27 Yoritomi here uses the term "Lamaism" ラマ教 (Rama kyō), which is still commonly used among older Japanese scholars, though younger scholars, especially those aware of recent Western scholarship, have come to regard it as impolite (or worse, derogatory). For an examination of the highly problematic history of the label "Lamaism," see Donald S. Lopez Jr., "'Lamaism' and the Disappearance of Tibet," *Comparative Studies in Society and History* 38, no. 1 (1996): 3–25.

28 Paul Harrison, *The Samādhi of Direct Encounter with the Buddhas of the Present: An Annotated English Translation of the Tibetan Version of the Pratyutpanna-Buddha-Saṃmukhāvasthita-Samādhi-Sūtra with Several Appendices Relating to the History of the Text* (Tokyo: International Institute for Buddhist Studies, 1990); Paul Harrison, trans., *The Pratyutpanna Samādhi Sutra* (Berkeley, CA: Numata Center for Buddhist Translation and Research, 1998); Toganoo Shōun 栂尾祥雲, *Himitsu bukkyō shi* 秘密佛教史 (Kōyasan: Kōyasan Daigaku shuppanbu, 1933), p. 81. For further discussions of the relevance of this text to both Tantric and Pure Land Buddhism, see Sharf, *Coming to Terms with Chinese Buddhism*, p. 315; Lopez, *Elaborations on Emptiness*, p. 129n27, citing Paul Harrison, "Buddhānusmṛti in the Pratyutpanna-buddha-saṃmukhāvastita-samādhi-sūtra," *Journal of Indian Philosophy* 6 (1978): 35–57, and Janet Gyatso, "Commemoration and Identification in Buddhānusmṛti," in *In the Mirror of Memory: Reflections on Mindfulness and Remembrance in Indian and Tibetan Buddhism*, ed. Janet Gyatso (Albany: State University of New York Press, 1992), pp. 215–238.

29 一切諸刹心不著無所適念。出於諸佛刹。無所復罣礙。悉入諸陀憐尼門。: "They appear in all buddha fields without hindrance; they enter the doors of the holding spells ('dhāraṇī gate')," T. 418:903c21–22; see Harrison, *Pratyutpanna Samādhi Sutra*, p. 11.

30 Harrison, "Buddhānusmṛti in the Pratyutpanna-buddha-saṃmukhāvasthita-samādhi-sūtra," pp. 35–57.

31 Warder, *Indian Buddhism,* p. 342.

32 Ibid., p. 345.

33 Ibid., pp. 147, 346; Williams, *Mahāyāna Buddhism,* p. 24.

34 菩薩於是間國土聞阿彌陀佛。數數念。用是念故。見阿彌陀佛。見佛已從問。當持何等法生阿彌陀佛國。爾時　画像阿彌陀佛。語是菩薩言。欲來生我國者。常念我數數。常當守念。莫有休息。如是得來生我國。佛言。是菩薩用是念佛故。當得生阿彌陀佛國。(T. 418:905b9–14).

35 T. 418:905a15–27; Harrison, *Pratyutpanna Samādhi Sutra,* p. 18.

36 Halkias, *Luminous Bliss,* p. 11.

37 Yoritomi, "Chūgoku mikkyō no nagare," p. 17.

38 Paul F. Copp, "Dhāraṇī Scriptures," in Orzech, Sørensen, and Payne, *Esoteric Buddhism and the Tantras in East Asia,* p. 178; Fujita, "Pure Land Buddhism in India," p. 36. In addition to T. 1011, see also T. 1009, pp. 1012–1018.

39 Yan Yaozhong 严耀中, *Hanzhuan Mijiao* 汉传密教 (Shanghai: Xuelin chubanshe, 2006), pp. 6, 116–117.

40 Erik Zürcher, *The Buddhist Conquest of China: The Spread and Adaptation of Buddhism in Early Medieval China* (1959; repr., Leiden: Brill, 2007), p. 50.

41 Paul F. Copp, "Voice, Dust, Shadow, Stone: The Makings of Spells in Medieval Chinese Buddhism" (PhD diss., Princeton University, 2005), p. 242.

42 McBride, "Is There Really 'Esoteric' Buddhism?," p. 337.

43 Sharf, *Coming to Terms with Chinese Buddhism,* pp. 263–264n6, 337–338.

44 T. 1161:662b1.

45 Douglas Osto, "Proto-tantric Elements in the Gaṇḍavyūha-sūtra*," *Journal of Religious History* 33, no. 2 (2009): 165–177.

46 Sharf, *Coming to Terms with Chinese Buddhism,* pp. 263–264n6, 337–338. This text was translated into English by Nobuyoshi Yamabe, "The Sutra on the Ocean-Like Samadhi of the Visualization of the Buddha: The Interfusion of the Chinese and Indian Cultures in Central Asia as Reflected in a Fifth Century Apocryphal Sūtra" (PhD diss., Yale University, 1999).

47 Yi-liang Chou, "Tantrism in China," *Harvard Journal of Asiatic Studies* 8 (1945): 243.

48 Toganoo, *Himitsu bukkyō shi,* p. 82, notes the importance of this *kanjō* text in the development of Chinese Vajrayāna.

49 T. 1331:507c4–13.

50 T. 1331:528c24–532b3.

51 Zürcher, *Buddhist Conquest of China,* pp. 128–129, 194–195.

52 Ibid., pp. 204–239.

53 Yan, *Hanzhuan Mijiao,* p. 118.

54 Ibid., p. 119; T. 368:352a12–13.

55 Toganoo, *Himitsu bukkyō shi,* pp. 85–86.

56 See the full discussion in Tanaka, *Dawn of Chinese Pure Land Buddhist Doctrine,* pp. 17–19; Stanley Weinstein, *Buddhism under the Tang* (Cambridge: Cambridge University Press, 1987), pp. 69–71; Roger J. Corless, "T'an-luan: Taoist Sage and Buddhist Bodhisattva," in *Buddhist and Taoist Practice in Medieval Chinese Society,* ed. David W. Chappell (Honolulu: University of Hawai'i Press, 1987), pp. 36–48; Roger J. Corless, "T'an-luan: The First Systematizer of Pure Land Buddhism," in *The Pure Land Tradition: History and Development,* ed. James Foard, Michael Solomon, and Richard K. Payne (Berkeley: University of California Press, 1996), pp. 107–137.

57 Tanaka, *Dawn of Chinese Pure Land Buddhist Doctrine,* p. 18, citing T. 2060:470–435.

58 Ibid., pp. 115–197.

59 Ibid., p. 56.

60 即得往生結明修益。上來明因。第二因成往生之中此人精進彌陀如來與觀音等彼來迎此。行者見已歡喜已下此往生彼。第三生彼得益之中事別有三。一生彼國見佛聞法得無生忍。二遍事諸佛從之受之受記。三還本國得陀羅尼總持之門。(T. 1749:184c29–185a5).

61 McBride, "Is There Really 'Esoteric Buddhism'?," p. 339; McBride examines the work of Jingying Huiyuan (523–592), Daoshi 道世 (ca. 596–683), and Amoghavajra (705–774) and how they understood dhāraṇī to see if they present dhāraṇī as belonging to a distinct bibliographic category—i.e., something that could be identified as tantric—and concludes that they did not. I am thus building upon observations made by McBride and others that dhāraṇī were ubiquitous in East Asian Mahayana Buddhism and are not tantric in orientation. See also McBride, "Dhāraṇī and Spells in Medieval Sinitic Buddhism," *Journal of the International Association of Buddhist Studies* 28 (2005): 85–86.

62 Weinstein, *Buddhism under the Tang,* pp. 70–72.

63 Michael Conway, "A Transformative Expression: The Role of the Name of Amituo Buddha in Daochuo's Soteriology" (paper presented at the 16th Biennial Conference of the International Association of Shin Buddhist Studies, University of British Columbia, Vancouver, May 31–June 2, 2013).

64 T. 1958:6c16–18.

65 Michael Conway, personal communication to author, June 6, 2014.

66 Charles B. Jones, *Chinese Pure Land Buddhism: Understanding a Tradition of Practice* (Honolulu: University of Hawai'i Press, 2019), pp. 20–27.

67 又言三昧者亦是西國語。此翻名爲定。由前三業無間。心至所感。即佛境現前。正境現時。即身心内悦。故名爲樂。亦名立定見諸佛也。 (T. 1981:448b21–23).

68 T. 1753:274a18–19.

69 T. 1981:452a24.

70 See Leon Hurvitz, *Chih-I* 智顗 *(538–597): An Introduction to the Life and Ideas of a Chinese Buddhist Monk* (Bruxelles: l'Institut Belge des Hautes Études Chinoises, 1962 (cited in McBride, "Is There Really 'Esoteric Buddhism'?," pp. 340–341n33).

71 McBride, "Is There Really 'Esoteric Buddhism'?," p. 342.

72 T. 1911:25c23–25; T. 1911:128c26–29; for an English-language translation of the *Mohezhiguan,* see Paul Swanson, Clear Serenity, Quiet Insight: T'ien-t'ai Chih-i's Mo-ho chih-kuan (Honolulu: University of Hawai'i Press, 2018).

73 Sakuma Ruriko 佐久間留理子, "Henge Kannon kyōten" 変化観音経典, in Takahashi Hisao, *Shoki mikkyō,* pp. 77–89; Ōtsuka Nobuo 大塚伸夫, "Fukūkensaku jinpen shingon kyō no jumon: Tayōna jumonkeitai ga mirareru kyōten" 不空羂索神変真言経の呪文: 多様な呪文形態が見られる経典, in Takahashi Hisao, *Shoki mikkyō,* pp. 121–133.

74 Yoritomi, "Chūgoku mikkyō no nagare," pp. 19–22. Yoritomi also includes a list of the major texts in this genre on pp. 19–21.

75 Yan, *Hanzhuan Mijiao,* p. 130.

76 T. 1043:34b11–c21.

77 T. 1093:399a13–400b9.

78 Yan, *Hanzhuan Mijiao,* p. 119.

79 T. 1340:713a3–714c9.

80 命終之後生無量壽國 (T. 1070:149a17–150a7).

81 得轉生他方淨土蓮華化生不受胎身濕卵之身 (T. 1060:108c27–110a1).

82 Copp, "Voice, Dust, Shadow, Stone," p. 223; T. 1060:109a.

83 無邊樂乘寶雲車速令往生安樂世界蓮華化生成佛 (T. 1059:105b18–23).

84 Toganoo, *Himitsu bukkyō shi,* p. 84, notes that this text promises a variety of benefits that came to characterize not only Chinese Esoteric Buddhist literature but also Chinese Buddhist literature more generally, such as the sudden attainment of Buddhahood 速得成仏, avoiding disaster and acquiring good fortune 除災招福, extinguishing sins、滅罪, and so on.

85 永離三塗即得往生阿彌陀佛國如來 (T. 1057A:88a6–11; T. 1057B:94c1–6).

86 往生十方淨土 (T. 1057A:85b19–25; T. 1057B:92a1–5).

87 欲生諸佛淨土 (T. 1035:18a1–28).

88 Toganoo, *Himitsu bukkyō shi,* p. 86.

89 往生十方淨土見一切諸佛聞說正法 (T. 1038:22b8–27).

90 誦根本真言作此印時爲彼一切諸衆生等臨命終時作此法印一心誦真言隨欲樂生何佛國土隨意往生 (T. 1103:466a19–22); Toganoo, *Himitsu bukkyō shi,* p. 84, also notes that this text includes the contemplation of a particular object of devotion, *honzonkan* 本尊観, as well as a different form of *bija* contemplation, *jirinkan* 字輪観 and *shujikan* 種字観.

91 命終生無量壽國面見觀世音菩薩 (T. 1103:461b9–16); 如是我聞一時薄伽梵住極樂世界爾時觀世音菩薩摩訶薩往詣佛所白佛言世尊我有隨心自在心王陀羅尼能爲未來一切衆生作大利益 (T. 1103:463b6–23).

92 Xuanzang, one of the most famous figures in Chinese Buddhist history, is renowned as a translator and as the systematizer of Faxiang 法相, a Chinese Yogācāra system. He traveled to India in defiance of the Chinese emperor to seek out new Buddhist texts, and his journey was recorded in the *Da Tang xiyu ji* 大唐西域記 (T. 2087).

93 得生極樂世界 (T. 1071:152b14–c22).

94 捨命已隨願往生諸佛淨國 (T. 1094:403b5–c3).

95 捨此身得生西方極樂世界 (T. 956:317a22–320a10).

96 見西方無量壽佛極樂世界及菩薩會補特勒伽山中觀世音菩薩宮殿. 其身清淨貴人供養衆人樂見罪障蓋纏無不清淨所生之處得宿命智蓮華化生一切妙具皆自寶思惟譯 (T. 1083:200b29–201a5).

97 This text was partially translated into English. C. Chang, *A Treasury of Mahāyāna Sūtras: Selections from the Mahāratnakūta Sūtra* (University Park: Pennsylvania State University Press, 1983).

98 T. 1058:98c7–13; 不受女身隨得往生阿彌陀佛國 (T. 1058:102a1–7).

99 命終當得往生西方極樂剎土蓮花化生 (T. 1080:190c24–25, 193b17–194a13).

100 T. 1092:390c4–391c28.

101 壽命長遠見於淨土一切諸佛菩薩摩訶薩衆阿彌陀佛前 (T. 1092:264a23–265a29).

102 Copp, "Voice, Shadow, Dust, Stone," p. 66, citing T. 970:361a.

103 往西方淨土蓮華受生住不退地 (T. 1092:393a22–c27).

104 臨命終時願生佛剎隨願往生諸佛淨剎蓮華化生 (T. 1092:228b23–c28).

105 胎身捨此生已直往西方極樂國土住受上品蓮花化生 . . . 乃至阿耨多羅三藐三菩提 (T. 1092:253a28–254c12).

106 命終已隨願往生諸佛淨土 (T. 1095:406a24–407b23).

107 Yoritomi, "Chūgoku mikkyō no nagare," p. 21.

108 Yan, *Hanzhuan Mijiao,* p. 120.

109 得往生種種微妙諸佛剎土 (T. 967:351c22–352a11); 得往生寂靜世界從此身已後更不受胞胎之身所生之處蓮華 (T. 967:351c11–15).

110 Toganoo, *Himitsu Bukkyōshi*, p. 86.

111 壽命往極樂國蓮華化生 (T. 969:356c9–357a10).

112 終時念此陀羅尼者即得往生諸佛國土 (T. 970:359a12–b5); 諸佛淨土乃至成就無上菩提 (T. 970:360a8–12).

113 Copp, "Voice, Shadow, Dust, Stone," p. 214, citing T. 970:360b5–7.

114 命終之後生極樂國若常念持此陀羅尼命終之後生諸淨土從一佛國至一佛國一切佛剎 (T. 968:354b19–c17).

115 諸佛淨土及諸天宮一切菩薩甚深行願隨意遊入悉無障礙 (T. 971:362a29–b26).

116 得解脫即得往生妙喜世界盡此身已後更不受胞胎之身所在之處蓮花化生 (T. 971:363b29–c14).

117 世間殊勝供養捨身往生極樂世界若常誦念復增壽命受諸快樂捨此身已即得往生種種微妙諸佛剎土常與諸佛俱會一處一切如來常爲演說微妙之法一切諸佛授菩提 (T. 971:363c15–c26).

118 安樂世界速趣菩提 (T. 1374:891b27–c14).

119 見諸如來樂生淨土. . . . 無病延壽 (T. 1374:892b8–c8).

120 無量十方淨土極樂世界 (T. 1374:893b13–21).

121 T. 1375:895a11–c18.

122 Chou, "Tantrism in China," p. 244.

123 Orzech, "Esoteric Buddhism in the Tang," pp. 268–269.

124 Ibid., p. 269.

125 Shinohara, *Spells, Images, and Mandalas.*

126 T. 901:800a2–803b23; see also T. 901:790a17, 797c18, 812b12, 824a18–25, 857b11–14.

127 T. 901:800a3–26.

128 隨意往生阿彌陀佛國. . . . 滅恒沙四重五逆之罪 (T. 901:801b1–10).

129 T. 901:801b23–c6.

130 T. 901:801b14–22.

131 T. 901:802b4–11.

132 T. 901:802b12–c13, T. 901:802c20–803b7.

133 T. 901:802c14–19.

134 T. 901:803b7–10.

135 T. 901:801c18–23.

136 T. 901:801c12–17.

137 T. 901:801c24–802b1.

138 命終之後生阿彌陀佛國 (T. 901:802a29).

139 十方淨土隨意往生 (T. 901:805a10–11, 806b9–10, 811c06).

140 The five unforgivable sins are to kill an arhat, to kill one's mother or father, to injure a buddha, and to cause a schism in the Buddhist community.

141 T. 901:812a22–26.

142 T. 901:813a12, 814a6, 823a6–b13, c16–17, 826b24–27, 828a2–5.

143 T. 901:808c3–6.

144 T. 2154:599b1–2.

145 Chou, "Tantrism in China," p. 256n27–28. The term "yoga" here means uniting the mind with the object of devotion. See MD, 2201a.

146 Chou, "Tantrism in China," pp. 250–272; T. 2061:714b1–716a17.

147 Orzech, "Esoteric Buddhism in the Tang," p. 276.

148 Yoritomi, "Chūgoku mikkyō no nagare," pp. 30–31.

149 T. 1796:579a7–593a25.

150 得此心時即知釋迦牟尼淨土不毀見佛壽量長遠本地之身與上行等 (T. 1796:593b6–605b23).

151 T. 1796:688a23–690b12.

152 T. 1796:627b10–628a26.

153 淨身故先取淨土 (T. 894:706b20–21).

154 定命終必隨願往生十方淨土 (T. 906:913c18–914b11).

155 T. 973:374a2–4.

156 不轉肉身 . . . 往四方淨土 (T. 1079:187c17–188a1).

157 T. 1141:592c21–23; T. 1141:594c29–595a02.

158 T. 1158:652b12–c2.

159 Chou, "Tantrism in China," pp. 273–284; T. 2061:711b6–712a22.

160 Chou, "Tantrism in China," p. 281.

161 T. 923:26a2–4, 27b19–c8, 28a25–c25.

162 T. 1075:174c7–12, 175a9–b10.

163 一切衆生地獄苦極樂往生 (T. 1149:607c22–608b28).

164 Chou notes that though this version of the story is often repeated it has been called into question by Matsumoto Bunzaburō 松本文三郎, "Tōbatsu bishamon kō" 兜跋毘沙門攷, *Tōhō gakuhō* 東方学報 10 (1939): 12–21. See Chou, "Tantrism in China," p. 305n103, for a summary of Matsumoto's argument.

165 Charles D. Orzech, *Politics and Transcendent Wisdom: The Scripture for Humane Kings in the Creation of Chinese Buddhism* (University Park: Pennsylvania State University Press, 2008).

166 Yoritomi, "Chūgoku mikkyō no nagare," pp. 30–32.

167 Yan, *Hanzhuan Mijiao*, p. 121.

168 This text was recently translated in Thomas Eijō Dreitlein, "Amoghavajra's Amitāyus Ritual Manual," in *Pure Lands in Asian Texts and Contexts,* ed. Georgios Halkias and Richard K. Payne (Honolulu: University of Hawaiʻi Press, 2019), pp. 223–268.

169 T. 930:71b1–18. Ōmori Gijō 大森義成, *Jisshu Shingonshū no mikkyō to shugyō* 実修真言宗の密教と修行 (Tokyo: Gakken, 2010), pp. 113–114, notes that the Amitāyus dhāraṇī was important for the development of the training regime in the Shingon, Tendai, and other traditions. Drawing on the *Dhāraṇīsaṃgraha-sūtra,* Ōmori references a section that discusses the dhāraṇī's power to purify evil karma and bring about rebirth in the highest levels of the Pure Land. Ōmori's text is intended for a general audience, as a guide for Shingon lay practitioners, so it serves as a good indication of the level of general interest in Pure Land thought and practice within an orthodox Shingon context. Indeed, while contemporary Shingon devotion is not widely known for aspiration to rebirth in Sukhāvatī or the practice of the *nenbutsu,* these elements remain important dimensions of the tradition today.

170 Sasaki Daiju 佐々木大樹, "San darani" 三陀羅尼, in Takahashi Hisao, *Shoki mikkyō,* p. 173.

171 Sasaki, "San darani," p. 175; 終決定得生極樂世界 (T. 930:72b12–14).

172 於定中見極樂世界無量壽如來在大菩薩衆會聞說無量契經臨命終時心不散亂三昧現前刹那迅速則生彼土蓮花化生證菩薩位 (T. 930:69b–12); 生極樂世界上品上生證菩薩位 (T. 930:71b19–28).

173 得生極樂世界見佛聞法速證無上菩提 (T. 930:72a1–12).

174 七寶莊嚴車輅往彼極樂世界 (T. 930:69b17–20).

175 Sasaki, "San darani," p. 175.

176 Sasaki, "San darani," pp. 174–175, notes that this dhāraṇī is found in various forms in a number of texts. He lists ten source texts, seven in Chinese and three in Tibetan. For the Chinese texts, I have identified the specific lines where the dhāraṇī appears:

(1) T. 366:348b02–06; (2) T. 368:351c08–12; (3) T. 901:801a17a–24; (4) T. 930:70b29–c05; (5) T. 934:80b08–16; (6) T. 978:408c02–408c06; (7) T. 1185A:792a24–27; (8) Deruge 版西藏大藏経, 東北目録, no. 595, Pha 237b4–242a6, cf. 東北目録, no. 594 and no. 596; (9) Deruge 版西藏大藏経, 東北目録, no. 677, Ba 222b1–6, cf. 東北目録, no. 864; (10) Deruge 版西藏大藏経, 東北目録, no. 679, Ba 223a1–5, cf. 東北目録, no. 851.

177 真言加持於淨土 (T. 950:201b5–18).

178 往極樂世界見無量壽如來 (T. 953:305a18–c2).

179 得往生無量壽佛極樂國土 (T. 961:333c14–334a7).

180 捨此身已往生西方安樂國土上品蓮臺證得無生不空王三摩地遊歷十方金剛界會禮拜承仕大日如來 (T. 961:334a9–18).

181 捨生死發往生意當得往生速證法身之位 (T. 962:335b18–336b2).

182 更隨志願亦得往生十方淨土見佛聞法 (T. 962:336c24–337a19).

183 T. 1039:23c19–30b17.

184 命終生極樂世界 (T. 1033:10b28–c10).

185 此命終當生淨妙佛刹 (T. 1037:21a6–17).

186 往十方淨土歴事諸佛速成無上菩提 (T. 1041:33a8–12).

187 修瑜伽人欲生西方極樂世界利益衆生 (T. 1042:33a27–33b10); 命終之後當得極樂上品之生 (T. 1042:34a23–26).

188 臨命終時本尊現前將往極樂世界蓮華胎中上品上生證菩薩位受無上菩提記 (T. 1056:82a1–23); see also T. 1056:74c7–8 for a discussion of Amitābha's *uṣṇīṣa.*

189 欲生何等佛土隨願皆得往生復白佛言世尊若諸衆生誦持大悲神呪墮三惡道者我誓不成正覺誦持大悲神呪者若不生諸佛國者我誓不成正覺 (T. 1064:115c23–116b12).

190 命終四者從此世界得生極樂國土 (T. 1069:140a1–b27); 七寶車輅至於極樂世界想請無量壽如來昇七寶車中央無量壽如來坐左大勢至右邊觀自在 (T. 1069:144c6–12).

191 不墮三惡道決定往生諸佛國土 (T. 1072A:169b14–c7).

192 命終之後生無量壽國 (T. 1110:484c11–485a21).

193 善趣欲生極樂國 (T. 1153:625b1–626a14).

194 修三密門證念佛三昧得生淨土 . . . 祕密法 (T. 1155:644b25–c29); 地獄變成淨土 (T. 1155:647b9–648a18).

195 得往生寂淨世界從此身已後更不受胞胎之身所生之處蓮華化生 (T. 1155:649a13–b9).

196 DZD, p. 331, mentions fasc. 7 and 9.

197 一者無生門。二者無動門。三者平等門。四者淨土門。五者解脱門 (T. 1177A:724c24–25); 四者牟尼世尊説入左字觀本淨妙行義。是觀自在王如來説。爲往昔千百億降伏瞋根。無量壽無忍自在佛説。是佛成道時。此佛因地作菩薩時。如來與説此左字觀。修入妙觀理趣淨土門 (T. 1177A:726a7–11); 何次第得入淨土門一者入左字觀本淨妙行義觀自在王如來説妙觀理趣淨土門就此門中説有二品一者先演不思議法界聖道如來真如法藏自在聖智 (T. 1177A:757a7–13). Also consult T. 1177A:728b4–753a18.

198 Hun Y. Lye, "Song Tiantai Ghost-Feeding Rituals," in Orzech, Sørensen, and Payne, *Esoteric Buddhism and the Tantras in East Asia,* pp. 521–524; Orzech, "Seeing Chen-yen Buddhism," pp. 101–109, describes the preta rituals found in T. 1319 and T. 1320, noting in particular the rituals' efficacy in delivering hungry ghosts to the heavens and/or Pure Lands.

199 Orzech, "Esoteric Buddhism under the Song: An Overview," in Orzech, Sørensen, and Payne, *Esoteric Buddhism and the Tantras in East Asia,*

pp. 427–430; George A. Keyworth, "The Esotericization of Chinese Buddhist Practice," in Orzech, Sørensen, and Payne, *Esoteric Buddhism and the Tantras in East Asia,* pp. 516–519.

200 Orzech, "Esoteric Buddhism under the Song," pp. 421–424.

201 Yan, *Hanzhuan Mijiao,* pp. 121–123.

202 Orzech, "Esoteric Buddhism under the Song," p. 426. See also Yoritomi, "Chūgoku mikkyō no nagare," p. 34.

203 Orzech, "Esoteric Buddhism under the Song," p. 426, citing ZDJ 73:420; Zhao Anren 趙安仁 (958–1018), comp., *Zhonghua da zang jing* 中華大藏經 (ZDJ 73:414–523).

204 *Dafangguang pusazangjing zhong wenshushiligenben yizi tuoluonijing* 大方廣菩薩藏經中文殊師利根本一字陀羅尼經 (T. 1181), corresponds to chapter 9 (DZD, 332); *Manshushilipusa zhouzangzhong yizi zhouwangjing* 曼殊師利菩薩咒藏中一字咒王經 (T. 1182) is an alternate version of T. 1181 (DZD, 332); *Dacheng fangguang manshushilipusa huayan benjiao yanman dejiafennuwang zhenyan daweideyiguipin* 大乘方廣曼殊室利菩薩華嚴本教閻曼德迦忿怒王真言大威德儀軌品 (T. 1215) corresponds to chapter 50 of the Sanskrit version and to chapter 33 of the Tibetan version held at Otani University (no. 162). One theory attributes this text to Amoghavajra (DZD, 339); *Dafangguang manshushili tongzhenpusa huayanbenjiaozhanyan mandejiafennuwang zhenyan apizhelujia yigui pin* 大方廣曼殊室利童真菩薩華嚴本教讚閻曼德迦忿怒王真言阿毘遮嚕迦儀軌品 (T. 1216) corresponds to chapter 51 of the Sanskrit (DZD, 339); *Wenshushilipusa genben dajiaowang jing jinchiniaowang pin* 文殊師利菩薩根本大教王經金翅鳥王品 (T. 1276) is a variant text of T. 1191 (DZD, 351).

205 速得往生極樂世界面見無量壽如來聽聞妙法 (T. 1050:50c8–9); see also T. 1050:53a14–28.

206 T. 890:582b5–10.

207 得見無量壽佛 (T. 934:80b6).

208 得具足極樂世界無量壽佛身口意 (T. 1051:65a28–29).

209 快樂命終之後當得生於極樂世界 (T. 1051:65c2–3).

Chapter 3

Early Japanese Esoteric Pure Land Buddhism

The transmission and development of East Asian Mahayana Buddhist culture in Japan took place in the context of continuous dialogue with developments on the Continent. The major power players in early Japanese history belonged to what some scholars refer to as "immigrant kinship groups" from the mainland (China) and the peninsula (Korea), which introduced continental material and intellectual culture throughout the early centuries of the formation of a centralized state on the archipelago of Japan. Official dates for the introduction of Buddhism to Japan are highly speculative.[1] Herman Ooms, Michael Como, and others argue that the famous conflagration in 587 between the Mononobe 物部 and Soga 蘇我 clans was not a contest between a "pro-Shinto" (and thus indigenous) Mononobe clan versus a "pro-Buddhist" (and thus foreign) Soga clan. Both groups were of relatively recent continental extraction and participated in and competed through the use of similar, recently imported continental traditions.[2] Buddhism was thus introduced to Japan in a context in which the Sinitic cultural "toolbox"—Buddhist, Daoist, Confucian, and more—was already in use by diverse groups in competition for ascendancy as the political center took shape.

Many of the available historical sources for the study of Buddhism before the eighth century, such as the *Nihonshoki* 日本書紀, the *Shōsōin monjo* 正倉院文書, the *Shoku nihongi* 續日本紀, and the *Nihon Ryōiki* 日本靈異記, actually date from later centuries, and many were written by Buddhist monks with clearly articulated political agendas. It is therefore difficult to gain an accurate picture of what Buddhism actually looked like at the time of its introduction and adoption in Japan. Many texts have been lost, and it is common practice in sectarian scholarship to discover evidence from this period that establishes precedent for later, especially medieval, developments. For example, scholars of Pure Land Buddhism often search for proto-Pure Land developments. Similarly, Esoteric Buddhism scholars often look to early Sino-Japanese dhāraṇī culture or "proto-Esoteric" rituals (referred to in some Japanese scholarship as *komikkyō* 古密教, or "old esotericism").

Mahayana Esoterica and Pure Land Aspiration in Early Japanese Buddhism

Shōtoku Taishi 聖德太子 (574–622), widely regarded as the grandfather of Japanese Buddhism, is also sometimes presented as a devout Pure Land Buddhist. Shōtoku came to power against the backdrop of continued tension between immigrant kinship groups on the Japanese archipelago. In 592, Soga no Umako 蘇我馬子 (551–626) arranged for the assassination of Emperor Sushun 崇峻天皇 (520–592; r. 588–592) and helped establish Empress Suiko 推古天皇 (554–628; r. 592–628) as the head of state, with Shōtoku as her regent. Shōtoku's life and career in some ways signify the beginning of Japan's full participation in continental Buddhist culture.[3] Three sutra commentaries are attributed to him: the *Hokke gisho* 法華義疏 (T. 2187), the *Yuimagyō gisho* 維摩經義疏 (T. 2186), and the *Shōmangyō gisho* 勝鬘經義疏 (T. 2185), though his authorship is now doubted. These texts show that by Shōtoku's time elite Japanese Buddhists were able to produce doctrinal works that demonstrate a sophisticated understanding of Mahayana scholarship. Hisao Inagaki notes that Shōtoku, the presumed author of the commentaries, recognized that "sentient beings have their own land of reward and retribution, whereas Buddhas dwell in no fixed lands; Bodhisattvas above the seventh stage are the same as Buddhas in that they have no abode. But Buddhas and those Bodhisattvas can manifest lands by their supernatural powers in order to save sentient beings."[4]

However, there is no definitive evidence for whether or not Shōtoku was personally an aspirant for rebirth in Sukhāvatī, as it would have been understood by later Buddhists. Robert Rhodes argues that it is more likely that his views could be classified as Buddhist-Daoist or perhaps even non-Buddhist in orientation.[5]

In any case, traditional sources credit the monk Eon 惠隱 (early seventh century) with delivering the first recorded lecture on Buddhism in the imperial palace. Eon was possibly of Chinese descent, and he was an early scholar in Japan of Madhyamaka, known as Sanron 三論 from the Chinese Sanlun, an exegetical tradition based on the "three treatises" translated into Chinese by Kumārajīva: the *Madhyamaka-śāstra* 中論 (T. 1564) and the *Dvādaśanikāya-śāstra* 十二門論 (T. 1568) attributed to Nāgārjuna and the *Śata-śāstra* 百論 (T. 1569) by Āryadeva 聖提婆, a disciple of Nāgārjuna. In 608, Eon accompanied Ono no Imoko 小野妹子 (late sixth to early seventh centuries) on a mission to China. On his return in 639, Eon delivered his now famous lecture. Out of the vast corpora of Chinese Mahayana texts, he chose the *Sukhāvatī-vyūha-sūtra.* He purportedly later delivered a similar lecture in 652 to over one thousand monks.[6] It is interesting to note that as with the early transmission of Mahayana to China, in Japan the philosophy of śūnyatā was transmitted by the very same people who also transmitted teachings about rebirth in Sukhāvatī.

It is difficult to say exactly how early Japanese Buddhists understood Sukhāvatī at this time. Instead of focusing on pursuing rebirth in Sukhāvatī for one's own personal salvation through cultivating a devotional relationship with Amitābha Buddha, Japanese Buddhists seem to have been especially interested in *tsuizen jōdo* 追善浄土, "Pure Land [rebirth through] pursuing the good," a practice in which one seeks to transfer merit for the benefit of a deceased relative or pacify the spirit of someone who has died, in some cases an enemy defeated in battle, to help send them along to the Pure Land.

Hayami Tasuku 速水侑 notes that some modern scholars have often derided this form of practice as superstitious and not authentically Mahayana in orientation. These scholars often suggest that Japanese Buddhists at this time still relied on pre-Buddhist folk traditions and superstition. Hayami critiques this point of view, however, and argues that while *tsuizen jōdo* may not fit the agendas of modernist thinkers, it is fully in line with how premodern and contemporary East Asian Mahayana Buddhists have traditionally interpreted and used their texts. Merit transference, cultivating good karmic roots, establishing karmically beneficial connections with buddhas and bodhisattvas through devotional practices, seeking fortunate future rebirth, and so on are fundamental features of many genres of Mahayana scripture and ritual texts.[7] Furthermore, the centrality of spellcraft and dhāraṇī texts in early Japanese Buddhist practice clearly demonstrates that rather than deviating from the norms of the broader East Asian Mahayana Sinosphere, Japanese Buddhists were already productive members of that cosmopolitan culture.

By the seventh and eighth centuries, ritual texts promoting various dhāraṇī, spells, and mantras, as well as tantras, circulated in China at the very pinnacle of elite Chinese Buddhist culture. As Beghi has demonstrated, at the same time monks in Japan worked to master numerous areas of Chinese Buddhist knowledge, including those texts and practices commonly labeled as "esoteric."[8] He notes that many of the texts and images commonly associated with so-called Pure Esotericism were imported intentionally and used by Japanese monks for over a century before Kūkai's career.[9]

Dōshō 道昭/道照 (629–700) is often credited with the transmission of Hossō, the Japanese rendering of Faxiang, the Chinese Yogācāra lineage. Dōshō studied under Xuanzang and Kuiji 窺基 (632–682) for seven years in China and on his return to Japan resided at Gangōji 元興寺 (the ancestral temple of the Soga clan). Like other monks of this period, Dōshō studied broadly and is said to have even studied Chan under Huiman 慧滿 (seventh century), a disciple of Huike 慧可 (487–593), the second patriarch of the Chinese Chan lineage.[10] Among the texts transmitted by Dōshō was the *Vajramaṇḍa-dhāraṇī-sūtra* 金剛場陀羅尼經 (T. 1345), translated by Jñānagupta.[11] This text presents a dialogue between the Buddha and Mañjuśrī Bodhisattva on the merits of the Dharma gate of the *vajramaṇḍa-dhāraṇī*. Like most dhāraṇī texts, it contains numerous declarations on the many benefits of the dhāraṇī itself, including a reference to the attainment of all *buddha-kṣetra*. In addition, one surviving edition of this text, dated 686, includes the following colophon:

> 歳次丙戌年五月川内國志貴評内知識為七世父母及一　切衆生敬造金剛場陀羅尼経一部籍此善因往生浄土 終成正覺教化僧寶林.
>
> In the fifth month of 686, in the Shiki *gun* of Kanai *kuni*, for the benefit of their mothers and fathers for seven generations, and all sentient beings, reverently, they sponsored the copying of the *Vajramaṇḍa-dhāraṇī-sūtra*, may the virtue of this act be the cause for rebirth in Sukhāvatī and the attainment of correct awakening. Written by the dharma teacher Hōrin.[12]

Like Xuanzang before him, Dōshō was also a devotee of Maitreya Bodhisattva. The brothers Vasubandhu 世親 and Asaṅga 無著 (fourth to fifth centuries) are said to have received the divine revelation directly from Maitreya that led to the establishment of the Yogācāra tradition. This established a trend for Maitreya devotion and perhaps even aspiration for rebirth in Tuṣita, regarded by many as a *buddha-kṣetra*. The early popularity of Maitreya devotion in East Asia helped lay the groundwork for the popularity of Amitābha devotion.[13]

According to traditional biographies, Dōshō helped in the construction of roads and bridges and promoted cremation and the use of spells to aid the departed in their transition to a better rebirth. As is common in the hagiographies of elite monks, miraculous signs were recorded upon his death, such as a luminous presence that moved through the temple in a westerly direction, signifying rebirth in Sukhāvatī.[14]

Dōji 道慈 (675–744), a Madhyamaka scholar, eventually took the position of head administrator in the monastic hierarchy.[15] Dōji studied in China for eighteen years, returning in 718. In China he had studied under Yuankang 元康 in Chang'an 長安, who is said to have transmitted to him the innermost secrets (*hitsugi* 秘奥) of the Chinese Sanlun tradition.[16] At Daianji 大安寺 in Yamato, Dōji promoted the *Renwang jing* and the *Suvarṇaprabhāsa-sūtra,* texts that contain a number of common Mahayana tropes: purification and pacification of the political realm, promises of this-worldly and otherworldly benefits, and future rebirth in Sukhāvatī, up to and including full Buddhahood for all sentient beings. Some scholars of Esoteric Buddhism have often regarded these two sutras as "proto-Esoteric/Tantric" in orientation.

Dōji also transmitted the *Xukongzang pusa wen qifo tuoluonizhou jing* 虛空藏菩薩諸問七佛陀羅尼呪經 (T. 1333), an important dhāraṇī text associated with Ākāśagarbha Bodhisattva. This text promises that its complex visualizations and spells will not only protect one from calamities, illnesses, and harm but also, through diligent practice, allow one to attain rebirth in the Pure Land.[17] Dōji is also credited with the transmission of the *Xukongzangpusa nengman zhuyuan zuishengxin tuoluoni qiuwenchifa* 虛空藏菩薩能滿諸願最勝心陀羅尼求聞持法 (T. 1145), another text dedicated to Ākāśagarbha and later made famous by Kūkai.[18] This text describes complex visualizations, gives descriptions of mudras and the five buddhas in one's crown, provides instructions on setting up an elaborate ritual altar, and more. Both of these texts are attributed to Śubhakarasiṃha, and some scholars speculate that Dōji may have studied under Śubhakarasiṃha in China, while others doubt this assertion.[19]

Emperor Shōmu and Japan as Vairocana Buddha's *Buddha-kṣetra*

Early Japanese Buddhism reached a new plateau during the reign of Emperor Shōmu 聖武天皇 (701–756; r. 724–749) and Empress Kōmyō 光明 (701–760), both of whom were prolific patrons of the Dharma. Employing the expertise of the monk Rōben (Ryōben) 良辯 (689–773), Shōmu and Kōmyo founded Tōdaiji 東大寺 in 741, establishing it as the administrative center of the national temple network, the *kokubunji* 國分寺. Tōdaiji is home to the famous Nara Daibutsu 大佛 (Great Buddha) statue of Vairocana Buddha 毘盧舍那佛, the central figure of the *Avataṃsaka-sūtra.*

Rōben studied under the Sillan monk Simsang 審祥 (?–742), a disciple of Fazang 法藏 (643–712), who is responsible for the systematization of Huayan, the Chinese *Avataṃsaka-sūtra* exegetical tradition known as Kegon in Japan. Rōben is credited with helping Emperor Shōmu in the construction of Tōdaiji and the Vairocana Buddha statue and may have encouraged the emperor to use the *Avataṃsaka-sūtra* as the organizing principle for the temple. Rōben promoted texts associated with Esoteric Buddhism, including the *Amoghapāśa-dhāraṇī* and the *Dhāraṇīsaṃgraha-sūtra.* At the Lotus Hall 法華堂 at Tōdaiji, Rōben installed the images of Amoghapāśa Avalokiteśvara Bodhisattva and Vajrasattva Bodhisattva 金剛薩埵菩薩, and at Tōshōdaiji 唐招提寺 he installed figures of the Thousand-Hand Avalokiteśvara Bodhisattva and Mahāvairocana Buddha.[20] Tōdaiji and other major temples in Japan at this time were not organized around a specific school or sect in the way they are today; instead they were often home to many different areas of study. While Tōdaiji is usually associated with Kegon studies, specialists in Madhyamaka, Yogācāra, Vinaya—and eventually Shingon and Tendai as well—practiced there.

To assist with the consecration of the Great Buddha at Tōdaiji in 752, the monk Daoxuan 道璿 (702–760) brought the Indian monk Bodhisena 菩提僊那 (704–760) to assist in the performance of the eye-opening ceremony. Daoxuan and Bodhisena brought the *Vajraśekhara-sūtra,* the *Mahāvairocanā-sūtra,* and the *Susiddhikāra-sūtra* with them to Japan.[21] These texts are usually associated with later Esoteric Buddhism, but it is possible that traditions associated with these texts were already informing the ritual culture at the highest levels of elite Japanese Buddhist society.

Vairocana Buddha, the central object of devotion at Tōdaiji, is associated with the *Avataṃsaka-sūtra* and the *Brahmajāla-sūtra* 梵網經 (T. 1484), commonly known as the *Brahma's Net Sutra.* Later, under Kūkai's influence, the image of Vairocana Buddha was eventually reimagined as Mahāvairocana Buddha of the *Mahāvairocana-sutra,* but this later development built upon what some scholars (and perhaps even Kūkai himself) may have identified as the proto-tantric qualities of the *Avataṃsaka-sūtra* and related texts that focus on Śākyamuni Buddha's apotheosis as Vairocana, the lord of the *buddha-kṣetra* of the ten directions. The importance of this imperial metaphor becomes obvious when considering Vairocana Buddha's placement as the central image at the head of the *kokubunji,* which was coextensive with the sphere of the emperor's influence. In a sense, the realm was transformed into a mandalic *buddhakṣetra* with Vairocana/Shōmu as the central Buddha/*cakravartin* (wheel-turning king).

Sukhāvatī-oriented practices were also an important dimension of these early religiopolitical institutions. The Amitābha Hall at Tōdaiji was built in 741. Shortly thereafter, Empress Kōmyō established Hokkeji in 745 as the head temple of the *kokubunniji* 國分尼寺, or national convent temple system. On the death of Empress Kōmyō in 761, a Pure Land Hall was built at Hokkeji, Pure Land tableaus were displayed at all state and provincial temples, and *Amida keka* 阿彌陀悔過 (Amitābha Buddha repentance rituals) were performed at all state temples throughout Japan. These rituals were intended to purify the past karma and sins of the patron or a deceased person, and to this day they are an important component of East Asian Buddhist ritual activity.[22]

Other monks at this time were instrumental in establishing rituals, images, and texts now associated with Esoteric Buddhism in the Buddhist repertoire of early Japan. Genbō 玄昉 (?–746), a Yogācāra scholar, was also involved with the construction of the Tōdaiji Daibutsu. After studying in China, he returned to Japan in 735 and, purportedly, received the purple robe from Emperor Xuanzong 玄宗 (685–762).[23] Like many other Yogācāra scholars, Genbō was a Maitreya devotee and an aspirant for rebirth in Tuṣita through the practice of dhāraṇī. Genbō's student Zenju 善珠 (723–797) was a scholar-monk at Kōfukuji 興福寺. Scholars of Pure Land Buddhism have generally been interested in Zenju's commentaries on the *Sukhāvatīvyūha-sūtra,* emphasizing his debt to Korean thinkers.[24] In addition to his interest in Sukhāvatī, Zenju also seems to have developed an interest in Esoteric Buddhism. In 754, Zenju's associate Nyohō 如寶 (?–815) received the precepts from Jianzhen 鑑真 (688–763), the famous Chinese precept master who established the precept platform at Tōdaiji, and studied at both Yakushiji and Tōshōdaiji. Both Zenju and Nyohō worked with Kūkai later in life.[25]

Kōmyō and Dhāraṇī Texts

While Empress Kōmyō's activities have often been overshadowed by those of her husband, she was also a major patron of the Dharma. For example, in 741 she promoted the Shakyōjo 寫經所, which was tasked with producing copies of the Buddhist canon for the major temples.[26] Texts attributed to Jñānagupta, Śikṣānanda, Bodhiruci, Śubhakarasiṃha,

Vajrabodhi, and Amoghavajra were not only included in these collections but actually read and circulated. Tōdaiji requested a copy of the *Mahāvairocana-sūtra* in 722, signifying, perhaps, that this text was already something of a known quantity within Japan at the time.[27]

Dhāraṇī texts were especially important for the ordination of monks. As part of their role in government, they were expected to memorize particular sutras and dhāraṇī and practice austerities for the safety of the realm and the long life of the emperor. Some of the most prominent examples of these texts include the *Uṣṇīsavijayā-dhāraṇī-sūtra*, the *Ekādaśamukha-dhāraṇī*, the *Adhyarthaśatikā-prajñāpāramitā-sūtra* 金剛頂瑜伽理趣般若經 (T. 241), the *Ṣaṇmukhī-dhāraṇī-sūtra* 六門陀羅尼經 (T. 1360), the *Guanding qiwanerjian shenwang hu biqiu zhou jing*, the *Qijuzhi fomuxin dazhunti tuoluoni jing*, the *Mahābala-dhāraṇī-sūtra* 大威德陀羅尼經 (T. 1341), and the *Dharmolkadhāraṇī-sūtra*.[28]

In addition to these texts, the *Dhāraṇīsaṃgraha-sūtra* was especially important in this period: Empress Kōmyō herself seems to have been especially interested in this text, and numerous rituals were drawn from it.[29] This text was examined in some detail in chapter 2, so here I briefly note that the *Dhāraṇīsaṃgraha-sūtra* is commonly regarded as an important transitional text situated between the diffuse dhāraṇī and spell texts found throughout South Asian religious literature and the more systematic tantric ritual systems. As previously discussed, it contains an interesting section in which Amitābha Buddha teaches Avalokiteśvara Bodhisattva secret mudras and mantras for the deliverance of beings from samsara, which is referenced in later ritual texts such as the *Gyōrin-shō* 行林抄 compiled in 1190 by Jōhen 靜然 (n.d.).[30]

Emperor Kōken/Shōtoku

In 749, when Emperor Shōmu and Empress Kōmyō abdicated and entered the cloister, their daughter ascended the throne and took the title Emperor Kōken 孝謙天皇 (718–770; r. 749–758; note that Kōken did not take the title "empress" but rather reigned as "emperor"). After almost ten years, she abdicated and took the tonsure at Hokkeji in 762. Emperor Junnin 淳仁天皇 (r. 758–764), who followed Kōken, only reigned for a short time due to ongoing struggles for political power. Kōken then regained the throne in 764, this time under the name Emperor Shōtoku 称徳天皇, and ruled until her death in 770.[31] In protest, Fujiwara no Nakamaro 藤原仲麻呂 (706–764) led a rebellion against the Kōken/Shōtoku regime, but the rebels were crushed, and Nakamaro's family was slaughtered.[32]

In order to pacify the spirits of her slain enemies and to further unify the realm, Emperor Shōtoku (Kōken) erected dhāraṇī stupas at the so-called Ten Great Temples,[33] enshrining the *Raśmivimala-viśuddhaprabhā-dhāraṇī* 無垢淨光大陀羅尼經 (T. 1024). This strategy for aiding the spirits of the departed (or of one's dispatched enemies) in attaining rebirth in Sukhāvatī was utilized to prevent their return to the world as vengeful spirits. Moreover, on a symbolic level, temples often served to demonstrate the extent of the government's power and reach, and the dhāraṇī stupas projected the image of a unified and pacified realm.[34]

The *Raśmivimala-viśuddhaprabhā-dhāraṇī* is said to extend one's life span, promises rebirth in various *buddha-kṣetra* such as Sukhāvatī, Tuṣita, and Abhirati, purifies sins, prevents future rebirth in hell, and so on. This dhāraṇī text remained important throughout the Heian and Kamakura periods; Kūkai and others imported new versions along with other texts.[35] In particular, this dhāraṇī came to be associated with and practiced alongside the Amitābha dhāraṇī.[36]

Kūkai and Esoteric Buddhism

Due to ongoing tensions at the political center throughout the eighth century, the capital was moved several times. Finally, in 794 Emperor Kanmu 桓武天皇 (736–806; r. 781–806) established a new capital, Heian-kyō 平安京, in present-day Kyoto. The Buddhist traditions that rose to prominence during the early ninth century, the Shingon and Tendai schools, are sometimes referred to as "Heian Buddhism." Ryūichi Abé critiques this notion, however, noting that the religiopolitical structure established in Nara remained powerful throughout the early Heian period and that the major temples continued to be major landholders active well into the medieval period (thirteenth century and after).[37]

In addition to establishing a new and stable capital, Emperor Kanmu also reestablished diplomatic relations with China and sent a delegation there in 804. Kūkai and Saichō, tasked with "updating" Japanese Buddhism, went to study abroad and later brought back texts and lineages then at the cutting edge of Chinese Buddhist practice. Both men had reputations as pure monks who followed the precepts; their biographies describe periods of individual study and ascetic practice in the wilderness. Hayami suggests that the court wanted monks with this balance of purity and power to bless and pacify the realm.[38]

In China, Kūkai studied at Qinglongsi 青龍寺, an important temple in the Chinese capital Chang'an, a thriving cosmopolitan stop along the

Silk Road. His teacher there was Huiguo 惠果 (746–806), a former student of Amoghavajra. Kūkai returned to Japan with a vast store of ritual and doctrinal texts, the latest and most important of the materials available in China and India at the time, and was eventually able to integrate what he had learned into the ritual culture of Japan. Kūkai studied in several ritual lineages and brought back many texts and ritual paraphernalia unknown to Japanese monks, as well as a comprehensive system for integrating the texts, images, and practices that had already been adopted in Japan before his time.

New visual and material culture was central to the practices Kūkai introduced, such as the so-called dual-mandala system, comprising the *Mahākaruṇā-garbhodbhava-maṇḍala* 胎藏界曼荼羅, or "Womb Realm mandala," and the *Vajradhātu-maṇḍala* 金剛界曼荼羅, or "Vajra Realm mandala." The Womb Realm mandala is said to symbolize the nature of reality as it truly is, the inherent Buddhahood of all things, while the Vajra Realm Mandala constitutes the wisdom practitioners acquire to see that reality.[39] These mandalas and the ritual systems associated with them circulated independently, but according to Kūkai, he had received initiation into a synthesized dual-mandala system.

The dual-mandala system constitutes a unified all-inclusive perspective on reality. The dual mandalas of the Womb and Vajra Realms correspond to the *Mahāvairocana* and the *Vajraśekhara* sutras, the respective textual lineages of Śubhakarasiṃha and Vajrabodhi. These mandalas and texts are focused on Mahāvairocana. All buddhas, bodhisattvas, gods, and ordinary beings and in fact all forms are seen as embodiments or aspects of Mahāvairocana; all sounds are the speech of Mahāvairocana; all thoughts are the mind of Mahāvairocana. This ultimate reality is all-encompassing and immanent, although beings are unaware that they are corporally constituted by the very Buddhahood they seek. In order to awaken beings to the true nature of reality, to this secret hidden in plain sight, the bodies, speech, and minds of beings must be engaged and awakened through corresponding ritual practices of mudra (body), mantra (speech), and "mandalic" visualization (mind) under the guidance of a qualified teacher. The union of these three practices is known as the "three mysteries," and through practice of the three mysteries one is able to realize Buddhahood in one's very body.

Dhāraṇī texts and many of the texts and deities Kūkai promoted had already been imported and in use in Japan before he went to China and returned.[40] He therefore had some precedent for his case that his ritual theory was latent, or "hidden," within Nara dhāraṇī culture.[41] However, without the technology of mantra, which Kūkai defined as a subcategory of dhāraṇī, these practices were essentially equivalent to "reading a medical textbook to someone who was ill."[42] Abé notes that part of Kūkai's argument entailed convincing his intended audience that "mantras show that *dhāraṇī* are not devoid of meaning but, on the contrary, saturated with it. It is through their semantic superabundance that Kūkai attempted to explain why *dhāraṇī* were impregnated with the power to condense the meaning of scriptures, to protect chanters, or to bring about supernatural effects."[43]

Given his reputation and authority as one who had studied at the center of Buddhist power in East Asia, Kūkai was eventually able to successfully integrate this theory into the highest monastic institutions in Japan.

Like other Mahayana systems, Kūkai's approach purported to reveal to the practitioner the true intent of the Buddha, the "secret teaching." As a result, Kūkai's doctrinal and ritual system is often referred to as *himitsu bukkyō* 秘密佛教, "Esoteric Buddhism," commonly abbreviated as *mikkyō.* However, as previously noted, *mikkyō* and other cognate terms are found widely throughout East Asian Mahayana lineages and are used as polemical designations to indicate the superiority of one's own lineage. In other words, though the term is commonly associated with Kūkai, it has a much broader application. Given the breadth of Kūkai's knowledge of Buddhist and non-Buddhist traditions and literature, his own usage of the term *mikkyō* should therefore be viewed in that broader context.

Besides *mikkyō,* Kūkai used various terms to describe the teachings and practices he introduced to Japan: mantra-*piṭaka,* secret-*piṭaka, saijōjō* 最上乘 (highest vehicle), and even Vajrayāna. In the *Daioshō hōi Heianjō taijōtennō kanjōmon* 大和尚奉爲平安城太上天皇灌頂文 (T. 2461), Kūkai presents a fivefold taxonomy of the Mahayana: sutras, Vinaya, Abhidharma, and Prajñāpāramitā and then, referring to his teachings, dhāraṇī-*piṭaka.*[44] Later in the same text, he presents an eightfold taxonomy and refers to his teachings as the "secret Vajrayāna."[45] According to Abé, Kūkai tended to use the Sanskrit terms *piṭaka* (J. *zō* 藏), "treasury," and *yāna* (J. *jō* 乘), "vehicle," but rarely used the term *shū,* commonly translated as "sect" today (but implying something more like essence or area of focus in premodern Japan). As Abé notes, this suggests that Kūkai may have wanted to present his teaching not as some new area of study but rather as a technique for accessing the power already inherent within established texts and practices.[46]

While regarded as the founder of the Shingon school of Japanese Buddhism, Kūkai did not necessarily found a new "school," as we might understand the term today, nor introduce a wholly new "kind" of Buddhism into Japan. Rather, to grasp Kūkai's main contribution to Japanese Buddhism we must consider how he worked within the Nara Buddhist establishment, eventually serving as the head of the monastic bureau itself.[47]

At the request of Emperor Junna 淳和天皇 (785–840; r. 810–823), Kūkai composed what is widely regarded as his magnum opus, the *Himitsu mandara jūjushinron* 秘密曼荼羅十住心論 (T. 2425), which lays out how the secret teaching fits into the bigger picture through a ten-stage system of the mind:[48]

1. *Ishō teiyō shin* 異生羝羊心, the mind of the unenlightened, one who pursues worldly pleasures with no concern for ethics or self-cultivation, like a worldly sheep
2. *Gudōji saijū shin* 愚童持齋心, the mind of a foolish child (associated with Confucians and materialist-nihilist philosophies)
3. *Eidō mui shin* 嬰童無畏心, the mind of a smart child (associated with those who aspire to higher spiritual truths, such as Daoists and Brahmans)
4. *Yuiun muga shin* 唯蘊無我心, the mind of one who understands the teachings on no-self and the five aggregates (associated with non-Mahayana Buddhists, especially *śrāvakas*)
5. *Batsugō inshu shin* 抜業因種心, the mind of one who has eliminated the causes of karma (non-Mahayana, *pratyekabuddhas*)
6. *Taen daijō shin* 他縁大乘心, the mind of one who understands the interconnectedness of all beings (Mahayana, associated with Yogācāra)
7. *Kakushin fusho shin* 覺心不生心, the mind of one who understands the nonarising of mind (Mahayana, associated with Madhyamaka)
8. *Ichidō mui shin* 一道無爲心 , the mind of one who grasps the unconditioned nature of mind and the One Vehicle (Mahayana traditions such as Tiantai/Tendai)
9. *Gokumujishō shin* 極無自性心, the mind of one who sees beyond the notion of self-nature (Mahayana traditions such as Huayan/Kegon)
10. *Himitsu shōgon shin* 秘密莊嚴心, the mind of mysterious adornment (the true intent of the buddhadharma, Buddhism from the perspective of ultimate reality)

Many interpreters of Kūkai seem to take these ten stations of the mind as a vertical hierarchy of teachings that gradually progress from the basest to the highest (Kūkai's own perspective). However, there are two ways of reading this taxonomy: vertical and horizontal. The vertical reading entails the hierarchical progression from base to sublime, superficial to profound. The horizontal reading regards all ten stations from the perspective of equanimity, with the lowest and highest as non-dual and on the same level. In other words, the nine "exoteric" paths contain the "esoteric" truth within them, only mediated by varying levels of *upāya.* Esoteric implies exoteric, and vice versa.

Through the practice of mantra, the practitioner of Madhyamaka, Yogacara, Tendai, or Kegon as well as practitioners of non-Mahayana paths, followers of non-Buddhist paths like Hinduism, Daoism, or Confucianism, and even a secular hedonist may be able to encounter ultimate reality. It is also interesting to note that while stages four through eight originate in the teaching of Śākyamuni Buddha, the tenth stage is the teaching of Mahāvairocana Buddha, the dharmakāya, "ultimate reality" itself.[49]

In order to become a member of this "loosely organized club" of mantra practitioners, one had to study under a qualified master in a recognized ritual lineage.[50] Since Kūkai's career was largely focused in Nara, many of the top monks in Nara became his disciples. For example, in 816 Kūkai initiated the Daianji monk Gonsō 勤操 (758–827), a prominent Nara scholar-monk. Enmyō 圓明 (d. 851) and Dōshō 道昌 (789–875), scholars of Prajñāpāramitā and Madhyamaka; Jōshō 定照 (906–983), the *bettō* 別當 (highest government administrative post in temples) of Kōfukuji and a Yogācāra scholar; Shōbō 聖寶 (832–909) of Gangōji, a scholar of Madhyamaka, the *Avataṃsaka-sūtra,* and Prajñāpāramitā; Shinkō 真皎 (934–1004) of Kōfukuji, a Yogācāra scholar; and many others soon helped spread Kūkai's ritual lineages.[51] Nara Buddhist institutions continued to dominate through the early Heian period and remained powerful even through the medieval period; Abé therefore emphasizes the importance of studying Nara ritual lineages for insight into the effects of Kūkai's introduction of this new ritual culture and discourse.[52]

Toward the end of his life, Kūkai ascended to the highest echelons of power in the Japanese Buddhist world.[53] His successful integration of Tang ritual into the Nara curriculum transformed the way monks were trained. In 816 Emperor Saga 嵯峨天皇 (785–842, r. 809–823) granted Kūkai land on the high plateau-mountaintop known as Kōyasan, far from the capital, to build a training center. In 822 Kūkai was also granted

Tōji in the capital, and he was allowed to establish an abhiṣeka hall at Tōdaiji.[54] With this move, Vairocana *became* Mahāvairocana Buddha.[55]

In 827 Kūkai was appointed head of the monastic bureau, and in this role he performed many important rituals at court and elsewhere. For example, in 834 he performed the *mishuhō* 御修法 (also called *mizuhō, mishihō*), a prayer for the health of the emperor held at the start of the new year, and this became an important recurring ritual in the annual court calendar. In 835 he built the Shingon-in 真言院 (mantra hall) in the imperial palace. *Shingon gyōnin* 真言行人 (practitioners of mantra) began to proliferate throughout the centers of elite ritual culture in Japan, just as they had in China—not as a school or a sect but as an area of specialization that blended into the broader Japanese religious environment.

Buddha-kṣetra and Sukhāvatī in Kūkai's Works

The recitation of dhāraṇī was an important component of early Japanese Buddhist practice, and remains so today. Rebirth in Sukhāvatī is one of the many benefits associated with various genres of dhāraṇī literature as well as many texts associated with Esoteric Buddhism. This dhāraṇī-centric theory of Buddhist ritual power served as the grist for Kūkai's reconceptualization of Buddhist theories of ritual speech, and dhāraṇī practitioners were one of the main audiences Kūkai taught. So it is somewhat surprising that so few scholars have examined the place of *buddha-kṣetra* in general, and Sukhāvatī in particular, in the writings attributed to Kūkai, which contain numerous references concerning rebirth in Sukhāvatī as a soteriological goal and *buddha-kṣetra* as a feature of Mahayana cosmology.

Certainly, following Kūkai's career, Buddhists in Japan did not suddenly abandon their understanding of Sukhāvatī nor the power of dhāraṇī to lead to rebirth there. Like Amoghavajra before him, Kūkai seems to have regarded mastery of these rituals as leading to the rapid attainment of progress along the bodhisattva path and Buddhahood, both of which, understood from the normative Mahayana Buddhist viewpoint, assume travel to the *buddha-kṣetra* of the ten directions, interaction with buddhas in various *buddha-kṣetra,* and so on.

For example, in the *Hokkekyō kaidai* 法華經開題 (T. 2190),[56] a commentary on the *Lotus Sutra,* Kūkai (or the author who attributed this work to Kūkai) discusses Sukhāvatī and the attainment of rebirth there at some length through the contemplation of the letter *A,* a Sanskrit *bīja* (seed syllable) associated with śūnyatā and Mahāvairocana, as the *ekayāna* 一乘

(one vehicle).[57] The text also discusses other paths to rebirth in Sukhāvatī, such as devotion to Avalokiteśvara Bodhisattva and the *Lotus Sutra*, visualization of *hrīḥ*, and the *bīja* of Amitābha Buddha.[58]

Another important Esoteric Pure Land text attributed to Kūkai is the *Muryōju nyorai sakuhō shidai* 無量壽如來供養作法次第,[59] a ritual commentary on Amoghavajra's *Wuliang rulai guanxing gongyang yigui.* Amoghavajra's text, which contains the famous Amitābha dhāraṇī, was significant in China and Japan, was transmitted multiple times by Kūkai and many others, and emerged as a foundational text in the development of training programs in Japanese ritual lineages. Nakamikado Keikyō 中御門敬教 notes that references to this text appear in Genshin's 源信 (942-1017) *Ōjōyōshū* 往生要集 (T. 2682) and Kakuban's *Gorin kuji myō himitsu shaku* 五輪九字明祕密釋 (T. 2514), and it serves as the base text for the *Tendai Amidahō sanbusaku* 天台阿彌陀法三部作.[60]

The ritual commentary attributed to Kūkai begins with preliminary invocations and mantras intended to purify and sanctify the ritual arena and the practitioner.[61] Next, the practitioner envisions an ocean of lapis lazuli. The seed syllable *hrīḥ* emerges, crimson in color, like Amitābha Buddha himself, illuminating the *buddha-kṣetra* of the ten directions. Next, the syllable transforms, taking the shape of Avalokiteśvara Bodhisattva, and then eventually becomes Amitābha Buddha, who has the mantra *Oṃ aṃṛta teje hara hūṃ,* inscribed in *siddhaṃ* 悉曇 (a script for writing Sanskrit), on a luminous moon disc at his heart-center. The practitioner then envisions a similar moon disc with the same mantra at the practitioner's own heart-center. Amitābha Buddha then begins chanting the mantra, sending the moon disc from his torso up through his mouth, and it enters the practitioner through the crown of the head. The practitioner then sends the practitioner's own moon disc up through the crown of the head, and it enters through the feet of Amitābha Buddha. This rite shows the confluence of two fundamental Mahayana concepts: the nonduality of buddhas and beings and the idea that through practice the buddhas respond to the needs of the practitioner in a transference of the Buddha's power. When I first read this ritual commentary, I was reminded of the popular Tibetan *phowa* practice wherein the practitioner prepares for the moment of death by visualizing the projection of their consciousness to Sukhāvatī.[62]

Next, the practitioner engages in a visualization practice very similar to that described in the *Contemplation Sutra,* including visualization of the light of Amitābha that permeates the ten directions. As with Amoghavajra's text, this commentary claims that through these practices one will purify not only all of one's past karma but also all of one's illness and suffering, and at the end of life, one will attain rebirth in the highest level of Sukhāvatī. Moreover, as in the *Pratyutpanna-samādhi-sūtra,* this practice leads one to comprehend the nonduality of buddhas and beings and, further, realize that all Dharmas are śūnyatā, that the bodhi mind is originally pure and nonarising, and that even the visions attained through this practice are ultimately śūnyatā, just as is the deluded mind of ordinary reality.

Kūkai's authorship of these two texts may be doubtful. In fact, there is disagreement about his authorship of even some of the major works commonly attributed to him. According to Matthew McMullen, the attribution of the *Benkenmitsu nikyōron* 辯顯密二教論 (T. 2427), generally assumed to be *the* foundational text in which Kūkai most clearly distinguishes between exoteric and esoteric approaches to Buddhism, has been called into question in some recent scholarship.[63] In any case the point of examining these two texts is not to position Kūkai as a proto-Esoteric Pure Land thinker or to suggest that Sukhāvatī aspiration was a central part of his teachings. Because *buddha-kṣetra* are fundamental to the soteriological cosmology in Mahayana sutras and tantras, it is not surprising that the *buddha-kṣetra* of the ten directions are mentioned throughout these texts, even in Kūkai's *Jūjūshinron.*[64] Nor is it surprising that later generations of devotees or members of Kūkai's lineages employed the ritual traditions he imported for the attainment of such a greatly sought-after soteriological goal as rebirth in Sukhāvatī.

Esoteric Pure Land in the Southern Capital

Following Kūkai's illustrious career, many ritual lineages proliferated throughout the major monastic institutions in Japan. Kūkai did not establish a distinctly new school or sect apart from the dominant institutional structure, so while the ritual practices he promoted grew in popularity, his doctrinal writings seem to have eventually fallen out of fashion. Kōyasan, the monastic training center and the site of his tomb, was eventually all but abandoned. From the eleventh to twelfth century on, however, a confluence of forces led to the revival of Kōyasan as a monastic training and pilgrimage site and the revitalization of "Kūkai studies" as an active area of dedicated scholastic inquiry. This development established Kūkai as a central figure around which a lineage identity and something like a distinct Shingon school formed.[65]

Aspiration for rebirth in Sukhāvatī was a significant factor in the revival of both Kōyasan and Kūkai studies. Before turning to consider the development of Esoteric Pure Land thought on Kōyasan and Kūkai's lineage, it is important to consider the careers of two key Esoteric Pure Land practitioners in the Nara capital, where Kūkai's ritual lineages first flourished.

Eikan of Zenrinji

Eikan took ordination at Tōdaiji's Tōnan-in 東南院 and studied under Jinkan 深觀 (1001–1050) at Zenrinji 禪林寺 in Heian-kyō. Zenrinji was founded by Kūkai's disciple, Shinshō 真紹 (797–873), and was under Tōdaiji's authority. This temple later came to be associated with the Seizan-ha 西山派 branch of the Jōdo-shū, which maintains close relations with the Tendai school even today and is regarded as the most "esoteric" of the lineages descending from Hōnen's Jōdo-shū. Eikan's teacher, Jinkan, also later served as *zasu* 座主 (abbot) of Kōyasan and *chōja* 長者 (the Tōji rank equivalent to *zasu*) of Tōji. At the time it was common for Kōyasan and Tōji to share *zasu* and for Nara temples to hold administrative roles over temples in Heian-kyō. Nara-based institutions remained quite powerful throughout the Heian and medieval periods, and from this the interconnected institutional environment of Eikan's early career is evident.

Eikan studied broadly in the evolving Buddhist scholastic culture. He studied *mikkyō* under Jingaku 深覺 (955–1043), an important monk associated with Tōdaiji and a former student of Jinkan, who retired to the Muryōju-in 無量壽院 (Temple of Amitāyus) on Kōyasan later in life (the same temple where Dōhan later passed away). Eikan was also known to have studied Madhyamaka under Yūgyō 有慶 (986–1071), but during his time in Nara he also apparently studied the *Avataṃsaka-sūtra*, Yogācāra, and more. His study of the Pure Land path under Chōyo 重譽 (d. ca. 1139–1143) at Kōmyō-san 光明山 in Yamato, a *bessho* 別所 (subsidiary temple) of Tōdaiji's Tōnan-in, seems to have left a lasting impression. At the age of forty, Eikan returned to Zenrinji and began lecturing on rebirth in Sukhāvatī. He eventually became strongly associated with Zenrinji, which is sometimes referred to as Eikan-dō 永觀堂 (Eikan's Hall).

Eikan is famous for having described himself as Eikan of the Nenbutsu-shū 念佛宗 and is perhaps the first monk in Japan to self-identify *buddhānusmṛti* as a distinctive lineage marker.[66] According to Inagaki, Eikan emphasized recitative *buddhānusmṛti* as an effective route to attaining rebirth in Sukhāvatī.[67] As was common at this time, his views were broadly informed by Madhyamaka and Yogācāra as well as *mikkyō* ritual practice. The *Ōjōjūin* 往生拾因 (T. 2683) is perhaps his most famous work.

In addition to promoting the recitative form of *buddhānusmṛti* as a simple practice that leads to rebirth in Sukhāvatī, Eikan also promoted recitation of dhāraṇī such as the Great Compassion Dhāraṇī and the *Uṣṇīṣavijayā-dhāraṇī*,[68] and in his works he draws upon the *Dhāraṇīsaṃgraha-sūtra*.[69] Eikan even promoted the recitation of the name of Amitābha as possessing even greater power than dhāraṇī.[70] He also declared that *buddhānusmṛti* is the highest practice, on par with if not surpassing the elite practices and doctrines of Shingon, Tendai, Madhyamaka, or Yogācāra. Through the Pure Land Dharma gate, Eikan suggested, there is neither high nor low: the *buddhānusmṛti* is the great equalizer.[71]

Chingai

Like Eikan, Chingai was a product of Tōdaiji's Tōnan-in. He studied broadly in Madhyamaka, Yogācāra, and logic and composed many works spanning the whole range of Mahayana scholasticism. Chingai also studied *mikkyō* under Jōkai 定海 (1074–1149) of the Sanbō-in 三寶院 lineage of Daigoji, which today houses one of the major lineages of the Shingon school (examined in greater detail in chapter 4). Chingai is regarded as one of the great painters of the late Heian period. His teacher Jōkai requested that he paint a mandala for the *Renwang jing*, the *Nin'ō gyōhō sokusai mandara* 仁王經法息災曼荼羅, as well as the mandala of the five directions, the *Gohō mandara* 五方曼荼羅, and many others.[72]

Chingai's writings on rebirth in Sukhāvatī, especially the *Ketsujō ōjō shū* 決定往生集 (T. 2684), were especially influential. Like Eikan, Chingai presents practices leading to rebirth in Sukhāvatī as embedded in a diverse ritual program, not somehow distinct or separate from mantra and dhāraṇī practices. He discusses the "essence of the pure [land] teachings," *jōkyō no shū* 浄教之宗, a phrase that may be taken as an early version of "Pure Land Buddhism" or "Pure Land school." This may indicate that, like Eikan, Chingai regarded the Pure Land gate as a distinct path within the broader program or perhaps that he saw himself as presenting the essence of the teachings on rebirth in Sukhāvatī.[73] Both meanings were possibly intended.

Chingai promoted a variety of practices said to lead to rebirth in Sukhāvatī: contemplation of images of Amitābha (an appropriate prescription from a revered artist), devotion to the *Lotus Sutra*, and recitation of the Amitābha spell (a common name for the mantra of the Buddha in Amoghavajra's *Wuliang rulai guanxing gongyang yigui*). Chingai regarded the latter as a practice promoted by Nāgārjuna, the patriarch of the Madhyamaka tradition.[74]

Drawing from the Korean monk Wŏnhyo 元曉 (617–686), Chingai also promoted the practice of the *Kōmyō Shingon* 光明真言, or Mantra of Light: *Oṃ amogha vairocana mahāmudrā maṇipadma jvāla pravarttaya hūṃ*. This mantra was famously used to "charge" sand to sprinkle over the body of a deceased person to purify the person's past karma and send the deceased to Sukhāvatī.[75] The Mantra of Light, which emerged as a popular practice in early medieval Japan, was closely associated with *buddhānusmṛti*.[76] Chingai noted that while attaining Buddhahood while still in samsara was difficult, one could quickly attain Buddhahood in Sukhāvatī, where one could engage in more advanced practices that lead rapidly to awakening.[77]

Discussing these practices in the context of the broader spectrum of Mahayana, Chingai emphasized the importance of reciting the name of Amitābha for those of lesser attainment. He saw the practice of *nenbutsu* as a means by which ordinary beings might be assured of rebirth in the Pure Land through even a single moment of faith and giving rise to the mind that seeks awakening (*bodhicitta*).[78]

The Fall and Rise of Kōyasan

In addition to the major Nara monastic centers, Kūkai also established Kōyasan as an ideal training center for dedicated meditation practice far away from the capitals in Heian and Nara. Kōyasan, literally, "high mountain plain," consists of a basin surrounded by higher peaks. Kūkai purportedly identified eight peaks as representing the eight petals of the lotus blossom at the center of the Womb Realm mandala, a fortuitous sign indeed. He was finally able to retire to Kōyasan shortly before his death in 835, spending his final days in meditation. Kūkai's disciple Shinzen 真然 (804–891) is believed to have built a temple on the site where Kongōbuji, the central administrative temple for the Kōyasan school of Shingon, now stands.

Some presentations of the history of Kōyasan downplay the prominence of Sukhāvatī aspirants, focusing instead on the life and teachings of Kūkai and the orthodox thinkers regarded by contemporary scholars as the "string of pearls" stretching back to the founder himself. In part, this redirecting of the narrative is intended to draw a clear line between the contemporary sectarian institutions and the founder. Yet this historiography has often left out the dynamic Esoteric Pure Land culture that developed on the mountain and ignores the fact that the revitalization of Kōyasan, the rebuilding of the mountaintop center, and its establishment as a major transsectarian pilgrimage center were due in large part to the widespread belief that Kūkai remained on Kōyasan as a bodhisattva-like savior figure capable of guiding beings to rebirth in Sukhāvatī, Tuṣita, or any of the other popular postmortem destinations.

From early on Kōyasan seems to have served as a site for meditation and devotion to Kūkai as a lineage ancestor. According to William Londo, due to its considerable distance from the vital center of political and economic power, an ongoing contentious relationship with Tōji, and a series of natural disasters and other problematic events, Kōyasan's early history is somewhat tragic, leading to a rapid decline by the tenth century. Jichie 實慧 (786–847), a direct student of Kūkai, oversaw Tōji and was followed by another of Kukai's disciples, Shinzei 真濟 (800–860). Shinzei petitioned the court to consolidate Kōyasan's and Tōji's yearly ordinands, effectively bequeathing Kōyasan's priests to Tōji. However, when Shinzen became the abbot of both Tōji and Kōyasan, he worked to once again guarantee that Kōyasan would continue to receive its own ordained monastics independent of Tōji's allocation.[79]

In 883, perhaps to further bolster Kōyasan's prominence, Shinzen encouraged Emperor Yōzei 陽成天皇 (869–948; r. 876–884) to make a pilgrimage to the site in order to attain salvation in Maitreya Bodhisattva's Tuṣita Heaven. It is unknown whether or not Kūkai actually promoted aspiration for postmortem rebirth in Tuṣita or devotion to Maitreya Bodhisattva. However, Hayami argues that evidence may indicate that at least some of Kūkai's early disciples believed he had a special relationship with Maitreya.[80] Soon after Kūkai's death, stories began to circulate that he had not actually died but had instead entered a state of eternal meditation, awaiting the descent of Maitreya to Kōyasan. Abiding between two worlds, neither alive nor dead, neither in this world nor removed from it, Kūkai thus was seen as a kind of spiritual conduit for the attainment of rebirth in Tuṣita.

In 877, Shinzen sent a collection of works attributed to Kūkai, the *Sanjūchō sasshi* 三十帖冊子, to Kōyasan in order to bolster the prestige of the mountain complex and its independence. This eventually led to another dispute between Tōji and Kōyasan. In 912 the abbot of Tōji, Kangen 觀賢 (853–925), demanded that the texts be returned. Mukū 無空 (d. 916), a respected ascetic and abbot of Kōyasan, refused. After a yearslong stalemate, Mukū resigned his position and abandoned the mountain with a large faction of monks in 916, and the group resettled in Yamashiro 山城. Following this series of events, Kōyasan was practically abandoned.[81] Mukū's auspicious rebirth in Sukhāvatī is recorded in the *Kōyasan ōjōden* 高野山往生傳, a collection of stories compiled by a monk named Nyojaku 如寂 (n.d.) in 1184 about people who were reborn in Sukhāvatī on Kōyasan.[82]

According to Londo, inconsistencies in funding and renovation, as well as a succession of natural and human-caused disasters throughout the tenth century, led to Kōyasan's decline and near extinction. In 952 Kūkai's mausoleum burned down. Gashin 雅真 (d. 999) was dispatched by Kankū 寛空 (884–972), abbot of Tōji, to rebuild the area. The reconstruction work was completed in only six months, but another fire in 994 decimated the complex yet again. In 998 the court stepped in and appointed Ōe no Kagemasa 大江景理, the governor of Kii Province 紀伊國 (present-day Wakayama Prefecture), to oversee the rebuilding efforts, but he embezzled and mismanaged the funds and the land revenue. After Gashin passed away, with the renovations incomplete, others attempted to complete the work, but ongoing obstacles, a lack of consistent funding, and so on led to the further decline of the mountain center. Emperor Uda 宇多天皇 (867–931; r. 887–897) visited Kōyasan in 900, but very few subsequent imperial trips were taken to the mountain until Fujiwara no Michinaga's pilgrimage in 1023. Kōyasan was not reborn as a major site of devotion and institutional vitality until the mid- to late eleventh century.[83]

Pure Land Preachers of Kōyasan

Arguably, one of the most important single individuals responsible for the revitalization of Kōyasan as a political, economic, and religious site was the itinerant Nara-based Kōfukuji monk Kishin Shōnin Jōyo 祈親上人定譽 (958–1047). Jōyo (also sometimes referred to as Kishin) belonged to a class of monks called *kanjinsō* 勸進僧, who were tasked with traveling throughout the country to fundraise and preach to the laity, two activities that often went hand in hand. He was especially well known as an accomplished reciter of the sutras (*jikyōsha* 持經者). From the beginning, Mahayana literature emphasized the many benefits said to arise from hearing or reciting the sutras. By traveling around disseminating the Dharma, itinerant ascetics were simultaneous spreading and accumulating merit.

Jōyo studied Yogācāra and Esoteric Buddhism at Kōfukuji and seems to have been a *Lotus Sutra* devotee. Like Xuanzang and Dōshō, he was also an aspirant for rebirth in Tuṣita. The popularity of Maitreya/Tuṣita devotion extended to Jōshō 定昭 (906–983), who served as abbot of Kōfukuji, Tōji, and Kongōbuji. Jōyo was able to build on the popularity of Maitreya devotion and aspiration for rebirth in Tuṣita to further establish ties to Kōyasan.

According to traditional narratives, Jōyo had a mystical vision at the famous Hasedera Temple 長谷寺 in which a mysterious figure carried him far through the air to the southwest, to a mountain site in a state of disrepair. In the dream Jōyo was inspired to build a stupa at the site. When he awoke, he sought counsel from the image of Avalokiteśvara Bodhisattva at Hasedera through ritual practice dedicated to the bodhisattva. This produced a vision of Jōyo's future rebirth in Tuṣita that would result from his efforts to rebuild Kōyasan.[84]

Londo suggests that Jōyo was in a unique position for his ultimately successful fundraising. Jōyo began to raise funds in 1016 and was initially able to tap official and nonofficial support networks, including temple priests and affiliated and nonaffiliated peripatetic ascetics and ritual practitioners, commonly referred to as *hijiri* 聖. Within a few years, construction was underway, and the halls of Kōyasan were once again ready to house priests performing rituals for state protection and for study in various ritual lineages, as well as aspirants for rebirth in the *buddhakṣetra* of the ten directions.[85]

Jōyo did not work in isolation, however; Gorai Shigeru 五来重 notes that even though Kōyasan had for the most part fallen by the wayside, some ascetics and hermits had remained at the site.[86] These *hijiri* continued to play an important role in the popularization of Kōyasan throughout its history. Londo also notes that Jōyo received some assistance from the Kōya *mandokoro* 高野政所, the office officially in charge of Kōyasan stationed at Jison-in 慈尊院 at the base of the mountain. However, it was unable to provide much in the way of financial support.[87]

Following Jōyo's career, the next figure to organize *hijiri* efforts on Kōyasan was the monk Kyōkai 教懐 (1001–1093), who established a lineage in the Odawara 小田原 area of Kōyasan in 1073.[88] Kyōkai's Esoteric Pure Land orientation was expressed through his simultaneous practice of Amitābha-focused deity yoga, recitation of the *Uṣṇīṣavijayā-dhāraṇī* and the Amitābha Buddha mantra, worship of the Vajra and Womb World mandalas, and so on. Just as Jōyo had tapped his high-level connections at Kōfukuji to aid his fundraising efforts, Kyōkai enlisted the help of

Emperor Shirakawa, leading the emperor to undertake a pilgrimage to Kōyasan in 1088 and 1091. This ultimately led to the rebuilding of the Great Stupa, further construction, and increases in Kōyasan's landholdings.[89]

Revival of "Kūkai Studies"

Coincidentally, a separate effort to rehabilitate Kōyasan and the legacy of Kūkai was underway at Ninnaji in the Heian capital. Ninnaji, founded by Emperor Uda, was regarded as an *omuro* 御室, a title for a temple closely affiliated with the imperial family. In fact, until 1869 Ninnaji abbots were members of the imperial family. Since its inception Amitābha has been the principle object of devotion in Ninnaji's main hall. There is also a hall dedicated to Kūkai near the main hall.[90] From the eleventh century onward, Ninnaji was also the site of a concerted effort to revive Kūkai studies as an area of dedicated Buddhist scholasticism.[91]

After Kūkai's influential career, the ritual manuals he worked to import into Japan continued to play an important role in the monastic curriculum at all major temples, but there was scant interest in his doctrinal writings until Ninnaji monks, perhaps in response to the rise of Hieizan as a dominant force, began to promote Kūkai as a lineage ancestor and object of study and devotion in his own right. Shōshin 性信 (1005–1085), Saisen 濟暹 (1025–1115), Kyōjin 教尋 (d. 1141), Jōson 定尊 (ca. 1118), Kakuban, and Jippan 實範 (d. 1144) were all major figures associated with Ninnaji and the revival of Kūkai studies. Many of these monks were also keenly interested in Amitābha Buddha devotion and wrote about rebirth in Sukhāvatī as well. Furthermore, Saisen, a student of Shōshin, was not only central to the revival of Kūkai studies; he is credited with the discovery and editing of several of the works now regarded as central to Kūkai's thought. Saisen apparently wrote a number of works on the *Contemplation Sutra,* but none has survived.[92]

Ningai 仁海 (951-1046), one of the most influential monks active at this time, established his reputation in 1018 by purportedly successfully performing a rainmaking ritual.[93] Ningai was supposedly also a mountain ascetic who encouraged other ascetics and promoted aspiration for rebirth in Sukhavati. Londo notes that Ningai also attempted to raise funds for the revitalization of Kōyasan, and he is credited with having led Fujiwara no Michinaga to the mountain in 1023. Despite his fame, Ningai failed in his initial attempt to revive

Kōyasan but lent his support and resources once he heard of Jōyo's success. The revitalization of Kōyasan was thus tied to both Nara- and Kyoto-based lineages that promoted devotion to Kūkai as a savior figure and the study of Kūkai's texts as the teachings of an enlightened being.[94]

Kakuban and Esoteric Pure Land Thought

Commonly regarded as the second founder of the Shingon school and the de facto founder of the Shingi-Shingon lineage 新義真言宗, Kakuban is also closely associated with the *himitsu nenbutsu* and Esoteric Pure Land Buddhism in Japan and was a major influence on Dōhan's Esoteric Pure Land thought. The reestablishment of Kōyasan as an active pilgrimage site, the creation of Kūkai studies as a significant area of Esoteric Buddhist scholasticism, the active engagement with powerful Nara- and Kyoto-based temples, and the dynamic role of peripatetic ascetics all had a significant impact on Kakuban's career. Before turning to Dōhan, I will briefly touch upon Kakuban's short but influential career. Like Kūkai and other important figures associated with the historiography of the Shingon school, Kakuban is usually presented in a fairly uncomplicated, clearly sectarian mode. However, his career is as complicated and his influences as diverse as the mountain complex he would eventually call home.

Like many monks at the time, Kakuban studied widely across many different lineages and at many institutions. He entered Jōju-in temple at Ninnaji, where he studied under Kanjo 寛助 (1057–1125), a student of Shōshin. Kanjo and Shōshin were both influential figures in Ninnaji Kūkai studies and promoted the practice of the *denbō kanjō*, which would have a lasting impact on Kakuban.[95] He later studied Yogācāra at Kōfukuji, as well as Kegon and Madhyamaka at Tōdaiji. At Daigoji he received initiation into the Hirosawa lineage 廣澤流 under Jōkai 定海 (1074–1149) of Sanbō-in 三寶院 and into the Ono lineage 小野流 from Kanjin 寛信 of Kanjūji 勸修寺. Kakuban also studied under Genkaku 賢覺 (1080–1156) of Daigoji's Rishō-in 理性院.

Daigoji, founded in 874 by Shōbō, takes its name from Emperor Daigo 醍醐天皇 (885–930; r. 897–930), who later retired to the monastery and whose ashes are interred there as well. Shōbō began his career in Nara, studying the *Avataṃsaka-sūtra* and Madhyamaka and Yogācāra, and established the Tōnan-in, a highly regarded site for Madhyamaka scholarship, at Tōdaiji. He maintained a close relationship with Daigoji, which was often administered by the same abbot. Shōbō is traditionally regarded as the patriarch of the Ono lineage, with which Daigoji is associated. Shōbō also studied under two famous disciples of Kūkai, Shinzen and Shinga 真雅 (801–879). Under Shinzen he studied rituals for the Vajra and Womb Realm mandalas. Under Shinga, who also taught Mukū, he studied rituals associated with Amitāyus Buddha.[96]

Daigoji is near the Kasatori mountains 笠取山 southeast of the Heian capital, a site, much like Kōyasan, populated by ascetic practitioners in pursuit of rebirth in Tuṣita Heaven. The Shugendō tradition claims Shōbō as an early Shugendō master at Kinpusen 金峯山 in Nara. The Sanbō-in lineage, the dominant lineage at Daigoji, is associated with the Daigoji Shugendō tradition; its principle object of devotion is Maitreya Bodhisattva.

In addition to Maitreya devotion centered at the Sanbō-in, as with Hieizan, Kōyasan, and Tōji, the main object of devotion for the Daigoji complex is the Medicine Buddha. The Medicine Buddha is revered not only as an emanation of dharmakāya capable of bestowing this-worldly benefits but also as a "cure" for one's negative karma through postmortem rebirth in the Pure Land of Lapis Lazuli in the eastern quarter and even rebirth in Sukhāvatī in the western quarter.

Shōbō is credited with the installation of images of Cintāmaṇi-cakra Avalokiteśvara and Cundī Avalokiteśvara, two popular "esoteric" emanations of the Bodhisattva of Compassion that remain popular as objects of devotion and pilgrimage today. Avalokiteśvara is commonly associated with Amitābha, and dhāraṇī texts devoted to Avalokiteśvara's many forms consistently reference Amitābha and Pure Land rebirth in Sukhāvatī. This association between Avalokiteśvara and Amitābha is on full display in the hall at Daigoji today, where the famous image of Cundī Avalokiteśvara resides. Before and around the figure is a diverse array of buddhas, bodhisattvas, and gods, but a large statue of Amitābha towers over the figure of Avalokiteśvara. Indeed, Amitābha looms large in this diverse ritual and devotional environment, and as the examples above show, various approaches to rebirth were practiced at Daigoji alongside training in elite ritual lineages.

In addition to Ninnaji and Daigoji, Kakuban also studied at Miidera, where he received abhiṣeka from Kakuyū 覺猷 (1053–1140).[97] Today, Ninnaji and Daigoji are usually regarded as Shingon school temples and Miidera as a Tendai temple. However, at the time all of these temples were "Shingon" in the same way that the major temples of Nara or Enryakuji on Hieizan were Shingon. In other words, these major temple complexes all had diverse lineages with monks who aspired to mastery of the "secret *piṭaka*." While Kakuban's diverse background seems to resist the categorization typical of contemporary sectarian thought, this breadth of lineage and praxis was typical of elite monks in Japan and East Asia at this time.

In 1115 Kakuban studied on Kōyasan and received further training. His Odawara lineage was one of the prominent and well-connected *hijiri* lineages on Kōyasan, but eventually Kakuban's Mitsugon-in 密嚴院 lineage became a popular site for Esoteric Pure Land Buddhist practice as well. Like Kyōkai, Kakuban's fortuitous relationship with an emperor was key to his future success. Thanks to the patronage of Emperor Toba, Kakuban established the Daidenbō-in in 1130 and eventually revived the *denbōe* 傳法會 (Dharma transmission ritual), which, as Abé argues, served a key role in solidifying Kūkai's vision of the mantra practitioner as establishing a direct link to the dharmakāya.[98]

Abé suggests that Shingon Dharma transmission, according to Kakuban's reading of Kūkai, transmits the potency of the Buddha "diachronically,"[99] directly from buddha reality to ordinary beings. Whether from Śākyamuni to his disciples or from Mahāvairocana to Vajrasattva Bodhisattva, as in the *Mahāvairocana-sūtra,* the potency of the Dharma is not diminished by its transmission through manifold forms such as stupas, sutras, and treatises by enlightened beings, as well as the various practices described in Buddhist literature. Ultimate reality, the dharmakāya, teaches beings through infinite Dharma gates.[100]

In 1134 the emperor granted Kakuban the position of abbot of Daidenbō-in and *inju* 院主 of Kongōbuji.[101] This rapid ascent through the ranks earned him the ire of conservative factions on the mountain, and Kakuban stepped down in 1135. Perhaps because of its remoteness from the center of power in the capital, or due to diverse interests competing for ascendancy on the mountain, Kōyasan has often been afflicted by violent factionalism. The struggle between Kongōbuji and Daidenbō-in is just one example, and ongoing conflagrations between these two institutions was formative not only for Kakuban but also for Dōhan later on. In 1140 the Kongōbuji faction made an attempt on Kakuban's life, and the Daidenbō-in was burned down. Kakuban retreated to Negoroji 根來寺 with a cadre of seven hundred loyal monastics.

Kakuban is commonly regarded as the founder of the Shingi lineage of Shingon, though this appellation seems to have been projected onto him later. The eruptions of factionalist violence on Kōyasan were a recurring problem before Kakuban's time, during Dōhan's lifetime, and after: the famous Shingon scholar-monk Raiyu 頼瑜 (1226–1304) fled Kōyasan and moved both the Daidenbō-in and the Mitsugon-in from Kōyasan to Negoroji. This newly established community came to view Kakuban as their founder. The Shingi and the so-called Kogi ("old") factions eventually came to promote two different interpretations of the nature of the dharmakāya's preaching. Monks associated with Shingi argued that accommodated forms are required for ultimate reality to meet beings of differing capacities. This teaching is referred to as *kajishinsetsu* 加持身説. Kogi monks promoted the *honji shinsetsu* 本地身説, the idea that Mahāvairocana preaches to beings directly. While the Shingi doctrinal position has traditionally been attributed to Kakuban, McMullen and others argue that this was a later development.[102]

Kakuban and Esoteric Pure Land Buddhism

Kakuban died at a fairly young age in 1143, yet he significantly influenced the Esoteric Pure Land culture of early medieval Kōyasan. By his time, *buddhānusmṛti* had already emerged as a major form of practice popular among elite monks throughout Japan and on Kōyasan as well as among the many *hijiri* who traveled between mountains and monastic centers seeking alms or awakening. Kakuban's Mitsugon-in temple was a *buddhānusmṛti* practice site to which *hijiri* apparently flocked, and *hijiri* in the Ōjō-in dani 往生院谷 area of Kōyasan later came to regard Kakuban as their lineage patriarch. Gorai notes that these *hijiri* may have been attracted to the thaumaturgical potential of *buddhānusmṛti* and related practices, as well as their capacity for purifying negative karma.[103]

Kakuban was associated around 1114 with the monk Aba Shōnin Shōren 阿波上人青蓮, a pilgrim who traveled throughout the Kii Province, including both Kōyasan and Kumano. Shōren eventually settled at the Ōjō-in at Henshōkō-in on Kōyasan. His lineage grew to prominence at Kayadō 萱堂 and Mitsugon-in.[104] Another *buddhānusmṛti* practice site on Kōyasan was established at Kakkō-in 覺皇院 by Kakuban's student Kenkai 兼海 (1107–1155).[105]

Kakuban's Esoteric Pure Land perspective is explained in the influential *Gorin kujimyō himitsu shaku* 五輪九字明秘密釋 (T. 2514), a text from which Dōhan draws frequently. Weaving together Chinese theories of the five viscera,[106] Indian theories of the "five *cakras*,"[107] and an esoteric exegesis of the Amitābha mantra, Kakuban conceives of the whole human person (unified in body and spirit) as a locus for the soteriological activity of the Buddha. Kakuban's *Amida hisshaku* 阿彌陀秘釋 (T. 2522), which

Dōhan also references, examines the relationship between Amitābha and Mahāvairocana, arguing that, as with all things, Amitābha is in essence but one aspect of ultimate reality. He also suggests that literal (or "exoteric") teachings about postmortem rebirth are intended to teach those of lesser capacities, but in fact, Sukhāvatī is accessible right here and now—"this" world and "that" world are not fundamentally separate. In other words, to conceive of Sukhāvatī, or any of the other *buddha-kṣetra,* simply as a far-distant, discrete world is in some sense taking the long way around. The attainment of Buddhahood in this very body through the practice of mantra (and according to Kakuban, the recitative *buddhānusmṛti* ultimately is a mantra) and going for rebirth in Sukhāvatī are not necessarily two inherently distinct goals. This notion is mirrored in Dōhan's Esoteric Pure Land writings.

Butsugon and the Mitsugon-in

Between Kakuban and Dōhan, Butsugon bō Shōshin 佛嚴房聖心 (late twelfth to early thirteenth century) serves as a link in the development of a kind of Esoteric Pure Land lineage. Butsugon was active in the Negoroji lineage and is associated with Kenkai and Daijō bō Shōin 大乘房證印 (1105–1187), but he eventually took up residence at the Mitsugon-in on Kōyasan. He was a student of Kyōjin 教尋 (?–1141), a devotee of Mañjuśrī Bodhisattva and an aspirant for Sukhāvatī rebirth whose miraculous deathbed experience is recorded in the *Kōyasan ōjōden.*[108] According to Wada Shūjō 和多秀乘, Butsugon's *Jūnen gokuraku iōshū* 十念極樂易往集, written for Go-Shirakawa 後白河法皇 (1127–1192) around 1176, concludes with a section titled *Ichigo taiyō rinjū mon* 一期大要臨終門, which bears a striking resemblance to a work traditionally attributed to Kakuban, the *Ichigo taiyō himitsu shū* 一期大要祕密集. Wada suggests that this demonstrates the popularity of Kakuban's Esoteric Pure Land thought after his death.[109]

As Japanese Buddhists engaged in cross-cultural dialogue with their counterparts on the continent, diverse texts and practices that do not easily fit into standard sectarian rubrics coalesced. Throughout the early history of Japanese Buddhism, Esoteric Buddhism and Pure Land Buddhism flowed together as mutually informative and internally diverse currents that pervaded the whole of Japanese Buddhism. In this overview and examination of early Nara and Heian period Buddhist traditions, I have attempted to decenter our understanding of Esoteric Buddhism and Pure Land Buddhism as monolithic, autonomous entities, highlighting areas of overlap and harmony and ultimately pointing to the diversity of approaches to Pure Land thought and practice through the early evolution of Japanese ritual culture.

Notes

Chapter 3: Early Japanese Esoteric Pure Land Buddhism

1 Kazuhiko Yoshida, "Religion in the Classical Period," in *Nanzan Guide to Japanese Religions,* ed. Paul L. Swanson and Clark Chilson (Honolulu: University of Hawai'i Press, 2006), pp. 145–146.

2 Herman Ooms, *Imperial Politics and Symbolics in Ancient Japan: The Tenmu Dynasty, 650–800* (Honolulu: University of Hawai'i Press, 2009); Michael Como, *Weaving and Binding: Immigrant Gods and Female Immortals in Ancient Japan* (Honolulu: University of Hawai'i Press, 2009).

3 Michael Como, *Shōtoku: Ethnicity, Ritual and Violence in the Japanese Buddhist Tradition* (Oxford: Oxford University Press, 2008); Kevin G. Carr, *Plotting the Prince: Shōtoku Cults and the Mapping of Medieval Japanese Buddhism* (Honolulu: University of Hawai'i Press, 2012).

4 Hisao Inagaki, *The Three Pure Land Sutras: A Study and Translation from Chinese* (Kyoto: Nagata bunshōdo, 1995), p. 141.

5 Robert F. Rhodes, "The Beginnings of Pure Land Buddhism in Japan: From Its Introduction through the Nara Period," *Japanese Religions* 31, no. 1 (2006): 1–22.

6 Inagaki, *Three Pure Land Sutras,* p. 143; MBD, 264b.

7 Hayami Tasuku 速水侑, *Jōdo shinkō ron* 浄土信仰論 (Tokyo: Yūzankaku shuppan, 1978), pp. 60–66.

8 Clemente Beghi, "The Dissemination of Esoteric Scriptures in Eighth Century Japan," in Orzech, Sørensen, and Payne, *Esoteric Buddhism and the Tantras in East Asia,* p. 663.

9 Beghi, "The Dissemination of Esoteric Scriptures," pp. 661, 675–681; James L. Ford, "Exploring the Esoteric in Nara Buddhism," in Orzech, Sørensen, and Payne, *Esoteric Buddhism and the Tantras in East Asia,* p. 777.

10 MBD, 3876b.

11 Beghi, "Dissemination of Esoteric Scriptures," p. 661.

12 T. 1345:855a4; Yoritomi Motohiro 頼富本宏, "Nihon mikkyō no seiritsu to tenkai" 日本密教の成立と展開, in *Nihon mikkyō* 日本密教, ed. Tachikawa Musashi 立川武蔵 and Motohiro Yoritomi 頼富本宏 (Tokyo: Shunshūsha, 2005), pp. 25–26.

13 Inoue Mitsusada 井上光貞, *Nihon jōdokyō seiritsushi no kenkyū* 日本浄土教成立史の研究 (Tokyo: Yamakawa shuppansha, 1956), pp. 7–27.

14 Inagaki, *Three Pure Land Sutras,* pp. 143–144.

15 Como, *Shōtoku: Ethnicity, Ritual and Violence,* p. 140.

16 MBD, 3871c–3872a.

17 T. 1333:563a21.

18 Abé, *Weaving of Mantra,* pp. 74–75.

19 Beghi, "Dissemination of Esoteric Scriptures," p. 661.

20 MBD, 5022c; Beghi, "Dissemination of Esoteric Scriptures," p. 663.

21 Beghi, "Dissemination of Esoteric Scriptures," p. 662.

22 Nakano Satoshi 中野聡, *Nara jidai no Amida nyoraizō to jōdo shinkō* 奈良時代の阿弥陀如来像と浄土信仰 (Tokyo: Bensei shuppan, 2013) examines in great detail the role played by the powerful women of the Nara period in establishing Pure Land faith and Amitābha devotion as a national phenomenon. Having read his book, I would argue that in order to truly understand the history of Pure Land Buddhism the central role of women cannot be ignored. This is an area I hope to explore in greater detail in the future.

23 Beghi, "Dissemination of Esoteric Scriptures," p. 662.

24 Kakehashi Nobuaki 梯信暁, *Jōdokyō shisōshi: Indo, Chūgoku, Chōsen, Nihon* 浄土教思想史:インド・中国・朝鮮・日本 (Kyoto: Hōzōkan, 2012), pp. 72–73.

25 Nemoto Seiji 根本誠二, *Nara Bukkyō to Mikkyō* 奈良仏教と密教 (Tokyo: Koshi shoin, 2011).

26 Beghi, "Dissemination of Esoteric Scriptures," p. 663.

27 Ibid., p. 666.

28 Ibid., pp. 665–666.

29 Ibid., p. 663.

30 T. 2409:33b13.

31 Abé, *Weaving of Mantra,* p. 21.

32 Emperor Shōtoku is often remembered for her controversial relationship with the monk Dōkyō 道鏡 (d. 772). A former student of Rōben at Tōdaiji, Dōkyō was revered for his powers as a healer, acquired through "esoteric" ascetic practices in the mountains. When Kōken became ill, Dōkyō was credited with helping her regain her health. As their relationship grew closer, Kōken/Shōtoku bestowed a series of titles on Dōkyō, eventually granting him the title *hōō* 法王 (Dharma king). On Shōtoku's death, rivals of the Shōtoku/Dōkyō regime, perhaps fearful that Dōkyō might become emperor, seized the opportunity to banish Dōkyō and propagated a smear campaign against him. Scholars speculate that some factions at court were angered by

Emperor Shōtoku/Kōken favoring Dōkyō and the sangha over other power holders. As the rumors of Dōkyō's evil ways spread, concern grew in the court over the role of the sangha and the importance of maintaining a pure priesthood that could harness the powers of the buddhas, bodhisattvas, and gods while working for the benefit of the realm (and the ruling elites).

33 The Ten Great Temples are Daianji 大安寺, Gangōji 元興寺, Kōfukuji 興福寺, Yakushiji 薬師寺, Tōdaiji 東大寺, Saidaiji 西大寺, Hōryūji 法隆寺, Kōfukuji 弘福寺 (Kawara-dera 川原寺), Shitennōji 四天王寺, and Sōfukuji 崇福寺.

34 Katsuura Noriko 勝浦令子, "Higashi Ajia no 'Mukujōkō daidaranikyō' juyō to hyakumantō 東アジアの『無垢浄光大陀羅尼経』受容と百万塔," in *Nara-Heian Bukkyō no tenkai* 奈良・平安仏教の展開, ed. Hayami Tasuku 速水侑 (Tokyo: Yoshikawa kōbunkan, 2006), pp. 2–31.

35 Katsuura, "Higashi Ajia no 'Mukujōkō daidaranikyō,'" p. 24.

36 Ibid., p. 8, citing the *Kakuzenshō* 覺禪鈔, DNBZ 54:93–96.

37 Abé, *Weaving of Mantra,* pp. 399–403.

38 Hayami Tasuku 速水侑, *Jujutsu shūkyō no sekai* 呪術宗教の世界 (1987; repr., Tokyo: Hanawa shinsho, 2007), pp. 41–50.

39 Thomas Eijō Dreitlein and Takagi Shingen, *Kūkai on the Philosophy of Language* (Tokyo: Keio University Press, 2010) pp. 374, 401–402; see p. 356 on the dharmakāya of truth and the dharmakāya of wisdom.

40 Abé, *Weaving of Mantra,* pp. 125–126.

41 Ibid., p. 271.

42 Ibid., p. 58.

43 Ibid., p. 6.

44 大分爲五。一蘇多覽藏。二毘那藏。三阿毘達磨藏。四般若藏。五總持藏。(T. 2461:3a8–9).

45 依佛説經判有五種別。至菩薩説人師談其流有八。一律宗。二倶舍宗。三成實宗。四法相宗。五三論宗。六天台。七花嚴。八真言。初三謂之小乘。次四謂之大乘。後一祕密金剛乘也。 (T. 2461:3a24–29).

46 Abé, *Weaving of Mantra,* pp. 191–194.

47 Ibid., pp. 386–388.

48 The list of the ten stages of the mind can be found at T. 2425:303c29–304a5, followed by a lengthy explanation.

49 I owe these insights to conversations with my former advisors at Kōyasan University, Nakamura Honnen and Thomas Eijō Dreitlein. Regarding Kūkai's reading of exoteric teachings as containing the esoteric truths, see Thomas Eijō Dreitlein, "An Annotated Translation of Kūkai's *Secret Key to the Heart Sūtra,*" *Kōyasan daigaku mikkyō bunka kenkyūsho kiyō* 高野山大学密教文化研究所紀要 24 (2011): 1–3.

50 Abé, *Weaving of Mantra,* p. 46.

51 Ford, "Exploring the Esoteric in Nara Buddhism," pp. 781–782.

52 Abé, *Weaving of Mantra,* p. 404.

53 Ibid., p. 13.

54 Ibid., p. 10.

55 Ibid., p. 374.

56 BKD 10:18. For a translation of the *Jūen shōkai* version of this text, very similar in content, see Dreitlein, "Annotated Translation of Kūkai's *Secret Key to the Heart Sutra,*" pp. 1–41.

57 T. 2190:174c1–4.

58

> 今真言宗意。據金剛頂經。擧人名妙法蓮華者。乃觀自在如來密號也。此佛名無量壽。淨妙國土現阿彌陀佛身。五濁世界號觀自在菩薩。此菩薩名曰一切法平等觀自在智印。若聞此名。讀誦思惟設住欲。猶如華蓮客塵不染。疾證無上正等菩提。故觀自在菩薩手持蓮華。觀一切衆生身中如來藏性自性淸淨。此菩薩以*hṛīḥ*字爲種子。此字*ha, ra, i, aḥ*以四字。合爲一字之*hṛīḥ*字。名爲懺悔義。若具慚心不爲一切惡。即具一切無漏善法故。蓮華部名法部。此字加持力故。極樂世界水鳥樹木皆演法音。若人持此*hṛīḥ*字念誦。能除一切災禍疾病。命終後極樂淨土上品蓮臺。法華經廣略無邊義皆含藏上*hṛīḥ* 字。故念持此字門誦受一部法華經功德。此法華經於法*hṛīḥ*字於三摩地八葉蓮花於人觀自在王如來也。(T. 2190:183a29–b15).

This text corresponds to the version of the *Hokke kaidai* in the *Teihon Kōbōdaishi zenshū* 定本弘法大師全集 (TKZ), 4: 155–168; the equivalent passage is on pp. 159–160. For an explanation of the Esoteric Pure Land content of this text and an explanation of the title of the *Lotus Sutra* as the samādhi of Avalokiteśvara Bodhisattva, see pp. 456–461.

59 Sofū Sen'yōkai 祖風宣揚會, ed., *Kōbō Daishi zenshū* 弘法大師全集, vol. 2 (Tokyo: Yoshikawa kōbunkan 吉川弘文館, 1910), pp. 495–521; BKDJ 10: 445, 447, 448.

60 Nakamikado Keikyō 中御門敬教, "Muryōju nyorai kengyō kuyō giki" 無量寿如来観行供養儀軌, in *Jōdokyōtenseki mokuroku* 浄土教典籍目録 (Kyoto: Bukkyō daigaku sōgō kenkyūjo, 2011), pp. 27–28.

61 The following description is an updated, revised, and expanded version of a section in a previously published paper: Aaron P. Proffitt, "Nenbutsu Mandala Visualization in Dōhan's *Himitsu nenbutsu shō:* An Investigation into Medieval Japanese Vajrayāna Pure Land," *Pacific World,* 3rd ser., 15 (2013): 155–157.

62 Patrul Rinpoche, *The Words of My Perfect Teacher: A Complete Translation of a Classic Introduction to Tibetan Buddhism* (San Francisco: HarperCollins, 1994), pp. 351–366.

63 McMullen, "Development of Esoteric Buddhist Scholasticism," pp. 18–62.

64 T. 2425:317b17, 338a13–14, 351b3–6.

65 Abé, "From Kūkai to Kakuban," pp. 301–302.

66 T. 2683:91a4–5.

67 Inagaki, *Three Pure Land Sutras,* pp. 166–168.

68 T. 2683:92a1.

69 T. 2683:95b10–14.

70 彌陀名號殆過大陀羅尼之德 (T. 2683:92a3).

71

> 夫以衆生無始輪迴諸趣。諸佛更出濟度無量。恨漏諸佛之利益猶爲生死凡夫。適値釋尊之遺法。盍勵出離之聖行。一生空暮再會何日。真言止觀之行道幽易迷。三論法相之教理奧難悟。不勇猛精進者何修之。不聰明利智者誰學之。朝家簡定賜其賞。學徒競望增其欲。暗三密行忝登遍照之位。飾毀戒質誤居持律之職。實世間之假名智者之所厭也。今至念佛宗者所行佛號。不妨行住坐臥。所期極樂。不簡道俗貴賤。衆生罪重一念能滅。彌陀願深十念往生。公家不賞自離名位之欲。壇那不祈亦無虛受之罪。況南北諸宗互諍權實之教。西方一家觸無方便之門。(T. 2683:102a12–25).

72 MBD, 3624c–3625a.

73 T. 2684:102b29.

74 大乘神呪 (T. 2684:110c16–22).

75 元曉云。以光明真言呪彼土沙 (T. 2684:114c13).

76 Kushida, *Shingon mikkyō seiritsu katei no kenkyū,* pp. 172–180.

77 依三昧門陀羅尼門速得菩提 (T. 2684:107c4–10).

78 Kakehashi, *Jōdokyō shisōshi,* p. 121.

79 William Londo, "The Other Mountain: The Mt. Kōya Temple Complex in the Heian Era" (PhD diss., University of Michigan, 2004).

80 Hayami Tasuku 速水侑, *Miroku shinkō—mō hitotsu jōdo shinkō* 弥勒信仰—もう一つの浄 土信仰 (Tokyo: Hyōronsha, 1971), pp. 91–94.

81 Abé, "From Kūkai to Kakuban," pp. 269–270.

82 ZJZ 6.

83 Londo, "Other Mountain," pp. 65–70, 65n29.

84 Ibid., pp. 86–87, 96.

85 Ibid., p. 109.

86 Gorai Shigeru 五来重, *Kōya hijiri* 高野聖 (1975; repr., Tokyo: Kadokawa bunko 角川文庫, 2011), p. 110.

87 Londo, "Other Mountain," pp. 102–103.

88 Gorai, *Kōya hijiri,* pp. 104–116.

89 Ibid., pp. 117–127.

90 MD, 1775–1779.

91 Abé, "From Kūkai to Kakuban," pp. 301–304, 317–320.

92 Horiuchi Noriyuki 堀内規之, *Saisen kyōgaku no kenkyū: Inseiki shingonmikkyō no shomondai* 済暹教学の研究: 院政期真言密教の諸問題 (Tokyo: Nonburu, 2009), pp. 307–345, esp. pp. 328–330; Satō, *Eizan jōdokyō no kenkyū,* pp. 11–14, 397–425.

93 MD, 1768.

94 Londo, "Other Mountain," pp. 120–122.

95 van der Veere, *Study into the Thought of Kōgyō Daishi Kakuban,* p. 21.

96 KS, 35–43.

97 MD, 225–227.

98 Abé, "From Kūkai to Kakuban," p. 261.

99 Ibid., p. 6.

100 Ibid., pp. 136, 182, 214–219.

101 van der Veere, *Study into the Thought of Kōgyō Daishi Kakuban,* p. 39.

102 Matthew D. McMullen, "Raiyu and Shingi Shingon Sectarian History" (MA thesis, University of Hawai'i at Manoa, 2008).

103 Gorai, *Kōya hijiri,* pp. 123–124.

104 Ibid., pp. 128–138.

105 Ibid., p. 16.

106 In traditional Chinese medical theory, the five organs are the heart, lungs, liver, kidneys, and spleen.

107 T. 2514:13a17. The "five wheels" may denote the elements of earth, water, fire, wind, and ether; the traditional *cakras,* the crown of the head, face, heart, stomach, and knees; and the correspondence of both.

108 ZJZ 6:175.

109 Wada Shūjō 和多秀乗, "Jūnen gokuraku iōshū nit suite" 十念極楽易往集について, *Indogaku Bukkyōgaku kenkyū* 印度学仏教学研究 63 (1983): 1–10.

Chapter 4

Dōhan and the Esoteric Pure Land Culture of Kōyasan

So far I have focused on providing the historical context for the development of Esoteric Pure Land Buddhist thought and practice in East Asia. Now it is time to examine the life and thought of Dōhan and the Esoteric Pure Land culture of early medieval Kōyasan. There is relatively little information on the life of Dōhan, and for the most part, it is preserved in Edo-period histories that were possibly redacted or embellished.[1] The narrative gaps in the available information may be an advantage, however, that allows for broader engagement in the context of Dōhan's education, training, and intellectual output. I examine Dōhan as a participant in a diverse ritual, devotional, and institutional environment, emphasizing that neither he nor his Esoteric Pure Land thought should be studied in isolation. Ultimately, examining Dōhan as a product of and participant in his environment will result in a better understanding of Kōyasan and Esoteric Pure Land culture.

Dōhan was not only an influential thinker in Japanese Esoteric Buddhist scholastic circles, drawing from and influencing the scholarship of monks working on Kōyasan, in the Heian and Nara capitals, and at Hieizan. His influence also extended to the early Pure Land and Zen traditions as well. While traditional and modern Japanese Buddhist historians seemingly regard Dōhan as one of the great thinkers of the medieval era, until fairly recently very little scholarship on this enigmatic figure or his early medieval environment on Kōyasan has been conducted. A primary reason for this is that many Buddhist studies scholars begin their academic careers under the influence of one or more contemporary sectarian historiographic or doctrinal perspectives; in fact, I am no exception. Yet early medieval Japanese Buddhism was not structured in the same way as contemporary Japanese Buddhism. Rather than focusing on a particular lineage or interpretive schema to the exclusion of all others, monks like Dōhan would take their particular perspective as a starting point for reading and thinking broadly across the Mahayana tradition.

Dōhan was a scholar of Kūkai's works, a devotee of Amitābha Buddha, and a theorist on the nature of the mantra path. He trained at various temples on Kōyasan as well as at Daigoji, Zuishin-in 随心院, and Ninnaji in the capital—temples that in the Kamakura period housed major Shingon lineages and today are associated with the Shingon school. During the Kamakura period, however, each of these temple complexes was also a site for the study of a wide range of Buddhist scholastic and ritual traditions, and particular lineages were emphasized over others as political currents changed.

Enryakuji, Tōdaiji, Kōfukuji, and other temples could be thought of as sites for Shingon study, so it is not a mistake to characterize Dōhan as a "Shingon" monk, but how we understand this term in the early medieval period requires some nuance. Dōhan was broadly educated, and his later work demonstrates his proficiency in Tendai doctrine, the *Avataṃsaka-sūtra,* Yogācāra, and Madhyamaka. He was also clearly aware of developments in Chinese Buddhism, and later taught monks who were influential in the newly imported Zen tradition in Japan. It is precisely this kind of fluidity that the anachronistically sectarian study of Japanese Buddhism precludes.

In presenting Dōhan as a window onto early medieval Japanese Buddhism, I have drawn from traditional Shingon school scholarship.[2] I want to make clear that my critique of the influence of sectarianism on contemporary scholarship is not directed at traditional scholarship as such or toward the work of scholars with clear sectarian affiliations. I have benefited greatly from dialogue with scholars, priests, and scholar-priests associated with various schools in Japan and the US.

Nevertheless, there are many shortcomings in much of the earlier scholarship on Dōhan that should be addressed. In some cases, aspects of Dōhan's writing that align with contemporary orthodoxies are emphasized at the expense of others. Contemporary Shingon-shū scholarship focuses on the interpretation of the doctrinal works of Kūkai, and Dōhan is understood primarily as a scholar of Kūkai, which he was, among other things. In other cases, scholars inspired by late medieval and early modern sectarian polemical writing emphasize Dōhan's connections to the Tachikawa-ryū 立川流, a late medieval heterodox lineage that purportedly promoted a form of sexual yoga as a vehicle for the attainment of Buddhahood in this very body and rebirth in Sukhāvatī.[3] The fact that Dōhan has been viewed as both orthodox and heterodox reveals not only the fluidity of orthodoxy as an ever-changing construct but also the complexity and breadth of his doctrinal thought.

One of the more contentious issues addressed in both traditional and more recent scholarship on Dōhan is his understanding of Pure Land Buddhism. Like Kakuban, Dōhan is often characterized as someone who "syncretized" Pure Land Buddhism and Esoteric Buddhism. I hope to refute once and for all such an overly simplistic, anachronistic, and ahistorical perspective by establishing the prominent role that Sukhāvatī as a soteriological goal and *buddhānusmṛti* as a form of practice played within major Shingon lineages at various high-ranking temples on Kōyasan and in the capital. For example, the primary object of devotion in many temples where Dōhan trained, such as Shōchi-in, Hōkō-in on Kōyasan, and Zenrinji and Ninnaji in Heian-kyō, was, and remains, Amitābha Buddha. Many monks at other temples associated with Dōhan, Daigoji, Zuishin-in, Keō-in, and others also focused their scholastic devotional efforts on various forms of ritual and practice, including Maitreya and Amitābha devotion. Pure Land Buddhism was thus a dominant feature of the Buddhist world within which Dōhan's career took place, and at each stage of Dōhan's Shingon education, he participated in or had the opportunity to observe diverse forms of practice concerning rebirth in Sukhāvatī and the practice of *buddhānusmṛti.*

Kōyasan attracted a diverse range of practitioners and devotees in the early medieval period. Due to pioneering work by itinerant ascetics and scholiasts, by the end of the eleventh century the mountain complex was rehabilitated as a devotional site, and Kūkai studies emerged as a major area around which lineages came to define their identities. Central to both efforts was the reimagining of Kōyasan as a *buddha-kṣetra* on Earth, or perhaps as a portal to various *buddha-kṣetra,* with Kūkai as a bodhisattva-like savior figure: Kōbō Daishi, the "Great Teacher Who Spreads the Dharma," a powerful spiritual guide who resides on the mountain, leading beings to their postmortem destination.

In the twelfth century, the "dual rule" shared by the aristocrats and the imperial family in the Heian capital and the samurai warrior government in Kamakura was established. As the political landscape began to shift, Kōyasan monks adapted quickly and sent delegates to establish connections to both centers of power, and throughout the early medieval period, the Kōyasan monks were often called on to perform rituals in both places.[4] In 1215 the Kōyasan monk Jōgyō 貞暁 (1186–1231)

traveled to Kamakura, and Dōhan's teacher Kakkai traveled to Heian. Both monks promoted devotion to Kōyasan and Amitābha.[5]

The relationship between Kōyasan and Kamakura inspired Hōjō Masako 北條政子 (1186–1231), the wife of Shogun Minamoto Yoritomo 源頼朝 (1147–1199), to take tonsure under Jōgyō. She also buried her hair on the mountain and built a temple called Zenjō-in 禪定院 in 1211, later renamed Kongōsanmai-in 金剛三昧院 in 1219. Dōhan's disciple Gyōyū 行勇 (1163–1241), an important early student of Zen in Japan, later presided over Kongōsanmai-in.[6] The stupa originally built by Masako still stands on Kōyasan today.

Taira no Kiyomori 平清盛 (1118–1181) helped rebuild the Great Stupa on Kōyasan after one of its many devastating fires, and Ashikaga Yoshimitsu 足利義満 (1358–1408) and Ashikaga Takauji 足利尊氏 (1305–1358) also visited the mountain. In addition to high-ranking warriors, aristocrats, poets, and peripatetic ascetics also cultivated a relationship with Kōyasan, further raising its profile as a site for this-worldly and otherworldly benefits. Fujiwara no Michinaga, Fujiwara no Yorimichi 藤原頼通 (992–1074), Emperor Shirakawa 白河上皇 (1053–1129; r. 1073–1087), Emperor Toba 鳥羽天皇 (1103–1156; r. 1107–1123), and others contributed their considerable resources to the economic and institutional revival of Kōyasan and its environs.

The poet and monk Saigyō 西行 (1118–1190) spent time on the mountain, which played an important role in his religious life. Today a hall dedicated to Saigyō stands at the entrance to the Garan 伽藍, the area where stupas and other halls surround the main hall on Kōyasan. Other famous monks, such as Chōgen 重源 (1121–1206), secluded themselves on the mountain, as did Myōhen 明遍 (1142–1224), a student of Hōnen. Local legends sprang up connecting Kamakura "New School" founders, such as Hōnen, Shinran, and Nichiren, to the mountain. Today the Saizen-in 西禪院 claims to possess Shinran's hat and staff, for example, and in the Okuno-in are grave markers dedicated to these and other major figures associated with Kamakura Buddhism.

Up to, during, and after the Kamakura period, both orthodox and heterodox peripatetic ascetics, often practitioners of *buddhānusmṛti,* were a major driving force central to Kōyasan's institutional development. By examining Dōhan's life in the broader context of the Esoteric Pure Land environment of early medieval Kōyasan, I hope to accomplish two interrelated goals: first, to lay a foundation for further study of the Esoteric Pure Land traditions of medieval Japan and, second, to emphasize the localized dimensions of Dōhan's religious identity over the ahistorical and retroactive application of contemporary sectarian designations to reveal the nuances of how identities and religious boundaries changed in early medieval Japan. When we consider Dōhan primarily as a Kōyasan monk, a participant in a heterogeneous local devotional cult centered on Kōbō Daishi Kūkai and a "catholic" Mahayana thinker, rather than simply as a Shingon school monk who wrote about Pure Land Buddhism, a more complicated and accurate picture emerges.

Dōhan's Early Education

Dōhan was born in Izumi no Kuni 和泉國, present-day southeast Osaka, which is relatively close to Kōyasan, and he entered monastic life at the age of fourteen on Kōyasan at the Shōchi-in Temple under the tutelage of Myōnin 明任 (1148–1229), who remained an important influence on him throughout his career. Dōhan eventually followed in Myōnin's footsteps and took up administrative positions at Shōchi-in, where he is regarded as an important patriarch even today.[7] I visited Shōchi-in while conducting field research on Kōyasan during the Obon お盆 holiday season in 2012. The temple happened to be open, and memorial portraits of the past abbots were on display. I was given a tour of the temple and was allowed a close look at Dōhan's image by candlelight but was not allowed to photograph it. Because images of lineage patriarchs are often treated as images of saints, bodhisattvas, or even fully awakened buddhas, photography is sometimes perceived as disrespectful, especially in ritual settings. Dōhan was depicted with a round face, gentle knowing eyes, and a wide, round nose. Having the opportunity to see the face of this figure to whom I had dedicated so much time and energy, in a candlelit room before an image of Amitābha Buddha said to date from the Heian period, was a truly moving experience.

Modern-day Shingon Buddhist home altars typically have Mahāvairocana Buddha in the center, with Kūkai and Acala on either side. Shingon temples, however, often have a more diverse assortment of main and tutelary deities, and those who pursue advanced training in Shingon meditation may take up devotion to any number of deities as part of their practice. On Kōyasan, historically, Amitābha Buddha has arguably been one of the most popular objects of devotion on the main altar of many temples. The place of Dōhan's early training, Shōchi-in, is one example. The figures of Amitābha Buddha and his attendant bodhisattvas, Avalokiteśvara and Mahāsthāmaprāpta, at Shōchi-in were purportedly carved by Kaikei 快慶 (n.d.), probably one of Japan's most famous sculptors of buddha images.

The main image installed in a temple is not insignificant and reveals quite a lot about the temple's ritual program. The various images must be cared for in specific ways, and there are prescribed practices associated with them. Buddha images are not mere symbols of awakening but concretizations of enlightened reality in this very world. Temples throughout the Buddhist world have legends about the miraculous events that have occurred due to the agency and power of an object of devotion. Dōhan's tonsure, early training, and later service at various temples where Amitābha Buddha is the main object of devotion would thus have given him a certain facility with Amitābha-centered practices.

Another important and relatively famous image of Amitābha Buddha at Shōchi-in is the *Guharishiki Amida nyorai* 紅頗梨色阿彌陀如來 (Crimson Crystal Body Amitābha Tathāgata),[8] dating from the Kamakura period. Amitābha is red in color, with a crown like Mahāvairocana, encircled by flames, like the wrathful figure Acala, and sits atop a *vajra*. Such an image may appear to some observers as distinctly "tantric." *Guharishiki Amida* is derived from Amoghavajra's influential deity yoga text dedicated to Amitābha/Amitāyus, the *Wuliang rulai guanxing gongyang yigui*, as well as a commentary on this text attributed to Kūkai, the *Muryōju nyorai sakuhō shidai* (previously discussed). This image would have been used in visualization and repentance rituals said to lead to rebirth in Sukhāvatī and the realization of the nonarising of Dharmas, as described in those texts.

Dōhan at Daigoji

Dōhan's teacher, Myōnin, traveled frequently to the capital, trained many students, and occupied high-ranking administrative posts on Kōyasan during his career. In 1225 he held the position of forty-seventh abbot for Kōyasan and in 1226 held the position of thirty-ninth *kengyō* 檢校 (administrator or overseer). His administrative roles apparently required him to travel to the capital on numerous occasions.[9] Dōhan also spent some time studying at temples in the capital and continued to interact with monks from Daigoji, Ninnaji, and so on even after he returned to Kōyasan. As Myōnin's and other's travels indicate, temple networks were complex and multinodal; competing factions within and between different institutions tried to outmaneuver one another through training students, acquiring and collecting lineage affiliations, forming patronage relationships with elite families, and so on.

Kōyasan played an interesting role in this because its marginality, which seemed to contribute to its initial fall, later served as an asset because elite lineage holders and aristocratic pilgrims envisioned it as yet another battleground in their own quests for power. This movement was a two-way street, however: monks from Kōyasan traveled to Kyoto and Kamakura and participated in regional and transregional networks even as the political and religious landscape continued to change throughout the Kamakura period.

At this point it is difficult to ascertain exactly when Dōhan was on Kōyasan and when he was in the capital and how much of his interaction with his interlocutors took place via correspondence or in person. Satō suggests that as additional documents are unearthed in temple archives and other collections, new pieces of the puzzle may come to light and provide a more complete chronology of Dōhan's life.[10]

Dōhan's time at Daigoji possibly left a lasting impression on his Esoteric Pure Land thought in particular. Sources indicate that he associated with the monk Jikken 實賢 (1176–1249) of Daigoji, but the exact date and locale of their interaction is unclear.[11] In 2014, Brian Ruppert fortuitously happened upon a reference to Dōhan and Jikken in the Daigoji Temple archive. According to this document, Dōhan received a secret oral transmission from Jikken at Sanbō-in, the main temple of the Daigoji temple complex, in 1193.[12] This would mean that soon after his ordination under Myōnin, Dōhan went to Daigoji and studied with Jikken.

Given Jikken's and Dōhan's later prominence in their respective institutions, it is possible that the two may have kept in touch. Jikken received *denbō kanjō* from Shōken 勝賢 (1138–1196), the abbot of Sanbō-in, in 1196.[13] Shōken also taught two of Dōhan's other teachers, Jōhen 靜遍 (1165–1223) of Zenrinji and Shukaku of Ninnaji, and also taught the monk Seigen 成賢 (1162–1231), an important Daigoji monk and Amitābha devotee.[14] Jikken also studied under Kenkai 賢海 (1162–1237) at Kongōō-in 金剛王院 in 1200.[15] Like other monks of this time, Jikken studied at other institutions as well, learning Yogācāra at Kōfukuji and training on Kōyasan later in life.[16] He later served as abbot of Daigoji from 1236.[17] Jikken also studied under Jōhen of Zenrinji, the figure who had the most impact on Dōhan's Esoteric Pure Land thought.

Later interpreters of Esoteric Pure Land have identified Dōhan's signature teaching as the idea that Amitābha Buddha is the "vital breath" of all beings, or *myōsoku* 命息. This vital breath was understood as the compassionate activity of the dharmakāya coursing through all beings as life itself. Nakamura Honnen and Kameyama Takahiko identify Jitsuun 實運 (1105–1160), Shōken, and Seigen as systematizers of this idea and the *Shūkotsushō* 宗骨抄 (SZ 22) by Kenjin 憲深 (1159–1263) of the Sanbō-in as an influential text that discusses this idea.[18] Seigen, who also studied under Shōken and later served as abbot of Daigoji, was an Amitābha devotee who installed images of Amitābha and performed rituals focused on Amitābha and Sukhāvatī.[19] Another *zasu* of Daigoji, also named Shōken 聖憲 (1242–1293), was a devotee of Amitābha as well and even earned the appellation Amida Daisōzu.[20] Is it possible that the content of Jikken's transmission to Dōhan, or perhaps one of the teachings that Jikken and Jōhen received from Shōken, included something about the vital breath, a concept that became so central to Dōhan's conception of Esoteric Pure Land?

Shukaku of Ninnaji

Dōhan also studied at Ninnaji, receiving initiation into the Hirosawa-ryū and the "secret teachings of yoga" (another common name for Esoteric Buddhism) from Shukaku, the son of Emperor Goshirakawa.[21] As Ruppert notes, Shukaku was one of the most important ritual masters of his generation, and further inquiry into his career reveals much about the relationships between aristocratic involvement in the sangha and the evolving Shingon tradition and the imperial family. Shukaku spent time on Kōyasan in 1177, two years before Dōhan was born, and also trained at Daigoji. As Shukaku's and Dōhan's educational experiences both demonstrate, the Ninnaji, Daigoji, and Nara institutions were interconnected in important ways that greatly affected Kōyasan's participation in the evolving religious environment of the early medieval period.[22]

Sonnin of Zuishin-in

Dōhan also studied in the Zennen 禪然 sublineage of the Ono lineage under Sonnin 尊仁 (n.d.) at Zuishin-in. He transmitted this lineage to Kakua 覺阿 (1143–?), who recorded the *Kakua mondō shō* 覚阿問答鈔, which includes notes on Dōhan's teachings on esoteric ritual, Zen, teacher-student dialogues, and so on (chapter 5 will examine this text in more detail).[23] Zuishin-in was founded by Ningai of Kyoto, under the name Mandara-ji 曼荼羅寺. According to temple legend, Ningai had a dream about his mother being reborn as a cow; when the cow died, he had the leather from the cow used to create images of the Womb and Vajra Realm mandalas. Zuishin-in is located northeast of Daigoji and has the same object of devotion, Cintāmaṇi-cakra Avalokiteśvara, also established by Ningai. In addition, Zuishin-in has a statue of Amitābha Buddha that dates from the Heian period. Like Dōhan, Zuishin-in represents the confluence of diverse traditions and lineages.[24]

Kenchō of Hōkō-in

Dōhan returned to Kōyasan in 1202 and entered the Hōkō-in. His new teacher, Kenchō 兼澄 (?–1202), was in the same cohort as Dōhan's first teacher, Myōnin, and, like Dōhan, was born in Izumi and began his career at Shōchi-in.[25] Hōkō-in also has Amitābha Buddha as its central object of devotion, as does Shōchi-in, so it is possible that Dōhan would have studied similar Amitābha-focused practices under Kenchō and Myōnin. Sources indicate that Kenchō's practice focused on the purification of negative karma and the pursuit of rebirth in Sukhāvatī. Traditional biographical notes relate that Dōhan studied and practiced so diligently at Hōkō-in that he sometimes forgot to eat and sleep.[26] After Kenchō passed away, Dōhan eventually took up an administrative role over this temple.

Dōhan's departure from Ninnaji seems to have coincided with the passing of Shukaku, and within one year of his arrival at Hōkō-in, Kenchō passed away as well. It is certainly plausible that Dōhan may have attended both funerals. Because Hōkō-in and Ninnaji both possess images of Amitābha Buddha as their primary object of devotion, it is also reasonable to assume that the two monks' funerals focused on their attainment of rebirth in Sukhāvatī. Having trained at temples that emphasized Amitābha Buddha devotion and Sukhāvatī aspiration and having witnessed funerals for two of his teachers within a year's time, it is reasonable to suspect that these events may have influenced Dōhan's devotional orientation.

Chū-in Lineage Initiation

Dōhan eventually studied with Myōnin again and in 1216 received the full precepts.[27] The main lineage on Kōyasan at the time was the Chūin-ryū 中院流. This was a synthetic lineage to some extent, serving to bring some coherence to the diverse training regimes on the mountain, where many different lineages competed. The main object of devotion for Chūin-ryū training is Mahāvairocana Buddha; other lineages may have

Acala, Avalokiteśvara Bodhisattva, Śākyamuni Buddha, or others.[28] Mahāvairocana is certainly an appropriate object of devotion for a lineage intended to coalesce diverse perspectives.

Dōhan also studied the *shido kegyō* 四度加行 under Myōnin. *Shido kegyō* is a fourfold ritual training regime signifying that one has begun one's training and is preparing to pursue more advanced ritual practices. Richard Payne and Robert Sharf have explored the Shingon *shido kegyō* in much greater depth, drawing from their own experiences while pursuing training in the *shido kegyō*,[29] so I give only a brief explanation here.

Essentially an introductory form of deity yoga, *shido kegyō* is rooted in a kind of "ritual grammar," a template wherein the practitioner engages with an object of devotion, merges with that being, and ultimately reveals the practitioner's contiguous relationship with that being. The rite begins with purificatory acts: the practitioner puts on clean clothes and performs incantations and visualizations aimed at purifying one's body, speech, and mind and the ritual arena. Next, the ritual practitioner invokes a variety of deities through mantras, mudras, visualizations, and contemplative practices, ultimately inviting the primary object of devotion to descend from the deity's *buddha-kṣetra* or heaven into the sanctified and fortified ritual space.

The first phase of the fourfold ritual is known as *jūhachi dōhō* 十八道法, which includes instruction in mudras, mantras, and so on, establishing the ritual grammar of esoteric practice. This basic template may be expanded for more advanced ritual regimes or contracted for preliminary novice practices. After mastering the *jūhachi dōhō*, the student studies rituals for the Vajra Realm and Womb Realm mandalas. Finally, the student is trained in the performance of the votive fire ritual, *goma hō* 護摩法.[30] The Japanese word *goma* is a transliteration of the Sanskrit term *homa* and ultimately derives from early Indo-Iranian fire worship practices.

This fourfold training regime is traditionally carried out only after a student has mastered foundational Buddhist doctrine because without this foundation the relationship between practice and doctrine would be unclear. Though I have found no explicit mention of Dōhan's training in these other disciplines, based on my reading of the *Himitsu nenbutsu shō* in the context of his oeuvre, Dōhan was clearly well versed in Yogācāra, Madhyamaka, Tendai, and other areas of doctrinal study. With this firm ritual and doctrinal foundation, as well as initiation into the major lineages in the capital and Kōyasan, Dōhan would go on to be an important ritual master in his own right, influencing the advanced ritual program of Kōyasan Shingon trainees even today.

Kakkai of the Keō-in and Jōhen of Zenrinji

While Dōhan wrote broadly across the spectrum of East Asian Esoteric Buddhism and Kūkai studies and was clearly fluent in other major areas of Buddhist study, he is arguably best known for his contributions to the study and practice of Esoteric Pure Land Buddhism. Two of his most important influential teachers also wrote on Esoteric Pure Land, Kakkai of Keō-in and Jōhen of Zenrinji. Both teachers articulated a Shingon identity rooted in the study of Kūkai's doctrinal works, and both responded to the Esoteric Pure Land culture of Kōyasan and the growing Pure Land movement of Hōnen. However, their views on the nature of Sukhāvatī-oriented thought and practice appear to differ. As a preliminary hypothesis, I suggest that Dōhan's own Esoteric Pure Land perspective may have been inspired by a desire to harmonize the perspectives of his two great teachers.

Kakkai of Keō-in served as the forty-fifth *zasu* of Kongōbuji in 1216.[31] Kakkai and his students are best known for articulating a doctrinal perspective known as *rokudai funimon shisō* 六大不二門思想, or "six elements nondualist thought," which postulates that the first five elements—earth, water, fire, wind, and space—are contiguous with, or permeated by, the sixth element, consciousness. Kūkai's nondualist Mahayana perspective was developed by later Shingon thinkers such as Kakkai and Dōhan, who argued that consciousness, or the "mind element," could be understood as the vital breath of the universe itself, which ultimately permeates all elements.[32] Throughout the early medieval period, Kakkai's students promoted the idea that "mind" and "matter" are contiguous, and by the time of the Kōyasan monk Chōgaku 長覺 (1340–1416) of Muryōju-in 無量壽院 (Dōhan's final resting place) in the Muromachi period, this view had emerged as the dominant doctrinal perspective in Shingon lineages.[33]

This view is rooted in Kūkai's *Sokushin jōbutsu gi* 即身成佛義 (T. 2428), in which the six elements are interconnected and nondual with the dharmakāya. Ultimate reality and conventional reality are not two and not separate discrete realities but aspects of a unified reality. Kūkai's view that ultimate reality is ultimately *effable* was a point of controversy when he first returned from China and began to teach his new theory of ritual speech and practice.[34] Buddhas and beings are ultimately one and, according to the theory of the six elements, composed of the very same stuff. Ignorant beings, however, are unaware of this "secret," which is revealed through empowerment and the practice of the three mysteries.

Mudra, mantra, mandalic visualization, body, speech, mind, buddhas and beings are all coparticipants in a contiguous reality, which may be referred to as Mahāvairocana.

Kakkai's perspective on Sukhāvatī similarly emphasizes the ontological nonduality of ultimate reality and provisional reality, buddhas and beings, and Sukhāvatī and samsara. Drawing from the *mitsugon jōdo* 密嚴淨土 teaching, Kakkai emphasized the "big picture," seeing all pure and impure *buddha-kṣetra* as ultimately within the ultimate *buddha-kṣetra* of Mahāvairocana. Like Kakuban before him, Kakkai promoted a this-worldly approach to Sukhāvatī, but perhaps more than his predecessor, he deemphasized postmortem rebirth in Sukhāvatī as a soteriological goal, possibly in response to the perceived excesses and dualistic thinking of members of the Pure Land movement and the *hijiri* lineage on Kōyasan. Robert Morrell's and George Tanabe's scholarship on Kakkai has brought more light to his this-worldly interpretation on Sukhāvatī.[35] Rather than assuming that Kakkai's perspective functions as the default sectarian perspective, we should remember that neither Shingon nor Kōyasan were univocal at this time but comprised diverse lineages, teachings, practices, and perspectives. Moreover, according to Jacqueline Stone, Kakuban and Dōhan promoted a more nuanced perspective in which both dualist and nondualist perspectives on Sukhāvatī coexist in a productive tension.[36] This tension is to varying degrees present in Chan, Tiantai, and the traditions that would come to be known as the Pure Land schools as well.

In 1221 Kakkai received buddha relics sent by Tōji, which he enshrined in the Okuno-in, and he retired from his administrative post that same year.[37] Kakkai died in 1223, and according to traditional biographies, due to his attainment of miraculous powers through his practice he attained rebirth in the Māra Heaven and nondual realization of union with Mahāvairocana Buddha.[38]

Jōhen of Zenrinji was Dōhan's other major influence after Kakkai.[39] As in the case of many high-ranking monks of this era, Jōhen was of aristocratic ancestry: his father was Taira no Yorimori 平頼盛 (1133–1186), and his grandfather was Taira no Tadayori 平忠盛 (1096–1153). Jōhen's uncle, Taira no Kiyomori 平清盛 (1118–1181), was the samurai who famously opened the doors for the emergence of the warrior aristocracy that would transform Japanese politics and culture for generations afterward.

Like Kakuban before him and Dōhan after, Jōhen trained at both Daigoji and Ninnaji. At Daigoji he studied under Shōken, the abbot at the time, who initiated him into the Ono-ryū. At Ninnaji he studied under

Ninryū 仁隆 (1144–1205), who initiated him into the Hirosawa-ryū. He also studied at Kōfukuji under the famous Gedatsu Shōnin Jōkei 解脱上人貞慶 (1155–1213).[40]

Jōhen's temple, Zenrinji, also has a diverse and illustrious background. Zenrinji was founded by Shinshō 眞紹 (797–873), a famous early disciple of Kūkai who also studied at Daianji 大安寺 and Tōdaiji. Due to Shinshō's association with the Shingon lineage, Zenrinji is sometimes referred to as a Shingon temple.[41] However, its primary affiliation during the Kamakura period was with Tōdaiji. Eikan and Chingai, Nara-based Esoteric Pure Land thinkers, were also associated with Zenrinji. The temple later became associated with the Seizan 西山 branch of Jōdo-shū, commonly regarded as the most Tendai or Esoteric branch of the Jōdo school. Yoshishige no Yasutane 慶滋保胤 (933–1002), author of the *Nihon ōjō gokuraku ki* 往生極樂記,[42] studied in the *kangakue* 勸學會 at Zenrinji. The *kangakue* was a kind of lay Buddhist study and practice association that promoted communal *buddhānusmṛti* in the tradition of Genshin.

Igarashi Takayuki 五十嵐隆幸 suggests that Zenrinji possessed all three contemporary "streams" of Pure Land Buddhism—those of Nara, Hieizan, and Shingon.[43] It is not entirely clear, however, how precisely a "Shingon" stream could be distinguished at this time. Certainly, because Nara and Hieizan are geographic locations we are on somewhat firmer ground in distinguishing these as identifiable "streams." Yet thinking of Shingon as a distinct stream with a particular perspective on Pure Land thought is somewhat complicated. Certainly, we see an evolving coalition between Ninnaji, Daigoji, Tōji, and Kōyasan and other related sites with lineage ties to Kūkai. However, these temple institutions were not entirely separate from Nara- and Hieizan-based Shingon lineages at sites such as Kōfukuji, Tōdaiji, and elsewhere. In other words, the idea that only three streams existed is overly simplistic. Rather, a deluge of currents, cross-currents, and flows were shaping and reshaping the landscape below the feet of traveling monks, official and unofficial.[44]

Jōhen was a Kūkai scholar who wrote several important treatises on Shingon practice. Some of these works, to be examined in chapter 5, were recorded by Dōhan. Rebirth in Sukhāvatī was Jōhen's other major area of interest. According to tradition, he sought to articulate an Esoteric Pure Land perspective in contradistinction to the perspectives he had gleaned from the so-called Pure Land movement. Zenrinji was, after all, in the environs of eastern Kyoto, where early Pure Land lineages under Hōnen first began to form.

In 1218 Jōhen apparently received a copy of the *Senchaku hongan nenbutsushū* 選擇本願念佛集 (T. 2608, hereafter cited as *Senchakushū*), Hōnen's major work, from Ryūkan 隆寛 (1148–1227). This text lays out Hōnen's radical approach to the Pure Land path as well as his critique of mainstream elite Buddhist culture. It was a potentially dangerous text kept secret at first and circulated only among Hōnen's closest disciples.[45] Jōhen supposedly initially intended to write a rebuttal to Honen's thought, but on reading the work closely, he was so inspired that he instead composed a *zoku* 續 (continuation) of the *Senchakushū*, the *Zoku senchaku mongi yōshō* 續選擇文義要鈔,[46] of which only the last of three fascicles has survived. This work clearly influenced Dōhan's thought. According to narratives about Jōhen's life, while he interacted with disciples of Honen he never met Hōnen in person. Yet he was moved enough by Hōnen's thought and writings to visit Hōnen's grave and pay homage, and he changed his name to Shin'en 心圓.[47]

Zenriji later became affiliated with the Seizan branch of Hōnen's lineage, founded by Shōkū 證空 (1177–1247), an important esoteric thinker in his own right. When Jōhen retired from Zenrinji, he relocated to Kōyasan and formed an important relationship with Myōhen, another Hōnen disciple. This admittedly circumstantial evidence nonetheless suggests a closer connection between the Kūkai scholar Jōhen and the early Pure Land movement, further indicating that for many Buddhists in medieval Japan the path of mantra and the Pure Land path were not necessarily in conflict.[48]

In 1221 the Jōkyū War broke out, resulting in an exodus of some monastics to Kōyasan. Jōhen took up residence at the Byōdoshin-in 平等心院 and the Shaka-in 釋迦院; Kōyasan records indicate he made a visit to Kūkai's tomb as well.[49] Myōhen also relocated to Kōyasan at this time and came to be known as the founder of the Rengesanmai-in 蓮華三昧院 lineage. The year Jōhen moved to Kōyasan, Dōjo of Ninnaji built the Kōdai-in 光台院 on Kōyasan as a buddhānusmṛti samādhi practice site.[50] Dōhan's interaction with Dōjo helped establish the former as an authority in debate, doctrine, and ritual studies. Jōhen began to work with Dōhan on Kōyasan, and the two traveled to Ninnaji, where Dōhan recorded Jōhen's lectures on Kūkai's *Benkenmitsu nikyōron* in his *Nikyōron tekagami shō* 二教論手鏡抄.[51] Dōhan also compiled Jōhen's *Hishū mongi yō* 祕宗文義要, a work that draws from Kūkai and Kakuban and summarizes the essence of the Esoteric teachings as understood in early medieval Japan.[52]

In 1223, within one year of the death of Kakkai, Jōhen passed away. Just as in 1202, when Shukaku and Kenchō both died within a year of each other, Dōhan again lost two of his Esoteric Pure Land teachers. In 1224 Dōhan composed the *Himitsu nenbutsu shō,* a text in which he draws from both Kakkai and Jōhen and elaborates on their ideas to produce a unique view of the role of Sukhāvatī aspiration for the practitioner of mantra.

The Conflagration at Daidenbō-in

Given its status as a place where diverse lineages vied for power, tension and even violence were recurrent features in the history of Kōyasan's institutional development. The reemergence of conflict between Daidenbō-in and Kongōbuji ultimately resulted in Dōhan's exile from Kōyasan, just as similar events had caused Kakuban to flee the mountain before him. Dōhan entered the Shōchi-in lecture hall in 1234 and was granted the position of head administrator of Kongōbuji in 1237. While serving as a lecturer and administrator, Dōhan continued his prolific output and ritual activities. The *Nanzan denpu* notes that in 1239 he lectured on the *Bodaishinron* at the request of Dōjo of Ninnaji, and these teachings were recorded in the *Bodaishinron dangiki* 菩提心論談義記.[53] In 1240 Dōhan composed the *Hizōhōyaku mondanshō* 秘蔵宝鑰問談鈔, a compendium of dialogues on Kūkai's *Hizōhōyaku.* That same year he also erected a stupa at Muryōju-in, the institution that later became his final resting place and with which his lineage remained affiliated.[54]

In 1240 the monk Myōken 明賢 became abbot of Kongōbuji, ultimately assuming the role of lead administrator in 1243. Dōhan was called to Rokuhara 六波羅 in 1242 to answer questions in an investigation into the unrest on the mountain between Daidenbō-in and Kongōbuji. In 1243 Kongōbuji monks allegedly burned down one of Daidenbō-in's buildings. Following this incident, both institutions launched suits against one another, and Myōken was forced out. Dōhan was part of a coterie of senior monks who were exiled from Kōyasan as part of the settlement.[55]

Dōhan's record of his time in exile and travelogue from this time, the *Nankai rurōki,* "A Record of Wandering along the Southern Sea," begins with an account of the conflict between the two factions.[56] According to this travelogue, a mysterious fire took place one night at the Daidenbō-in. Because of its inappropriate disregard for the chain of command and Kongōbuji's superior position, Daidenbō-in had been flagrantly profiting from patronage that should have belonged to Kongōbuji. As a karmic recompense for these evil actions, fire spontaneously fell from the sky and destroyed the building.[57] Dōhan finds no fault on the part of those who judged the case, however.

Exile in Sakuni

The *Nankai rurōki* begins with an introduction in which Dōhan lays out the circumstances of the dispute between Kongōbuji and Daidenbō-in and the legal case mentioned above. The text shifts to a more informal narration in the travelogue, which begins in 1243 as he travels downriver from Kyoto. Some of the literary qualities of Dōhan's travelogue, or diary, arc worth noting. The *Nankai rurōki* is written in a mixture of classical Japanese and classical Chinese (J. *kana-kanbun zuihitsu* 仮名漢文随筆 or *wakan konkōbun* 和漢混交文), and the writing frequently flows in and out of each, with sentences sometimes beginning in one language and ending in the other. Describing his travels in the province of Sanuki, the narrative is punctuated with Chinese and Japanese poetry—*kanshi* and *waka,* respectively. The diary covers all seven years of his exile, and though actually quite brief, it nevertheless provides a wealth of information on Dōhan's activities and Buddhist practice during this time. Moreover, scholars of ancient Shikoku hold his diary in high regard because Dōhan mentions both place names and the distance traveled between each stop, noting important landmarks along the way, and thus offers a fairly clear picture of the early medieval geography of the regions where he traveled.[58]

As was customary in travelogue literature,[59] Dōhan's poetic compositions punctuate key events. For example, Dōhan writes the following *waka* on embarking for Shikoku:

都をは
霞の余所に
かへり見て
いつち行らん
淀の川なみ

Oh, the capital!
To the mists of this faraway place,
looking back,
where am I going?
—the waves of Yodo River.[60]

Introductory works on Japanese literature sometimes note that men's diaries tend not to convey emotion, while the diaries of women are often more expressive. One of the interesting features of this short, and relatively unpolished, diary is how frequently Dōhan does in fact describe his feelings. The reader is carried along with him as he floats down the river, expressing his longing for the capital as well as for Kōyasan.

Poetic composition in the Kamakura period was always already deeply connected to Esoteric Buddhism. Keller Kimbrough, for example, notes that *waka* often functioned like dhāraṇī,[61] and Ryuichi Abé's discussion of the poet-priest Saigyō suggests that he viewed poetic and mantric language as inherently connected.[62] Dōhan even mentions Saigyō by name; Saigyō was not only closely associated with Kōyasan but also spent time in Sanuki. Dōhan also employs poetry to establish a connection between his exile and Saigyō's peripatetic wandering.

At that time, exile could very well mean a death sentence. It was therefore imperative that those cut off from their social network through exile find another means of support. Dōhan's travel was sponsored by the Naganuma family 長沼氏 of Sanuki at the behest of the Miura family 三浦氏, whose head was the governor of Sanuki Province.[63] So prolific were Dōhan's efforts and activities at this time—composing treatises, conducting rituals, and teaching monastic and lay students—that he is still associated with Shikoku and the pilgrimage of Kūkai devotees.

Dōhan's diary records the names of students he trained in Shikoku: Nōhen Hōshinbō 能遍法信房, Shōen 清圓, Ryūben 隆辯, and Yūnin 祐仁.[64] Pol van den Broucke has produced a translation of the *Dōhan shōsoku* 道範消息, a guide to contemplation of the letter *A*, an important form of Esoteric Buddhist meditation.[65]

In 1245, Dōhan's close associate Hosshō 法性 (?–1245) died in exile. Like Dōhan, Hosshō was regarded as one of the great thinkers in the history of Kōyasan, and both studied under both Myōnin and Kakkai. He was exiled alongside Dōhan and ended up in Izumo 出雲 (present-day Shimane Prefecture 島根県).[66] According to Dōhan's travelogue, in response to the news of Hosshō's passing he conducted a fifty-day-long fire ritual dedicated to Amitābha Buddha, likely in supplication of Hosshō's postmortem fate. At the conclusion of the ritual, Dōhan recounts, he experienced a vision of Amitābha before him.[67]

That same year, the monk Shōso 尚祚 (d. 1245), also a student of Kakkai alongside Dōhan and Hosshō, passed away. He died peacefully while in a state of meditative absorption, chanting a mantra and forming a mudra before an image of Amitābha Buddha.[68] Dōhan's patron and interlocutor, Dōjo Hosshinō of Ninnaji, also died while chanting before an image of Amitābha Buddha while residing at Kōdai-in 光台院 on Kōyasan.[69]

While in exile Dōhan stayed at Zentsūji, which had purportedly been built at the birthplace of Kūkai. Even though he had been cast out from Kōyasan, the place of Kūkai's eternal meditation, Dōhan established himself at the place of Kūkai's birth. Dōhan built an image of Kūkai at Zentsūji in 1248.[70] Though the modern inclination is to conceive of Kūkai primarily as the founder of a sect of Japanese Buddhism, he was much more than that for Dōhan: Kūkai was an important object of devotion in his own right, a soteriological conduit for Buddhist power. We should therefore view Dōhan's founder devotion in some sense as a localized form of Buddhist "ancestor" worship, as well as devotion to one progressing along the bodhisattva path. By establishing and maintaining karmic connections with such beings, ancestors, and buddhas (all of which may be combined or conflated), one's own salvation is further guaranteed.

Today Shingon Buddhists chant the *hōgō* 寶號 (treasure name) of Kūkai as part of the daily liturgy: *Namu Daishi Henjō Kongō* 南無大師遍照金剛. Just as one might chant the name of a buddha or bodhisattva in order to draw on the deity's storehouse of merit, so, too, might one call upon a revered lineage patriarch who also possesses a vast storehouse of merit. Different versions of this chant are found in various Shingon lineages; however, according to Hinonishi Shinjō 日野西眞定, the earliest instance of the most commonly used version, *Namu Daishi Henjō Kongō,* is from Dōhan's *Himitsu nenbutsu shō.*[71]

Return to the Pure Land

Dōhan was officially pardoned and given permission to return to Kōyasan in 1249. There he resided at Hōkō-in and immediately resumed his prolific scholastic and ritual activity, enshrining an image of Kūkai and performing various ceremonies for Shōchi-in monks.[72]

As mentioned, Dōhan remains closely associated with Shōchi-in. There is a garden behind the temple with a prominent rock formation emerging from a hillside. Temple lore relates that Dōhan had a vision of the protector god of the mountain at this site. According to the *Henmyōin Daishi Myōjin gotakusenki* 遍明院大師明神御託宣記, which has been examined in detail by Elizabeth Tinsley, in 1251 a temple acolyte began to receive an oracle, which was purportedly recorded by Dōhan. Tinsley's analysis of this text situates this event in the context of the political life of lineage competition and reveals the complicated nature of power and lineage identity formation on Kōyasan at this time.[73]

Dōhan passed away at Hōkō-in in 1252.[74] One of his final acts was the copying of a manuscript of the *Avataṃsaka-sūtra* that was attributed to Kūkai.[75] He completed this in the fifth month of Kenchō 4, the same month he died. How might Dōhan have directed his final moments? In the colophon of the *Avataṃsaka-sūtra,* he mentions Kūkai and his connection to the Maitreya cult on Kōyasan. At the end of the *Himitsu nenbutsu shō,* Dōhan constructs a deathbed ritual wherein one directs one's mind to the place of Kūkai's eternal meditation so that he may guide one to rebirth in Sukhāvatī. A deathbed ritual recently edited at Kōyasan University presents what may have been Dōhan's final deathbed instructions and practice. According to Yamaguchi Shikyo 山口史恭, there is no way to know for certain whether Dōhan explicitly aspired for rebirth in Sukhāvatī. One account of his death notes simply that he passed away while in seated meditation, in deep samādhi, chanting a mantra.[76] Dōhan's grave was established at Muryōju-in.[77]

Reorienting Sukhāvatī

The study of Dōhan's life and context and the Esoteric Pure Land Buddhist culture of early medieval Kōyasan reveals not only the heterogeneous nature of Kōyasan as a devotional site but also "Shingon/*shingon*" as a mode of practice. Before, during, and after his time, communities of practice as well as solitary practitioners aspiring for rebirth in one of the many *buddha-kṣetra* of the ten directions flocked to Kōyasan. Amitābha Buddha, Mahāvairocana, the Medicine Buddha, and the bodhisattvas Avalokiteśvara, Maitreya, and others all "purify" their spheres of influence, and all of their *buddha-kṣetra* were believed to be accessible through Kōyasan.

Over time, however, a more founder-centric and hierarchically organized, top-down approach to practice came to dominate the mountain complex. In this process, unorthodox communities of Sukhāvatī aspirants were either coopted, destroyed, or ignored. As a result of this systematic eradication, the prominence of Pure Land Buddhist thought and practice has too often been excluded from the historiography of the Shingon school.

Beginning in the fourteenth century, scholar-monks in positions of power imposed a three-tiered monastic hierarchy on Kōyasan, with themselves at the top followed by practitioners pursuing a course of study deemed orthodox by the scholar-monks. On the lowest tier were the various *hijiri.* Monks such as Chōkaku and Yūkai 宥快 (1345–1416),

who worked to suppress unorthodox lineages like the Tachikawa-ryū and to articulate an orthodox Shingon school perspective, helped lay the groundwork for the Kūkai-centric view of Shingon Buddhism that would eventually be used to corral the at-times disruptive activities of the unorthodox groups. In 1413 the *Kōyasan gobanshū ichimi keijō* 高野山五番衆一味契狀 edicts banned unorthodox forms of practice, including ecstatic dancing, loud communal chanting, and more.[78]

Yamanaka Takahiro 山中嵩裕 notes that around this time, recitation of the *Amida Sutra* was also replaced by recitation of the equally brief *Rishukyō,* which is still part of the Kōyasan Shingon school morning practice. Similarly, the widely attested Amitābha samādhi practice, which grew out of Hieizan lineages, was replaced by the *Rishu sanmai* 理趣三昧, and recitation of the name of Amitābha was replaced by recitation of the treasure name of Kūkai.[79] In 1606 the Tokugawa shōgunate issued an edict requiring all Buddhist clergy to officially register with a specific sectarian lineage. On Kōyasan, this seems to have entailed choosing between Shingon and the Jishū 時宗 school of Pure Land Buddhism.

Ippen 一遍 (1239–1289), the founder of the Jishū school, is yet another illustrious example of an itinerant practitioner who pursued practice on Kōyasan. He studied Zen under the monk Kakushin 心地覺心 (a.k.a Muhon Kakushin 無本覺心 or Hottō Kokushi 法燈國師; 1207–1298), who had also been a student of Dōhan and Dōgen. Ippen's lineage was associated with the Senju-in dani 千手院谷 lineage on Kōyasan.[80] Like other *hijiri,* Ippen was a practitioner of an ecstatic, perhaps even shamanistic, form of "dancing" *buddhānusmṛti,* the *odori nenbutsu* 踊念佛. While dancing through the marketplaces, for example, Ippen and other *odori nenbutsu* practitioners would bestow *o-fuda* 札, slips of paper or silk inscribed with the name of Amitābha Buddha. *O-fuda*-type objects have a long history in East Asian religion and were often regarded as talismans or charms that helped devotees establish a tangible connection with an object of devotion. Gorai notes that during this period a form of *nenbutsu o-fuda,* copies of *o-fuda* purportedly written by Kūkai, were quite popular in the region.[81]

From this period, it seems that the *hijiri* and the unorthodox buddhānusmṛti practitioners were vanquished. However, Gorai notes that the recorders of history may have simply stopped writing about them so the historical record would reflect an idealized homogeneity.[82] The necessity of such repeat edicts reveals that the fluidity of these communities continued despite top-down pressure and that Esoteric Pure Land culture on

Kōyasan was so pervasive that the boundaries between practitioners of Jishū and Kōyasan Shingon may not have been clear-cut.

Shingon school sectarian historiography often attempts to explain away the important role that unorthodox *buddhānusmṛti* practitioners played in the lives of the systematizers of the Shingon tradition, broadly conceived. Furthermore, this line of scholarship also attempts to dismiss the influence of aspiration for Sukhāvatī rebirth on the revitalization of Kōyasan as a cultic site. Situating Dōhan in his historical, ritual, and localized context demonstrates the centrality of Amitābha devotion in the foundations of Dōhan's Shingon education and training.

Notes

Chapter 4: Dōhan and the Esoteric Pure Land Culture of Kōyasan

1 Dōhan is regarded as one of the "eight great ones" (*hachitetsu* 八傑) of Kamakura-period Kōyasan, along with Hōsshō 法性 (d. 1245) and others. See entries in MD, 549a; MBD, 4612b.

Sources for Dōhan's biography may be found in Nakamura Honnen, "Kakuhon bō Dōhan no seibotsu nen nitsuite" 覚本房道範の生没年について, *Sangaku shugen* 山岳修験 60 (2017): 121–136; Satō Mona 佐藤もな, "Dōhan ni kan suru kisoteki kenkyū—denki shiryō wo chūshin toshite" 道範に関する基礎的研究 伝記史料を中心として, *Bukkyō bunka kenkyū ronshū* 仏教文化研究論集 7 (2003): 85–95 (L); Yamaguchi Shikyo 山口史恭, "Dōhan cho Himitsu nenbutsu shō no hihan taishō nitsuite" 道範著『秘密念仏鈔』の批判対象について, *Buzankyōgaku taikaikiyō* 豊山教学大会紀要 30 (2002): 81–122, esp. pp. 81–82n1, 115–116; and Matsuzaki Keisui 松崎惠水, *Heian mikkyō no kenkyū: Kōgyō Daishi Kakuban wo chūshin toshite* 平安密教の研究: 興教大師覚鑁 を中心として (Tokyo: Yoshikawa kōbunkan, 2002), pp. 739–752, 785–790.

Primary sources for further investigation into Dōhan's life include *Azuma no kuni kōsōden* 東國高僧傳, fasc. 9, DNBZ 104; *Hōkōin sekifuki* 寶光院析負紀, *Kongōbuji shoinke sekihushū* 金剛峰寺諸院家析負輯, fasc. 1, ZSZ 34; *Honchō kōsōden* 本朝高僧傳, fasc. 14, DNBZ 102; *Jike Shōchiin* 寺家正智院, *Kii zokufūdoki* 紀伊續風土記, fasc. 4, ZSZ 37; *Kitamuroin rekidai keifūsshi* 北室院歴代系譜寫, *Kongōbuji shoinke sekifushū,* fasc. 10, ZSZ 34; *Kongōchō mujōshū dendōroku zokuhen* 金剛頂無上正宗傳燈廣錄續編, fasc. 6, ZSZ 33; *Kōsō gōjō Shōchiin Dōhan den Kōsō gōjō Shōchiin Dōhan den* 高僧行狀正智院道範傳, *Kii zokufudōki* 紀伊続風土記, fasc. 10, ZSZ 39; *Kōya shunjū hennen shūroku* 高野春秋編年輯錄, fasc. 8, DNBZ 131; Mikkyō bunka kenkyūjo seikyō bunsho chosa han 密教文化研究所聖教文書調査班, ed., "Kōyasan shinnō seikyō bunsho chosa gaiyō—suke, shiryō kaishō 'Dōhan nikka rinjū higi" 高野山親王院聖教文書調査概要—付、資料紹　介『道範日課臨終秘儀』, *Kōyasan daigaku mikkyō bunka kenkyūjo kiyō* 高野山大学密教文化研究所紀要 16 (2003): 79–92; *Nanzan chūin shingon hihōshoso denpu* 南山中院真言秘法諸祖伝譜, fasc. 2, ZSZ 32; *Shōchiin ruiyō senshi meibo* 正智院累葉先師名簿, *Kongōbuji shoinke sekihushū* 金剛峰寺諸院家析負輯, fasc. 1, ZSZ 34; and *Yahō meitokuden* 野峯名徳伝, fasc. 2, DNBZ 106.

2 For traditional scholarship on Dōhan, see Ueda Shinjō 上田進城, "Hairyū no Ajari Dōhan" 配流の阿闍梨道範, *Misshū gakuhō* 密宗学報 161 (1912): 617–642; Hasuzawa Jojun 蓮沢浄淳, "Kakkai sonshi no monka" 覚海尊師の 門下, *Mikkyō bunka* 密教研究 10 (1922): 151–166, 167–228; Ōyama Kōjun 大山公淳, "Dōhan daitoku no Kōya hiji" 道範大徳の高野秘事, *Mikkyō bunka* 11 (1923): 116–135; Toganoo Shōun 栂尾祥雲, *Nihon Mikkyō gakudōshi* 日本密教学道史 (Kōyasan: Kōyasan Daigaku shuppanbu, 1942).

By and large, most English scholarship currently available on Dōhan's Esoteric Pure Land thought draws on Kushida's "Himitsu nenbutsu shisō no bokkō," also found in the *Shingon mikkyō seiritsu katei no kenkyū.*

Scholars writing in English who have drawn from Kushida's approach include Sanford, "Breath of Life: The Esoteric Nenbutsu"; Tanabe, "Kōyasan in the Countryside"; and Stone, "Secret Art of Dying."

3 For scholarship that connects Dōhan to the Tachikawa-ryū, see Kōda Yūun 甲田宥吽, "Dōhan ajari no jagisōden ni tsuite" 道範阿闍梨の邪義相伝について, *Mikkyōgaku kaihō* 密教学会報 19, no. 20 (1981): 36–47 (L), and "Chūin-ryū no jaryū wo tsutaeta hitobito" 中院流の邪流を伝えた人々, *Mikkyōbunka* 密教文化 135 (1981): 19–37. See also Nobumi Iyanaga, "Secrecy, Sex and Apocrypha: Remarks on Some Paradoxical Phenomena," in *The Culture of Secrecy in Japanese Religion,* ed. Bernard Scheid and Mark Teeuwen (London: Routledge, 2006), pp. 204–228, and "Tachikawa-ryū," in Orzech, Sørensen, and Payne, *Esoteric Buddhism and the Tantras in East Asia,* pp. 803–814.

4 KS, fasc. 7, 8, 9.

5 KS, 137–140.

6 MD, 690.

7 Yamamoto Nobuyoshi 山本信吉, ed., *Shōchiin monjo* 正智院文書 (Tokyo: Yoshikawa kōbunkan, 2004).

8 *Hari* (Skt. *spaṭika*) is one of the seven precious jewels. Regarding the ritual use of this particular form of Amida, see Tomabechi Seiichi 苫米地誠一, "Guhari shoku Amidazō wo megutte" 紅頗梨色阿弥陀像をめぐって, *Chizan gakuhō* 智山学報 44 (1995): 53–79.

9 KS, 135–148.

10 Satō Mona, "Dōhan ni kansuru kisoteki kenkyū—denki shiryō wo chūshin toshite," pp. 86–87.

11 MBD 4:3218–3222; Jikken is also pronounced Jitsugen. MD, 983–984.

12 *Daigoji monjo* 醍醐寺文書 144.3.1: 秘鈔団 十一団. 建久四年六月廿日、於三宝院伝受了、 合点ハ道範受実賢ニ口決云々本ハ裏付也云々、/一校了、花押 [（憲深）]. I thank Brian Ruppert for this reference, from a personal communication, August 31, 2014.

13 SN, 237.

14 MD, 1329–1330.

15 SN, 242.

16 MD, 983.

17 SN, 279.

18 Kameyama Takahiko 亀山隆彦, "Chūsei Shingonshū ni okeru myōsoku shisō no tenkai—Shūkotsushō wo chūshin ni" 中世真言宗における命息思想の展開—『宗骨抄』を中心に, *Indogaku Bukkyōgaku kenkyū* 印度学仏教学研究 59 (2011): 651–654; Nakamura Honnen, "Shingon kyōgaku ni okeru shōshikan" 真言教学における生死観, *Nihon Bukkyōgaku nenpō* 日本仏教学会年報 75 (2010): 169–184 (R). For an overview of Dōhan's perspective, see Sanford, "Breath of Life," pp. 161–190.

19 MD, 1329–1330.

20 MD, 1138.

21 NBJT 6888, MD 1666, etc., suggest that Dōhan did indeed study in Kyoto at various locations, as does the *Honchō kōsōden* and the *Yahō meitokuden.* The *Honchō kōsōden* states that Dōhan studied under Kakuhō 覺法 (1091–1153) of Ninnaji, but Kakuhō passed away twenty-six years before Dōhan was born. This error has been repeated by several scholars who have not read all of the available resources and compared them against one another. The *Yahō meitokuden* is regarded as the most authoritative, and earliest, record, and it correctly lists Shukaku.

22 MBD 3:2428; for a concise introduction to Shukaku, see Brian D. Ruppert, "Dharma Prince Shukaku and the Esoteric Buddhist Culture of Sacred Works (Shōgyō) in Medieval Japan," in Orzech, Sørensen, and Payne, *Esoteric Buddhism and the Tantras in East Asia,* pp. 794–800. See also Ninnaji Konbyōshi Kozōshi Kenkyūkai 仁和寺紺表紙小双紙研究会, ed., *Shukaku hosshinnō no girei sekai: Ninnajizō konbyōshi kozōshi no kenkyū* 守覚法親王の儀礼世界: 仁和寺蔵紺表紙小双紙の研究, 2 vols. (Tokyo: Benseisha, 1995); Tsuchiya Megumi 土谷恵, "Chusei shoki no Ninnajji omuro" 中世初期の仁和寺御室, *Nihon rekikishi* 日本歴史 451 (1985): 46–63; Abe Yasurō 阿部泰郎, "Shukaku hosshinnō to inseiki no Bukkyō bunka" 守覚法親王と院政期の仏教文化, in *Inseiki no Bukkyō* 院政期の仏教, ed. Hayami Tasuku 速水侑 (Tokyo: Yoshikawa kōbunkan, 1998), pp. 118–142; Abe Yasurō and Yamasaki Makoto 山崎誠, eds., *Shukaku hosshinnō to Ninnaji goryū no bunkenteki kenkyū,*

ronbunhen 守覚法親王と仁和寺御流の文献学的研究, 論文編, 2 vols. (Tokyo: Benseisha, 1998).

23 MD, 1365.

24 MD, 1316–1317.

25 MD, 481; *Yahō meitokuden,* fasc. 1, DNBZ 106.

26 Nakamura Honnen, *Shingon mikkyō ni okeru anjinron,* p. 215; *Yahō meitokuden,* fasc. 2, DNBZ 106.

27 Satō Mona, "Dōhan ni kan suru kisoteki kenkyū—denki shiryō wo chūshin toshite," p. 88; KS, 136.

28 Gorai, *Kōya hijiri,* p. 117.

29 Richard K. Payne, "The Fourfold Training in Japanese Esoteric Buddhism," in Orzech, Sørensen, and Payne, *Esoteric Buddhism and the Tantras in East Asia,* pp. 1024–1028; Robert Sharf, "Thinking through Shingon Ritual," *Journal of the International Association of Buddhist Studies* 26, no. 1 (2003): 51–96, esp. pp. 59–86; MD, 1010–1011; MBD 2:1969–1970, 1024–1028.

30 MD, 638–645.

31 MD, 215.

32 MD, 2320–2325; MD, 1958–1960; Morita Ryūsen 森田竜僊, "Mikkyō no jōdo shisō" 密教の浄土思想, *Mikkyō kenkyū* 密教研究 6 (1921): 19–20.

33 MD, 1602. Thomas Conlan, *From Sovereign to Symbol: An Age of Ritual Determinism in Fourteenth-Century Japan* (Oxford: Oxford University Press, 2011), argues that Shingon lineages came to dominate during the Muromachi period.

34 Abé, *Weaving of Mantra,* pp. 148–150, 199–220, etc.

35 NKBT 83; Robert Morrell, "Shingon's Kakukai on the Immanence of the Pure Land," *Japanese Journal of Religious Studies* 11, no. 2–3 (1984): 195–220; Tanabe, "Kōyasan in the Countryside."

36 Stone, "Secret Art of Dying," pp. 155–162.

37 KS, 141.

38 KS, 144.

39 MD, 1195; Matsuzaki Keisui 松崎惠水, "Kakuban to Jōhen no Jōdo ōjō shisō" 覚鑁と静遍の浄土往生思想, *Buzan gakuhō* 豊山学報 53 (2010): 1–18; Satō Mona 佐藤もな, "Dōhan no kyōshugi ni tsuite" 道範の教主義について, *Nihon Bukkyō sōgō kenkyū* 日本仏教綜合研究 5 (2006): 67–78 (R); Nasu Kazuo 那須 一雄, "Myōhen kyōgaku to Jōhen kyōgaku" 明遍教学 と静遍教学, *Shūkyo kenkyū* 宗教研究 363 (2010): 359–360 (R); Nasu Kazuo 那須 一雄, "Hōnen to sono monka ni okeru 'senju' 'zasshu' rikai—tokuni Ryūkan, Shōkū, Jōhen ni tsuite" 法然とその門下における「専修・雑修」理解—特に隆寛・証 空・静遍について, *Shinshū kenkyū* 眞宗研究 52 (2008): 42–62; Nasu

Kazuo 那須 一雄, "Jōhen to Hōnen Jōdokyō" 静遍と法然浄土教, *Indogaku Bukkyōgaku kenkyū* 印度学仏教学研究 106 (2005): 80–85; Ito Shigeki 伊藤茂樹, "Jōhen no shūkyō katsudō" 静遍の宗教活動, *Indogaku Bukkyōgaku kenkyū* 印度学仏教学研究 117 (2009): 55–59 (R); Ito Shigeki 伊藤茂樹, "Jōhen no shōgai ni tsuite" 静遍の生涯について, *Jōdokyō kenkyū* 浄土宗学研究 34 (2008): 93–94 (R); Kumata Junshō 熊田 順正, "Jōhen 'Zoku sentaku mongi yōshō' ni okeru Amida no busshin butsudokan ni tsuite" 静遍『続選択文義要鈔』における阿弥陀仏の仏身仏土観について, *Indogaku Bukkyōgaku kenkyū* 印度学仏教学研究 106 (2005): 86–89; Kumata Junshō 熊田 順正, "Jōhen kyōgaku no tokuisei ni tsuite—shoshi o hihan wo tooshite" 静遍教学の特異性について—諸師の批判 を通して, *Tōyōgaku kenkyū* 東洋学研究 (2008): 97–121; Kumata Junshō 熊田 順正, "Jōhen Jōdokyō ni mieru shichi hachi kushiki setsu ni tsuite kōsatsu" 静遍浄土教に見える七八九識説についての考察, *Bukkyōgaku* 仏教学 48 (2006): 69–92; Kumata Junshō 熊田 順正, "Tōkoku no genshi Shinshū kyōdan e no himitsu nenbutsu shisō no eikyō ni tsuite" 東国の原始真宗教団への秘密 念仏思想の影響について, *Ryūkoku kyōgaku* 竜谷教学 (2004): 9–25; Nakamura Honnen, "Zenrinji Jōhen no sōmokuhihō jōbutsu ni tsuite" 禅林寺静遍の草木非情成仏説について, *Nihon Bukkyōgakkai nenpō* 日 本仏教学会年報 68 (2003): 281–304; Nakamura Honnen (under his preordination name, Nakamura Shōbun 中村正文), "Jōhen sōzu no shinkō no ichi sokumen ni tsuite" 静遍僧都の信仰の一側面について, *Mikkyō gakkaihō* 密教学会 報 31 (1992): 1–49; Nakamura Shōbun 中村正文), "Zenrinji Jōhen no teishōshita kyōgaku ni tsuite" 禅林寺静遍の提唱した教学について, *Kōyasan daigaku ronsō* 高野山大学論叢 26 (1991): 73–97; Ishida Mitsuyuki 石田充之, "Mikkyōkei Jōdo ganshōsha Jōhen sōzu no Jōdokyō tachiba" 密教系浄土願生者静遍僧都の浄土教的立場, *Ryūkoku daigaku ronshū* 龍谷大学論集 336 (1949): 36–62.

40 Nakamura Honnen, *Shingon mikkyō ni okeru anjinron,* pp. 211–215; Igarashi Takayuki 五十嵐隆幸, *Seizan Jōdokyō no kiban to tenkai* 西山浄土教の基盤と展開 (Kyoto: Shibunkaku shuppansha, 2010), pp. 52–67. Jōkei has received more attention in English in recent years; see James Ford, *Jōkei and Buddhist Devotion in Early Medieval Japan* (Oxford: Oxford University Press, 2006) and "Competing with Amida: A Study and Translation of Jōkei's Miroku Koshiki," *Monumenta Nipponica* 60, no. 1 (2005): 43–79.

41 MD, 1284.

42 ZJZ 6.

43 Igarashi, *Seizan Jōdokyō no kiban to tenkai,* pp. 52–55.

44 Abé, *Weaving of Mantra,* pp. 375–376. Regarding the intersections between Tōmitsu (Shingon) lineages and Taimitsu (Tendai) lineages, see Kagiwada Seiko 鍵和田聖子, "Tōmitsu to Taimitsu no sōgo eikyō kara mita juyō to kensan no tenkai" 東密と台密の相互影響から見た受容と研鑽の展開 (PhD diss., Ryūkoku University, 2014).

45 Yamaguchi, "Dōhan cho Himitsu nenbutsu shō," pp. 102–103.

46 Jōhen, *Zoku Senchaku mongi yōshō* 続選択文義要鈔 (Tokyo: Kokusho kankōkai, 1984).

47 Nasu, "Jōhen to Hōnen Jōdokyō," p. 81.

48 Ibid., pp. 80–85.

49 KS, 143.

50 KS, 141.

51 ZSZ 18; Yamaguchi, "Dōhan cho Himitsu nenbutsu shō," p. 103.

52 SZ 22.

53 Satō Mona, "Dōhan ni kan suru kisoteki kenkyū—denki shiryō wo chūshin toshite," p. 88; ND 24 (1916), 47 (1975); variant titles: *Bodaishinron shitta shō* 菩提心論質多抄, *Shitta shō* 質多抄, BKD 9:427d–428a; Nakamura Honnen, "Dōhan ki 'Bodaishin ron dangi ki' ni tsuite 道範記『菩提心論談義記』について," in *Mandara no shosō to bunka: Yoritomi Motohiro hakase kanreki kinen ronbunshū* マンダラの諸相と文化: 頼富本宏博士還暦記念論文集, ed. Yoritomi Motohiro hakushi kanshiki kinen ronbunshū kankōka 頼富本宏博士還暦記念論文集刊行会 (Kyoto: Hōzōkan 法藏館, 2005), pp. 395–430.

54 Kaneoka Shūyū 金岡秀友, ed., *Toganoo korekushon kenmitsu tenseki monjoshūsei* 栂尾コレク ション顕密典籍文書集成 5 (*Kyōsōhen* 教相篇 5) (Tokyo: Heika shuppansha, 1981).

55 KS, 154.

56 GR 18:468–476.

57 GR 18:468.

58 For a complete list of the places Dōhan visited, see Satō Mona, "Dōhan ni kan suru kisoteki kenkyū—denki shiryō wo chūshin toshite," p. 90; Tanaka Kenji 田中健二, "Komonjo kaitoku kōza, Kamakura jidai no ryūjin no nikki, 'Nankai rurōki' ni miru Sanuki no sugata" 古文書解読講座 鎌倉時代の流人の日記「南海流浪記」に見る讃岐の姿, *Kagawa kenritsu monjokan kiyō* 香川県立文書館紀要 15 (2011): 1–13.

59 Regarding medieval Japanese travel diaries, see Kendra Strand, "Aesthetics of Space: Representations of Travel in Medieval Japan" (PhD diss., University of Michigan, 2015).

60 GR 18:468b.

61 R. Keller Kimbrough, "Reading the Miraculous Powers of Japanese Poetry: Spells, Truth Acts, and a Medieval Buddhist Poetics of the Supernatural," *Japanese Journal of Religious Studies* 32, no. 1 (2005): 4.

62 Abé, *Weaving of Mantra*, pp. 2, 390–392.

63 Tanaka Kenji, "Komonjo kaitoku kōza, Kamakura jidai no ryūjin no nikki," p. 1.

64 KS, 155; Satō Mona, "Dōhan ni kan suru kisoteki kenkyū—denki shiryō wo chūshin toshite," p. 89.

65 NKBT 83:76–83; Pol K. van den Broucke, "Dōhan's Letter on the Visualization of Syllable A," *Shingi Shingon kyōgaku no kenkyū* 新義真言教学の研究 10 (2002): 65–87.

66 KS, 154.

67 GR 18:472b–473a.

68 MD, 1179; KS, 155. Like Dōhan and Hosshō, Shōso was also a student of Kakkai and is regarded as one of the "eight greats" of Kōyasan.

69 KS, 157.

70 Yamamoto, *Shōchiin monjo,* p. 349.

71 Hinonishi Shinjō, "The Hōgō (Treasure Name) of Kōbō Daishi and the Development of Beliefs Associated with It," trans. William Londo, *Japanese Religions* 27 (2002): 5–18.

72 KS, 157; Satō Mona, "Dōhan ni kan suru kisoteki kenkyū—denki shiryō wo chūshin toshite," p. 89.

73 KS, 159; *Henmyōin Daishi Myōjin gotakusenki* 遍明院大師明神御託宣記, reconstructed in Abe Yasurō 阿部泰郎, *Chūsei Kōyasan engi no kenkyū* 中世高野山縁起の研究 (Nara: Gangōji bunkasai kenkyūjo 元興寺文化財研究所, 1982), pp. 104–112 (cited in Elizabeth N. Tinsley, "Notes on the Authorship and Dating of the 13th Century Henmyōin Daishi Myōjin Go Takusen Ki (attributed to Dōhan)," *Indogaku bukkyōgaku* 印度学仏教学 58 (2010): 168–171. For an excellent overview of this oracle and its place in the historical context of the competition between lineages, see Elizabeth Tinsley, "Indirect Transmission in Shingon Buddhism: Notes on the Henmyoin Oracle," *Eastern Buddhist* 45, no. 1–2 (2016): 77–111.

74 KS, 159.

75 *Dainihon komonjo* 大日本古文書, *Kōyasan monjo* 高野山文書2:289–290 (cited by Satō Mona, "Dōhan ni kan suru kisoteki kenkyū—denki shiryō wo chūshin toshite," p. 93).

76 *Dentōkōroku* 傳燈廣錄, fasc. 6, ZSZ 33:387–388 (cited in Yamaguchi, "Dōhan cho Himitsu nenbutsu shō no hihan taishō ni tsuite," pp. 115, 122). See also Yamamoto Nobuyoshi 山本信吉, "Kōyasan Shōchi'in shozō Ajari Dōhan jihitsubo (nishu)" 高野山正智院所蔵阿闍梨道範自筆本 (二種), in vol. 2, *Kodai chūsei shiryō kenkyū* 古代中世史料学研究, ed. Minagawa Kanichi 皆川完一 (Tokyo: Yoshikawa Kōbunkan, 1998), pp. 342–372.

77 MD, 2147, notes that after Chōkaku at Muryōju-in and Yūkai at Hosshō-in (the former temple of Hosshō) established a strong doctrinal studies relationship between their respective temples, the two temples were officially renamed Hōju-in 寶寿院 in 1913.

78 Yamakage Kazuo 山陰加春夫, "Chūsei Kōya kyōdan soshiki shōkō" 中世高野山教 団組織小考, *Kōyasan daigaku ronsō* 高野山大学論叢 19 (1984): 1–21.

79 Yamanaka Takahiro 山中嵩裕, "Kōyasan niokeru nenbutsu shinkō to sono tenkai—nenbutsu sanmai kara risshu sanmai e" 高野山における念仏信仰とその展開—念仏三昧から理趣三昧へ, *Mikkyō gakkai hō* 密教学会報 (2013): 13–28.

80 Gorai, *Kōya hijiri,* pp. 300–314.

81 Ibid., pp. 83–84.

82 Ibid., pp. 23–24, 84.

Chapter 5

Dōhan's Major Works and Kamakura Buddhism

Dōhan's writings provide an important window into aspects of the early medieval Japanese Buddhist environment that remain largely unstudied by Anglophone scholars. Situating Dōhan's scholarship in the broader context of "Kamakura Buddhism" reveals important connections between the so-called new schools—Pure Land, Zen, Nichiren, and so on—and the old schools—Shingon, Tendai, and more. It also demonstrates the links between *hongaku* doctrinal thought and Esoteric ritual practice as shared paradigms within premodern Japanese religion and the contours of Esoteric Buddhism both as a widespread area of study and the evolving and distinct tradition of Shingon. One of Dōhan's main concerns as a scholar of the doctrinal and ritual texts that are now associated with the East Asian Esoteric Buddhist tradition was clarifying what it means to be a practitioner of the mantra path.

Through the Heian and into the Kamakura periods, Esoteric Buddhism and *shingon* were to some extent synonyms, and neither was necessarily associated with or owned by a single "school," as we understand that term today. What scholars today might label Esoteric Buddhism functioned broadly as one of many disciplinary areas, a repository of ("Esoteric") ritual and doctrinal knowledge from which many different competing lineages, sublineages, and traditions emerged, across various major monastic institutions. The metaphor of a tree and its branches has often been employed to conceptualize this situation. From this view, the founder is the base, or trunk, of the tree, and the various lineages that grew and evolved from this base are the branches. On closer inspection, however, a much more complex picture emerges of a tangled mass of bushes, vines, and weeds, or perhaps even a rhizome, with the occasional forest fire that thins the undergrowth, only for it to grow again.

Staying with this metaphor, *shingon* as an area of study was just one pervasive species of flora that pervaded the dense thicket of early medieval Japanese religious, political, and philosophical culture. The premodern Japanese Buddhist landscape was devoid of "sects" or "schools" as we understand them today; instead it comprised localized institutions, lineages, and cultic sites populated by monks who employed their mastery of a wide range of ritual and doctrinal tools to compete with one another. Though the Shingon school is commonly imagined to have begun with Kūkai in the early ninth century, Kūkai himself did not envision Shingon Esoteric Buddhism as a distinct school or sect, and even by the late medieval period, something we could identify as the Shingon "school" was instead

> a loose affiliation of monasteries, in which Shingon was one of several disciplines practiced. The Shingon Schools at these monasteries were connected through diverse master-disciple lineages, some based on doctrinal studies, others on ritual training, and yet others on the transmission of meditative secrets. The resultant primary-branch relationship between monasteries had no hierarchical structure and was fluid, to say the least.[1]

Daigoji, Tōji, Ninnaji, and Kōyasan were important Esoteric Buddhist centers, as were Enryakuji, Onjōji, Tōdaiji, and Kōfukuji. Today only some of these are technically associated with the Shingon school, yet to this day each of these temples maintains a rigorous training regime in Esoteric Buddhist ritual.

Why has mantra practice come to be associated with one school in particular? Why is it not considered a pan-Japanese area of ritual specialization and knowledge? First, during the mid- to late medieval period (late Kamakura to Muromachi), after Dōhan's lifetime, the aristocratic temple-shrine complexes experienced the same social and political instability as aristocrats and warriors in the so-called Warring States period (1467–1600). In 1571 Oda Nobunaga burned down Enryakuji and the temple-shrine complexes on Hieizan, the headquarters of the Tendai Buddhist tradition, which, until that time, had remained a dominant force in the evolution of Japanese Esoteric Buddhism. Thousands of monks were slaughtered. What had been regarded as the "Vatican of Japan" suddenly disappeared.

As the Tokugawa regime established control over religious institutions throughout Japan, Kōyasan and other temples associated with Kūkai's lineage served to fill the lacuna of expertise in Esoteric ritual caused by the destruction of Enryakuji. Yet this was not an entirely sudden shift: for some time during the medieval period, from the late Heian on, lineages claiming descent from Kūkai had been in competition with Enryakuji to establish mastery of Esoteric scripture and ritual. The complex evolution of the Shingon school in the medieval period was thus a dependently arisen and interconnected process. Buddhist sectarian literature from the modern period tends to attribute a degree of *svabhāva* (inherent existence) to sects and lineages, utilizing Protestant Christian historical teleological models to essentialize the teachings of a founder strategically in order to appropriate the cultural power of a founder or teaching.

Abé notes further that in 1611 Kōyasan, Ninnaji, Jingoji, Tōji, and Daigoji were designated as "Shingon-shū" head temples with branch temples. Throughout the early modern Japanese world, the previously fluid relationship between temples and lineages became rigid and defined by such sectarian hierarchies. Within this environment, scholar-monks focused their attention on the key texts associated with founders and patriarchs. With the advent of the Meiji era (1868–1912), Japanese Buddhist institutions adapted to the European-style university model, and the sectarian taxonomy that had begun in the Tokugawa era came to be applied to the whole of Japanese Buddhist history.[2]

The fluidity of Dōhan's early medieval context has often been ignored because it is simply incompatible with this taxonomic, founder-sect framework. His thought, and the thought of others like him—in other words, the mainstream of early medieval Japanese Buddhism—has often been left out of the picture. For this reason, further inquiry into the work of figures like Dōhan is extremely important for understanding medieval Japanese religion. In the world of Shingon sectarian studies, Dōhan sits between Kakuban, the "second founder" of Shingon Buddhism, and Raiyu, the founder of the Shingi branch of Shingon. Dōhan drew from Kakuban extensively, and Raiyu critiqued Dōhan as his Daidenbō-in faction moved away from Kōyasan. Dōhan's works are particularly important for studying these more well-known figures.

Kamakura Buddhism and the *Kenmitsu* System

The Kamakura period (1195–1333) has been the focus of much of the scholarship on Japanese religion. Today's largest schools of Japanese Buddhism, including the Zen schools of Rinzai Zen-shū, founded by Eisai, and the Sōtō Zen-shū, founded by Dōgen; the Pure Land schools of Jōdo-shū, founded by Hōnen, Jōdo Shinshū, founded by Shinran, and Ji-shū, founded by Ippen; and the "Lotus school" (Hokke-shū) founded by

Nichiren (more commonly known as the Nichiren-shū), all emerged during this time. As a result, the powerful sectarian institutions that claim descent from the "new school" founders dominate scholarly and popular writing on Buddhism and have pioneered the international spread of Japanese Buddhism.

It has been noted that the founders of these schools were marginal figures and were not representative of the religious mainstream in their own time. Despite the plethora of scholarship on the Kamakura period, the fact that most of this scholarship focuses on figures whose thought became influential only in later centuries indicates that there is still much more to uncover in this fascinating era of Japanese history. For this reason, the perspectives and ideas of scholar-monks such as Dōhan must necessarily receive further attention.

One of the most important contributions of Kuroda Toshio, who was one of the most influential scholars of early medieval Japan, was his effort to reorient the study of medieval Japanese religion and culture around the so-called old schools by demonstrating that the institutions based in Kyoto and Nara dominated Buddhism in the Kamakura period.[3] Kuroda thus shifted the conversation from old schools versus new schools to orthodoxy versus heterodoxy.[4] According to him, the dialogic exoteric-esoteric system (*kenmitsu taisei*) served as the religious justification for the established order, balancing the power blocs of the warrior, aristocratic, and temple communities. Kuroda referred to this interconnected religiopolitical power structure as the gates of power (*kenmon taisei*).

These two systems were mutually supportive. On the institutional level, the *kenmon taisei* ruled the land and economy, while the *kenmitsu taisei* ruled hearts and minds, supporting the former. Another key concept addressed by Kuroda is *ōbō buppō sōi* 王法佛法相依, or the mutual dependence of secular and religious law: "The king's law and the Buddha's dharma rely upon one another." Kuroda's approach to the history of medieval Japan and its religious traditions was heavily influenced by Marxist theories of history, as was quite common in his time.

From the 1970s to the 1990s, Anglophone scholars of Japanese Buddhism began publishing works that were heavily influenced by Kuroda's perspective. Previously, such scholars had largely uncritically taken as gospel the sectarian teleological rhetoric of the Kamakura Buddhism model. Kuroda's *kenmitsu taisei* thus emerged as a foundational concept in premodern Japanese studies.[5] As James Ford observes somewhat more recently, there remain essentially two basic approaches to the study of early medieval Japanese religion. The first scholars are those holdovers from "pre-Kuroda" scholarship who remain content to take an essentialist, sectarian, founder-centric, doctrinal view. The second are scholars who have built upon, and occasionally critique and elaborate on, Kuroda's sociohistorical and institutional approach to the study of Japanese religion.[6]

As influential as Kuroda's critique of the dominant paradigm has been, a number of scholars, including Ryuichi Abé, Jaqueline Stone, Sueki Fumihiko, and others, have offered critiques that further refine his theories. Abé considers the ambiguity inherent in Kuroda's use of the term "exo-esoteric" Buddhism, noting that Kuroda never clearly defines exactly what he means by "Esoteric Buddhism." Abé also contends that Kuroda does not clearly distinguish between *hongaku* thought and Esoteric Buddhism. Though there are many areas of overlap, their intellectual lineage and function in Japanese religion are different.[7] Finally, Abé points out that focusing on the institutions, teachers, and movements associated with the major temples based in Nara is one way to address these issues because these temples, such as Tōdaiji, Kōfukuji, and others, were major landholding institutions and so were highly influential upon Buddhist culture at both the elite and popular levels.[8]

Stone, followed by James L. Ford, David Quinter, and others, discusses some of the possible critiques of the very idea of a *kenmitsu* "system." Taira Masayuki 平雅行, one of Kuroda's most prominent students, suggests that it may be problematic to conceive of *kenmitsu* thought as a unified ideology or force.[9] Sasaki Kaoru 佐々木馨 further nuances the early medieval period by distinguishing between *taisei* Bukkyō 體制佛教 (establishment Buddhism), *han-taisei* Bukkyō 反體制佛教 (antiestablishment Buddhism), and *chō-taisei* Bukkyō 超體制佛教 (transestablishment Buddhism). Quinter suggests that monks such as Saigyō, Chōgen, and Ippen may be seen as representatives of *chō-taisei* Bukkyō.[10] Dōhan likely sits somewhere between the establishment and transestablishment spheres due to his position as a high-ranking monastic administrative official who also wrote broadly on a variety of topics and endured a period of exile, though for reasons unrelated to doctrine or religious practice.

Though less well known than Kuroda, Tanaka Hisao's scholarship has been especially influential for this book. In *Kamakura Bukkyō* 鎌倉仏教 (Kamakura Buddhism), Tanaka considers the major traditions associated with Kamakura Buddhism and Buddhism in the Kamakura period from multiple innovative and overlapping angles. For example, instead of Tendai Buddhism he sometimes refers to Hokurei 北嶺, the Northern Peak, a common term for Hieizan, the seat of Tendai Buddhism. In this way Tanaka localizes and grounds the commonly used and abstract sectarian monikers. Furthermore, Tanaka refers to the "Nara schools" by the name Nanto 南都, the "Southern Capital," and Kōyasan as Nanzan 南山, the "Southern Mountain." This may not seem that significant, yet by displacing such widely used labels and replacing them with less familiar terms commonly used in the source material, a subtle shock is rendered that may encourage readers to approach the tradition under consideration from a new vantage point. The emphasis on place and geography allows a better perspective on the fluidity among cultic sites and the people and ideas associated with them.

Tanaka also performs an interesting bait and switch with chapter titles, such as "Zen" or "Shingon *mikkyō*" (this by itself stands out as Shingon *mikkyō* is rarely discussed in Kamakura-period scholarship); rather than narrate the standard sectarian teleology of founder-doctrine-sect, he instead reveals the diverse range of practices and teachings that were actually associated with each tradition during the Kamakura period. For example, in the chapter on Zen he considers the early Zen movement's debt to Esoteric Buddhism. In brief, Tanaka reveals how each area of study is actually deeply intertwined.[11]

Over the last few decades, a number of studies examining mainstream Kamakura Buddhist figures (the so-called old schools) have helped establish the foundation on which my investigation into Dōhan's thought stands. James Ford has examined the life and career of Jōkei, revealing the importance of eclectic cultic practice and catholic devotion to a diverse range of Buddhist deities as well as Pure Land aspiration, Esoteric ritual, and so on.[12] Lori Meek's study of Hokkeji and female monastic networks reveals the dynamic activities of medieval Japanese nuns, eschewing the often patriarchal history of Japanese Buddhism. Meek's work also highlights the institutional and devotional agency of medieval Japanese Buddhist women.[13] David Quinter's study of Eison 叡尊 (1201–1290) and his Shingon-risshū lineage 眞言律宗, including Nishō Ryōkan 忍性良観 (1217–1303), Shinkū 信空 (1229–1316), and Monkan 文観 (1278–1357), shows just how indistinct the lines between the "old" and "new" schools are and how the activities of monks and nuns in the early Kamakura period reveal them to be complex social actors working between the worlds of elites and commoners.[14] George Tanabe and Mark Unno's scholarship on Myōe 明恵 (1173–1232) examines the importance of dreams and visionary experiences in early medieval religion,[15] as well as important areas of overlap between *Avataṃsaka-sūtra* studies and Esoteric Pure Land ritual and thought. Scholarship on Gyōnen 凝然 (1240–1321) by Mark Blum examines the ways in which scholar-monks of this period understood the relationship between the various areas of study, such as Shingon, Tendai, Pure Land, and more.[16]

Janet Goodwin explores the pilgrimage and patronage networks of major institutions and the diverse economic and religious systems that served as the foundation for Kamakura-period religious activity.[17] Tanabe discusses the neglect of Esoteric Buddhism and the cultic site of Kōyasan in particular and situates Kōyasan as a marginal site that attracted devotees from elite and commoner backgrounds alike, thus serving as a new "center" where institutional and devotional relationships were formed. He discredits the claim that Esoteric Buddhism was too "esoteric" for ordinary people, referencing the universal appeal of pageantry and the intrigue of secrecy.[18]

Emerging scholarship on Buddhism in the Kamakura period successfully counters the rhetoric of decline associated with the Kamakura Buddhism historiographic model, which has often mischaracterized the dynamic and vital world of the so-called old schools as out of touch or in a state of decline.

Stone, Ford, and Quinter, however, note that as the contemporary academic consensus has moved away from doctrine and charismatic individuals, focusing instead on institutions, some aspects of the old/new dichotomy remain intact and unchallenged:[19] "Whether from Marxist orientations, postmodern methodologies, Protestant influences, or a distinctively American emphasis on pioneers and individualism—the 'new,' 'reform,' 'heterodox,' and 'anti-establishment' classifications of Buddhist schools continue to lend themselves to positive valuations and their counterparts to negative valuations."[20]

Brian Ruppert and James Dobbins similarly observe that instead of essentialist sect, founder, and doctrinal histories, or the deterministic study of faceless institutions, scholars might more productively focus their attention on specific cultic sites and the fluid figures and practices associated with them. This is arguably another useful way to engage in the study of doctrine and practice as well as institutions.[21]

Dobbins provides several examples, such as Chion'in 知恩院 (associated with Jōdo-shū), Honganji 本願寺 (associated with Jōdo Shinshū), Shōjōkōji 清浄光寺 (associated with Jishū), Eiheiji 永平寺 and Sōjiji 總持寺 (associated with Sōtō-shū), Daitokuji 大德寺 (associated with Rinzai-shū), and Minobusan 身延山 (associated with Nichiren-shū). Though each of these institutions is now firmly situated within the new schools, they all maintained close and complicated relationships with their parent traditions even into the Tokugawa period. Thus, further study of these cultic sites would further nuance and complicate the often teleological sectarian historiography.

For example, Jōdo Shinshū was closely connected to Shōren'in 青蓮院, where Shinran took tonsure.[22] Shōren'in served as the place where many Shin Buddhist priests received ordination, and some also trained in Nara. Additionally, this temple acted on the Honganji's behalf in the event of legal disputes and more.[23] By looking to the concrete institutional life of these groups and the ways in which new and old were intimately bound to one another, a more complex and accurate picture emerges. Dobbins also emphasizes a balanced approach that employs inquiry into institutional matters as well as the more abstract facets of religious life, including popular narratives, relic worship, pilgrimage, and the effect that charisma and compelling doctrine may exert on these.[24]

Hongaku as Shared Paradigm

However the *kenmitsu* "system" is defined or understood, Esoteric ritual lineages and doctrine permeated medieval Japanese culture. As Jacqueline Stone has demonstrated, *hongaku* (original enlightenment) thought also exerted significant influence upon Japanese Buddhism as a whole. However, as Abé notes, the relationship between *kenmitsu* and *hongaku* is sparsely studied. *Hongaku* is usually associated with the idea that, in contradistinction to traditional perspectives assuming that practice facilitates progress along the Buddhist path, instead all beings are understood to already, or originally, be "awakened." The teachings associated with this notion of original enlightenment were passed down through secret oral transmission (*kuden* 口傳). Stone notes that *hongaku* thought is rooted in the Chinese Tiantai philosophy of Zhiyi and followed established precedent regarding the interrelationship between the "provisional" and "true" nature of different teachings. Zhiyi argued that the purported binaries proposed in Chinese and Buddhist philosophical systems, including provisional and true, phenomena 事 and principle 理, essence 體 and function 用, and nature 性 and form 相, were ultimately not separate from one another. Furthermore, each pair of concepts may initially purport to establish hierarchies or a strictly vertical relationship, but each is nondual, with mutually interpenetrating facets.[25]

Other threads contributing to the development of this way of thinking about Buddhism include the *Avataṃsaka-sūtra*, the *Vimalakīrti-sūtra*, the *Benevolent King Sutra*, the *Vajra-samādhi-sūtra*, and the confluence and pervasive influence of tathāgata-*garbha* thought, as well as Madhyamaka and Yogācāra concepts. In Japan the notion of *hongaku* first appeared in Kūkai's nondualistic Mahayana thought, especially in his *Shakumakaenron shiji* 釋摩訶衍論指事 (T. 2284), a commentary on the *Shimoheyanlun* 釋摩訶衍論 (T. 1668), which is itself a commentary attributed to Nāgārjuna on the *Awakening of Faith.*[26] In the early Japanese environment, which was eventually dominated by an esotericized Tendai tradition, *hongaku* doctrine evolved organically in dialogue with Esoteric ritual practice and theory.

Several key concepts prevalent in *hongaku* literature exerted broad influence on the whole of early medieval Japanese Buddhism. For example, while traditional Mahayana and non-Mahayana traditions take for granted a mechanistic approach to practice and enlightenment (i.e., practice leads to enlightenment), *hongaku* presents a "nonlinear" view. Ordinary ignorant beings and enlightened buddhas abide in a fundamentally nondual relationship; therefore, cause and effect are effectively collapsed into a single moment of practice and faith. Some of Hōnen's disciples believed that a single heartfelt recitation of Amitābha's name would lead one to attain rebirth in the Pure Land. Dōgen spoke of the "eternal now" and famously characterized practice as the performance of one's state of awakening, rather than being the act that leads one to awakening. Nichiren proposed that the attainment of awakening is present in the very moment in which one embraces the *Lotus Sutra.*

Hongaku also emphasizes the efficacy of simple practices, or a "single condition." Reciting one mantra or spell or performing a single practice (*zazen, nenbutsu, daimoku*) was said to be all that was required to attain awakening. I suggest that this perspective may ultimately derive from the *Lotus Sutra,* which asserts that the eternal Śākyamuni is always working behind the scenes to aid beings in the attainment of awakening. The fact that someone is in the position to encounter the Mahayana teachings therefore indicates that the person has already set down good karmic roots and is close to awakening. Thus, a single moment of faith or an act of practice may be all that is needed to complete the journey.

These simple practices are also "all-inclusive," containing the whole of the bodhisattva path in themselves. For example, Shinran suggests that recitation of the name of Amitābha and the mind of confidence that gives rise to spiritual transformation in this life are ultimately the working of Amitābha as the compassionate activity of dharmakāya. Finally, and perhaps most controversially, *hongaku* thought emphasizes the "nonobstructing" nature of bad karma. In other words, being a bad person, even an *evil* person, is no longer an inherent obstacle to the realization of awakening right here and now. This interpretation of the teaching may have been designed to alleviate the anxiety of those who lived in the tumultuous Kamakura period, though later critics suggest that it was simply a way to excuse bad behavior.[27]

Traditional Buddhism is based in the triad of wisdom-morality-meditation, and according to its critics, *hongaku* seems to eliminate all three. From the Meiji period on, scholars appear to have seen the dynamic fluidity and hermeneutical flexibility of *hongaku kuden* texts as evidence of the decadence of the old-school thinkers.[28] Dōhan was clearly influenced by *hongaku* modes of thinking, so it is easy to speculate that this is one more reason for the scholarly neglect of his thought.

Certain aspects of Dōhan's thought confirm Ford's supposition that *hongaku* modes of thought extended well beyond Tendai Buddhism and the so-called new schools (Pure Land, Zen, Nichiren) to the evolving Shingon school and Nara institutions as well.[29] In previous chapters I demonstrated that the Kōyasan revival of the eleventh century resulted from concerted efforts by Nara- and Heian-kyō-based institutions, and forms of practice such as the *fudan nenbutsu* (continuous *buddhānusmṛti*) first pioneered on Hieizan also spread to Kōyasan and other major monastic practice sites. In the same way, Kōyasan scholar-monks, including Dōhan, drew from multiple areas of disciplinary specialization, including *hongaku* thought.

As Stone notes, the founders of the Kamakura new schools were all trained in the Tendai tradition, and modern scholars have long pondered the nature of such Tendai influence on the thought of these founders. She suggests that there are three basic approaches to this issue:[30] First, some scholars regard Tendai *hongaku* thought as the matrix from which, or perhaps the environment within which, the Kamakura founders built their views. Second, other scholars read the thought of the Kamakura founders as having been established in a "radical break" from the purportedly elitist Tendai *hongaku* tradition. Scholars associated with the Nichiren and Sōtō schools in particular have emphasized the discontinuities between their respective founders' views and *hongaku* thought. However, this approach, rooted in the founder-centric views of the Tokugawa period, in some sense requires the dismissal of contextual evidence to the contrary.[31] Finally, other scholars still regard *hongaku* as fundamentally heretical and non-Buddhist and an affront to universally understood views on ethics and morality; thus, the Kamakura reformers were trying to restore Japanese Buddhism to a more orthodox, "pure" perspective.[32] Furthermore, more recent critics of *hongaku,* influenced by Marxist historiography, have dismissed *hongaku* as well as *kenmitsu* thought as nothing more than ideological support for oppressive regimes. Stone finds all of these views to be flawed in crucial ways. In particular, Stone notes that *hongaku* does not in fact obviate the need for practice and ethics and that each of the critiques mentioned presupposes the inherent superiority of the new schools over the so-called old schools and regards *hongaku* thought as elitist and out of touch with the concerns of ordinary people.

Drawing on the work of Tamura Yoshirō 田村芳朗, Stone presents and further develops a "dialectical emergence" theory, a view that seeks to address the deficiencies and biases inherent in the other views and arrive at a more nuanced perspective. She notes that antecedents to *hongaku* are pervasive throughout East Asian Mahayana Buddhist culture, Kamakura founders included. What distinguishes the Kamakura founders within this context, and from one another, is the degree to which they adopted or critiqued some of those basic assumptions. Stone refers to this as dialectical engagement and suggests that the nonduality inherent in *hongaku* thought can be considered to be the "thesis" and Hōnen's seemingly dualistic approach to Buddhist soteriology, premised on the gulf between samsara and the Pure Land, the "antithesis." It is important to note that Hōnen was born in 1133, and the Kamakura period began in 1195. Much of his life and thought therefore fall within what historians refer to as the Heian period. Later thinkers, chronologically and developmentally, were responding to a different time altogether.

Based on this, Shinran, Dōgen, and Nichiren may perhaps be seen as the "synthesis" of thesis and antithesis.[33] Like Hōnen's other disciples, Shinran professed to be simply presenting the teachings he had received from Hōnen, and as with his other disciples, Shinran's views develop, elaborate on, and in some ways further advance Hōnen's thought. Meanwhile, Dōgen's understanding of the nonduality of practice and awakening, as well as Nichiren's understanding that faith in the *Lotus Sutra* is sufficient to purify this world, is clearly indebted to ideas prevalent in *hongaku* thought. In other words, both "Tendai as matrix" and "radical break" theories are insufficient to explain the complex relationship between the new school founders and the *hongaku* context of early medieval Japan. Ultimately, both old and new "may be seen as participating in the articulation of an emerging paradigm of Buddhist liberation."[34]

Dōhan and Zen

It is sometimes assumed that elite scholar-monks like Dōhan were out of touch with changes in the early medieval religious environment, but in addition to his work on Pure Land thought and practice, Dōhan taught a number of monks who were important to the early Japanese Zen lineages and indeed had his own opinion of this newly imported approach to Buddhism. According to scholar-priests on Kōyasan today, from the early medieval until the postwar period Zen meditation was a vibrant "transsectarian" area of focus, bridging the gulfs among monks of disparate lineages and sects.[35]

William Bodiford has noted the importance of Esoteric Buddhist ritual culture to the early Japanese Zen tradition. Enni Ben'en 圓爾辨圓 (1202–1280), Mujū Ichien 無住一圓 (1226–1312), and Dōgen's successor Keizan Jōkin 瑩山紹瑾 (1264–1325) all drew on the pervasive influence of Esoteric Buddhism in their articulation of Zen in Japan.[36] For example, there existed a close relationship, or perhaps a "family resemblance," between Esoteric secret transmissions and the Zen transmission of lineage. The "shared body of esoteric lore" often overlapped as lineages overlapped: the widely popular Mantra of Light was present in both Zen and Esoteric lineages. Esoteric Buddhism and Zen could be viewed as rival "esoteric" traditions, as Bodiford suggests.[37]

Bodiford also notes that (sectarian) scholars of Esoteric Buddhism and Zen quibble over "pure" and "mixed" varieties, seeking to establish an unadulterated form of their respective traditions. This was not a major concern for medieval monks, however, who availed themselves of various elements in their environments.[38] For example, in this competitive environment, Zen and Esoteric ritual masters employed their respective mastery of dhāraṇī to claim the superiority of their particular lineages.[39] Zen temples sometimes performed rituals commonly associated with Shingon and Tendai traditions, such as feeding the hungry ghosts, creating talismans, and conducting votive fire ceremonies. After all, many early Zen monks, including Dōgen and Eisai, began their careers as Tendai monks who were well versed in Esoteric traditions.[40]

Two important figures in the early transmission of Zen studied under Dōhan. Shinji Kakushin studied at Tōdaiji and relocated to Kōyasan in 1225. Kakushin studied Esoteric Buddhism under Dōhan's tutelage and

Zen under Gyōyū at the Zenjō-in of Kongōsanmai-in; as mentioned previously, Gyōyū was another Zen teacher who had studied under Dōhan. During his time on Kōyasan, Kakushin was also affiliated with the Kayadō lineage of the Mitsugon-in, Kakuban's *nenbutsu* practice site.[41] Kakushin later traveled to Song China and on his return to Japan promoted Zen.[42] Kakushin received the bodhisattva precepts from Dōgen. Ippen, regarded as the founder of the Jishū Pure Land lineage, also studied under Kakushin and received *inka,* or "recognition of awakening," from him.

Gyōyū, Kakushin's Zen master, lived on Kōyasan for nine years. He helped establish the Kongōsanmai-in with the help of the patronage of Hōjō Masako, the wife of Minamoto no Yoritomo, founder of the Kamakura shogunate. During his time on Kōyasan, Gyōyū studied under Dōhan as well as a monk named Kakubutsu who was affiliated with the Daidenbō-in.[43] Gyōyū was also active in Kamakura, traveling to the new capital in 1241.[44]

Dōhan's Major Works

Dōhan was a prolific scholar whose vast oeuvre may be variously categorized: debate manuals, works on ritual praxis and doctrinal theory, commentaries, subcommentaries, sub-subcommentaries, and so on. Here I will briefly outline some of his major works around the following themes: works emerging from Dōhan's devotion to Kōbō Daishi Kūkai and the holy mountain Kōyasan, works emerging from Dōhan's productive relationship with Ninnaji monks, introductory or "simple practice" works that present various aspects of Esoteric Buddhism, works inspired by Dōhan's study under Kakkai and Jōhen, and deathbed ritual texts.

Approaching Dōhan's work in this way has several advantages, beginning with situating Dōhan's thought in the shared *hongaku* and *kenmitsu* paradigms of early medieval Japanese Buddhist culture. By grounding Dōhan's thought in relation to specific lineages, cultic sites, and methods and discourse on praxis, some of the issues discussed above can be avoided, building on recent insights that have opened up new avenues for inquiry.

Kōbō Daishi and Kōyasan

Devotion to Kōbō Daishi Kūkai as a bodhisattva-like savior figure is central to Dōhan's thought. This is not simply a function of Dōhan belonging to something called the Shingon school; it is also based in his identity as a longtime resident of Kōyasan. It is more useful to think of Dōhan as a devotee of a particular object of devotion and the cultic site associated with that object of devotion: the legacy of Kūkai and the power of Kōyasan.

Control over and the authority to speak for the cult of Kūkai conferred economic and social advantages, as did the administration of Kōyasan as a site for interpretive contestation and institutional competition. During Dōhan's lifetime, administrators, ritual masters, and preachers on the mountain worked to establish connections with the important power centers in Kyoto, quickly adapting to the changing political landscape and sending missions to Kamakura, and also strove to maintain control over the dynamic and fluid lineages on the mountain. In examining what Dōhan says about Kōyasan or Kūkai, it is important to keep in mind what effects his views may have had, as well as the political effects of piety and the struggle for authority.

Nanzan hiku

The *Nanzan hiku* 南山秘口 is a very brief text in which Dōhan clearly outlines his understanding of Kōyasan and Kūkai as the savior figure associated with the sacred mountain. According to Dōhan, Kōyasan, if not a *buddha-kṣetra* in its own right, is a conduit to the *buddha-kṣetra* of various buddhas and bodhisattvas. As a Mahayana Buddhist thinker, Dōhan took for granted the idea that as practitioners progress along the bodhisattva path they course throughout the manifold *buddha-kṣetra* of the ten directions. Today the primary focus on Kūkai has been his doctrinal writings, especially those features that mark him as different or distinct from his surrounding environment. Although Dōhan was clearly an avid reader of and commentator on Kūkai's writings, Kūkai was much more than just a Buddhist intellectual to him. Kūkai was in fact a source of Buddhist power capable of leading beings to the *buddha-kṣetra* of the ten directions.

Drawing from Kūkai, Dōhan's understanding of Buddhism is rooted in a fundamentally nondualist understanding of the world. One way he articulates this is through the *santen* 三點 (three-point) exegetical technique. In the Siddham script for writing Sanskrit, the letter *I* is written in the form of three circles that form an upside-down triangle. This was used to describe the relationship between essence, phenomena, and wisdom. This tripartite hermeneutic is mapped onto the three characters of the word "Kō-ya-san," bestowing esoteric significance to the very name of the mountain. Dōhan also incorporates a nondual reading of the dual mandalas of the Shingon tradition and of male and female bodies joined in cosmic sexual union.[45]

Kōbō Daishi ryaku joshō

The *Kōbō Daishi ryaku joshō* 弘法大師略頌鈔 is a commentary on Enmyō's 圓明 (d. 851) eighteen-verse poetic retelling of the major events in Kūkai's life. In this text Dōhan mainly provides source text citations for each of these events as well as some additional biographical detail. What is interesting about this text is how it reveals that by Dōhan's time miraculous narrative events, such as Kūkai throwing a *vajra* from China that landed on Kōyasan, as well as what modern scholars take for granted to be biographical events in the life of Kūkai, were clearly already in place. In the section on the *Sokushin jobutsugi,* Kūkai's attainment of Buddhahood in this very body is portrayed as a justification for both the transsectarian nature of Shingon practice and Kūkai's position as the leader of disciples from the various schools.

At the end of this text, Dōhan describes a miraculous encounter experienced by a Kūkai devotee who visited Kūkai's tomb. As a result of touching Kūkai's knee, the devotee's hand emitted a mysterious fragrance for the rest of his life. Furthermore, the scent of divine flowers grew in intensity when this devotee died, and he attained rebirth in Sukhāvatī.[46]

Dōhan and Dōjo of Ninnaji

In his youth Dōhan trained at Ninnaji, and after he went back to Kōyasan, Ninnaji monks continued to request his return to Ninnaji to teach. Many of Dōhan's most important extant works were produced through his interactions with Dōjo, an imperial prince and abbot of Ninnaji who later retired to Kōyasan. That so many of Dōhan's works survive may be due to his longtime association with such an important capital institution.

Jōōshō

The *Jōōshō* (a.k.a *Teiōshō*) 貞応抄 (T. 2447) was compiled by Dōhan in response to the inquiries of Dōjo of Ninnaji, who consulted him to clarify the buddha-body theory, the exoteric and esoteric interpretations of the five viscera, the relationship between sudden and gradual enlightenment, the attainment of Buddhahood in this very body, and other topics. Dōhan's discussion of the *raigō* and its significance in relation to *sokushin jōbutsu* is particularly interesting. According to Dōhan the two are not distinct but correspond to the inner and outer experience of the moment of death.[47] This text also draws from works by Jippan, Jōhen, Kakkai, and Yūgen 融源 (1120–1218), a monk from Kakuban's Daidenbō-in 大傳法院.[48]

Chiba Tadashi 千葉正 has examined this text and the concept of *shukuzen* 宿善 in the medieval Japanese context. *Shukuzen* refers to the importance of establishing good karma in past lives, which renders one's present practices efficacious and allows one to achieve religious goals. Perhaps influenced by Genshin's discussion of the efficacy of the *nenbutsu,* Dōhan notes the importance of *shukuzen* for the achievement of *sokushin jōbutsu.*[49]

Yugikyō kuketsu

The *Yugikyō kuketsu* 瑜祇經口決 is a collection of orally transmitted teachings on Vajrabodhi's *Jingangfeng louge yiqie yujia yuqi jing* 金剛峯樓閣一切瑜伽瑜祇經 (T. 867), known in Japanese by its abbreviated title, *Yugikyō* 瑜祇經. One of the most important texts in the East Asian Esoteric tradition, the *Yugikyō* contains many rituals dedicated to various deities and teachings on the nonduality of principle and wisdom and the practice of deity yoga. Dōhan's work includes the teachings of Kūkai, Annen 安然 (841-915?), Ennin 圓仁 (794-864), Ningai, Jōhen, Jikken, Dōhan, and others, and the *Yugikyō kuketsu* was circulated widely, with some sections circulating independently.

This text also discusses the notion that the first stage of the bodhisattva path and the final stage, the stage of Buddhahood, are ultimately nondual. This teaching is based on the *Mahāvairocana-sūtra* and the *Vajraśekhara* cycle, where the ten stages of the bodhisattva path as outlined in the *Avataṃsaka-sūtra* and other texts are understood to have two meanings, according to Exoteric and Esoteric interpretations. From the Exoteric perspective, the ten bodhisattva stages are hierarchically oriented, beginning with the first stage and working up to the buddha stage.[50] From the Esoteric perspective, the first and final stages are completely nondual; ultimately, there is no hierarchy. This concept features prominently in Dōhan's thought. According to Ōshika Shinō, in this work Dōhan seeks to establish the superiority of the Shingon tradition over the Tendai tradition, countering the dominance of earlier Tendai commentaries on the *Yugikyō.*[51]

Dainichi kyōsho joanshō

The *Dainichi kyōsho joanshō* 大日經疏除暗鈔 is a subcommentary on Yixing's famous *Commentary on the Mahāvairocana-sūtra.* The *Dainichi kyōsho joanshō* is another important text by Dōhan that was influential on later generations of Shingon scholiasts. In the early modern period, because Kōyasan lacked a complete version, Jōshin 浄信 of Jiganji 慈眼寺 in Awaji 淡路 traveled around Japan for several years in search of one, which he eventually found at Jingoji 神護寺 in Yamashiro, Yamasaki 山城山崎. Dōhan's work focuses on the first chapter and provides a secret explication of the title of the *Mahāvairocana-sūtra.* This text was originally compiled by Dōhan at Dōjo's request after he attended a lecture by Dōhan on Kōyasan. In other words, this text may be something akin to Dōhan's lecture notes. The Kōyasan *kengyō* Shūzen 宗禅 gathered a large assembly of students to hear Dōhan's lectures. The teachings of Jōhen and Kakkai feature prominently in this text. Dōhan was forty-seven years old at the time.[52]

Bodaishinron dangiki

The *Bodaishinron dangiki* 菩提心論談義記 is a commentary on Amoghavajra's *Jingangding yujia zhong fa anouduoluosanmiaosanputi xin lun* 金剛頂瑜伽中發阿耨多羅三藐三菩提心論 (T. 1665), traditionally attributed to Nāgārjuna and more commonly known in Japan by the abbreviated title, *Bodaishinron* 菩提心論. The *Bodaishinron* describes various practices and the nature of *bodhicitta,* and it also discusses the concept of the *Mitsugon jōdo,* the land of mystical adornment, the totality of all *buddha-kṣetra* conceived as the ever-eminent *buddha-kṣetra* of Mahāvairocana. Dōhan's text is written in the style of a *dangi* 談義, a "dialogue and debate" text in which questions are posed by a hypothetical interlocutor and the answers provided for students to memorize for debates. As discussed previously, Dōhan was often called upon to teach students in debate skills, testing their knowledge and ability to refute unorthodox views.[53]

Rishushaku hidenshō

The *Rishushaku hidenshō* 理趣釋祕傳鈔 is a subcommentary on the *Dale jingang bukong zhenshi sanmeiye jing bore boluomiduo liqushi* 大樂金剛不空眞實三昧耶經般若波羅蜜多理趣釋 (T. 1003), which is Amoghavajra's commentary on the *Adhyarthaśatikā-prajñāpāramitā-sūtra* 大樂金剛不空眞實三摩耶經 (T. 243), commonly known in Japanese as the *Rishukyō* 理趣經. Today the *Rishukyō* is chanted as part of Shingon Buddhist liturgy every morning. In the text Mahāvairocana explains the fundamental wisdom of the Esoteric path to Vajrasattva. One of its main teachings is that beings are fundamentally pure and awakened. Dōhan's work was composed at the request of Dōjo of Ninnaji and was completed shortly before he passed away. Dōhan explores Jōhen's notion that principle-wisdom-phenomena are ultimately nondual.[54]

Shakumakaenron ōkyōshō

The *Shakumakaenron ōkyōshō* 釋摩訶衍論應教鈔 (T. 2288) was another work composed by Dōhan at the request of Dōjo. This is a commentary on Kūkai's *Shakumakaenron shiji,* mentioned above. Thus, this work may be considered a "sub"-subcommentary. Dōhan's text was originally composed in three fascicles, but at present only one survives. Many scholars of Shingon Buddhism are unaware of just how important the *Shimoheyanlun* was in the articulation of Kūkai's nondualist Mahayana thought. The thought of Dōhan's teachers Kakkai and Jōhen feature prominently in this text; further study may reveal yet more of their teachings.[55]

In one section Dōhan considers the meaning of the forty-eight vows of Amitābha Buddha and also discusses the concept *kimyō* 歸命. This term means literally to "take refuge," but the two characters can also be understood to mean "returning (*ki*) to life (*myō*)." By taking refuge in Amitābha Buddha, one returns to the very source of life and the universe itself: Mahāvairocana Tathāgata.

Hizōhōyaku mondanshō

Dōhan's *Hizōhōyaku mondanshō* 祕藏寶鑰問談鈔 is a compilation of notes taken during his lectures on Kūkai's *Hizōhōyaku* 祕藏寶鑰 (T. 2426), which is commonly regarded as an abbreviated summary of the *Jūjūshinron,* Kūkai's magnum opus on the ten stages of mind. Dōhan's work was again composed at Dōjo's request and is based on lecture notes taken by Shōnagon Risshi Bōshin 少納言律師房信. Dōhan's examination of this important text was held in esteem by Shingon scholar-monks and remains an authoritative commentary.[56]

Kongōchōgyō kaidai kanchū

The *Kongōchōgyō kaidai kanchū* 金剛頂經開題勘註 is a commentary on Kūkai's *Kongōchōgyō kaidai* 金剛頂經開題 (T. 2221), which is an Esoteric reading of the title of the *Vajraśekhara.* In the Shingon tradition, it is commonly stated that doctrine derives from the *Mahāvairocana-sūtra,* while ritual theory derives from the *Vajraśekhara.* Kūkai wrote many *kaidai,* a fascinating and understudied genre that may provide more nuanced insights into Kūkai's thought than the works commonly referenced in cursory overviews. In these *kaidai* Kūkai examines the Esoteric meaning inherent within the very title of a text, often discussing such texts as the *Lotus Sutra* or the *Heart Sutra,* works not normally thought of as "esoteric" but that may be said to have esoteric layers, as do all Mahayana sutras. Thomas Eijō Dreitlein has translated and analyzed several of Kūkai's *kaidai.*[57] Nakamura Honnen's study of this commentary notes the importance of the *santen setsu.*[58]

Sokushin jōbutsugi kiki gaki

The *Sokushin jōbutsugi kiki gaki* 卽身成佛義聞書 is composed of three fascicles. The first two constitute Dōhan's commentary and lecture notes on the *Sokushin jōbutsu gi* 卽身成佛義 (T. 2428), traditionally attributed to Kūkai, which deals with the notion of becoming a buddha in this very body. The *Sokushin jōbutsu gi* argues on ontological grounds that just as the fundamental elements of reality are interconnected, so, too, is the reality of buddhas and ordinary beings. Beings and buddhas are made of the same "stuff"; therefore, through empowerment and the cultivation of the three mysteries, one is able to realize one's always-already present unity with ultimate reality.

Dōhan's commentary consists of a sustained explication of key terms, concepts, and passages found in the *Sokushin jōbutsu gi.*[59] The third fascicle comprises a series of dialogues between Dōhan and several interlocutors, including, for example, Hōsshō 寶性, Shinshō 真性, and Genchō 源朝.[60] According to the *Nihon Bukkyō tenseki daijiten,* this text is especially important for providing insight into the state of early medieval Kūkai studies and doctrinal thought, as each interlocutor offers his own unique perspective.[61] Because Dōhan often provides very clear and straightforward explanations, as well as "esoteric"-inspired readings and the parsing of major concepts in the Shingon tradition, this text would be useful for further study into the evolution of Shingon orthodoxy.

Shōji jissōgi shō

The *Shōji jissōgi shō* 聲字實相義鈔 is a rich commentary on Kūkai's *Shōjijissōgi* 聲字實相義 (T. 2429), in which Kūkai lays out his theory of the power of language and the nonduality of signifier and signified. As Nakamura notes, in his commentary Dōhan considers the methods by which Mahāvairocana teaches sentient beings, as well as Zen's and Shingon's unique approaches to nonduality, among other things.[62]

Dōhan as Scribe: Jōhen's and Kakkai's Shingon Thought

As mentioned previously, Dōhan may be considered a window onto the world of early medieval Buddhist scholasticism not simply because of his prolific output or because he was an intellectual "prime mover" but because some of his scholarship is the product of key relationships with important teachers and members of major lineages. One of Dōhan's other important roles is as the editor and interpreter of the teachings of Jōhen and Kakkai, influential scholars of Shingon thought in the early Kamakura period whose legacies greatly influenced Dōhan and, through him, Kōyasan Shingon and beyond.

Benkenmitsu nikyōron shukyō (tekagami) shō

The *Benkenmitsu nikyōron shukyō (tekagami) shō* 辯顯密二教論手鏡鈔 is a record of Jōhen's lectures on the *Benkenmitsu nikyō ron* 辯顯密二教論 (T. 2427) held at Shōrenge-in 勝蓮華院. By the early medieval period, members of the Shingon lineage wishing to invoke Kūkai as a lineage patriarch cited this text to assert the purported superiority of Esoteric Buddhism over "Exoteric Buddhism," which in some cases may have merely served as a polemical or pejorative label applied to anyone perceived as an opponent or competitor for patronage and authority over Mahayana esoterica. Dōhan's text concludes with a valuable dialogue between Dōhan and Jōhen over sixty-nine key points related to Shingon doctrine and practice.[63]

Hizōki shō

The *Hizōki shō* 祕藏記鈔 is a record of Jōhen's teachings on the *Hizōki* 祕藏記,[64] a text dating to the ninth to tenth century attributed to Kūkai, which purportedly contains Kūkai's record of Huiguo's teachings and Huiguo's account of the teachings of Amoghavajra. Dōhan's account covers various topics, including the Womb Realm mandala, the three truths, seed syllables, and contemplation and visualization. There are many interesting illustrations outlining the visualizations to be used in this form of meditation, employing the five elements, the five wisdom buddhas, Chinese *wuxing* theory, and so on. The text also discusses Yogācāra philosophy and doctrine, the nature of Mahāvairocana's relation to the three mysteries, the idea that buddha bodies and the infinite *buddhakṣetra* also abide within the practitioner's own body, and more.

The *Hizōki* is quoted at length several times in the *Himitsu nenbutsu shō*, clearly demonstrating that as Dōhan worked to synthesize Jōhen's views on the Pure Land, his interpretation of this text attributed to Kūkai played a major role.[65]

Chō kaishō

The *Chō kaishō* 聴海抄 is a record of Kakkai's teaching on various topics related to Esoteric Buddhist theory and practice. Some of the major concepts encountered in Dōhan's text include the practice of mantra, the fundamental meaning of the letter A, the five wisdom buddhas, and more. Of particular importance is "nondualist six elements thought." Dōhan's lineage through the Muryōju-in Temple influenced later generations, in particular in their articulation of the notion that the mind element is nondual with the other five elements.

Though only two fascicles survive, this record may be especially important for understanding how Kūkai's seemingly materialist philosophy (the notion that the physical elements that constitute all of reality are themselves "buddha") contributed to the medieval notion of Buddhahood even for insentient beings.[66]

Himitsu (shū) nenbutsu shō

The *Himitsu nenbutsu* (a.k.a *Himitsushū nenbutsu shō*) represents Dōhan's major contribution to medieval Japanese Pure Land Buddhist thought. In this he articulates the nuances of the diverse range of teaching and practices on Amitābha Buddha, *buddhānusmṛti,* and Sukhāvatī in Japan at the time. Like the other works mentioned above, the *Himitsu nenbutsu shō* can be viewed as an attempt to synthesize the views held by Jōhen, Kakkai, and others. As will be explored in subsequent chapters and the annotated translation, Dōhan cites Kakkai and Jōhen throughout this work— several times without clear citation or attribution.[67]

Dōhan's Teachings in Exile

Dōhan was a prolific author and sought-after ritual master, and yet his biography is often reduced to a brief mention of his exile to Sanuki.

Before, during, and after his seven years in exile, he continued to write, teach, and train students. The *Nankai rurōki,* explored in some detail in the previous chapter, indicates Dōhan was very active in Sanuki.

Dainichi kyōsho henmyō shō

Dōhan composed the *Dainichi kyōsho henmyō shō* 大日經疏遍明鈔 at Zentsūji, at the request of Zenkaku 禅閣 of Hosshōji. Like the *Jōanshō,* this text is another subcommentary on Yixing's *Commentary on the Mahāvairocana-sūtra.* However, this text was written approximately twenty-two years later and is almost four times longer than the former. As with other texts associated with Dōhan, the teachings of Jōhen and Kakkai feature prominently.[68]

Dōhan shōsoku

The *Dōhan shōsoku* 道範消息 is a vernacular Japanese composition written at the request of the monk Kōyasan Ōmuro-yō Ren'i 高野山御室葉蓮以 during Dōhan's period in exile. Scholars have speculated on the identity of the recipient. Pol K. van den Broucke, referencing Miyasaka Yūshō, notes that the only Kōyasan "Ōmuro" still alive during Dōhan's time in exile was Dōjo.[69] This discourse was translated into English by van den Broucke and may be the first of Dōhan's texts rendered in English.[70]

The thrust of this text is the explanation of and introduction to Aji-kan practice. According to Dōhan, the letter *A* is all-encompassing: it unites and transcends good and evil, Sukhāvatī and samsara. Even Mahāvairocana, the anthropomorphic form of the dharmakāya, may be understood as an external function of *A.* In one interesting passage, Dōhan gives a metaphor of the waves of the sea. The waves that reach the shore and the waves far out at sea may be likened, respectively, to the cause-and-effect relationship held by the phenomenal universe and the nonarising mind. They are one yet they are not the same. They are of the same substance, but their relationship is not directly one of cause and effect.[71]

Gyōhō kanyō shō

The *Gyōhō kanyō shō* 行法肝葉 (alternately, 要)鈔; T. 2502) was also composed during Dōhan's exile. Each fascicle appears to have been composed at different times. The first fascicle does not include a date, while the second fascicle is dated to 1244 and the third fascicle to 1248. The first two fascicles include secret oral transmissions on practice, including discussion of mudra, mantra, ritual paraphernalia, and the adornment of the ritual arena. Fascicle 3 concerns mainly the performance of the votive fire ceremony, *goma.*

This text was apparently composed (or compiled) at the request of Shōnin Kanyū 上人勧誘 from Yataniji 彌谷寺 in Awaji. Scholars theorize that it is a synthetic composition, compiled into a single work by later disciples and lineage descendants. Early modern Shingon scholiasts held this text in particularly high esteem.[72]

Hannya shingyō hiken kaihō shō

The *Hannya shingyō hiken kaihō shō* 般若心経秘鍵開宝鈔 is a commentary on the *Hannya shingyō hiken ryakuchū* 般若心經祕鍵略註 (T. 2203B), Kūkai's Esoteric explication of the *Heart Sutra.*[73] This text, composed while Dōhan was in exile, cites the teachings of Jōhen and Kakkai and Kūkai's *Jūjūshinron* and discusses the idea that the five wisdoms are manifested by Prajñā Bodhisattva 般若菩薩, a female deity symbolizing wisdom (*prajñā*), regarded as the "mother of all buddhas."[74]

Simple Practice

One of the important characteristics of Kamakura Buddhism is the prominence of so-called simple practices, which have often been forced into a false dichotomy with Esoteric Buddhism, said to be too "esoteric" to be relevant for ordinary people. As with the *Dōhan shōsoku* mentioned above, the rich doctrinal and ritual treasure trove of Esoteric Buddhism may address the needs of neophytes as well as elite scholar-monks and ascetic practitioners. Seemingly simple practices have many layers of interpretation; the ultimate teaching is not that the deep practice is the superior practice but rather that seemingly simple practices may hold great efficacy for many different kinds of practitioners, as Dohan shows in the *Himitsu nenbutsu shō.* Some of Dōhan's other texts dealing with simple practices are outlined below.

Shoshin tongaku shō

Dōhan's *Shoshin tongaku shō* 初心頓覺鈔 is a relatively short introduction to Esoteric Buddhist practice written in vernacular Japanese. One of the interesting issues revealed in this text is Dōhan's somewhat ambivalent view of Zen, then an emerging new religious movement in Japan. Dōhan, it seems, believes that the benefits attributed to Zen are already to be found within Esoteric Buddhism, which he takes to be primary. In the first fascicle, he discusses the unitary identity of Mahāvairocana Tathāgata and the Sun Goddess Amaterasu, the mythic progenitor of the imperial family. He also considers other "combinatory" identities: Amaterasu and Avalokiteśvara Bodhisattva, Kōbō Daishi Kūkai, Maitreya Bodhisattva, and others. Dōhan also discusses Kūkai's *Jūjū shinron*, Sukhāvatī, and other topics.

In fascicle 2, the *Shōryōshū* 性霊集 and the Esoteric precepts are discussed.[75] In fascicle 3, Dōhan considers the relationship between Exoteric and Esoteric approaches to Buddhism, noting that Esoteric Buddhism is not only appropriate for monastic practitioners but may be especially efficacious for laypeople and beginning practitioners. Here he notes that the negative karma accumulated from even the five "unforgivable" sins is not an insurmountable obstacle to effective practice and the attainment of liberation. Tanaka Hisao and Nakamura Honnen have examined this text closely.[76]

Kōmyō shingon shijū shaku

The Mantra of Light, explored by Mark Unno in his study of the monk Myōe,[77] was a popular Esoteric Pure Land practice. In the *Kōmyō shingon shijū shaku* 光明真言四重釈, Dōhan gives a fourfold secret explication of the Mantra of Light. The fourfold secret explication seems to have been one of Dōhan's favorite hermeneutical devices, as it appears in several of his works and in the introduction to the *Himitsu nenbutsu shō*. This text is written in a style and format very similar to the *Himitsu nenbutsu shō* such that I have begun to wonder if it actually belongs in the *Himitsu nenbutsu shō* as a section that circulated independently due to the popularity of this mantra practice. The Mantra of Light is (Skt.) *Oṃ amogha vairocana mahāmudrā maṇipadma jvāla pravarttaya hūṃ* (Ch. 唵阿謨伽尾盧左曩摩訶母捺囉麼抳鉢納麼入嚩攞鉢囉韈哆野吽, Jp. *On abokya beiroshanō makabodara mani handoma jinbara harabaritaya un*).

Dōhan's discussion of the mantra is broken down into four levels. According to level one (the shallow interpretation), this mantra reveals the true nature of the relationship between Amitābha and Mahāvairocana. Of particular interest is that this interpretation seems to relate to the second and third level of his examination of *buddhānusmṛti* in the *Himitsu nenbutsu shō.* The way Dōhan uses the terms "shallow" and "deep" may shift depending on the needs of a particular text or audience. Level two (the deep interpretation) provides an explanation for each of the twenty-three letters that compose the mantra. Level three (the secret within the secret) intimates that the Mantra of Light actually encompasses the mantras of the five wisdom buddhas associated with the mandala. In other words, this mantra is all-inclusive because the five buddhas are the ultimate source of *all* buddhas, bodhisattvas, and gods. Level four (deep interpretation of the secret within the secret) takes level three to its logical (or, perhaps, "esoteric") conclusion, revealing that the Mantra of Light truly is all-inclusive, encompassing the six elements, all Dharmas, all mantras, and more. Dōhan thus proposes that the Mantra of Light is an appropriate practice for beginners and elite practitioners alike.[78]

Kakua mondō shō

The *Kakua mondō shō* 覚阿問答鈔 is purportedly a record of Dōhan's dialogues with the monk Kakua 覚阿 (1143–?), a Zen practitioner who was his student. Dōhan argues that Zen's sudden enlightenment is subordinate to Esoteric Buddhism.[79]

Unjigi shakukanchū shō

Compiled by Ryūgen 隆源 (1342–1426), the *Unjigi shakukanchū shō* 吽字義釋勘註抄 is a commentary and exegesis of Kūkai's *Unjigi* 吽字義 (T. 2430), in which Kūkai outlines the basic approach to mantra, seed syllable contemplation, and his theory of language. This work seems to be written to provide guidance to beginning Esoteric Buddhist practitioners.[80]

Deathbed Rituals

As Jacqueline Stone recently noted, deathbed practices grew in importance in Japanese Buddhism, and rituals for personal and communal preparation for death proliferated. In a context in which Esoteric and Pure Land Buddhism functioned as diverse repertoires upon which practitioners might draw, Dōhan's writings often dealt with the problem of the final moments of death. The texts discussed below present simple practices and teachings for the final moments of life and may be productively read in dialogue with the *Himitsu nenbutsu shō,* as many of the themes discussed in that text appear in these works as well. Indeed, many texts may "spill over" beyond their pages to reveal important connections to other works in a given time frame or in the totality of an author's oeuvre.

Aun gōkan

The *Aun gōkan* 阿吽合観 is a guide to the practice of the contemplation of the letters *A* and *UṆ* that can help lead one to a peaceful death. These two letters are popular objects of meditation in the Shingon tradition. The letter *A* typically symbolizes the origin in all things as originally "unborn," or nonarising, or emptiness, and *UṆ* is the culmination. Here, they are presented first as a dyad that ultimately collapses perceived dualities between provisional and ultimate reality, body and mind, ordinary beings and Mahāvairocana, the in-breath and out-breath, and so on.

Dōhan's discussion of Vajra and Womb mandalas and the breath in this work is mirrored in the *Himitsu nenbutsu shō*'s discussion of the two forms of the *nenbutsu: A-MI-TA* and *NAMO-A-MI-TA-BU.* Next, Dōhan breaks down *A* and *UṆ* into a triadic structure: *A* is composed of *A, Ia,* and *Ua; UṆ* is composed of *U, N,* and *M.* This is then used as an organizing heuristic to read in (*eisegesis*[81]) deeper meanings and correspondences, through which this "simple" practice comes to incorporate and possess various aspects of Buddhist practice and thought. Dōhan explains, for example, connections to the organs of speech (throat, tongue, and lips), the three bodies of buddha reality, the three divisions of the dual mandalas (Buddha, Lotus, Vajra), and more. Here again are heuristic and methodological approaches similar to those found in the *Himitsu nenbutsu shō.*[82]

Dōhan nikka rinjū higi

A recently discovered text attributed to Dōhan, the *Dōhan nikka rinjū higi* 道範日課臨終秘儀, is another deathbed practice text; however, this work is more complete and systematic and reads more like a ritual manual, with clear parallels to standard Esoteric Buddhist ritual templates. As in the final section of the *Himitsu nenbutsu shō,* Dōhan recommends an image of Kōbō Daishi Kūkai as the object of contemplation for one's final moments of life. One interesting feature of this ritual manual is the range of practices that may be incorporated into the general outline or template depending on the practitioner's inclinations or needs. Dōhan mentions, for example, the performance of a *goma* ritual for Amitābha Buddha; a rite dedicated to Aizen Myōō; flower offerings before an image of Kōbō Daishi Kūkai; and chanting the *Rishukyō*, the *Uṣṇīṣa Vijaya Dhāraṇī*, and the *Daishi Myōgo* (Treasure Name of the Great Teacher, *Namu Daishi Henjō Kongō*, which first appears in Dōhan's *Himitsu nenbutsu shō*), the names of the gods of Kōyasan, the seed syllables of the holy ones of Sukhāvatī (Amitābha Buddha, Avalokiteśvara Bodhisattva, and Mahāsthāmaprāpta Bodhisattva), and the Mantra of Light.

As noted previously, Dōhan employs the *santen setsu* here as well. Finally, he instructs the practitioner nearing the end to lie facing east with the head to the south. This is the exact opposite of Śākyamuni's bodily orientation when he passed, facing west with his head to the north. Recent scholarship speculates that perhaps this configuration for the deathbed posture may have a secret meaning for Dōhan's students.[83]

Rinjū yōshin ji

Dōhan's *Rinjū yōshin no koto* 臨終用心事 is actually the final section of the *Himitsu nenbutsu shō*, appearing in the *Shingonshū anjin zensho* as a standalone text. This work describes a deathbed ritual in which the primary object of devotion is Kōbō Daishi Kūkai, a savior figure who guides beings to the Pure Land. This text will be examined in detail, and a complete translation is given in this book, so here I briefly mention some of its main points.

According to Dōhan, the experience of rebirth in Sukhāvatī and the perception of the descent of Amitābha Buddha and his retinue of bodhisattvas are but one aspect of the experience of death; there are deeper meanings, including the attainment of Buddhahood in this very body. The text provides descriptions of practices for people in different states of illness near the time of death: first, those whose illness is so advanced that they cannot sit up or walk to the hall for practice; second, those who have been ill for some time and are unable to clean their bodies or rinse their mouths (i.e., preparatory purification practices for worship); and finally, those who have been ill for an extended period of time.[84]

Dōhan wrote extensively on both doctrine and practice, and this is one way in which his work can be seen as participating in two major shared paradigms: *hongaku* thought and *kenmitsu* ritual culture. Broad erudition was certainly an asset in a competitive environment in which scholar-monks contended for patronage and prestige, and economic and spiritual benefits were not mutually exclusive.

Notes

Chapter 5: Dōhan's Major Works and Kamakura Buddhism

1 Abé, *Weaving of Mantra,* pp. 412–413.

2 Ibid., pp. 409–416.

3 Ibid., pp. 404–406.

4 Jacqueline I. Stone, *Original Enlightenment and the Transformation of Medieval Japan* (Honolulu: University of Hawai'i Press, 1999), p. 61.

5 Abé, "Post-Script," in *Weaving of Mantra,* pp. 399–428; James C. Dobbins, "Envisioning Kamakura Buddhism," in Richard K. Payne, ed., *Re-visioning "Kamakura Buddhism* (Honolulu: University of Hawai'i Press, 1998), pp. 28–38; James H. Foard, "In Search of a Lost Reformation: A Reconsideration of Kamakura Buddhism," *Japanese Journal of Religious Studies* 7, no. 4 (1980): 261–291; Neil McMullin, "Historical and Historiographical Issues in the Study of Pre-modern Japanese Religions," *Japanese Journal of Religious Studies* 16, no. 1 (1989): 3–40; Payne, *Re-visioning "Kamakura" Buddhism.*

6 Ford, *Jōkei and Buddhist Devotion,* pp. 185–186.

7 David Quinter, "The Shingon Ritsu School and the Mañjuśrī Cult in the Kamakura Period: From Eison to Monkan" (PhD diss., Stanford University, 2006), pp. 20–21, citing Sueki Fumihiko, "A Reexamination of the *Kenmitsu Taisei* Theory," *Japanese Journal of Religious Studies* 23, no. 3–4 (1996): 449–466.

8 Abé, *Weaving of Mantra,* pp. 424–426.

9 Quinter, "Shingon Ritsu School and the Mañjuśri Cult," pp. 19–20, citing Taira Masayuki, "Kuroda Toshio and the *Kenmitsu Taisei* Theory," *Japanese Journal of Religious Studies* 23, no. 3–4 (1996): 427–448. See also Ford, *Jōkei and Buddhist Devotion,* p. 193; Stone, *Original Enlightenment,* p. 62.

10 Quinter, "Shingon Ritsu School and the Mañjuśri Cult," p. 21, citing Sasaki Kaoru 佐々木馨, *Chūsei kokka no shūkyō kōzō: Taisei bukkyō to taisei-gai bukkyō no sōkoku* 中世国家の宗教構造―体制仏教と体制外仏教の相剋 (Tokyo: Yoshikawa kōbunkan, 1988).

11 Tanaka Hisao 田中久夫, *Kamakura Bukkyō* 鎌倉仏教 (1980; repr., Kōdansha gakujutsu bunko, 2009), pp. 13–20.

12 Ford, "Competing with Amida," pp. 43–79; James L. Ford, "Buddhist Ceremonials (kōshiki) and the Ideological Discourse of Established Buddhism in Early Medieval Japan," in *Discourse and Ideology in Medieval Japanese Buddhism,* ed. Richard K. Payne and Taigen Daniel Leighton (New York: RoutledgeCurzon, 2006), pp. 97–125; James L. Ford, "Jōkei and Kannon: Defending Buddhist Pluralism in Medieval Japan," *Eastern Buddhist* 39, no. 1 (2008): 11–28; Ford, "Exploring the Esoteric in Nara Buddhism," pp. 776–793.

13 Lori Meeks, *Hokkeji and the Reemergence of Female Monastic Orders in Premodern Japan* (Honolulu: University of Hawai'i Press, 2010).

14 Quinter, "Shingon Ritsu School and the Mañjuśrī Cult," pp. 29–30.

15 Hayao Kawai and Mark Unno, *The Buddhist Priest Myōe: A Life of Dreams* (Venice, CA: Lapis Press, 1992); Mark T. Unno, "As Appropriate: Myōe Kōben and the Problem of the Vinaya in Early Kamakura Buddhism" (PhD diss., Stanford University, 1994) and *Shingon Refractions: Myōe and the Mantra of Light* (Somerville, MA: Wisdom, 2004); George J. Tanabe, *Myōe the Dreamkeeper: Fantasy and Knowledge in Early Kamakura Buddhism* (Cambridge, MA: Harvard University Press, 1992).

16 Mark L. Blum, *The Origins and Development of Pure Land Buddhism: A Study and Translation of Gyōnen's Jōdo Hōmon Genrushō* (New York: Oxford University Press, 2002).

17 Janet Goodwin, *Alms and Vagabonds: Buddhist Temples and Popular Pilgrimage in Medieval Japan* (Honolulu: University of Hawai'i Press, 1994).

18 Tanabe, "Kōyasan in the Countryside," p. 43.

19 Quinter, "Shingon Ritsu School and the Mañjuśrī Cult," p. 31.

20 Ibid., p. 30.

21 Brian D. Ruppert, *Jewel in the Ashes: Buddha Relics and Power in Early Medieval Japan* (Cambridge, MA: Harvard University Press, 2000), pp. 12–13; Dobbins, "Envisioning Kamakura Buddhism," pp. 28–38.

22 Dobbins, "Envisioning Kamakura Buddhism," p. 31.

23 Ibid., pp. 29–31.

24 Ibid., pp. 29–37; Ford, *Jōkei and Buddhist Devotion,* pp. 202–203.

25 Stone, *Original Enlightenment,* pp. 5–10.

26 Jacqueline I. Stone, "Medieval Tendai *Hongaku* Thought and the New Kamakura Buddhism," *Japanese Journal of Religious Studies* 22 no. 1–2 (1995): 18–19. Nakamura Honnen has investigated Kūkai's contributions to *hongaku* thought: "Shakumakaenron niokeru huni makaenhō ni tsuite—kenge to mike no chūshakusho no hikaku wo chūshin toshite" 『釈摩訶衍論』における不二摩訶衍法 不二摩訶衍法について一顕 家と密家の註釈疏の比較を中心として, *Mikkyōgaku kenkyū* 密教学研究 15 (1983): 129–144.

27 Stone, *Original Enlightenment,* pp. 61–62, 215–217, 228–236; Ford, *Jōkei and Buddhist Devotion,* pp. 187–190.

28 Stone, *Original Enlightenment,* pp. 63–65.

29 Ford, *Jōkei and Buddhist Devotion,* 198–199.

30 Stone, *Original Enlightenment,* p. 63.

31 Ibid., pp. 66–73.

32 Ibid., p. 85.

33 Ibid., pp. 84–86, 89–92.

34 Ibid., p. 229.

35 According to anecdotal evidence that calls for further investigation, Zen monks in the Sōtō tradition continued to practice on Kōyasan alongside Shingon monks until the postwar period, when conservative factions at the major Zen centers withdrew support for such transsectarian situations. In any case, several temples on Kōyasan today, such as the Rengejō-in, teach Zen meditation on a regular basis.

36 Lucia Dolce and Shinya Mano, "Yōsai and Esoteric Buddhism," in Orzech, Sørensen, and Payne, *Esoteric Buddhism and the Tantras in East Asia,* p. 834.

37 William M. Bodiford, "Zen and Esoteric Buddhism," in Orzech, Sørensen, and Payne, *Esoteric Buddhism and the Tantras in East Asia,* pp. 926–935.

38 Bodiford, "Zen and Esoteric Buddhism," pp. 924–935.

39 Ibid., p. 930.

40 Ibid., pp. 930–933, citing William M. Bodiford, *Sōtō Zen in Medieval Japan* (Honolulu: University of Hawai'i Press, 1993), pp. 111–121, 173–179.

41 Gorai, *Kōya hijiri,* pp. 282–299.

42 KS, 145, 157.

43 KS, 139.

44 KS, 153.

45 *Nanzan hiku* 南山秘口, 1 fasc., ZSZ 41; ZSZ 42:198.

46 *Kōbō Daishi ryaku joshō* 弘法大師略頌鈔, 1 fasc. (1234). Available editions include printed editions produced from 1658 (Manji 万治1). See also KDZ 3; *Kōbō Daishi ryakujo* 弘法大師略頌 (治田七兵衛, 1658); *Kōbō Daishi ryaku joshō* 弘法大師略頌鈔 (Tokyo: Kōyasan shucchō sho 高野山出張所, 1882), http://kindai.ndl.go.jp/info:ndljp/pid/819290. See also *Kōdenryaku* 弘伝略頌鈔, BKD 2:355d; *Kōbō Daishi ryakuju narabini gyōjō ki* 弘法大師略頌並行状記, BKD 3:330; NBTD 164.

47 Nakamura Honnen, "Dōhan no Jōdokan," pp. 149–202, esp. 201–202.

48 *Jōōshō* (a.k.a *Teiōshō*) 貞応抄, 3 fasc., 1225 (貞応 4); T. 77:2447. A manuscript from 1303 (Kengen 乾元2) is held at Kanshūji 勸修寺; BKD 8:88b; NBTD 386. For some preliminary research on variant manuscripts, see Satō Mona, "Dōhan cho *Jōō shō* ni kansuru ichikōsatsu tōji kanchiin shozōhon wo chūshin toshite" 道範著『貞応抄』に関する一考察—東寺観智院所蔵本を中心として, *Indogaku Bukkyōgaku kenkyū* 印度学仏教学研究 102, no. 51–52 (2003): 655–657.

49 Chiba Tadashi 千葉正, "Dōhan sen Teiōshō niokeru shukuzensetsu" 道範撰『貞応抄』における宿善説, *Indogaku Bukkyōgaku kenkyū* 60, no. 2 (2012): 609–614.

50 FD 419.

51 *Yugikyō kuketsu* 瑜祇經口決, 5 fasc., 1241 (Ninji 仁治 2), 1224 (Jōō 貞応3), SZ 5. Alternate and abridged versions include 地祇経伝授口伝、瑜祇秘密口伝抄, *Yoga sūtraṃ* ユギスートラン, *kukestu* 口決, *Yugikyō kuden* 瑜祇口傳, 2 fasc., manuscript from 1650 (Keigan 慶安 3) held at Hōju-in 寶寿院, composed in 1218 (Kenpo 建保 6); *Yugikyō kuden* 瑜祇口傳1224 (貞応3) and so on; *Yoga sūtraṃ kuden* [ユギスートラン]口傳, 2 fasc., Teihon, manuscript ed. from 1297 (Einin 永仁5) from the archive of Shinbessho 眞別處 at Kōyasan University Library; ZSZ 7 (ZSZ 42:40), which appears to be a portion of Dōhan's five-fascicle work; BKD 11:84a; NBTD 525c–d; MD 2206b–c; SZ 43:11. See also Ōshika Shino, "Chūsei tōmitsu kyōgaku ni okeru Yugikyō kaishaku no tenkai" 中世東密教学における『瑜祇経』解釈の展開, *Indogaku Bukkyōgaku kenkyū* 63, no. 1 (2014b): 92–96.

52 *Dainichi kyōsho joanshō* 大日經疏除暗鈔, 7 fasc., 1224 (Jōō 貞応3), BT (*Bukkyō taikei* 仏教大系) 19; ZSZ 5:1–97, based on a manuscript held at Kōyasan University Library dating from 1752 (Hōreki 寶暦, year 2) and compared with an edition from the archives of Hōju-in held at the Reihō-kan (Kōyasan Museum). Variant titles include *Daisho joanshō* 大疏除暗鈔 and *Jōanshō* 除暗鈔. BKD 5:287c; BKD 7:400c; NBTD 368b; MD 1516a; ZSZ 42:29–34; ZSZ 42:29–34 provides a detailed list of all of the subsections of this text.

53 *Bodaishinron dangiki* 菩提心論談義記, 2 fasc., 1240 (En'ō 延応 2), ND (*Nihon Daizōkyō* 日本大蔵経), 24 (1916 ed.), 47 (1975 ed.); printed editions are available from 1723 (An'ei 安永 2) at the Ōtani and Ryūkoku Universities. Variant titles include *Bodaishinron shitta shō* 菩提心論質多抄 and *Shitta shō* 質多抄. BKD 9:427d–428a; Nakamura Honnen 中村本然, "Dōhan ki Bodaishinron dangiki ni tsuite," pp. 395–430.

54 *Rishushaku hidenshō* 理趣釋祕傳鈔, 2 fasc., 1250; ND 17; BKD 11:192b; MD 2266c.

55 *Shakumakaenron ōkyōshō* 釋摩訶衍論應教鈔, 1 fasc., 1226 (Karoku 嘉禄 2), T. 2288. An edition from 1265 (Bunei 文永2) is held at Hōju-in 寶寿院, and Kōyasan University has editions from 1849–1850 (Kaei 嘉永 2–3) and 1889 (Meiji 22). Alternate titles include *Shakuron ōkyōshō* 积論応教抄 and *Ōkyōshō* 応教抄. BKD 5:25b; MD 176c (*Ōkyōshō*).

56 *Hizōhōyaku mondanshō* 祕藏寶鑰問談鈔, 2 fasc., 1240 (Ninji 仁治 1), manuscript ed. from 1718 (Kyōho 享保 3) held at Hōki-in 寶龜院. A manuscript edition from 1811 (Bunka 文化8) is held at Kōyasan University, and another manuscript is held at Kyoto University. See also Mori Shigeki 森重樹, ed., *Toganō korekushon kenmitsu tenseki monjo shūsei* 栂尾コレクション顕密典籍文書集成, vol. 5 (Tokyo: Hirakawa shuppansha, 1981); BKD 9:110a; MD 1862a.

57 For a discussion of the *kaidai* attributed to Kūkai, see Dreitlein, "Annotated Translation of Kūkai's *Secret Key to the Heart Sūtra*," pp. 1–41.

58 *Kongōchōgyō kaidai kanchū* 金剛頂經開題勘註, 1 fasc., ZSZ 7, based on a manuscript from 1841 (Tenpō 天保12) from Kōdai-in's 光臺院 archive and held at Kōyasan University; BKD 3:478b; ZSZ 42:37; Nakamura Honnen 中村本然, "Dōhan sen 'Kongōchōkyō kaidai kanchū' ni tsuite" 道範撰『金剛頂経開題勘註』について, *Kōyasan daigaku Mikkyō bunka kenkyūjo kiyō* 高野山大学密教文化研究所紀要 21 (2008): 29–52.

59 Fukuda Ryōsei 福田亮成, "Sokushinjōbutsugi kikigaki nitsuite" 即身成佛義聞書『について』, *Kawasaki Daishi kyōgaku kenkyū kiyō* 川崎大師教学研究所紀要 1 (2016): 1–60.

60 *Sokushin jōbutsugi kiki gaki* 卽身成佛義聞書, 3 fasc., ZSZ 17, is based on a two-fascicle manuscript edition from the archive of Kōdai-in 光臺院 held at Kōyasan University from 1728 (Kyōho 享保13). Mori, *Toganō korekushon;* BKD 7:76d; ZSZ 42:68.

61 NBTD, 342.

62 *Shōji jissōgi shō* 聲字實相義鈔, 2 fasc., 1240, SZ 14; BKD 5:401b–d; MD 403b; SZ 43:61; Nakamura Honnen 中村本然, "'Shōji jissō gi shō' (Dōhan ki) ni tokareru nyogi gensetsu ni tsuite–sono ichi, 'Shaku makaen ron' to Kūkai no chosa ni miru nyogi gensetsu wo chūshin toshite" 『声字実相義抄』(道範記)に説かれる如義言説について—その1、『釈摩訶衍論』と空海の著作にみる如義言説を中心として, *Mikkyō bunka* 密教文化203 (1999): 1–20.

63 *Benkenmitsu nikyōron shukyō (tekagami) shō* 辯顯密二教論手鏡鈔, 3 fasc., completed in 1223–1224 (Jōō 貞応 2–3). ZSZ (*Zoku Shingonshū zensho* 続真言宗全書) 18:273–323 is based on a manuscript titled *Nikyōron shukyō shō* 二教論手鏡鈔 from 1225 (Gennin 元仁2) from Sanbō-in's 三寶院 archive and is held at Kōyasan University. This edition was compared with a manuscript from 1529 (Kyōroku 享禄 2) also from Sanbō-in's archive and held at Kōyasan University. A manuscript held at Kyōto University from Ninnaji's 仁和寺 archives dating from 1272 (Bunei 文永 9) is titled *Benkenmitsu nikyōron shukyō shō.* An edition printed between 1716 and 1736 (Kyōho 享保) is also known. BKD (*Bussho kaisetsu daijiten* 仏書解説大辞典) 9:377d, 8:299b; MD (*Mikkyō daijiten* 密教大辞典) 1978c; ZSZ 42:75. See also Nakamura Honnen 中村本然, "Kenmitsu nikyōron tekagami shō ni tsuite, tokuni 'Shakumakaenron' kaishaku ni kansuru shomondai wo chūshin to shite" 『顕密二教論手鏡鈔』について特に『釈摩訶衍論』解釈に関する諸問題を中心として, in *Bukkyō kyōri shisō no kenkyū: Satō Ryūken hakushi koki kinen ronbunshū* 仏教教理思想の研究: 佐藤隆賢博士古稀記念論文集, ed. Satō Ryūken hakushi koki kinen ronbunshū kankōkai 佐藤隆賢博士古稀記念論文集刊行会 (Tokyo: Sankibō busshori, 1998), pp. 333–263 (R).

64 KDZ (*Kōbō Daishi zenshū* 弘法大師全集) 5.

65 *Hizōki shō* 祕藏記鈔, 1 fasc. ZSZ 15:35–58 is based on a manuscript from 1774 (An'ei 安永3) held at Ōtani University, which was compared with an edition

from 1872 (Meiji 3) from Sakuraike-in 桜池院 on Kōyasan. Variant titles include *Hissō denshō* 非相伝抄 and *Hissō denjushō* 非相伝受抄. BKD 9:106a; ZSZ 42:62.

66 *Chō kaishō* 聴海抄, 2 fasc. Kanayama Maboku 金山穆韶, "Chōkaishō (Dōhan ajari ki)" 聴海抄 (道範阿闍梨記), *Mikkyō kenkyū* 密教研究 10 (1922): 167–228, reproduces the two remaining fascicles of this work, fasc. 5 and 8, both of which were preserved at Kongōsanmai-in and Shōchi-in. An alternate title is *Daisho chōkaishō* 大疏聴海抄 (BKD 7:264c). Further information on this edition is found in Kanayama, "Chōkai shō ni tsuite" 聽海抄に就, *Mikkyō kenkyū* 密教研究 10 (1922): 229–231.

67 *Himitsu shū nenbutsu shō* 秘密宗念佛鈔/*Himitsu nenbutsu shō* 秘密念佛鈔, 3 fasc., 1223 (貞応 2); DNBZ 70:51–82; ZJZ 15:79–110; SAZ 2:225–266; *Himitsu shū nenbutsu shō* 秘密宗念佛鈔 (Kyoto: Nagata chōbee 永田長兵衛, 1686); *Himitsu shū nenbutsu shō* 秘密宗念仏鈔 (Kyoto: Rokudai shinhōsha insatsubu 六大新報社印刷部, 1907); Himitsu nenbutsu shō kenkyūkai 秘密念仏抄研究会, ed.,"Dōhan cho 'Himitsu *nenbutsu* shō' no kenkyū—honbun kōtei to kaki kudashi gochū" 道範著 '秘密念仏抄' の研究—本文校訂と書き下し・語註, *Buzan gakuhō* 豊山学報 39 (1996): 105–130. Printed editions from 1645 (正保 2) are relatively widely available; BKD 9:119–120 (other relevant works through 117–120); NBTD 446.

68 *Dainichi kyōsho henmyō shō* 大日經疏遍明鈔, 21 fasc., 1245 (寛元 3), ZSZ 5:99–444, is based on a manuscript held at Kōyasan University dating from 1659 (Manji 萬治2), which was compared with editions held at Kanazawa Bunko 金澤文庫 and Hōju-in 宝寿院. Other manuscripts are held at Ryūkoku and Ōtani universities. Variant titles include *Daibirushana jōbutsukyō henmyō shō* 大毘盧遮那成佛經疏遍明鈔, *Daisho henmyōshō* 大疏遍明鈔, *Henmyōshō* 遍明鈔, and *Dainichikyō daisho henmyōshō* 大日經大疏遍明鈔. BKD 7:403c; NBTD 369c; MD 1517b; ZSZ 42:34–35.

69 Van den Broucke, "Dōhan's Letter," pp. 65–66.

70 Van den Brouck, "Dōhan's Letter," pp. 73–74.

71 NKBT (*Nihon koten bungaku taikei* 日本古典文学大系) 83:76–83 is based on a text held at Shōchi-in titled *Shōsoku Ajikan* 消息阿字観, which was compared with several other editions on Kōyasan (van den Broucke, "Dōhan's Letter," p. 66); *Shōsoku Ajikan* 消息阿字観, in *Ajikan hiketsu shū* 阿字観秘決集, ed. Rai Mitsuun 雷密雲 (Yao, Japan: Jōkō-in 定光院, 1912; repr., Yao, Japan: Moriyama Kamon 守山嘉門, 2010). Originally printed in 1678 (Enhō 延寶6). Early printed editions are also available at Ōtani, Ryūkoku, and Taishō universities. This was the first text by Dōhan to be translated into English (as *Shōsoku ajikan*, BKD 5:346d); see van den Broucke, "Dōhan's Letter," pp. 65–87.

72 *Gyōhō kanyō shō* 行法肝葉 (alternately, 要)鈔, 3 fasc., completed ca. 1243–1249 (Kangen 寛元 to Hōji 宝治). SZ 23:147–178 is based on a Tokugawa

printed edition, but the year is unknown. This was also compared with manuscripts from Kongōsanmai-in's archive, held at Kōyasan University, from the Muromachi period. T. 78:2502 was also consulted. Other manuscripts known to be at Kanchi-in 観智院 and Ishiyamadera 石山寺 date from the Ashikaga 足利 period. Printed editions are held at Ryūkoku, and the Tokugawa edition is held at Kōyasan, the Tokyo universities, etc. Other manuscripts are at Ōtani and Kōyasan. BKD 2:302a, 12:144a; NBTD 124; MD 307b; SZ 43:161–162.

73 Dreitlein, "Kūkai's Secret Key to the Heart Sūtra."

74 *Hannya shingyō hiken kaihō shō* 般若心経秘鍵開宝鈔, 2 fasc., 1247. ND 10 (1916 ed.), 20 (1975 ed.). The printed edition from 1781 (Tenmei 天明 1) is held at Taishō and Ryūkoku. Alternate titles include *Shingyō hiken kaihōshō* 心経秘鍵開宝鈔, *Hiken kaihōshō* 秘鍵開宝鈔, and *Shingyō kaihōshō* 心経開宝鈔. BKD 9:73d; MD 1836a.

75 NKBT 71.

76 *Shoshin tongaku shō* 初心頓覺鈔, 3 fasc., SZ 22, based on an edition published in 1648 (Keian 慶安 2) held at Taishō University; BKD 5:246c; NBTD 298; MD 1226c; SZ 43:142. Tanaka Hisao, "Dōhan no 'Shoshin tonkaku shō' ni tsuite" 道範の「初心頓覚鈔」について, *Nihonrekishi* 日本歴史172 (1962): 87–89; Nakamura Honnen, "Dōhan ki 'Shoshintongaku shō' ni tsuite" 道範記『初心頓覚鈔』について, in *Mikkyō to shobunka no kōryū: Yamasaki Taikō kyōju koki kinen ronbunshū* 密教と諸文化の交流: 山崎泰広教授古稀記念論文集, ed. Yamasaki Taikō kyōju koki kinen ronbunshū kankōkai 山崎泰広教授古稀記念論文集刊行会 (Kyoto: Bunkōdo, 1998), pp. 151–184.

77 Mark Unno, "Recommending Faith in the Sand of the Mantra of Light," in Payne, *Re-visioning "Kamakura" Buddhism,* pp. 167–218.

78 *Kōmyō shingon shijū shaku* 光明真言四重釈, 1 fasc., SAZ 2:74–81; NBTD 165; BKD 3:338c.

79 *Kakua mondō shō* 覚阿問答鈔, *3* fasc. (1252). Mori, *Toganō korekushon kenmitsu tenseki monjo shūsei,* vol. 1. There is also an edition held at Zentsūji 善通寺 (1663), http://base1.nijl.ac.jp/iview/Frame.jsp?DB_ID=G0003917KTM&C_CODE=XSE1-00113. Other editions include a printed edition from 寛文3 at Taishō, Ryūkoku, Ōtani, and Kōyasan. BKD 2:63a; MD 212b.

80 *Unjigi shakukanchū shō* 吽字義釋勘註抄, 3 fasc., SZ 7; BKD 1:230a; NBDT 68.

81 Stone, *Original Enlightenment,* p. 158.

82 Mitsuun 密雲; Moriyama Kamon 守山嘉門, ed., *Ajikan hiketsushū* 阿字観秘決集 (1912, repr., Yao, Japan: Jōkō-in 定光院, 2010), pp. 19–20, http://kindai.ndl.go.jp/info:ndljp/pid/819152/3. English translation by Richard K. Payne, "Ajikan: Ritual and Meditation in the Shingon Tradition," in Payne, *Re-visioning "Kamakura" Buddhism,* pp. 232–233.

83 Mikkyō Bunka Kenkyūjo Shōgyō Bunsho Chosahan 密教文化研究所聖教文書調査班, "Kōyasan shinnōin shōgyō bunsho chosa gaiyō—suke, shiryō kaishō 'Dōhan nikka rinjū higi'" 高野山親王院聖教文書調査概要—付、資料紹介『道範日課臨終秘儀』, *Kōyasan daigaku mikkyō bunka kenkyūjo kiyō* 高野山大学密教文化研究所紀要 16 (2003): 79–92.

84 *Rinjū yōshin no koto* 臨終用心事, *1* fasc., SAZ 2:792–795; printed edition available at Kyoto University; BKD 11:277c; see Stone, *Right Thoughts at the Last Moment,* 391–392.

Chapter 6

Toward an Introduction to the *Himitsu nenbutsu shō*

As a prolific scholar and theorist, ritual master, and administrator, Dōhan and his thought may be approached by many avenues. In this book I have chosen as the primary focus Dōhan's Esoteric Pure Land thought and a single (relatively minor) work among dozens that survive down to the present. This is in some ways less a reflection of Dōhan's main area of interest as it is of my particular (perhaps idiosyncratic) interests.

A recent trend among scholars seeking to counterbalance the prevalent sectarian approach to the study of Japanese Buddhism is to look for various ways to subvert normative historiographical approaches in order to reveal ideas, practices, and peoples that have traditionally been excluded from the conversation. By presenting the historical context of a particular text, individual, and family of practices, this book is a contribution to this revisionist trend. As the previous chapters demonstrate, however, the particular text highlighted here, the *Himitsu nenbutsu shō,* samples, summarizes, and synthesizes a vast range of other texts in dealing with the various areas of Buddhist study and practice.

Dōhan was a member of several lineages, studied at various institutions, and paid close attention to the interconnected environment of medieval Japan. He certainly saw himself as a devotee of Kōbō Daishi Kūkai and as a resident of Kōyasan, and as a participant in a cosmopolitan East Asian Mahayana Buddhist culture, he contributed to the prestige of his mountain home and its saint. Dōhan likely did not see himself as a Pure Land Buddhist, however; separating Pure Land teachings and practices from the rest of Mahayana soteriology and culture would have made no sense to him. By studying his Pure Land thought, we have the opportunity to reconsider how we approach Pure Land soteriology and Esoteric rhetoric and polemics.

Finally, the so-called Esoteric Pure Land prescription provided in the *Himitsu nenbutsu shō* does not simply represent the "syncretism" of Pure Land Buddhism and Esoteric Buddhism or the orthodox perspective of the Shingon school; rather, it is a hermeneutic construct employed by Dōhan (which I have borrowed) for engaging with the diversity and ubiquity of techniques for achieving rebirth in the Pure Land of Amitābha Buddha. In some sense this study is an experiment in the "great man and his book" genre (arguably, the dominant style for works in Buddhist studies scholarship) by situating Dōhan and the *Himitsu nenbutsu shō* in the broader context of twelfth- and thirteenth-century Japanese Buddhism and beyond.

In this chapter I briefly describe the content of the *Himitsu nenbutsu shō* as a whole to help orient the reader in the investigation into the text itself and to guide the reader through the following chapters that investigate Dōhan's perspective on Amitābha Buddha, *buddhānusmṛti,* and Sukhāvatī. It is my sincere hope that readers intrigued by Dōhan and this text will engage in this dialogue, contributing to and critiquing my attempt to bring this particular "great man and his book" into the conversation.[1]

Text Critical Information

Numerous printed and manuscript versions of the *Himitsu nenbutsu shō* are mentioned in the *Nihon Bukkyō tenseki daijiten* 日本仏教典籍大辞典.[2] Manuscripts (*shahon* 寫本) belonging to Hōjō-in 寶城院 on Kōyasan date from 1606. Print editions (*kanpon* 刊本) from 1645, 1686, and 1907 are also widely available. Volume 6 of the *Kokusho sōmokuroku* 国書総目録 mentions numerous Edo-period editions held at Ryūkoku University 龍谷大学, Ōtani University 大谷大学, Kōyasan University 高野山大学, Taishō University 大正大学, Tōyō University 東洋大学, and others. The Eizan Bunko 叡山文庫 archives possess a version dating from 1616.

As will be discussed, Dōhan clearly draws from Tendai texts. It would be interesting to examine how this text was received on Hieizan and if any members of this Buddhist school wrote a response.[3] Further research into print culture in the Edo and Meiji periods, as well as into Shingon Buddhism–affiliated publishers, may reveal why so many editions of the text were produced. It is reasonable to speculate that as Jōdo Shinshū and Jōdo-shū grew in popularity, eventually dominating the Japanese

Buddhist landscape from the early Edo period on, other schools such as Shingon may have dug more deeply into their own textual tradition to formulate a response, inspiring Shingon scholiasts to dust off the *Himitsu nenbutsu shō.* A cursory survey of the text contained in the *Shingonshū anjin zensho* 真言宗安心全書 (SAZ) anthology, a rich collection of Esoteric Pure Land texts, seems to bear this out.

The first fascicle of the *Himitsu nenbutsu shō,* which arguably contains the main points and key arguments, has received a fair amount of close study. A critical *kanbun* 漢文 (classical Chinese text annotated so that it may be read as classical Japanese) edition compiled by Takeuchi Kōzen 武内孝善 is based on a version held at Jimyō-in 持明院 from the Muromachi period (1392–1573), dated to 1548, as well as a version held at Hōjō-in dated to 1606.[4] Scholars associated with the Buzan branch of Shingon used Takeuchi's *kanbun* edition to produce a *kakikudashi* 書き下し, a classical Japanese rendering of the *kanbun.*[5] Both the *kanbun* and *kakikudashi* versions of the first fascicle mention an early version titled *Amidajō* 阿彌陀帖 dated to 1391.

Widely available printed editions include the *Dai Nippon Bukkyō zenshō* 大日本佛教全書 (DNBZ) 70:51–82, the *Zoku jōdoshū zenshō* 續淨土宗全書 (ZJZ), 15:79–110, and the *Shingonshū anjin zensho* 眞言宗安心全書 (SAZ), 2:225–266. The DNBZ and ZJZ editions are identical; the latter is available online.[6] Scholars seem to prefer the SAZ edition that was used as the base text for the *kakikudashi* version, along with Takeuchi's version. Furthermore, this version was recommended to me by Nakamura Honnen, the foremost scholar of Dōhan and Esoteric Pure Land Buddhist thought. In producing the translation of the *Himitsu nenbutsu shō* that appears in this book, I relied on the SAZ edition, noting significant variants, mistakes, additions, and omissions with reference to the ZJZ/DNBZ version. I have also had the opportunity to procure copies of and consult the editions held at the Ryūkoku and Kōyasan University libraries.[7] In future research I hope to return to this text with additional manuscripts to produce a truly comprehensive critical edition.

Title Exegesis

Traditional East Asian Buddhist scriptural exegesis often begins with a character-by-character exegesis of the title of a work. I have adopted this approach to introduce the reader to the semantic range of key terms and concepts encountered throughout the text. Dōhan very well may be telling the reader something important about the text even in its title: the purportedly "shallow" interpretation of *buddhānusmṛti* is actually itself an expression of the "deepest" levels at which *buddhānusmṛti* functions as an expression of enlightened buddha reality within and all around sentient beings. Moreover, by utilizing this traditional approach I wish to illustrate how the academic study of religion and the traditional study of religion may be mutually informative and influential.

Himitsu

The term *himitsu* (Ch. *mimi*) can be translated as "secret," "esoteric," "inner," "hidden," "profound," "mysterious," and so on. This term is one of the ways in which East Asian Buddhists rendered the Sanskrit term *guhya,* which has the basic meaning of secret, mysterious, concealed, or hidden. *Guhya* was also translated in East Asia as "inside" 内, "subtle" 妙, "profound" 深, "mysterious" 陰, "inner" 奥, and "hidden" 隱密.[8] Though the term *himitsu* is commonly associated with so-called Esoteric Buddhism and Esoteric Buddhism is commonly assumed to be the East Asian equivalent of Indo-Tibetan Tantric Buddhism, in fact there is nothing inherently Tantric about the term. Rather, scriptural texts such as the *Lotus Sutra* and the *Nirvana Sutra* and commentaries such as the *Dazhidulun,* among others, employ the term *himitsu* to indicate "esotericism," as well as to serve as a generalized Buddhist hermeneutical and polemical strategy to designate some teachings as provisional and others as ultimate, some as superficial and others as profound, some as revealing and others as secret.[9]

In some cases the term *himitsu* is used simply as a synonym for the Mahayana itself, purportedly the highest and most sublime teaching of the Buddha. In ideal religious terms, buddhas and great bodhisattvas understand the true meaning of the Dharma. In social human terms, secrecy is a way to maintain power over ideas and people and may also be used to claim and maintain the superiority of certain lineages and factions. The *Mikkyō daijiten* 密教大辭典, a six-volume dictionary produced by the Shingon school, also discusses the broad semantic range of the term *himitsu.* As with Dōhan himself, however, its discussion of *himitsu* is grounded in a Kūkai-centered perspective, simultaneously addressing the breadth of this term's application while also arguing for the superiority of one particular view.[10] As Dōhan's discussion of *buddhānusmṛti* reveals, these two objectives are not necessarily mutually exclusive. The term *himitsu nenbutsu* may be more accurately translated as "secret *buddhānusmṛti,*" yet the term might also imply something like "the secret of *buddhānusmṛti.*"

Himitsu-shū

While I prefer the title *Himitsu nenbutsu shō* for this text that has survived in multiple print and manuscript versions, some versions have an alternate title, *Himitsu-shū nenbutsu shō* (Compendium on the Buddha Contemplation of the Secret Teaching/Lineage).[11] As with *himitsu*, the term *himitsu-shū* 秘密宗 is generally assumed to be synonymous for Esoteric Buddhism or the Shingon school.[12] Indeed, the term appears frequently, for example, in Yixing's *Commentary on the Mahāvairocana-sūtra*. This text states that following the *himitsu-shū* (Ch. *mimizong*) will lead one to crosswise traverse the three limitless kalpas of practice necessary for the attainment of Buddhahood. *Himitsu-shū* also appears in the works of important Japanese commentators, including Saisen, Kakuban, and Raiyu, citing the text.[13]

The semantic range of this term is more expansive than merely referring to the Shingon school or Esoteric Buddhism, however. In its broader context, *himitsu-shū* may also carry the connotation of equalizing the early stages of the bodhisattva path with the attainment of Buddhahood. Furthermore, the term may also signify the power of the truths realized by buddhas to transform the "low" into the "high," inverting hierarchies assumed to be real or inherent. Ōshika Shinnō has examined the concept of *shoji sokugoku* 初地卽極 ("the first stage of the bodhisattva path is none other than the attainment of Buddhahood"), noting its importance in Dōhan's thought.[14] Whether or not the title originally contained the term *himitsu* or *himitsu-shū*, Dōhan may actually be hinting at the actual meaning of the text itself. Throughout this work Dōhan takes established hierarchies and inverts them, playing upon and subverting readers' expectations. The part is the whole, and the whole is in the part. The simple practice of *buddhānusmṛti* is awakening in action.

I would suggest that *Himitsu nenbutsu shō* is the older or original title. The term *himitsu-shū nenbutsu* does not actually appear in the text, while the term *himitsu nenbutsu* appears several times. Why might the term *shū* have been added? A reasonable assumption is that *himitsu-shū* was added in later versions to serve as a synonym for the Shingon school; some later scribe perhaps read the sectarianism of Edo-period Buddhism into Dōhan's early Kamakura intellectual context.

The term *shū* has been examined in detail in previous chapters; the term today tends to be used to indicate a distinct school, sect, religious organization, institution, or group. In premodern times *shū* indicated areas of study or specialization, lineage, especially the "essence" or inner meaning of the teachings of a particular lineage, and so on. The term "Shingon-shū," for example, may have once meant something like "the essence of mantra," but it eventually came to mean the "mantra sect," reflecting that as particular institutions grew in prominence they branded themselves as representatives of a major area of concern, mastery of the mantra path. In reading the *Himitsu nenbutsu shō,* it is clear that Dōhan was contributing to this effort.

In other words, in some contexts the meaning and polemical impact of the term *shū* is not far removed from the meaning of the term *himitsu.* Thus, if we entertain for a moment the idea that the character *shū* did originally appear in the title, it seems that Dōhan may have intended to imply that his interpretation revealed not simply the "Shingon school *buddhānusmṛti,*" as we might understand it today, but perhaps the true meaning of the hidden essence (*himitsu-shū*) of *buddhānusmṛti.* In the context of the work as a whole, another interpretation could be that by understanding the true meaning of the diversity of approaches to *buddhānusmṛti,* all may be understood as contextual approaches ultimately leading to the same goal: rebirth in Sukhāvatī and/as the attainment of Buddhahood. According to Dōhan, it seems, the practitioner of mantra is uniquely positioned to see this bigger picture.

Nenbutsu

The term *nenbutsu* 念佛 is generally assumed to denote chanting of the name of Amitābha: *Namo Amida Butsu.* However, *nenbutsu* as *buddhānusmṛti* may have much broader, even generic, connotations, including mindfulness of a buddha and remembrance of a buddha. There are *buddhānusmṛti* practices for Avalokiteśvara, Śākyamuni, and more.

Dōhan, for example, explores two mantra versions, *A-MI-TA* and *NAMO-A-MI-TA-BU,* written in the Siddhaṃ script in addition to the more common Chinese characters. He first situates the *nenbutsu* in the context of mantra and dhāraṇī culture (two terms he consistently uses interchangeably). Dōhan later imbues vocal *buddhānusmṛti* with the meaning of speech itself, manifesting not only as the vocal utterance in three or five parts but also as the speech organs and the breath that renders speech and even life itself possible. *Buddhānusmṛti* is ultimate reality active in the world as Amitābha Buddha (Amitābha is Mahāvairocana), as well as the mind of awakening that is always-already present within all beings. Thus, the meaning of *buddhānusmṛti* is eventually expanded to include all aspects of reality, collapsing the duality between buddhas and beings, all Dharmas, and all actions. According to Dōhan, ultimately there is nothing that is not *buddhānusmṛti.*

Shō

Among various genres of Buddhist commentarial literature, a *shū* 集 is a compilation, a *sho* 疏 is a commentary, and so on. Dōhan's text is a *shō* 抄/鈔, which may be translated as a compendium or collection of excerpts, extracts, or notes. The character itself seems to evoke the image of a small sample held in the hand (手+少) or a small metal scoop (金+少). *Shō* is an explicitly synthetic or composite genre that, like *shū* and *sho,* draws upon and samples texts (at times quite "liberally" or "strategically") to support a claim or amplify the potency of a line of argumentation. The author or compiler of a *shō* may draw from the authority of others to further establish the credibility of the author's views. In these kinds of works, it is therefore not always clear where the text being sampled ends and the compiler's own views begin. The writing style in some ways is similar to the literature review section of a dissertation. Or it might resemble the way a modern author quotes or name-drops prestigious theorists (in humanities scholarship Foucault and Derrida are the most obvious examples), not because the work deals at length with that theorist but because the name confers prestige (in other words, power) to that style of writing.

Dōhan draws upon a great many sources in the *Himitsu nenbutsu shō.* What is striking about them is that Dōhan freely samples from texts regarded as classics in the Shingon, Tendai, and Pure Land traditions, as well as concepts associated with diverse philosophical traditions. Dōhan's compendium on one of the most simple forms of Buddhist practice, the recitation of the name of the Buddha, thus taps into the entirety of the Mahayana tradition, and it may be considered a point of departure for thinking more broadly about the diversity of Pure Land thought and culture not only in medieval Japan but also in East Asia in general.

An Overview of the *Himitsu nenbutsu shō*

The *Himitsu nenbutsu shō* comprises three fascicles and is subdivided into numerous subsections, which address a wide range of topics that will be familiar to scholars of Pure Land Buddhism and especially scholars of Tendai Pure Land literature. The format of the *Himitsu nenbutsu shō* follows a question and answer (J. *mondō* 問答) style, with Dōhan responding to the questions of an imagined interlocutor. I have previously speculated that this work may have functioned as a way for Dōhan to place his two teachers, Jōhen and Kakkai, in dialogue with one another. He completed a version of the *Himitsu nenbutsu shō* around 1224, within a year of the passing of both men, and these monks exerted a powerful influence on Dōhan's thought. They had different perspectives on the nature of the Pure Land and the growing Pure Land "movement": Kakkai had a more skeptical view, while Jōhen adopted a more sympathetic view.

Speculation aside, Dōhan as a teacher, lecturer, and ritual master was often called upon by elite monks at Ninnaji and Kōyasan to summarize and explain the major texts of the emerging Esoteric tradition. The *mondō* format may have been utilized in this text so that it could serve as a manual for debate preparation. After all, this is precisely the context in which many of Dōhan's extant texts were produced.

Fascicle One

1.1 The Name 名號事

Like the title, the opening passage of the *Himitsu nenbutsu shō* may very well impart to the reader exactly what the work as a whole is actually about. Dōhan begins with a rhetorical question: Why do laypeople and monastics alike, regardless of affiliation or area of specialization, rely on Amitābha Buddha, the "primal vow," the *buddhānusmṛti* samādhi, and so on? Is it because *buddhānusmṛti* is easy or because within its seeming simplicity, many layers and shades of meaning and power are hidden? In response to his own questions, Dōhan lays out a *shijū hissaku* 四重秘釋 (fourfold secret explanation).

This exegetical strategy will be examined in some detail in the following chapter, so I will only briefly explain it here: At level one we encounter Dharmākara Bodhisattva, who embarked upon the bodhisattva path under the direction of Lokeśvararāja Buddha and ultimately achieved awakening as Amitābha/Amitāyus Buddha. As the story goes, whoever calls the name of this buddha will attain rebirth in Sukhāvatī. This is what could be termed the literal level of meaning, which Dōhan calls the "shallow" view. Level two indicates that Amitābha Buddha is but one aspect of Mahāvairocana and the dual mandalas. Level three reveals that Amitābha Buddha is in fact the compassionate activity of ultimate reality, the universal gate through which all beings attain liberation. At level four, the deepest secret within the profound secret,

Dōhan reveals that Amitābha is in fact active within/as the body-mind, the true nature, of all beings.

The first named individual Dōhan cites is Jippan, a contemporary and possible associate of Kakuban to whom Dōhan is commonly compared. Jippan is well known as a specialist and reviver of the monastic precepts and a Shingon theorist. Less commonly discussed, however, is Jippan's facility in Tendai and Pure Land (especially the Tendai perspective on Pure Land).[15] This is another clue to Dōhan's intellectual lineage. Dōhan's thought is rooted in the prevalent *hongaku* thought of his time, yet nevertheless he emphasized the importance of following the precepts and maintaining standards of morality. Dōhan was versed in Shingon and Tendai, and based on the broad range of sources quoted in the *Himitsu nenbutsu shō,* he was well versed in Tendai Pure Land perspectives as well.

From Jippan's *Byōchū shugyōki* 病中修行記,[16] Dōhan cites the *Amida-santai-setsu* 阿彌陀三諦說, a Tendai-Madhyamaka hermeneutic technique in which the three characters *A-MI-TA* are treated as a three-syllable mantra (or a mantra composed of three one-syllable mantras) that is associated with the three truths: the truth of śūnyatā, the provisional truth, and "the middle." Stone and Sueki note that this was an important discursive strategy in early *hongaku* thought. Dōhan consistently employs this tripartite structure throughout the text, rearranging, shifting, and imbuing each syllable with different meanings. This approach is common in the explication of mantras in various traditions, in Japan and elsewhere.

Indeed, for Dōhan the vocal recitation of the name of Amitābha is a mantra, and throughout the text he quotes Kakuban and Kūkai to establish the parameters of a mantra theory of *buddhānusmṛti.* In addition to the three-syllable mantra, Dōhan employs a five-"syllable" mantra, *NAMO-A-MI-TA-BU.* Five buddhas, five wisdoms, five hindrances, and more are all subsumed within, and produced by, the name.[17] Again, for Dōhan there is nothing that is not *buddhānusmṛti.*

1.2 Calling the Name and the Primordial Vow 稱名本願事

In the next section, Dōhan explores the relationship between reciting the name of the Buddha and the mystery of speech. Again employing a tripartite *santaisetsu* interpretive structure, Dōhan lays out the three bodies of buddha, the three mysteries, the three kinds of *buddhakṣetra,* and more. The dharmakāya, *mitsugon,* and Mahāvairocana correspond, respectively, to the saṃbhogakāya, Sukhāvatī, and Amitābha and to the nirmāṇakāya, samsara, and Śākyamuni. Thus, in the same way that speech is the "middle way" between body and mind, encompassing both, so, too, are the saṃbhogakāya, Sukhāvatī, and Amitābha ultimately revealed to be the unity of ultimate and provisional reality and "high" and "low" Buddhologies.

In other words, Amitābha Buddha as a saṃbhogakāya emanation of buddha reality and Sukhāvatī are the ultimate manifestation of the "middle" of the *santaisetsu*.[18] The middle, though not the "highest" truth of the three, is certainly the ultimate truth because it is from within the middle that we realize the interdependence of ultimate and provisional reality. Furthermore, it is because of Amitābha's mysterious relationship with speech, the middle of body and mind, that this buddha selected the vocal act as the object of his primal vow. This idea is explored and elaborated on throughout the text.

1.3 The *Buddhānusmṛti* Samādhi 念佛三昧事

The next section examines the *buddhānusmṛti* samādhi, a state of meditative absorption attained through dedicated contemplation of Amitābha Buddha, a fundamental practice in China and Japan. Dōhan's understanding of the *buddhānusmṛti* samādhi establishes that the compassionate activity of buddha reality is all-pervasive, like wind. This "wind" is life itself, the "breath" of all beings and thus, consciousness. Life, consciousness, and contemplation (*smṛti*) of the buddha reality (*buddha*) are one. In other words, the recitation of the name of the Buddha as a mantra, the contemplation of this mantra/Buddha, and the wind-breath-life that *is* Amitābha Buddha are unified.[19]

1.4 The Ten [Moments of Mindfulness] 十念事

Fascicle 1 concludes with a discussion of the ten moments of mindfulness said to lead to rebirth in Sukhāvatī, described in the *Sukhāvatīvyūha-sūtra*.[20] According to Dōhan, these ten moments are but one moment, just as the levels of Sukhāvatī and the stages of the bodhisattva path are fundamentally collapsible. Drawing from Kūkai's nondualist Mahayana philosophy, Dōhan suggests that the perspectives on Sukhāvatī that establish or literally believe the hierarchies described in the texts, or the notion of progression through stages, are merely provisional (Exoteric) views. However, as understood from the enlightened Buddha's perspective (the Esoteric view), there is no distinction between the first stage of the path and the completion of the path. Thus, the first and ninth levels of the Pure Land are ultimately one and the same.[21]

Fascicle Two

2.1 The Lotus Samādhi 蓮華三昧事

Fascicle 2 begins with a discussion of the dual-mandala system and Amitābha's position as the lord of the lotus division of the mandala. The lotus is a perennial image in Buddhism, so Dōhan has quite a lot of material to work with in establishing Amitābha/lotus correspondences. For example, in Shingon meditation one visualizes a moon disc at the heart-center and imagines a lotus blossom opening and producing seed syllables, buddhas, bodhisattvas, mantras, and more, depending on the practice. The "heart-lotus" in meditation, the mind that produces these visions, and the physical heart organ, a symbol for vitality throughout the world, are all identified by the same character, *shin* 心. Dōhan exploits this ambiguity to great effect. Having established connections between the mind, wind, breath, and life force of the universe as the compassionate activity of buddha reality in the form of Amitābha, Dōhan further connects the physical organ of the heart with the mind, the heart-lotus, and the lotus division of the dual-mandala system.

Dōhan reiterates the correspondences between the buddha bodies, lands, three mysteries, and others. Here and in the conclusion, Dōhan likens Sukhāvatī to an ocean and sentient beings to the various rivers and tributaries that naturally flow into the sea and are purified.[22] Buddha-nature is that aspect of sentient beings that binds them, always-already, to buddha reality. Throughout the second fascicle, Dōhan draws from Yogācāra concepts to establish correspondences between the letters of the mantra, buddhas, forms of wisdom, and Sukhāvatī. This complex system of correspondences makes the second fascicle the most challenging of the three to read, and it will be examined in greater detail in the following chapters.

2.2 The Great Compassion Samādhi 大悲三昧事

Next, Dōhan discusses the Great Compassion Samādhi usually associated with Avalokiteśvara and its connection to Amitābha. As noted, Amitābha is the wind-breath of beings that gives rise to this buddha's connection to the mystery of speech. The "wind" of the Buddha is all-pervasive as the great compassion of buddha reality guiding all beings to awakening, serving as that force that opens the heart-lotus of beings, a psychophysical event that indicates awakening. Finally, here Dōhan notes that the mind, buddha, and "ordinary" beings are ultimately nondifferentiated: they are one.[23]

2.3 The Name of Sukhāvatī 極樂名字事

Some of the main objects of Dōhan's critique are those whose understanding of Buddhist literature is not informed by a deeper understanding of the practices that reveal the fundamental unity of buddhas and beings. In other words, his objects of critique are practitioners who take the sutras at face value without looking deeper into the true nature of the reality that these texts purport to reveal. For example, Dōhan notes that some regard Amitābha as having a limited life span, and after his ultimate demise, Avalokiteśvara will take over. Dōhan is unsatisfied with this view, which he likely regarded as an overly literal reading that puts limits on that which should be unlimited: the compassion of the buddhas. This applies to Sukhāvatī as well. Rather than view Sukhāvatī as a particular location, distinct and far away (in other words, "limited"), Dōhan emphasizes the all-pervasive nature of Sukhāvatī through an analysis of the name itself. He takes Sukhāvatī to mean ultimate bliss, the bliss of awakening, an all-pervasive force that is not limited to the "western" quarter, or any quarter. Sukhāvatī is the Lotus Blossom Treasure World 蓮華藏世界 described in the *Brahma's Net Sutra* and the *Avataṃsaka-sūtra;* Dōhan suggests it is equivalent to the Womb Realm mandala, Tuṣita Heaven, the *Mitsugon Jōdo* (which he equates with the Vajra Realm mandala), and others. Ultimately, these are all one, fully present within every being's own heart-mind and body. Any distinctions drawn between these realms are merely provisional designations, not the ultimate truth.[24]

2.4 The Western Direction 西方事

Continuing from the previous section, Dōhan interrogates the idea that Sukhāvatī is limited to the "western" quarter of the universe. He notes that Sukhāvatī's association with the western direction also includes associations with autumn, love, and desire. These are certainly elaborations on the association of the western direction with the sunset, the ending of things, and the sense of comfort and peace that arises from the deep reddish orange of the setting sun, a color widely associated with Amitābha and mentioned in the *Wuliangshou yigui,* a text consistently referenced by Dōhan. Again, employing concepts related to the various levels of the mind, Dōhan establishes complex connections between the cardinal directions and aspects of Sukhāvatī and Buddhahood. He also draws from the *Contemplation Sutra,* which some propose as a base text for the *Wuliangshou yigui*—itself one of the base texts for Shingon ritual training.[25]

2.5 The Innumerable [Buddha] Lands 十万億土事

Further elaborating on the universality of Sukhāvatī (now redefined, like Amitābha, to encompass all things), Dōhan reiterates his earlier point that all *buddhakṣetra* ultimately reside within one's body-mind as well. It should be noted that this does not negate the vast and complex traditional Buddhist cosmology but simply means that what lies beyond is found within as well.[26]

2.6 The Forty-Eight Vows 四十八願事

In this relatively short section, Dōhan simply asks: Why did Dharmākara Bodhisattva make the forty-eight vows? While different versions of the *Sukhāvatīvyūha-sūtra* give different numbers of the vows—as few as twenty-four—Dōhan relies on the *Shimoheyanlun* and, with some creative math, arrives at forty-eight virtues of the mind that correspond to the vows.[27]

As discussed in chapter 5, the *Shimoheyanlun* is a commentary on the *Awakening of Faith* attributed to Nāgārjuna. Kūkai held this text in high esteem and composed a subcommentary; Dōhan later wrote a sub-subcommentary. For many East Asian Buddhists, the great śūnyatā philosopher Nāgārjuna named in virtually all Mahayana Buddhist patriarch lists is understood to be an aspirant for rebirth in Sukhāvatī and an Amitābha devotee. This brings to mind the *Pratyutpanna-samādhi-sūtra,* in which *buddhānusmṛti* is a technique that leads to the true understanding of śūnyatā and rebirth in Sukhāvatī. This is one reason why Zhiyi references this text in particular in the "constant walking" part of his scheme of the fourfold samādhi, and Dōhan also draws from this text throughout the *Himitsu nenbutsu shō.*

2.7 The Sixteen Contemplations 十六想觀事

In this section Dōhan illustrates the correspondences between the sixteen contemplations in the *Contemplation Sutra* and the dual mandalas. He accomplishes this by bringing in the five elements, the nine consciousnesses, the dual mandalas, and the sixteen bodhisattvas. Dōhan ultimately suggests that these contemplations reveal the light of the Buddha that is always-already within oneself.[28]

2.8 [The Buddha] Coming and Greeting [One at Death] 来迎事

Next, Dōhan addresses the widely popular hope that upon one's deathbed one may experience a *raigō* 来迎 (vision) of Amitābha Buddha and his retinue of twenty-five bodhisattvas descending to escort one to the Pure Land on a lotus blossom pedestal. Devotional images of Amitābha often depict this very moment.

According to Dōhan, Amitābha's light is always-already present in/as the very heart of beings. He later indicates that the deathbed experience is merely perceived by the mind in the moment of attaining Buddhahood in this very body. In other words, for Dōhan the *raigō* and *sokushin jōbutsu* (attainment of Buddhahood in this very body) are attained/experienced simultaneously. The moment of death, the moment of rebirth in Sukhāvatī, the moment of achieving Buddhahood in Sukhāvatī, and the moment of attainment of Buddhahood in this very body may all be simultaneously occurring events understood from different perspectives.[29]

2.9 The Twenty-Five Bodhisattvas 二十五菩薩事

Dōhan continues in this section to build correspondences between the twenty-five bodhisattvas depicted in the *raigō* and the five buddhas of the mandala, each with their attendant bodhisattvas—five groups of five. Thus, the *raigō* may signify the attainment of the five wisdoms of the five buddhas. Further correspondences are made between the six realms and the various manifestation bodies of Avalokiteśvara.[30]

2.10 Revealed as Avalokiteśvara in Sahā and Amitāyus in Sukhāvatī 娑婆示現觀世音極樂稱爲無量壽之事

Throughout the previous sections in fascicles 1 and 2, Dōhan consistently addresses the closely associated Avalokiteśvara Bodhisattva and

Amitābha Buddha. This close relationship is explored in discussions of the Lotus Samādhi, the Great Compassion Samādhi, and so on. Here Dōhan reaches the logical conclusion of this line of inquiry. In a very short passage, he suggests that as the title indicates, what we might identify as "Avalokiteśvara" from within samsara and what we might identify as Amitābha/Amitāyus from within Sukhāvatī are in fact one and the same.[31]

Fascicle Three

3.1 The Nine-Level Lotus Dais 九品蓮台事

Fascicle 3 begins with a discussion of the nine levels, or grades, of Sukhāvatī, seemingly picking up where the first fascicle left off. Again Dōhan emphasizes that for one who truly understands the mantra path, the seeming hierarchies between buddhas and beings and the various levels of the Pure Land are all merely provisional. He critiques those who take as absolute a passage in the *Sukhāvatīvyūha-sūtra* stating that those who commit the five unforgivable sins will not attain rebirth in Sukhāvatī. Citing the *Dazhidulun*, Dōhan says that the Esoteric practices of the dhāraṇī-*piṭaka* may eliminate the negative karma caused by such actions.

Here Dōhan identifies the *himitsu nenbutsu* as the highest technology of the "secret *piṭaka*." In this section he plays into the ambiguity between dhāraṇī, mantra, and *buddhānusmṛti*, as well as the relationships among Mahayana esotericism, dhāraṇī literature, and Esoteric Buddhism/*shingon*/Shingon, in order to claim this nebulous area of Buddhist inquiry as the ultimate vector for the transmission of the highest teaching of the Mahayana.[32]

3.2 Exclusive Practice and Incessant Practice 專修無間修事

In the next section, Dōhan elaborates on just what he means by the term *himitsu nenbutsu* by investigating the idea of constant practice. For some Pure Land practitioners, the goal of reciting the name of Amitābha is to attune oneself to the higher reality of Sukhāvatī or to purify one's negative karma through reciting the holy name as many times as possible: the more one practices, the better one's chances for future rebirth in Sukhāvatī. Numerous stories survive in monastic biographies of practitioners chanting the name tens of thousands of times on a daily basis.

Dōhan takes a different view. According to his understanding, the true *buddhānusmṛti,* the *himitsu nenbutsu,* is already a constant thing, just as is the breath of all beings. Whether asleep or awake, beings are always-already engaged in *buddhānusmṛti.* Because it is already the foundation of all practices, all activities, the *himitsu nenbutsu* is not limited to the consciously directed act of chanting the name.[33]

3.3 Routine Practices 尋常行儀事

Next Dōhan clarifies his implicit critique of exclusive perspectives on *buddhānusmṛti.* From his understanding of *buddhānusmṛti* as all-pervasive, which is perhaps a slight critique of Hōnen (whom he does not address by name), Dōhan rejects the notion of "exclusive practice." Instead he proffers a view of practice that is customizable to meet the needs and abilities of each practitioner. Furthermore, if all actions are already imbued with *buddhānusmṛti,* then there is no logic in selecting a particular practice and rejecting others. Like other contemporary critics of the Pure Land movement, Dōhan argues that *buddhānusmṛti* is meant to be carried out as part of a broader regime of practice, not as a distinct area of specialization in its own right. From Dōhan's perspective this is even more the case because, in fact, *all* practices are always-already *buddhānusmṛti.*

In this rather lengthy section, Dōhan outlines specific instructions for the establishment of a diverse and integrated ritual regime. While for Dōhan Amitābha Buddha and *buddhānusmṛti* are central, he references the *Dhāraṇīsaṃgraha-sūtra* as precedent in asserting that this prescription can certainly be oriented around any object of devotion. Dōhan begins with a description of the tenfold contemplation gate (*jisshu kanmon* 十種觀門) and the six kinds of auxiliary practice (*rokushu jogyō* 六種助行) for a total of sixteen, a number that again may correspond to the sixteen contemplations mentioned above. The tenfold gate of contemplation comprises the following:

1. Contemplation of the limitless heart and the unity of one's own mind and buddha reality
2. Contemplation of equanimity and the unity of one's own mind and the object of devotion, which is equal to all buddhas
3. Contemplation of the unity of the dual mandalas and other dualities, such as body and mind, matter and consciousness, male and female, yin and yang, heaven and earth, Womb and Vajra, and so on

4. Contemplation of the five *cakras*
5. Contemplation of the moon disc used in Esoteric visualization practices
6. Contemplation of the letter *A*
7. Contemplation and counting of the breath, seed syllable contemplation and chanting, and *zazen* (seated meditation)
8. Contemplation of the inner *homa*
9. Contemplation of *sokushin jōbutsu*
10. Contemplation of the ten illusions (*jūenshō* 十緣生), including a mirage, a shadow, bubbles, and more, which Dōhan takes from the *Mahāvairocana-sūtra*[34]

Next, Dōhan describes the six auxiliary practices:

1. Precepts
2. Empowerment and contemplation
3. Preaching to the gods who, while revered, have taken unfortunate rebirth, especially those of the Nippon-kuni 日本國, such as Amaterasu Ōmikami 天照大神
4. Cultivation of a sense of gratitude toward one's lineage ancestors and the great masters of the past who have transmitted the Dharma and Exoteric and Esoteric perspectives as well
5. Practices for the protection of the realm
6. Transference of merit

Through this practice scheme, mantra practitioners are able to transform all activities into Buddhist practice and permeate their own environment with the compassion of buddha reality, thus bringing benefit to all beings near and far. Beginning with the section on the transference of merit, Dōhan continually praises Kōbō Daishi Kūkai. This is the earliest mention of the *daishi myōgō,* essentially a "Kūkai *nenbutsu,*" currently still used in Kōyasan Shingon.

Dōhan concludes this section with a discussion of the vital importance of the cultivation of faith, and what may be implied here is an admonition to have faith in Kōbō Daishi Kūkai as the one who will lead beings to the Pure Land. Of particular interest here is Dōhan's critique of those who regard faith as simply a prescription for beginners or those of limited capacity, arguing that advanced mantra practitioners understand well the central role that faith plays in the life of a Buddhist. Finally, he states that despite the diversity of the many forms of practice one might pursue, all are ultimately expressions of the limitless compassion of buddha reality and the fundamental letter *A*.[35]

3.4 End of Life Mindfulness Practice 臨終用心事

The SAZ edition of the *Himitsu nenbutsu shō* concludes with a deathbed meditation ritual manual dedicated to Kōbō Daishi Kūkai as a bodhisattva-like savior being who guides beings to the Pure Land. By directing one's thought to Kōbō Daishi Kūkai, one may draw upon his great store of merit and escape samsaric rebirth. Dōhan's dual devotion to both Amitābha and Kūkai is on full display in this systematic, and customizable, approach to end-of-life meditation. There is some speculation that this final section may not have been originally included in the *Himitsu nenbutsu shō.* Whether it was originally written by Dōhan or an interpreter of this text, this section is certainly one of the most interesting pieces in the work as a whole. Its inclusion as a separate text in the SAZ anthology demonstrates that this part "lifts out" very easily.[36]

Additional Excerpts

The SAZ edition of the *Himitsu nenbutsu shō* comes to a close with the Amitābha/Kūkai deathbed ritual manual. The edition's colophon, dated 1907, includes the term *kenmitsu nenbutsu*, indicating the breadth of Dōhan's approach to *buddhānusmṛti.* The *himitsu nenbutsu* is not just the Esoteric Buddhist's *buddhānusmṛti,* not just the Shingon school *buddhānusmṛti,* but a way of thinking about all *buddhānusmṛti.* Perhaps, after all, this is the "secret" to Dōhan's *himitsu nenbutsu:* unity in diversity and diversity in unity.

While the SAZ edition ends here, the DNBZ/ZJZ version includes additional excerpts and sections, outlined below, not found in the SAZ, though some lines actually appear in previous sections of the text.

3.5 The Pure Round and Bright Three Turnings 清淨圓明三轉之事

The DNBZ edition includes several short passages; in the first Dōhan discusses the nature of awakening, again employing a threefold structure, linking such concepts as essence 性, the lotus 蓮, embodiment 體, and more.[37]

3.6 The Hundred Rivers Enter the Sea and Are Purified 百川入海淸淨事

Here we see the repetition of a line noted above in which Dōhan likens the relationship of beings and Amitābha Buddha and Sukhāvatī to the rivers and tributaries, large and small, pure and defiled, that all eventually reach and enter the ocean and are purified. All beings return to their fundamental source. The term Dōhan uses for purity, *shōjō* 淸淨, is also used as a synonym for Amitābha Buddha in some Esoteric texts.[38]

3.7 The Three Hindrances 三障事

The DNBZ concludes with an incomplete line mentioning the three hindrances (greed, hatred, and ignorance) and a very brief description of an Amitābha altar from the *Shiyimian guanzizai pusa xinmiyan niansong yigui jing*, with Mahāsthāmaprāpta on the left and Avalokiteśvara on the right. No commentary on this line is provided.

Other Additions: The Hōjō-in and Jimyō-in Editions

As noted in the Buzan edition, the Hōjō-in and Jimyō-in editions of the text include another passage quoting Shandao on Pure Land rebirth and a passage from a text titled *Seiryūji ōshō rinjū kengyō* 靑龍寺和尙臨終觀行 held at the Zentsūji archives.[39] The *Seiryūji ōshō rinjū kengyō* purports to include the teachings of Huiguo, a Chinese patriarch of the Shingon school and Kūkai's teacher, revealing him to have been a Sukhāvatī aspirant.

Notes

Chapter 6: Toward an Introduction to the *Himitsu nenbutsu shō*

1 This introduction is a revised and expanded version of the introduction that appears in Aaron P. Proffitt, "Dōhan's *Compendium on the Secret Contemplation of Buddha,* Fascicle One," in *Pure Land in Asian Texts and Contexts,* ed. Georgios T. Halkias and Richard K. Payne (Honolulu: University of Hawai'i Press, 2019), pp. 269–275.

2 NBTD 446.

3 On this issue, see my recent article: Aaron Proffitt, "*Nenbutsu* Orthodoxies in Medieval Japan," *Japanese Journal of Religious Studies* 47, no. 1 (2020): 135–160.

4 Takeuchi Kōzen 武内孝善, "Dōhan cho, 'Himitsu nenbutsu shō,' honbun kōtei (ichi)" 「道範著『秘密念仏抄』本文校訂(一)」, *Kōyasan daigaku ronsō* 高野山大学論叢 20 (1985): 13–71.

5 Himitsu Nenbutsu Shō Kenkyūkai, ed., "Dōhan cho 'Himitsu nenbutsu shō' no kenkyū—honbun kōtei to kaki kudashi gochū" 道範著 '秘密念仏抄'の研究—本文校訂と書き下し・語註," *Buzan gakuhō* 豊山学報 39 (1996): 105–131.

6 Jodo Shu Buddhist Denomination (website), accessed May 13, 2019, http://jodoshuzensho.jp/.

7 I would like to thank Nasu Eishō of the Ryūkoku University in particular for his help in acquiring copies of the versions held at the Ryūkoku University library.

8 Ogiwara Unrai 荻原雲来, ed., *Kan'yaku taishō bonwa daijiten* 漢譯對照梵和大辭典 (Tokyo: Kan'yaku taishō bonwa daijiten hensan kankōkai, 1940–1943), 431.

9 MBD, 4330.

10 MD, 1868–1869.

11 The SAZ edition uses the term *shū,* while the edition used by Takeuchi does not; see "Dōhan cho, "'Himitsu nenbutsu shō,' honbun kōtei (ichi)," p. 106n1–2. I follow Takeuchi in using the title *Himitsu nenbutsu shō.*

12 MD, 1870.

13 T. 1796:602a1–10; see also Kakuban's *Shingonshū sokushinjōbutsu gishō* 眞言宗即身成佛義章 (T. 2511:3b15–17) and Raiyū's *Taizō nyūzōnyūri shō* 胎藏入理鈔 (T. 2534:148b14–23).

14 Ōshika Shinnō, "Tōmitsu ni okeru shoji sokugokusetsu no tenkai" 東密における初地即極説の展開, *Tōyō no shisō to shūkyō* 東洋の思想と宗教 29 (2012): 71–89.

15 Satō, *Eizan Jōdokyō,* 22–24.

16 SAZ 2:781–787.

17 SAZ 2:231–235.

18 SAZ 2:235.

19 SAS 2:235–237.

20 The ten thought moments are discussed in the *Sukhāvatīvyūha-sūtra* 佛說無量壽經 (T. 360:268a26–28) and the *Contemplation Sutra* 佛說觀無量壽經 (T. 365:346a18–20).

21 SAZ 2:237–238.

22 SAZ 2:238–245.

23 SAZ 2:245–246.

24 SAZ 2:246–247.

25 SAZ 2:247–248.

26 SAZ 2:248.

27 SAZ 2:249.

28 SAZ 2:249–250.

29 SAZ 2:250.

30 SAZ 2:250–251.

31 SAZ 2:251.

32 SAZ 2:252–253.

33 SAZ 2:253–255.

34 T. 848, 3c11–14.

35 SAZ 2:255–263.

36 SAZ 2:263–266.

37 DNBZ 43:64–65.

38 DNBZ 43:64–65.

39 I located a text under the same title in the Zentsūji 善通寺 archive online, accessed December 15, 2020, http://base1.nijl.ac.jp/iview/Frame.jsp?DB_ID=G0003917KTM&C_CODE=XSE1-21704.

Chapter 7

The Buddha Amitābha in the *Himitsu nenbutsu shō*

The *Commentary on the Mahāvairocana-sūtra* states, "Like the four great rivers of Jamudvīpa, each comprised of five hundred smaller tributaries, all together these various water sources are variously impure, but they enter the great ocean and, therein, they are all purified."—T. 1796:39.608c11–13

Nianfo zhe shishei 念佛者是誰?

A well-known Chan *gong'an* 公案 (J. kōan) asks the meditator to inquire about who engages in *buddhānusmṛti: nianfo zhe shishei* 念佛者是誰. "Who contemplates the Buddha?" Is it 'I?' Is it 'Thou?' Is it both? Is it neither? Or is it something else altogether, thus rendering the premise behind the question problematic? The Chan/Zen, Tiantai/Tendai traditions, and the East Asian Esoteric Buddhist traditions as well, all have patriarchs who have promoted contemplation and devotion to Amitābha Buddha and the Pure Land mythos as a nuanced philosophical-soteriological dimension of the Mahayana.

The fundamental question of what exactly *is* Amitābha Buddha actually offers an opportunity to apply the philosophical insights of Mahayana Buddhism in a dynamic way. Buddhas are not just abstract symbols, however; in a sense they are also resources from which Buddhists might draw in their pursuit of the path. The Buddhist studies assumption has often been that Pure Land devotion is a kind of "Buddhism for dummies," a practice for unrefined peasants who lack the intelligence to appreciate the subtle philosophy of Gautama Buddha. Yet throughout the history of Mahayana Buddhism, many of the philosophical systems deemed worthy of Western Buddhologists' academic attention in fact already had quite a lot to say about Amitābha Buddha and Sukhāvatī.

In this chapter I examine Dōhan's understanding of Amitābha, an object of devotion and meditation for him throughout his life. As a scholar-monk and interpreter of the works of Kūkai, who is one of the most famous and important monastics in Japanese history (and perhaps one of the most popular objects of modern academic devotion), Dōhan fits well within the realm of what Buddhologists have typically found worthwhile of scholarly inquiry. Therefore, perhaps, an ontological, epistemological, or metaphysical (a term that may or may not be appropriate in the case of Dōhan's monistic worldview) investigation into Dōhan's views on Amitābha may enlighten those skeptical of the importance of the Pure Land path and inspire them to inquire further.

Who/What Is Amitābha Buddha?

The *Himitsu nenbutsu shō* begins with a question: Why have so many chosen to rely on the *buddhānusmṛti* samādhi? To this rhetorical question, Dōhan replies that whether exploring Amitābha Buddha, *buddhānusmṛti,* or Sukhāvatī, in all cases they may be understood to have four levels.[1] Dōhan, who derived his fourfold secret explication from Yixing, uses it in many of his texts, such as his commentary on the Mantra of Light.[2] The four levels are (1) shallow or abbreviated 淺略, (2) the deep secret 深秘, (3) the deep secret within the secret 秘中深秘, and (4) the deepest secret within the secret 秘秘中深秘.

Dōhan's initial inquiry and the text as a whole are largely concerned with *buddhānusmṛti,* broadly conceived indeed, and the various levels by which this practice might be engaged or understood. The first section of the *Himitsu nenbutsu shō,* however, begins with an exploration of the fourfold secret explication of Amitābha Buddha, which Dōhan explicitly indicates should serve as a model for further inquiry.[3]

The first level, which Dōhan refers to as the shallow-abbreviated level, is what might be referred to as the surface level: the "exoteric," literal, or even "literary" level of the narrative of the sutras. This familiar story can be summarized as follows: In the remote past lived a bodhisattva named Dharmākara who met Lokeśvararāja Buddha. Under the tutelage of this buddha, Dharmākara studied the *buddha-kṣetra* of the ten directions and undertook a series of forty-eight vows and, by doing this, created the very best *buddha-kṣetra,* Sukhāvatī, the Land of Bliss. Having accomplished these vows, Dharmākara Bodhisattva became what we now refer to as Amitābha/Amitāyus Buddha, the Buddha of Infinite Light and Life. And if anyone calls upon this buddha even as few as ten times with sincere faith, they will be reborn in Sukhāvatī after death and pursue the bodhisattva path to Buddhahood.

This narrative proved to be an attractive soteriological path that has been pursued by lay and monastic Buddhists, commoners and peasants, and cultural and economic elites alike. From this perspective, Amitābha Buddha and Sukhāvatī, his Pure Land of Bliss, are *really real*—more real than our illusory world of suffering and ignorance. If one could fly in a rocket to the western quarter of the Buddhist "multiverse," after passing through many parallel universes one would eventually land in Sukhāvatī, meet Amitābha face-to-face, and shake hands (or bow). Regrettably, too many scholars have not only unfairly dismissed this particular Mahayana Buddhist perspective as inauthentically Buddhist but have also mistakenly taken the entirety of the Pure Land dimensions of Mahayana Buddhism to consist only of this interpretation. For Dōhan and many other Mahayana Buddhists before and after him, however, this narrative is simply one component of a broader soteriology and worldview, an essential part of the "setup" for a "punch line" that distills the whole of the Mahayana.[4]

The second level, the deep secret, seems to introduce but not fully explore basic concepts generally associated with Esoteric Buddhism. According to this perspective, Amitābha Buddha is not simply some enlightened being who exists far away; rather, this buddha is an aspect or dimension of ultimate reality itself, abiding in mysterious union with all sentient beings. This particular facet of ultimate reality is depicted in the dual mandala system, the Vajra and Womb Realm mandalas. Aside from Mahāvairocana Buddha, the anthropomorphization of ultimate reality in the center, Amitābha Buddha is the only other buddha who appears on the central dais of both mandalas. In the Vajra Realm, Dōhan notes, Amitābha appears as the wisdom of subtle discernment 妙觀察智, and in the Womb Realm, Amitābha appears as the gate of the awakening to bodhi 證菩提門.

This perspective, contrasted with the shallow-abbreviated interpretation, is thus called the deep-secret level of understanding Amitābha Buddha. Here Dōhan notes that for Buddhists whose perspective is limited to the Exoteric view, Amitābha Buddha is a kind of mechanistic byproduct of Dharmākara Bodhisattva's practice. From that perspective, practice *leads to* awakening. For Buddhists who grasp the Esoteric truth, however, all of the holy ones contained in the dual mandalas—the manifold buddhas, bodhisattvas, gods, wrathful deities, and so on—are revealed to be aspects of one's own practice. Buddhas and beings are not separate; thus, ultimately, practice *is* awakening. This is the deep-secret interpretation. However, as this is only the second of four levels of ever-deepening meaning,[5] I suggest we think of this level as neophyte Esoteric Buddhism.

The third level expands on level two, conceiving of Amitābha Buddha as an ever-present, all-pervasive quality of ultimate reality, the very living wisdom of the dharmakāya. This buddha's other name, Amitāyus (Limitless Life), encompasses this meaning. Limitless beings, when taken together in the holistic, interconnected Mahayana multiverse, constitute a life force that is truly limitless: limitless beings = limitless lives. Given the infinite capacity of ultimate reality's compassion, this then necessarily means that these infinite lives are connected to the limitless life embodied by Amitāyus.

From this perspective, Amitābha/Amitāyus is merely another name for the boundless, eternally evolving vital force that, when correctly understood, is none other than the compassionate activity of the dharmakāya, within and all around sentient beings, awakening within beings and guiding them along the path. Amitābha Buddha therefore encompasses all buddhas and all paths. Dōhan describes this as the "secret within the deep secret." Even though level three elaborates on the second level, the deeper meaning of the deep understanding, it is still not the whole picture.[6]

Level four, the "deepest secret within the deep secret," seems to reverse course. The second and third levels elaborated on the "exo-esoteric" perspective on Amitābha Buddha described in the sutras and tantras, expanding this buddha to encompass ultimate reality itself. Yet at level four Amitābha seems at first to shrink to the size of a fist: the anatomical heart that beats within the chests of sentient beings. Throughout the *Himitsu nenbutsu shō,* Dōhan plays on the ambiguity between *shin* 心 as mind or essence and/or the physical heart organ, all of which are present in the meaning of the Sanskrit term *hṛdaya.* Dōhan thus identifies Amitābha Buddha as an aspect of the mind/body (heart) of beings. The abstract "cosmic" Amitābha Buddha of levels two and three is in this way expanded further, somewhat paradoxically, by "shrinking" it to the size of a human heart.

Here Amitābha Buddha is revealed not only as an object of soteriological devotion but also as the very life force of all beings, perhaps life itself—a radical philosophical proposition that ultimately transforms what *buddhānusmṛti* can mean. With level four, moreover, Dōhan also reveals Amitābha Buddha to reside within and function as an aspect of one's own body, the physical expression of this life force. The Buddha is the body-mind of beings, not far away at all but in fact closer than beings typically imagine the Buddha to be. When ignorance subsides, Amitābha Buddha is revealed to have always-already been present, literally active within one's own body. Dark clouds may obscure one's view, but the light of buddha reality is ever luminous.[7]

Is Amitābha Buddha Limited or Limitless?

Dōhan suggests that those who have penetrated to the Esoteric truth are able to fully grasp both the inner realization and the outer application of Amitābha Buddha. According to Yixing's *Commentary on the Mahāvairocana*, at the level of outer application Amitābha Buddha is the form that ultimate reality takes as *upāya* (skill in means) to reach limitless beings in limitless realms.[8] Limitless lives = Limitless Life/Amitāyus. The level of inner realization is identified in Kūkai's *Dainichikyō-kaidai*, which describes Amitābha as an all-pervasive dimension of ultimate reality, unifying inner and outer, matter and spirit.[9]

One way in which Dōhan distinguishes between Exoteric and Esoteric levels of engagement is through an assessment of the various interpretations of Amitābha Buddha's life span. Though the name Amitāyus might imply a buddha whose life span is in fact infinite, another common reading suggests that though this buddha's life span is immeasurable, it is not necessarily infinite. However, because of Dōhan's association of Amitābha with ultimate reality itself, the life span of Amitāyus/Amitābha is taken to be literally infinite. According to Dōhan, only those who rely solely on the Exoteric reading of the sutras take them literally when they state that at the end of Amitāyus's life span Avalokiteśvara will take over as the Lord of Sukhāvatī.[10] For Dōhan, Amitābha/Amitāyus truly is limitless.

Amitābha: Unity and Difference

Dōhan considers the different forms in which Amitābha Buddha is represented, examining the meaning of the names Amitābha (Limitless Light), Amitāyus (Limitless Life), and *amṛta* (the nectar of immortality), as well as the name Lokeśvararāja Tathāgata, which appears as an alternative name for Amitābha in texts associated with the *Vajraśekhara* cycle, and the Crimson Crystal Body Amida, which appears in the *Wuliangshou yigui*. While Dōhan tends to focus on and emphasize the unity of

Amitābha, at times he also emphasizes different perspectives, noting their importance in laying out the capacity of ultimate reality to reach beings in diverse ways. Dōhan notes three different views of Amitābha:

1. Amitābha may be conceived as the one gate that reveals all virtues.
2. Amitābha may be understood as an aspect of Mahāvairocana.
3. Amitābha may be encountered as the essence of one's own body-mind.[11]

Amitābha and the Mystery of the "Middle"

The *Mahāvairocana-sūtra* identifies the element of wind and breath with life itself.[12] The element of wind is also associated with Amitābha and takes the form of the breath of beings. Breath is the basis for the production of speech, the middle aspect of the three mysteries (body, speech, and mind). Dōhan notes that all beings in the six realms or the ten realms produce speech or sound, and through the speech act of intoning the *nenbutsu*, Amitābha aids beings in the attainment of awakening.[13] In the section titled "On the Primal Vow of Calling the Name," Dōhan's hypothetical interlocutor asks about the connection between the primal vow and calling the name. Why is the name of Amitābha so special? Why did Amitābha select such a seemingly simple practice, the vocal recitation of the name, as the object of the primal vow to save all beings? Dōhan replies by invoking a tripartite hermeneutic structure rooted in the three mysteries of body, speech, and mind.[14]

Dōhan identifies Amitābha Buddha as the buddha of the mystery of speech, and for this reason Amitābha chose the act of speech as the ultimate tool for liberating beings. Speech is the "middle way" because it lies between and unifies body and mind, both of which are necessary for the performance of a speech act.[15] Because of Amitābha's association with the middle way, Sukhāvatī-oriented speech acts serve as the path that unifies the dharmakāya Mahāvairocana (the mystery of mind) and the nirmāṇakāya Śākyamuni (the mystery of body) through the saṃbhogakāya Amitābha (the mystery of speech). These three buddhas, three dimensions of ultimate reality, and three mysteries overlap through the one buddha: Amitābha.

Amitābha, identified with the mystery of speech, is also associated with the lotus division of the mandala, the Lotus Samādhi, and the sixth consciousness, which unifies body and mind. From this perspective, recitation of the name of the Buddha signifies the opening of the heart-lotus of beings, the pure mind of beings, awakening to Buddhahood in this very body. Amitābha is the mystery of speech as the wind element, and in Chinese *wuxing* thought the west corresponds with metal and wind. Wind is the breath of all beings, the life force that enlivens beings and makes possible the act of speech known as the *nenbutsu*. This wind/breath/life/*nenbutsu* is thus none other than Amitāyus, Limitless Life. The seed syllable of the lotus division of the mandala is *hrīḥ*, and the essence of *hrīḥ* is the syllable *ha*, which signifies "wind." According to Dōhan, when taken all together, this evidence necessarily leads to the conclusion that *buddhānusmṛti* is efficacious because of forces both beyond and within sentient beings.[16]

Dōhan also imagines a question about the capacities of beings who cannot speak. If the vocal recitation of the name is all-encompassing, is salvation possible for those who cannot speak? In response, Dōhan notes that body, speech, and mind are neither fundamentally discrete nor mutually exclusive. Rather, each is mutually inclusive of the others. Mind has traces of body and speech. Furthermore, because Dōhan's main argument is essentially that true *buddhānusmṛti*, the *himitsu nenbutsu*, is the very breath of beings, all living beings are in this way already fundamentally engaged in *buddhānusmṛti* with every breath. The external vocalization of the name of the Buddha is beside the point. He also asserts that one should not be concerned about the number of times one recites the Buddha's name.[17]

Amitābha Is the Lotus Samādhi

Dōhan identifies Amitābha as the lord of the lotus division of the mandala, so he therefore has a close connection with the widely practiced Lotus Samādhi. The Lotus Samādhi 法華三昧 (Skt. *saddharma-pundarīka-samādhi*) refers to a form of repentance practice commonly performed in the third stage of the fourfold samādhi of the Chinese Tiantai and Japanese Tendai traditions, which consists of ninety-day periods of sitting, walking, both sitting and walking, and neither sitting nor walking. The third part, both sitting and walking, may be divided into the *vaipulya*-samādhi 方等三昧 and the Lotus Samādhi practices.[18]

According to Dōhan, the Lotus Samādhi is none other than the realization of awakening, experienced by beings as the opening of the heart-lotus, which is a concretization of their pure Buddha-nature.[19] When Dōhan refers to the heart-lotus, he is conflating both the heart-lotus that is visualized in Buddhist practice and the physical heart organ. Here again, human biology is reimagined as an integral aspect of the experience of awakening. Attaining Buddhahood in one's physical body is taken to its logical conclusion, and awakening is located in the biological reality of death. Dōhan also notes the differences between male and female in connection to the heart-lotus, stating that a man's heart-lotus faces up and a female's faces downward.[20] The anatomical and gendered heart-lotus is none other than the activity of Amitābha Buddha as the compassionate activity of the dharmakāya. This dimension of ultimate reality also employs the Exoteric teachings as *upāya* to reach beings. In other words, even the shallow interpretation is an active extension of Amitābha's vow to save all beings.[21]

According to Dōhan, practices centered on Amitābha are especially efficacious because this buddha is the embodiment of the wisdom of subtle discernment. This form of wisdom is understood to be the result of the purification of the sixth consciousness (Skt. *mano-vijñāna*), described in Yogācāra thought, which functions to unify body and mind and serves as the faculty that discerns the truth.[22] The first five consciousnesses (those related to the sense bases of the eyes, ears, nose, tongue, and body) are associated with the body and Śākyamuni as the nirmāṇakāya. The sixth consciousness, which synthesizes the sensory input arising from the five consciousnesses, is associated with speech and Amitābha as the saṃbhogakāya. The seventh consciousness, which gives rise to the sense of self, the eighth consciousness, which facilitates karmic continuity between lives, and the ninth consciousness, recognized as pure consciousness, are associated with the mind and the three bodies of Mahāvairocana ("the essential nature, the enjoyment body, the sphere of the wisdom of inner realization"), the dharmakāya.[23]

Here again, Amitābha plays an important role as the "middle," revealing the inherent unity of body and mind, nirvana and samsara, buddhas and ordinary beings. Associated with the sixth consciousness and the mystery of speech, this buddha occupies an important position between body and mind, unifying both. Furthermore, the sixth and seventh consciousnesses are linked and nondual, just as the saṃbhogakāya stands between Śākyamuni as the nirmāṇakāya and Mahāvairocana as the dharmakāya.[24] Sukhāvatī plays a similar role, unifying samsara, with which Śākyamuni as the nirmāṇakāya is associated, and the "three points" of Mahāvairocana as the dharmakāya.[25]

Amitābha Buddha, as the mystery of speech, the wisdom of subtle discernment, the sixth consciousness, and the saṃbhogakāya, thus occupies a central position from which buddha reality is able to work in coordination with Śākyamuni, who, as the mystery of the body, the nirmāṇakāya, and the five consciousnesses, is able to teach beings in samsara through the five senses. Śākyamuni Buddha teaches beings about Sukhāvatī. From Sukhāvatī, Amitābha Buddha reaches out to beings in samsara. In this way, Śākyamuni and Amitābha function together to guide beings to awakening.[26]

This integrated view of unity in diversity, and diversity in unity, is explained here again, as in the introduction, as all gates are one gate.[27] In other words, to conceive of Śākyamuni and Amitābha as separate from one another, or separate from one's own mind, is merely a provisional (Exoteric) perspective. The Esoteric perspective purports to locate both within this very body. However, this is not simply to assert that the Esoteric view is "better" but rather to explain that the Exoteric and Esoteric work together to guide beings to awakening, as do the two buddhas Śākyamuni and Amitābha. These are two approaches among many that are part of a larger "force" working to bring beings toward the recognition of their true place within the Mahayana Buddhist multiverse.[28]

The sixth consciousness is also connected to the Lotus Samādhi, which reveals the very essence of life and death. Because this consciousness functions to "process" the sensory input from the five (sense) consciousnesses (the resultant consciousnesses that arise from the contact of the eyes, ears, nose, tongue, and body with their respective objects), it is therefore within the sixth consciousness that the mechanism by which beings become attached and "stuck" in the muck of samsara operates. Conversely, this aspect of the mind seems to simultaneously possess the key to liberation from samsara. Dōhan suggests that this apparent "duality" reveals that the "lotus" (here meaning the psychophysical heart-lotus of beings, the inherently pure nature) *requires* the "mud" of samsara because it is needed for the lotus to open.[29] The lotus not only needs the mud but, in fact, the mud and lotus are ultimately one. In the same way, beings seemingly "stuck" in samsara are always-already in perfect and complete union with ultimate reality.[30]

Both the inherent, or original, awakening of all beings and the process by which this potential is realized are allowed to stand and function together when seen from the perspective of ultimate reality.[31] Amitābha is ultimately an aspect of buddha reality that guides beings along the path. As an aspect of body-mind, Amitābha reveals that external and internal realities are one. Dōhan compares Amitābha to the father in the parable of the burning house in the *Lotus Sutra,* who uses various devices to guide beings out. For the practitioner of mantra, awakening may be achieved right here and now, without waiting to "go" to Sukhāvatī.[32] Amitābha Buddha thus has a certain kind of reality: a manifestation of the dharmakāya, acting on behalf of beings to aid in their progress. Yet many remain stuck in samsara, and so Amitābha reaches out to aid them into gradually cultivating the path as well. The mantra practitioner has the power to directly and immediately use the name of Amitābha to realize right here and now the manifold virtues of the Buddhist path; Sukhāvatī is right here for those who are karmically predisposed to use the right techniques. Yet for those who are not yet at such an advanced stage of practice, the Buddha remains active in the world to guide them.

Amitābha as the Lotus of Inherent Purity

The Lotus Samādhi reveals that the three poisons and five desires are, in essence, inherently pure. For one who is awakened, all things are possible, even when committing seemingly evil acts, but one who is not awakened should continue to practice and observe proper conduct. Dōhan notes that discussions over the inherent purity of beings and the realization that even within the essence of sin great virtue may be found is not license to engage in evil acts. One who is awakened to one's inner nature sees these evils as contiguous with the greater buddha reality, but for one who is not awakened to one's true nature, the indiscriminate commission of evil acts will lead to unfortunate rebirth.[33]

The lotus is associated with the water element, a symbol of purity. It takes root in muddy water but rises above and reveals its inherent purity. This symbol is meant to compel beings to take refuge in their own inherently pure nature. The water element is also associated with the west, the direction of Sukhāvatī.[34] The wind element signifies the activity of the Buddha revealing one's inherent nature.[35] Wind and water thus work together. Dōhan likens beings attaining birth in Sukhāvatī to "one hundred rivers enter the ocean and are purified." This means that infinite beings of infinite universes will find peace through rebirth in Sukhāvatī because Amitābha is the buddha reality within beings, guiding them to awakening.[36]

Amitābha as Wisdom and Compassion

The buddha known as Amitābha/Amitāyus is sometimes referred to in English as "the Buddha of Infinite Life and Light," or some variation thereof. Amitābha (Infinite Light) and Amitāyus (Infinite Life) are also often linked with the twin virtues of wisdom and compassion, which are often described as the "two wings" of Buddhism. Dōhan also considers the way in which wisdom and compassion are interconnected and how devotion to Amitābha may serve to engage both virtues. Great compassion (Skt. *mahākaruṇā*) and great wisdom (Skt. *mahāprajñā*) correspond to the Womb Realm and the Vajra Realm mandalas, respectively. These ultimately nondual aspects of buddha reality further correspond to the six elements. The great compassion/Womb Realm mandala corresponds to the five physical elements, and the great wisdom/Vajra Realm mandala corresponds to the element of consciousness. Thus, the relationship between wisdom and compassion signifies the nonduality of matter and spirit, body and mind.

Wisdom and compassion correspond further to the lotus and the moon discs, signifying principle and wisdom, respectively, used together in Esoteric meditation/visualization. Great compassion examines all things, embraces all beings, and is everywhere at once. Great wisdom makes it possible to realize great compassion, and great compassion makes it possible to cultivate great wisdom; the two are one. Great compassion is represented by all beings; great wisdom is represented by all buddhas. The wisdom of all buddhas is the principle of all beings. The universal great compassion of all buddhas is none other than Amitābha Buddha, who manifests as the heart-lotus beating within all beings and the breath-speech of the *nenbutsu* as well.[37]

Great compassion may be further divided into two meanings: *mahā-maitrī* and *mahā-karuṇā*. *Maitrī* is commonly translated as "loving-kindness," and *karuṇā* may be translated as "mercy" or "pity." Dōhan connects *maitrī* and *karuṇā* to wisdom and principle, father and mother, heaven and earth, meditation and wisdom, the Vajra Realm mandala and the Womb Realm mandala. *Maitrī* is associated with kindness, wisdom, father, heaven, meditation, principle, and the Vajra Realm. *Karuṇā* is associated with pity, principle, mother, earth, wisdom, and the Womb Realm. Amitābha Buddha is the unity of these two, the one universal gate of principle and wisdom and the Womb and Vajra Realm mandalas.[38]

Amitābha Is Avalokiteśvara, Avalokiteśvara Is Amitābha

Dōhan's investigation into the relationship between Amitābha and Avalokiteśvara, as encountered in the visualizations in the *Wuliangshou yigui*, the Amitābha mandala, and so on, reveals that the dichotomous relationship between buddha and bodhisattva transforms into an occasion to meditate on the perceived relationship between cause and effect, inherent and partial awakening, Sukhāvatī and samsara, and so on. Amoghavajra's *Wuliangshou yigui* states:

> On entering the *samādhi* of Avalokiteśvara Bodhisattva [c]lose your eyes and clear your thoughts. Visualize in your body a perfect circle of pure white, like a pure moon, lying face up within your heart. Above the pure moon [disc] visualize the letter *hrīḥ* emitting a great radiance. The letter transforms into an eight-petaled lotus. On the center of the lotus is Avalokiteśvara Bodhisattva. His beautiful appearance is distinct. In his left hand he holds a lotus, and with his right hand he makes the gesture of opening the petals of the lotus. Have this thought, "All sentient beings fully possess within their bodies this lotus of awakening. The pure *dharmadhātu* is not tainted by afflictions." On each of the eight petals of the lotus is a *tathāgata,* sitting in *samādhi* in the full cross-legged position. Their faces are turned toward Avalokiteśvara Bodhisattva.[39]

According to Dōhan, the lotus held by Avalokiteśvara is the heart-lotus of all beings, a concretization of enlightenment within one's own body. In visualizing Amitābha and Avalokiteśvara, Amitābha is at the center of the mandala surrounded by Avalokiteśvaras on each petal, and Avalokiteśvara is at the center of the mandala surrounded by Amitābhas on each petal, each honored one becoming the other, each surrounded by the other. Here again is an articulation of the nonduality between Buddha-nature as a capacity within beings and the realization and actualization of that capacity.[40]

Amitābha is none other than the Buddha-nature of all beings, inherently possessed by all beings. This nature is like the lotus because even when submerged in the "mud" of samsara, it remains pure and unsullied. This womb-like capacity is likened to the Womb Realm mandala. Amitābha Buddha, as the wisdom of subtle discernment, the purification of the sixth consciousness, not only signifies the ability to discriminate between phenomena, thus leading to wisdom, but also indicates the capacity for beings to develop revulsion toward this afflicted world and aspire to Sukhāvatī. This is the shared essence of the heart-lotus and the Womb mandala.

Going further, Dōhan indicates that Amitābha represents not only the capacity for awakening that is synonymous with the life force of all beings but also the capacity for awakening that renders beings capable of practicing Buddhism at all. Visualizing the heart-lotus and engaging in visualization practices help beings realize their inherent connection with their Buddha-nature, their own innate capacity for awakening. This is ultimately like looking in a mirror to see one's true face.

Amitābha is working not only within beings but also as an external force or dimension of reality that reaches out in the form of the Buddhist teachings. Ultimately, however, the inner and outer forces are unified.[41] The complete Buddhahood of all things is not something that simply arises from striving for perfection and rejecting the imperfections of the world; rather, it is inherent within them all along. Moreover, from the level of absolute reality that which is perceived to be imperfect and thus rejected is ultimately recontextualized.

Amitābha, Avalokiteśvara, and Mahāsthāmaprāpta

Further inquiry into the relationship between Amitābha and his attendant bodhisattvas in Sukhāvatī, Avalokiteśvara, and Mahāsthāmaprāpta illustrates the nonduality between cause and effect on the Buddhist path to awakening. These two bodhisattvas symbolize wisdom and meditation, cause and effect, yang and yin. Taken together, the three honored ones of Sukhāvatī may signify the three divisions of the Womb Realm mandala.

Dōhan next examines the Esoteric meaning of the arrangement of an altar with these three objects of devotion and their connection to the mandala: Mahāsthāmaprāpta is on the right side of the altar and signifies the lotus division, principle, and meditation; Avalokiteśvara is on the left side of the altar and signifies the vajra division of the mandala, method, and wisdom; Amitābha Buddha in the center signifies phenomenal reality.

This configuration ultimately signifies the nonduality of conventional and ultimate reality, spirit and matter, and form and emptiness.[42] Avalokiteśvara's association with great compassion also has the meaning of principle, an interpretation that may serve to destabilize and shift this hierarchy further.[43]

Awakening is not strictly "spiritual" but also corporeal because matter and spirit/consciousness are ultimately one. One way of illustrating this relates to Amitābha's connection, again, not only to the mystery of speech but also to the physical basis of speech: the throat, tongue, and lips. Returning to a tripartite structure, Dōhan establishes connections between the three-syllable mantra (*A-MI-TA*), the honored ones of Sukhāvatī, the organs of speech, and the divisions of the mandala:

> *A-* is Amitābha, the throat, the Buddha division;
> *MI-* is Avalokiteśvara, the tongue, the lotus division;
> *TA-* is Mahāsthāmaprāpta, the lips, the vajra division.[44]

Amitābha and the mandala are located in the body, manifesting as the capacity for speech and the speech act itself. The honored ones of Sukhāvatī are expressions of the mandala that manifest in samsara as the organs of speech. As Dōhan establishes throughout, Amitābha is the mystery of speech, the sixth consciousness, and the wisdom of subtle discernment. Each part of this scheme can be seen as an avenue by which beings discern and differentiate phenomena in the world and thus awaken to their true nature, which is a fundamental expression of buddha reality. This is the purpose of the preaching of the Dharma.

Amitābha Buddha may also be found in the three mysteries. As the mind, Amitābha is the sixth consciousness and the vital breath that sustains life.[45] As the body, Amitābha manifests as the organs of speech production (throat, tongue, lips) and the heart-lotus within every living being. As the act of speech, Amitābha manifests as the mystery of speech. Thus, Amitābha may be located in the body, speech, and mind of all beings. Each of these interconnected aspects corresponds to the three buddha bodies, or bodies of buddha reality: with Amitābha as saṃbhogakāya, Śākyamuni as nirmāṇakāya, and Mahāvairocana as dharmakāya.

Through the connection between the mystery of speech and the sixth consciousness, Amitābha may be understood as the mind that processes sensory input. This activity leads to the acquisition of wisdom. Wisdom leads to the preaching of Dharma, which takes the form of speech. Thus, Amitābha is the connection between mind and speech.

Śākyamuni is associated with the physical body. The five senses (eye, ear, nose, tongue, and body) encounter the world and give rise to the five consciousnesses.

The universal, or perhaps multiverse, buddha, Mahāvairocana is none other than the awakening within the mind and is thus associated with the mystery of mind.[46]

Amitābha in Sukhāvatī Is Avalokiteśvara in Samsara

Again emphasizing the connection between Amitābha and Avalokiteśvara, Dōhan suggests that the perceived difference between these deities is simply a matter of perception. Beings in samsara perceive Avalokiteśvara, while beings who see the (ultimate) truth are able to perceive the unity of what seem to be "two" different entities. Indeed, Avalokiteśvara and Amitābha are very closely related. In texts devoted to Avalokiteśvara, this bodhisattva sometimes consults Amitābha for advice. In texts devoted to Amitābha, Avalokiteśvara is identified as one of Amitābha's attendants, and in some instances the texts go so far as to say that Avalokiteśvara will take over after Amitābha passes into final nirvana. For Dōhan, however, these are merely Exoteric understandings of a more subtle reality.

In the *Lotus Sutra*, chapter 25, the Bodhisattva of Compassion may take on whatever form is most effective, and most appropriate, for the specific capacities and inclinations of the beings to whose aid they are going. From Dōhan's perspective, Amitābha as Avalokiteśvara is active in the six realms in six different emanation bodies in order to meet the specific needs of the beings born into each realm. Dōhan draws from and quotes at length Zhiyi's description from the *Mohezhiguan*,[47] which states in brief:

(1) Sahasrabhuja Sahasranetra Avalokiteśvara Bodhisattva 千手千眼觀音菩薩 (Thousand Hands, Thousand Eyes Bodhisattva of Compassion) comes to the aid of beings in the hells.
(2) Āryāvalokiteśvara Bodhisattva 聖觀音菩薩 (Noble Bodhisattva of Compassion) comes to the aid of beings born as hungry ghosts.
(3) Hayagrīva Avalokiteśvara Bodhisattva 馬頭觀音菩薩 (Horse-headed Bodhisattva of Compassion) comes to the aid of beings born as animals.
(4) Ekādaśamukha Avalokiteśvara Bodhisattva 十一面觀音菩薩 (Eleven-headed Bodhisattva of Compassion) comes to the aid of beings born as Asura.
(5) Cundī Avalokiteśvara Bodhisattva 准胝觀音菩薩 (Fierce Bodhisattva of Compassion) comes to the aid of beings born as humans.
(6) Cintāmaṇicakra Avalokiteśvara Bodhisattva 如意輪觀音菩薩 (Wish-granting Jewel Wheel Bodhisattva of Compassion) comes to the aid of beings born as devas.

This list, taken from Zhiyi, remains the standard for the Shingon tradition, while the Tendai tradition tends to replace the fifth, Cundi Avalokiteśvara, with Amoghapāśa Avalokiteśvara Bodhisattva (Unfailing Lance Bodhisattva of Compassion).[48] Amitābha's manifest form in Sukhāvatī and Avalokiteśvara's various manifestation bodies in samsara are ultimately contiguous, connected, nondual expressions of an underlying buddha reality reaching out to guide beings to awakening.[49] From the gods in heaven to the beings suffering in hell, and all those in between, Amitābha Buddha is active within and through them all.

There is a duality present in Dōhan's understanding of Amitābha Buddha that is never fully resolved, perhaps intentionally so. Indeed, this seeming duality is present throughout Mahayana tradition. On the one hand, the Buddha is perceived as external to beings, and they aspire to establish a connection through calling out the name or contemplating the attributes of Amitābha and Sukhāvatī, offering flowers and images on an altar. Amitābha is that to which beings attribute all virtues and goodness. Furthermore, Amitābha is a force of nature, an extension of buddha reality that reaches out and guides beings along the path to awakening. This is reminiscent of the "eternal" Śākyamuni described in the chapter "Buddha's Life Span" in the *Lotus Sutra.* At the same time, Amitābha is also active within beings as the "breath of life," the mystery of speech uniting body and mind, the wisdom of subtle discernment that not only unifies body and mind but also reveals the path from within. Amitābha is also the heart-lotus that opens at the moment of death and/ as awakening. Amitābha is thus both within and without.

Drawing on Dōhan, the metaphorical relationship between breath and speech serves as another image to convey the simultaneously dual/ nondual nature of Amitābha. We tend to conceive of speech as a willed act (except perhaps when one vocalizes when one has stubbed one's toe or has been surprised or startled). However, this willed act is rooted in something automatic and unconscious: the breath. In the same way that the willed act of speech is fundamentally rooted in the unwilled act of breath, the ability of beings to attain awakening on the Buddhist path is premised on their underlying always-already present connection to buddha reality. Practice is therefore not really divisible into "self-power" or "other-power"—it is both and neither simultaneously, just as Amitābha Buddha is both within and beyond.

Dōhan does not necessarily resolve this tension. His disquisition on the *himitsu nenbutsu* is yet another way of framing the broader nondual Mahayana view of the Pure Land path that is present within diverse traditions such as Chan/Zen, Tiantai/Tendai, and Huayan/Kegon.

Notes

Chapter 7: The Buddha Amitābha in the *Himitsu nenbutsu shō*

1 SAZ 2:226.

2 SAZ 2:74–81; BKD 1:230a; NBTD 68.

3 SAZ 2:226.

4 SAZ 2:226.

5 SAZ 2:226.

6 SAZ 2:226.

7 SAZ 2:226.

8 SAZ 2:234; T. 1796:622c20–23.

9 SAZ 2:234; T. 2211:6c15–17; TKDZ 4:35.

10 SAZ 2:234–235.

11 SAZ 2:243.

12 T. 848:17b29.

13 SAZ 2:235.

14 SAZ 2:235.

15 SAZ 2:235.

16 SAZ 2:241.

17 DNBZ 86–87; omitted in SAZ 2:235–236.

18 FD 3396.

19 SAZ 2:238.

20 SAZ 2:239.

21 SAZ 2:239.

22 SAZ 2:239.

23 SAZ 2:239.

24 SAZ 2:239.

25 SAZ 2:239.

26 SAZ 2:239.

27 SAZ 2:240.

28 SAZ 2:240.

29 SAZ 2:240.

30 SAZ 2:240.

31 SAZ 2:241.

32 SAZ 2:241.

33 SAZ 2:244.

34 SAZ 2:244.

35 SAZ 2:244.

36 SAZ 2:244.

37 SAZ 2:246.

38 SAZ 2:246.

39 SAZ 2:242; T. 930:19.0071a10–14; for the translation of this passage of the *Wuliangshou yigui,* I have relied on Thomas Eijō Dreitlein's full translation of the *Wuliangshou yigui* found in Thomas Eijō Dreitlein, "Amoghavajra's Amitāyus Ritual Manual," in *Pure Lands in Asian Texts and Contexts: An Anthology,* ed. Georgios T. Halkias and Richard K. Payne (Honolulu: University of Hawai'i Press, 2019), pp. 242–243.

40 SAZ 2:242.

41 SAZ 2:242.

42 SAZ 2:243.

43 SAZ 2:244.

44 SAZ 2:244.

45 SAZ 2:244.

46 SAZ 2:244.

47 T. 1911:46.15a28–15b14.

48 FD 1314.

49 SAZ 2:251.

Chapter 8

Buddhānusmṛti in the *Himitsu nenbutsu shō*

According to Dōhan, practitioners of *śamatha-vipaśyanā* and mantra almost universally rely on the practice of the *buddhānusmṛti* samādhi. The phrase he uses in his initial inquiry, *shikan-shingon, śamatha-vipaśyanā* and mantra, respectively, could be read as indicating Tendai and Shingon schools of Japanese Buddhism. Tendai is often associated with *shikan,* and Shingon is named after the Japanese translation of the word for mantra, *shingon.* However, as stated previously, Dōhan would not necessarily have been thinking in terms that are familiar to us today. Rather, at this time *shikan-shingon* was a stock phrase indicating the contiguous exo-esoteric Buddhist culture of early medieval Japan. In other words, Dōhan's question could be paraphrased as "Why does everyone practice *buddhānusmṛti?*" Dōhan clearly centers the conversation on the cult of Kōbō Daishi Kūkai, as both a lineage ancestor and object of devotion, yet his aim is not simply to articulate the Shingon school's perspective on *buddhānusmṛti,* as we would understand that today. Rather, Dōhan sets out to explore the contours and diversity of medieval Japanese culture and thought regarding *buddhānusmṛti.* Toward that end, Dōhan answers his hypothetical interlocutor by explaining that *buddhānusmṛti* has multiple levels of deeper nuance and meaning, as do Amitābha Buddha as an object of devotion and meditation and the Pure Land Sukhāvatī as a soteriological goal.[1]

Indeed, practice of *buddhānusmṛti* was from its inception, and remains so today, a nearly ubiquitous form of Mahayana Buddhist practice. *Buddhānusmṛti* is often reduced to the East Asian practice of reciting the name of Amitābha Buddha out loud. However, across the Mahayana world this term could refer to a wide range of practices, including visualization, contemplation, devotion, and, indeed, the vocal recitation of the name of a buddha or bodhisattva. Throughout the *Himitsu nenbutsu shō,* Dōhan employs this ambiguity to explore the possible meanings and shades of nuance, positing the practice as fundamental to the whole of Buddhism. This strategy, part meditation manual and part strategic universalizing polemic, ultimately encompasses the whole of the Buddhist cosmos, the six realms, the ten realms, the dual mandala, and so on, as well as diverse schools of Buddhist philosophy and doctrinal study.

The Fourfold *Nenbutsu*

After considering the four levels of Amitābha (described in chapter 7), Dōhan begins an exploration of the name of Amitābha. Throughout, he presents two interconnected forms of the name rendered in Siddhaṃ, a script for writing Sanskrit: *A-MI-TA* and *NAMO-A-MI-TA-BU.* These two forms of the name, plus the form with which most people are familiar, *Namu Amida Butsu,* are ultimately vocal technologies for the transformation of ignorant karma-bound beings into awakened buddhas. Practice is the mechanism for this, but what is practice? How does it work? Why does it work? Just as Amitābha Buddha has four levels, Dōhan suggests, so, too, does the name. While he does not explicitly present a "fourfold secret explication" of this sacred mantra, Dōhan goes into considerable detail examining the name from multiple perspectives. It is thus possible to extrapolate what a fourfold secret explication of the name might look like, based on his presentation of Amitābha Buddha, and indeed Dōhan recommends that the reader do exactly that.

Based on my interpretation of Dōhan's fourfold secret explication of Amitābha, I propose the following secret explication:

- Level 1. According to the major Pure Land sutras, the *Sukhāvatīvyūha-sūtra,* the *Contemplation Sutra,* and so on, *buddhānusmṛti* is the recitation of the name of Amitābha Buddha. On its surface, this is a practice that delivers you to the Pure Land after death—period. Following this hypothetical interpretation, according to the vows of Dharmākara Bodhisattva/Amitābha Buddha, if one calls upon this buddha *even just* ten times (which can mean fewer than that or none), at the moment of death one will be greeted by Amitābha Buddha and a retinue of bodhisattvas, attain rebirth in Sukhāvatī, and progress quickly along the bodhisattva path. This view, simply stated, holds that if you say the name of the Buddha, you will go to Sukhāvatī.

- Level 2. According to this view, which I have suggested could be called an introductory Shingon view, the holy name is actually a mantra and should be understood within the particular context of the tantric systems grounded in mandalic contemplation and mantric recitation and/or the broader context of the normative Mahayana incantatory culture of spells, dhāraṇī, mantra, and more. This level may perhaps be conceived of as the level of ritual application of the Pure Land mythos that transforms the mechanistic view of practice. The name of Buddha is a vehicle for the activation of the mystery of speech, which points to the nonduality of enlightened buddhas and benighted beings. Rather than performing a practice that necessarily *leads one to* awakening, this practice actually reveals the unity of practice and attainment: path and goal are always-already one.
- Level 3. At this level we move deeper into Esoteric Buddhist thought. According to this view, the name is the "breath of life" of all beings united in the ultimate buddha reality, the dharmakāya. Correctly understood, *buddhānusmṛti* is the compassionate activity of ultimate reality in the form of Amitābha Buddha, working through/as beings in the world: infinite beings = infinite lives = "Infinite Life," Amitāyus. This perspective recognizes the vocal recitation as breath, wind, or *ki* (Ch. *qi*; breath, wind, energy, life). As the vital activity of universal compassion, *buddhānusmṛti* is therefore a practice in which all beings are always-already engaged.
- Level 4. In this view the symbolic, subjective, and interpretive views of the first three levels are inscribed within the very body/mind of sentient beings. *Buddhānusmṛti* is then an expression of that which unifies dualities and opposites, serving as the site for realizing and embodying the equanimity of body and mind, "spirit" and matter, buddhas and beings, Sukhāvatī and this world, nirvana and samsara. From this perspective, even the "shallow" view presented in level one may be understood to have real efficacy for those who subscribe to that particular perspective. It may not be the entire picture, but it is nonetheless part of a greater whole.

Exploring the Name of Buddha

Dōhan begins his examination of *buddhānusmṛti* with the thought of Jippan, who, like Saisen and Kakuban, trained in the Ninnaji lineage, which is noteworthy for its dual emphasis on Kūkai studies and ritual practice focusing on Amitābha Buddha. Jippan also trained in various other traditions and seems to have emphasized Tendai thought and the precepts. Dōhan quotes a long passage from Jippan's *Byōchū shugyōki*.[2] It is interesting to note that the *Himitsu nenbutsu shō* practically begins and ends with texts for deathbed practice. According to Jippan, all sound is rooted in the fundamental mantra of the dharmakāya: the letter A, which signifies not only the original source of all sound and thus all things but also the śūnyatā of all Dharmas and the fundamental nonarising of Buddha-nature. Dharmas, the constituent elements of mental and physical reality, are empty of any inherent qualities. They are impermanent, composite, context bound, and dependent on causes and conditions. Furthermore, causes and conditions are also impermanent, composite, context-bound, and dependent on yet other causes and conditions, and so on, and so on. Ultimately, all Dharmas, the "atoms" that compose phenomena, are empty of inherent existence.

That Buddha-nature is nonarising means that awakening is not some tangible "thing" that one lacks or that can be attained somewhere else. Buddhahood, or inherent Buddha-nature, is always-already present; in some sense it is that which is fundamentally present. Like śūnyatā—or, perhaps, *as* śūnyatā?—Buddha-nature is a fundamental dimension of being itself. Ultimate reality is equated with śūnyatā, which the practitioner apprehends from meditation on conditioned arising. In this way both śūnyatā and Buddha-nature are one, and śūnyatā and the mundane ordinary reality of the physical world are also ultimately one. Buddha reality is what there is.

For Jippan the important point here is that this observation extends to include those afflictions that beings imagine to be insurmountable obstacles to their awakening. In other words, in all cases that which seems to keep beings bound to samsara, as well as the virtues to which beings aspire—Sukhāvatī, Amitābha Buddha, and so on—are all fundamentally śūnyatā. This truth destroys fixed notions about suffering, the body, the self, the nature of defilement, afflictions, and "sin"; thus, according to Jippan, *buddhānusmṛti* is the ambrosia that liberates beings from cyclic suffering.[3] In this context, the holy name of Amitābha Buddha is a technology for liberation because it unfolds like a lotus blossom, revealing multiple levels of reality and truth ordinarily beyond our purview.

Next, Dōhan continues this line of thought and engages in his first act of destabilizing hierarchies, positing what we may consider to be the central point of the text as a whole: "For the mantra practitioner, it is precisely the shallow [understanding] that penetrates [and is not separate from] the most profound secret, and it is precisely the easy [practice] that immediately attains [and is not separate from] awakening."[4]

In the *Himitsu nenbutsu shō,* Dōhan consults and critically assesses diverse perspectives on *buddhānusmṛti,* walking a fine line between universalism and particularity of perspectives. Even the shallow and abbreviated interpretation of *buddhānusmṛti,* exactly as it is, constitutes a fully realized path to awakening. The shallow penetrates the most profound secret. The "easy" practice reveals the highest attainment. Underlying these diverse expressions of Buddhist practice is the fundamental truth that buddhas and beings are not separate. Samsara and nirvana are but two perspectives on one reality. For those with eyes to see and ears to hear, even simple practices and sincere acts of faith may reveal the abundance that is always-already present.

Dōhan seems to anticipate readers' assumption that "the point" is that there is a shallow or ordinary *buddhānusmṛti* counterposed with the deeper, extraordinary, secret *buddhānusmṛti.* Indeed, there are times when Dōhan, like Kakuban before him, critiques those who cling to limited and limiting perspectives, but he does not necessarily deny the viability or validity of those approaches. Rather, he sees them as expressions of both the inherent inclination toward buddha reality and the activity of buddha reality that actively reaches out to aid beings.

Amida santai setsu

Beginning with the above-mentioned passage quoting Jippan and throughout the first fascicle in particular, Dōhan employs a tripartite heuristic device, the *Amida santai setsu* (explanation of the three truths through *A-MI-TA*), to explore the various shades of meaning contained within the three character mantra *A-MI-TA.* For example,

> *A* is nonarising as the middle path.
> *MI* is self-nature as perfect freedom.
> *TA* is reality itself as awakening.[5]

The three letters *A-MI-TA* are thus imbued with multifarious interpretive layers, allowing the name itself to become a virtually kaleidoscopic exegetical tool. In particular, *A-MI-TA* is often used to explain the three truths articulated by Zhiyi. This expands on the Mahayana Buddhist postulate that śūnyatā, the ultimate truth, and the conventional reality within which ordinary beings operate are actually nondual. For Zhiyi, the perspective from which both realities may be experienced simultaneously is the "middle"; thus, śūnyatā, conventional reality, and the middle are understood as the "three truths." The insights arising from the three truths are harnessed through the three syllables *A-MI-TA* to address the complex relationship between the sublime *buddhakṣetra* Sukhāvatī and our decadent human world or between enlightened buddhas and ignorant sentient beings: Are they two? Are they one? Are they both? Are they neither?

Dōhan employs this exegetical tool to encompass the whole of the Buddhist tradition, as well as the entire universe. Drawing from Kūkai, Dōhan notes that just as a single syllable may contain innumerable meanings, the three-syllable mantra is like infinity times infinity. Drawing from Kakuban, Dōhan observes that one should not simply adopt the shallow view. One must also understand that because all sounds are "mantra," the very speech of ultimate reality, *buddhānusmṛti* is an even more potent technology because it comprises several syllables and is infinite mantras simultaneously.[6]

Three Divisions of the Mandala: Buddha, Vajra, Lotus

Throughout the *Himitsu nenbutsu shō,* Dōhan references popular notions that associate Amitābha Buddha with the Womb Realm mandala, also known as the Womb of Great Compassion mandala, the lotus division of the mandala, and so on. The center of the Womb Realm mandala is a large lotus blossom with eight petals and a central dais on which sit five buddhas and four bodhisattvas (see table 1).

Northeast Maitreya Bodhisattva 彌勒菩薩	East Ratnaketu Tathāgata 寶幢如來	Southeast Samantabhadra Bodhisattva 普賢菩薩
North Divyadundubhimeghanirghoṣa Tathāgata 天鼓雷音如來	Center Mahāvairocana Tathāgata 大日如來	South Saṃkusumitarāja Tathāgata 開敷華王如來
Northwest Avalokiteśvara Bodhisattva 觀自在菩薩	West Amitāyus Tathāgata 無量壽佛	Southwest Mañjuśrī Bodhisattva 文殊菩薩

The mandala is divided into three main divisions of buddha, lotus, and vajra and thirteen subdivisions, which will be explored below. The buddha division comprises the buddhas and bodhisattvas sitting on the eight-petal lotus blossom. The lotus division is situated to the north of the Buddha division and is associated with Avalokiteśvara Bodhisattva (and/as Amitābha Buddha, according to Dōhan). The vajra division is to the south of the Buddha division and is associated with Vajrasattva Bodhisattva, Mahāvairocana Tathāgata's interlocutor.[7] Dōhan uses the three syllables of the *nenbutsu* to encompass the mandala, assigning each division to one syllable:

> *A,* as the Buddha division 佛部, signifies the eternal middle way.
>
> *MI,* as the vajra division 金剛部, signifies the ungraspable nature of self that, when transcended, leads to the knowledge that sentient beings and Dharmas are inherently empty.
>
> *TA,* as the lotus division 蓮華部, signifies the ungraspable nature of purity, of true reality.[8]
>
> Furthermore,
>
> *A* (Buddha), as ultimate reality, signifies the fundamental union of wisdom and principle.
>
> *MI* (Vajra) is the wisdom that is indestructible, like a *vajra.*
>
> *TA* (Lotus) is the principle (ultimate reality) that is the purity of one's own nature.[9]
>
> Again,
>
> *A* (Buddha) is the Buddha, signifying the unity of being (existence) and śūnyatā (emptiness/nothingness) as the middle way.
>
> *MI* (Vajra) is the wisdom that pervades being as śūnyatā itself, *as* the element of consciousness.
>
> *TA* (Lotus) is the principle that pervades being *as* the other five elements.[10]

Three Truths: Emptiness, Provisional Reality, Middle

Next, Dōhan examines *A-MI-TA* as embodying the three truths of śūnyatā, provisional reality, and the middle. Even as Dōhan references Zhiyi and various Chinese Tiantai and Japanese Tendai masters, he establishes a (provisional) polemic that distinguishes between the three truths as understood within purportedly Exoteric Tendai and Esoteric Buddhism. Of course, Tendai Buddhism, as such, comprised diverse competing lineages on and around Hieizan and Onjōji, including many important esoteric lineages as well. Therefore, this seeming ambivalence likely stems from Dōhan's efforts to contribute to the ongoing conversation around Esoteric Buddhism. Dōhan suggests that the Exoteric, or standard, view of the three truths is as follows:

> *A*—śūnyatā;
> *MI*—provisional reality;
> *TA*—the middle.

However, Dōhan presents an alternate Esoteric reading:

> *A*—the middle;
> *MI*—śūnyatā;
> *TA*—being/provisional reality.

Dōhan justifies this interpretation by suggesting that *A-MI-TA* as a vehicle for articulating the three truths has both "inner" and "outer" meanings. The Exoteric approach may mistakenly take the outer meaning of the text as the final word, but in fact each letter has within it multiple inner meanings as well.[11]

> *A*—The outer meaning corresponds to śūnyatā (Exoteric), while the inner meaning corresponds to the middle, the synthesis of śūnyatā and provisional reality (Esoteric). This is arguably a "higher" truth.
>
> *MI*—The outer meaning corresponds to provisional reality (Exoteric), while the inner meaning corresponds to śūnyatā (Esoteric).
>
> *TA*—The outer meaning corresponds to the middle (Exoteric), while the inner meaning corresponds to being, or provisional reality (Esoteric).

I suggest that Dōhan here reveals a synopsis of his understanding of the subtleties of the Buddhist path. At several points throughout the text, Dōhan inverts the letters *A-MI-TA*, placing special emphasis on *TA;* in other cases he inverts awakening and delusion, this world and Sukhāvatī, and ordinary beings and the Buddha to make the case that from the starting point—the perspective of ordinary deluded beings stuck in samsara—awakening is always-already present and fully embodied. Thus, the "highest" truth of the middle and the "lowest" truth of provisional reality simultaneously frame the starting point, the process of Buddhist practice, and the result as interconnected.

In order to help establish consistency across these various inspired correspondences, Dōhan makes connections between the Exoteric understanding of *TA* as interdependence and "initial enlightenment" and the Esoteric understanding of *TA* that relates it to "being" and "original enlightenment." The Exoteric perspective is rooted in the view held by initial enlightenment, whereas the Esoteric view is rooted in original enlightenment; practitioners of mantra hold the latter view.[12]

Three Bodies: Dharmakāya, Saṃbhogakāya, Nirmāṇakāya

One of the teachings that scholars associate with Kūkai and the Shingon tradition is *hosshin seppō* 法身說法, the idea that the Esoteric teachings originate not with Śākyamuni but with Mahāvairocana, an anthropomorphized representation of dharmakāya, "ultimate reality." All speech is the sound of dharmakāya, all bodies are forms of dharmakāya, and all mentation is the mind of dharmakāya. This "monistic" perspective was initially seen as controversial because normative Mahayana scripture tends to portray dharmakāya as ineffable and beyond speech, form, and characteristics. Kūkai famously argued that dharmakāya actively employs speech and images to teach beings as appropriate.

Esoteric Buddhist thinkers on Hieizan in particular systematized the view that the dharmakāya may take on many different forms, including visionary reward bodies (saṃbhogakāya), such as Amitābha Buddha or the Medicine Buddha, or corporeal emanation bodies (nirmāṇakāya), such as Śākyamuni Buddha. According to this view, the Exoteric texts emanate from Śākyamuni Buddha, an accommodated form, while the Esoteric texts emanate directly from ultimate reality itself. Ultimately, all of these buddhas are really aspects of one buddha reality. This three bodies (trikāya) scheme for organizing the diversity and unity of Buddhism has been elaborated on and revised throughout East Asian Buddhist history. In the *Himitsu nenbutsu shō,* Dōhan consistently employs the standard formulation outlined here:

The three letters *A-MI-TA* encompass and correspond to the trifold body of buddha reality:

> *A* as nirmāṇakāya signifies the buddha division of the mandala, as well as the unity of meditation/wisdom, principle/wisdom, and fundamental nonarising.
>
> *MI* as saṃbhogakāya signifies the vajra division of the mandala, as well as insight (wisdom) into the śūnyatā of beings and Dharmas. Thus wisdom and śūnyatā are one.
>
> *TA* as dharmakāya signifies the lotus division of the mandala, as well as the inherent purity of the fundamental self (non-self), thusness/fundamental reality, and ultimately signifies one's connection with the dharmakāya.

Here we see another interesting reversal. One might expect that *A*, commonly associated with Mahāvairocana, śūnyatā, and more, would correspond to the dharmakāya. However, Dōhan subverts the reader's expectations with this inversion (presented as *TA-MI-A* in the text), associating the dharmakāya with *TA*, the "lowest" of the three. This is another instance in which Dōhan presents the lowest as the highest—a way of presenting ideas that seems intended to impart the notion that even the shallow view, the "exoteric" teaching, may itself be a mode for accessing the highest form of awakening. This text is especially interesting for the study of Esoteric Buddhism because of the way in which Dōhan plays upon readers' expectations (Esoteric = best/highest) by revealing the value inherent in even "Exoteric" approaches to Buddhism.[13]

Three Points: Principle, Wisdom, Phenomena

One of the main ideas associated with Dōhan's thought, the "three points," derives from his teacher Jōhen of Zenrinji. The three points refer to the Sanskrit letter *I*, which is rendered in the Siddham script as three circles in a triangular shape; thus, it is three-sided or has three points. This letter is taken to be an expression of nonduality: all three points are interconnected, but depending on one's perspective, only two line up in view. Dōhan/Jōhen, drawing from the *Nirvana Sutra* and the East Asian Esoteric tradition, identify the three points with principle 理, or ultimate reality; the wisdom 智 that is required to understand principle; and the phenomenal world 事, which appears separate from principle from the perspective of ordinary beings when in fact the three are unified. The perspective promoted by Dōhan/Jōhen sees these "three" as ultimately one, which corresponds to *A-MI-TA* in the following way:

> A as dharmakāya is the principle that permeates all things.
> *MI* as saṃbhogakāya is the wisdom that is indestructible like a *vajra*.
> *TA* as nirmāṇakāya is the liberation through awakening to the true nature of phenomena.[14]

Three Mysteries: Body, Speech, Mind

The "three mysteries" concept is another major feature of Esoteric Buddhist thought and practice, to the degree that some scholars regard this idea as the fundamental teaching that distinguishes Esoteric Buddhism as a distinct tradition. Normally, the body, speech, and mind are understood to be the sites of karmic production. Beings commit bodily actions, speech acts, and mental acts (thoughts) while mired in samsara and afflicted by the three poisons of greed, hatred, and ignorance. In Esoteric Buddhism, the bodies, speech, and minds of ordinary beings are revealed as abiding in a nondual relationship with ultimate reality through cultivation of the three mysteries. Through Esoteric practice and empowerment, these sites of karmic production become the three mysteries. Practicing the yoga of the three mysteries, one realizes that the dharmakāya and suffering beings are fundamentally one. Referring back to the three divisions of the Womb Realm mandala, Dōhan establishes connections between *A-MI-TA* and the three mysteries:

> *A* as the buddha division of the mandala is the mystery of body.
> *MI* as the vajra division of the mandala is the mystery of mind.
> *TA* as the lotus division of the mandala is the mystery of speech.

Notice that *TA*, the "lowest" of the three, is associated with speech. The importance of this association was established in chapter 7: it is through speech that one encounters the Dharma and through speech that Amitābha Buddha acts in the world, guiding beings to awakening. Amitābha embodies both as the act of speech itself and as the breath of life that renders all speech and practice possible.[15]

Three Jewels: Buddha, Dharma, Sangha

Dōhan further associates *A-MI-TA* with the well-known idea of the Three Jewels of Buddhism in his exploration of the many layers of the three mysteries.

> *A* as the mystery of body signifies the Buddha.
> *MI* as the mystery of mind signifies sangha.
> *TA* as the mystery of speech signifies Dharma.

Given this configuration, one may intuit an Exoteric view based on well-established hierarchies: the Buddha is mind, Dharma is speech, and sangha is body. However, here again Dōhan employs a kind of reversal of the usual or expected configuration, associating sangha with mind and the Buddha with body. This may also serve to illustrate the notion that even provisional corporeal reality is an aspect of buddha reality. Also, as *TA* is (semicovertly) associated with Amitābha Buddha, the association of speech with the Dharma illustrates the importance of the Dharma as that which liberates beings from suffering.[16]

Three Truths and Three Wisdoms: Unimpeded Wisdom, All Wisdom, Spontaneously Arising Wisdom

Next, Dōhan returns to the *Amida santai setsu* and references unimpeded wisdom, all wisdom, spontaneously arising wisdom,[17] and commonly held notions about the inherent nature of awakening. What scholars commonly call *hongaku* thought is based on the notion that all beings are always-already, just as they are—"warts and all"—fully awakened. This controversial idea is typically associated with the Tendai school; however, like Esoteric Buddhism, *hongaku* thought permeated medieval Japanese Buddhism. Here Dōhan connects *A-MI-TA* with the three truths, the three forms of wisdom, and the synthesis of original awakening and initial awakening.

> *A*, as the truth of the "middle," signifies unimpeded wisdom 無礙智, which reveals that initial and original enlightenment are nondual.
>
> *MI*, as the truth of śūnyatā, signifies all wisdom 一切智 or omniscience, which is associated with the initial realization of awakening.
>
> *TA*, as the truth of being, of provisional reality, signifies the spontaneously arising wisdom 自然智, which is associated with original awakening.

Three Organs of Speech and Three Divisions of the Mandala: Throat, Tongue, Lips

According to the nondualist Mahayana philosophy from which Kūkai drew, nirvana and samsara, buddhas and beings, path and destination, practice and attainment, and awakening and delusion are all understood to be ultimately nondual. The corporeality of awakening, the physical unity of buddhas and beings as seen from the perspective of the three mysteries, opens the door for deeper engagement with the body itself as a locus for attainment. At various points in the *Himitsu nenbutsu shō,* Dōhan argues that all buddhas, bodhisattvas, gods, and virtues of the path are ultimately present within the practitioner's own body. In one section he identifies the three divisions of the mandala and the three syllables *A-MI-TA* with the organs of speech, suggesting that Amitābha Buddha is present not only in/as the practice of vocal *buddhānusmṛti* but also within the organs of speech that make it possible to chant:

> *A* as the buddha division of the mandala is the throat.
> *MI* as the vajra division of the mandala is the lips.
> *TA* as the lotus division of the mandala is the tongue.

Dōhan also notes that this arrangement means that *A-MI-TA* is in fact Mahāvairocana Tathāgata of the Vajra Realm mandala, thus establishing a nondual connection between the Womb Realm and the Vajra Realm mandalas.[18] Going deeper still, Dōhan examines the process of speech production and the beginning, middle, and end of the vocalization of *A-MI-TA:*

> *A* is the "beginning," the origin of the speech act in the throat.
> *TA* is the "middle," as the tongue touches the roof of the mouth, between *A* and the final syllable, *MI.*
> *MI* is the "end," as the lips close.

Dōhan describes the initial act of speech *A,* moving forward from the throat to the mouth and manifesting as *MI,* just as Amitābha Buddha manifests in the world as Avalokiteśvara Bodhisattva and the opening of the heart-lotus of all beings. *MI* then returns to the middle of the mouth (or the end of the mantra) as *TA* and the realization of one's inherently awakened mind.[19] Uttering the *A-MI-TA* mantra progresses from inner to outer and then from outer to inner. Dōhan does not spell this out explicitly, but here he seems to refer to the dialogic resolution of the relationship between practice and awakening, the give-and-take of progress along the path. If awakening is inherent, how do we understand practice? This is a question with which the Zen tradition has long struggled, and here, too, we see the resolution of two seemingly contradictory aspects of medieval Japanese religion: practice is necessary yet awakening is inherent; awakening is inherent and thus practice is necessary.

Three Mystery Bodies 三秘密身: Letter 字, Mudra 印, Form 形

A-MI-TA may also be said to correspond to the three mystery bodies, which are described in the *Mahāvairocana-sūtra:* "All objects of devotion possess a threefold body: letter, mudra, and form."[20] In the text these three are referred to as the threefold body 三種身. As discussed in Jōhen's *Benkenmitsu nikyōron tekagami shō* 弁顕密二教論手鏡鈔, a text recorded by Dōhan, the threefold body also corresponds to the three points described above. Dōhan has already discussed the dual mandala, the Womb Realm and the Vajra Realm, but these two views of ultimate reality may be presented in different forms. The Womb and the Vajra Realm mandalas with which the reader is most likely familiar correspond to the first of four methods for depicting ultimate reality in mandalic form:

1. The *mahā* maṇḍala 大曼荼羅 presents ultimate reality in the form of anthropomorphic deities.
2. The *samaya* maṇḍala 三昧耶曼荼羅 presents ultimate reality in the form of implements and tools associated with each deity and the deity's vows.
3. The *dharma* maṇḍala 法曼荼羅 presents ultimate reality in the form of the *bīja,* the Sanskrit seed syllables associated with each deity.
4. The *karma* maṇḍala 羯磨曼荼羅 depicts the deities in question in the form of three-dimensional images.

Letter, mudra, and form correspond to items 2–4. Letter signifies the *bīja* mandala, or dharma maṇḍala; mudra signifies the *samaya* maṇḍala; form signifies the karma maṇḍala. These three are also understood to correspond to the three buddha bodies mentioned above.

A—*bīja*—dharmakāya.
MI—*samaya*—saṃbhogakāya.
TA—*karma* (form of the object of devotion)—nirmāṇakāya.

In this way, *A-MI-TA* expands to encompass not only the dual mandalas but all four forms that the dual mandalas may take, as well as the three bodies of buddha.[21]

Three Honored Ones of Sukhāvatī: *Honji suijaku* and Reverse *Honji suijaku*

Employing *A-MI-TA* to explore the relationship between Amitābha Buddha, Avalokiteśvara Bodhisattva, and Mahāsthāmaprāpta Bodhisattva, Dōhan presents the relationship of the three honored ones as follows, noting their correspondences with the three buddha bodies:

A (dharmakāya) is Amitābha Buddha.
MI (saṃbhogakāya) is Avalokiteśvara Bodhisattva.
TA (nirmāṇakāya) is Mahāsthāmaprāpta Bodhisattva.

However, this presentation is merely the setup to the punch line that the Three Revered Ones are not in fact separate from one another. Dōhan suggests that if Amitābha is likened to a bird, then Avalokiteśvara and Mahāsthāmaprāpta are the bird's two wings—they function together to guide beings to Sukhāvatī.[22]

In addition, Dōhan takes this nondual relationship between the one buddha and the two bodhisattvas as an expression of the doctrine of *honji suijaku* (fundamental ground and trace manifestation). As has been explored elsewhere, one of the defining characteristics of Japanese Buddhism is the frequency with which the identities of buddhas, bodhisattvas, and the various Indian, Chinese, Korean, and Japanese gods adopted into the tradition blend into one another. In many cases the god (kami) of a local Japanese shrine would be revealed as the manifestation of an Indian buddha. Throughout the medieval period, a form of "reverse" *honji suijaku* developed in Shintō lineages, in which an Indian buddha might be revealed as the trace manifestation of a local Japanese kami, thus inverting the normative hierarchy. Here Dōhan presents both *honji suijaku* and reverse *honji suijaku* to describe the nondual relationship between these Three Honored Ones of the Pure Land:

> *A*—Amitābha is the source from which the two bodhisattvas originate.
> *MI-TA*—Avalokiteśvara and Mahāsthāmaprāpta are trace manifestations of the one buddha, Amitābha.

Next, in the reverse configuration:

> *MI-TA*—Avalokiteśvara and Mahāsthāmaprāpta are the original ground from which Amitābha Buddha arises.
> *A*—Amitābha Buddha is thus a trace manifestation of the two bodhisattvas.

These three are then likened to the three points (principle, wisdom, phenomena): different yet one. Sentient beings may perceive ultimate reality (principle) as distinct from phenomena and the wisdom that penetrates through the veil of phenomena to perceive principle, but ultimately they are all contiguous and undifferentiated.[23]

Moreover, assumptions about the cause-and-effect relationship between practice and attainment are also implied here. "Cause" and "effect" have a more complicated relationship than commonly supposed, arising together as features of a contiguous unified reality. In some cases, practice may be described as a mechanistic or gradual process through which deluded beings progress to become enlightened beings. However, nondualist soteriologies may conflate path and goal, practice and attainment, and so on. Furthermore, Dōhan's hierarchical inversion, which prioritizes the "lowest" over the "highest," may serve to illustrate his understanding of the problem of religious diversity and the differing capacities of beings. It seems that according to Dōhan, while perspectives on the nature of Sukhāvatī, the role and agency of Amitābha Buddha in the context of practice, and the role of practice itself on the path to awakening may vary, ultimately, all beings, whether high or low, are actively guided to Sukhāvatī.

Three Poisons: Greed, Anger, Delusion

If practice and attainment can be recognized as nondual, what about the relationship between the afflictions and the inherently enlightened mind? Here, too, Dōhan references a well-established Mahayana nondualist philosophical precedent that conflates, or perhaps plays into, the delicate tension between delusion and awakening. Dōhan first considers the "three poisons" and their correspondence to *A-MI-TA:*

> *A* (buddha): Delusion may be taken to mean not grasping things correctly, and therefore is associated with the nongrasping of nonduality.
>
> *MI* (vajra): Anger may be taken to signify the act of rejecting or doing away with phenomena. It may therefore be associated with the wisdom of śūnyatā that rejects the notion of *svabhāva.*
>
> *TA* (lotus): Greed may be taken to mean grasping onto things, or a fixation on being. It may therefore be associated with the Buddha's compassion, always "grasping" onto beings (i.e., never abandoning them) and principle.[24]

Delusion, properly understood, or perhaps understood from the perspective of an enlightened buddha, is in fact always-already awakening. There is no delusion apart from awakening and no awakening apart from delusion. To explain why this is the case, Dōhan here establishes a correspondence between *A-MI-TA* and delusion, anger, and greed. *A,* delusion, in essence, is the inability to grasp the truth. This can be likened to the concept of equanimity or nonduality, in which one does not grasp onto things. Therefore, nonduality may be taken as the root of that which expresses itself as delusion. Fully cultivated or matured, even this affliction, this "poison," is revealed to naturally lead to the realization of nonduality. *MI,* anger, also translated as "hatred," is in essence the rejection of things; the inclination to reject is thus linked to the realization of śūnyatā in that when one sees the śūnyatā of all things, the tendency to construct an unchanging inherent essence, or *svabhāva,* does not arise. A rejection of or an aversion toward things, in anger or hatred, is in other words an expression of a deeper inclination to move beyond clinging to (imaginary) essences. *TA,* greed, means clinging, grasping, not differentiating between that which is good and that which is bad. Therefore, greedy clinging may point toward the compassionate activity of buddha reality, always "grasping" beings and never abandoning them regardless of their capacities, inclinations, or afflictions. The three poisons are thus reimagined as their opposites.

Three Evils: Afflictions, Karma, Suffering

Dōhan continues his exploration of the connection between *A-MI-TA* and the fundamental flaws of the human condition:

> *A* as dharmakāya is the [true nature of the] path of suffering.
> *MI* as wisdom is the [true nature of the] path of the afflictions.
> *TA* as liberation is the [true nature of the] path of karma.

"Samsara is nirvana" is an oft-repeated notion in textbook presentations of Mahayana Buddhism, and this construction appears frequently in East Asian Buddhist texts.[25] What does it actually mean? Here it seems that Dōhan is promoting the idea that even as sentient beings course through samsara—afflicted by the consequences of their negative karma and acquiring afflictions through negative actions of the body, speech, and mind, all of which lead to more and more suffering—buddha reality is in fact always active behind the scenes, guiding them to acquire wisdom and realize their inherently enlightened nature and potential. Dōhan notes that this view is the same as that in Exoteric Tendai, and it may derive in some sense from the "eternal Śākyamuni" concept explored in the *Lotus Sutra.* According to Dōhan, however, the Tendai view tends to focus on doctrine and phenomena, whereas the Esoteric view focuses on the breath/*ki,* the essence, thus revealing the true meaning.

As the compassionate activity of ultimate reality working through the very body/mind of all sentient beings, *A-MI-TA* pervades both sentient and nonsentient existence. It is present in the six elements, the eternal yoga of the five elements that compose the corporeal world, and the consciousness that permeates the world. It is expressed through the three mysteries, the sites of karmic production in beings that abides in a nondual relationship with buddha reality. It constitutes the body itself (manifesting as the elements of earth, water, and fire), our capacity for speech (manifesting as the element of wind), and the mind (manifesting as the element of consciousness).[26] Wind, the "vital breath," is life and consciousness.[27] *A-MI-TA* pervades all things: there is nothing that is not *A-MI-TA,* the three mysteries of the dharmakāya.

The Five-Syllable Name: *NAMO-A-MI-TA-BU*

Following his exploration of the three-syllable nembutsu *A-MI-TA,* said to be an expression of the Womb Realm mandala, Dōhan then considers the five- (or sometimes six-) syllable version of the name of Amitābha Buddha, which he suggests is an expression of the Vajra Realm mandala. In this section Dōhan presents a syllable wheel commonly used in mantra visualization practices in deity yoga. This syllable wheel contains a rendering of the Japanese pronunciation of the name in the Siddhaṃ script rendering of the name of Amitābha: *NAMO-A-MI-TA-BU.* Of course, this construction contains within it *A-MI-TA.* Dōhan thus eventually uses this connection to discuss the nonduality of the Womb and Vajra mandalas. After establishing connections between *NAMO-A-MI-TA-BU* and a long list of groups of five—five buddhas, five wisdoms, and so on—the overlap with the three-syllable name allows Dōhan to intuit even more correspondences.

According to Dōhan, the five buddhas and five wisdoms of the mandala produce all buddhas and all wisdoms, and in all cases they are expressions, aspects, or dimensions of dharmakāya.[28]

	TA (4)	
MI (3)	*NAMO* (1)	*BU* (5)
	A (2)	

NAMO is situated in the central dais, corresponding to Mahāvairocana Buddha. The form of enlightening wisdom associated with Mahāvairocana is the wisdom of the fundamental nature of the universe, *dharmadhātu-svabhāva-jñāna* 法界體性智, which perceives the true nature of all Dharmas that constitute the mental and physical realities of all beings and worlds in the Mahayana multiverse, thus signifying the boundless nature of dharmakāya in/as all Dharmas. This form of wisdom is connected to the ninth consciousness (*amalavijñāna* 阿摩羅識), the pure consciousness, also called the undefiled consciousness, buddha consciousness, or the consciousness of ultimate reality. It is also commonly connected with the Buddha division of the Vajra Realm mandala and signifies the principle and wisdom that ordinary beings do not yet grasp but which is revealed upon awakening.

Further expanding upon the meaning of *NAMO*, Dōhan notes that though we tend to think that all sutras begin with the famous words "Thus have I heard" (*evaṃ mayā śrūtaṃ* 如是我聞), in fact most sutra texts begin with the Sanskrit words *Oṃ Namaḥ*. Therefore, *NAMO* takes the center position, just as would *Oṃ* in other syllable wheel contemplations. Moreover, *NAMO* is the act of refuge itself, also translated as *kimyō* 歸命, which, when rendering the two Chinese characters separately, literally means "return to life." This observation fits perfectly with Dōhan's position that Amitābha/Amitāyus Buddha, as "Infinite Life," is the eternally abiding compassionate activity of dharmakāya as the vital life force of all beings. To take refuge in Amitābha/dharmakāya is thus to take refuge in the ultimate source of all life—to "return to life." This central position of *NAMO* also signifies principle or ultimate reality.[29]

The letter *A* is positioned in the eastern quarter (*bottom of mandala/diagram*) and is associated with Akṣobhya Buddha. The form of wisdom associated with Akṣobhya is the wisdom that is like a great round mirror, *ādarśa-jñāna* 大圓鏡智. This wisdom accurately and completely reflects all things as they truly are, signifying the originally pure nature of the mind. This wisdom results from the purification of the eighth consciousness (*ālayavijñāna* 阿賴耶識), the fundamental consciousness of beings in which karmic seeds take root, leading to continuity between lives and experience. This wisdom is connected with the vajra division of the mandala and signifies the fundamental nature of the mind that even though mired in samsara is ever able to destroy the afflictions. Dōhan also states that *A* may signify the act of giving rise to *bodhicitta*.[30]

The syllable *MI* is positioned in the southern quarter (*left*) and is associated with Ratnasaṃbhava Buddha 寶生佛. The form of wisdom associated with this buddha is the wisdom of equanimity (Skt. *samatā-jñāna* 平等性智), which is able to see things as fundamentally equal and unified. This form of wisdom arises from the purification of the seventh consciousness (*manas-vijñāna* 末那識), the consciousness that builds upon the consolidated consciousness of the sixth consciousness. It is due to the seventh consciousness that beings give rise to the concept of a self. This wisdom is associated with the ratna division 寶部 of the mandala, which signifies the boundless merit of the buddhas. Dōhan elaborates that since *MI* is associated with the constructed self it may also be seen as the unity of *NAMO-A*, center and east, meaning the unification of principle and wisdom in the form of the enlightened being.[31]

The syllable *TA* is positioned in the western quarter (*top*) and is associated with Amitābha Buddha. As we have previously seen, Dōhan placed special emphasis on the syllable *TA* in his discussion of the three-syllable *nenbutsu*. The form of wisdom associated with Amitābha is the wisdom of subtle discernment (Skt. *pratyaveksanā-jñāna* 妙觀察智), a form of wisdom that is able to clearly distinguish between things and see them as they truly are. This wisdom is said to arise through the purification of the sixth consciousness (*mano-vijñāna* 意識), which gathers the sensory input arising from the five consciousnesses (eyes, ears, nose, tongue, body). This wisdom is associated with the lotus division of the mandala, signifying the inherently pure nature of all beings that remains pure and bright even while mired in samsara.[32] The correspondence between Amitābha, the lotus division, and the inherent purity of all beings is later revealed to have special significance.

The syllable *BU*, an abbreviation of *butsu* (buddha), is placed in the northern quarter (*right*) and is associated with Amoghasiddhi Buddha 不空成就佛 (who is commonly associated with Śākyamuni Buddha). This buddha is associated with the wisdom of unimpeded activity (kṛtyānuṣṭhāna-jñāna 成所作智), which is able to accomplish all things without any hindrance or obstruction. This wisdom arises through purification of the five consciousnesses, the consciousnesses of the so-called five senses: sight, hearing, smell, taste, and touch. The wisdom of unimpeded activity is associated with the karma division 羯磨部 of the mandala, signifying the Buddha's compassion that makes it possible for beings to accomplish all things. Dōhan also suggests that *NAMO* corresponds to the concept of inner realization, while the syllable *BU* corresponds to outer manifestation. Thus, beginning and end are nondual.[33]

Five Wisdoms and Five Elements

As an embodiment of the five buddhas and the five wisdoms (or the source from which these arise), *NAMO-A-MI-TA-BU* unfurls like an opening lotus to reveal a host of other correspondences and associations, further establishing the manifold ways in which the seemingly simple *nenbutsu* may be employed to encompass all things. After introducing the Siddham *nenbutsu* "mandala" and the correspondences between the syllables of the *nenbutsu* and the five buddhas and five wisdoms, Dōhan uses this visualized heuristic device to establish connections between respective Indian and Chinese theories of the five elements.

First, Dōhan mentions a list based on Amoghavajra's view of the connections between the five syllables and the Chinese five elements (*wuxing* 五行)

> *NAMO* (center): earth;
> *A* (east): wood (which takes as its essence void);
> *MI* (south): fire;
> *TA* (west): metal (which takes as its essence wind);
> *BU* (north): water.

It is important to note how *TA*/west, both of which are associated with Amitābha, are connected to the wind element. Amitābha's connection to wind/air/breath/speech is very important, as will be revealed below. The "wind as essence of metal" designation made by Dōhan here anticipates a line of inquiry he pursues to great effect later.[34]

Next, Dōhan draws from Śubhakarasiṃha's presentation of the five elements, which references the four continents around the central great cosmic mountain, Sumeru. Here the direction of progression changes, moving from the center to the north (*center to the right position, then counterclockwise*):

> *NAMO* (center): void;
> *BU* (north): earth;
> *TA* (west): water;
> *MI* (south): fire;
> *A* (east): wind.

According to Dōhan, the five wisdoms permeate the five elements. Higher truths are not distinct from physical reality; they are connected. This extends to all sentient and nonsentient things.[35]

In This Very Body: Five Senses, Five Elements

Furthermore, Dōhan makes connections among the five senses, the five elements, the mystical seed syllables of the five buddhas, and thus the five buddhas. In this way Dōhan again connects the human body to the activity of the buddhas. The five buddhas and the five wisdoms are not simply abstract, otherworldly objects of devotion or contemplation. In line with the principle of "Buddhahood in this very body," each of these is understood to correspond to an element, a sense, and so on, and this aligns with the notion that enlightenment is fundamentally rooted in the body and corporeal human experience.

NAMO invokes Mahāvairocana Tathāgata in the central position of the mandala and the wisdom of the fundamental nature of the universe. The buddha is associated with the corporeal body and the sense of touch. This is because from this central position Mahāvairocana is able to encompass all other elements, senses, and forms of wisdom. This buddha is connected to the spleen and the earth element. His seed syllable is *vaṃ*.[36]

A invokes Akṣobhya Tathāgata in the eastern quarter of the mandala and the great round mirror wisdom that fully reflects all things. Therefore, Akṣobhya is associated with the eye and the faculty of sight. This buddha is also connected to the liver and the wood element, and the seed syllable is *hūṃ*.[37]

MI invokes Ratnasaṃbhava Tathāgata in the southern quarter and the wisdom of equanimity. This form of wisdom is able to see all things as being "of one taste." Therefore, this buddha is associated with the tongue and the faculty of taste. This buddha is also connected with the heart and the fire element, and the seed syllable is *trah*.[38]

TA invokes Amitābha Tathāgata in the western quarter and the wisdom of subtle discernment. This buddha is associated with the element of metal, which takes as its essence the element of wind, as noted above. According to Dōhan, this is because Amitābha is also associated with the nose and the faculty of smell. Amitābha employs the wind to spread the Dharma like a fragrance that permeates in all directions. The association with Amitābha and wind will become more important later, when Amitābha is presented as the buddha who activates the breath of life within beings. It makes sense, therefore, that this buddha is also associated with the element of wind. The seed syllable is *hrīḥ*, which is shared in common with Avalokiteśvara, the bodhisattva who is most closely connected with Amitābha.[39]

BU invokes Amoghasiddhi Tathāgata in the northern quarter and the wisdom of unimpeded activity. This buddha is associated with the water element and the kidneys. This buddha is also associated with the ear and the faculty of hearing and sound. In this way, this buddha manifests the sound of the Dharma, similar to the beating of a heavenly drum or the blowing of a conch shell, and the seed syllable is *aḥ*.[40]

Five Afflictions and the Five Faculties

The buddhas and forms of wisdom correspond not only to facets of the body but also to the various human flaws that arise through sensory contact with the world: ignorance, clinging, and so on. The five senses give rise to desires for the objects of sight, sound, scent, taste, and touch. All of this, in its most basic sense, is simply part of the embodied human experience. However, even as beings mingle in and are seduced by sensory experience, project onto their experiences a whole host of unskillful views, and then act on these views and generate negative karma, their fundamental purity remains unaffected, like that of the lotus blossom rising from the mud. According to Dōhan, this is because all afflictions actually have as their fundamental essence one of the five wisdoms. This goes beyond the popular phrase "no mud, no lotus." The afflictions and the muck of samsara are not simply rank impurity that must be neutralized; rather, even the afflictions have a role to play in the realization of awakening. This goes to the heart of nondualist Mahayana philosophy, and Dōhan takes it even further, asserting that the mud *is* the lotus.

Next, even the five afflictions, which include the three poisons of greed, anger, and ignorance, may be said to reveal the five-syllable mantra:

> *NAMO:* greed;
> *A:* anger;
> *MI:* ignorance;
> *TA:* doubt;
> *BU:* pride.

In a previous discussion, Dōhan established correspondence between the afflictions and the three-syllable mantra letters; here he emphasizes in particular the connection between subtle discerning wisdom and doubt. Again, notice the association with *TA*. Doubt as an affliction prevents beings from grasping the subtle truths of the Dharma. The ability to discern and analyze, however, is not fundamentally separate from this affliction. Similarly, the affliction of pride is associated with the wisdom of unimpeded action. When one has accomplished awakening, is there not a kind of pride in that? Again it is evident that from the perspective of beings seemingly mired in samsara the afflictions of the human condition are sometimes seen merely as expressions of a sinful nature. However, when viewed from the perspective of awakening, the all-encompassing perspective of buddha reality, even the afflictions themselves serve as channels to higher wisdom.[41]

It would seem that this way of thinking about human flaws and the human condition would give one the ability to look with compassion, rather than in judgment, on people who are struggling with anger, greed, or ignorance. Writing in the Kamakura period as an elite scholar-monk who exhibited a clear awareness of and engagement with changing religious trends, Dōhan no doubt was aware of the widespread chaos of early medieval Japan. One of the common issues that thinkers of this time addressed was how to comprehend a chaotic world and consider the obstacles faced by people experiencing violence, poverty, and social instability. How can the eternal and omnipresent compassion of the Buddha extend even to those incapable of practice? Thinking through the corporeal nature of buddha reality was certainly one way to address this issue.

Five Realms: Hell, Hungry Ghosts, Animals, Humans, Gods

The five afflictions lead to rebirth in particular realms of samsara. Even in the three lowest evil paths, which result in rebirth in the realms of hell, hungry ghosts, and animals, one is not apart from buddha reality.

> *A:* anger, hell realms;
> *NAMO:* greed, the realm of hungry ghosts;
> *MI:* ignorance, the animal realm;
> *TA:* doubt, the human realm;
> *BU:* pride, the heavenly realms.

Giving in to anger leads to rebirth in hell. Greed leads to rebirth as a hungry ghost. Willful ignorance leads to rebirth in the animal realm. Doubt leads to rebirth as a human. Pride leads to rebirth in the heavens. Yet these destinies are not eternal, and from this perspective even rebirth in an unfortunate realm may be understood as part of a path toward awakening that is ultimately guided by the manifold forms of wisdom arising from buddha reality. From the perspective of karma-bound beings, samsara appears to be full of pain and suffering. From the perspective of enlightened reality, "samsara is nirvana," and "the afflictions are awakening." Beings must give rise to faith in the buddhas and bodhisattvas working behind the scenes to guide them along the path. The five wisdoms pervade all: there is nothing that is not *NAMO-A-MI-TA-BU.*

Dōhan suggests that while the Exoteric perspective may articulate similar ideas the Esoteric perspective is essential for grasping the true essence of these ideas.[42]

Dual Mandalas and the Three- and Five-Syllable Mantra

As noted above, the Japanese Shingon tradition presents the Womb and Vajra Realm mandalas as nondual, all-inclusive representations of dimensions of ultimate reality. In the same way, as expressions of these mandalas *A-MI-TA* and *NAMO-A-MI-TA-BU* are also nondual. There is a long tradition of establishing correspondences between the two mandalas, and Dōhan weaves these correspondences and associations together in his discussion of these mantras. In particular, he draws heavily from the *Contemplation Sutra,* which some scholars have described as a "proto-tantric" text, based on the complex nature of the visualizations it describes. Furthermore, this text's teaching on the nonduality of the mind and the buddha realized in the mind (through visualization) is clearly an expression of nondual Mahayana philosophy, from which texts identified as tantric also draw. Perhaps Dōhan is simply noticing a "family resemblance" that modern scholars have since also identified.

Dōhan first connects the mantras to the five wisdoms and the three-points doctrine previously discussed:

> *A-MI-TA* = five wisdoms.
> *NAMO-A-MI-TA-BU* = three points (principle, wisdom, phenomena).

Next, Dōhan shows how *A-MI-TA* corresponds to the Womb Realm mandala and the bodies of beings. The thirteen subsections of the Womb Realm mandala correspond to the thirteen meditations of the *Contemplation Sutra. NAMO-A-MI-TA-BU* corresponds to the Vajra Realm mandala and the minds of beings. The nine assemblies of the Vajra Realm mandala correspond to the nine levels of the Pure Land, which are the last three contemplations in addition to the thirteen mentioned above:

The thirteen courts 十三院 of the Womb Realm mandala are as follows:

1. The court of the central dais with eight petals 中臺八葉院 includes the five wisdom buddhas described above and four bodhisattvas: Samantabhadra (southeast), Mañjuśrī (southwest), Avalokiteśvara (northwest), and Maitreya (northeast). The eight-petaled lotus is

said to resemble the segmentation of the valves of the human heart. Thus, this division of the mandala imparts the teachings that the very heart of beings is awakening and contains the buddhas and bodhisattvas of the lotus. This division of the mandala may also reveal the teaching of fundamental nonarising and the letter *A*.

2. The court of the all-pervasive wisdom of the buddhas 遍智院, also known as the buddha mind court 佛心院, is positioned above the central court. It includes the "mother of all buddhas," the embodiment of wisdom itself, Buddhalocanī 佛眼佛母. This division of the mandala reveals the all-pervasive wisdom of the buddhas and the inherent capacity of sentient beings to give rise to that wisdom.
3. The court of Avalokiteśvara Bodhisattva 觀音院, also known as the lotus hand court 蓮華手院, includes Mahāvairocana and thirty-seven other objects of devotion. This division of the mandala is positioned north of the central dais and denotes the compassion of the Buddha reaching out to aid beings.
4. The Vajra hand court 金剛手院, also known as the [Vajra]sattva court 薩埵院, contains thirty-three Esoteric deities led by Vajrasattva Bodhisattva. This bodhisattva, Mahāvairocana Tathāgata's interlocutor in the *Mahāvairocana-sūtra,* is a very important deity in Esoteric traditions across Asia. This division of the mandala is located south of the central dais and reveals the capacity of beings to attain the great wisdom of the buddhas.
5. The court of the *vidyādhara*s 持明院, or "upholder of mantra," is also known as the court of the five great ones 五大院. In addition to Prajñāpāramitā Bodhisattva, this court includes Trailokyavijaya 勝三世明王, Acala, Yamāntaka 大威德明王, and Vajrahūṃkara 降三世明王 and indicates the ability of beings to subdue evil and acquire merit. This court is located below the central dais.
6. The court of Śākyamuni Tathāgata 釋迦院 is located above the court of all-pervasive wisdom. With Śākyamuni as its lord, it contains thirty-nine objects of devotion and indicates the activity of enlightened reality in the form of this buddha who employs wisdom and compassion to guide beings to the other shore of awakening.
7. The court of the removal of obstacles 除盖障院 is located south of the *vidyādhara* court. This court reveals the *vajra*-like wisdom that removes obstacles.
8. The court of Kṣitigarbha Bodhisattva 地藏院, located north of the Avalokiteśvara court, contains nine additional objects of

devotion in addition to Kṣitigarbha. This court indicates the great compassion that works for the salvation of beings in the nine realms of hell, hungry ghosts, animals, Asuras (demigods), humans, gods, *śrāvakas, pratyekabuddhas,* and bodhisattvas.

9. The court of Ākāśagarbha Bodhisattva 虚空藏院, located below the *vidyādhara* court, includes twenty-eight objects of devotion in addition to this bodhisattva. This court indicates the unity of compassion and wisdom and contains all of the manifold virtues of the Buddhist path.
10. The court of Mañjuśrī Bodhisattva 文殊院 is located above the Śākyamuni court. In addition to Mañjuśrī, whose great wisdom is able to eliminate all conceptual constructs, there are twenty-five objects of devotion.
11. The court of excellent accomplishment 蘇悉地院 is located below the court of Ākāśagarbha Bodhisattva. This court has Eleven-Head Avalokiteśvara and eight other objects of devotion and indicates the accomplishment of benefit for self and other.
12. The court of the *vajra* perimeter 外金剛部 contains numerous deities, both Buddhist and non-Buddhist, who encircle and offer protection. This court indicates the teaching that the holy and the mundane are nondual.
13. The court of the four great guardians 四大護院, the protectors of the four directions.[43]

The nine assemblies of the Vajra Realm mandala are as follows:

1. The attainment of the form of perfection assembly 成身會 corresponds to the *māha-maṇḍala* and is composed of a configuration of five moon discs, one in the center and the other four at the cardinal directions. Upon each moon disc are positioned the five buddhas with their attendant bodhisattvas. This division of the mandala indicates the reality of the attainment of awakening.
2. The *samaya* assembly 三昧耶會 corresponds to the *samaya* maṇḍala and contains the various implements associated with each of the buddhas and bodhisattvas, such as bells, jewels, *vajras,* and others according to the primal vow of each object of devotion.
3. The subtle assembly 微細會 corresponds to the dharma maṇḍala and indicates that each individual object of devotion completely possesses within it all the virtues of the mandala.

4. The offering assembly 供養會 corresponds to the karma maṇḍala and indicates the idea that all of the holy ones are united in their practice. Other than the five buddhas, all of the bodhisattvas form a fist with their left hand and hold a lotus in their right. Above them is placed their *samaya* form, which indicates their unique vow.
5. The four seals assembly 四印會 indicates the nonduality of the four mandalas. Mahāvairocana is in the center, surrounded by assemblies of bodhisattvas and *samaya* implements.
6. The one seal assembly 一印會 indicates that all the objects of devotion depicted in the four mandalas in all cases take refuge in the nondual oceanic essence of buddha reality. The five buddhas are all white in color, wearing crowns, and form the wisdom fist mudra, indicating their fundamental unity in dharmakāya.
7. The maxim assembly 理趣會, also referred to as either the Vajrasattva assembly or the Samanthabadra assembly, symbolizes Mahāvairocana's manifestation as Vajrasattva in order to teach sentient beings.
8. The *trailokya-vijaya* (triple-world conqueror) assembly 降三世會 indicates Mahāvairocana's manifestation as wrathful deities in order to subdue beings who are difficult to teach.
9. The *trailokya-vijaya* samādhi assembly 降三世三昧耶會 indicates Mahāvairocana's fundamental vow to subdue Śiva and that the light of wisdom reveals that one's nature is inherently pure. The inclusion of Śiva here should not be surprising. As Buddhism moved beyond India, the gods of the Hindu pantheon were carried with it. As Buddhism grew in popularity within India, especially in the context of tantric systems, tensions arose between devotees of Śiva and Buddhist tantric practitioners.[44]

The sixteen visualizations in the *Contemplation Sutra* (T. 365) are given below. Again Dōhan connects the thirteen courts of the Womb Realm mandala with the first thirteen visualizations, while the last three (the three levels of Sukhavati, each of which has three divisions) are connected to the nine assemblies of the Vajra Realm mandala. The *Contemplation Sutra* thus reveals the nonduality of the dual mandalas:

1. The setting sun (T. 365:341c27–342a6)
2. The water of the Pure Land (T. 365:342a6–a23)
3. The land (T. 365:342a23–b1)

4. The jeweled trees (T. 365:342b1–23)
5. The jeweled ponds (T. 365:342b23–c6)
6. The jeweled towers (T. 365:342c6–14)
7. The lotus throne of the Buddha (T. 365:342c14–343a18)
8. The marvelous body of the Buddha (T. 365:343a18–b15)
9. The light of the Buddha (T. 365:343b15–c12)
10. Avalokiteśvara Bodhisattva (T. 365:343c12–344a18)
11. Mahāsthāmaprāpta Bodhisattva (T. 365:344a18–b14)
12. Envisioning one's own rebirth in the Pure Land (T. 365:344b14–24)
13. The extent of the Buddha's influence and various aspects of the Pure Land (T. 365:344b24–c8)
14. Beings of the highest capacity (T. 365:344c9–345b7), subdivided into high, middle, or low categories
15. Beings of middling capacities (T. 365:345b8–c9), subdivided into high, middle, or low categories
16. Beings of lower capacities (T. 365:345c10–346a26), subdivided into high, middle, or low categories[45]

In considering how the iconography of the mandala and the Pure Land mythos may be expanded and integrated, we again see how both the Pure Land path and Esoteric Buddhist thought and ritual culture may function together, like threads in a tapestry, connecting diverse perspectives, lineages, and traditions of Buddhist practice and thought. This elasticity is not novel. It is built into the very fabric of the East Asian Mahayana textual and ritual tradition stretching as far back as we can see.

The Part Equals the Whole

Whether in the form of *A-MI-TA* or *NAMO-A-MI-TA-BU,* the name of Amitābha Buddha not only encompasses the power of a particular object of devotion but also unfolds to reveal the entirety of the Buddhist universe, including buddhas, bodhisattvas, gods, and so on, along with the so-called eight classes of supernormal beings: *devas, nāgas, yakṣas, gandharvas, Asuras, garuḍas, kiṃnaras,* and *mahoragas.*[46] All of this is in service to Dōhan's broader point that "the part equals the whole." The seemingly simple recitation of the name of Amitābha is a powerful soteriological tool because, in fact, it possesses infinite layers. As the *Mahāvairocana-sūtra* states, "The lotus eyes of Avalokiteśvara are equal to all buddhas,"[47] and as Tiantai Zhiyi says in his *Mohezhiguan,* "When one chants [the name of] Amitābha Buddha, it is equal in virtue to chanting the names of the buddhas of the ten directions. Solely take Amitābha Buddha to be the lord of this Dharma gate."[48]

On this point Dōhan also references Kūkai's *Shōji jissō gi* 聲字實相義 (T. 2429) to draw the connections between the ultimate buddha reality (as reality 實相), which is nondual with the five wisdoms (letter 字), which are similarly nondual with *A-MI-TA* and *NAMO-A-MI-TA-BU* (voice 聲). In other words, the recitation of the name itself, a seemingly finite and simple vocal act, fully encompasses all of buddha reality.[49]

Extending this view to Shandao's emphasis on vocal recitation, Dōhan notes: "The transformation buddha that Shandao encountered within the *qi* ('breath') of his recitation of the name is the true body [of Amitābha Buddha], the *voice* that is *reality*. For this reason, however, there is no sense in merely constructing a vision coming from the western direction."[50]

What are we to make of this statement? Is Dōhan saying that beings should not seek rebirth in Sukhāvatī? Or that seeking to go to Sukhāvatī is not a worthy goal? No, he simply notes that there is ultimately no need to exclusively pursue that goal in those terms because there is more to the picture: the connection of the other world with this world, the outer world with the inner world. This is because, as Dōhan contends, Amitābha Buddha is fully present within/as the very *qi*/breath of the recitation of the name. This is perhaps the true "secret" of the *himitsu nenbutsu.*

Three Names in Three Bodies

Next, Dōhan considers three different Sanskrit names for the buddha known in Japanese as Amida.

The first, Amitāyus as "Limitless Life," is the deep interpretation of Amitāyus to which Dōhan continually returns. He equates Amitāyus with the dynamic compassionate activity of the dharmakāya: it is both the "vital force" that enlivens all beings and the gravity-like force that guides them to awakening. This correspondence begins with the idea that if beings are infinite, then those infinite beings possess infinite lives. Even as beings mistakenly perceive themselves as isolated individuals possessing *svabhāva* ("own-being," an unchanging eternal essence), in fact all lives are unified with and expressions of buddha reality. The unity of these infinite lives may therefore be called Amitāyus, "Limitless Life."

Dōhan also briefly mentions a tradition within Tendai that connects the name Amitāyus to the "Life Span of the Tathāgata" chapter 如來壽量品 of the *Lotus Sutra* and elaborates on additional nuances of the name

Amitāyus.[51] Again, this is further evidence that in his text Dōhan supposes a Tendai interlocutor, or perhaps an interlocutor for whom the Pure Land path has primarily been defined in relation to the Tendai interpretive tradition.

Next, Amitābha as "Limitless Light" is a manifestation of the wisdom of ultimate reality, in the form of the saṃbhogakāya, a form of ultimate reality encountered in deep states of meditation (e.g., in the *Pratyutpanna-samādhi-sūtra*), after the moment of death (in the *Contemplation Sutra*), or through the stages of rebirth along the bodhisattva path.

Amṛta: Both names, Amitāyus and Amitābha, theoretically derive from the Sanskrit root *amṛta*, "ambrosia" or "nectar." This mysterious substance is described in the Hindu Vedas as the nectar of the gods that delivers immortality and freedom from suffering. The word itself originally means immortality or "no death." The teaching manifestations that emanate from this corporeal form of the Buddha are like medicine, remedies for particular ailments. Therefore, this form of the activity of ultimate reality corresponds with the nirmāṇakāya.[52]

Three Levels of *Buddhānusmṛti* Samādhi

In the section on the *buddhānusmṛti* samādhi, Dōhan identifies three different approaches to this practice. Initially pioneered by Hieizan monks, by Dōhan's time this practice had spread across traditions and institutions.

1. The *buddhānusmṛti* samādhi as taught by the nirmāṇakāya signifies the initial level, the Exoteric approach. Dōhan identifies the practice described in the *Avataṃsaka-sūtra*, wherein the youth Sudhana encounters Meghaśrī *bhikṣu*.[53]
2. The *buddhānusmṛti* samādhi as taught by the saṃbhogakāya is the approach outlined in the *Pratyutpanna-samādhi-sūtra*, in which the practice of chanting the name in order to encounter and learn from a living buddha is extolled. This text offers a sophisticated view, revealing the connection between the Pure Land mythos and śūnyatā. This view, which was adopted by Zhiyi in his "constant walking samādhi," may be viewed as the Exoteric Tendai view.
3. The *buddhānusmṛti* samādhi as taught by the dharmakāya is the approach found in the dhāraṇī, or mantra, gate. It is notable that here Dōhan explicitly conflates the diversity of approaches to dhāraṇī and mantra practices. In particular, he invokes the

> *Wuliangshou rulai guanxing gongyang yigui*, a deity yoga text devoted to Amitāyus that adapts the themes and imagery of the *Contemplation Sutra* to the Esoteric three mysteries framework. Some scholars regard this text as belonging to the category known as "miscellaneous esotericism."

However, as discussed above, dividing Esoteric Buddhism into "pure" and "miscellaneous" categories is anachronistic. In other words, in the same way that he conflates dhāraṇī and mantra, Dōhan also plays into the ambiguity between the more diffuse Mahayana esotericism and the "systematic" tantras.

In the conclusion to this section, having established a kind of hierarchy of the different kinds of *buddhānusmṛti* samādhi, Dōhan then collapses these divisions and asserts that the apparent differences between these three approaches are not inherent; rather, all paths are taught as appropriate to different audiences and, in essence, are simultaneously aspects of the mantra path. The vocal recitation of the name of the Buddha is a mantra, "the secret dhāraṇī *buddhānusmṛti* samādhi."[54] In other words, even though Dōhan denies the distinctions to some extent, he still acknowledges that diverse views ultimately have their place. Unity does not negate diversity.

Ten Thought Moments

Deathbed rituals said to lead to rebirth in Sukhāvatī often emphasized reciting the name of the Buddha ten times. This led to a pervasive concern about the literal number of times one recited the name. During Dōhan's lifetime there was some debate over how many times one had to recite it for it to be efficacious. Dōhan draws from the *Hizōki*, a text attributed to Kūkai, and compares the ten thought moments to the ten stages of the bodhisattva path. The ten thought moments, the ten stages of the bodhisattva path, and the nine levels of Sukhāvatī may all be understood horizontally or vertically. According to Dōhan, while the Exoteric teaching emphasizes the vertical, progressive, mechanistic, hierarchical approach, the Esoteric emphasizes the nonduality of the initial stage and the goal of practice and attainment.[55]

First, it was believed that those of lower capacities and those who committed evil acts must literally recite the name ten times at the moment of death to attain rebirth in Sukhāvatī. The result is rebirth in the lowest level, where one will pass many eons in a kind of suspended animation awaiting one's chance to pursue the bodhisattva path in the Pure Land. Second, in the lowest level of Sukhāvatī, evil ones receive the special *amṛta* that cures them of their afflictions. Third, according to the Esoteric reading of the ten thought moments (the view Dōhan is promoting), rebirth in Sukhāvatī is in fact equal to the first stage of the bodhisattva path, which is itself equated with the attainment of full awakening as a buddha. Therefore, the teachings about various levels and grades are merely *upāya,* skillful means for teaching practitioners of varying capacities. There are actually no levels or hierarchies in Sukhāvatī, high or low—there is only awakening.[56]

Dōhan later states that the *himitsu nenbutsu* reveals that the Exoteric "ten thoughts" are none other than this secret ambrosia.[57] The *himitsu nenbutsu* is a mantra/dhāraṇī through which one can recontextualize even the simple recitation of the name of the Buddha as a technology for distilling the entirety of the Buddhadharma.

Buddhānusmṛti and the Lotus Samādhi

Like Amitābha Buddha, *buddhānusmṛti* may also be understood as an expression of the Lotus Samādhi—it, too, is a practice that reveals the inherently pure nature of beings as well as the path to nirvana and that mind, beings, and buddha are one. Having realized this, practitioners of *buddhānusmṛti* can then extend the great compassion associated with the Lotus Samādhi (which is connected to the Great Compassion Samādhi and Avalokiteśvara) to all beings. *Buddhānusmṛti* itself acts like the wind, extending to all beings, opening the heart-lotus of all. One's own practice is thus the practice of all beings. Dōhan recommends that one contemplate *buddhānusmṛti* as the wind that bestows great compassion and aid to all beings. In their own attainment of awakening, all buddhas and beings turn to the practitioner of *buddhānusmṛti,* bestowing benefits that further empower themselves. One's own awakening is therefore the awakening of all beings, and the awakening of beings and buddha alike is connected as well—the "three" are "one."[58]

Elsewhere, Dōhan notes that, in essence, *buddhānusmṛti* and the awakening mind are one and the same. When correctly understood, the mind that awakens is none other than bodhi. Dōhan explains that "mind" here refers to the heart-lotus within all beings. The Lotus Samādhi is connected to the lotus division of the mandala, visualization practices associated with Amitābha, and the central lotus dais of the Womb Realm mandala. These are also embodied in the heart-lotus of all beings, the originally unborn nature of mind that is the mind of awakening.[59]

Buddhānusmṛti as a Single-Minded, Exclusive, and Uninterrupted Practice

Buddhānusmṛti is sometimes described as a "single-minded" practice. Some Buddhists apparently attempted to cultivate *buddhānusmṛti* as an uninterrupted practice. Dōhan quotes Shandao, who explains the different ways to cultivate practices focused on Amitābha, including those that lead to uninterrupted practice in which one orients all one's actions toward the Buddha.[60] He also quotes Eikan, who, drawing from Shandao, emphasizes the importance of pursuing practice until it becomes an all-pervasive aspect of one's daily life.[61] Thus, Dōhan reiterates a long-standing East Asian Mahayana perspective that *buddhānusmṛti* may become an all-encompassing practice.[62] He then counters this view by asking whether or not ignorant beings can ever truly achieve such an exalted state.

Ultimately, he argues that the truly continuous and uninterrupted *buddhānusmṛti* is the *himitsu nenbutsu*. Dōhan identifies *nen-* (Skt. *smṛti,* "mindfulness") with wisdom and the ability to praise the Buddha. *Butsu* (buddha) corresponds with principle, that which is perceived through wisdom, and that which is praised. Referring back to Kūkai's construction of voice, letter, and reality, Dōhan identifies *nen-* with letter and *-butsu* with reality. Thus, this mind that is mindful of the Buddha, *buddhānusmṛti,* is one with the Buddha.[63] This manifests as the vital breath that is the embodiment of Amitābha and the nonduality of the Womb and Vajra mandalas, of principle and wisdom, of body and mind, and of inner realization and outer manifestation. The vital breath is the truly uninterrupted *buddhānusmṛti,* the "true reality" of the bodies and minds of beings.

> Inbreath: Womb, inner realization, principle, body.
> Outbreath: Vajra, outer manifestation, wisdom, mind.

Dōhan proclaims that beings who hear this teaching and have even one moment of sincere faith will attain liberation from samsara immediately. All teachings have this teaching as their essence; all teachings are but different expressions of Amitābha's Esoteric speech. There is no sense, therefore, in separating out the Pure Land gate from the path of sages. If all practices are *buddhānusmṛti,* how could one practice be singled out as good while all others are rejected? The *himitsu nenbutsu* is the true single-minded practice, the "brilliant light that universally illuminates" all things in all worlds;[64] it embraces all sentient beings and never lets them go.[65] How could there be any limits on such a broad-scope practice as this?[66] Though some say that the three minds of faith, which are hard to achieve, are required, Dōhan counters that the *himitsu nenbutsu* already inherently includes the three minds of faith because *A-MI-TA* is none other than principle, wisdom, and phenomena.

Buddhānusmṛti as the Foundation of Buddhist Practice

While Dōhan critiques Hōnen/Shandao on philosophical grounds, he does not disagree with the basic premise that it is useful to distinguish between the "gate of the path of sages" and the "Pure Land gate" in order to teach ordinary beings. Those with few good roots or who carry the burden of bad karma are not able to cultivate more advanced practices. For them, a simplified form of practice is most appropriate and perhaps even necessary. However, those who are able to encounter and practice the Esoteric path should focus on that path. The dhāraṇī path, which Dōhan regards as a synonym for "Esoteric Buddhism," and the path of *buddhānusmṛti,* is certainly complementary. For example, Dōhan recommends the practice of the Akṣobhya dhāraṇī and the Amitābha dhāraṇī for the purification of even grave or unforgivable sins, as well as for rebirth in Sukhāvatī. In this way, rebirth is indeed a suitable soteriological goal for practitioners of mantra/dhāraṇī.[67]

Dōhan notes that *buddhānusmṛti* is a good practice and that dhāraṇī are inherently powerful, so when practiced together, *buddhānusmṛti* and dhāraṇī cultivation leads to vast merits. In other words, *buddhānusmṛti* practitioners should aim for a robust practice that incorporates various practices as appropriate for their abilities and inclinations, drawing from the breadth and depth of the Mahayana tradition. He recommends that those of lower or middling capacities take mantra as primary and *buddhānusmṛti* as secondary while acknowledging that those of superior capacity comprehend the fundamental truth that *buddhānusmṛti* and mantra are really one.

Because Dōhan recognizes that *buddhānusmṛti,* the *himitsu nenbutsu,* is the "vital breath" of all beings, it is in fact *buddhānusmṛti* that undergirds *all* practice. He outlines a basic template for practice, describing various primary and secondary forms of self-cultivation while also recommending that one should at times simply abide in the *himitsu nenbutsu.* One should practice one to three times daily and perform rites such as the *goma* regularly. One's practice should expand and increase over time so that over several years of cultivation it includes the diverse range of deities in the Mahayana pantheon. This is because all buddhas are one and all practices are one. Continuous cultivation establishes ties with the deep stores of merit held by the holy ones. Liberation is at hand; practice is liberation. Therefore, one's perspective on practice should be all-inclusive, not based in the selection or rejection of certain practices to the detriment of a well-rounded and robust engagement with the Mahayana. Dōhan is clearly calling out those who promote so-called single-practice perspectives. Ultimately, he contends, it is not enough merely to cultivate a diverse set of practices—these practices will finally transform even mundane everyday tasks into forms of Buddhist practice. Mantra practice ultimately encompasses all ordinary daily activities. All practice is *himitsu nenbutsu.*[68]

Ten Primary and Six Auxiliary Practices

Dōhan recommends a tenfold approach to one's contemplative practice along with six auxiliary practices:

1. As Buddhahood is inherently within oneself and all beings, the bodhisattva therefore vows to aid all beings by cultivating the four immeasurables: kindness (Skt. *maitrī*), compassion (Skt. *karuṇā*), sympathetic joy (Skt. *muditā*), and equanimity (Skt. *upekṣa*).
2. One should contemplate the three forms of equanimity—the equanimity of body, speech, and mind (mudra-mantra-mandala) of buddhas and ordinary beings. All things in the universe are characterized by this equanimity; Buddhist practice serves to remind one of the always-already present reality of this unity. Cultivated to maturity, this realization naturally gives rise to altruism. Therefore, mantra practice automatically leads to the ethical treatment of all beings and the vow to save them. First, one sees that the Buddha and oneself are unified. Second, one sees that this unity pervades all beings. Third, one naturally employs this insight to aid beings in the realization of their own awakening.
3. Through contemplation of the Womb and Vajra mandalas, one realizes that every aspect of human experience and the natural world may be recognized within the dual mandala system. Dōhan provides a list of prominent dualities and shows how they relate to their

respective mandalas. The nonduality of these mandalas, and their related aspects, are put into practice through simple breathing meditations. Dōhan recommends that when preparing for sleep, the practitioner should envision the eight petals of the central dais of the Womb Realm mandala as corresponding to the divisions of the body and imagine the moon disc and the thirty-seven deities of the Vajra realm. Such visualization and breathing meditation enlighten the practitioner to the truth that all beings are always-already imbued with the reality of the dual mandalas in this very body. Next, one should intone the letter *A* with the in- and out-breaths. Thus, even sleep becomes a meritorious practice. The state of sleep becomes the samādhi of the object of devotion, producing great merit. Indeed, due to the insight arising from the *himitsu nenbutsu,* every aspect of one's life becomes a form of practice.

4. One should contemplate the five elements.
5. One should contemplate the moon disc at one's heart center.
6. One should contemplate the letter *A* upon this moon disc.
7. One should contemplate the letter *A* on the in-breath and the out-breath.
8. One should contemplate the inner *goma,* as described in the *Yugikyō.* Dōhan notes here that additional practice may be made available to those who have not yet been initiated or who have a heavy burden of bad karma.
9. One should contemplate the true nature of one's corporeal form. The six elements, the enlightened buddhas, and the ordinary beings in their fourfold mandalas are all interconnected. The cultivation of the three mysteries reveals the true interconnections of Indra's Net.[69]
10. One should contemplate the ten illusions: "Illusion, mirage, dream, reflection, a *gandharva* city, an echo, the reflection of the moon in water, a bubble, a flower in empty space, and a spinning wheel of fire."[70] This practice leads to the dissolution of false notions of self, revealing the truth.[71]

The six auxiliary practices are as follows:

1. One should follow the Exoteric and Esoteric precepts. Here Dōhan departs from some of his controversial Kamakura-period contemporaries who disregarded the precepts, but this prescription is well in line with his more mainstream contemporaries, who in

some cases actively promoted precept revival movements. Referencing Kūkai's *Sanmaiyakai jo* 三昧耶戒序 (T. 2462), Dōhan quotes a passage that explains that due to the aid granted by the buddhas, earnest practitioners will naturally be drawn toward virtuous behavior.[72] One should work for the benefit of self and others such that the boundary between the two collapses. By keeping the precepts, one is enacting one's connection to buddhas and ordinary beings. If one breaks a precept, one should earnestly repent, and eventually, such bad habits will cease.[73]

2. Many different forms of practice may be appropriate in various circumstances. One should employ dhāraṇī and *bīja* contemplation and chanting to empower and bless the environment and all beings inhabiting it. One should chant from a mountaintop to bless the beings below. One should intone a spell over sand and rocks, and (mentally) inscribe the *bīja vaṃ* and *hrīḥ* on the surface of the water to bless the beings living therein.[74] One should practice dhāraṇī as one travels from place to place to bless those encountered and aid them in the attainment of awakening. Charity and generous giving establish a tie between one's practice and the object of one's compassion. Chanting while bathing creates an offering for hungry ghosts. Chanting while passing by flowers will cause them to "perfume" good merit to others who pass by.[75]
3. One should preach to the gods and spirits, as they may become Dharma protectors. Dōhan mentions the sun goddess Amaterasu in particular as the protector of the emperor and the islands of Japan. In his time Amaterasu was widely regarded as a manifestation of Mahāvairocana, whose name in Sino-Japanese characters means "great sun" 大日.[76]
4. One should also cultivate gratitude in reverence for past teachers who preserved and transmitted the Dharma. Conduct memorial services for the lineage ancestors.
5. One should conduct nation-protection ritual practices, just as the Esoteric and Exoteric masters of the past did. This is because such practices benefit all beings.[77]
6. One should practice the dedication of merit to all beings. Here Dōhan presents a verse dedicated to Kōbō Daishi Kūkai:

   Namu Daishi Henjō Kongō 南無大師遍照金剛

   The practices and vows of Samathabadra, may they all be fulfilled. Now, I, with one mind, vow to transfer all of my merit, life after life, world after world, in accordance with thy command. In whatever place

> I find myself, I will directly encounter the Esoteric teachings. In this life my practice is perfumed by the subtle karma of the three mysteries. In whatever place that I am born, I will remember and not neglect to work for the awakening of beings that fundamentally have good roots so that they may give rise to the mind [that seeks awakening], to practice, and attain *bodhi* and nirvana, and the purification of the buddha land.[78]

As discussed previously, this is the oldest datable occurrence of the *Daishi myōgō,* the "treasure name of the Great Teacher." Different Shingon lineages developed different versions of this "Kūkai *nenbutsu*"; the Kōyasan lineage still uses this version. This is not to claim that Dōhan "invented" it but rather that of the various versions in circulation, this form became the preferred practice on Kōyasan.

Finally, Dōhan notes that cultivating faith in Buddhism is a major part of practice, suggesting that only Exoteric Buddhists relegate the cultivation of faith as a "beginner's" practice. Those who comprehend the Esoteric truth of Buddhism realize that sincere faith is absolutely central to a robust Buddhist practice. This is another perspective from which one might recommend *buddhānusmṛti,* which is often understood as a devotional practice closely connected to Buddhist notions of faith. Dōhan writes that a single moment of true faith is precisely the attainment of awakening. A single moment of faith is thus precisely *buddhānusmṛti,* "mindfulness of buddha."[79] According to Dōhan, the *buddhānusmṛti* samādhi and *bodhicitta* are united: one moment of mindfulness is the immediate attainment of awakening. Through deep faith, even a single moment of *buddhānusmṛti* is the attainment of awakening.[80]

According to Dōhan, *buddhānusmṛti* is an all-inclusive practice. Scholars often note that *buddhānusmṛti* includes buddha contemplation as well as the recitation of the name of Amitābha, which Dōhan expands to ultimately include all Buddhist practice. Dōhan employs the very letters of Amitābha's name, appearing in the Siddhaṃ script for writing Sanskrit, to emphasize the nonduality between buddhas and beings, practice, and awakening. Dōhan contends that while followers of Exoteric approaches to Buddhism might squabble over the merits of contemplative or vocal forms of *buddhānusmṛti* or over whether or not one must say the name of the Buddha exactly ten times at the moment of death, in fact the true *buddhānusmṛti,* the *himitsu nenbutsu,* is already working within beings, even while they sleep. This is because the Buddha Amitābha is *buddhānusmṛti* itself, the breath of life of all beings, rendering practice and attainment possible with every breath. In other words, there is nothing that is not the *himitsu nenbutsu.*

Notes

Chapter 8: *Buddhānusmṛti* in the *Himitsu nenbutsu shō*

1 SAZ 2:226.

2 SAZ 2:781–788; Jippan's *Byōchū shugyōki* may have been of interest to Dōhan because of its discussion of the contemplation of the letter *A*, which is cited in fascicle 1 of the *Himitsu nenbutsu shō*. Jippan's version, the *Ajigi* 阿字義 (T. 2438), for example, contains a colophon that indicates it was copied by Dōhan (T. 2438:551c10).

3 SAZ 2:227.

4 SAZ 2:227.

5 SAZ 2:228.

6 SAZ 2:228.

7 SAZ 2:228.

8 SAZ 2:228.

9 SAZ 2:228.

10 SAZ 2:228.

11 SAZ 2:228.

12 SAZ 2:228.

13 SAZ 2:228.

14 SAZ 2:228.

15 SAZ 2:229.

16 SAZ 2:229.

17 SAZ 2:229. This list of three wisdoms is presented in the *Avataṃsaka-sūtra* (T. 279:272c6). This passage also appears in Amoghavajra's *Jin'gangding yujia zhong fa anouduoluo sanmiaosanputi xin lun* 金剛頂瑜伽中發阿耨多羅三藐三菩提心論 (T. 1665:572c24), Saisen's *Dainichi kyō jūshin bonsho shiki* 大日經住心品疏私記 (T. 2215:737b3), and Yūkai's 宥快 (1345–1416) *Dainichikyō shoshō* 大日經疏鈔 (T. 2218:36c20–21).

18 SAZ 2:229.

19 SAZ 2:229.

20 T. 848:44a16–17.

21 SAZ 2:230.

22 SAZ 2:230.

23 SAZ 2:230.

24 SAZ 2:231.

25 SAZ 2:231.

26 SAZ 2:231.

27 SAZ 2:237.

28 SAZ 2:232.

29 SAZ 2:232.

30 SAZ 2:232.

31 SAZ 2:232.

32 SAZ 2:232.

33 SAZ 2:232.

34 SAZ 2:232.

35 SAZ 2:232.

36 SAZ 2:232–233.

37 SAZ 2:232–233.

38 SAZ 2:232–233.

39 SAZ 2:232–233.

40 SAZ 2:232–233.

41 SAZ 2:233.

42 SAZ 2:233.

43 MD, 863c.

44 MD, 663–664, 668–669; for a more detailed explanation, see Robert Sharf, "Visualization and Mandala in Shingon Buddhism," in *Living Images: Japanese Buddhist Icons in Context,* ed. Robert Sharf and Elizabeth Horton Sharf (Palo Alto, CA: Stanford University Press, 2001), pp. 167–180.

45 SAZ 2:233.

46 SAZ 2:234.

47 T. 848:53c14.

48 T. 1911:12b22–24.

49 SAZ 2:234.

50 SAZ 2:234.

51 T. 1719:328b. I wish to thank Professor Robert Rhodes of Ōtani University for helping me find this reference: T. 1718, fasc. 9, pt. 2, starting at T. 1718:127a15. See, especially, T. 1718:127b12–15. The relevant chapter in the *Lotus Sutra* can be found at T. 262:42a29. For an English translation of this passage, see Leon Hurvitz, trans., *Scripture of the Lotus Blossom of the Fine Dharma (The Lotus Sutra)* (New York: Columbia University Press, 2009), p. 219.

52 SAZ 2:234.

53 The relevant passage may be found in the *Avataṃsaka-sūtra* (T. 278:689c17–690b25) and in Zhiyan's *Dafangguangfo huayanjing souxuanfenqi tongzhifanggui* 大方廣佛華嚴經搜玄分齊通智方軌 (T. 1732:91b10–97b21). Meghaśrī *bhikṣu* is Sudhana's first teacher along the bodhisattva path. Shandao also makes reference to this aspect of the *nenbutsu* samādhi in his commentary on the *Contemplation Sutra*, the *Guan Wuliangshoufo jingshu* (T. 1753:249c15–16).

54 SAZ 2:236.

55 TKDZ 5:148; see also Saisen's *Kongōchō hotsu bodaishinron shishō* 金剛頂發菩提心論私抄 (T. 2292:20a10–20).

56 SAZ 2:237–238.

57 SAZ 2:253.

58 SAZ 2:245.

59 SAZ 2:236.

60 T. 1753:272b6–11.

61 Eikan here quotes Shandao's *Wangsheng lizan jie* 往生禮讚偈 (T. 1980:439a16–17), which is also quoted by Hōnen in the *Senchakushū* (T. 2608:12c8–9).

62 SAZ 2:253.

63 SAZ 2:254.

64 Kōmyō Henjō 光明遍照 is also an appellation for Mahāvairocana.

65 T. 365:343b26.

66 SAZ 2:254–255.

67 SAZ 2:256.

68 SAZ 2:256.

69 SAZ 2:258.

70 DDB 十緣生句; T. 848:3c12–14.

71 SAZ 2:259.

72 SAZ 2:259; T. 2462:6a13–16; for the complete passage, see T. 2462:6a1–16.

73 SAZ 2:260.

74 SAZ 2:260.

75 SAZ 2:261.

76 SAZ 2:261.

77 SAZ 2:262.

78 SAZ 2:262.

79 SAZ 2:262.

80 SAZ 2:236.

Chapter 9

Sukhāvatī in the *Himitsu nenbutsu shō*

Having considered Dōhan's interpretation of Amitābha Buddha and *buddhānusmṛti,* I will briefly examine Dōhan's description of how different perspectives on Sukhāvatī fit together. Using this approach, he interrogates the ontology and meaning of Sukhāvatī and rebirth itself: Is Sukhāvatī a distant land, or is it somehow present within this world or within our very experience of reality? Is Sukhāvatī a soteriological goal taught to those of lesser capacities, a path for those of insufficiently pristine karmic roots or wisdom, or the central object of Śākyamuni Buddha's teaching career? Is it an object of contemplation or a postmortem destination? Is it truly another world arisen from the mind and vows of Dharmākara Bodhisattva/Amitābha Buddha, or is Sukhāvatī in some sense the true state of this world when perceived by the purified minds of awakened beings? Different Mahayana Buddhist traditions, lineages, and cultures may subscribe to one, several, all, or none of these options. Dōhan does not necessarily reject the idea held by some Mahayana Buddhist thinkers that Sukhāvatī is a remote place removed from samsara. Rather, he insists that there is much more to the picture.[1]

What Is Sukhāvatī?

Citing Kūkai, Dōhan notes, "Sukhāvatī and Tuṣita are from the very beginning within your very breast."[2] Yet he also notes that in some cases to "despise this defiled world and aspire for rebirth in the Pure Land" may be a useful perspective or focal point for practice.[3] While these disparate views on the proximity of awakening to the human condition may seem incompatible, placing them in the context of the diversity of Mahayana soteriologies clarifies their compatibility. Whether Sukhāvatī, the Lotus Store World of the *Avataṃsaka-sūtra,* the "highest bliss" described in the tantras, the Tuṣita Heaven, or the Mitsugon Jōdo—all of these are *ultimately* one and the same. Each of these various soteriological goals may seem distinct, but once coordinated in the dualist/nondualist framework of Esoteric Buddhist associations and correspondence, their unity *and* differences are allowed to stand.[4]

Sukhāvatī corresponds to the Lotus Store World, principle (ultimate reality), the mind, and the earth. Just as the earth produces all beings, it thus produces all bliss.

Tuṣita corresponds to Mitsugon Jōdo, wisdom, the body, and the sky. Like space (the sky), wisdom eliminates ignorance, purifies the self, and reveals the śūnyatā of all things.

The proposition that Sukhāvatī and Tuṣita are nondual is thus used as a way to coordinate different soteriological goals, virtues, and so on. Dōhan rather pointedly states that it is utterly meaningless to argue over which soteriological destination, or perspective, is better or more desirable.

Furthermore, Dōhan also suggests that aspiration for rebirth in Sukhāvatī actually reveals not only the true nature of Śākyamuni's Pure Land but also the Mitsugon Jōdo. These "three" lands are one. This realization is also framed in terms of the three mysteries of body, speech, and mind. Śākyamuni Buddha, the lord of the seemingly ordinary "defiled" world of samsara, corresponds to the mystery of the body. Amitābha Buddha, lord of Sukhāvatī, is the mystery of speech. Mahāvairocana Buddha, lord of the Mitsugon Jōdo, is the mystery of mind. Thus, in the same way that speech is the yoga (union) of body and mind, so, too, is Sukhāvatī the yoga of samsara and the Mitsugon Jōdo. Sukhāvatī, as the "middle" of the three truths, abides between and unifies all three.

Sukhāvatī-oriented practices, though initially directed toward a relatively simple and straightforward soteriological goal, can be seen to ultimately connect the mundane reality of this world with the metareality, or ultimate reality.[5] Moreover, through this configuration Dōhan establishes interconnections between the soteriological goals described in various Mahayana textual traditions. Indeed, reverence for the *Lotus Sutra,* aspiration for rebirth in Sukhāvatī, and the use of Esoteric ritual techniques for this-worldly and otherworldly benefits were certainly some of the dominant aspects of early medieval Japanese religion in general. Here again we find a complex interplay between "multiple logics," as well as another perspective on the context within which these logics functioned.

Attributes of Sukhāvatī

Through an investigation of the various attributes said to characterize Sukhāvatī, Dōhan considers different perspectives on what exactly it is and how these different perspectives may stand together. For example, why is Sukhāvatī associated with the western quarter? According to Dōhan, the west is associated with autumn, the end of things, completion, and fruition, as well as warmth, love, and compassion. Thus, Sukhāvatī is associated with the Great Compassion Samādhi and the lotus division of the mandala, as well as the Womb Realm mandala itself. All of these are manifest within beings as the psychophysical heart-lotus, which, when opened, signifies the attainment of awakening.[6]

Dōhan notes that those who read the sutras literally imagine that Sukhāvatī is one hundred million *buddha-kṣetra* to the west. Drawing from a text attributed to Ennin, he counters that the "distance" of Sukhāvatī is directly proportional to the severity of one's own afflictions. If one is only able to conceive of Sukhāvatī as far away, their afflictions are great. If one is able to conceive of Sukhāvatī as right here and now, their afflictions are somewhat less severe. Self-cultivation is apparently the path to bridging this gulf. As the mind is purified, Sukhāvatī reveals itself.[7] This view is reminiscent of a scene in the first chapter of the *Vimalakīrti-sūtra* in which Śākyamuni Buddha merely touches his toe to the ground to reveal the purity of our world to his audience. The monks are amazed to realize that the defiled world of ordinary existence is in fact the *buddha-kṣetra* of Śākyamuni, and it is only because beings are so afflicted that they cannot see the world as it truly is.

Sukhāvatī's various attributes are also explained through the establishment of correspondences between the dual mandalas and the sixteen contemplations of the *Contemplation Sutra.* The first contemplation, the sun disc, has both superficial and deep interpretations. The sun disc meditation appears in different forms in East Asian Pure Land, Zen, and Esoteric lineages. Here Dōhan draws from Shandao: "In Shandao's *Commentary on the Contemplation Sutra* they have three meanings, and among those three, the 'mind mirror/mind and objects of perception' resemble the deep secret [teaching]."[8]

According to his understanding of the *himitsu nenbutsu,* Dōhan asserts that he and Shandao are basically in agreement. He adds that the sun disc contemplation may also be understood as the *katsuma* form of Amitābha, an emblem that signifies the buddha's vow. The second visualization, the red setting sun, represents the deep red of *mahā-karuṇā* (great compassion). These together symbolize the warmth and compassion of Amitābha Buddha.[9] Furthermore, depictions of Amitābha Buddha within the *Wuliang shou yigui* and other Esoteric texts and commentaries often portray Amitābha as deep red or crimson in color, signifying great compassion.

The sixteen contemplations also correspond to the sixteen bodhisattva attendants to the five buddhas:[10]

1. Akṣobhya Buddha (in the eastern quarter of the mandala) is attended by the bodhisattvas Vajrasattva 金剛薩埵, Vajrarāja 金剛王, Vajrarāga 金剛愛, and Vajrasādhu 金剛喜.
2. Ratnasaṃbhava Buddha (south) is attended by the bodhisattvas Vajraratna 金剛寶, Vajratejas 金剛光, Vajraketu 金剛幡, and Vajrahāsa 金剛笑.
3. Amitābha Buddha (west) is attended by the bodhisattvas Vajradharma 金剛法, Vajratīkṣṇa 金剛利, Vajrahetu 金剛因, and Vajrabhāṣa 金剛語.
4. Amoghasiddhi Buddha (north) is attended by the bodhisattvas Vajrakarma 金剛業, Vajrarakṣa 金剛護, Vajrayakṣa 金剛牙, and Vajrasaṃdhi 金剛拳.

The dual mandalas also correspond to these sixteen visualizations. The Womb Realm mandala corresponds to the first thirteen contemplations; the nine assemblies of the Vajra Realm mandala correspond to the nine levels of the Pure Land. Furthermore, Dōhan connects the Womb Realm to the five elements, the goodness that arises from meditation, and the outer manifestation of that goodness. The Vajra Realm corresponds to the element of mind, the gate of wisdom, and the inner realization of awakening. Again, these are all nondual aspects revealing the connection between practice and attainment, body and mind, buddhas and beings, and so on.[11]

Dōhan also connects the nine grades in three levels of the Pure Land to the nine consciousnesses of the Yogācāra philosophical-psychological interpretive tradition.[12] As Dōhan notes in the introduction to the *Himitsu nenbutsu shō,* according to the Exoteric view the buddha body and land received at the completion of awakening are a direct result of the bodhisattva's practice. The bodhisattva is the cause, and the buddha and land are the result. Furthermore, buddhas and their lands are nondual. The Esoteric view conceives of all buddhas and bodhisattvas as realized within one's own practice, within one's own body. Amitābha is Sukhāvatī, and

Sukhāvatī is Amitābha. Furthermore, Amitābha is the very breath and heart-mind of beings, and Sukhāvatī is none other than this defiled world.

However, just as buddha bodies can be conceived of in multiple ways (three bodies, four bodies, ten bodies), so, too, are there many ways to conceive of the corresponding *buddha-kṣetra.* Dōhan states that practitioners who take the Esoteric perspective attain rebirth in the dharmakāya land, while those who take the Exoteric view attain birth in the appropriate lands of accommodated manifestations. The conception that Sukhāvatī is located in the western quarter of the universe is merely the result of provisional designations. The true Sukhāvatī is the whole of the multiverse of the *buddha-kṣetra* of all buddhas. Thus, multiplicity and diversity abide together in a kind of unity.[13]

Furthermore, Buddhists who rely on the Exoteric interpretation take literally the description of Sukhāvatī as having nine levels, as well as the ten-stage conception of the bodhisattva path. But Dōhan contends that in Sukhāvatī there is in fact only one level: the nine levels of the Pure Land and the ten stages of the bodhisattva path are ultimately collapsed; they are identical to one another. Rebirth in Sukhāvatī is thus none other than the attainment of Buddhahood.[14]

Heart-Lotus: Setup and Punch Line

Amitābha-centered practices begin with the premise, the setup, that the practitioner aspires for rebirth in a Sukhāvatī divided into levels and divisions. Various practices establish hierarchies and dichotomies: buddhas and beings, this world and that world, this mind and the mind of Buddha, and so on. Because this soteriology is framed in terms of Mahayana philosophical concepts like emptiness, nonduality, equanimity, and so on, over time a kind of dialogical tension emerges. An interesting facet of Mahayana soteriology is that this tension is not necessarily resolved. Dōhan's explanation allows for recognition of the inherent value of overlap and diversity in Buddhist practices and perspectives. At times he establishes a hierarchy, Esoteric versus Exoteric, yet this hierarchy is highly unstable, and throughout Dōhan alternately establishes and subverts this tension. Dōhan's engagement with Exoteric and Esoteric Buddhisms as heuristic constructs draws on widely established precedent in East Asian Mahayana and beyond.

The productive tension produced by the overlap of multiple logics is exemplified in Dōhan's discussion of the heart-lotus, which could be seen as the punch line to the setup. The heart-lotus within one's very body is none other than the innumerable virtues of all buddhas, more numerous than grains of sand in the Ganges.[15] The heart-lotus, like the syllables of a mantra, simultaneously holds multiple meanings. First, the heart-lotus is the physical heart organ, the chambers of which are said to resemble a closed lotus blossom. The heart-lotus is also the envisioned lotus and moon disc of Esoteric visualization practices: when the heart-lotus opens, a moon disc appears, producing *bīja,* buddhas, bodhisattvas, or *samaya* forms that transform into one another. The heart-lotus symbolizes the buddha division of the Womb Realm mandala, comprising nine components (eight petals and a central dais). The heart-lotus also represents the moon discs in the nine assemblies of the Vajra Realm mandala. These further correspond to the nine consciousnesses, the structure of the mind as conceived in the Yogācāra tradition, and the nine levels of the Pure Land. These various narratives, multiple logics, and multiple "realities" are interwoven with the body, with the Womb and Vajra mandalas, with the mind, and with Sukhāvatī itself. The heart-lotus is the site for the convergence of body and mind, samsara and Sukhāvatī, the dual mandalas, rebirth in Sukhāvatī, and the attainment of nirvana right here and now.

Dōhan emphasizes the corporeality of rebirth and presents miraculous accounts of great Buddhist figures who attained rebirth to emphasize the diversity of how rebirth is made manifest. For example, he considers how some great beings, such as Nāgārjuna, cast off their physical bodies and ascended to Sukhāvatī. Like other East Asian Buddhists, Dōhan considered Nāgārjuna to be an aspirant for rebirth in Sukhāvatī.[16] Others, Dōhan notes, actually ascend bodily or, like Kūkai, maintain their mortal form. Along with many other Buddhists on Kōyasan, Dōhan believed that Kūkai abides on Kōyasan, waiting for Maitreya Bodhisattva to descend. While physically present in our world, in a state of "eternal meditation," Kūkai is also in a liminal space between our world and Tuṣita. Certainly, Kūkai and Nāgārjuna were both great and fully realized masters. Nāgārjuna cast off his body but Kūkai did not. Dōhan explains that the differences between them are due to mysterious and unknowable karmic conditions,[17] thus sidestepping the potential for a postmortem hierarchical arrangement of these two great masters. They are different but their differences do not mean that one is correct and the other is not.

What Is Rebirth?

Rebirth in Sukhāvatī is often described in terms of a mystical vision of Amitābha Buddha and a retinue of twenty-five bodhisattvas that appear to the devotee on the deathbed and usher the practitioner to the Pure Land atop a floating lotus blossom. By Dōhan's time there were various mantra, dhāraṇī, prayers, contemplations, and so on believed to lead to one of these visions, called *raigō,* assuring the dying person of an immanent rebirth in paradise. One of the primary questions of this book has been how exactly this ideal is connected to attaining Buddhahood in this very body. Dōhan argues that the mystical experiences of *raigō* and *sokushin jōbutsu* are ultimately the same event viewed from two different perspectives. Thus "going" to the Pure Land is in fact "nongoing"—"here" and "there" are ultimately contiguous dimensions of one reality.[18]

In order to explain this idea, Dōhan draws on the well-established East Asian Mahayana concept of "sympathetic resonance": Buddhist practices resonate with buddha reality, which in turn responds and empowers the practitioner. What may initially be perceived as "self-power" is actually also "other-power"; the two are in fact one. Dōhan connects the visionary experience of Amitābha and the bodhisattva retinue with *adhiṣṭhāna,* variously translated as "empowerment" or "grace," which results from the establishment of a link with buddha reality. He quotes Kūkai's *Sokushin jobutsugi:* "The word *adhiṣṭhāna* [Ch. *jiachi* (加持), 'adding and holding'] demonstrates the universal compassion [that is 'added' by] the tathāgatas and the mind of faith [that is held by] beings. *Jia,* to 'add,' means that the radiance of the Buddha reflects in the minds of beings, as the sun reflects on water. *Chi,* to 'hold,' is when the practitioner perceives the radiance of the Buddha in his mind as though reflected on water."[19]

The afflictions and delusions acquired by beings as they course through rounds of rebirth may for a time obscure the luminous and pure Buddha-nature that is always-already present. So at the moment of death, one may perceive Amitābha Buddha "descending" from beyond, but what is descending is one's very own mind in its awakened Buddha-nature. What practitioners experience at the moment of death and what Esoteric theorists describe as awakening in one's own body are in fact the very same event: the attainment of Buddhahood, merely experienced from different perspectives.

Dōhan states that at the opening of the heart-lotus, Mahāsthāmaprāpta Bodhisattva reaches out and takes one's hand.[20] As we have seen previously, Dōhan at times inverts hierarchies, and here again special importance is placed on Mahāsthāmaprāpta, the object of devotion often ranked lowest after Amitābha and Avalokiteśvara.

Dōhan's hypothetical interlocutor asks whether or not rebirth is a literal event for practitioners of both Exoteric and Esoteric perspectives. Is it that Exoteric practices lead to rebirth, while Esoteric practices lead to Buddhahood here and now? Is it both? Is it neither? If both Exoteric and Esoteric practices may lead to "rebirth," what is the difference between the two? In response to this potential question, Dōhan says that aspirants for rebirth do experience rebirth in Sukhāvatī as a provisional attainment. Indeed, the widely acknowledged Mahayana view suggests that rebirth in Sukhāvatī is one step along the path to Buddhahood. Because the mantra teachings come from the dharmakāya, mantra practice leads to the attainment of Amitābha's dharmakāya, the "own-nature" of Amitābha Buddha. Mantra practitioners with superior karmic roots are therefore able to reach a higher state of realization more quickly. The very fact that one has the ability to encounter and practice the mantra path is already a sign of superior karmic roots, yet some mantra practitioners may still have some work to do. Some mantra practitioners may also aspire to birth in Sukhāvatī, and once reborn they will quickly reach the highest realization. Mantra practice has the same power as having performed various good deeds in past lives; it purifies past karma. Negative karma is therefore only a temporary stumbling block.[21]

Dōhan critiques the notion put forth by the Tendai monk Zenyu 禅瑜 (913?-990), who suggests that upon rebirth in Sukhāvatī the devotee will still undergo kalpas of effort before attaining Buddhahood.[22] Dōhan asserts that those of inferior capacity who have no other recourse than to rely upon Amitābha Buddha may become acquainted with the Esoteric teachings in Sukhāvatī, and thus even they may quickly attain Buddhahood. Furthermore, for those who study the Esoteric teachings in this life, rebirth in Sukhāvatī may be synonymous with Buddhahood in this very body. In other words, Dōhan recognizes the reality of rebirth and reassures readers that those who have not laid down the good karmic roots that lead to mastery of the Esoteric teachings in this life may, once reborn in Sukhāvatī, begin their education in the mantra path and thus attain Buddhahood quickly.[23]

Taking the Vajrayāna to Sukhāvatī: A Deathbed Practice

Dōhan concludes the *Himitsu nenbutsu shō* with a deathbed ritual in which the practitioner visualizes Kōbō Daishi guiding the devotee to Sukhāvatī.

> *Namaḥ*, I humbly bow my head, and take refuge in the assemblies of the Womb and Vajra mandalas, honored ones beyond number. [I take refuge] in Amitābha Tathāgata and the holy ones of Sukhāvatī in the west: Avalokiteśvara, Mahāsthāmaprāpta, and the holy ones [who abide in] all nine levels [of Sukhāvatī]. With humility I repent the transgressions of my six senses (i.e., eyes, ears, nose, tongue, body, and mind) [produced] of my negative karma since beginningless time. I enter the gate of the letter A, the originally unborn. I enter the gate of the letter *hrīḥ*, the originally pure.

Continuing to play into the tension between dualist and monist views, he offers the following prayer:

> May the sublime merits [I have accumulated] be used to foster good roots for beings throughout the universe, and through the mystical powers of the Tathāgata's empowerments may all beings attain rebirth in Sukhāvatī.

As previously discussed, some modernist scholars argue that faith in Sukhāvatī is rooted in the theory of merit transference, which is somehow not a full expression of Mahayana thought. However, merit transference is arguably one of the cornerstones of devotional and memorial practices across many Buddhist cultures.

Turning his attention finally to his primary object of devotion, Dōhan recommends that before an image of Kōbō Daishi Kūkai, one should pray that he comes in one's moment of need:

> *Namu Daishi Henjō Kongō!* Have pity on me and empower me to attain rebirth in Sukhāvatī. Now, drawing on the good karma received from Kōbō Daishi's transmission of the Dharma, seeking solace in the accomplishments of Kōbō Daishi's deep meditative practice, at the end of your life [you will go to] Kōbō Daishi's compassionate abode. Since we already possess deep connections to Kōbō Daishi in the past and present, who would be abandoned? Simply make this vow and Kōbō Daishi will lead you to Sukhāvatī.[24]

From this we see that not only one's own karmic roots and not only the storehouse of merit granted by the Buddha but also Kōbō Daishi Kūkai himself, the bodhisattva-like savior figure, may bestow merit that will aid one in the attainment of rebirth in the Pure Land.

One of the interesting features of this short deathbed ritual prescription is Dōhan's insistence that even though the best-case scenario is that one has trained the mind beforehand to meet the moment of death calmly, he pragmatically recognizes that for many practitioners this may be impossible. So he continually restates that one should perform whatever practice is most appropriate—simple or complex—be consistent, and stick with it.

Dōhan regards all things as expressions, dimensions, facets of buddha reality, the dharmakāya, and Mahāvairocana. The ten realms of the "multiverse," those of buddhas, bodhisattvas, arhats, *pratyekabuddhas,* gods, humans, Asuras, animals, hungry ghosts, and hell beings, are all composed of the six primordial elements. These six elements are in eternal yoga. As beings are reborn, the functioning of their minds encounters objects of sense perception and may become ensnared as consciousness flows from one reality to another. However, by simply breathing in and out the syllables *A* and *HUM,* the spontaneously arising mantra of all beings is activated. These syllables embody the dual mandalas, embodying multiple realities within each breath.

According to Dōhan, the aspect of ultimate reality that guides lost beings back to the path is none other than Amitābha Buddha. Beings course through samsara, but just as all rivers and tributaries ultimately return to the sea, all beings, too, eventually make their way to Sukhāvatī, the Land of Bliss, where their afflictions are purified. This teaching is perhaps the object of faith described by Dōhan. The "secret" is not just that Sukhāvatī has been here all along and not just that all perspectives are ultimately unified; it is that perhaps these multiple perspectives are necessary because the infinite beings of infinite worlds require infinite approaches and paths to ultimate reality. These diverse views all cohere within the big picture, the "no-self" that is the great self, the dharmakāya, which is itself the ultimate *buddhakṣetra.*[25]

Notes

Chapter 9: Sukhāvatī in the *Himitsu nenbutsu shō*

1 SAZ 2:246.

2 SAZ 2:247; *Chūjukankyōshi* 中壽感興詩並序 in the *Shōryōshū* 性靈集, TKDZ 8:43. I was able to locate this reference thanks to Satō Mona, "Dōhan cho Himitsu nenbutsu shō inyō bunken shutten chūki" 道範著『秘密念仏抄』引用文献出典注記, *Bukkyō bunka kenkyū ronshū* 仏教文化研究論集 4 (2000): 137. On this text, see Sakai Shiro 酒井紫朗, "Kōbō Daishi no *Chūjukankyōshi* nitsuite" 弘法大師の中寿感興詩並序について, *Mikkyō bunka* 密教文化 147 (1984): 13–25. I would also like to note that I have seen this phrase on a pamphlet-size practice book at Tōji Temple in Kyoto.

3 SAZ 2:265.

4 SAZ 2:247.

5 SAZ 2:235.

6 SAZ 2:247.

7 SAZ 2:248.

8 T. 1753:260c3–4, 262b12–13; SAZ 2:250.

9 SAZ 2:250.

10 DDB: 十六大菩薩. See Amoghavajra's *Putixinlun* 菩提心論 (T. 1665:573c22).

11 SAZ 2:249.

12 SAZ 2:250.

13 SAZ 2:252.

14 SAZ 2:237.

15 SAZ 2:252.

16 SAZ 2:249.

17 SAZ 2:253.

18 SAZ 2:264.

19 T. 2428:383b26–27. The translation of this passage is adapted from Dreitlein and Takagi, *Kūkai on the Philosophy of Language*, p. 66.

20 SAZ 2:250.

21 SAZ 2:252.

22 SAZ 2:252.

23 SAZ 2:252–253.

24 SAZ 2:264.

25 SAZ 2:265.

Conclusion

I began this book with a critical assessment of the history of the field of Buddhist studies, considering the processes by which the categories called Mahayana Buddhism, Pure Land Buddhism, and Tantric/Esoteric Buddhism came to be constructed as discrete areas of academic inquiry. Mahayana Buddhism was described by early scholars in the field as a "developed" form of Buddhism—at the time a derogatory term. Similarly, Indian Tantric and Chinese Pure Land texts and traditions were initially framed as deviations from the simple moral philosophy of the human Buddha. Scholarship on "original" Buddhism tended to dismiss or overlook the importance of soteriology and ritual culture in the history of Buddhist practice. The study of Esoteric Pure Land Buddhism, as a new heuristic device, may help open up space for rethinking the diversity of the Pure Land path within the broader Mahayana Buddhist tradition.

In chapters 2 and 3, I investigated what many scholars have recognized as the "overlap" between Pure Land Buddhism and Esoteric Buddhism in Chinese and Japanese Buddhist literature, focusing on broader trends across sutras, dhāraṇī and spell texts, tantric ritual manuals, and texts that do not fit neatly into these categories. This investigation intentionally integrated the "string of pearls" narrative common in both Pure Land and Esoteric Buddhist studies to reveal that scholars in these distinct fields are not necessarily working on different materials. Therefore, to speak of an overlap between Esoteric Buddhism and Pure Land Buddhism reflects that one's starting position mistakenly assumes them to be separate. One of my goals in these chapters was to emphasize the importance of taking broader East Asian trends as the default framework from which to engage Japanese Buddhism.

Chapters 4 and 5, building on the foundational research in the previous chapters, considered Dōhan's life and thought. Chapter 4 discussed Dōhan's educational context, especially the diverse connections in various lineages and institutions within the early medieval environment, and grounded his thought and religious identity in the cult of Kōbō Daishi (Kūkai) on Kōyasan. The discussion also highlighted the significant role that Dōhan's dual devotion to both Kōbō Daishi and Amitābha played from the very beginning and throughout his education as a scholar-monk in the evolving early medieval Shingon tradition, revealing that this form of devotion was not in any way an outlier. Chapter 5 considered Dōhan's major extant works within the intellectual context of Kamakura Buddhism, showing again that, like other important thinkers of his time, Dōhan does not so easily fit into any one category. The lines between old-school and new-school approaches, Shingon and Tendai, and Esoteric Buddhism and Pure Land Buddhism are not as sharply etched as some modern scholarship holds. In particular, in this chapter I emphasized Dōhan's participation in the dominant shared paradigms of early medieval Japan, *hongaku* and *kenmitsu* thought.

Chapter 6 offered an overview and general explanation of the content of the *Himitsu nenbutsu shō,* noting in particular the complex and shifting interpretive strategies Dōhan employs in blending together diverse threads of Mahayana Buddhist philosophy, ritual, and devotional practices. Chapters 7, 8, and 9 analyzed particular themes in the *Himitsu nenbutsu shō:* Amitābha Buddha, *buddhānusmṛti,* and Sukhāvatī. Even as Dōhan argues for a vision of the mantra path rooted in the lineage of Kōbō Daishi, he also synthesizes the diverse approaches to Pure Land Buddhism found in various traditions and lineages. In this way, Dōhan exemplifies the general Mahayana tendency toward dialogic engagement with particularism and universalism, diversity and unity, and one's own views and perspectives and those of others.

Today numerous scholars continuously produce works on Dōgen, Shinran, and Nichiren, the recognized "heavy hitters" of Japanese Buddhism. It may be too much to hope that Dōhan is as thoroughly investigated as Dōgen one day. Yet as a contemporary of the more famous Kamakura founders, Dōhan's thought in its own right holds great potential for further research. Further investigation into Dōhan's works in particular, as well as their reception in later generations, will broaden our understanding of early medieval Shingon practice and scholasticism, the evolution of the cult of Kōbō Daishi, and Shingon Buddhism's connections to, interactions with, and responses to rival institutions and competing interests.

Furthermore, Dōhan's works on the *ajikan,* the Mantra of Light, and so on reveal much about how Shingon neophytes were instructed in these old-school "easy practices." His perspective on *hongaku* might be productively compared with Dōgen's thought—both emphasize the inherent identity of practice with awakening. Like Nichiren, Dōhan drew from

Kakuban and responded to the prevailing trends in medieval Japanese Esoteric Pure Land Buddhism, especially as it was influenced by Tendai Buddhism. In contrast to the "single-practice" new schools of the Kamakura era, Dōhan argues passionately for the importance of developing a robust, comprehensive, and inclusive practice regime while also emphasizing that practitioners should choose appropriate practices in accord with their inclinations and abilities.

Of potential interest to readers in Pure Land Buddhist studies, Dōhan's understanding of the Pure Land path may be productively compared and contrasted with Shinran, one of the most influential Buddhist thinkers in world history. As a contemporary of Shinran, though not directly involved in the so-called Pure Land movement, Dōhan nevertheless responded to the Pure Land movement as well as the older and more pervasive *kenmitsu* Pure Land culture of early medieval Japan. He may thus serve as a productive "partner in dialogue" for Shin Buddhist scholars as well.

In building this project, I hoped to enter into a conversation on medieval Japanese Buddhism and introduce the field to a fascinating and long-ignored figure. Working within our various areas of study and specialization, Buddhist studies scholars tend to grow comfortable in our own pastures, neglecting to look around at what others are doing. By engaging in new conversations and building relationships across areas of specialization, new connections may appear, new areas of inquiry may open, and even well-tread ground may be productively illuminated.

Appendix

Himitsu nenbutsu shō 秘密念佛鈔 (SAZ 2:226)

Fascicle One

(This should not be shown to those who have not yet received abhiṣeka.)[1]

By Dōhan (1179–1252)

[1.1] On the Name [of Amitābha Buddha]

Question: It is widely known that these days among practitioners of mantra and *śamatha-vipaśyanā,* there are many who rely upon the practice of chanting of the name of Amitābha Buddha, with the hope of being reborn in Sukhāvatī. As for the *buddhānusmṛti* samādhi, it is a practice that does not depend upon the various conditions of time or place [into which sentient beings are born and may thus be cultivated by all]. But why have so many taken refuge in the primal vow of Amitābha Buddha? Is it perhaps because [*buddhānusmṛti*] is an easy practice that possesses the virtues of uninterrupted cultivation? Or is it perhaps that the chanting of the name has superficial and profound, apparent and hidden meanings?

Answer: Practitioners of *śamatha-vipaśyanā* rely in particular upon the *buddhānusmṛti* samādhi within the fourfold samādhi discussed in the *Mohezhiguan,* and their main practice is the chanting of the name of Amitābha Buddha.[2] The practitioner of mantra employs the purport of the fourfold secret explanation in their contemplation and cultivation of the buddha bodies, names, and lands, etc.[3]

The Fourfold [Secret Explanation of the Buddha Amitābha]:

1. Long ago, before attaining enlightenment, [the being that would become Amitābha Buddha] first set out on the [Buddhist] path as King Araṇemin,[4] giving rise to the mind that seeks enlightenment before Ratnagarbha Buddha.[5] Then, as the *bhikṣu* Dharmākara,

made the forty-eight vows before Lokeśvararāja Buddha. As a result of these vows, this Buddha is called Amitābha. These and other things are explained in the *Karuṇāpuṇḍarīka-sūtra,*[6] the *Contemplation Sutra,* and others. This may be regarded as the shallow, or abbreviated [meaning of Amitābha Buddha].

2. Amitābha Buddha is but one of the manifold virtues of the universal gate of *dharmakāya,* Mahāvairocana Buddha. Amitābha Buddha is found among the five wisdoms of the Vajra Realm mandala as the wisdom of subtle discernment.[7] Amitābha Buddha is also found in the eight petals of the Womb Realm mandala,[8] where this buddha is understood to be the gate of realizing awakening, as is explained in the two great sūtras [the *Mahāvairocana* and the *Vajraśekhara*]; this is the deep secret [meaning of Amitābha Buddha]. In general, within the exoteric teachings, the buddhas of the ten directions are the products of a past bodhisattva's practice and ultimate awakening. According to the mantra teachings, however, the tathāgatas of the ten directions and the fourfold mandala[9] are understood to be the revealed within the infinite virtues of the practitioner.
3. Amitābha Buddha is the living wisdom[10] of the *dharmakāya* Mahāvairocana Buddha, ever abiding in the three worlds. Amitābha Buddha is therefore also referred to as Amitāyus, or Limitless Life. Amitābha Buddha is Mahāvairocana Buddha. One gate is all gates. This may be taken to be the secret within the deep secret.
4. Amitābha Buddha is the true nature of the body-mind of all sentient beings, the essentially pure, perfectly bright embodiment of the wisdom that sees all things as equal. The eight-petaled heart-lotus of sentient beings[11] is the three-point mandala of Amitābha Buddha.[12] Though submerged in the muck of ignorance, [this enlightened mind] is neither defiled nor obscured. Though revealed by our initial awakening, the Buddha's light is uncreated and inexpressible. It is unchanging in the past, present, and future. The manifold virtues are thus steadfast. This may be taken as the deepest secret within the deep secret. When contemplating the name of Amitābha, Sukhāvatī, etc., one should immerse one's thoughts deeply in these four levels. In the examination that follows, one should rely upon these four levels.

[The patriarchs and teachers of the ordinary path of *buddhānusmṛti* established the secret teachings of rebirth by relying upon the meaning of the first level. Vinaya Master Dazhi 大智律師 (Yuanzhao 元照, 1048–1116) and [Tiantai Pure Land masters], though they established the teaching of the self-nature of Amitābha Buddha, the one gate of the essence of principle, they did not necessarily convey the true teachings of ritual practice. The practitioner of mantra wholly abides within the fourfold secret meaning of Amitābha Buddha, penetrates both the revealed and secret [teachings], and perfectly realizes the four bodies of the *dharmakāya*].[13]

[Therefore,] according to the esoteric understanding, *buddhānusmṛti* is actually a secret mantra. Though this secret mantra and *buddhānusmṛti* of the ordinary path may both take the form of the chanting of the name (SAZ 2:227), in fact, it is wholly different than the shallow understanding of the ordinary path.

Jippan Shōnin's *Byōchū shugyō ki*[14] states:

> Employ the empowerment[15] of the three mysteries[16] to attain [liberation through] *siddhi*.[17] One should assume the fundamental mudra of the object of devotion (i.e., Amitābha Buddha), recite the fundamental mantra of that object of devotion, and in your mind contemplate the meaning of the mantra's letters. The essence of mantra is the letter *A*.[18] The letter *A* has three meanings: śūnyatā, being, and original nonarising. You should contemplate the three meanings as [having] one essence, and take it to be the *dharmakāya* of the object of devotion. *Dharmakāya* is not different from one's very own mind. That mind is the essence of the three meanings. In accordance with the inconceivability of śūnyatā, the obstructions [to rebirth in Sukhāvatī] that arise from unskillful actions are extinguished in accordance with the teaching [of the Dharma]. In accordance with the inconceivability of being, the Sukhāvatī that is sought after is attained in accordance with the vow. That which is referred to as "original nonarising" is none other than the middle way. Through this middle way, the fixed characteristics of both Sukhāvatī and the obstruction are "nonexistent." Because there are no fixed characteristics, the practice is in accordance with principle. Because the practice accords with principle, the highest accomplishment is thus attained. (One should practice like this three or four times a day.) Whenever there is free time, or when your body is weak [from illness], arrange the body in a respectful posture; this is regarded as the mystery of the body. Vocal recitation of the name of the object of devotion may be regarded as the mystery of speech. Of all bodily movements there is not that which is not mudra. How much more so those reverential meditative postures? Of all speech, there is not that which is not a mantra. How much more so the intoning of the name of Amitābha Buddha? The mind, relying upon the [deep] meaning of the name, is taken to be the mystery of mind. As for

the [deep] meaning of [*A-MI-TA*], the three letters that comprise the Buddha's name are all mantras. The meaning of the word itself is actually *amṛta,* ambrosia. This is because Amitābha Buddha is naturally able to separate [beings] from all of the bile and poison of the obstacles of confusion so that they realize the cooling serenity of nirvana. Moreover, this buddha causes sentient beings who keep this mantra in mind to [realize that they are] the same as buddha. This is called *amṛta.* If you rely upon the [inner] meaning of the letters, they constitute a three-letter mantra. First, *A* is taken to be the essence. The rest is a developed exegesis.

> *A* is the doctrine of nonarising and is none other than the middle path.
> *MI* is the self and the doctrine of sovereignty 自在 (Skt. *vaśitā*).[19]
> *TA* is suchness and the doctrine of extinction.

The manifold virtues of the middle path of the unborn are free from all extremes: there is neither "this" nor "that." In the great self of no-self,[20] there is not that which is not sovereign. Upon being able to understand the sovereignty grasped by no-self, the mind is awakened and grasps thusness. This is none other than extinction. (Though the letters have many meanings, here I have presented but one corner. [For example,] with the letter MI, one can add "meditation" to its fundamental meaning, which is "wisdom." Thusly, it also reveals the virtues of sovereignty. Meditation and wisdom are its adornment. Even though the Sanskrit employs the letter *mṛ,* it is abbreviated in accordance with the [traditional] chanting pronunciation.) When the end has come, and one's eyes are beginning to close, abide in the meditative mudra of the object of worship, intone the name, and with one mind, take refuge in the manifold virtues of the middle path.[21]

Kakuban's *Gorinkujimyō himitsu shaku* says, "Practitioners of the mantra path, as for the Buddha's Name, *NA-MO A-MI-TA Butsu,* do not establish a shallow understanding. If one enters the mantra gate, all speech and all words are in all cases mantra. How much more so the [mantra] *A-MI-TA?*"[22]

Fascicle seven of the *Mahāvairocana-sūtra* says, "The *Vajraśekhara-sutra* explains that the lotus blossom eyes of Avalokiteśvara embody limitless adornments equal to that of all the buddhas. Moreover, in accordance with the sovereign dharma taught by contemporary masters, you should employ this one name and establish the empowerment of one's fundamental nature."[23] (Take this passage as a model for how to understand the name of Amitābha.)

For the mantra practitioner, it is precisely the shallow [understanding] that penetrates [and is not separate from] the most profound secret, and it is precisely the easy [practice] that immediately attains [and is not separate from] awakening. Therefore (SAZ 2:228), the buddha name in which monks and laypeople alike have taken refuge is the none other than the primal vow associated with the chanting of Amitābha Buddha's name.

Question: What about the profound secret meaning of the name [of the Buddha]?

Answer: A mantra is something that in "one letter can encompass one thousand principles, and in its very form realizes the thusness of dharmas."[24] Therefore, the name in three letters possesses countless virtues. That which is called the three letters *A-MI-TA*, as described below, are the *bīja* mantras for the three divisions of [the mandala]: buddha, vajra, and lotus.[25]

> *A* is the fundamentally uncreated middle way; it is therefore the buddha division.
>
> *MI* is the ungraspable meaning of the self. When the self is transcended, it becomes the wisdom that beings and dharmas are both śūnyatā; it is therefore the vajra division.
>
> *TA* is the teaching of the ungraspable doctrine of suchness. This is the principle of thusness as fundamentally pure. It is taken to be the lotus division.

In general, regarding these three divisions:

> The lotus is the principle of the original purity of one's own self-nature.
>
> The vajra is indestructible wisdom.
>
> The buddha is the *dharmakāya* in which principle and wisdom are mutually joined.

Principle universally pervades all of existence and is therefore taken to be wondrous being (as the five elements: earth, water, fire, wind, and space). Wisdom severs the attachment to the [mistaken view that] self and dharmas possess "self" and is therefore taken to be the truth of śūnyatā (as the element of consciousness). In the buddha division [of the mandala], principle and wisdom, being and emptiness are wholly embodied, and it may therefore be taken to be the middle way. For this reason, *A, MI,* and *TA* is also the three truths.[26]

Question: According to the ordinary path, *A-MI-TA* corresponds to the three truths of śūnyatā, provisional reality, and the middle. Just now [you suggested] middle, śūnyatā, and provisional reality. Why the difference in order?

Answer: Śūnyatā, provisional reality, and the middle accord with the outer characteristic of each letter, while middle, śūnyatā, and provisional reality accords with the inner meaning.[27]

The outer characteristic of the letter *A* is śūnyatā.

[The outer characteristic of the letter] *MI* is the self. Self is being.

The outer characteristic of the letter *TA* is thusness. Thusness is the middle. The inner meaning of the three truths is like the aforementioned three divisions.

Question: In comparing the outer characteristics and inner meaning, the outer characteristics are shallow, and the inner meaning is deep. But now, the outer characteristic of the letter *TA* is thusness; this is the middle, which may be taken as the deep. As for the inner meaning, that of the lotus division is being, and being is therefore taken to be shallow. Why is there this discrepancy?

Answer: The middle of the outer characteristics is interdependence, and therefore the middle may be taken to have the meaning of the gate of initial enlightenment.[28] The inner meaning of being is fundamental being, so being may therefore be taken to have the meaning of the gate of fundamental enlightenment. When emptiness [as understood by] the three truths of initial awakening is taken as the basis, this is the three truths of the exoteric teaching. When being [as understood by] the three truths of original awakening is taken as the basis, this is the three truths of the mantra gate. Therefore, indeed, with regard to the doctrine of the three truths, there are certainly shallow and deep [levels of understanding].

Moreover, these three divisions of the mandala are none other than the three bodies: the *dharmakāya,* the *saṃbhogakāya,* and the *nirmāṇakāya.*

The buddha division is the *nirmāṇakāya.* This is because meditation and wisdom are nondual, and principle and wisdom are united. (*A*)

The vajra division is the *saṃbhogakāya.* This is because of the wisdom of the emptiness of beings and dharmas. (*MI*)

The lotus division is the *dharmakāya.* This is because of the principle of the fundamentally pure self-nature. (*TA*)

Also, these three letters also correspond to the *dharmakāya, saṃbhogakāya,* and *nirmāṇakāya.*

> *A* is the principle of original non-arising and may therefore be taken to be the *dharmakāya.*
>
> *MI* is the wisdom of great emptiness and may therefore be taken to be the *saṃbhogakāya.*
>
> *TA* is thusness and may therefore be taken to be the *nirmāṇakāya.* In this way it possesses the meaning of establishing a connection with the *nirmāṇakāya.*

Also, these three letters may be taken to represent the three points [of principle, wisdom, and phenomena].

> *A* is the *dharmakāya.* This is because it represents the principle that universally [penetrates] every corner [of the universe].
>
> *MI* is wisdom. This is because it represents the wisdom that is indestructible like a vajra.
>
> *TA* is liberation (SAZ 2:229). The outer characteristic of the letter *TA* is awakening to thusness. That is to say, it is liberation from the dual hindrances of *kleśas* and mental hindrances [and leads to] the realization of the dual reality of bodhi and nirvana. This is taken to be the liberation of the stage of Buddhahood (or the buddha body of liberation).

Also, the three letters are the three mysteries [of body, speech, and mind].

> *A,* as the buddha division, is the mystery of body.
> *MI,* as the vajra division, is the mystery of mind.
> *TA,* as the lotus division, is the mystery of speech.

These three letters are also the three jewels [of Buddha, Dharma, and Sangha].

> *A,* as the mystery of body, is the Buddha jewel.
> *MI,* as the mystery of mind, is the sangha jewel.
> *TA,* as the mystery of speech, is the Dharma jewel.

(The mutual relation between the three mysteries and the three jewels may be seen in the teaching of the fourfold mandala. The mind, taken to be the sangha, signifies the mutual interpenetration of principle and wisdom and may be taken to be the one taste of subject and object. The meaning of this jewel is that the essence of mind pervades the middle way. The middle is nonduality. Nonduality is the mutual harmony of principle and wisdom. For this reason, it is called sangha.)

These three letters may also be taken to be the three wisdoms.

> *A* is unimpeded wisdom. Unimpeded wisdom is the wisdom of [realizing] that initial and inherent awakening are not two. ([This is the truth of the] middle.)
>
> *MI* is all-knowing wisdom. All-knowing wisdom is the wisdom of initial awakening. ([This is the truth of] śūnyatā.)
>
> *TA* is the wisdom of spontaneous arising. The wisdom of spontaneous arising is inherent awakening. ([This is the truth of] being).

These three letters are also the three organs of speech: the throat, the tongue, and the lips.[29]

> *A* is the throat, the voice of the buddha division.
> *MI* is the lips, the voice of the vajra division.
> *TA* is the tongue, the voice of the lotus division.

Question: Speaking of the three organs of speech,[30] the throat, tongue, and lips are [examined] in the order by which the voice flows out. In the *Mahāvairocana-sūtra*[31] the three letters *A-SA-VA* are the three divisions [of the mandala]; in this way [these divisions] are the throat, tongue, and lips. And now with the three letters of *A-MI-TA:*

> Throat, *A,* is the beginning.
> Lips, *MI,* is the middle.
> Tongue, *TA,* is the end.

How might we understand this teaching?

Answer: The three organs of speech correspond to the three divisions [of the mandala], and the three divisions have two orders:

> First according to the Vajra Realm mandala: buddha, vajra, lotus.
> Second, according to the Womb Realm mandala: buddha, lotus, vajra.

In the *Mahāvairocana-sūtra* the order is explained according to the Womb Realm mandala, in which the order is:

> *A,* buddha, throat.
> *SA,* lotus, tongue.
> *VA,* vajra, lips.

However, here in accordance with the order of the Vajra Realm mandala, the order is taken to be:

> *A,* buddha, throat.
> *MI,* lotus, tongue.
> TA, vajra, lips.

[This order is chosen] because A-MI-TA is the gate of the realization of awakening and possesses the meaning of Mahāvairocana of the Vajra Realm mandala.

This also has an extremely deep meaning. First, these three organs are the beginning, middle, and end of the voice's outward production.

A is the throat because it abides within the throat, having not yet arisen as speech.

TA is the tongue because it is produced by the tongue touching the roof of the mouth.

MI is the lips because it is produced by the meeting of the lips.

In this way, the order of throat, tongue, and lips [correspond] to the inner, middle, and outer [components] of the voice. Inner may be taken to be inner realization, and outer may be taken to be outer manifestation.

Lips, *MI,* is being-middle.
Tongue, *TA,* is the end.

From *A, MI* is produced, which is the fundamental *dharmakāya* of Amitābha Buddha as Avalokiteśvara Bodhisattva. This is the opening of the heart-lotus of sentient beings in saṃsāra. Next, *MI* enters *TA,* signifying the opening of the heart-lotus of sentient beings, and this means the returning to the lotus of inherently awakened nature.

In the *Commentary on the Mahāvairocana,* Mahāsthāmaprāpta Bodhisattva is interpreted as the unopened lotus, saying, "This unopened lotus is the Tathāgata's jeweled basket. It is like one that has already opened, and yet it is still closed."[32] Therefore, the order of these three letters [progresses] from the roots (SAZ 2:230) to the branches, and from outer to inner. From origin to trace manifestation, from cause to effect, these two virtues[33] are revealed by the vocalization of these three letters, and this is the profound mystery of perfect virtue. Keep this in mind and think about it deeply.

These three letters may also be taken to be the three mysterious bodies of letter, mudra, and form.[34]

A is the *bīja* and the *dharmakāya.*

MI is *samaya,* the original vow that is based in wisdom. This is the *saṃbhogakāya.*

TA may be taken as the form of the object of worship, the *nirmāṇakāya,* the Buddha who points to liberation.

These three secret bodies are the fourfold mandala. The Womb Realm mandala explains the three secret mudras. The Vajra Realm mandala propounds the fourfold mandala. The fourfold mandalas are as follows: the *mahā-mandala,* the *samaya-mandala,* the *dharma-mandala,* and the *karma-mandala.* Among these, the *karma-mandala* pervades the above three mysterious bodies and is therefore the fourfold mandala and three mysterious bodies. [The difference between the fourfold mandala and three mysterious bodies is that one is concise and one is detailed].

These three letters are also the three honored ones of Sukhāvatī.

> A is the *dharmakāya* and Amitābha.
> MI is the *saṃbhogakāya* and Avalokiteśvara.
> TA is the *nirmāṇakāya* and Mahāsthāmaprāpta. Therefore, one buddha is the three honored ones, and the three honored ones are of one buddha essence.

Question: Before, when discussing the three divisions, it was said that *TA* is the lotus division and that the lotus division is the *dharmakāya.* Now you are saying that *TA* may be taken as Mahāsthāmaprāpta and that Mahāsthāmaprāpta is the *nirmāṇakāya.* How can this one letter *TA* possess the two meanings of *dharmakāya* and *nirmāṇakāya?*

Answer: These three honored ones also possess two meanings. First, Amitābha is taken as the origin, and the two bodhisattvas are taken to be the trace manifestation.[35] From the nondual original source, they will appear as the two wings [of a bird]. Here, the buddha division is taken to be the Dharma body, and the two other divisions, [vajra and lotus,] are the *saṃbhogakāya* and *nirmāṇakāya.* Of the two honored ones who correspond, respectively, to meditation and wisdom, meditation is the principle, and principle pervades all of existence; therefore this means that being is connected to the *nirmāṇakāya.* And so Mahāsthāmaprāpta is to be taken as the *nirmāṇakāya.*

Second, the two honored ones may be taken as the origin, and the one Buddha is the trace manifestation. From the origin, which possesses principle and wisdom, the cultivated virtues of the oceanlike fruition of awakening arise. This cause is the fundamental cause of original awakening and may be taken as the *dharmakāya* and the *saṃbhogakāya.* The resultant revealed virtues and expedient results may be taken as the *nirmāṇakāya.* For this reason, the two letters *A-TA* together possess the meaning of *dharmakāya* and *nirmāṇakāya.*

Also, the three divisions and three objects of devotion also possess this meaning: these three letters not only wholly embody nirvana and bodhi. They are also the true nature of saṃsāra and the *kleśas.* That which is called "three letters" is the fundamental true nature of the three poisons.

> *A* is the true nature of delusion.
> *MI* is the true nature of anger.

> *TA* is the true nature of greed. Greed is attachment to desired objects and is therefore the nature of being.

This is the essence of the Tathāgata's great compassion, and it is of the same essence as the lotus division and principle. Hatred is the rejection of unfavorable objects, and because it [expresses] the desire to do away with those phenomena, it is therefore the nature of emptiness.

This is the nature of the Tathāgata's great wisdom and is of the same nature as the vajra division and wisdom. Because delusion neither attaches to nor rejects the various objects of sense perception, being the nature of foolishness, for this reason it is of the same essence as the non-duality of the buddha division, [neither grasping nor rejecting].

For this reason, these three letters are the true nature of the three poisons. These three poisons are of the same essence as the three bodies [of the Buddha]. Therefore, by means of the causes and conditions [that give rise] to the chanting and contemplation of these three letters, the nature of "delusion is bodhi" is revealed. In this way, the fundamental three poisons of sentient beings [that afflict them] throughout beginningless transmigration are none other than the attainment of pure self-nature (SAZ 2:231) and the resultant virtues of the fundamental nature of the heart-lotus.

According to the *Rishushaku*, drawing from the *Rishukyō*, "The attainment of pure self-nature is a level of the mandala. The three gates establish the form of the three poisons, which are established in the three gates of the mandala. This northern gate establishes the form of the lotus. This indicates the originally pure self-nature of the three poisons."[36]

These three letters are also the true nature of the three [evil] paths of the afflictions, karma, and suffering.

> *A,* as the *dharmakāya,* is the [true nature of the] path of suffering.
> *MI,* as wisdom, is the [true nature of the] path of the afflictions.
> *TA,* liberation, is the [true nature of the] path of karma.

The three paths have the meaning of the three points, which is the same as a Tendai interpretation, but theirs is concerned with the nature of principle [the doctrinal interpretation], the [outer] characteristics of phenomena. The three paths are the three letters, and the three letters are the three points, and therefore, within the *qi* of the chanting of the name in three letters, the true virtue of "saṃsāra is none other than nirvana" is revealed. The Buddha's intention in teaching about the attainment of Pure Land rebirth by those who have committed the [five] evil sins in the *Contemplation Sutra,*[37] and others, is like this.

Also, the three letters not only universally pervade the world of sentient beings but also nonsentient grasses and trees. That which is referred to as the six elements become the four mandalas and the three types of worlds [sentient, insentient, and enlightened].[38] Therefore, the collected aggregates and phenomenal world are composed of these six elements. [Moreover,] these six elements are the three mysteries. Earth, water, and fire may be taken to be the mystery of body. Wind[39] and space may be taken to be the mystery of speech, and the element of consciousness may be taken to be the mind.

According to the *Unjigi*,

> The three mysteries of the *dharmakāya* may fit into something the size of a mustard seed, and yet they cannot be reduced. They encompass the great void and yet cannot be expended. They make no distinction between clay tiles and grasses and trees, nor the human, *deva, preta,* or animal realms. What is not illuminated by them? What do they not embrace? They are therefore known as *samādhi.*[40]

The three mysteries of the *dharmakāya* pervade the universe. There is not that which the three letters *A-MI-TA* do not reach, [and so on].

[(On the back of the [scroll] is this inscription: "Letter-mudra-form may be taken as body-speech-mind. Speech = mantra, body = Dharma mudra, and mind = the object of devotion. This is called the triple harmonious union of body, speech, and mind.) The body [employs] the mudra, speech the mantra, and mind the object of devotion.][41]

The preceding has been the general outline of the inner and outer meaning of the three letters. If one were to explain every detail, even through the duration of a kalpa it would be difficult to [explain] it fully. And so, the meaning of these three letters is solely to take refuge in the one letter *A*. The letter *A* is the basis for all sounds, the mother of all letters, the seed of all buddhas, the essence of all dharmas, and therefore, it is the manifold virtues of the three divisions [of the mandala] and the three [buddha] bodies, and so on. Using only the letter *A*, contemplate the sequential revolution [of the letters][42] and the inverse, the one letter encompassing all letters, all letters encompassing one, and so on. This is what is called the teaching of the sixteen mysterious gates.[43] The three letters together possess three letter meanings, and therefore each grasps limitless virtues. Vast and without border, like the multifarious layers of Indra's net they cannot be exhausted. For this reason, it signifies the three bodies, and so on. Depending on the meaning, they are sometimes in opposition and sometimes encompass each other. Grasp the meaning and forget the net!

"Na-mo A-mi-ta bu" in the Siddham script for writing Sanskrit mantras. From the Shōhō 2 (1645) edition of the *Himitsu nenbutsu shō*. Image courtesy of Ryūkoku University. This image appeared in Aaron P. Proffitt, "Dohan's *Compendium on the Secret Contemplation of Buddha,* Fascicle One," in *Pure Lands in Asian Texts and Contexts: An Anthology,* ed. Georgios T. Halkias and Richard K. Payne (Honolulu: University of Hawai'i Press), p. 269.

Next, [I will here] reveal the meaning of the six characters: *Na-mo A-mi-da butsu.*

These six characters [encompass] the five wisdoms, five buddhas, etc. (SAZ 2:232). In constructing this kind of mandala by means of the mantras of all objects of devotion, use *OṂ* as the central dais. This is a common aspect of all mentally constructed mandala. *Namaḥ* and *OṂ* both [serve as phrases for] taking refuge. Therefore, *namaḥ* is to be established in the central position.

Moreover, the [*Dainichikyō kaidai*] says, "At the beginning of all sutras, before the two characters *rushi* 如是, there are in all cases the two character *NA-MO,* and the translators abbreviate this. If we follow the Sanskrit text, then these two characters *NA-MO* should be present."[44] Refuge (literally, "return to life") is called Amitāyus, the Buddha of Limitless Life. Refuge is [also] the one who relies. Limitless Life has the virtue of the eternally indestructible *dharmakāya;* its body pervades the infinite space of the *dharmadhātu.* As mind, it is present as the essence and appearance of principle and phenomena. This body, this mind—in what place is it not present? What is not included in it? It is therefore called refuge (return to life). For this reason, one uses this refuge verse and establishes it on the central dais as the totality of the ever-abiding life of the *dharmakāya*. The four wisdoms of the four directions return to this center, the fundamental basis for the *dharmakāya* of Limitless Life.

> *A*, to the East [bottom position], gives rise to the bodhi mind and the wisdom [that is like a] great round mirror.
>
> *MI*, to the South [left side], is the seventh consciousness, the self. East and Center are the harmonious unity of principle and wisdom, joined together in the "true person." This is the wisdom of the nature of equanimity.
>
> *TA*, to the West [upper position] is the wisdom of the lotus of thusness (the wisdom of subtle discernment).[45]
>
> [*BU*/butsu/buddha] in the North [right side] is the wisdom of the karma-body that performs actions.
>
> *NA-MO* is inner realization, and Buddha/North is the outer manifestation.

The [Kongōchōgyo kaidai] elaborates: "The buddhas of the five wisdoms [may be referred to as] all tathāgatas. Gathering together all dharmas, they collectively constitute the bodies of these five buddhas; these five buddhas are seen to be the [fundamental essence of the source of all the myriad buddhas and the primordial origin of all dharmas]."[46]

The *Benkenmitsu nikyōron* (hereafter, *Nikyōron*), says, "The five wisdoms are the wisdoms attained by the five great elements."[47]

There are two explanations for the way in which the five elements may be taken to be the five wisdoms: First, taking the earth element as the middle, [followed by] wood (void), fire, metal (wind), water. The order is east, south, west, north [down and clockwise].

This is the order according to the five phases [Chinese *wuxing* theory].

The essence of wood is void, and the essence of metal is wind.

(This is Amoghavajra's explanation, wherein earth may be taken as the center of the mandala.)

Second, void as the center, [followed by] earth, water, fire, and wind.

The order is north, west, south, and east [from center, to right, and counterclockwise].

This is the order of the four continents [surrounding Mount Sumeru].

(This is Śubhakarasiṃha's explanation.)

The five wisdoms and five buddhas are positioned according to these two explanations, with the same center, east, south, west, north [center, down, and clockwise], in the following order: Mahāvairocana, Akṣobhya, Ratnasaṃbhava, Amitābha, and Amoghasiddhi.

The five phases and the five elements, though different in name, are one in essence. The five great elements permeate all sentient and non-sentient things and all dharmas. Therefore, the five wisdoms permeate everything, and moreover, the five sense faculties of all sentient beings, coursing without beginning through samsara, are the five wisdoms and the five elements.

Eye, ear, nose, tongue, and body correspond, in order, to wood, water, metal, fire, and earth. These are the five wisdoms as *hūṃ, aḥ, hrīḥ, traḥ,* and *vaṃ.*

The five viscera within the body (SAZ 2:233) are also the five buddhas: liver, heart, spleen, lungs, kidney, corresponding, in order, to wood, fire, earth, metal, and water, which has the order of the five buddhas of the east, south, center, west, and north, [respectively].

That which is bound to the five objects of perception is also the five wisdoms:

Sight, sound, scent, flavor, and touch correspond to wood, water, metal, fire, and earth.

The five wisdoms [correspond to the senses] in the following way:

Sight in the eastern direction is the wisdom like a perfectly round mirror because myriad forms are reflected therein.

Sound in the northern direction is the wisdom of unencumbered accomplishment of all things because it is the sound of the Dharma being preached like the heavenly drum and the conch shell.

Scent employs the power of the wind to be able to reach everywhere. This is the western direction, the wisdom of subtle discernment that has the meaning of preaching the Dharma, which is compared with fragrant wind. Therefore, fragrance and wind are together the western direction.

Taste in the southern direction is the wisdom of equanimity [perceiving all things as being] the same and having one taste.

Touch is the object of the bodily sense organs. The body employs the four faculties (sight, sound, smell, taste), and feeling possesses the four great elements (earth, water, fire, wind). Touch may be taken as the center.

(As outlined above, the five wisdoms, the five viscera, and the five phases are distributed in accordance with the explanation in the

Mohezhiguan.[48] The five wisdoms, five buddhas, according to the mantra teachings, also, *adhiṣṭhāna* body,[49] five accomplishments,[50] and five wisdoms, etc., are not included because their meanings are manifold.)

The five sense fields give rise to the five desires. Desires relate to the five objects of sense perception. These are in essence the five wisdoms. They should be known in accordance with the realm of perception (referring to previous section).

Moreover, the five fundamental afflictions of the five faculties, which are the cause of the suffering of beginningless transmigration in samsara, are also these five wisdoms. That which is referred to as greed, anger, and ignorance, in the order of center, east, and south, are the three points and the three wisdoms (as above). Doubt is based in wisdom and corresponds to the western direction (the wisdom of subtle discernment). Because pride is in its essence the ability to accomplish all things, it is in the north.

The activities of sentient beings that result in the five rebirths are also embodiments of the five wisdoms.

> That is to say, the fruits of anger is the hell realm.
> Greed results in the preta realm.
> Ignorance results in the animal realm.
> Doubt results in the human realm.
> Pride results in the heavenly realm.

The five wisdoms correspond to the above[-mentioned] afflictions. In this way, the resultant virtues of the five wisdoms pervade all places, and therefore the six characters of the name also pervade the universe. This is because when these six characters are intoned, this is the attainment of the manifold virtues of the five wisdoms, five buddhas, and so on.

The manifestation of the innate virtues of "birth and death is nirvana" and "the afflictions are awakening," etc., should be understood in accordance with these three letters discussed above. While in the exoteric teaching there is the interpretation that recitation of the name encompasses the manifold virtues, they are unable to point to its essential aspects. One should have faith in the secret teachings of dhāraṇī.

Now, the three letters and the three divisions of the mandala presented above are the doctrine of the Womb Realm mandala, and the six characters and five wisdoms are the doctrine of the Vajra Realm mandala. This dual mandala is the body-mind of the practitioner. The three divisions of one's body, the five wisdoms of one's mind, and still more may be apprehended. This is because the inexhaustible Dharma gate of Amitābha cannot be [fully] explained even over countless eons.

The three letters grasp the doctrine of thirteen, revealing the thirteen courts of the Womb [Realm mandala].[51] They also correspond to the [first] thirteen virtuous meditations of the [*Contemplation Sutra.*][52]

The six characters grasp the doctrine of nine, revealing the nine assemblies of the Vajra Realm [mandala] and the nine levels [of rebirth in the Pure Land] in the *Contemplation Sutra.*[53]

However, [just as] body and mind are nondual, the dual mandalas are of one essence; therefore, the three letters and the six characters together employ the manifold virtues of the principle and wisdom of both mandalas. For this reason, the chanting of the three letters is the five wisdoms. Intoning the six characters is the three points.

Moreover, the name of this one buddha, Amitābha, is equal to the names of countless honored ones as numerous as grains of sand contained within the dual *dharmadhatū* mandala (SAZ 2:234). The dual mandala is all the buddhas and bodhisattvas of the ten directions and in the three times (past, present, and future), the two vehicles, the eight [kinds of beings: *devas, nāgas, yakṣas, gandharvas, Asuras, garuḍas, kiṃnaras,* and *mahoragas*], etc.,[54] and the round wheel of the ten worlds, inner realization and outer application, the perfectly round altar of the *dharmadhatū.* This is because when one chants the name of one buddha, [one is in fact] chanting the names of all the buddhas of the ten directions.

Therefore, the *Mahāvairocana-sūtra* says, "The lotus eyes of Avalokiteśvara are equal to all buddhas."[55]

And accordingly, the one name is taken up and identified as the *adhiṣṭhāna* of fundamental nature, [which reveals the fundamental nonduality between buddhas and beings and that the mind of the Buddha is none other than the mind of sentient beings].

Tiantai [Zhiyi's] *Mohezhiguan* says, "When one chants [the name of] Amitābha Buddha, it is equal in virtue to chanting the names of the buddhas of ten directions. Solely take Amitābha Buddha to be the lord of this Dharma gate."[56]

Also, according to the explication in [the *Shōji jissō gi*], the voice that intones the three letters or six characters is called "voice." The three or six characters, Amitābha Tathāgata, the three bodies, the name [received by the bodhisattva upon the attainment of awakening], and the five wisdoms are called "letter." This is because the name is "letter." This "voice-letter" is the embodiment of the buddhas and may be taken as the "true nature."

[Kōbō] Daishi, in the *Shōji jissō* [*gi*,] establishes the five levels of analysis for the *tat-purusa* and the *karma-dhāraya* [of the terms according to the six types of linguistic compound analysis of Sanskrit]. Within this analysis, the *karma-dhāraya* may be taken to be the deep and profound [meaning]. The *karma-dhāraya* is the [idea that] "voice" is "letter." This "voice-letter" is the "true nature." This is because intoning the "voice-letter" of the six characters is the embodiment of the Tathāgata's true nature.[57]

Using this idea, [one can see that] the transformation buddha that Shandao encountered within the *qi* (breath) of his *buddhānusmṛti* is the true body [of the Buddha], the *voice* that is *true nature*. For this reason, there is no sense in merely constructing a vision coming from the western direction.

Moreover, as for the meaning of the phrase, there are three levels of the translation of the name *A-MI-TA*.

The first is called Amitāyus, "Limitless Life"; this is the eternally abiding life of *dharmakāya*.

The second is called Amitābha, "Limitless Light"; this is the wisdom of luminous [supernatural cognition] of the *saṃbhogakāya*.

The third is called the Lord of *Amṛta;* this is the *nirmāṇakāya*, whose teachings are like medicine.

Moreover, as for the name "Limitless Life," it possesses three bodies. This accords with the explanation in Tendai scholar [Zhanran's 湛然 (711–782) *Fahua wenjuji* 法華文句記 (T. 1719) based on Zhiyi's *Miaofa lianhuajing wenju* 妙法蓮華經文句 (T. 1718) in the commentary on the "Tathāgata's Life Span" chapter from the *Lotus Sutra*[58]].

Our tradition explains as well that "Limitless Life" has the meaning of inner realization and outer application. The *Commentary on the Mahāvairocana* says, "In the western direction, contemplate Amitāyus, the Buddha of Limitless Life. This is the *upāya* wisdom of the Tathāgata. Because the realms of beings are without limit, therefore, the *upāya* of Buddha is also without end. For this reason, it is called 'Limitless Life.' This interpretation refers to the extent of the [Buddha's ability] to convert beings. This is called Limitless Life."[59]

The *Dainichikyō-kaidai* says: "[The Buddha of] Limitless Life is the eternally indestructible virtue of the *dharma-kāya*, whose body pervades the space of the universe, and whose mind is mutually [inner] nature and [outer] characteristics of principle and phenomena.[60] According to this, inner realization is called 'Limitless Life.'"

Exoteric scholars regard Amitāyus/Amitābha as having a [limited life span, at the end of which the attendant bodhisattvas will rule], and therefore as a result they establish names that have limit or do not have limit. This is the shallow, abbreviated view. There is also the deep and profound meaning whereby Amitābha is taken to be none other than the life force of sentient beings. Therefore, the Buddha is called "Limitless Life."

Amitābha is referred to as the essence of the lotus division of the mandala and of the mysteries of speech. Therefore, the language and speech of beings born into the six realms [through an egg, a womb, condensation, and transformation[61]], the sounds of the words of the enlightened and deluded beings of the ten realms, are without exception the essence of the *dharmadhātu* of Amitābha. The sound and speech of [these beings], among the six elements, [may be taken to be] the element of wind, which is the in- and out-breath of all sentient beings. This breath-wind may be taken as the fundamental life-force of sentient beings.

The *Mahāvairocana-sūtra* explains, "Life is that which is called wind (Skt. *prāṇa*)."[62]

The *Yugikyō* says, "The fundamental basis of life is *vajra*."[63]

In all cases, the breath-wind is taken to be the basis of life (SAZ 2:235). By means of this, Amitābha is the life-force of sentient beings, and because the realms of beings are limitless, Amitābha is called "Limitless Life." The ultimate reason for Amitābha's great compassion stems from the nature of the union Buddha and all beings. Sound and speech expound this truth and wisdom. Keep this in mind and think on it deeply.

Next is the explanation of the name Amitābha, "Limitless Light." There are twelve names that express the light of Amitābha. The secret explanation of them is found in Kakuban's *Amida hisshaku*.[64] There is also an explanation for the name Amṛta. This also has ten meanings; however, [listing them all] would be cumbersome.

[1.2] On the Primal Vow of the Calling of the Name

Question: Why does Amitābha Buddha use the calling of the name as the object of the primal vow?

Answer: This revered one is the buddha of the mystery of speech within the universal gate of the three mysteries. Name is speech; therefore, [the Buddha] employs the chanting of the name for the primal vow.

Question: As for the mystery of speech, what efficacy does it possess? What efficacy does *buddhānusmṛti* possess that this particular buddha's name is taken as the object of reverence for freeing oneself from birth and death and attaining awakening?

Answer: Speech possesses the efficacy of the middle way because the middle way is the true road for entering the stage of the buddhas. Speech abides in the center of the three sites of karmic production: [body, speech, and mind] and is also endowed with the two sources of karmic production, body and mind, prior and subsequent. Vocal utterances give rise to speech-karma, the movement of the tongue gives rise to bodily karma, and mental karma relates to mental cogitation. ([This accords with] the interpretation of Jiaxiang's 嘉祥 (549–623) (a.k.a. Jizang 吉藏, the Chinese Madhyamaka scholar).

The body is something that can be seen and takes up space; the mind is something that cannot be seen and takes up no space; the voice cannot be seen and yet takes up space. Thus, the voice conjoins being and nonbeing, grasping both and yet ungrasped by either. It is nonbeing and yet not nonbeing. This is the meaning of the middle.

According to [Kūkai's *Nikyōron,* where he quotes the *Yugikyō*]:

> The indestructible *vajra* is extolled as the eternally abiding body, and the mind of brilliant light is praised as the awakened virtue of the mind. The palace is revealed to be the place where in turn the body and mind become both abode and that which abides [mind arising from body, and body arising from mind]. The middle is the mystery of speech, which, moreover, has the significance of being unattached to either extreme.[65]

According to the *Rishushaku,* "Take the mystery of speech to be the virtue of the middle."[66]

The meaning of this teaching is that the buddha bodies and buddha lands associated with the *trikāya* are the three mysteries.

Śākyamuni is the mystery of the body (the ordinary world).

Amitābha is the mystery of speech (Sukhāvatī).

Mahāvairocana is the mystery of mind (the Land of Mystical Adornment).

Amitābha abides as the middle in Sukhāvatī, [between] this world and the Land of Mystical Adornment, extracting sentient beings from the muck of samsara so that they may enter the pure lotus dais of perfect quiescence. In this way, the mystery of speech possesses the efficacy of the middle way, penetrating inner realization and outer application.

In the [*Fahua wenju*], the notion of "abiding by the side of the gate" is explained as follows: "The practitioner of the perfect middle [way] arrives at the gate and correctly sees the *samādhi* of emptiness. The wisdom eye of the [path] of partial truth perceives but one side of the Dharma body."[67]

Accordingly, the middle way may be taken as the correct path to enlightenment, and therefore the mystery of speech and/as Amitābha may be taken to be the object of devotion for liberating [beings] from [samsara] and entering nirvana. The Womb Realm mandala opens the common approach to liberation from the western direction. This is the profound meaning. And so on.

[Question: *MI-TA* is the buddha of the mystery of speech and therefore has taken the calling of the name as the primary object of devotion. What of those, however, in this world who are deaf or unable to speak and cannot call upon the name—are they unable to attain awakening or rebirth in that land?

Answer: If one considers the details closely, each of the three sources of karmic production (body, speech, and mind) each have aspects that correspond to body, speech, and mind. Just as with the karma accrued from the act of murder, there is [karma accrued from all acts of body, speech, and mind]. In contemplative practice (i.e., deity yoga),[68] there is lotus, vajra, and samādhi, and so on. Therefore, for those who lack the capacity to hear or speak, if they learn of the primal vow of Amitābha Buddha and rejoice deeply in great faith and contemplate *Namu Amida Butsu* in their minds, this is precisely [the intent] of the term "vocal recitation." Because [vocal recitation] can grasp the karma of speech, the name takes speech to be its basis. In general, the three mysteries are used together. You should inquire into this further.[69]]

[1.3] The *Buddhānusmṛti* Samādhi

The *buddhānusmṛti* samādhi has three levels:

First is the samādhi of the *nirmāṇakāya.* This is the first among the eighty-four thousand Dharma gates of the many [concepts presented in the exoteric teachings].[70] [In the *Avataṃsaka-sūtra*] Sudhana received the *buddhānusmṛti* samādhi from Meghaśrī *bhikṣu.* This was the initial Dharma gate [that they attained].[71]

Second is the *buddhānusmṛti* samādhi of the *saṃbhogakāya.* This is what is referred to as the samādhi of contemplating Amitābha and calling the name. According to the *Pratyutpanna-samādhi-sūtra,* "Whoever desires to be born in my land, if they constantly contemplate my name without rest they will attain birth there."[72]

Third, is the *buddhānusmṛti* samādhi of the *dharmakāya*. This is what is referred to as the all-encompassing dhāraṇī gate or mantra. There are many different kinds of mantra, [such as] dhāraṇīs in the sūtras, or the names [of buddhas and bodhisattvas] that may be used as mantras, or a single *bīja* that may be used as a mantra. The [*Wuliangshou rulai guanxing gongyang yigui* (hereafter, cited as *Wuliangshou yigui*)] and other texts [say], "Through cultivation of the gate of the three mysteries, one attains the *buddhānusmṛti samādhi*." This is the third, the dhāraṇī gate.[73]

However, the [differences between the] three kinds of samādhi are just variations of teachings. In reality the name of Amitābha is a mantra, and therefore, the samādhi of chanting the name is in fact the secret *dhāraṇī buddhānusmṛti samādhi*.

[The *Commentary on the Mahāvairocana-sūtra*] says: "Through the purification of the three karmas [of body, speech, and mind], the practitioner perceives the unobstructed marks of the buddha. The pure bodhi-mind and the *buddhānusmṛti samādhi* arise together, fully illuminated and unencumbered [and those with pure minds are able to perfectly see the buddha before them even when others are not able to]."[74]

As for the pure bodhi mind, according to the *Mahāvairocana-sūtra*, "What is *bodhi*? It is to know correctly one's own mind as it truly is."[75]

The *Commentary on the Mahāvairocana-sūtra* says:

> [Bodhi] is precisely that which reveals the site of the treasure of the Tathāgata's virtue. It is like if someone intends to open a treasure storehouse but does not know where it is located, they will not progress [toward their goal]. For this reason, I will reiterate that it is none other than the practitioner's very mind. If one truly knows one's own mind, this is none other than the attainment of awakening immediately upon first giving rise to the mind that seeks awakening. By way of metaphor, it is like the prodigal son of the householder [in the *Lotus Sutra*]—from the moment the son recognized his father how could he have ever again been an impoverished guest?[76]

"To truly know one's mind" [means] to know that in fact one's very own mind is none other than bodhi. "One's [own] mind" here means the heart-lotus. By means of the Lotus Samādhi, this heart-lotus opens, and the myriad virtues of the nine honored ones on the eight petals of the mandala are revealed and attained, [and this] is the awakening to the originally unborn nature of one's own mind. This is called bodhi. The pure bodhi mind and the *buddhānusmṛti* samādhi are unified in [yoga]. If one believes deeply in this way, one moment of mindful recollection and intoning of the name [of the Buddha] is none other than the opening of the inherent virtue of the lotus dais. Therefore, it is referred to as the attainment of awakening immediately upon the initial arousal of the mind that seeks awakening.[77]

Question: What is the difference between *shō* 稱 ("intoning the name") and *nen* 念 ("mindful recollection")?

Answer: Tiantai [Zhiyi's] *Mohezhiguan* says:

> With the voice constantly intone the name of Amitābha Buddha, with the mind constantly contemplate Amitābha Buddha, [and with the body constantly embody the Amitābha Buddha[78]]; or alternate chanting and contemplating together, or first contemplate and then chant, or first chant and then contemplate.[79] This is the difference between [*buddhānusmṛti* as] chanting and contemplation. According to the meaning of Shandao's explication, ten thought-moments are ten vocal acts.[80] These explanations accord with the ordinary common teaching.

The intent of the mantra teachings is that the three mysteries are equal and universally pervade the *dharmadhatū* (SAZ 2:237). Because the three mysteries are bound together, that which is referred to as [the body is present in all three mysteries. It is the same for speech and mind as well].

Therefore, the *Commentary on the Mahāvairocana-sūtra* says: "Body is equal to speech, speech is equal to mind; thus, like the great ocean, they universally pervade all places and together they all possess the same taste. Therefore, they are called equal."[81]

The *Mahāvairocana-sūtra* says, "Life is that which is called the wind."[82]

The *Commentary on the Mahāvairocana-sūtra* elaborates, "Wind is ideation, and ideation is contemplation."[83]

(A note on the back [of the scroll] reads: "The [*Sanzhong xidi podiyuzhuanyezhang chusanjie mimituoluonifa* 三種悉地破地獄轉業障出三界秘密陀羅尼法 (T. 905)] says, 'Among the five aggregates,[84] the aggregate of ideation possesses the essence of wind, and this essence of ideation arises from consciousness.'"[85])

In fact, when one [chants the name of the Buddha] with one mind, body-mind are connected by speech. Therefore, vocal recitation and contemplation are one. This teaching says, however, that the three mysteries are equal and pervade all places, and therefore the three mysteries mutually embrace one another—they are mixed, but not disordered. Therefore, vocal recitation and contemplation are the same yet different. It is like the two meanings of garden. With the Amitābha samādhi, however, contemplation is vocal recitation because Amitābha is the embodiment of voice-speech.

[1.4] On the Ten Thought Moments

The *Hizōki* says:

> According to the secret teaching, the accomplishment of the ten thought-moments is [the same as] the full accomplishment of the ten perfections [of the bodhisattva path]. Or, in greater detail, the sūtra notes that through the accomplishment of ten thought-moments one may attain rebirth in the Western Pure Land, which is the land into which bodhisattvas of the first stage are born. The ten perfections are cultivated according to each stage, and completed according to each stage. Therefore, taking the accomplishment of ten thought-moments to grasp the ten perfections, when one is born into Sukhāvatī one will surely realize the tenth stage. Why is this land referred as a place where bodhisattvas of the first stage are born? The answer may be stated as follows: that which is referred to as the secret teaching is the horizontal teaching. This is because between the first and tenth stages there is neither high nor low. Therefore, it is only the doctrine of progression [or gradual enlightenment] that you criticize. This is the exoteric teaching of progression through stages. Now, according to the secret teaching, that which is referred to as the stages of the bodhisattva path is but one's very mind, the Dharma, the buddhas, the bodhisattvas. In general, other teachings differ on the particulars.[86]

Question: Regarding the matter of the ten thought moments as it appears in the *Contemplation Sutra,* therein the ten thought moments are said to result in rebirth in the very lowest grade [of Sukhāvatī]. Now, according to the *Hizōki,* Sukhāvatī is the land into which bodhisattvas of the first stage are born. The ten thought moments are said to be the cause of this. According to the *Contemplation Sutra,* the nine levels [are as follows]: the upper division (levels 7–9) is for bodhisattvas, the middle division (levels 4–6) is for those who believe in the two vehicles, and the lower division (levels 1–3) is for ordinary beings. According to this, how [can one understand] the similarities and differences between the *Contemplation Sutra* and the *Hizōki?*

Answer: For the mantra practitioner, being born into Sukhāvatī is merely the first stage. The [*Wuliangshou yigui*] says: "Through this Dharma teaching, if one practices diligently with a focused mind, one will certainly be born in the highest level of the realm of Sukhāvatī and assuredly achieve the first stage of the bodhisattva path."[87]

As for the first stage, in my tradition, the first stage is the beginning of the fundamental stage of the *buddhayāna.* This is different from the "stage of bliss," which is referred to in the exoteric teachings because the first stage is none other than the buddha stage. For this reason, in reality, in Sukhāvatī there is only the highest level of rebirth at the first stage.

In the *Contemplation Sutra,* at the first stage (SAZ 2:238) that which opens is the inherent virtue of the heart-lotus; all nine levels open [immediately] in vertical succession, and this may be taken as the adornments of the response land. The nine levels are the total goodness of all worldly and otherworldly things associated with the three virtuous deeds[88] [as described in the *Contemplation Sutra*] and the three vehicles.

The ten thought moments of the lower birth in the lower level [may be understood to possess] the following three meanings:

1. According to the superficial [reading], ten thought moments may be taken to be [the cause of rebirth in] the lowest grade.
2. The people who are reborn in the lowest stage of the lowest level are those who committed extremely evil acts; therefore, they enter the ten thought moments of secret ambrosia and it is the precious elixir [that they require]. This accords with the explanation in the *Liuduji jing* 六度經 (T. 152).[89] The "esoteric ten thought moments" may be taken as the cause of the first stage, and in the *Wuliangshou yigui,* rebirth in the highest level is contrasted with the nine levels as given in the common interpretation. The subtle practice of mantra may be taken as the highest level, or perhaps the highest level may be taken to be the teachings of the incomparable unsurpassable [truth], whereby there is no opposition to the lower eight levels. This is what is meant by "highest level." Therefore, the *Hizōki* says, "Abiding within the most wonderful bliss, this is called Sukhāvatī." This is its intended [meaning].[90]
3. The nine levels [as described in the] *Contemplation Sutra* are in reality all the true causes of the ten thought moments. Moreover, the upper six levels possess additional goodness, and therefore *buddhānusmṛti* is not revealed. In the lower three levels, however, it is explained to evil [beings]. Vocal recitation may be taken to be the cause [of rebirth], also of the nine levels that opened the three virtuous acts. As a result, even the lower three levels possess good. Accordingly, there are hidden and revealed explanations for the upper, middle, and lower levels, of which you are probably unaware. The nine levels of the *Contemplation Sutra* possess exoteric and esoteric, "horizontal and vertical" meanings. In the *Hizōki,* relying on the horizontal [esoteric] teachings, the ten thought moments are

taken to be the common cause of Sukhāvatī, possessing bliss, and may be taken as the first stage. The superficial aspects of the *Contemplation Sutra* explain the ten thought moments to those of the lowest level in accordance with the vertical [exoteric] teaching.[91]

End of fascicle one
Himitsu nenbutsu shō

Himitsu nenbutsu shō

Fascicle Two
(This should not be shown to those who have not yet received abhiṣeka.)

By Dōhan

[2.1] The Lotus Samādhi

Question: Taking Amitābha Buddha as the lord of the lotus division of the mandala, what is the meaning of the dharma gate of awakening known as the Lotus Samādhi?

Answer: All sentient being possess a fundamentally pure heart-lotus, and the Lotus Samādhi causes it to open.

The *Commentary on the Mahāvairocana-sūtra* says: "Envision at one's own heart a lotus blossom with eight petals. The heart (Skt. *hṛdaya*) of ignorant beings is like a lotus that is closed, (SAZ 2:239) and not yet opened. The muscle and sinews appear to have eight divisions, [just like a lotus]. For men, it faces upward, and for women it faces down. First, one should contemplate this blossom opening [in the form of] a white lotus with eight petals."[92]

The lotus blossom that is envisioned is none other than the *dharmakāya* of Amitābha Buddha. Moreover, the *upāya* that reveals the provisional teaching is an expression of Amitābha's fundamental vow. This is because Amitābha is the lord of the lotus division.

Question: Why is it the Amitābha samādhi that opens the heart-lotus?

Answer: Amitābha is the Buddha of the transformation of the sixth consciousness (Skt. *manovijñāna*) through the attainment of the wisdom of subtle discernment. The tathāgatas of the three worlds and the ten directions in all cases use this wisdom to open the fundamental ground of the heart-lotus, which becomes the lotus dais of the resultant virtues [of the bliss of nirvana]. Why is this so? As when the provisional teachings of the nine consciousnesses and five wisdoms were set aside so that their ultimate truth may be taught, [I have explained that] the three consciousnesses (nine, eight, and seven), the three wisdoms (center, east, and south), the three points of the mind's inner essential purity, which is round and bright [like a mirror] all correspond to the three bodies fundamentally possessed by Vairocana (essential nature, the enjoyment body, and the sphere of the wisdom of inner realization). The other two consciousnesses (six and five) and the other wisdoms (west and north) correspond to the two bodies of the Buddha perceived to be outside of the mind. These are none other than the *saṃbhogakaya* that teaches the Dharma (Amitābha) and the *nirmāṇakāya* (Śākyamuni).

The sixth consciousness and the inner mind as the basis for the *manas* (seventh consciousness) are of one essence. Therefore, the conditions within the mind correspond to that which appears to be outside the mind. Because of this, one can rely on the unified essence [of the fifth, sixth, and seventh consciousnesses].

According to [Kūkai's] discussion on the wisdom of subtle discerning consciousness: "From the perspective of the buddha eye, the highest of the five eyes, neither right nor wrong are mistaken."[93]

The term "five eyes" here means Amitābha,[94] the one gate that includes the five wisdoms. The phrase "neither right nor wrong are mistaken" is the wisdom of equanimity, in the southern direction [of the mandala]. Because within [the teaching of] mind only, [that which is provisionally designated as] "this" and "that" are [ultimately] the same.

Therefore, not seeing [the difference between] samsara and nirvana, the wisdom of subtle discernment permeates inner and outer, whereupon it perceives and distinguishes the differences between samsara and nirvana, beings and buddhas, delusion and awakening. [Because it encompasses both inner and outer realities,] it therefore says that "neither wrong (samsara) nor right (nirvana) are mistaken."

In the teaching on the three bodies:

> Śākyamuni Buddha in this defiled world may be taken as the *nirmāṇakāya.*
> Amitābha Buddha in the Pure Land may be taken as the *saṃbhogakāya.*
> The three points of Mahāvairocana may be taken as the *dharmakāya.*

Therefore, the *Rishushaku* says: "Through the practice of yoga, when the heart is purified with a single thought, one immediately apprehends the truth but one does not reject great compassion. Therefore, in both pure and defiled lands, the *saṃbhogakāya* and the *nirmāṇakāya* attain buddhahood."[95]

The "practice of yoga" refers to the central dais of the mandala, the ninth consciousness.

"When the mind is purified with a single thought" refers to the eastern direction, the eighth consciousness (wisdom that is round and bright like a mirror).

"When the truth is immediately attained" refers to the southern direction and the seventh consciousness. The association of principle and wisdom [may be taken] as the essence of equanimity.

The *saṃbhogakāya* buddha in Sukhāvatī is Amitābha Buddha, and the *nirmāṇakāya* buddha of this defiled realm is Śākyamuni Buddha. Amitābha Buddha resides in Sukhāvatī and employs the wisdom of subtle discernment to see samsara. Giving rise to great compassion, Buddha guides ignorant beings in the six realms to take delight in Buddha's appearance, expounding the Dharma as appropriate.

Śākyamuni Buddha is the buddha of the five spheres of consciousnesses (eyes, ears, nose, and so on). Therefore, Buddha employs the realm of sense perception and immediately causes ignorant beings to see, hear, touch, and know [the truth]. Through relying on the power of hearing the Dharma of Śākyamuni Buddha, therefore, beings see the *saṃbhogakāya* buddha in Sukhavati. Through relying on Amitābha Buddha's opening up the teachings and indicating the truth, beings enter the lotus dais of inner realization.

If one relies on the gate of the ordinary teachings (SAZ 2:240), [both] Śākyamuni Buddha, who preaches the Dharma, and Amitābha Buddha, the buddha one sees as a *saṃbhogakāya,* are comprehended as separate from oneself in terms of birth and awakening.

[However,] if one relies on the secret teachings, the three bodies and the three lands are [found] within one's own breast. Relying on this teaching, and practicing with right mindfulness, one will very quickly attain [Buddhahood] in a single lifetime.

In this way, the Amitābha Buddha that is taken to be outside of oneself and Śākyamuni Buddha are of the same essence (same body), just as Ratnasaṃbhava Buddha may be taken to be within oneself. [These buddhas are all] of the same essence (same body).

Inner and outer are interpenetrated, unobstructed, and sovereign. Pulling the deluded mind of the ordinary being, [which perceives the Buddha as] external, into the lotus dais within the heart of Vairocana is called "Lokeśvararāja Tathāgata" 觀自在王如來.[96] Like the letter *Ī* among the four letters that comprise *hrīḥ,* the teaching of sovereignty is like this.

In the *Yugikyō* it is called the great *samaya* of sovereignty.[97] Sovereignty means "high" or "uppermost." The great *samaya* is like the opening of the lotus and entry into the awakening of the original vow. For all buddhas and bodhisattvas of the ten directions and three worlds, the two vehicles, the eight kinds of beings,[98] and so on, all gates are one gate. Awakening to the mundane and transmundane, ascending to the wisdom of the Buddha, [realizing] that there is nothing to be attained, is therefore called great *samaya.* This is like how the half-opened lotus that Avalokiteśvara holds in her hand signifies the bestowal of strength. In Shandao's *Commentary on the Contemplation Sutra,* this is referred to as the "opening lotus *samādhi.*"[99] Isn't this a deep secret teaching?

Question: Why is it that within the eight consciousnesses the sixth consciousness is distinguished as the opening of the Lotus Samādhi?

Answer: The sixth consciousness is distinguished as the essence of life and death, and therefore, the opening of the heart-lotus of one's essential nature reveals this defiled realm to be Sukhāvatī. That which is called the sixth consciousness perceives dharmas as outside of the mind. In response to external objects and the six defiled sense fields,[100] the mind gives rise to the perception of, and attachment to, the afflictions, as well as to the performance of karmic actions that result in either sins or merit. This causes the distinction between life and death and defilement and the fundamentally pure essence of the mind. Within the muck [of samsara] there is no muck; there is no defilement. This is just like the lotus, which grows in brackish water yet emerges pure. In this way, unchanging defilement, in the very muck of life and death, where purity cannot appear, the sixth consciousness, the pure heart-lotus, the fundamentally awakened essence opens.

This heart-lotus is the inner nature of mind that is pure like a lotus, in principle perfectly round and bright like the moon, the wisdom in three points.[101]

As for the lotus that emerges from the muck of samsara, the heart-lotus, the muck of the three poisons is none other than the essence of the lotus division of the three divisions of the mandala. Ignorant beings perceive the poisons as external, and this becomes the muck of samsara; the opening of the awakened eye within the mind illuminates this. The muck is the lotus. Therefore, within the bodies of all sentient beings, in the corporeal eight divisions of the [heart] that have the form of eight petals, is the cause of seeing that this fundamental essence, the heart-lotus, is not only the [heart/mind lotus as the heart in eight divisions] that is fundamentally pure, but also the five divisions of the body are the five wisdoms of the Buddha, the pure essence of the lotus.

Therefore, Yixing's *Commentary on the Mahāvairocana-sūtra* says, "The true nature of the body and mind of all sentient beings are always already constantly abiding in a state indistinguishable from the body of Mahāvairocana."[102]

([*Commentary on the Mahāvairocana-sūtra* further states:] "The reality of the body-mind of all sentient beings, the body is the five elements, which are principle, and the mind is consciousness which is wisdom. Reality is the body-mind that is the non-dual buddha essence. This may be taken as the pure nature that is perfectly round and bright in three points. Always, this is the body of the wisdom of equanimity of Vairocana. This is not when bodhi is attained. Strengthen ones understanding of the emptiness of all dharmas, and this will cause one to attain the *dharma-dhātu.*"[103])

As for Vairocana, the first part [of the name] means "inherent *sattva.*" From the view of cause it is called *sattva,* and from the view of effect it is called *shana.* Equanimity is the *dharmakāya.* Wisdom is *prajña.* Body is liberation. Sentient beings arise fundamentally endowed with this buddha wisdom, undefiled by the muck of samsara, but unknowing and unawakened [to this], they encounter manifold forms of suffering. Now, Amitābha Buddha uses great compassion to contain the manifold virtues of ghee, the merits of awakening, in the purified milk of the name (SAZ 2:241). Buddha causes the ignorant children caught in the six realms, who are like ignorant unknowing children, to receive the milk and water of the name of Amitābha. Maturing in the *dharmakāya,* at the end of their lives they are born in the Land of Eternal Life (Land of Amitāyus) in an open lotus blossom, thereupon giving rise to the mind that seeks enlightenment. If one such as this were a mantra practitioner, they could directly distill the ghee of liberation from the milk of the name of Amitābha Buddha and suddenly uncover its essential virtues.

Question: The sixth consciousness reveals the meaning of the lotus. What is the purport of this exactly? The calling of the name reveals the meaning of the flower. Could you please clarify this matter?

Answer: Amitābha is the Buddha of the mystery of speech and the lotus division of the mandala. Buddha therefore employs the calling of the name (speech and wind) to reveal the lotus dais of one's own mind.

Within the *wuxing* system there is the western direction. Therein, the element of metal corresponds to wind. Also, "Limitless Life" is none other than the breath-wind (i.e., life) of all sentient beings. Also, the fundamental essence of the lotus seed syllable *hrīḥ* is *ha,* which means "wind." This is because wind reveals the arising of one's inherent nature.

Yixing's *Commentary on the Mahāvairocana-sūtra* says, "Great compassion is the element of wind, that which reveals [one's Buddha-nature]."[104]

This *bīja* possesses the fundamental essence that reveals one's innate potential, and therefore it takes the form of the calling of the name (speech and wind) as its outer manifestation. It reveals the essential virtue of the heart-lotus. Avalokiteśvara uses their right hand (wind and space) and disseminates power. Contemplate this deeply.

Question: The opening of the flower, what meaning does this have?

Answer: The flower petals spread, and thus the lotus is revealed. "The lotus is revealed" means fully possessing the virtues of enlightenment.

The *Commentary on the Mahāvairocana-sūtra* says: "At the heart of the Lotus Samādhi, when the flower opens, of the manifold dharmas there are none that are not fully grasped. This includes the six *pāramitās,*[105] the eighteen aspects of emptiness,[106] the thirty-seven factors of enlightenment,[107] the liberation of meditative absorption, the gate of the 108 *samādhis,*[108] or the 500 *dhāraṇī* gates,[109] and others such as these, endless and without limit; there are none that are not fully grasped. You should know that all dharmas arise from the mind and being."[110]

The open lotus dais is the Amitābha mandala with eight petals and the nine honored ones. These nine honored ones encompass the limitless manifold virtues of all [buddhas, bodhisattvas, their trace manifestations such as the gods, inner and outer, ultimate and conventional realities], cause and effect, and so on.

The *Wuliangshou yigui* says:

> Then enter the *samādhi* of Avalokiteśvara Bodhisattva. Close your eyes and clear your thoughts. Visualize in your body a perfect circle of pure white, like a pure moon, lying face up within your heart. Above the pure moon [disk] visualize the letter *hrīḥ* emitting a great radiance. The letter transforms into an eight-petaled lotus. On the center of the lotus is Avalokiteśvara Bodhisattva. His beautiful appearance is distinct. In his left hand he holds a lotus, and with his right hand he makes the gesture of opening the petals of the lotus. Have this thought, 'All sentient beings fully possess within their bodies this lotus of awakening. The pure *dharmadhātu* is not tainted by afflictions.' On each of the eight petals of the lotus is a *tathāgata,* sitting in *samādhi* in the full cross-legged position. Their faces are turned toward Avalokiteśvara Bodhisattva.[111]

(In the Womb Realm mandala envision the *vajra* practice.)

The *Rishushaku* says: "At that time visualize in one's body the gate of the seed syllable *hrīḥ*, which becomes the eight-petaled lotus, in the womb visualize the *vajra* dharma. Above the eight petals visualize the eight buddhas."[112]

Jippan's [*Rishushaku kuketsushō* 理趣釋口決鈔] says, "The eight petal lotus (SAZ 242) is the Lotus of Awakening."[113]

Also, the *Rishushaku* says: "Avalokiteśvara Bodhisattva holds the lotus in their hand. Contemplate all sentient beings as possessing in their bodies an essence that is *tathāgatagarbha*. Their self-nature is pure, luminous, and bright and cannot be defiled."[114]

Therefore, know that the *tathāgatagarbha* essence is called the lotus of awakening. Tathāgata is the Buddha. The Buddha calls awakening *garbha;* the essence is the lotus. The lotus holds the Tathāgata's manifold virtues and is called *garbha. Garbha* may be taken as the Tathāgata's self-essence and is called essence. Essence is pure and undefiled and is therefore named lotus. "In the left hand holding a lotus" is the Great Compassion Samādhi, contemplation of sentient beings' Buddha-nature. "The right hand holding an open lotus" is the skillful *upāya*, the revelation of wisdom. This is the buddha-nature that causes the manifestation of the attainment of the Bodhisattva sitting on the dais. The Tathāgata on the petal is Avalokiteśvara Bodhisattva, representing the great compassion of all buddhas. "The great compassion of all buddhas" helping others is the main [idea]. Self and other, the merits of awakening—all of these are your companions, therefore Avalokiteśvara Bodhisattva who sits on the central dais is your companion, therefore the virtues of awakening for others is present on the petals.

Question: These buddhas on the petals, what of the unity of their name and form?

Answer: A record says:

> The eight buddhas of the eight petals are the *samaya* of the heart-king of the eight consciousnesses (except the sixth consciousness). Avalokiteśvara Bodhisattva sits on the central dais as the sixth consciousness. Usually, cause takes the position of the ninth consciousness together with the fetters, even though the function of wisdom has not yet been revealed. The sixth consciousness is the consciousness that discriminates and clearly distinguishes [between things], and therefore despises the realm of death and rebirth and aspires for *bodhi*. This sixth consciousness is the tool of the wisdom of subtle discernment. For this reason, it takes the central position.

It also says:

> The eight buddhas are the honored ones that sit atop the petals of the Womb Realm mandala, the four wisdoms and the four practices. These eight petals are the crimson lotus, which is none other than the eight petals of the *hṛdaya* of the practitioner [(the lotus opens, unfurling eight petals, the *tathāgata* appear and declare the *hṛdaya* is the heart of sentient beings)[115]], together with the *samaya* of Amitābha Buddha, which is red in color.

The passage above is based on the *Commentary on the Mahāvairocana-sūtra,* which says, "First contemplate this lotus, which opens to form an eight-petal white lotus."[116]

This heart-lotus also has the teaching of white and red, [or male and female]. Red is the color of great compassion, and white is the doctrine of the fundamentally pure.

Also, a secret discourse says:

> There are two types of Amitābha mandala. One has Amitābha in the central dais, with the eight bodhisattvas on the eight petals of the lotus. This is the explanation according to the *Dhāraṇī-saṃgraha-sūtra.* The second type has Avalokiteśvara at the center, and on the eight petals are eight [buddhas]. This is the explanation according to the *Wuliangshou yigui.* [The first is for] the novice, revealing the mandala of the resultant stage and the eight bodhisattvas that course in the causal stage. Take refuge in the central dais of the resultant virtues of Amida. The former fundamentally possesses the essence of the virtues of the causal stage mandala. Therefore, the Buddha's virtues all turn, and fundamentally they already possess the causal stage of Kannon (Avalokiteśvara). These two mandalas with nine objects of devotion are all the lords of the nine stages of Sukhāvatī. Cause and effect may be differentiated; the nine consciousness that arise from the minds of sentient beings are the fetters as understood at the first stage.

Furthermore, the flower, dais, and petals together have the meaning of cause and effect. It is said that the flower and its eight petals may be taken as the cause, and the central dais may be taken to be the effect. Effect is the Vajra Realm. Cause is the Womb Realm mandala. The dais and petals each have a central dais and may be taken as effect. Effect also may be taken to mean "seed" and has the meaning of the cause of cause and effect (SAZ 2:243). Therefore, both mandalas are nondual. Also, each of these cause-effect has the meaning of the fundamental source-trace (J. *honji suijaku*). Trace-cause, trace-effect, cause and effect all arise together. Origin-cause, origin-effect, cause and effect all accord with the law of the universe. This is because fundamentally cause and effect, the "flower-effect" and the fundamental being, dais, and petal do not arise together.

Kakuban's [*Himitsu sōgon ryōbu isshin ju* 秘密荘厳両部一心頌], says, "Manifest phenomena are described as complete and beautiful. The cause of this is not unhappiness and confusion."[117]

Furthermore, rely on this doctrine of the nonduality of cause and effect. A secret record also mentions that in addition to these two kinds of mandalas, there is also the mandala of the nonduality of cause and effect. This is Lokeśvararāja Tathāgata of the *Vajraśekhara*.[118] This is called the seat of Crimson Crystal Body Amitābha Buddha, *vajra* lotus mandala. (Inquire further into the doctrine of nonduality.)

Also, the mandala of the nine honored ones has three different interpretations. First, Amitābha Buddha is the manifold virtues of the one gate. Second, it is the manifold virtues of the one gate of Amitābha Buddha, which are the manifold virtues of the universal gate of Mahāvairocana Buddha. Third, it is the corporeal mandala in eight segments of sentient beings' own minds. These different teachings are not all the same. Think about this.

Question: The dais-petal/cause-effect mandala contains only Avalokiteśvara Bodhisattva and Amitābha Buddha. There is no discussion of Mahāsthāmaprāpta Bodhisattva. What is the meaning of this?

Answer: These two bodhisattvas, after attaining enlightenment, may be taken to be the two wings of meditation and wisdom, helping Amitābha Buddha in converting beings and leading them [to liberation in the Pure Land]. Their fundamental being may be taken to be the principle and wisdom of the *dharmakāya,* the cause of awakening. Therefore, this meditation and wisdom transform into two. One's own awakening is nondual. Therefore, with Amitābha Buddha as the effect, these two bodhisattvas gathered together are the cause. The fundamental being of principle and wisdom, therefore, the cause of that which is awakened, is the one Avalokiteśvara Bodhisattva who upholds and contains the principle of Mahāsthāmaprāpta Bodhisattva. Though there are three honored ones, they contain the meaning of the dual mandala. This question leaves out the issue of fundamental being, therefore it is added.

Question: [Concerning] these three honored ones, Avalokiteśvara Bodhisattva and Mahāsthāmaprāpta Bodhisattva are on the left and right [of Amitābha], respectively, yet when they appear in images they are not the same. What is the intention behind this?

Answer: Avalokiteśvara Bodhisattva on the left and Mahāsthāmaprāpta Bodhisattva on the right is the explanation we find in the *Contemplation*

Sutra and others. In the *Dhāraṇīsaṃgraha-sūtra* we find Mahāsthāmaprāpta on the left and Avalokiteśvara on the right.[119]

[(On the backside it mentions that the eleven-headed [Avalokiteśvara] ritual manual says, "In the center is Amitāyus Tathāgata, on the left is Mahāsthāmaprāpta and on the right is Avalokiteśvara.")[120]]

As for the meaning behind this, these two bodhisattvas are Amitābha Tathāgata's two wings of meditation and wisdom, and so left and right have these two meanings of meditation and wisdom. One explanation takes left to be meditation and right to be wisdom. If *yang* is wisdom, then *yin* would be meditation. This is the ordinary explanation, which is also found in the *Dhāraṇīsaṃgraha-sūtra.*

Another explanation takes the three divisions of the Womb Realm mandala to be the lotus division as principle, on the right, and the vajra division as wisdom on the left. This "realm of principle" (i.e., the Womb Realm mandala) therefore has principle on the right. The feminine aspect on the right is according to conventional reality, which is the truth that phenomenal reality is no different from ultimate reality. Amitābha, the buddha of the lotus gate, therefore employs Mahāsthāmaprāpta Bodhisattva as meditation on the right and Avalokiteśvara Bodhisattva as wisdom on the left. This accords with the three divisions of the Womb Realm mandala.

Question: Are there instances where Avalokiteśvara Bodhisattva is taken as meditation and Mahāsthāmaprāpta Bodhisattva is taken as wisdom?

Answer: The *Contemplation Sutra* says: "This bodhisattva is also called Boundless Light, because it employs wisdom to illuminate universally, shining upon all [sentient beings], causing them to be liberated from the three evil paths (hell, hungry ghosts, animals), and attain that unsurpassable power. For this reason, this bodhisattva (SAZ 2:244) is named Mahāsthāmaprāpta ('Possessor of Great Power')."[121]

Therefore, Mahāsthāmaprāpta Bodhisattva can [also be taken as] wisdom.

As it is said, the great compassion of all buddhas is possessed by Avalokiteśvara Bodhisattva. For this reason, Avalokiteśvara Bodhisattva may be taken as principle. Great compassion is principle; therefore, a secret transmission says to take the three letters of the name *A-MI-TA* as corresponding in order to the three honored ones Amitābha Buddha, Avalokiteśvara Bodhisattva, and Mahāsthāmaprāpta Bodhisattva.

By means of this correspondence,

Mahāsthāmaprāpta Bodhisattva is the lips (within which is contained the vajra division of the mandala),

Avalokiteśvara Bodhisattva is the tongue (within which is contained the lotus division of the mandala)

[Amitābha would therefore be the throat, which contains the buddha division of the mandala[122]].

[Just as we see in the Tendai tradition,] the three truths perfectly interpenetrate. [(These three objects of devotion are nondual, therefore two teachings are exactly right.)[123]]

Question: In the primal vow of Amitābha Buddha held up the calling of the holy name. For this reason, Amitābha is taken to be the buddha of the mystery of speech. Yet here in this explanation of the Lotus Samādhi, you have suggested that Amitābha is also the buddha of the sixth consciousness. Is this not contradictory?

Answer: Discerning consciousness differentiates between objects; language explains. Both rouse the masses, causing their eyes to open, and they awaken to the one essence of the wisdom of the buddhas. The wisdom of subtle discernment is the wisdom that removes all doubt through the preaching of the Dharma. The Dharma preaching is language. Doubt is mentation (*mano,* the sixth consciousness). For this reason, [Amitābha Buddha] pervades [both] language and mentation.

When divided broadly into the three bodies and the three mysteries, however:

Amitābha/"*mano*-mentation" is also part of the wisdom that preaches the Dharma and therefore part of speech.

Śākyamuni preached the Dharma of the karma gate and therefore part of bodily activity.

Mahāvairocana preaches the Dharma within the inner awakening of the mind. Thus, Mahāvairocana belongs to the mystery of mind.

Question: From the perspective of the mind in the Lotus Samādhi, the three poisons and the five desires[124] are inherently pure. They are none other than the three bodies and the five wisdoms. Does this mean, then, that the practitioner is permitted to just continue to engage in evil activity?

Answer: For one who is already awakened, the three poisons and the ten evils become [recognized as dimensions of] inconceivable awakening. For one who is not yet trained, who has not yet mastered the gate of the contemplation of reality, if they commit these sins of body and mind, they will be cast about in samsara by karma. [Therefore, one who has not yet attained awakening should] exert themselves, and they should not commit these [negative actions].

(Should one be pulled into negative karma and lose one's mind and become confused and engage in confused or evil actions and suddenly give rise to the three poisons or ten evils, one should repent one's sins and enter the Lotus Samādhi and chant the name of Amitābha, and all of one's transgressions will be eliminated. Contemplate the fundamental basis of the three sources of karmic production as fundamentally pure. The movement of the tongue and mouth is phenomena [encompassing wisdom and principle]. Or one could intone the one letter.)[125]

Question: As for the heavenly ones in the mandala, they are distinguished by their flowers, jasmine and *campaka,* and other excellent sublime flowers, of which there are many. Why is the lotus taken to indicate the purity of the fundamental essence [of all beings]?

Answer: The lotus is born in [muddy] water. At first the bud is submerged, and it is therefore called "water-born." For this reason, the flower possesses water as its essence. So, of the five elements (earth, water, fire, wind, space), only water is taken to signify purity.

The *Commentary on the Mahāvairocana-sūtra* says, "The water element (or perhaps water and fire) are called the essence of purity, undefiled and unsullied."[126]

Also: "It is said to be like rain in the sky, the water with eight virtues,[127] the single unadulterated taste (of camphor?). According to the receptacle, they are distinguished into various kinds: bitter, sour, warm water, or mud. In this way, the essence of the eight virtues [of water] is not [recognizable in the same way in each one]. Warm water washes away mud and when it subsides, it is as if the water was never dirty."[128]

Also, the hundred rivers enter the ocean and are purified. For this reason, all sentient beings in the muddy swamp [of samsara] take refuge in the "water" of their fundamental nature. The western direction is the direction of water. In the western states, the character for water is a circle.

Therefore, [fascicle twenty] of the *Commentary on the Mahāvairocana-sūtra* says: "Next, when you recite the characters *san-bo-dai* all practices lead to highest complete awakening. That buddha is named Amitābha, the western direction, the attainment of *bodhi,* and the color white. In the end it is perfectly bright. In addition to this meaning, it has the meaning of water."[129]

Also, the [*Sanzhong xidi podiyu zhuan yezhang chu sanjie mimi tuoluonifa* 三種悉地破地獄轉業障出三界祕密陀羅尼法 (T. 905)] says: "The letter *vaṃ* is the lord of the lotus division, and corresponds to the lungs; the circle transforms to explain the letter *A,* which has the meaning of Mahāvairocana's ocean of wisdom. It is the seed syllable of the great water disc.[130] The mystical powers of sovereignty in the dharma are called the wisdom of the *dharmakāya.* [This is also called the *saṃbhogakāya*[131]] and the lotus division of the mandala."[132]

It also says, "The letter *A* is in the east, is Akṣobhya Buddha. The letter *vaṃ* is in the west, is Amitābha Buddha."[133]

Again: "Next, recite the characters, the western direction is *san-bo-dai.* All practices therefore become perfect awakening. The color white means is perfectly bright. It also has the meaning of water, and Amitābha Buddha. This Amitābha is also translated as nectar (*amṛta*), which can also mean water."[134]

[Fascicle twelve] of the *Commentary on the Mahāvairocana-sūtra* says:

> Through the gate of the yoga of *hrīḥ* you may understand all dharmas and bring great benefit to all sentient beings. First, you should contemplate this letter above your head, white like snow or flowing milk, pouring into one's heart. Then it fills your entire body, which is purified inside and out. All that one sees is the same as the body of the Buddha. From your body it flows out, universally permeating the bodies of all sentient beings, causing them to be purified. A secret commentary says this is the water of great compassion. Next contemplate the [beings in] the world of great torment as also benefited in this way. Whatever they drink or touch, they will ultimately have their suffering removed and will attain the highest awakening. This water is the same as nectar.[135]

For this reason, the lotus reveals one's pure nature in samādhi. Now, the western direction has wind and water, two spheres. In *wuxing* it corresponds to metal and wind. In the four continents[136] it has the appearance of the element of water. Both confirm that it is the one essence of the yoga of the Lotus Samādhi. Water signifies the purity of one's nature. Wind reveals the fundamental essence.

[2.2] On the *Mahākaruṇā* Samādhi

Question: The Dharma gate of Amitābha Buddha is called the mind of the *mahākaruṇā* samādhi. Why is this?

Answer: According to Kōbō Daishi's [*Hannya shingyō hiken* 般若心經祕鍵 (T. 2203A)], "This 'Tathāgata who attains the purity of self-nature' opens and demonstrates [the Buddha's insight] to beings, and frees them from suffering and distress."[137]

The opening of the heart-lotus reveals the resultant virtues [of Buddhahood]. At that time, one is liberated from samsara, suffering, and distress and awakens to nirvana and permanent bliss. It is therefore called the *mahākaruṇā* samādhi, which accords with the Lotus Samādhi.

When the practitioner single-mindedly follows the breath in and out in the yoga of calling the name, they should contemplate themselves employing this *mahākaruṇā*. The words of the calling of the name become like the wind that permeates the ten directions, without a single world excluded. The heart-lotus of all sentient beings blossoms. The practitioner who has accomplished the resultant virtues of the eight-petaled lotus dais turns toward [all] sentient beings and bestows *mahākaruṇā*. All buddhas turn toward this practitioner and perform the *adhiṣṭhāna*. The mind, buddhas, and sentient beings—these three are without distinction. The heart-lotuses of self and other blossom simultaneously.

Question: Regarding the *mahākaruṇā* samādhi that accords with the Lotus Samādhi (SAZ 2:246), is it the case that *mahākaruṇā* is the lotus? Is *mahākaruṇā* inherently connected with the wisdom of sentient beings? [The *Abhidharmakośa-bhāṣya* 阿毘達磨俱舍論 (T. 1558)] says, "*Mahākaruṇā* is simply mundane cognition (as opposed to sublime wisdom)."[138] The lotus is that which reveals the principle. What is called the one substance?

Answer: The principle and wisdom of the inseparability of all dharmas is contained within the dual mandala. The Womb Realm mandala is *mahākaruṇā*, the lotus. (The principle of the five elements.) The Vajra Realm mandala is *mahāprajñā*, the moon disc. (The wisdom of the consciousness element.)

Wisdom has as its essence distinguishing and deciding, and therefore it signifies cutting off deluded thinking, the realization of principle, and so on. Principle means universally grasping, and therefore it permeates everywhere. For this reason, the gate of *mahākaruṇā* not only does not reject any [beings] it embraces all equally. As for the connection of the heart of sentient beings to *mahākaruṇā*, the thusness of the six elements and the body-mind [of sentient beings] is nondual. Therefore, the body has principle-wisdom. The body reveals the (wisdom) form (principle). This is it. Mind has principle and wisdom. The mind-compassion (principle) wisdom is therefore the union of wisdom and principle, the nondual mind of *mahākaruṇā*. *Mahākaruṇā* is connected to sentient beings. Great wisdom is connected to all of the buddhas, and all of the buddhas' wisdom is connected to the principle of sentient beings. This is the nonduality that is called *mahākaruṇā*. Thus, *mahākaruṇā* is the lotus.

Question: Both have as their essence *mahākaruṇā*. What does this mean?

Answer: The *mahākaruṇā* that arises from the fundamental unity of all buddhas is what Amitābha Buddha truly is. The six realms, the beings born in four ways, the nine realms and the buddha realm, including crickets, ants, mosquitoes, horseflies, and so on—all sentient beings, each and every one, has a corporeal [heart] divided into eight segments, and this is the heart-lotus, which is none other than Amitābha Buddha. Based on the aforementioned discussion, when you call out the name in three letters (*A-MI-TA*) and five wisdoms (*NAMO-A-MI-TA-BU*), in the realms of the buddhas and of sentient beings there is not [one entity] that is not the "letter" of Buddha's "voice," the "outer expression" to Buddha's "truth." For this reason, take Amitābha to be the great compassion that arises from the fundamental unity of all.

Question: *Mahāmaitrī* (great kindness) and *mahākaruṇā* (great compassion), what are their similarities and the differences between them?

Answer: The words *maitrī* and *karuṇā* are distinguished as corresponding to wisdom and principle, respectively. It is also said that *maitrī* corresponds to the father and *karuṇā* to the mother. The father decisively takes up practice; the mother wholly embraces and nourishes. This is the essence of wisdom and compassion (*karuṇā*), heaven and earth, and meditation, wisdom, kindness (*maitrī*), and pity (*karuṇā*). Meditation accords with wisdom as *maitrī* accords with *karuṇā*. *Karuṇā* and wisdom are of the fundamental dichotomies.[139]

Sometimes it is revealed that *maitrī* and *karuṇā* correspond to principle and wisdom, with the Womb Realm mandala taken to be *mahakaruṇā* and the Vajra Realm mandala as *mahamaitrī* (and so on).

Amitābha Buddha is both *mahamaitri* and *mahakaruṇā*. This has two meanings: One, *karuṇā* within is used by wisdom. This is the one gate of principle-wisdom. Two, this is the universal gate of principle-wisdom. This honored one (Amitābha Buddha) has taken the nondual practice of the dual mandalas to its completion. Think about this.

[2.3] On the Characters "Utmost Bliss"

The *Smaller Amitābha Sutra* says, "In that land sentient beings never experience suffering, but rather experience all forms of bliss. For that reason, it is called Sukhāvatī, the Land of Utmost Bliss."[140]

According to the minds of exoteric Buddhist thinkers, Sukhāvatī is the entryway to the Pure Lands of the ten directions. In contrast to the defilement, evil, and extreme suffering [of beings] in this *sahā* world, that land is called Sukhāvatī. For that reason, they say to feel revulsion toward this defiled land and joyfully seek the Pure Land.[141]

Tiantai Zhiyi's *Amituojing yiji* 阿彌陀經義記 (T. 1755) says: "In this way, in regards to the noble ones, [those born in the Pure Land], initially they are still in the lower level [of the Pure Land], but when compared to this *sahā* world it is therefore called Sukhāvatī."[142] This the shallow abbreviated explanation.

Next, the deep and secret explanation: According to the *Hizōki:* "The Lotus Store World, therein lies the highest sublime bliss; for that reason it is called Sukhāvatī. You should know that Sukhāvatī and the Lotus Store World, though they have different names, are not different locations."[143]

The meaning of this secret teaching is that the Lotus Store is principle, the Womb Realm mandala. The Realm of Esoteric Splendor is wisdom, the Vajra Realm mandala. Sukhāvatī is the Lotus Store. Tuṣita is the Realm of Esoteric Splendor.

Principle includes the store of the manifold virtues, just as the great earth produces manifold forms of life, and therefore it possesses bliss that is like an inexhaustible array of marvelous jewels. Thus it is called Sukhāvatī.

Wisdom eliminates and purifies the delusion of a "self" in objects in the world or a human being and causes one to attain the emptiness of both, revealing the manifold virtues. Like space, including the manifold things, Tuṣita is in the sky, and Sukhāvatī is of the earth. One should consider deeply the profound meaning that Tuṣita is "in the heavens." Also, the meaning of the word Tuṣita is "satisfaction" (Skt. *saṃtuṣṭi*).

The Abhidharmakośa-bhāṣya says, "In the body it is called bliss, in the mind it is called happiness."[144]

The Womb Realm mandala is connected to the body, and the Vajra Realm mandala is connected to the mind. Therefore, the names Utmost Bliss (Sukhāvatī) and Satisfaction (Saṃtuṣṭi) reveal the teaching of the dual mandala of body and mind. Both principle and wisdom are endowed with the manifold virtues, encompassing the two truths of being and emptiness. Thus, Sukhāvatī has thirty-three levels of adornments, and Tuṣita has seventy-seven layers of wonders. Think about this.

One should not discourse on the relative merits of Sukhāvatī as opposed to Tuṣita. One should not separate Amitābha Buddha from Maitreya Bodhisattva. From time immemorial we fundamentally have in our body and mind both principle and wisdom, the body [of Amitābha Buddha and Maitreya Bodhisattva], and the lands [Sukhāvatī and Tuṣita]. For this reason, [Kōbō] Daishi said, "Sukhāvatī and Tuṣita are from the very beginning within your very breast."[145]

[2.4] On the Western Direction

Question: Why is it that Amitābha resides in the western direction?

Answer: West is the direction of autumn, where all things come to fruition. People take delight in this, and therefore it is also seen as the direction of reverential love. Reverence is *mahakaruṇā;* therefore, the western direction reveals the gate of the *mahakaruṇā* samādhi. Also, Amitābha is the buddha of the gate of awakening to bodhi. For this reason, regarding the direction of fruition, fascicle twenty of the *Commentary on the Mahāvairocana-sutra* says, "Next, chant *san-bo-dai,* employ the manifold practices to attain perfect enlightenment.[146] The buddha is named Amitābha and is in the western direction."[147]

It also says: "Next, why is the open flower called Amitābha? This is the Buddha outwardly manifesting the results [of enlightenment]. This is the limitless inconceivable bliss of Dharma. That is why it has this name."[148]

Question: Of the five divisions [of the center of the mandala], the western direction is the lotus division of the mandala. The lotus is the Womb Realm mandala. The dual mandala takes the Womb Realm mandala as the East, and the Vajra Realm mandala as the West. Does this mean that Lotus-Womb/East-West has two meanings?

Answer: In the dual mandala the Lotus-Womb Realm has some similarities and differences in meaning in regard to the three divisions and the five divisions. You should look to Kakuban's *Himitsu sōgon funigi shō* 祕密莊嚴不二義章 (T. 2524). However, regarding the lotus division of the mandala and the Lotus-as-Womb Realm mandala, though in general there are differences and they are not the same, on the level of principle they are one. The meaning of east and west in the dual mandala moreover has two gates. One is the gate of the dichotomy of cause and effect. Womb and Vajra, respectively, mean cause and effect. Womb is east, and that which is called east is the direction of spring. Grasses, trees, and buds move, and therefore mean "cause." West is the direction of autumn, the fruition of all things, and therefore means "effect" (and so on).

The gate of the dichotomy between both meditation and wisdom, Womb and Vajra, respectively, [correspond] to meditation and wisdom, and therefore Womb is west and east is Vajra. That which is called east is the direction of *yang,* and therefore taken to be wisdom-man, west is the western direction, *yin,* meditation, and woman. For this reason, meditation is established in the western direction.

Question: West is also named the gate of wisdom-compassion. How is this similar or different from meditation and wisdom?

Answer: In the east is the great round mirror wisdom, which we may call the Vajra division; it is the wisdom of the buddhas that cuts off delusion and causes beings to attain awakening. Turning toward the self-realization in the west, the wisdom of subtle discernment, which we may call the gate of wisdom and compassion, is the wisdom of the Dharma preaching that cuts off doubts. It is connected to the conversion of others; therefore the wisdom and compassion of the western direction is also connected to the wisdom of the gate of great compassion.

Also, *bodhicitta,* practice, bodhi, nirvana, *upāya* possess the five points (of the mandala), which may be engaged, in order, in the following three ways. First: east, west, south, north, middle. Second: center, east, west, south, north. Third: center, south, north, west. Thus, when west has the full meaning of *upāya,* therefore, together with the other five points, meditation, (wisdom), in the east and so on, the meaning between these is not in conflict (i.e., they are the same).

[2.5] On the [Notion That Sukhāvatī Lies beyond] Ten Thousand Million Buddha Lands

(This section may contain mistakes.[149])

The *Golden Sands Discourse* mentioned in Enchin's 圓珍 (814 -891) *Catalogue of Works Brought from China* says:

> Question: In the western direction does there exist, over one hundred thousand million buddha lands away, Sukhāvatī?
>
> Answer: As for the western direction, [which you perceive to be one hundred thousand million buddha lands away,] it is a function of the one hundred thousand million afflictions. Through the adornment of myriad good deeds one is able to see the sublime essence of the enlightened mind, and this is called Sukhāvatī.[150]

A secret transmission conveys that the hundred thousand million afflictions are composed of the ten fundamental afflictions that possess one hundred thousand million connected afflictions. Also, as for those who are liberated [from the afflictions by virtue], as explained above, and as for those who discourse on the attainment of the virtues, this is the mudra of the wisdom that distinguishes the tens of buddha realms as numerous as particles of dust.

Regarding the Buddha's ten powers of wisdom, one by one, each wisdom has one buddha land [composed of buddha lands as] numerous as dust particles; they are therefore called tens of buddha lands as numerous as dust particles. Thus, though in truth they are limitless, in order to explain the ten wisdoms they are provisionally described in this way, as having a finite number. Now, this number "one hundred thousand million" is also like this; with one of the powers of [the Buddha's] wisdom, you raise the wisdom mudra of ten thousand million, and also manifest one hundred thousand million.

[2.6] On the Forty-Eight Vows

Question: When Amitābha Buddha was still at the causal stage, giving rise to the mind that seeks enlightenment, for what reason did the Bodhisattva make forty-eight vows, no more, no less?

Answer: In Nāgārjuna's *Shi moheyan lun*, regarding buddha reality, it reveals 84,048 kinds of virtues [so that beings may] take refuge in the 84,000 forms and attributes of those virtues and the forty-eight kinds of virtues of the mind. Nāgārjuna was a great gentleman of the first stage, a sage in Sukhāvatī. The buddha in whom he took refuge was the *saṃbhogakāya,* Amitābha Buddha. The 84,000 forms and attributes are the [84,000] major and minor marks of the Buddha. The forty-eight kinds of virtues, how could they be the *nirmāṇakāya?* Hence, take the forty-eight vows of the causal stage as the full attainment of the kinds of virtue associated with the forty-eight vows. Now, the resultant virtues have forty-eight [kinds]; therefore the vow to attain awakening is "six times eight."

An esoteric text says:

> The *Wuliangshou yigui* explains the Amitābha mandala. On the central dais is Avalokiteśvara. On the eight petals of the lotus are eight buddhas. The great compassion of Avalokiteśvara causes the truth of the resultant virtues of the eight wisdoms of Amitabha to be revealed. Avalokiteśvara has six kinds of bodies, and these are the great compassion which is of the same substance as the six realms. For this reason, sentient beings of the six realms all have as their fundamental nature the eight-petaled heart-lotus, for this causes the arousal and opening of the six [realms?], the eight [petals of the mandala of Amitābha], and the forty-eight vows.

[2.7] On the Sixteen Contemplations [in the *Contemplation Sutra*]

Question: What is the meaning for the sixteen contemplations in the *Contemplation Sutra?*

Answer: The resultant virtues of Amitābha Buddha's [awakening], perfect and complete, give rise to sixteen bodhisattvas. The Buddha's absolutely perfect virtue is no more than the sixteen stages of birth [in the Pure Land], just as the sixteen phases of the moon [altogether compose the full moon]. From Vajrasattva Bodhisattva to Vajrasaṃdhi Bodhisattva[151], these are called the sixteen great bodhisattvas that are born. Being born means the arising of virtue, not the meaning of [samsaric] rebirth [where one forgets one's past knowledge].

These sixteen contemplations possess the [sixteen] manifold virtues of the dual mandala. The first thirteen constitute the goodness arising from meditation, which is the gate of meditation of the Womb Realm mandala. The latter three constitute the three levels of the Pure Land [in nine divisions], which is the gate of wisdom of the Vajra Realm mandala. Goodness arising from meditation, beginning with the contemplations of the earth and water and so on, relies on the orthodox Womb Realm mandala, employing the five elements as [its outer manifestation], together with principle and wisdom.

Goodness arising in ordinary life [outside of meditation] follows the conduct of body and mind, which is divided into nine classes [of karmic activity], together with meditation and wisdom. Form is without distinction and is therefore connected to meditation. The mind [of the sixth consciousness] perceives objects and is therefore associated with [one's conduct outside of meditative absorption, in contact with the world].

In this way, the thirteen forms of goodness arising from meditation correspond to the thirteen great courts of the Womb Realm mandala, and the nine grades of rebirth in the Pure Land are the nine assemblies of the Vajra Realm mandala.

According to Paramārtha (499–569),[152] the expansion and contraction of the three grades of the Pure Land in nine levels include the nine consciousness as three:

(1) *ādāna* (SAZ 2:250) (or *manas*, the seventh consciousness)
(2) *ālaya* (the eighth consciousness)
(3) *amala* (the ninth consciousness)

Therefore, [just as the three grades of the Pure Land contain the nine levels, so, too,] do the three consciousness and the nine consciousnesses also expand and contract.

Question: Both of the dual mandalas are regarded as these sixteen births. What evidence is there for this?

Answer: The Buddha's perfect and complete [virtue] is no more than these sixteen; what then is not principle and wisdom? [The same goes for] the five wisdoms, the sixteen honored ones, the seventeen honored ones, and so on. As for the discourse on the connections between the dual mandalas, one should devote oneself to further inquiry into this matter.

First off, the sun disc meditation, and so on, have both shallow and deep meanings. The shallow interpretation is the common way.

In Shandao's *Commentary on the Contemplation Sutra* they have three meanings, and among those three, the "mind mirror/mind and objects of perception" (T. 1753:260c3–4, 262b12–13) resembles the deep secret [teaching].

In our tradition, in the sun disc meditation the sun disc itself is the *katsuma* body of Amitābha Tathāgata. When one grasps the setting sun (the next stage in the contemplation), one imagines that the sun disc takes on the color of deep crimson, the color of great compassion. The deep secret sun disc contemplation is performed throughout the twelve divisions of day and night [and so on], excluding the earth and water contemplation, and so on. Think about this deeply.

[2.8] On the [Descent of the Buddha to Usher Beings into the Pure Land]

The [descent of the Buddha to usher beings into the Pure Land] signifies the Buddha's sympathetic response to the practices of sentient beings and the empowerment of the Buddha.

The *Commentary on the Mahāvairocana-sūtra* says: "The practitioner cultivates the *pratyutpanna-samādhi* within and externally receives the protection and support of all buddhas, attaining a vision of the adornments without limit, which are the revelations signifying the Buddha's empowerments."[153]

The *Sokushin jobutsugi* says: "The word *adhiṣṭhāna* [expressed in Chinese as *jiachi* (加持), meaning 'adding and holding'], demonstrates the universal compassion ['added' by] the tathāgatas and the mind of faith [held by] beings. *Jia,* to 'add,' means that the radiance of the Buddha reflects in the minds of beings, just as the sun is reflected on the water's surface. *Chi,* to 'hold," is when the practitioner perceives the radiance of the Buddha in their mind as though reflected on water."[154]

When the mind of the practitioner is gradually purified of defilements, the original enlightenment of one's own mind is reflected [as if in a clear mirror], and one's identity with the *dharmakāya* is also reflected. This harmonization of the water of the floating mind is called the reflection facing the Buddha. [Therefore,] the Buddha that descends [seemingly from the Pure Land to usher beings to that other land] is none other than your very mind reflecting the image of the Buddha. At the end of one's life, in a single moment of mindfulness, attain a vision of the adornments without limit, which are the revelations signifying the Buddha's empowerments. This is called [the Buddha that descends].

If one is a practitioner of the ordinary methods of the exoteric vehicle, having not yet discovered the inner awakening of one's own mind, you will [perceive] the descent of the Buddha and the lotus dais as being outside your mind, and therefore you will be reborn in a lotus blossom in the Pure Land and see the Buddha.

If you are a practitioner of mantra, this miraculous birth upon the lotus dais is understood to be none other than the very lotus of one's own inner realization; therefore you will instantaneously discover the wisdom of the buddhas.

If one practices the contemplation of the Buddha in the ordinary path, and if one has the good karmic roots of mantra, however, you should think of this Buddha's welcoming descent as being none other than the mudra and mantra of discerning the mind.[155] This indicates the lotus dais of one's own mind and grasping the hand of Mahāsthāmaprāpta Bodhisattva.

[2.10] On the Twenty-Five Bodhisattvas [in Amitābha's Retinue]

Amitābha Buddha has five wisdoms, and these five wisdoms each have five wisdoms. This is like the five discs of liberation [visualized in] the assemblies of the Vajra Realm mandala. Each disc has five honored ones, and these tathāgata discs are perfectly round and full of virtue, containing only this. These (SAZ 2:251) twenty-five bodhisattvas of the Pure Land give rise to these five wisdoms of the five directions, and so on. They are also the embodiment of great compassion. As there are six realms, there are six forms of Avalokiteśvara. Revealed within these six realms are the twenty-five forms of being.[156]

The six forms of Avalokiteśvara each produce twenty-five samādhis. The twenty-five bodhisattvas are the true nature of these twenty-five forms of being, and using their innate realization they open their eyes and see the five discs of liberation in the five directions and the five wisdoms.

The *Mohezhiguan* says:

> The "*dhāraṇī* of six-syllable phrases" have the power to destroy the obstacles of passionate afflictions; without a doubt they purify the [senses of] the poisons [of greed, anger, and delusion], and consummate the path to buddhahood. The "six syllables" refer to the six [incarnations of] Avalokiteśvara, who have the power to destroy the three kinds of obstacles in the six [lower] destinies.
>
> (1) [*Dōhan identifies Avalokiteśvara with Ten Thousand Hands 千手觀世音 with] Avalokiteśvara as Great Compassion 大悲觀世音destroys the three obstacles in the destiny of hell. The suffering in this destiny is intense—therefore it is appropriate to apply great compassion.
> (2) [*Dōhan identifies Ārya Avalokiteśvara 正觀音 with) Avalokiteśvara as Great Mercy 大慈觀世音 destroys the three obstacles in the destiny of hungry ghosts. This destiny entails starvation and thirst—therefore it is appropriate to apply great mercy.
> (3) [*Dōhan identifies Hayagrīva Avalokiteśvara 馬頭觀世音 with] The Fearless Lionlike Avalokiteśvara 師子無畏觀世音 destroys the three obstacles in the destiny of animals. The king of beasts is majestic and fierce [and can thus face the untamed ferociousness of beasts]—therefore it is appropriate to apply fearlessness.
> (4) [*Dōhan identifies eleven-faced Avalokiteśvara 十一面觀世音 with] Avalokiteśvara as Universally Shining Great Light 大光普照觀世音 destroys the three obstacles of the destiny of the *asuras*. This destiny entails envy and distrust—therefore it is appropriate to apply universal illumination.
> (5) [*Dōhan identifies Cundi Avalokiteśvara 准胝觀世音 with] Avalokiteśvara as the Divine Hero 天人丈夫觀世音 destroys the three obstacles in the destiny of human beings. The human destiny involves both mundane affairs 事 and [the capacity] to understand the principle [of reality] 理. He is called "divine" because he uses mundane means to overcome [human arrogance]; he is called a "hero" in [that he helps human beings understand] the principle [of reality], that is, to perceive buddha-nature.
> (6) [*Dōhan identifies Wish-Granting Jewel Avalokiteśvara 意輪觀世音 with] Avalokiteśvara as Mahābrahmā the Profound 大梵深遠觀世音 destroys the three obstacles in the destiny of divine beings. Brahmā is the lord of divine beings—by indicating the lord, one includes the vassals as well.

Expanding on this further, the six [incarnations of Avalokiteśvara may signify the twenty-five *samādhis*. [Avalokiteśvara as] Great Compassion corresponds to the *samādhi* of nondefilement [#1]. [Avalokiteśvara as] Great

Mercy corresponds to the *samādhi* of a blissful mind [#3]. Fearless Lionlike [Avalokiteśvara] corresponds to the *samādhi* of nonretrogression [#2]. [Avalokiteśvara as] Great Light corresponds to the *samādhi* of joy [#4]. [Avalokiteśvara as] Hero corresponds to the four *samādhis* up to that which is like a mirage [#5–#8]. [Avalokiteśvara as] Mahābrahmā corresponds to the seventeen *samādhis* [that remain], starting with that which is immobile [#9–#25].[157]

[2.11] On *Sahā* Revealing Avalokiteśvara and Sukhāvatī Being Called Limitless Life

Avalokiteśvara Bodhisattva is the cause, and Amitābha Buddha is the effect. This defiled world is the cause, and the Pure Land is the effect. This is why Avalokiteśvara Bodhisattva abides within *sahā,* in the muck, among the evil defilements, revealing [to beings] their fundamental self-nature, the heart-lotus. Amitābha Buddha is that which is contemplated; it is the "reward name." Avalokiteśvara Bodhisattva is able to call upon the virtues of that name. Therefore, to *sahā,* in the world of sounds, Avalokiteśvara Bodhisattva reveals the voice of liberation in the primal vow.

End of Fascicle Two

Himitsu nenbutsu shō

Fascicle Three

[3.1] On the Lotus Daises of the Nine Levels [of the Pure Land]

Kakuban says:

> If [one practices] in accordance with the shallow and abbreviated teachings, then they [will be reborn] in the *nirmāṇakāya* land manifested for others by the Buddha. If one relies on the deep secret [teaching] then they [will be reborn] in the buddha land of the self-nature of the *dharmakāya*.[158] That which is provisionally named the western direction is in reality the universal *dharmadhātu*. Giving rise to the vow desiring birth, this mind and that land, the nine-level lotus dais is the opening of the heart-lotus of your essential virtue. The infinite adornments are revealed to be already possessed and as numerous as grains of sands of the Ganges.[159]

Therefore, it is revealed that fundamentally the nine levels of the lotus dais are the nine levels of consciousness, and that which is called the heart organ of eight segments, and so on, include the essential characteristics of the dual mandala. Contemplate the eight-petal dais as the Womb Realm mandala, and contemplate the nine-level moon disc as the Vajra Realm mandala. The eight-petal lotus is round like the moon.

Question: The practitioner of the three mysteries takes the adornment of the buddha land of the pure mind as rebirth in the Pure Land. This is the Lotus Repository. But for those practitioners who follow the ordinary path that is shallow and abbreviated, will they truly be born in the Pure Land outside their own minds?

Answer: Amitābha's *dharmakāya* has four levels. Sukhāvatī has four lands (this is Annen's interpretation); therefore, for the practitioner of the ordinary path, since they [think] that the Pure Land is something beyond their own minds they will experience the bliss of birth in the response land of Sukhāvatī.

Because the mantra teachings are the teachings of the *dharmakāya,* certainly this Dharma [leads to the] direct realization of the body and land of Amitābha's own nature. The revealed teachings are the teachings of the *nirmāṇakāya* buddha; therefore, those who rely on these teachings are born to the *nirmāṇakāya* and land of Amitābha.

For those who practice the mantra vehicle, however, whose good karma is not quite ripe and who have not yet been able to immediately enter [awakening], [they may be] born in that *nirmāṇakāya* land and enjoy the many blessings revealed by Amitābha. [There they will] discover the lotus dais of Mahāvairocana. Those who fall into this category can only make a connection [with the Buddha], but through the practice of mantra, they will become like those who have performed good karmic deeds.

Question: Those who practice *nenbutsu* according to the ordinary path and those who have established connections with mantra practice both attain rebirth in the Pure Land. Is there then no difference between exoteric and esoteric [paths]?

Answer: Those who are born in that land through exoteric practice must pass through many kalpas in a womblike lotus, and after this lotus blossom opens and they see the Buddha, they will pass through kalpas without number before they enter the stage of the Buddha.

Therefore, according to the Tendai monk Zenyu's [*Amida shinjū gi* 阿彌陀新十疑]: "After rebirth in Sukhāvatī you may pass through thousands of kalpas to attain the first stage. After the first stage you may still pass through one thousand kalpas. This is called the marvelous awakening of becoming a buddha."[160]

Shandao's *Commentary on the Contemplation Sutra* says, "Riding the power of the Buddha's vow until the attainment of rebirth, you will directly give rise to the *bodhi* mind upon the opening of the lotus blossom."[161]

The meaning of these commentaries suggests that going for rebirth in Sukhāvatī is merely for those ordinary beings who [have not yet ascended the ten *bhūmis* (grounds) of the bodhisattva path], and once born there in the land of nonretrogression, they will then pursue bodhisattva practices and be able to attain Buddhahood.

Practitioners of the mantra gate fundamentally accord with the gate of sudden entry [into Buddhahood]. Therefore, [for mantra practitioners] birth in that land is exactly the opening of the lotus dais of self-realization.

The *Wuliangshou yigui* says, "Rely on this Dharma teaching practice with correct mindfulness and you will certainly be born in the realm of Sukhāvatī in the very highest level, attaining the first stage [of the bodhisattva path]."[162]

Now, in the exoteric vehicle, [the notion of] attaining Buddhahood after passing through many kalpas is a provisional explanation given within that teaching gate. In regard to true practice, after being born in that land if you then enter into the mantra gate, you will realize entry into the lotus dais of Mahāvairocana Buddha.

Question: Now, [regarding] practitioners of mantra who do not realize entry [into Buddhahood] in this life but instead attain rebirth in Sukhāvatī and cast off this body, are they like those of this defiled realm who do not attain sudden awakening in this very body?

Answer: Through the direct perception of the [nature] of delusion, one cannot doubt the truth of the realm of awakening. As for those who suddenly attain awakening, there are some who cast off their bodies, and some who do not, in accordance with their [karmic background and environment]. Nagarjuna cast off his body, whereas Kōbō Daishi did not. In all cases, it is due to mysterious karmic factors. This is something about which the unenlightened cannot know.

Question: According to the *Contemplation Sutra,* in the levels of the nine grades the lowest level of the lowest grade is for those who have committed the five unforgivable sins, and so on, yet through reliance on the ten moments of mindfulness at the end of their lives they attain rebirth. Does the ordinary *nenbutsu* [possess] the power to extinguish even such sins as these?

Answer: There are two explanations. The *Larger Sukhāvatīvyūhasūtra* says that those who commit such sins are excluded. The *Contemplation Sutra* says those transgressors [will] attain rebirth. These differing interpretations are like fire and ice; they cannot be completely resolved. However, this does not pertain to the *himitsu nenbutsu* 秘密念佛 [as this is not its purpose]. One cannot wholly extinguish the five unforgivable sins.

The *Liuduji jing* gathers a repository of Dharma from all past and present buddhas, up to the fifth repository, the dhāraṇī repository. This alone may eliminate the five grave unforgivable sins. The other four cannot accomplish this. Relying on this as precedent, the ten thought moments discussed in the *Contemplation Sutra* are none other than the esoteric ghee. The explanation of the subtle Dharma is none other than the secret subtle Dharma.

The *Contemplation Sutra* says:

> As for those born into the lowest level of the lowest grade, those who have committed the five grave offenses and the ten evil acts, and various other unvirtuous acts: at the end of their lives they will meet a *kalyāṇa-mitra* (good spiritual friend) who lifts their spirits and teaches them the Dharma, instructing them in contemplation of the Buddha. Such a person, however, suffers to the degree that they are unable to contemplate the Buddha. Therefore, the good friend tells them that if they are unable to contemplate the Buddha, they should call upon the Buddha wholeheartedly, continuously chanting *Namo Amitābhāya* ten times. In this way, they will be liberated from past negative karma, as much as that acquired in eight *koṭis* of *kalpas,* and will immediately attain rebirth.[163]

[3.2] On Exclusive (Single-Minded) Practice and Uninterrupted Practice

Shandao's *Commentary on the Contemplation Sutra* says:

> Also, then, within this correct [form of contemplation] there are moreover two kinds: First is with a single-minded contemplation, exclusively contemplating the name of Amitābha Buddha. Whether walking, standing, sitting, or lying down, without concern for practicing at a set time, whether long or short, constantly contemplating the Buddha without ceasing—this is called the correct meditative activity.
>
> Second, following in accordance with this the Buddha's vows, if one were to rely upon worshiping [the Buddha], chanting [the sutras], and so on, then this is called auxiliary actions. Besides these the two practices of main and auxiliary, there are also the practices carried out before and after. [These practices contain] manifold good [merits] and are all called miscellaneous practices. If practicing before the main and auxiliary practices, then one's mind is constantly practicing, in a state of constant contemplation without ceasing. This is called uninterrupted [practice].[164]

Eikan's *Ōjō jūin* says:

> Question: The minds of ordinary practitioners are like wild horses. Through the sole practice of contemplating or chanting the name of the Buddha, how can one achieve uninterrupted practice?
>
> Answer: Those who we refer to as beginning practitioners are not all confused or giving rise to distraction in their contemplation. Master

> Shandao says (SAZ 2:254), "When the afflictions of greed, hatred, [and ignorance], and so on arise, as sins are followed by repentance [then] contemplate without separation, separation of time, separation of days. Always endeavor to purify [oneself]; this is also called uninterrupted practice."[165]

Also, for those whose minds are confused, it is difficult to successfully practice contemplation. Out of compassion the Great Sage taught the practice of calling the Name. This is because calling the Name is easy to practice continuously, day or night without rest. How could it not be uninterrupted?[166] Also, do not compare bodies as being pure or unpure. Do not discourse on whose minds are focused and whose are not. Call the Name without ceasing, and you will certainly attain rebirth. Also, [this constant practice is the correct contemplation of the Buddha].[167]

It is also says, "Relying on this, the practitioner sets aside all other desires, vows only [to be reborn], and only practices the one practice of *nenbutsu*. Among those who are scattered and sluggish, out of a thousand not one will attain birth. Among those who are single-minded in their practice, out of ten thousand not one will be lost."[168]

The true meaning of passages like this is that you should take up the single-minded recitation of the name and never let it go. Single-mindedly chant the name and constantly contemplate [the Buddha]. The name that is single-mindedly cultivated is the name that is cultivated without ceasing.

But what of the ignorant being? How can they achieve a mind that is continuously good?

One may continuously chant the name, but then commit offenses and repent. This is not truly continuous. What about when one is asleep, or unconscious, or absent-minded, or unfocused, or your chanting or contemplation is interrupted? How can this be called unceasing?

In all cases, [you should] rely on the *himitsu nenbutsu*. This is the truly unceasing practice. [Within the phrase] *nenbutsu*, the character *nen* ("contemplation") refers to the ability to praise [the Buddha] with sound and letters; the character *butsu* ("buddha") refers to the true reality of that which is praised. The ability to praise [the Buddha] is wisdom, and that which is praised is principle. This wisdom and principle is the dual mandala.

At all times the practitioner breathes in and out. This breath-wind is none other than the essence of the name of Amitābha Buddha (name and essence). The in- and out-breath is none other than the dual mandala. The out-breath may be taken to be the Vajra [Realm mandala], the outward manifestation [of the Buddha's activity]; the in-breath may be taken to the Womb [Realm mandala], the inner realization [of the buddhas].

The out-breath is the wisdom that one is able to realize. The in-breath is the principle that one contemplates. Therefore, the in- and out-breath of the practitioner is precisely the uninterrupted contemplation of Buddha. Also, grasping the five *skandhas*, sentient beings realize that the five *skandhas* are both body and mind, and body and mind are precisely the dual mandalas [as well]. This is because the mind is the wisdom that one is able to contemplate, and the body is the principle that is praised.

Also, in this teaching, the voice-letter is none other than the true reality. [Just as] the dual mandalas are inseparable, the name [of the Buddha arises] together with the esoteric name [or mantra] of the Buddha. Because of this, [the *himitsu nenbutsu*] is the true reality of the bodies and minds of sentient beings. The naturally arisen contemplation of Buddha is the ever-present calling of the name.

If, on hearing this teaching even once, the practitioner has faith in this principle even once and afterward contemplates calling the name a single time, then this is the [true] uninterrupted contemplation of Buddha. This is the truly unceasing practice.

Also, all of the holy teachings are in their essence Amitābha Buddha's secret speech. How then can you separate the path of sages from the Pure Land gate? All of the sublime practices are the six characters, [*Namu A-mi-da-butsu*]. How then can you separate primary and auxiliary practice from miscellaneous practice?

You should know that all teachings, in principle, practice, and results, are in all cases the Dharma gate of Amitābha Buddha and Sukhāvatī. Therefore this is called the single-minded practice. This [*himitsu nenbutsu*] is the absolute single-minded practice.

To put it another way, *nenbutsu* is the "brilliant light that universally illuminates"[169] the world-systems of the ten directions, embracing sentient beings, never letting go of them.[170] How then can one place limits on [even the] chanting of the name according to the ordinary path?

Question: If even a single moment of mindful recitation of the name possesses the virtue of eternal uninterrupted practice, can it not also convey the merits of one who strives diligently in their practices?

Answer: The mantra practitioner is one who has very good karma from previous lives. That good karma has come to fruition through the yoga of the three mysteries [of body, speech, and mind]. The heart-lotus that opens after only one thought is therefore the complete achievement of enlightenment upon the first arising of the mind [that seeks awakening].[171] From this, all subsequent actions of body, speech, and mind will become *upāya* for the attainment of awakening. If a practitioner of the mantra gate who, even though they have heard this teaching, is still separated from the attainment of the stage of good karma and does not immediately attain enlightenment, they will certainly amass in one lifetime the merits of the stage of nonretrogression.

Question: In the *Contemplation Sutra*, the cause of rebirth is taken to be the "three minds." [Shandao's] *Commentary* [*on the Contemplation Sutra*] says, "If one only has a little bit of one of the three minds, that is not enough to attain birth."[172] Now, what is the esoteric meaning behind this statement?

Answer: The ordinary path is intended for ordinary sentient beings who are profoundly confused and for whom it is difficult to muster the three minds. According to the esoteric meaning, however, calling the name with one mind naturally employs all three minds. As for the "three minds": The mind that is perfectly sincere [in the aspiration for rebirth in the Pure Land] is the mind of true reality, [the mind of the Buddha]. The mind of profundity, [deeply immersed in the pursuit of awakening], is the mind of faith. The mind that vows to offer all of one's merit to other beings is the transference of past and present good karma of body, speech, and mind [directed toward the goal of attaining birth in] Sukhāvatī.

So, in my own tradition, these three minds are the three letters *A-MI-TA*. These three letters are the three points of principle, wisdom, and phenomena.

First, the mind of true reality, the *hṛdaya* (heart) [of the Buddha], is principle. Therefore, fascicle three, [chapter 5,] of the *Mahāvairocana-sūtra* says: "And using the contemplation of the mind-field, the mind will reveal things as they are: undefiled, sublime, pure. Like a perfectly round mirror always reflecting what is before it, this is the mind of true reality. This is as explained by ancient buddhas."[173]

Fascicle twelve of the *Commentary on the Mahāvairocana* says: "This mind-field is undefiled and pure. Furthermore, it is like a perfectly round mirror always present before you. You should know that this is none other than that which has been explained by the buddhas of the past, the mind of true reality. In this way, the essence of mind is always abiding, it is unmoving and indestructible. Because it is none other than the *mahāparinirvāṇa* of all buddhas (the *dharmakāya*), it is called true reality."[174]

The "mind" of the mind-field is the *hṛdaya* of the mind. *Mahāparinirvāṇa* is principle. Next, the mind of faith is the wisdom of the *citta* mind.[175] Therefore, the *Commentary on the Mahāvairocana* says, "The pure *bodhi*-mind is the pure white mind of faith."[176] The *bodhi*-mind is the wisdom of the *citta*-mind. Therefore, these two "minds" are the two points of *dharmakāya* and *prajñā*.[177]

[As discussed in Shandao's *Commentary on the Contemplation Sutra*], the first of these minds [is] "the good roots of the practices [that benefit] one's self and others, [which are all provided[178]] by the mind of true faith in accordance with the vow of transference of merit for rebirth in the Pure Land."[179] These two minds are completely good. The arousal of the vow to transfer merit is therefore the point of liberation [through] the union of principle and wisdom [that compliment the two points of *dharmakāya* and *prajñā*]. As for the three points, they are like the above holy name; therefore, call the three letters and one will be naturally endowed with the three minds.

[3.3] On Ritual Practices for the Everyday [Contemplation of the Buddha]

Question: These days practitioners of buddha contemplation take mantra and *śamatha-vipaśyanā* as the path of sages [and, contrasting them with] the Pure Land gate, they cast them aside. Both primary and ancillary practices are taken to be [merely] "miscellaneous practices," and these are not taken up. What is the meaning of this?

Answer: Shandao and other masters take the world to be degenerate and in the age of the end of the Dharma. For those who have not yet learned the true Dharma, they selected one method for converting beings and divided the Dharma into two gates and two modes of practice. This is certainly an appropriate means for [teaching] the unenlightened. It is therefore inappropriate to argue [over it]. Therefore, relying on one's good karma, those who enter into the practices of the mantra gate single-mindedly cultivate the three mysteries and are able to practice the buddhānusmṛti samādhi.

Therefore, fascicle three of the *Dhāraṇīsaṃgraha-sūtra* says:

> Everyday you should chant the *dhāraṇī* of Akṣobhya Buddha, the *dhāraṇī* of Amitābha Buddha, and so on, to be rid of the five unforgivable offenses (i.e., killing one's mother, killing one's father, killing an arhat, injuring a buddha, sowing discord in the sangha), the four *pārājikas* (killing, stealing,

> lying, sexual misconduct) and so on, including the burden of all sins. If you hope to attain birth in Amitābha's land, you should perform this practice every day. Perform the *dhāraṇī* practice and constantly perform these other practices. These dharmas will certainly lead to birth in Amitābha's Pure Land after death. If you practice [in this way] every day the merit will be extremely great, beyond description. [Indeed,] the merits of contemplation of the Buddha are incomparable. The merits of chanting the spells [and *dhāraṇī* are great], like the light of the moon and the sun, while the virtue of the contemplation of the Buddha is a lamp in the night. It is not the same. If daily you simultaneously practice both the spells [and *dhāraṇī*] alongside contemplation of the Buddha, the virtues will be like an ocean as deep as Mt. Sumeru is tall. If one practices only the contemplation of the Buddha contemplation and does not also practice the spells and other incantations, then the virtue will be small as the Aromatic Mountain [in comparison to Mount Sumeru], or as narrow as Anavatapta (a great cosmic mountain and great lake from which the major rivers all flow). It will not measure up.[180]

Relying on the explanation in this sutra, take mantra as the primary practice and Buddha contemplation as the secondary practice. (This explanation, however, is targeted at those who have the ordinary [simplistic] understanding of the contemplation of the Buddha. It should be understood that the "secret contemplation of the Buddha" is what is meant here by mantra.)

Therefore, the practitioner of mantra should ordinarily practice one to three times a day with determination, either at a *sanmitsu* altar, a fire altar, or when doing other practices. On other occasions, you should abide in the *himitsu nenbutsu.* Over the years, as you continue to pursue these practices, making offerings of flowers and incense before the various buddhas, bodhisattvas, *vidyarājas,* and so on, [or to one's individual object of devotion], never retreating from this practice, it will serve as the cause of your birth [in the Pure Land]. Why is this so? All the vows and practices of the manifold buddhas are one, and they cause beings to escape from samsara and attain awakening. The essential gate [for rebirth in the Pure Land] is the samādhi of the contemplation of Amitābha Buddha. Therefore, all of the manifold buddhas aid in this vow. How could they possibly abandon one so "perfumed" by their practices? How much more so when all buddhas are but the one *dharmakāya* of Amitābha? All practices are the one practice of calling the name. Quickly, open your eyes to this revelation of unity! Do not conceive of [your Buddhist practice in exclusive terms], selecting [some] and rejecting [others]!

Now, for the practitioner of mantra there are the ordinary practices, such as those carried out in one's quarters, the ceremonies for entering the main hall, the evening chants, the procedures for bodily protection, and so on. There are also [practices associated with] the eating, wearing clothes, bathing, going to the bathroom, also walking, standing, sitting, lying down, and so on. In short, you should [practice] the gate of the tenfold contemplation and the sixfold supplementary practices.

The Gate of the Tenfold Contemplation

1. The Four Immeasurables[181]

The [four immeasurables] are like the ritual practices of the Vajra Realm [mandala] and do not arise apart from it. The practitioner of mantra knows when they encounter this teaching that their own mind fundamentally is Buddha, therefore does not toil [seeking to find] one's own (SAZ 2:257) awakening but turns toward teaching others, relying always on the practice of contemplating the four immeasurables.

The [*Yugikyō*] says:

> Everywhere, all dharmas give rise to the four methods for saving beings, with kindness (Skt. *maitrī*) arising as the hook, compassion (Skt. *karuṇā*) as the pull, joy (Skt. *muditā*) as the thread, equanimity (Skt. *upekṣa*) as abiding, and so on. Give rise to kindness for all that you see. Give rise to compassion for all that you see. Give rise to joy for all that you see. Give rise to equanimity for all that you see. For the practitioner of mantra, having met this teaching always give rise to the four immeasurable minds for all things in this world. Treat all things the same, and you will quickly achieve highest enlightenment.[182]

(The four immeasurable minds are the same as the four methods for saving beings.)

2. Contemplation of the Three [Kinds] of Equanimity

The *Hizōki* says:

> As for the contemplation of the three [kinds] of equanimity: first, contemplate the main object of devotion upon the altar, then contemplate that one's body is the *mudra,* one's speech is the mantra, and one's mind is the main object of devotion. This equanimity of the three mysteries universally permeates the *dharmadhātu* equally. This is called the three kinds of equanimity of self. The three kinds of equanimity of self and the main object of devotion are unified in cause and outer aspect. This is called the three kinds of equanimity of other. This is not only the unity of cause and outer aspect of the object of devotion and the self, but also the [unity of] complete

[attainment of Buddhahood] and incomplete [attainment of Buddhahood] of all buddhas. Their three kinds of equanimity are also unified in cause and outer aspect. This is called the simultaneous three kinds of equanimity. They are one in cause and outer aspect, as are the mantra, *mudra,* and so on. Drawing into one's body the manifold buddhas is called "entering the self." Drawing into the body of all buddhas the self is called "self-entering," "Entering self, self-entering." The virtues acquired by all of the buddhas in their three incalculable *kalpas* of cultivation are completely present in one's own body. Also, within the very bodies of all sentient beings there fundamentally abides the principle of self-nature, and one's own self and the manifold buddhas own principle of self-nature—they are indistinguishable and unified. Sentient beings are unaware and unawakened [to this fundamental unity], and so course through the cycle of death and rebirth. Because of this, I give rise to compassion for sentient beings, and the virtues [of the buddhas] become the virtues of all beings. This is what it means for the mantra practitioner to practice for the benefit of others. The mantra practitioner performs the *mudra* with their hands, entones the mantra [with their mouth], and constantly practices this contemplation.[183]

3. Contemplation of the Dual [Mandala]

Envision the limbs and divisions of the body as the Womb Realm mandala, with eight petals, nine revered ones, three divisions, and the fourfold round altar. At your heart envision a moon disc, and the five wisdoms and thirty-seven honored ones of the Vajra Realm mandala. Perform the mudras and chant the mantras of the dual realm mandala, bestow empowerments upon the sentient beings of the *dharmadhātu,* and secretly extend mysterious benefits.

(If you are unable to contemplate extensively the fourfold and nine assembly, you should merely contemplate the [nine honored ones[184]] and the eight petals of the Womb Realm mandala, the seed syllables of the five buddhas of the Vajra [Realm mandala], and the revered forms of their *samaya.*)

One can also think of the forms of all sentient beings as the Womb, and their minds as the Vajra; men as Vajra, and women as Womb; front as Vajra, back as Womb; left as Womb, right as Vajra; walking and standing meditation as Vajra, and sitting and lying meditation as Womb; heaven as Vajra and earth as Womb; the sun as Womb and moon as Vajra; southeast as Vajra and northwest as Womb. [Contemplate] all things in this way. The first of the celestial stems as Vajra and the second celestial stem as Womb; yin as Womb and yang as Vajra, and so on for all dharmas; they are in all cases [aspects of the] dual [mandalas].

When it is time for sleep, [contemplate] at your heart a lotus, the three divisions, and the manifold honored ones of the Womb [Realm mandala][185] (SAZ 2:258) (and the eight petals). Imagine that you and all beings together abide in self-realization free from thoughts and intone the one-letter [*A* mantra] with the in- and out-breath as you gradually close your eyes.

When it is time to rise, [contemplate] at your heart a moon disc containing the thirty-seven honored ones of the Vajra [Realm mandala and the five wisdoms]. Imagine that you and all beings together produce the faculty of wisdom that converts others, and intone the one-letter [*A* mantra] with the in- and out-breath as you gradually wake up.

(There are additional contemplative practices to be used when you are lying down. You should inquire into this.)

(On the back it says,

> [The *Dapiluzhenajing gongyang cidifashu* 大毘盧遮那經供養次第法疏 (T. 1797), says,] "When you want to go to sleep, use the *bīja* within the in- and out-breath. Why is this? In your sleep you will automatically enter the *samādhi* of the object of devotion. This is because the breath of the object of devotion is a mantra. If you sleep in this way, you will attain *samādhis* as numerous as dust-motes, and awaken to merits as numerous as grains of sand in the Ganges. Whether sleeping or awake, you are never separated from the oceanlike assembly of the buddhas, and are one with the *mudra* of the palace of the Vajra *dharmadhātu*."[186])

4. Contemplation of the Five [Elements] Disc

In one's body, visualize the five letters of the five elements (earth, water, fire, air, and space) disc. This ritual is explained elsewhere.

5. Moon Disc Contemplation

At one's heart, contemplate a perfectly round bright moon disc. This ritual is explained elsewhere.

6. The *A* Letter Contemplation

At one's heart, contemplate the letter [*A*], the fundamentally uncreated. This ritual is explained elsewhere.

7. Contemplation of the Breath

Intone the one letter [*A*] with the in-breath and out-breath (there are secret transmissions associated with that one letter [*A*]). As is explained in the *Commentary on the Mahāvairocana*,[187] and so on, whenever practicing mindful recitation, just as contemplation relates to the voice, so too does the in-breath relate to the out-breath. (For the three kinds of [practice] mentioned above, one should use the protocols for seated meditation.)

8. Contemplation of the Inner *Goma*

The contemplation of the inner *goma* is as explained in the *Yugikyō.* Therein, it explains that this ritual has other explanations which those who have not [received initiation] are unable to practice. This is because they have not yet destroyed their delusions and attained entry into the fundamental.[188]

A commentary on the *Yugikyō* says:

> Taking the deluded attachments and the 160 forms of mind accumulated through three *kalpas* of transmigration to be the cause of the karma of the five delusions,[189] and this causative karma as the fuel, the thirty-seven wisdoms as the fire, the great *bodhicitta* [in the form of] a perfectly round and bright moon disc as the blaze, the mouth as the fire altar, the *dharmadhātu* as the amount [of the offering?], the mantra-voice as the burning, the form of the *mudra* as the form of the flame that is pervasive, like empty space.[190]

9. Contemplation of This Very Body

The verse on the

> Attainment of Buddhahood in this Very Body" [in Kūkai's *Sokushinjōbutsugi* (T. 2428)] says: "The six elements in unobstructed eternal yoga, and the four mandalas are each inseparable. The empowerments of the three mysteries quickly reveal the interconnections of Indra's net (SAZ 2:259), and are known as this very body. Naturally and completely [one possesses the wisdom of the buddhas]. The mental faculties of the mind-king [Vairocana] surpass lands as numerous as particles of dust, each fully possessing the five wisdoms, boundless wisdom like the power of a perfect[ly round mirror]. Therefore [they are like] the wisdom of true awakening.[191]

The essence of the body-mind of ignorant beings (the six elements), in aspect (four mandalas) and function (the three mysteries), fundamentally is none other than the true meaning of Buddha (as is explained in the *Sokushinjōbutsugi*).

10. Contemplation of the Ten Illusions Arising from Conditions

The *Mahāvairocana-sūtra* explains the ten illusions that arise from conditions. The sutra says, "What are the ten illusions that arise from conditions? They are called illusion, a mirage, a dream, a reflection, a *gandharva* city, an echo, the reflection of the moon reflected in water, a bubble, a flower in empty space, and a spinning wheel of fire."[192] (This is just as explained in the commentaries.) The practitioner, immediately on seeing these objects of perception, performs this contemplation that they are illusions, like a dream, and so on, is freed from grasping onto concepts like "I" and "mine," and does not give rise to concepts like desire or pride (and so on).

The ten contemplations described above are the path of yogic practice and contemplation whereby the pure *bodhi*-mind is to truly know within one's mind. The gates of the practice and contemplation of mantra are limitless; these ten [contemplative] gates together reveal the inexhaustible!

The Six Auxiliary Practices

1. Following the Precepts
Kōbō Daishi Kūkai's *Yuikai* 遺誡[193] says:

> Giving rise to the desire to set out on a long journey without taking a single step, it will be impossible to achieve your goal. In the same way, [if one] turns to the Buddhist path without honoring the precepts, it will be impossible to attain awakening. One must hold firmly to exoteric and esoteric precepts[194] and not transgress them.
>
> The exoteric precepts include the three refuges [in Buddha, Dharma, and Sangha], the five precepts [do not kill, steal, engage in sexual misconduct, lie, or imbibe intoxicants], up to and including the precepts of the *śrāvaka* and bodhisattva [paths], and so on. The four assemblies [of monks, nuns, and male and female lay Buddhists] as well all have their own fundamental precepts. The esoteric precepts are called *samaya* precepts. They are also called the Buddha precepts, the giving rise to the mind of awakening precepts, as well as the unconditioned precepts, and so on. All precepts are fundamentally based in the ten virtues (no killing, stealing, sexual misconduct, lying, harsh, divisive and frivolous speech, greed, anger, and wrong views). Of the ten views, three pertain to the body, four pertain to speech, and three to mind. Gathering the branches and returning to the source, taking the one mind as the source, the essence of the one mind is no different from the Buddha. The mind of one's self, all sentient beings, the mind of the Buddha—these are not [fundamentally] distinct from one another. Abiding in this mind is the practice of the Buddhist path. Embark on this jeweled vehicle, and you will directly arrive at the [seat of enlightenment].[195]

Also, on the bodhisattva precepts of the exoteric vehicle, I say read the *Mahāvairocana-sūtra* subchapter on upaya training on the ten virtues and precepts.[196] The *samaya* precepts concern the four *pārājika* offenses (grave offenses that result in expulsion from the monastic order: sexual misconduct, stealing, murder, lying about one's spiritual attainments), ten grave prohibitions (the sins that the ten virtues protect against), the three groups of pure precepts (doing what is good, not doing what is bad, and benefiting others), and so on.

(The essence of the precepts is explained elsewhere.[197])
The [*Sanmaiyakai jo*] says:

> All buddha tathagatas use the *samādhi* of the ultimate truth of great compassion and do not forget it even for an instant. . . .[198] Due to [the Buddha's] vow to practice great compassion (Skt. *mahāmaitrī-mahākaruṇā*), therefore beings naturally depart from the ten unvirtuous states of mind. Relinquishing the ten unvirtuous states of mind and the karma associated with them, this is the practice of the precepts. Due to the abandonment of that mind of wickedness, therefore, beings attain purity and tranquility in their minds; this is [the practice of] the precepts. This is also precisely [the meaning of] precepts to benefit sentient beings.[199]

Fascicle five of the *Commentary on the Mahāvairocana* says: "Now, the practitioner should deeply contemplate the ten illusions that arise from conditions. Fully cognize that the three karmas are fundamentally nonarising. Ultimate reality naturally creates without ever moving. This is what is called abiding in the unconditioned precepts."[200]

The two kinds of benefits [for self and others] of the precepts should be taken as fundamental. They protect against the three karmas and the various evils. Even though you know that the three karmas are fundamentally pure, you should not violate the precepts or give in to the three poisons. Even though you know that the three karmas are fundamentally nonarising, throughout your whole life do not commit any of the actions associated with the ten nonvirtuous deeds. If you commit any wrongdoing, repent quickly and the [stain] will be removed. Instead, uphold the precepts, abide only in the mind of compassion, and [work for the] benefit of sentient beings, and [the inclination to commit even minor sins will naturally abate]. This is called the Buddha precepts.

2. Practicing as Appropriate in Different Situations

In accordance with the appropriate time, place, kind, and capacity, establish benefit of sentient beings in [the realms of the] visible and invisible. Perhaps one may climb a tall mountain or plateau and chant the Great Compassion Dhāraṇī,[201] the *Baoqieyin tuoluoni jing* 寶篋印陀羅尼經 (T. 1022B), and other dhāraṇī. Employ the self-nature and [establish] the practice of *adhiṣṭhāna,* the mantra for liberation from the six realms of samsara, the *hrīḥ* one-letter mantra, and so on; the *adhiṣṭhāna* of the eye, up to the [faculties of all beings in] towns and villages, thereby all people, men and women, and all of the infinite beings who walk, crawl, or fly will all be liberated and attain awakening.[202] Or [if you go] to a river or seashore, intone a spell on the sand and pebbles, and when you enter the water write the letters *vaṃ* and *hrīḥ,* causing the water and so on to become the Dharma-nature *vaṃ* water, and even the fish and shellfish and so on will open the heart-lotus of their self-nature.

(On the back of the text it says: "The *Baoqieyin tuoluoni jing* says, "If the practitioner climbs to the top of a high mountain peak and chants the [Great Compassion Dhāraṇī], the eye faculty and so on of beings near and far throughout the world, mountains and valleys, forests and plains, streams, lakes, rivers, and oceans, and so on, and therein, all those that have fur, feathers, scales (fish and reptiles), sentient beings of all kinds, [it will] destroy their afflictions and enlighten their ignorance, revealing that they fundamentally possess three kinds of buddha-nature, and fundamentally that place is within the great [ocean of] nirvana."[203]

The *Uṣṇīṣavijayā-dhāraṇī-sūtra* says, "All of the birds that fly and the beasts, all creatures that have consciousness (i.e., all sentient beings) that hear this *dhāraṇī,* if it even only once passes their ears, will never again be born [into the body of an animal]."[204])

[It also says, "This *dhāraṇī* has the power of Jambudvīpa, and can bring about the liberation of even the various beings in hell and other evil realms, the various beings coursing through samsara, those of little merit, those who do not differentiate between good and evil or do not believe in karma, and those who have lost the righteous path."[205]]

When you are in a place where many people are gathered together, using the self-nature *adhiṣṭhāna* of the one-letter ritual, the *hrīḥ* letter mantra, and so on, the *adhiṣṭhāna* will cause the many myriads [of beings] to be mysteriously permeated with secret benefits. Or when you encounter snakes, deer, and so on, birds, sparrows, doves, etc., all kinds of sentient beings that have taken birth as an animal, chant the three refuges or the mantra of *bodhicitta,* or chant the *hrīḥ* mantra, and this will cause them all to attain liberation.

(The other side of the text says, "According to the second fascicle of the *Fanwan jing*: If the disciple of the Buddha constantly awakens the mind of great compassion, when they enter a city, village, inn, or home, for all of the sentient beings they encounter they should chant the words; all of you should certainly day or night receive the three refuges and the ten precepts. If one sees a cow, a horse, a pig, a sheep, or any animal, you should contemplate in your mind and with your mouth intone, 'All of you animals, give rise to the mind that seeks awakening.' Or, when you enter the mountains, rivers, forests, or plains, you will make all sentient beings give rise to the mind that seeks awakening."[206])

Or when you see a beggar or a monk asking for alms, if you give even one item of charity you create a secret bond [for them] to the incantations, the mandalas (altar), the *pāramitas*, the mudras, the mantras, and cause them to accomplish vast merits.

Or when taking a bath, the run-off [wastewater], even one's own saliva, can be fashioned into offerings for the hungry ghosts.

Or when seeing the flowers of spring, fall, summer, or winter, if one practices contemplation, you should intone a vow that the sublime flowery clouds pervade completely the realms of the ten directions, performing practice for all buddhas, the Dharma, and bodhisattvas, then [offer] sandal[wood] incense and other fragrances again to perfume that place in this way.

Or when you approach a stupa or place of worship, use the "opening door" mudra and mantra, and imagine that all sentient beings together open their hearts and enter the stupa of the Dharma.

Or when you go to a place where the Buddha has been seen, perform the mudra and mantra of universal reverence and imagine that all sentient beings together revere everywhere the buddhas embodied throughout the universe.

Or when you go to a place to hear Dharma preaching, intone the mantra of all wisdom and imagine that all sentient beings of all kinds acquire the various causes [that bring about awakening].

Or when you come across an ancestral temple, intone the Mantra of Light, and so on, and you will cause all of the spirits to be liberated from the path of karma.

Or, for the seen and unseen beings of the six realms in the limitless worlds of the ten directions, use the mantra for liberation from the six realms, *mahāmaitrī-mahākaruṇā,* that removes suffering and bestows bliss.

Or when you chant the letter *raṃ,* you melt the ice of the eight cold hells, and with the letter *vaṃ* you extinguish the fire of the eight hot hells.

Or, in this ordinary world comprised of the elements of earth, water, fire, wind, and space: contemplate these as the five seed syllables (*a, va, ra, ha, ka*) and the five great elements (earth, water, fire, wind, space). Indeed, the phenomenal world is not apart from ultimate reality.

Or, [when encountering] sights, sounds, fragrances, flavors, or tactile objects, you should imagine them as the virtues of the round disc of the fourfold mandala and three mysteries.

Thus, these particular practices cannot be exhausted, as the mind responds in accordance with one's contemplative practices.

(The above mudras, mantras, and so on cannot be explained fundamentally. Simply by attaining the mind, you may use whatever you touch.)

3. Preaching the Dharma to the Spirits

Now, while the buddhadharma abides in the world, one should rely on the spirits as protectors of the Dharma so that the Dharma may prevent disaster. Open the eye of wisdom so that the spirits may delight in the Dharma. The monks who protect the emperor (J. *gojisō* 護持増/護持僧) therefore use their power, first protecting the body and chanting the *Rishukyō*, the *Heart Sutra*, and so on; intone the mantra of the limitless repository of wisdom, the Mantra of Light, and others, for the gods of heaven and earth abiding in the three reams, including Amaterasu and others, all of the large and small gods of the realm known as Nippon, and the manifold great luminous gods that protect the king's palace, those with power and those without, their manifestations and true forms. Continuously preach to the spirits so that they too may attain the Way. (More on teaching the Dharma to gods and spirits is found elsewhere.) (SAZ 2:262).

4. Debts of Gratitude

Even in one hundred million kalpas it is difficult to encounter one verse of the subtle Dharma or even one character of the Buddha's name, such an excellent cloud that is beyond compare. How much more so the object of devotion and the mudra that connects one to the Buddha as if to your own parents, or [to have] the opportunity to receive ordination and the awareness that it is within one's very own body that awakening is achieved. There is no way to repay such a debt of gratitude for the virtues of the transmission of the *kenmitsu* Dharma.

(On the back, a note says, "According to the *Shōryōshū*, two, it says, 'One object of devotion and one *mudra* (connection) is the direct route to awakening to the Way. Through one character or one verse, one enters into the very parents of the Buddha.'")[207]

Therefore, the secret transmission of the eight great masters, conveyed through the three countries (India, China, and Japan) by many *ācārya*, are linked to one another by the intimate transmission of the teaching of the Dharma on the ordination platform, the study of exoteric and esoteric under the teacher's direction. On the memorial days for these virtuous ancestral teachers who came before, you should chant the sutras and incantations, as [it is due to their kindness] that one is able to practice in this way and fully realize awakening.

5. Protecting the Realm

The eight [Esoteric] masters and those of the Eight Schools who transmitted the lamp through the history of the three countries all took the protection of the realm as fundamental. The gist of this may be found in the *Zhufo jing jie shezhenshi jing* 諸佛境界攝眞實經 (T. 868) and the *Āryadhāraṇīśvararāja-sūtra* 守護國界主陀羅尼經 (T. 997), and others. Therefore, the cultivation of all good merits should be transmitted to the pacification of the realm and for the benefit of the people (and so on).

6. Vowing to Transfer Merit

Before an image of the treasure [name] of Kōbō Daishi, present flowers, candles, and incense, and chant the sutras and incantations. First chant the *Rishu kyō* reverently, then the *Uṣṇīṣavijayā-dhāraṇī,* the treasure name, and so on. With a pure mind, pray and chant this verse:

> *Namu Daishi Henjō Kongō* 南無大師遍照金剛
> The practices and vows of Samathabadra, may they all be fulfilled.
> Now, I, with one mind, vow to transfer all of my merit, life after life, world after world, in accordance with your command.
> In whatever place I find myself I will directly encounter the Esoteric teachings.
> In this life my practice is perfumed by the subtle karma of the three mysteries.
> In whatever place that I am born, I will remember and not neglect to work for the awakening of beings who fundamentally possess good roots so that they may give rise to the mind [that seeks awakening], to practice, and attain *bodhi,* nirvana, and the purification of the buddha land.

Regarding the above sixteenfold contemplation practice, you should employ noble faith as the foundation for the practice of each. Practitioner of mantra, if you lack the foundation of faith, your practice will be unsupported.

The *Commentary on the Mahāvairocana* says, "Therefore, *bodhicitta* is precisely the meaning of the mind of pure faith."

And a sutra commentary [by Zhili 知禮 (906–1028), in the *Jin'guangming jing wenju ji* 金光明經文句記 (T. 1786)], says, "It is by faith that one is able to enter the great ocean of the buddha-dharma."[208]

The *Commentary on the Mahāvairocana* also says:

> [Even though you] have not yet seen a true one, and have not yet been able to produce manifold mystical transformations like Vairocana, and so on, nevertheless, mental contemplation leads to accomplishments. Really there is one thing that is true and unerring, that which is referred to as self. The self is precisely the true faith of certainty. The self is the *dharmadhātu.* The self is Vairocana. The self is the universal gate of many bodies. This is for certain.[209]

Therefore, the manifold practices all employ this true faith as their foundation. The exoteric approach to Buddhism takes faith as the gate for beginners. In our tradition, faith is taken to be the immediate attainment of awakening. Therefore, take this true understanding of one's own mind and establish true faith as the essence of one's practice, and do not stray from this gate.

Question: The six characters of the name of Amitābha are perfectly and completely endowed with manifold virtues. Calling the name single-mindedly, one will be reborn in Sukhāvatī. What afflictions are remedied through this contemplative practice?

Answer: One may engage in ten thousand forms of practice and never depart from the gate of the letter *A*. The many follow from the essential desire to reveal the gate of *upāya*. This is the teaching that is the path to all wisdom. True wisdom and *upāya* are both complete and perfect. This is called the perfect circle (mandala).

The *Commentary on the Mahāvairocana* Nagarjuna is recorded as saying:

> *Prajñā* and *upāya* are fundamentally of one essence, but the uses to which they are put may differ. The way the teacher skillfully employs *upāya* may be compared to metallurgy. From metal many different things are created, and while they are all in essence metal, they each have different names. Vairocana is like this; being able to extend universally, the *vajra* [metal] (a play on words referring to the sentence above) of truth, the essence of wisdom, the many vehicles are constructed.[210]

Of the first ten contemplative practices explained above, however, the beginning practitioner may not be able to practice them all completely. The contemplation of the perfectly bright five circles (mandala) and so on accord with the preferences of the practitioner. It is important not to neglect the many forms of preparation for contemplative practice. Also, it is only by means of the single-minded recitation that one is able to completely cultivate and dedicate the merits [gained through practice].

[3.4] Mindfulness at the End of Life

Now, for those practicing mindfulness at the end of their life, the fundamental purpose of the buddha-dharma is the destruction of samsara. Relying on this, practitioners investigate deeply through their practice and enter the [treasure] storehouse of the mind. How can dyed paper and a confident brush not leave a mark?

However, in the instruction of beginner's questions it is especially important to explain the basic points of the great teachings. If the practitioner has been afflicted with an illness for many days, unable to go to the hall to practice, they should wash their hands and rinse their mouths, perform rituals for the protection of the body and establishment of a ritual space, and take refuge and perform repentance rites. Recite, saying:

> *Namaḥ,* I humbly bow my head, and take refuge in the assemblies of the Womb and Vajra mandalas, the honored ones beyond number. [I take refuge] in Amitābha Tathāgata and the holy ones of Sukhāvatī in the west: Avalokiteśvara, Mahāsthāmaprāpta, and the holy ones [who abide in] all nine levels [of the Pure Land]. With humility I repent the transgressions of my six senses (eye, ear, nose, tongue, body, mind, [produced] from my negative karma since beginningless time. I enter the gate of the letter *A,* the originally unborn. I enter the gate of the letter *hrīḥ,* the originally pure.
>
> Next, may all beings from beginningless time make the virtuous vow to transfer their merit.

Recite, saying:

> May the sublime merits [I have accumulated] be used to foster good roots for beings throughout the universe, and through the mystical powers of the Tathāgata's empowerments, may all beings attain rebirth in Sukhāvatī.

Next, contemplate the three *vajras* [in which the six elements are realized to be nondual with the three mysteries].[211]

Next, perform the mudra and mantra of the transmission of the Dharma abhiṣekha.

Next, perform the mudra and mantra of the fundamental [dhāraṇī] of Amitābha.

Next, chant the name of Amitābha [an unlimited number of times, such that the question of purity or impurity is beyond question].

Next, worshiping before an image of Kōbō Daishi, respectfully offer a (SAZ 2:264) pure prayer, "*Namu Daishi Henjō Kongō,* have pity on me and empower me to attain rebirth in Sukhāvatī." Now, drawing on the good karma received from Kōbō Daishi's transmission of the Dharma, and seeking solace in the accomplishments of Kōbō Daishi's deep meditative practice, at the end of your life [you will go to] Kōbō Daishi's compassionate abode. Since we already possess deep connections to Kōbō Daishi in the past and present, who would be abandoned? Simply make this vow, and Kōbō Daishi will lead you to the Pure Land.

Next, contemplate the fundamental source of birth and death. Birth is birth of that which is unborn; there is no place from which it originates. Death is the extinction that is nonextinction; there is no place to which you go. Instead, know that the causes and conditions of the letter *A* give rise to being as birth, but from the perspective of *A* as the unborn, śūnyatā, it may be taken as death. Therefore, birth and death are simply this letter *A*. The *Commentary on the Mahāvairocana* says, "You should know that the [true meaning of the] *A* gate is also said to encompass the meaning of all dharmas."[212]

The infinite dharmas arise due to causes and conditions. All of these causes and conditions have their beginning, their base. Now contemplate this arising from causes and conditions, then again contemplate the numberless causes and conditions that cause a thing to arise. At its base there is only this continuous arising based on conditions. In this way, when practicing *vipaśyanā* you will know fundamentally that things are inherently nonarising. This is the base of all dharmas. It is just as when you hear all forms of speech, in fact you are hearing the sound of the letter *A*. In the same way, when you perceive the arising of all dharmas, this is fundamental nonarising. If you see that which is fundamentally nonarising, they you truly know your own mind. Thus, all wisdom is Mahāvairocana. Take this one letter [*A*] as your mantra.

Ignorant worldly beings do not contemplate the origin of the manifold dharmas, and so they perceive things as arising. Because of this, subsequently they are born into samsara again and again and are unable to get out. It is as if they are unaware that they are the creator [of their own reality]. Within one's very own [mind], one carries the images with which the form of the fearsome *yakṣa* (flying flesh-eating ghosts) is constructed. These creations return to their source when contemplated. The mind that produces fear [can make such frightening things] fall to the ground. Sentient beings are also like this. Within their own minds, they carry the origination of all dharmas; creating the triple world and returning to its source, they are destroyed therein. One's own mind is burning up and suffering in various ways. The Tathāgata is a wise painter who is completely aware of this, and so freely manifests the Great Compassionate [Womb] mandala.

The Great Compassionate [Womb] mandala is the Great Compassionate Womb of the ten realms. It fundamentally possesses three divisions and four kinds of mandalic platforms. The ten realms are originally nonarising. Therefore, Ācala and the nine realms of unenlightened beings is the perfect circle (mandala) of Mahāvairocana. If you rely on the gate of the letter *A* and contemplate the source of samsara, the three poisons and the five destinies are fundamentally pure. *Kleśa* are *bodhi,* samsara is nirvana. The Vajra and Womb mandalas are mother and father; the harmony of principle and wisdom is sentience. (A fully detailed explanation is not provided here.)

Also, the harmony of the six great elements becomes sentience. The first five are principle, and the element of consciousness is wisdom. The mind in one thought moment falls into delusion and produces the twelvefold chain of dependent origination and samsaric existence. But by contemplating the nonduality of body and mind, transmigration through the twelvefold chain becomes the twelve mantra kings of Mahāvairocana and the Great Katsuma mandala. This is because samsara is merely the transformation of the six elements in accordance with causes and conditions (SAZ 2:265). Principle becomes earth (soil), which is the letter *A* and the great earth element. Fire produces smoke just as the letter *raṃ* realizes the great fire element. Contemplate the immutability of the six great elements, neither arising nor perishing, and the spontaneity of the buddha essence of the fourfold mandala.

Also, when not practicing the Buddha name recitation, at all other times when the mouth opens intone the letter *A*, and when the lips meet intone the letter *hūṃ*. These two letters are the secret uncreated spontaneous mantra of all sentient beings. The dual mandala is the essential source of manifold virtues.

Also, when one has been afflicted with illness for a long time and your strength has gradually wasted away, if you are unable to bathe at your heart visualize the letter *hrīḥ* and contemplate the purity of the three karmas, and perform the mudras and mantras.

Now, at the end of life, within your mind contemplate the lotus dais of the nine grades of the Sukhāvatī, and [you will] enter the jeweled lotus of the western land. Rest your mind in the *dharmadhātu* of the five great elements, and end the transmigration of the eight consciousnesses. Contemplate the ten realms as nondual, as are samsara and nirvana. [Envision] the one letter covering the five points of the body, and your body is now the *dharmakāya.* The dual mandalas disappear and return to the unified mind. Grasping all minds, in the end they are no mind. (The above six verses all have mudras that can be practiced along with reciting them.)

The body of the ritual practitioner, whether sitting or laying down, facing west or another direction, if you are able, perform secret mudras and visualizations, turning to the Buddha in your mind (form the mudra with your hands and [mantras] with your speech).

For the karma of speech, perhaps intone the essence of Amitābha, or that one's awakening is fundamentally nonarising, or one segment of the eight-petaled white lotus blossom, or take refuge in the fundamentally awakened mind of the *dharmakāya*, or when seeking the wisdom of the Buddhas, etc.

Also, the form of the *dharmakāya* is the six great elements of the *dharmadhātu*, the essence of each particle, the true nature of each iota. Their true nature is the omnipresent ocean of the *dharmadhātu*. The *dharmadhātu* is the fourfold mandala. The essence of these mandalas is the one thought moment. The mind in one thought moment is precisely the essence of the three mysteries. The three mysteries are the mind of no-thought (beyond conceptual/delusional thought).

Also, the six elements are unobstructed, in constant yoga. (The above essential points can be used as an object of contemplation and chanted.)

Also, you should only do such practices as you are able. For a mantra, perhaps the name [of Amitābha] in six characters, or the five-character mantra. These may be regarded as the true cause of [rebirth in the] nine grades [of the Pure Land], which may be taken to be the five *cakra*s [that reveal that Mahāvairocana] comprises one's very body.

Or the one letter *hrīḥ*, or the one letter A, by opening the heart-lotus of the fundamental source, by entering the quiescence of nonarising, the mudra is at the mouth.

The above may be practiced together with the yoga of the in- and out-breath, until one's breath ceases.

Now, one should contemplate deeply this matter. If the practitioner is not as ill as before, they should continue to cultivate the mind for practice. If death occurs quickly, at that time simply employ the mudra, the ten thought moments, or the one mudra and one letter. Also, as one initiates this practice, whether with this text or some other ritual or ceremony, [do not become fixated on the particulars; rather,] practice in accordance with your abilities.

As one prepares the mind through this Dharma practice, they may supplement or abbreviate as they see fit. As for the cultivation of such things as despising [this defiled world] and seeking [the Pure Land], the adornment of the site of practice, the mental preparation for the *kalyāṇa-mitra,* and other things regarding the proper care for and instruction for the one who is ill are not fully explained here, as they are the same as in the ordinary path.

[SAZ edition ends here]

[The DNBZ edition contains the following supplementary passages:

1. The Inherently Pure and Perfectly Bright Three Turnings

One's inherent nature is the essence of the lotus, and purity is its outer aspect. Being perfectly round is the essence of the moon, and its shining brilliance is its outer aspect. The Buddha is the perfect embodiment of principle and wisdom. Having principle and wisdom one must then have the ability to be a complete person. This is known as the three turnings.

Also, inherent nature is wisdom. Purity is principle. When distinguishing between essence and inherent nature, take wisdom as the inherent nature. This is the stable abode of one's *vajra*-like inherent nature. Also, Kōbō Daishi's *Shingon mondō, Nikyōron,* and the [*Yugikyō*] mention that "purity is indicated by principle."[213] This is because inherent nature and purity correspond respectively to wisdom and principle. Perfection (lit., "roundness") and brilliance (lit., "brightness") correspond to principle and wisdom, and perfection and completeness [correspond] to Buddha and essence. The Buddha is the face of wisdom, therefore it is called perfectly bright. The inherently pure and perfectly bright three turnings appear in the *Commentary on the Mahāvairocana.*[214]

2. The Hundred [Rivers] Enter the Ocean and Are Purified

The *Commentary on the Mahāvairocana-sūtra* says: "It is like the four great rivers of Jamudvīpa, each comprised of five hundred smaller tributaries. All together these various water sources are variously impure, but they enter the great ocean and therein are all purified.[215]

3. The Three Hindrances

The hindrance of retribution, the hindrance of karma, the hindrance of *kleśa* (ignorance, hatred, and greed) . . .

In another edition it says that the [*Shiyimian guanzizai pusa xinmiyan niansong yigui jing*] says, "[On your altar, place] Amitāyus at the center, Mahāsthāmaprāpta on the left, and Avalokiteśvara on the right.[216]]

[SAZ's Meiji-era colophon of the SAZ edition here omitted]

Written in the second year of Jōō, second month, twenty-first day (March 14, 1224)

End of Fascicle Three

Himitsu nenbutsu shō

Notes

Appendix

An earlier and abridged version of fascicle one of this translation appeared in Aaron P. Proffitt, "Dohan's *Compendium on the Secret Contemplation of Buddha,* Fascicle One," in *Pure Lands in Asian Texts and Contexts: An Anthology,* ed. Georgios T. Halkias and Richard K. Payne (Honolulu: University of Hawai'i Press), p. 269. Reprinted by permission.

1 The DNBZ omits this phrase.

2 T. 1911:1a–140c, esp. 4a11–12, 12b24–25.

3 MD 931 explains that the fourfold secret explanation 四重秘釋 is an exegetical technique in which a teaching is examined according to the shallow-abbreviated level 淺略, the deep-secret level 深秘, the secret within the deep-secret level 秘中深秘, and the deepest secret within the deep-secret level 秘々中深秘. The first level is the literal or common understanding. The second is the inner meaning beyond what is immediately apparent. The third level penetrates to the fundamental nature of dharmas. The fourth level, the reality of things as they truly are, reveals the profundity of the first level. This appears to be one of Dōhan's hallmark strategies.

4 Ujitani Yūken 宇治谷祐顯, "Hikekyō no Amidabutsu honjō setsuwa" 悲華経のアミダ佛本生說話考, *Indogaku bukkyōgaku kenkyū* 印度學佛教學研究 33, no. 1 (1968): 74–80.

5 Ratnagarbha is the Buddha who inspired both Amitābha and Śākyamuni. See MBD, 72.

6 T. 157:185a24–186a24, and so on.

7 The five buddhas and five wisdoms 五智 (Skt. *pañca-jñānāni*) are as follows: (1) Mahāvairocana Tathāgata 大日如来 in the center of the mandala corresponds to *dharmadhātu-svabhāva-jñāna* 法界體性智 (the wisdom that sees things in their essential nature, reality as it truly is). This corresponds to the ninth consciousness, *amala-vijñāna* 菴摩羅識, or pure consciousness. (2) Akṣobhya Tathāgata 阿閦如来 in the eastern quarter of the mandala corresponds to *ādarśa-jñāna* 大圓鏡智 (the wisdom that reflects all things simultaneously, like a great round mirror). This corresponds to the eighth consciousness, the *ālaya-vijñāna* 阿賴耶識, or storehouse consciousness. (3) Ratnasaṃbhava Tathāgata 寶生如來 in the southern quarter corresponds

to *samatā-jñāna* 平等性智 (the wisdom that sees the equanimity of all things and sees all things as one). This corresponds to the seventh consciousness, *manas-vijñāna* 末那識, from which arises the sense of self. (4) Amitābha Tathāgata 阿彌陀佛如來 in the western quarter corresponds to *pratyavekṣaṇā-jñāna* 妙觀察智 (the wisdom of subtle discernment). This corresponds to the sixth consciousness, *mano-vijñāna* 意識, the unified consciousness of the five-sense consciousness of eye, ear, nose, tongue, and body. (5) Amoghasiddhi Tathāgata 不空成就如來 in the northern quarter corresponds to *kṛtya-anuṣṭhāna-jñāna* 成所作智 (the omnipotent wisdom for benefiting beings). This corresponds to the five-sense consciousness 五識 of eye, ear, nose, tongue, and body. See also Dreitlein and Takagi, *Philosophy of Language*, pp. 361–362; NKBD, 493b–c; MD, 620c–621a; DDB 五智 and 五智如來, and so on.

8 The dual mandala 兩部曼荼羅 comprises the *Vajradhātu-maṇḍala* 金剛界曼荼羅, translated as "Vajra Realm mandala," and the *Mahākaruṇā-garbhodbhava maṇḍala* (sometimes rendered as *garbhadhatu-maṇḍala*) 胎藏界曼荼羅 (J. Taizōkai mandara), is translated here as "Womb Realm mandala." According to Dreitlein and Takagi, *Kūkai on the Philosophy of Language*, pp. 356, 374, 401–402, these two mandalas are understood to represent two nondual aspects of reality, the fundamental Buddhahood of reality (Womb) and the wisdom through which this is reality is attained (Vajra).

9 The fourfold mandala 四種曼荼羅 represents reality from four different perspectives: (1) the *mahā-maṇḍala* 大曼荼羅 is constituted by all beings composed of the five elements (earth, water, fire, wind, and space). This includes all buddhas, bodhisattvas, gods, humans, and nonhuman entities, as well as the other three mandalas listed below; (2) the *samaya-maṇḍala* 三昧耶曼荼羅 is constituted by the mudras and symbolic implements held by the buddhas, bodhisattvas, gods, and other beings in graphic depictions of mandalas and visualization practices. These mudras and implements symbolize the vows of these beings; (3) the *dharma-maṇḍala* 法曼荼羅 is represented by the sacred Sanskrit *bīja* of all buddhas, bodhisattvas, gods, and so on. These sacred syllables are said to symbolize the speech and sounds of all beings; (4) the *karma-maṇḍala* 羯磨曼荼羅 comprises the activities of all beings and symbolizes the activity to benefit all beings taken up by buddhas, bodhisattvas, gods, and so on. See Dreitlein and Takagi, *Kūkai on the Philosophy of Language*, pp. 363–364; MD, 943b, 1024b–1026a; NKBD, 664b.

10 NBD, 134a–b. *Emyō* 惠命 signifies that Buddha-nature and life itself are connected.

11 The chambers of the heart were traditionally believed to resemble the eight petals of the lotus. The spiritual heart and the physical heart are one and the same (MD 1818).

12 The *santen* may refer to the "three points of the Sanskrit letter *I*, which is written with three small circles, somewhat in the form of a triangle. Because

neither a horizontal nor vertical line may encompass them all, it signifies the multiplicity of reality—neither one nor not one. In the *Mahāparinirvāṇa-sūtra* it signifies the nonduality of dharmakāya, prajñā, and mokṣa. In *mikkyō* circles, Dōhan's *Dainichi kyōso henmyō shō* 大日経疏遍明抄 (ZSZ 5) and the *Yugikyō kuketsu* 瑜祇経口決 (SZ) established a standard understanding of the nondual relationship between principle 理, wisdom 智, and phenomena 事. See NKBD 598a; MD, 817a, 58.

13 The SAZ omits this passage.

14 SAZ 1:781–787.

15 *Adhiṣṭhāna* 加持 (empowerment) is achieved through yogic practice (the union of body, speech, and mind) with an object of devotion. In this ritual context, it is believed that once unified with the object of devotion one acquires one's supernormal abilities (*siddhi*) and may harness that power to effect change in the world. This concept also indicates the fundamental always-already manifest nonduality that beings have with awakened reality. *Adhiṣṭhāna* has also been translated as "grace," as these powers are understood to be given by the buddhas or bodhisattvas. See MD, 234a–b; NKBD, 203d–204a; Dreitlein and Takagi, *Philosophy of Language,* pp. 346–347.

16 The three mysteries 三密 concept signifies the notion that through the coordinated practice of mudra (body) and mantra and mantra/dhāraṇī (speech), ordinary beings may come to realize that their three sources of karmic production (*sangō* 三業; MD, 788a) are in fact unified with the body, speech, and mind of enlightened buddhas. See MD, 839b–840b.

17 *Siddhi* 悉地 (accomplishment) refers to the powers attained through the mastery of deep states of awakening. Commonly sought-after *siddhi* may include so-called mundane goals such as avoiding disaster, having good luck, acquiring wealth, succeeding in love, and so on, as well as so-called divine *siddhi,* which may include the attainment of rebirth in a heaven, a Pure Land, or the Realm of Esoteric Splendor 密嚴國土 and ultimately, awakening (MD, 984b–c).

18 The Sanskrit letter *A* is an important object of devotion and meditation in the Japanese Shingon tradition. In traditional Sanskrit linguistics, the "a-" prefix signifies negation and is also the first letter of the alphabet. The letter *A* signifies emptiness, the "unborn," and the original nonarising of dharmas. *A* is the mother of all letters, all sounds, the original source to which all things return, and so on. According to Dreitlein (personal communication with author), in the Shingon tradition the *ajikan* 阿字観 (contemplation of the letter *A*) is a popular form of meditation, perhaps the Shingon answer to the popularity of Zen. However, traditionally, *ajikan* was, and largely remains, an advanced practice. See Dreitlein and Takagi, *Philosophy of Language,* pp. 344–345.

19 *Jizai* 自在, which means something close to "sovereignty," refers to the ability of enlightened beings to accomplish tasks unimpeded. Having realized the fundamental emptiness of all things, one is able to do anything (see NKBD, 648a–b). It is perhaps reminiscent of Nāgārjuna's famous statement in the *Mūlamadhyamakakārikā* 24.14: "For whom emptiness is possible, all things are possible" (cited in Donald S. Lopez Jr., *A Study of Svatantrika* (Boulder, CO: Snow Lion, 1987), p. 54). Dōhan is saying here that on realizing that one is originally unborn, one still exists as a self—not the usual self but as a *jizai* self who is fully supported by Buddhahood and able to work for the benefit of all sentient beings.

20 Kūkai discusses the concept of *muga daiga* 無我大我, "the no-self that is the great self," which is the idea that when one casts the limitations of one's limited sense of self aside, one identifies with the whole universe and thus attains the omnipotence of buddha reality. See *Hokke kaidai* 法華經開題, T. 2190:182a1–4; *Dainichikyō kaidai* 大日經開題, T. 2211:7a3–5.

21 SAZ 1:784–785.

22 T. 2514:22b10–12. Perhaps one reason why Dōhan uses Siddhaṃ is to suggest that each syllable in and of itself may be thought of as possessing the power of a mantra. In this way the *nenbutsu* in three or five syllables would be rendered infinitely powerful and would encompass infinite meanings. See Kūkai's esoteric commentary on the *Heart Sūtra, Hannya shingyō hiken* 般若心經祕鍵: "One character encompasses one thousand *ri* 一字含千理," T. 2203A:12b23. See also Dreitlein, "Annotated Translation of Kūkai's *Secret Key to the Heart Sūtra,*" 38.

23 T. 848:53c14–17.

24 T. 2203B:18a8.

25 The three divisions, or three families 三部 (J. *sanbu*), of the *Mahākaruṇāgarbhodbhava-maṇḍala* are as follows: (1) the buddha division, led by Mahāvairocana Buddha and represented by the mystery of body; (2) the lotus division, led by Avalokiteśvara Bodhisattva (and/or Amitābha Buddha) and represented by the mystery of speech; (3) the vajra division, led by Vajrapaṇi and represented by the mystery of mind. See Dreitlein and Takagi, *Kūkai on the Philosophy of Language,* pp. 396–397.

26 The three truths 三諦 are developed in Zhiyi's *Mohezhiguan,* based on a creative reading of Nāgārjuna's two truths (emptiness and provisionality, or ultimate and apparent reality). Zhiyi's three truths add the position of the middle, the perspective from which emptiness and provisionality may be understood together: 空假中 (J. *ku-ke-chū*). Swanson, *Clear Serenity,* pp. 47–49.

27 *Jisō* and *jigi* 字相字義 signify the outer meaning (*sō,* "aspect") of a character and its inner meaning, respectively. See Kūkai, *Dainichikyō kaidai* 大日經

開題: 次據梵名釋者。初MA字 有二義。一字相二字義。字相者我義。字義者我不可得義又空義。此亦有無量我義。神我假我實我等是。毘盧遮那則名大我。我則大自在義。故又云内心之大我。我一切本初等。; T. 2211:1c16–20. See also Dreitlein and Takagi, *Philosophy of Language,* pp. 382–383, on the "profound meanings of letters," in which they note that the "inner meaning" attributed by Kūkai uses the interpretation of the form and meaning of Siddhaṃ letters as a metaphor for how exoteric and esoteric approaches to Buddhism differ. The exoteric reading of a text merely describes the form, while the esoteric gets to the meaning. While each "letter" might be different, at their core they all possess the letter *A,* the original nonarising, or emptiness. See *Dainichikyō kaidai,* TKDZ 4:47–48; *Kongōchō kaidai,* TKDZ 4:89, and *Himitsu mandarajūjūshinron,* TKDZ 2:144–445.

28 Initial enlightenment 始覺 signifies the first glimpse of awakening attained through Buddhist practice, contrasted with original enlightenment 本覺, the fundamental Buddhahood of all beings. Both of these concepts appeared in the *Awakening of Faith* 大乘起信論, T. 1666.

29 On *naishō* 内聲, see MD 1695, as well as other related concepts in 1693–1697. See also Kukai, *Shōjissōgi,* T. 2429:402b28.

30 T. 2438:522a21–25, 522b6–9.

31 T. 848:30b3, and so on. For the corresponding section in the *Commentary on the Mahāvairocana-sūtra,* see T. 1796:722c11, c27–23a1, and so on.

32 T. 1796:39.718b21–22. This was identified thanks to Mona Satō, "Dōhan cho 'Himitsu nenbutsu shō,' inyō bunken shutten chūki," p. 132. Identifying more obscure references has been made much easier thanks to Satō's pioneering research.

33 *Nitoku* 二德 may indicate either the dual virtues of wisdom and compassion or the virtues that are inherent (like Buddhahood) or acquired by practice. See NKBD, 1299.

34 *Ji-in-gyō* 字印形 signifies the "*bīja* mudra" and the form of the object of devotion. Using these three levels or aspects of the physical form signifies the dharma-, samaya-, and mahā-maṇḍalas present within the karma-maṇḍala. See *Mahāvairocana-sūtra,* T. 848:44a16–22; MD, 847b; Dōhan, *Gyōhōkanyō shō* 行法肝葉鈔, T. 2502:888a4–12, 889b8, and so on.

35 The concept of *honji suijaku* 本地垂迹, whereby a buddha may be taken to be the fundamental basis (*honji*) and a bodhisattva, god, or some other being may be taken to be the trace manifestation (*suijaku*), has been examined in Mark Teeuwen and Fabio Rambelli, eds., *Buddhas and Kami in Japan: Honji Suijaku as a Combinatory Paradigm* (London: RoutledgeCurzon, 2003).

36 While referencing the *Dalejin'gangbukong zhenshisanmoye jing* 大樂金剛不空眞實三摩耶經, T. 243:784c, the quote actually appears to come from the *Rishukyō* commentary, *Dale jingang bukong zhenshi sanmeiye jing*

banruo boluomiduo liqushi 大樂金剛不空眞實三昧耶經般若波羅蜜多理趣釋, T. 1003:612a10–b6.

37 T. 365:345c. See also T. 365:345b10, 341a25, 346a13.

38 *Seken* 世間, NKBD 1004.

39 T. 2438:521a26.

40 T. 2430:406c29–407a3; TKDZ 3:65, 10–12; Yoshito S. Hakeda, *Kūkai: Major Works. Translated with an Account of His Life and a Study of His Thought* (New York: Columbia University Press, 1972), pp. 258–259.

41 DNBZ.

42 MD 1105b.

43 Dreitlein, "Annotated Translation of Kūkai's *Secret Key to the Heart Sūtra,*" pp. 37–38, n130, directs the reader to consult Dreitlein and Takagi, *Kūkai on the Philosophy of Language,* pp. 150–151; *Hokkekyō kaidai* 法華經開題, TKDZ 4:185–186; *Hokkekyō shaku* 法華經釋, TKDZ 4:201, and also provides a translation of T. 1796:656a:

> There are sixteen gates for interpreting the entire Tripiṭaka. They are: (1) counteracting delusions (negating) and (2) revealing virtues (affirming), (3) the shallow and incomplete and (4) the profound and hidden, (5) the superficial meanings of letters and (6) the profound meanings of letters, (7) one letter encompassing many and (8) many letters returning to one, (9) one letter interpreting many and (10) many letters interpreting one, (11) one letter establishing many and (12) many letters establishing one, (13) one letter refuting many and (14) many letters refuting one, and (15) revolving clockwise and (16) revolving counter clockwise.

See also, in the Taishō canon, Kūkai, *Hokkekyō kaidai* 法華經開題, T. 2190:178a11–a16, which is cited by Kakuban in the *Hokkekyō hishaku* 法華經秘釋, T. 2191:189a19–22 and the *Gorinkujimyō himitsushaku* 五輪九字明秘密釋, T. 2514:21c18–21, as well as again by Dōhan in the *Gyōhōkanyōshō,* T. 2502:886c18–19.

44 T. 2211:3a6–8; TKDZ 4:34.

45 *Nyonyo rengechi* 如如蓮華智 is another name for the wisdom of subtle discernment. See MD 1744.

46 T. 2221:2c25–27; TKDZ 3:77–78.

47 T. 2427:380b23; TKDZ 3:105.

48 T. 1911:107a–108b.

49 *Adhiṣṭhāna* body 加持身(J. *kajishin*) signifies the body of the *dharmakāya* made manifest for the benefit and teaching of sentient beings. See MD 236.

50 MD 607.

51 The thirteen courts 十三院 of the Womb Realm mandala are the following:

1. The court of the central dais with eight petals, Chūdai Hachiyō-in 中台八葉院, containing the five wisdom buddhas mentioned above and four bodhisattvas: Samantabhadra (southeast), Mañjuśrī (southwest), Avalokiteśvara (northwest), and Maitreya (northeast).
2. Henchi-in 遍智院 sits above the center dais and depicts Cundi Avalokiteśvara.
3. Jimyō-in 持明院 sits below the center dais and depicts Buddhalocani 佛眼佛母 and other deities.
4. Kannon-in 觀音院 sits to the left of the central dais and is led by Avalokiteśvara Bodhisattva.
5. Satta-in 薩埵院 sits to the left of the central dais and is led by Vajrasattva Bodhisattva.
6. Shaka-in 釋迦院 sits above the Henchi-in and is led by Śākyamuni Buddha.
7. Monju-in 文殊院 sits above the Śākyamuni pavilion and is led by Mañjuśrī Bodhisattva.
8. Kokūzō-in 虛空藏院 sits below the Jimyō-in and is led by Ākāśagarbha Bodhisattva.
9. Soshitsuji-in 蘇悉地院 sits below the Kokūzō-in and conveys the accomplishments (*siddhi*).
10. Ksitigarbha 地藏院 sits to the left of the Kannon-in and is led by Ksitigarbha Bodhisattva.
11. Jogaishō-in 除蓋障院 sits to the right of Satta-in and depicts Karunāmreditah 悲愍菩薩. FD 4341, 4954.
12. Outer *vajra* 外金剛部 circles the perimeter of the mandala and depicts various deities.
13. Shidaigo-in 四大護院 indicates the deities that protect the four gates (FD 1658), but in contemporary depictions of the mandala, this last one is omitted, making twelve courts. MD 863c; FD 3935.

52 The *Contemplation Sutra* (T. 365) describes sixteen aspects of the Pure Land that one should contemplate upon seeking rebirth there: (1) the setting sun (T. 365:341c27–342a6); (2) the water of the Pure Land (342a6–23); (3) the land (342a23–b1); (4) the jeweled trees (342b1–23); (5) the jeweled ponds (342b23–c6); (6) the jeweled towers (342c6–14); (7) the lotus throne of the Buddha (342c14–343a18); (8) the marvelous body of the Buddha (343a18–b15); (9) the light of the Buddha (343b15–c12); (10) Avalokiteśvara Bodhisattva (343c12–344a18); (11) Mahāsthāmaprāpta Bodhisattva (344a18–b14); (12) envisioning one's own rebirth in the Pure Land (344b14–24); (13) the extent of the Buddha's influence and various aspects of the Pure Land (344b24–c8); (14) beings of the highest capacity (344c9–345b7); (15) beings of middling capacities (345b8–c9); (16) beings of lower capacities (345c10–346a26).

53 The Vajra Realm mandala is divided into nine "assemblies" in a three-by-three square: (1) *jōjin-e* 成身會, (2) *sanmaya-e* 三昧耶會, (3) *misai-e* 微細會, (4) *kuyō-e* 供養會, (5) *shiin-e* 四印會, (6) *ichiin-e* 一印會, (7) *rishu-e* 理趣會, (8) *gōsanze-e* 降三世會, and (9) *gōsanze sanmaya-e* 降三世三昧耶會. MD, 663–664, 668–669. For a detailed explanation, see Robert Sharf, "Visualization and Mandala in Shingon Buddhism," in *Living Images: Japanese Buddhist Icons in Context*, ed. Robert Sharf and Elizabeth Horton Sharf (Palo Alto, CA: Stanford University Press, 2001), pp. 167–180. The Pure Land is divided into three grades, each of which is divided into three levels, making a total of nine levels. See also the last three contemplations from the *Contemplation Sutra* listed in the previous note.

54 NKBD 1357.

55 T. 848:53c14.

56 T. 1911:12b22–24.

57 Dōhan appears to be providing his summary of the introduction to the *Shōji jissō gi* 聲字實相義, T. 2429:401c6–402a12. The tatpuruṣa 依主釋 (Ch. *yizhushi*, J. *eshushaku*) is a "dependent compound" wherein one noun modifies another noun—e.g., "mountain temple"; a karma-dhāraya 持業釋 (Ch. *chiyeshi*, J. *jigōshaku*) is a compound wherein an adjective modifies a noun—e.g."high mountain." In both cases, the coherence of the term is fundamentally dependent on the compound; if separated, the meaning is lost. See the DDB 六合釋, summarized here, which lists all six compound forms; NKBD 1762.

58 T. 1719:328b. I wish to thank Professor Robert Rhodes of Ōtani University for helping me find this reference; T. 1718, fasc. 9, pt. 2, beginning at T. 1718:127a15. See, especially, T. 1718:127b12–15. The relevant chapter in the *Lotus Sutra* is found at T. 262:42a29. For an English translation of this passage of the *Lotus Sutra*, see Hurvitz, *Lotus Sutra*, p. 219.

59 T. 1796:622c20–23.

60 T. 2211:6c15–17; TKDZ 4:35.

61 NKBD 665.

62 T. 848:17b29.

63 T. 867:267a3–4.

64 T. 2522:48b1–27: (1) Limitless Light Buddha 無量光佛, (2) Boundless Light Buddha 無邊光佛, (3) Unobstructed Light Buddha 無礙光佛, (4) Peerless Light Buddha 無對光佛, (5) King Blazing [Light] Buddha 炎王光佛, (6) Joyous Light Buddha 歡喜光佛, (7) Wisdom Light Buddha 智慧光佛, (8) Unceasing Light Buddha 不斷光佛, (9) Inconceivable Light Buddha 難思光佛, (10) Inexplicable Light Buddha 無稱光佛, (11) Pure Light Buddha 清淨光佛, (12) Light That Surpasses the Sun and Moon Buddha 超日月光佛. For a similar list, see *Sukhāvatīvyūha-sūtra*, T. 360:27a27–b3.

65 *Nikyōron,* T. 2427:380a18–c1; TKDZ 3:104, quoting *Yugikyō,* T. 867:253c19–254a17. See also Kūkai, *Himitsu mandara jūjūshinron,* T. 2425:360c29–b9).

66 T. 1003:608b3.

67 This passage notes Zhanran's commentary, but the quote actually comes directly from Zhiyi's text, T. 1718:82b10–15: 見父之處者即是門側。二觀爲方便即門二邊。圓中之機當門止見。二乘偏眞故言門側。但空三昧偏眞慧眼。傍窺法身耳。遙見其父。正見有二種。一近見。二遠見。今言大機始發扣召事遠。是故言遙。又機微非應赴。名之爲遙也。. The term 但空 (NKBD 1157) is contrasted with 不但空 (NKBD 1449). According to Tendai doctrine, the perfect middle path 圓中 (NKBD 143) is able to perceive both the essential emptiness and the being of things simultaneously. This text quotes the famous *Lotus Sutra* parable about the prodigal son who, upon seeing his father, becomes frightened and runs from the middle path to the side of the gate. Noticing this, the father puts on humble clothing so that he can reach out to his son. This illustrates the two teachings. Biased views are understood to perceive the truth from a limited perspective and thus only perceive the Dharma body from one side. Attached to the truth of emptiness, they see only part of the truth, whereas those within the perfect teaching correctly see the nature of emptiness and substance. T. 262:16b07–19a11; Hurvitz, *Lotus Sutra,* 84–100.

68 MD 1782.

69 See DNBZ 86–87. Passage omitted in SAZ 2:235–236.

70 MD, 1562, explains that the revealed teachings present many words, discourses, and concepts to establish a doctrine, whereas the secret teachings use a single letter to encompass all meanings; T. 2203A:12b22–12c10.

71 This passage is found in the *Avataṃsaka-sūtra* 大方廣佛華嚴經, T. 278:689c17–690b25, and the *Dafangguangfo huayanjing souxuanfenqi tongzhifanggui* 大方廣佛華嚴經搜玄分齊通智方軌 by Zhiyan 智儼 (602–668), T. 1732:91b10–97b21. Virtuous Cloud Bhikṣu is the first teacher that Sudhana encounters on the bodhisattva path. Shandao also makes references to this aspect of the *nenbutsu* samādhi in the *Guan Wuliangshoufo jingshu* 觀無量壽佛經疏, T. 1753:249c15–16.

72 T. 417:899a9–899c3, T. 418:904b24–906a7.

73 T. 930:67b29–67c22.

74 T. 1796:388c.

75 T. 848:1c1–3.

76 T. 1796:587b11–22. The passage in the *Lotus Sutra* is found at T. 262:16b25–19a11.

77 This phrase 初發心時便成正覺 is an important concept in the *Avataṃsaka-sūtra* 大方廣佛華嚴經, T. 278:449a13–449c15, and is quoted in numerous

other texts from which Dōhan draws, such as Yijing, *Dapiluzhena chengfo jingshu* 大毘盧遮那成佛經疏, T. 1796:579a7–593a25; Zhiyi, *Mohezhiguan* 摩訶止觀, T. 1911:59b14–69c27, 94a16–97a10, 97a15–101c22; Kūkai, *Himitsu mandara jūjūshinron* 秘密漫荼羅十住心論, T. 2425:353b5–356c25; Kūkai, *Hizohō yaku* 秘藏寶鑰, T. 2426:371c24–372b8; Kūkai, *Unjigi* 吽字義, T. 2430:406c11–408a29; Saisen, *Benkenmitsu Nikyōron kenkyōshō* 弁顯密二教論懸鏡抄, T. 2434:444c16–446c25; Saisen, *Kenmitsu shabetsu mondō* 顯密差別問答, T. 2435:484c19–485c2, 491a22–492a29, 497c1–498b15; and Dōhan, *Jōōshō* 貞應抄, T. 2447:706b5–706c1.

78 This line is omitted in the SAZ.

79 T. 1911:12b18–22.

80 Though Shandao does indeed discuss the ten vocal utterances and ten thought moments in various places, I have not yet found an instance where he addresses them in the same passage. The phrase 十念即十聲 does, however, actually appear in the work of the Tiantai Pure Land scholar Yuanzhao, mentioned previously by Dōhan; see *Amituojing yishu* 阿彌陀經義疏, T. 1761:361c17. A similar phrase is found in Yuanzhao's *Guan Wuliangshoufo jing yishu* 觀無量壽佛經義疏, T. 1754:304b12.

81 T. 1796:583a15–16.

82 T. 848:17b29.

83 T. 1796:689b08.

84 The five aggregates 五蘊 include form (Skt. *rūpa*), feeling (Skt. *vedanā*), perception (Skt. *saṃjñā*), volition (Skt. *saṃskāra*), and consciousness (Skt. *vijñāna*). Here the phrase 五陰 is used.

85 T. 905:910a1–2.

86 TKDZ 5:148. See also Saisen, *Kongōchō hotsu bodaishinron shishō* 金剛頂發菩提心論私抄, T. 2292:20a10–20.

87 T. 930:67c5–6.

88 T. 365:341c9–14: "One, honor your parent and respect teachers, practice compassion and do not kill, cultivate the ten virtuous deeds (refrain from killing, stealing, lust, deceit, criticizing others, sowing discord, idle speech, greed, anger, wrong views). Two, take refuge in the three jewels (Buddha, Dharma, Sangha), keep all of the precepts, not breaking etiquette. Three, give rise to the mind that seeks awakening, have deep faith in the law of cause and effect, read and chant the Mahayana sutras, encourage others to practice."

89 T. 152:868b.

90 TKDZ 5:144–145. Fascicle 1 ends at this point in the DNBZ edition, while the SAZ edition continues for another paragraph.

91 TKDZ 5:148.

92 T. 1796:623a5–9.

93 T. 2428:389c14.

94 The DDB 五眼 states:

> 肉眼, the earthly, physical eye, which sees the material aspects of things (*mâṃsa-cakṣus*). 天眼, the heavenly eye, possessed by devas, as well as humans in the form realm who are in meditation; this eye can see far and near, past and future, inside and outside. Celestial eyes see in detail the causes and effects of things (*divya-cakṣus*). 慧眼, the wisdom eye, possessed by Hinayana sages who can discern the lack of inherent existence in all things (*prajñā-cakṣus*). 法眼, the Dharma eye, possessed by bodhisattvas which illuminates all teachings in order to save sentient beings; the Dharma eyes sees the impermanence of all things (*dharma-cakṣus*). 佛眼, the Buddha eye, which includes all of the prior four (*buddha-cakṣus*).

95 T. 1003:608b13–15.

96 MD 394. Guanzizaiwang Rulai, or Lokeśvararāja Tathāgata, is another name for Amitābha in Amoghavajra's *Jin'gangding* 金剛頂經觀自在王如來修行法 (T. 931) and other texts associated with the *Vajraśekhara* cycle.

97 See the discussion beginning at T. 867:254a1.

98 DDB 八部: gods 天 (Skt. *devas*), snakes/dragons 龍 (Skt. *nāgas*), flying flesh-eating ghosts 夜叉(Skt. *yakṣas*), ghostly musicians 乾闥婆 (Skt. *gandharvas*), titans 阿修羅 (Skt. *Asuras*), divine birds 迦樓羅 (Skt. *garuḍas*), heavenly musicians 緊那羅 (Skt. *kiṃnaras*), snake spirits 摩睺羅迦 (Skt. *mahoragas*).

99 T. 1753:264a15.

100 DDB 六根: perception of form, sound, smell, taste, touch, and conception of sense perception.

101 At the end of fascicle 3, the DNBZ edition contains supplementary passages. The first of these passages appears here as well as in the DNBZ as a supplement written on the back of the scroll. See the end of fascicle 3 for this passage.

102 T. 1796:585b28–9.

103 T. 1796:585b28–c01. This note is found in the DNBZ version. I have translated the version of this passage that appears in the Taisho canon. The order in the DNBZ is slightly different.

104 T. 1796:587a24–25.

105 DDB 波羅蜜: generosity, morality, perseverence, effort, meditation, and wisdom.

106 DDB 十八空.

107 DDB 三十七道品.

108 DDB 百八三昧; *Foguangshan dacidian,* p. 2480; *Dazhidulun* 大智度論 (Skt. *Mahāprajñāpāramitā-śāstra*), T. 1509:361a12.

109 *Foguang dacidian,* p. 1081.

110 T. 1796:706a17–21.

111 T. 930:19.0071a10–14; Dreitlein, "Amoghavajra's Amitāyus Ritual Manual," pp. 242–243.

112 T. 1003:612b10–11; see also Kūkai, *Hokkekyō kaidai* 法華經開題, T. 2190:176a12–13.

113 ND 31:296–363. I was able to locate this reference thanks to Satō, *Himitsu nenbutsu inyo bunken,* p. 136.

114 T. 1003:612b16–19.

115 DNBZ.

116 T. 1796:623a8. This section follows the earlier reference to the differing anatomical heart-lotus buds within men and women.

117 KDZ, 1:200; Satō, "Dōhan cho Himitsu nenbutsu shō Inyō bunken shutten chūki," p. 136.

118 T. 931:73c16; Satō, "Dōhan cho Himitsu nenbutsu shō Inyō bunken shutten chūki," p. 136.

119 Possibly referring to the line at T. 901:801c24.

120 This line appears here in the DNBZ version and appears again at the very end of the *Himitsu nenbutsu shō.*

121 T. 365:344a23–25.

122 This line does not appear in the text. I added it in because it appears to be implied by the two previous sentences.

123 DNBZ.

124 DDB 五欲: the desires of the five senses are form, sound, fragrance, flavor, and touch.

125 DNBZ.

126 T. 1796:586b13.

127 DDB 八功德水: the eight attributes of the lotus pond in the Pure Land included sweetness 甘美, freshness 淸冷, softness 安和, lightness 輕軟, purity 澄淨, scentlessness 潤澤, cleansing 除饑渴, and nourishing 長養諸根.

128 T. 1796:588c7–10. Following this quote, the second supplementary passages found at the end of the text are found here in the DNBZ edition.

129 T. 1796:788b1–3; Satō, "Dōhan cho Himitsu nenbutsu shō Inyō bunken shutten chūki," p. 136.

130 DDB 五輪: the five great discs under Mt. Sumeru were space, wind, water, metal, and earth.

131 DNBZ.

132 T. 905:909c20–24. Jinjua Chen argues that this text is possibly a Japanese Tendai apocrypha, perhaps written by Annen; see Jinjua Chen, "The Construction of Early Tendai Esoteric Buddhism: The Japanese Provenance of Saichō's Transmission Documents and Three Esoteric Buddhist Apocrypha Attributed to Śubhākarasiṁha," *Journal of the International Association of Buddhist Studies* 21, no. 1 (1998): 21–76.

133 T. 905:910b22–23.

134 T. 905:911c14–16.

135 T. 1796:704a5–14.

136 DDB 四州: Jambudvīpa, Pūrvavideha, Aparagodānīya, and Uttarakuru.

137 T. 2203A:12a22–24. I am here quoting the English translation of the passage from Dreitlein, "Annotated Translation of Kūkai's *Secret Key to the Heart Sūtra*," pp. 31–32. See also notes 111–113, which explain in greater detail some of the references contained in this short line. In particular, Dreitlein writes in note 112 that the "Tathāgata who attains the purity of self-nature" is an epithet for Amitāyus in T. 243:784c.

138 *Abhidharmakośa-bhāṣya* 阿毘達磨俱舍論, T. 1558:141a11.

139 DDB 十對.

140 T. 366:346c13–14.

141 See Genshin, *Ōjōyōshū*, T. 2682:33a11.

142 T. 1755:306c5–6; however, a closer match to the actual line quoted here appears in Genshin, *Amidakyō ryakki*, T. 2210:680a3.

143 TKDZ 5:144–145. An abbreviated version of this line is cited above at the end of fascicle 1 of the DNBZ edition.

144 T. 1558:14c7–20ff.; Satō, "Dōhan cho Himitsu nenbutsu shō Inyō bunken shutten chūki," p. 137. While searching for this reference, I happened upon Ryōson's 了尊*Shittan rinryaku zushō* 悉曇輪略圖抄, T. 2709, compiled in 1287, in which this line appears exactly as written in Dōhan's text. This is interesting because, as Satō notes, Dōhan's version somewhat paraphrases the *Kusha ron* passage. As a near contemporary of Dōhan (who died in 1252), it is interesting to note how often the 兩部事 section (T. 2709:711b20–712a23) in Ryōson's text is nearly verbatim to the passages found in the second fascicle of the *Himitsu nenbutsu shō*. More inquiry into this text is needed.

145 *Chūjukankyōshi* 中壽感興詩並序, in the *Shōryōshū* 性靈集, TKDZ 8:43. I was able to locate this reference thanks to Satō, "Dōhan cho Himitsu nenbutsu shō Inyō bunken shutten chūki," p. 137. On this text, see Sakai Shiro 酒井紫朗, "Kōbō Daishi no *Chūjukankyōshi* ni tsuite," pp. 13–25.

146 The Sanskrit term *saṃbodhi* is transliterated in East Asian languages as 三菩提 and also may be translated as 正等覺. Here Dōhan draws from an

exegetical strategy that employs both translation and transliteration simultaneously.

147 T. 1796:788b1–3.

148 T. 1796:789c17–19.

149 The reader might notice the numerous parenthetical statements and marginalia in this work. I have endeavored to render passages such as this one as they appear in the text.

150 Satō, "Dōhan cho Himitsu nenbutsu shō Inyō bunken shutten chūki," p. 138, was also unable to locate this text, noting that it is mentioned in Enchin's text catalogues, *Nihon biku Enchin nittō guhō mokuroku* 日本比丘圓珍入唐求法目録, T. 2172:1101a3; *Chishō daishi shōrai mokuroku* 智證大師請來目録, T. 2173:1106b27; and *Fukushū onshuū daishū gutoku kyō ritsu ron sho ki gesho tō mokuroku* 福州温州台州求得經律論疏記外書等目録, T. 2170:1094a19.

151 DDB 十六大菩薩: (1) Akṣobhya Buddha (in the eastern quarter of the mandala) is attended by the bodhisattvas Vajrasattva 金剛薩埵, Vajrarāja 金剛王, Vajrarāga 金剛愛, and Vajrasādhu 金剛喜; (2) Ratnasaṃbhava Buddha (south) is attended by the bodhisattvas Vajraratna 金剛寶, Vajratejas 金剛光, Vajraketu 金剛幡, and Vajrahāsa 金剛笑; (3) Amitābha Buddha (west) is attended by the bodhisattvas Vajradharma 金剛法, Vajratīkṣṇa 金剛利, Vajrahetu 金剛因, and Vajrabhāṣa 金剛語; (4) Amoghasiddhi Buddha (north) is attended by the bodhisattvas Vajrakarma 金剛業, Vajrarakṣa 金剛護, Vajrayakṣa 金剛牙, and Vajrasaṃdhi 金剛拳. See Amoghavajra, *Putixinlun* 菩提心論, T. 1665:573c22.

152 The DDB 眞諦 has a substantial entry on Paramartha and his prolific career. He is recognized alongside Kumārajīva, Xuanzang, and Amoghavajra as the "four great translators."

153 T. 1796:583c12–13.

154 T. 2428:383b26–27. The translation of this passage is adapted from Dreitlein and Takagi, *Kūkai on the Philosophy of Language*, p. 66.

155 The 徹心印明 (mudra and mantra for discerning the mind) is associated with the first component of the *gosō jōshin* 五相成身, a fivefold practice associated with the Vajra Realm mandala. MD 613 contains a full description of the practice: (1) visualization of the mind as the full moon, symbolizing *bodhicitta;* (2) visualization of the cultivation of *bodhicitta;* (3) the attainment of the *vajra* mind; (4) realization of the *vajra* body; (5) complete attainment of the buddha body. The mantra associated with the first visualization is *Oṃ citta pratvedham karomi,* intoned while visualizing the moon disk at one's heart's center, which symbolizes Buddhahood. DDB 五相成身.

156 DDB 二十五有: "Four evil destinies 四惡道, the four continents 四洲, the six heavens of desire 六欲天, the four meditation heavens 四禪天, the heaven

of the five pure abodes 五淨居天, and the four spheres of the formless realm 四空處天."

157 *Mohezhiguan*, T. 1911:15a28–15b14. The translation of this passage adapted from the *Mohezhiguan* is in Swanson, *Clear Serenity*, pp. 339–344. See also p. 1931, where he references T. 1911:15a25–29 and the *Sutra on Petitioning Avalokiteśvara*, T. 20:36a6–12. For a complete list and explanation of the twenty-five samādhis, see pp. 342–343; for more on the dhāraṇīs of six-syllable phrases, see pp. 339–340. Dōhan also identifies particular manifestations of Avalokiteśvara with these six forms discussed by Zhiyi. I have indicated Dōhan's note with an asterisk in brackets.

158 Dōhan also quotes this part of this passage in his *Jōō-shō* 貞應抄, T. 2447:77.700b04–05.

159 Satō, "Dōhan cho Himitsu nenbutsu shō Inyō bunken shutten chūki," p. 138, was also unable to identify this reference.

160 Satō, "Dōhan cho Himitsu nenbutsu shō Inyō bunken shutten chūki," p. 138, identifies Satō Tetsuei, *Eizan Jōdokyō*, pp. 236–237.

161 T. 1753:249b3–5.

162 T. 930:67c5–6.

163 Corresponds roughly to T. 365:346a12–22.

164 T. 1753:272b6–11.

165 Eikan here quotes Shandao, *Wangsheng lizan jie* 往生禮讃偈, T. 1980:439a16–17; this is also quoted by Hōnen, *Senchakushū*, T. 2608:12c8–9.

166 My suspicion is that here Dōhan is riffing off Shandao—not necessarily as a critique of him or Hōnen being merely "exoteric" but rather to "clarify" the esoteric implications of these seemingly exoteric views.

167 T. 2683:93a5–14.

168 T. 2683:97c05–07.

169 光明遍照 is also an appellation for Mahāvairocana.

170 T. 365:343b26.

171 T. 278:449c14.

172 This passage from Shandao, *Wangsheng lizan jie*, T. 1980:438c12, is also quoted in Genshin, *Ōjōyōshū*, T. 2682:58a29; Hōnen, *Senchakushū*, T. 2608:12a26–12b2; and Shinran, *Kyōgyōshinshō*, T. 2646:628c28–29. The second part of the quote in the *Senchakushū* is very similar to this line. Could it be that Dōhan is actually quoting from a copy of the *Senchakushū*?

173 T. 848:22a15–17.

174 T. 1796:707a28–b2.

175 DDB: the base of the mind—the *ālayavijñāna* in Yogâcāra.

176 T. 1796:587a4–5.

177 Zhili 知禮 (960–1028), *Guan wuliangshoufo jing shumiaozong chao* 觀無量壽佛經疏妙宗鈔, T. 1751:206b2–10; and Guanding 灌頂 (561–632), *Dabanniepanjing xuanyi* 大般涅槃經玄義, T. 1765:6a3–10.

178 This passage is missing in the SAZ.

179 觀無量壽佛經疏, T. 1753:272b16–17.

180 T. 901:812a22–b3.

181 The "four immeasurables" are kindness (*maitrī*), compassion (*karuṇā*), sympathetic joy (*muditā*), and equanimity (*upekṣa*).

182 T. 867:257b23–c2. The corresponding passage in the Taishō is somewhat longer.

183 TKZ 5:133–134.

184 DNBZ.

185 In the DNBZ, the note below appears here.

186 T. 1797:806c24–28.

187 T. 1796:785a21–787a6.

188 The discussion of inner *goma* in the *Yugikyō* is at T. 867:264b1–268c3.

189 *Foguang dacidian*, 547, 2492.

190 It is possible that Dōhan here quotes Annen, *Kongōbu rōkaku issai yugi kyō shugyō* 金剛峰樓閣一切瑜祇經修行法, T. 2228:498b11–14.

191 T. 2428:381c16–21 (end quote).

192 DDB 十緣生句: "Ten illusions arising from environmental conditions: sleight of hand 幻, a mirage 陽焰, dreams 夢, reflections or shadows 影, *gandharva* cities (or cities of the sirens, seen in the seamist) 乾闥婆城, echoes 響, the moon reflected in water 水月, floating bubbles 浮泡, motes (muscae volitantes) 虛空華, a fire-wheel (made by revolving a flare) 旋火輪." Giebel's translation of *The Vairocanābhisaṃbodhi Sutra* (online version at T. 848:3c12–14) states: "What are the ten [propositions about dependent arising]? They are, namely, that [dependent arising] is like an illusion, a mirage, a dream, a reflection, a *gandharva* city, an echo, the moon [reflected] in water, bubbles, a flower in empty space, and a whirling wheel of fire."

193 TKDZ 7:391–393.

194 The TKDZ uses the term "teaching" 教 here.

195 TKDZ 7:392–393.

196 This section begins at T. 848:39a3; see, especially, from 39a21. See also Yixing's commentary at T. 1796:756c7.

197 The DDB entry for 戒體 references the 梵網經, T. 1484:998a24.

198 T. 2462:6a1–3.

199 T. 2462:6a13–16; for the complete passage, see T. 2462:6a1–16.

200 T. 1796:629c4–6.

201 *Qianshou qianyan guanshiyin pusa daveixin tuoluoni* 千手千眼觀世音菩薩大悲心陀羅尼, T. 1057, 1058, 1060:162a–b, 1063, 1064.

202 In the DNBZ edition, the following note appears here, and the next sentence is placed after the note. I follow the SAZ version here.

203 T. 1022B:714c5–7. In the original, the line before the passage quoted mentions the attainment of Pure Land rebirth.

204 T. 967:351c9–10.

205 T. 967:351a9–11.

206 T. 1484:1009a24–29.

207 This passage is missing from the DNBZ.

208 T. 1786:117c25–26, T. 1796:587a4–6.

209 T. 1796:789b4–7.

210 T. 1796:585b14–17.

211 MBD 1684b.

212 T. 1796:651c8–10.

213 *Nikyōron,* T. 2427:380b20. I am unable to locate this phrase in the *Yugikyō;* however, perhaps the *Sōōkyō* mentioned in the original text here, a common alternate name for the *Yugikyō,* is in fact a mistake referencing Dōhan's major work appearing in the Taishō canon, the *Jōōshō* 貞應抄, T. 2447:698c13, which does contain this phrase and again quotes the *Nikyōron.*

214 T. 1796:620c14.

215 T. 1796:608c11–13.

216 T. 1069:144c7–8.

Bibliography

Selected Major Extant Works of Dōhan 道範 (1179–1252)

Aun gōkan 阿吽合觀. Mitsuun 密雲 (1817–1884) and Moriyama Kamon 守山嘉門, eds. *Ajikan hiketsushū* 阿字観秘決集. 1912. Reprint, Yao: Jōkō-in 定光院, 2010, pp. 19–20. English translation by Richard K. Payne, "Ajikan: Ritual and Meditation in the Shingon Tradition." In Payne, *Re-visioning "Kamakura" Buddhism*, pp. 232–233.

Benkenmitsu nikyōron shukyō shō 辯顯密二教論手鏡抄. ZSZ 18:273–323. 3 fasc. Jōhen 靜遍 (1165–1223). Compiled by Dōhan, ca. 1223–1224 (Jōō 貞應 2–3).

Bodaishinron dangiki 菩提心論談義記. ND 24 (1916 ed.), 47 (1975 ed.). 2 fasc. Compiled 1240 (En'ō 延應 2).

Chō kaishō 聽海抄. 2 fasc. Kakkai/Kakukai 覺海 (Nanshōbō 南勝房; 1142–1223). Compiled by Dōhan. Kanayama Bokushō 金山穆韶. "Chōkaishō (Dōhan ajari ki) 聴海抄 (道範阿闍梨記). *Mikkyō kenkyū* 密教研究 10 (1922): 167–228.

Dainichi kyōsho henmyō shō 大日經疏遍明鈔. ZSZ 5:99–444. 21 fasc. 1245 (Kangen 寬元 3).

Dainichi kyōsho joanshō 大日經疏除暗鈔. BT 19; ZSZ 5:1–97. 7 fasc. 1224 (Jōō 3).

Dōhan nikka rinjū higi 道範日課臨終祕儀. *Kōyasan Daigaku mikkyō bunka kenkyūjo kiyō* 高野山大学密教文化研究所紀要 16 (2003): 79–92.

Dōhan shōsoku 道範消息. NKBT 83:76–83. 1 fasc. Pol Van den Broucke. "Dōhan's Letter on the Visualization of Syllable A." *Shingi Shingon kyōgaku no kenkyū* 新義真言教学の研究 10 (2002): 65–87.

Gyōhō kanyō shō 行法肝葉鈔. SZ 23:147–178. 3 fasc. Compiled ca. 1243–1249 (Kangen 1 to Hōji 寶治 3).

Hannya shingyō hiken kaihō shō 般若心經祕鍵開寶鈔. ND 10 (1916 ed.), 20 (1975 ed.). 2 fasc. 1247.

Himitsu nenbutsu shō 祕密念佛鈔. DNBZ 70:51–82; ZJZ 15:79–110; SAZ 2:225–266. 3 fasc. 1223 (Jōō 2); *Himitsushū nenbutsu shō* 秘密宗念佛鈔. Kyoto: Nagata chōbee 永田長兵衛, 1686; *Himitsu shū nenbutsu shō* 秘密宗念仏鈔. Rokudai shinhōsha insatsubu 六大新報社印刷部, 1907; Himitsu Nenbutsu Shō Kenkyūkai 秘密念仏抄研究会, ed. "Dōhan cho 'Himitsu *nenbutsu* shō' no kenkyū—honbun kōtei to kaki kudashi gochū 道範著 '秘密念仏抄' の研究—本文校訂と書き下し・語註. *Buzan gakuhō* 豊山学報 39 (1996): 105–130. Printed editions from 1645 (正保 2) are relatively widely available.

Hizōhōyaku mondanshō 祕藏寶鑰問談鈔. 2 fasc. Compiled ca. 1240; Mori Shigeki 森重樹, ed. *Toganō korekushon kenmitsu tenseki monjo shūsei* 栂尾コレクション顕密典籍文書集成. Vol. 5. Tokyo: Hirakawa shuppansha, 1981.

Hizōki shō 祕藏記鈔. ZSZ 15:35–58. 1 fasc.

Joōshō (*Teiōshō*) 貞應抄. T. 2447. 3 fasc. 1225 (Jōō 4).

Kakua mondō shō 覺阿問答鈔. 3 fasc. 1252. Mori Shigeki 森重樹, ed. *Toganō korekushon kenmitsu tenseki monjo shūsei* 栂尾コレクション顕密典籍文書集成. Vol. 1. Tokyo: Hirakawa shuppansha, 1981.

Kōbō Daishi ryaku joshō 弘法大師略頌鈔. KDZ 3. 1 fasc. 1234. *Kōbō Daishi ryakujo* 弘法大師略頌. 治田七兵衛, 1658; *Kōbō Daishi ryaku joshō* 弘法大師略頌鈔. Tokyo: Kōyasan shucchō sho 高野山出張所, 1882.

Kōmyō shingon shijū shaku 光明眞言四重釋. SAZ 2:74–81. 1 fasc.

Kongōchōgyō kaidai kanchū 金剛頂經開題勘註. ZSZ 7:1–18. 1 fasc.

Nankai rurōki 南海流浪記. GR 18:468–476. 1 fasc.

Nanzan hiku 南山秘口. ZSZ 41:99–102. 1 fasc. 1243 (Kangen 1).

Nichi sotsu toba daiji 日率都婆大事. Kōyasan Hachiyō Gakkai 高野山八葉学会, ed. *Chūinryū sakuhōshū* 中院流作法集. Kōyasan 高野山八葉学会, 1918, pp. 27–29.

Rinjū yōshin ji 臨終用心事. SAZ 2:792–795. 1 fasc.

Rishushaku hidenshō 理趣釋祕傳鈔. ND 17. 2 fasc. 1250.

Shakumakaenron ōkyōshō 釋摩訶衍論應教鈔. T. 2288. 1 fasc. 1226 (Karoku 嘉禄 2).

Shōji jissōgi shō 聲字實相義抄. SZ 14:9–36. 2 fasc. 1240. (Ninji 仁治 1).

Shoshin tongaku shō 初心頓覺鈔. SZ 22:149–175. 3 fasc.

Sokushin jōbutsugi kiki gaki 卽身成佛義聞書. ZSZ 17:1–37. 2 fasc.

Unjigi shakukanchū shō 吽字義釋勘註抄. SZ 15:11–54. 3 fasc. Dōhan's oral transmissions, later compiled by Ryūgen 隆源 (1342–1426).

Yoga sūtraṃ kuden 口傳. ZSZ 7:91–134. 2 fasc. 1224 (Jōō 3).

Yugikyō kuketsu 瑜祇經口決. SZ 5:27–136. 5 fasc. 1224 (Jōō 3).

Primary Sources

Achufoguo jing 阿閦佛國經 (Skt. *Akṣobhyavyūha-sūtra*, J. *Ashuku bukkokkyō*). T. 313. Lokakṣema 支婁迦讖 (second century; Ch. Zhi Loujiachen, J. Shi Rukashin).

Ajigi 阿字義. T. 2438. Jitsuhan/Jippan 實範 (d. 1144).

Aliduoluo tuoluoni alulijing 阿唎多羅陀羅尼阿嚕力經 (J. *Aritara darani aroriki kyō*). T. 1039. Amoghavajra 不空金剛 (705–774; Ch. Bukong Jin'gang, J. Fukū Kongō).

Amida hisshaku 阿彌陀祕釋. T. 2522. Kakuban 覺鑁 (1095–1143).

Amidashinjūgi 阿彌陀新十疑. SEJ 2:221–258. Zenyu 禅瑜 (913?–990).

Amituo gu yinsheng wang tuoluoni jing 阿彌陀鼓音聲王陀羅尼經 (Skt. *Aparimitāyurjñānahṛdaya-dhāraṇī*, J. *Amida ku onjō ō darani kyō*). T. 370.

Anantuo muqunihelituo jing 阿難陀目佉尼呵離陀經 (Skt. *Anatamukhasādhāka-dhāraṇī*, J. *Ananda mokukyanikarida kyō*). T. 1013. 1 fasc. Guṇabhadra 求那跋陀羅 (394–468; Ch. Qiunabatuoluo, J. Gunabaddara).

Anleji 安樂集 (J. *Anrakushū*). T. 1958. Daochuo 道綽 (562–645; J. Dōshaku).

Azuma no kuni kōsōden 東國高僧傳. DNBZ 104.

Bajikunantuoluoni jing 拔濟苦難陀羅尼經 (J. *Bassai kunan daranikyō*). T. 1395. Xuanzang 玄奘 (602–664; J. Genjō).

Baming pumi tuoluoni jing 八名普密陀羅尼經 (J. *Hacimyōhumitsu daranikyō*). T. 1365. Xuanzang.

Banzhousanmei jing 般舟三昧經 (Skt. **Pratyutpanna-buddha-saṃmukhāvasthita-samādhi-sūtra*, J. *Hanjusanmai kyō*). T. 418. Lokakṣema.

Baoxidi chengfo tuoluonijing 寶悉地成佛陀羅尼經 (J. *Hōshicchijōbutsu daranikyō*). T. 962. Amoghavajra.

Baoxing tuoluonijing 寶星陀羅尼經 (Skt. *Mahāsaṃnipāta-Ratnaketudhāraṇī*, J. *Hōsei daranikyō*). T. 402. Prabhākaramitra 波羅迦頗蜜多羅 (564–633; Ch. Boluojiapomiduoluo, J. Harakaramittara).

Bayiqie yezhang genben desheng jingtu shenzhou 拔一切業障根本得生淨土神呪 (J. *Batsuissai gosshō konpontokushō jōdojinju*). T. 368. Guṇabhadra.

Beihua jing 悲華經 (Skt. *Karuṇā-puṇḍarīka-sūtra*, J. *Hike kyō*). T. 157. Dharmakṣema 曇無讖 (385–433; Ch. Tan Wuchen, J. Don Musen).

Benkenmitsu nikyōron 辯顯密二教論. T. 2427. Kūkai 空海 (774–835).

Bukongjuansuo shenbian zhenyan jing 不空羂索神變眞言經 (Skt. *Amoghapāśa-kalparāja*, J. *Fukūkenjaku jinpen shingon kyō*). T. 1092. Bodhiruci 菩提流志 (d. 727; Ch. Putiliuzhi, J. Bodairushi).

Bukongjuansuo shenzhouxin jing 不空羂索神呪心經 (Skt. *Amoghapāśakalpa-hṛdayadhāraṇī*, J. *Fukū kenjaku jushinkyō*). T. 1094. Xuanzang.

Bukongjuansuo tuoluoni zizai wangshoujing 不空羂索陀羅尼自在王呪經 (Skt. *Amoghapāśa-dhāraṇī*, J. *Fukūkenjaku darani jizaiō kyō*). T. 1097. Maṇicinta 寶思惟 (?–721; Ch. Baosiwei, J. Hōshiyui).

Bukongjuansuo zhouxinjing 不空羂索呪心經. T. 1095. Bodhiruci.

Bukongjuansuo zhuojing 不空羂索呪經 (Skt. *Amoghapāśa-hṛdaya*, J. *Fukūkenjaku shukyō*). T. 1093. Jñānagupta 闍那崛多 (523–600; Ch. Shenajueduo, J. Janakutta).

Byōchū shugyō ki 病中修行記. SAZ 2. Jippan/Jitsuhan.

Chang ahan jing 長阿含經 (Skt. *Dīrghāgama*, J. *Jō agonkyō*). T. 1. Buddhayaśas 佛陀耶舍 (fifth century; Ch. Fotuoyeshe, J. Buddayasha) and Zhu Fonian 竺佛念 (fourth century; Ch. Zhu Fonian, J. Chiku Butsunen).

Chishi tuolunijing 持世陀羅尼經 (Skt. *Vasudhārā-dhāraṇī*, J. *Jisedarani kyō*). T. 1162. Xuanzang.

Chusheng wubianmen duoluonijing 出生無邊門陀羅尼經 (Skt. *Anatamukhasādhāka-dhāraṇī*, J. *Shusse muhenmon daranikyō*). T. 1009. Amoghavajra.

Chusheng wubianmen duoluonijing 出生無邊門陀羅尼經 (Skt. *Anatamukhasādhāka-dhāraṇī*, J. *Shusse muhenmon daranikyō*). T. 1018. Zhiyan 智嚴 (early fifth century).

Cishipusa lüexiuyu'e niansong fa 慈氏菩薩略修愈誐念誦法 (J. *Jishibosatsuryakushūyuganenjuhō*). T. 1141. Śubhakarasiṃha 善無畏 (637–735; Ch. Shanwuwei, J. Zenmui).

Da banniepan jing 大般涅槃經 (Skt. *Mahāparinirvāṇa-sūtra*, J. *Nehan gyō*). T. 374, T. 375. Dharmakṣema (T. 375); Huiyan 慧嚴 (363–443; J. Egon).

Dabaojijing 大寶積經 (Skt. *Ratnamegha-sūtra*, J. *Daihōshakukyō*). T. 310. Bodhiruci.

Dacheng fangguang manshushilipusa huayan benjiao yanman dejiafennuwang zhenyan daweideyiguipin 大乘方廣曼殊室利菩薩華嚴本教閻曼德迦忿怒王真言大威德儀軌品 (J. *Daijō hōkō manjushiribosatsu kegon pongyō enman tokkyahunnuō shingon daiitokugikihon*). T. 1215. 1 fasc. Attributed to Amoghavajra.

Dacheng yujia jingangxinghai manshushili qianbiqianbo dajiaowangjing 大乘瑜伽金剛性海曼殊室利千臂千鉢大教王經 (J. *Daijō yuga kongōshōkai manjushiri senpi-senpotsu daikyōōgyō*). T. 1177A. Amoghavajra.

Dafaju duoluoni jing 大法炬陀羅尼經 (Skt. *Dharmolkadhāraṇī-sūtra*, J. *Daihōko darani kyō*). T. 1340. Jñānagupta.

Dafangdeng dayunjing qingyupin diliushisi 大方等大雲經請雨品第六十四 (J. *Daihōdō daiun kyō shōubon dairokujūshi*). T. 992. 1 fasc. Jñānayaśas 闍那耶舍 (sixth century; Ch. Shenayeshe, J. Shanayasha).

Dafangdeng rulaizang jing 大方等如來藏經 (Skt. *Tathāgatagarbha-sūtra*, J. *Daihōdō nyorai zōkyō*). T. 666. Buddhabhadra.

Dafangdeng tuoluoni jing 大方等陀羅尼經 (J. *Daihōdō darani kyō*). T. 1339. Fazhong 法衆 (J. Hōshu).

Dafangdeng wuxiang jing 大方等無想經 (J. *Daihōdō musō kyō*). T. 387. Dharmakṣema.

Dafangguangfo huayan jing 大方廣佛華嚴經 (Skt. *Avataṃsaka-sūtra*, J. *Daihōkōbutsu kegon kyō*). T. 278. Buddhabhadra 佛陀跋陀羅 (early fifth century; Ch. Fotuobatuoluo, J. Buddabaddara).

Dafangguangfo huayan jing 大方廣佛華嚴經 (Skt. *Avataṃsaka-sūtra*, J. *Daihōkōbutsu kegon kyō*). T. 279. Śikṣānanda 實叉難陀 and Yijing 義淨 (635–713; J. Gijō).

Dafangguangfo huayan jing 大方廣佛華嚴經 (Skt. *Avataṃsaka-sūtra*, J. *Daihōkōbutsu kegon kyō*). T. 293. Prajñā 般若 (early ninth century; Ch. Bore, J. Hannya).

Daifangguangfo huayanjing jinshizi zhang 大方廣佛華嚴經金師子章 (J. *Daihōkōbutsu kegonkyō Konjishishō*). T. 1881. Fazan 法藏 (643–712; J. Hōzō).

Dafangguangfo huayanjing souxuanfenqi tongzhifanggui 大方廣佛華嚴經搜玄分齊通智方軌 (J. *Daihōkō butsu kegonkyō sōgen bunsei tsūchi hōki*). T. 1732. Zhiyan 智儼 (602–668; J. Chigen).

Dafangguang manshushili tongzhenpusa huayanbenjiaozhanyan mandejiafennuwang zhenyan apizhelujia yigui pin 大方廣曼殊室利童真菩薩華嚴本教讚閻曼德迦忿怒王真言阿毘遮嚕迦儀軌品 (Skt. *Āryamañjuśrīmūlakalpa*, J. *Daihōkōmanjushiri dōshinbosatsu kegonhongyōsan enmantokkyahunnuō shingon abisharokya giki hon*). T. 1216. Attributed to Amoghavajra.

Dafangguang pusazangjing zhong wenshushili genben yizi tuoluonijing 大方廣菩薩藏經中文殊師利根本一字陀羅尼經 (J. *Daihōkō bosatsu zōkyōchū monjushiri konpon ichiji daranikyō*). T. 1181. Manicinta.

Dafangguang pusazang wenshushili genben yiguijing 大方廣菩薩藏文殊師利根本儀軌經 (Skt. *Mañjuśrīmulakalpa*, J. *Daihōkōbosatsu monjushiri konpon gikikyō*). T.1191. Tianxizai 天息災 (d.u.–1000; J. Tensokusai).

Daibirushanakyō shiki 大毘盧遮那經指歸. T. 2212. Enchin 圓珍 (814–891).

Dainichikyō jūshinbon shoshiki 大日經住心品疏私記. T. 2215. Saisen 濟暹 (1025–1115).

Dainichikyō kaidai 大日經開題. T. 2211. Kūkai.

Daioshō hōi Heianjō taijōtennō kanjōmon 大和尚奉爲平安城太上天皇灌頂文. T. 2461. Kūkai.

Dajinsekongquewang zhoujing 大金色孔雀王呪經 (J. *Daikonjiki kujakuōjukyō*). T. 986. Śrīmitra.

Dajiyi shenzhoujing 大吉義神呪經 (J. *Daikitsugi shinjukyō*). T. 1335. Tanyao 曇曜 (fifth century; J. Donyō).

Dalejin'gang bukong zhenshi sanmeiye jing banruo boluomiduo liqushi 大樂金剛不空眞實三昧耶經般若波羅蜜多理趣釋 (J. *Dairaku kongō fukū shinjitsu sanmaya kyō hannya haramitta rishushaku*). T. 1003. Amoghavajra.

Dalejin'gang bukong zhenshi sanmoye jing 大樂金剛不空眞實三摩耶經 (J. *Dairaku kongō fukū shinjitsu sanmaya kyō*). T. 243. Amoghavajra.

Dapiluzhena chengfo jingshu 大毘盧遮那成佛經疏 (J. *Daibirushana jōbutsu kyōsho*). T. 1796. Yixing.

Dapiluzhena chengfo shenbian jiachi jing 大毘盧遮那成佛神變加持經 (Skt. *Mahāvairocanābhisaṃbodhi-sūtra*, J. *Daibirushana jōbutsu jinben kajikyō*). T. 848. Śubhakarasiṃha and Yixing 一行 (683–787; J. Ichigyō).

Dasheng qixin lun 大乘起信論 (J. *Daijō kishin ron*). T. 1666. Aśvaghoṣa 馬鳴 (second century; Ch. Maming, J. Memyō).

Dasheng yizhang 大乘義章 (J. *Daijō gishō*). T. 1851. Jingying Huiyuan 淨影慧遠 (523–592; J. Jōyō Eon).

Da Song sengshi lüe 大宋僧史略 (J. *Daisō sōshiryaku*). T. 2126. Zanning 贊寧 (920–1001; J. Sannei).

Datang xiyu qiufa gaoseng zhuan 大唐西域求法高僧傳 (J. *Daitō saiiki guhō kōsō den*). T. 2066. Yijing 義淨 (635–713; J. Gijō).

Datuoluoni mofa zhong yizixinzhoujing 大陀羅尼末法中一字心呪經 (J. *Daidarani mappōchū ichiji shinjukyō*). T. 956. Maṇicinta.

Daweide tuoluonijing 大威德陀羅尼經 (Skt. *Mahābala-dhāraṇī-sūtra*, J. *Daiitoku daranikyō*). T. 1341. Jñānagupta.

Dayunjing qingyupin diliushisi 大雲經請雨品第六十四 (J. *Daiunkyō shōubon dairokujūshi*). T. 993. Jñānayaśas.

Dayunlun qinyujing 大雲輪請雨經 (J. *Daiunrin shōukyō*). T. 991. 2 fasc. Narendrayaśas 那連提耶舍 (517–589; Ch. Naliantiyeshe, J. Narenteiyasha).

Dazhidulun 大智度論 (Skt. *Mahāprajñāpāramitā-śāstra*, J. *Daichidoron*). T. 1509. Attributed to Nāgārjuna 龍樹 (ca. second century; Ch. Longshu, J. Ryūju). Translated by Kumārajīva 鳩摩羅什 (344–413; Ch. Jiumoluoshe, J. Kumarajū).

Dentōkōroku 傳燈廣錄. ZSZ 33.

Dizangpusa yigui 地藏菩薩儀軌 (J. *Jizō bosatsu giki*). T. 1158. Śubhakarasiṃha.

Fahua sanmei jing 法華三昧經 (J. *Hokke sanmaikyō*). T. 269. Zhiyan.

Fahua wenjuji 法華文句記 (J. *Hokke monguki*). T. 1719. Zhanran 湛然 (711–782; J. Tannen).

Fanwangjing 梵網經 (J. *Bonmō kyō*). T. 1484. Attributed to Kumārajīva.

Foding zuisheng tuoluoni jing 佛頂最勝陀羅尼經 (J. *Bucchō saishō daranikyō*). T. 969. Divākara (late seventh century; Ch. Dipoheluo, J. Jibakara).

Foding zunsheng tuoluonijing 佛頂尊勝陀羅尼經 (Skt. *Uṣṇīsavijayā-dhāraṇī*, J. *Bucchō sonshō daranikyō*). T. 967. Buddhapāla (a.k.a. Buddhapālita 佛陀波利, late seventh century; Ch. Fotuoboli, J. Buddahari); T. 968. Attributed to Du Xingkai 杜行顗.

Foding zunsheng tuoluonijing 佛頂尊勝陀羅尼經 (Skt. *Uṣṇīṣavijayā-dhāraṇī*, J. *Bucchō sonshō daranikyō.* T. 968. 1 fasc. Du Xingkai 杜行顗 (late seventh century; J. Togyōgi).

Foding zunshengxin podizhuan yezhang chusanjie mimisanshen fogou sanzhong xidi zhenyan yigui 佛頂尊勝心破地獄轉業障出三界祕密三身佛果三種悉地眞言儀軌 (J. *Bucchō sonshō shinhajigoku tengosshōshutsusangai himitsusanjinbukka sanshushijji shingon giki*). T. 906. Śubhakarasiṃha.

Foshuo Amituo sanyesanfo saloufotan guodurendao jing 佛説阿彌陀三耶三佛薩樓佛檀過度人道經 (Skt. *Sukhvativyuha-sūtra*, J. *Bussetsu Amida sanyasanbutsu sarubutsudan kadonindō kyō*). T. 362. Zhi Qian 支謙 (fl. 223–253; J. Shiken).

Foshuo anan tuomuquniheli tuolinnijing 佛說阿難陀目佉尼呵離陀鄰尼經 (Skt. *Anatamukhasādhāka-dhāraṇī*, J. *Bussetsu ananda mokukyanikari darinnikyō*). T. 1015. Buddhaśānta 佛陀扇多 (early sixth century; Ch. Fotuoshanduo, J. Buddasenta).

Foshuo bajixiang shenzhou jing 佛說八吉祥神呪經 (J. *Bussetsu hachikichi jōjinshu kyō*). T. 427. Zhu Luyan 竺律炎 (late third–early fourth century; Ch. Zhu Lüyan, J. Chiku Ritsuen).

Foshuo chiju shenzhoujing 佛說持句神呪經 (J. *Bussetsu jiku jinju kyō*). T. 1351. Zhiqian 支謙 (fl. 223–253; J. Shiken).

Foshuo chusheng wubianmen duoluoni yigui 佛說出生無邊門陀羅尼儀軌 (Skt. *Anatamukhasādhāka-dhāraṇī*, J. *Bussetsu shusshō muhenmon daranikyō*). T. 1010. Amoghavajra.

Foshuo chusheng wulianmen chijing 佛說出生無量門持經 (Skt. *Anatamukhasādhāka-dhāraṇī*, J. *Bussetsu shusshō muryōmon jikyō*). T. 1012. Buddhabhadra.

Foshuo dabeikongzhi jingang dajiaowang yiguijing 佛說大悲空智金剛大教王儀軌經 (Skt. *Hevajra-tantra*, J. *Bussetsu daihikūchi kongō daikyōō gikikyō*). T. 892. Tianxizai.

Foshuo dacheng shengwuliangshou jueding guangmingwang rulai tuoluonijing 佛說大乘聖無量壽決定光明王如來陀羅尼經 (Skt. *Aparimitāyur-mahāyānasūtra*, J. *Bussetsu daijō shōmuryōju ketsujō kōmyō nyorai daranikyō*). T. 937. Dharmadeva 法天 (973–981; Ch. Fatian, J. Hōten).

Foshuo dacheng zhuangyan baowang jing 佛說大乘莊嚴寶王經 (Skt. *Kāraṇḍavyūha*, J. *Bussetsu daijōshōgon hōō kyō*). T. 1050. Tianxizai, Dānapāla 施護 (late tenth century; Ch. Shihu, J. Sego), and Dharmadeva.

Foshuo foding zunsheng tuoluoni jing 佛說佛頂尊勝陀羅尼經 (J. *Bussetsu bucchō sonshō daranikyō*). T. 971. Yijing 義淨 (635–713; J. Gijō).

Foshuo guanding qiwanerqian shenwang hubiqiuzhoujing 佛說灌頂七萬二千神王護比丘咒經 (Skt. *Abhiṣeka Sūtra*, J. *Bussetsu kanjō shichiman nisen shinnō gobiku jukyō*). T. 1331. Śrīmitra 戸梨蜜多羅 (d. ca. 343; Ch. Shilimiduoluo; J. Shirimittara).

Foshuo guanyaowang yaoshang erpusa jing 佛說觀藥王藥上二菩薩經 (Skt. *Bhaiṣajyarāja-bhaiṣajya-samudgata-sūtra*, J. *Bussetsu kanyakuōyakujō nibosatsu kyō*). T. 1161. Kālyaśas 畺良耶舍 (early fifth century; Ch. Jianglianggyeshe, J. Kyōryōyasha).

Foshuo huaji tuoluoji shenzhou jing 佛說華積陀羅尼神呪經 (J. *Bussetsu keshaku darani jinjukyō*). T. 1356. Zhi Qian.

Foshuo jiuba yankou egui tuoluoni jing 佛說救拔燄口餓鬼陀羅尼經 (J. *Bussetsu kubatsuenku gaki daranikyō*). T. 1313. Amoghavajra.

Foshuo jiumianran egui tuoluoni shenzhoujing 佛說救面然餓鬼陀羅尼神咒經 (J. *Bussekkumennen gaki darani shinshukyō*). T. 1314. Śikṣānanda 實叉難陀 (late seventh century; Ch. Shichananuo, J. Jisshananda).

Foshuo moniluodanjing 佛說摩尼羅亶經 (J. *Bussetsu maniradan kyō*). T. 1393. 1 fasc. Tanwulan 曇無蘭 (late fourth century; J. Donmuran).

Foshuo qijuzhi fomuxin dazhunti tuoluonijing 佛說七俱胝佛母心大准提陀羅尼經 (Skt. *Cundīdevī-dhāraṇī*, J. *Bussetsu shichi kutei butsumoshin daijuntei darani kyō*). T. 1077. Divākara.

Foshuo qijuzhifomu zhuntidaming tuoluoni jing 佛說七俱胝佛母准提大明陀羅尼經 (J. *Bussetsu shichikutei butsumojundai daimyō daranikyō*). T. 1075. Vajrabodhi.

Foshuo renwang banruoboluomi jing 佛說仁王般若波羅蜜經 (J. *Bussetsu ninnō hannya haramitsu kyō*). T. 245. Kumarajiva.

Foshuo shierfoming shenzhou jiaolianggongde chuzhang miezuijing 佛說十二佛名神呪校量功德除障滅罪經 (J. *Bussetsu jūnibutsu myōjin jukyōryō kudoku joshō metsuzai kyō*). T. 1348. Jñānagupta.

Foshuo suiqiu jide dazizai tuoluoni shenzhoujing 佛說隨求即得大自在陀羅尼神呪經 (J. *Bussetsu zuigusokutokudaijizaidarani jinshukyō*). T. 1154. Maṇicinta.

Foshuo tanteluomayoushujing 佛說檀特羅麻油述經 (J. *Bussetsu dantokuramayujutsu kyō*). T. 1391. Tanwulan.

Foshuo weimojie jing 佛說維摩詰經 (Skt. *Vimalakīrtinirdeśa-sūtra*, J. *Bussetsu yuimakitsu kyō*). T. 474. Zhi Qian.

Foshuo wenshushili fabaozang tuoluoni jing 佛說文殊師利法寶藏陀羅尼經 (J. *Bussetsu monjushiri hōhōzō daranikyō*). T. 1185A. T. 1185B. Bodhiruci.

Foshuo wuliang gongde tuoluoni jing 佛說無量功德陀羅尼經 (J. *Bussetsu muryōkudoku daranikyō*). T. 934. Dharmabhadra 法賢 (d.u.–1001; Ch. Faxian, J. Hōken).

Foshuo wuliang qingjing pingdeng juejing 佛說無量清淨平等覺經 (Skt. *Sukhāvatīvyūha-sūtra*, J. *Bussetsu muryōshōjō byōdō kakyō*). T. 361. Lokakṣema.

Foshuo wuliangshou jing 佛說無量壽經 (Skt. *Sukhāvatīvyūha-sūtra*, J. *Bussetsu muryōju kyō*). T. 360. Buddhabhadra.

Foshuo wulianmen weimi chijing 佛說無量門微密持經 (Skt. *Anatamukhasādhāka-dhāraṇī*, J. *Bussetsu muryōmon mimitsujikyō*). T. 1011. Zhiqian.

Foshuo xuanshi futuosuoshuo shenzhoujing 佛說玄師颰陀所說神呪經 (J. *Bussetsu genshi batta jinjukyō*). T. 1378A. Tanwulan.

Foshuo yiqie foshe xiangying dajiaowangjing Shengguanzizai pusa niansong yigui 佛說一切佛攝相應大教王經聖觀自在菩薩念誦儀軌 (Skt. *Samāyoga-tantra*, J. *Bussetsu issai butsu jōsōō daikyōōgyō shōkanjizaibosatsu nenjugiki*). T. 1051. Dharmadeva.

Foshuo yiqie gonde zhuangyanwang jing 佛說一切功德莊嚴王經 (J. *Bussetsu issai kudoku shōgonōkyō*). T. 1374. Yijing.

Foshuo yiqie rulai jingang sanye zuishang mimi dajiaowangjing 佛說一切如來金剛三業最上祕密大教王經 (Skt. *Guhyasamāja-tantra*, J. *Bussetsu issainyorai kongōsangō saijōhimitsu daikyōōkyō*). T. 885. Dānapāla.

Foshuo yiqie rulai zhenshi shedashengxianzheng sanmei jiaowangjing 佛說一切如來眞實攝大乘現證三昧大教王經 (Skt. *Sarvatathāgata-tattvasaṃgrahaṃ nāmamahāyāna-sūtra*, J. *Bussetsu issainyorai shinjitsu shōdaijō genshōzanmai daikyōōkyō*). T. 882. Dānapāla.

Foshuo yixiang chusheng pusa jing 佛說一向出生菩薩經 (Skt. *Anatamukhasādhāka-dhāraṇī*, J. *Bussetsu ikkō shusshō bosatsukyō*). T. 1017. Jñānagupta.

Foshuo yujia dajiaowang jing 佛說瑜伽大教王經 (J. *Bussetsu yuga daikyōō kyō*). T. 890. Dharmabhadra.

Foshuo zhuangyanwang tuoluoni zhoujing 佛說莊嚴王陀羅尼呪經 (J. *Bussetsu shōgonō darani jukyō*). T. 1375. Yijing.

Genkō shakusho 元亨釋書. DNBZ 101. Kokan Shiren 虎關師錬 (1278–1346).

Gokuraku jōdo kuhon ōjōgi 極樂淨土九品往生義. JZ 15. Ryōgen 良源 (912–985).

Gorin kuji myō himitsu shaku 五輪九字明祕密釋. T. 2514. Kakuban.

Guanfo sanmei hai jing 觀佛三昧海經 (J. *Kanbutsu sanmai kai kyō*). T. 643. Buddhabhadra.

Guanshiyin Pusa mimizang ruyilun tuoluoni shenzhoujing 觀世音菩薩祕密藏如意輪陀羅尼神呪經 (J. *Kanzeonbosatsu himitsuzō nyirin darani shinjukyō*). T. 1082. Śikṣānanda.

Guanshiyin Pusa ruyi moni tuoluoni jing 觀世音菩薩如意摩尼陀羅尼經 (J. *Kanzeonbosatsu nyoi mani daranikyō*). T. 1083. Maṇicinta.

Guanwuliangshuo jing 觀無量壽經 (J. *Kanmyryōju kyō*). T. 365. Kālayaśas.

Guan wuliangshou jing yishu 觀無量壽經義疏 (J. *Kanmuryōjukyō gisho*). T. 1749. Jingying Huiyuan.

Guanzizai pusa dabeizhiyin zhoubian fajie liyi zhongshengxunzhenrufa 觀自在菩薩大悲智印周遍法界利益衆生薫眞如法 (J. *Kanjizaibosatsu daihichiin shūhen hokkai ryakushujō kun shinnyo hō*). T. 1042. Amoghavajra.

Guanzizai pusa shuo puxian tuoluonijing 觀自在菩薩說普賢陀羅尼經 (J. *Kanjizaibosatsu setsu fugen daranikyō*). T. 1037. Amoghavajra.

Guanzizai pusa suixinzhoujing 觀自在菩薩隨心呪經 (J. *Kanjizaibosatsu zuishinshu kyō*). T. 1103. Zhitong 智通 (d.u.–653; J. Chitsū).

Guanzizai pusa xinzhenyan yiyin niansong fa 觀自在菩薩心眞言一印念誦法 (J. *Kanjizaibosatsu shinshingon ichiin nenjuhō*). T. 1041. Amoghavajra.

Hakke hiroku 八家秘録. See *Shoajari shingon mikkyō burui sōroku.*

Hannya shingyō hiken 般若心經祕鍵. T. 2203. Kūkai.

Hannya shingyō hiken ryakuchū 般若心經祕鍵略註. T. 2203B. Kakuban.

Heike monogatari 平家物語. NKBT 32–33, SNKBT 44–45.

Henjōhokki shōryōshū 遍照発揮性霊集. TKDZ 8. Kūkai.

Himitsu mandara jūjushinron 秘密曼荼羅十住心論. T. 2425. Kūkai.

Hishūnongiyō 祕宗文義要. SZ 22. Jōhen.

Hizōhōyaku 祕藏寶鑰. T. 2426. Kūkai.

Hizōki 祕藏記. TKDZ 5. Kūkai.

Hokke gisho 法華義疏. T. 2187. Shōtoku Taishi 聖德太子 (574–622).

Hokkekyō hishaku 法華經祕釋. T. 2191. Kakuban.

Hokkekyō kaidai 法華經開題. T. 2190. Kūkai.

Hōkōin sekifuki 寶光院析負紀, *Kongōbuji shoinke sekihushū* 金剛峰寺諸院家析負輯. ZSZ 34. fasc. 1.

Honchō kōsōden 本朝高僧傳. DNBZ 103.

Ichigo taiyō himitsu shū 一期大要祕密集. KDS 1. Kakuban.

Jike Shōchiin 寺家正智院, *Kii zokufūdoki* 紀伊續風土記. ZSZ 37, fasc 4.

Jin'gang chang tuoluonijing 金剛場陀羅尼經 (Skt. *Vajramaṇḍa-dhāraṇī*, J. *Kongōjōdaranikyō*). T. 1345. Jñānagupta.

Jin'gangding yiqierulai zhenshishe dacheng xianzheng dajiaowangjing 金剛頂一切如來眞實攝大乘現證大教王經 (Skt. *Sarvatathāgata-tattvasaṃgrahaṃ nāma mahāyāna-sūtra, Vajraśekhara-sūtra;* J. *Kongōchō issainyorai shinjitsushō daijō genshō daikyōōkyō*). T. 865. Amoghavajra.

Jin'gangding yujia liqubanruojing 金剛頂瑜伽理趣般若經 (Skt. *Adhyartha-śatikāprajñāpāramitā sūtra*, J. *Kongōchō yuga risshu hannyakyō*). T. 241. Vajrabodhi (671–741; Ch. Jin'gang zhi, J. Kongōchi).

Jin'gangding yujia qianshouqianyan Guanzizai pusa xiuxing yiguijing 金剛頂瑜伽千手千眼觀自在菩薩修行儀軌經 (J. *Kongōchō yuga senjusengen kanjizaibosatsu shugyō gikikyō*). T. 1056. Amoghavajra.

Jin'gangding yujia zhong fa anouduoluo sanmiaosan putixin lun 金剛頂瑜伽中發阿耨多羅三藐三菩提心論 (J. *Kongōchō yuga chū hotsu anokutara sanmyakusan bodaishin ron*). T. 1665. Amoghavajra.

Jin'gangding yujia zhong luechu niansong jing 金剛頂瑜伽中略出念誦經 (Skt. *Sarvatathāgata-tattvasaṃgrahaṃ nāma mahāyāna-sūtra, Vajraśekhara-sūtra;* J. *Kongōchō yuga chūryakujutsu nenju kyō*). T. 866. Vajrabodhi.

Jin'gangding yujia zuisheng mimi chengfo suiqiujide shenbian jiachi chengjiu tuoluoni yigui 金剛頂瑜伽最勝祕密成佛隨求即得神變加持成就陀羅尼儀軌 (J. *Kongōchō yuga saishō himitsujōbutsu zuigusokutoku jinpen kaji jōju daranigiki*). T. 1155. Amoghavajra.

Jin'gang fengluoge yiqieyujia yuqijing 金剛峯樓閣一切瑜伽瑜祇經 (J. *Kongōbu rōkaku issai yuga yugi kyō*). T. 867. Vajrabodhi.

Jin'gang kongbu jihui fangguang guiyi Guanzizai pusa sanshi zuisheng xinmingwangjing 金剛恐怖集會方廣儀軌觀自在菩薩三世最勝心明王經 (J. *Kongō kuhu shūe hōkō kigi kanjizaibosatsu sanze saishōshin myōōgyō*). T. 1033. Amoghavajra.

Jinguangming zuisheng wanging 金光明最勝王經 (Skt. *Suvarṇaprabhāsa-sūtra*, J. *Konkōmyō saishō ōkyō*). T. 665. Yijing.

Jingu lun 浄土論 (J. *Jōdo ron*). T. 1963. Jiacai 迦才 (fl. 645; J. Kazai).

Jiupin wangsheng amituosanmodiji tuoluonijing 九品往生阿彌陀三摩地集陀羅尼經 (J. *Kuhon ōjō amida sanmaji shū daranikyō*). T. 933. Amoghavajra.

Jubosatsukaigi 授菩薩戒儀. T. 2378. Enchin.

Jūgan hosshin ki 十願發心記. SEJ 2:159–220. Senkan 千觀 (918–984).

Jūnen gokuraku ioushū 十念極樂易往集 (*Taishō shinshū daizōkyō kankō yotei shomoku* 大正新修大藏經刊行豫定書目; Tōji Kanchi-in 東寺観智院 manuscript. Butsugon (late twelfth century).

Kakukai(Kakkai) hokkyō hōgo 覺海法橋法語. NKBT 83:55–58. Kakkai/Kakukai 覺海 (Nanshōbō 南勝房; 1142–1223).

Kakuzenshō 覺禪鈔. DNBZ 45–51. Kakuzen 覺禪 (1143–?).

Kechimyaku ruishūki 血脈類聚記. SZ 39.

Ketsujō ōjōshū 決定往生集. T. 2684. Chingai/Chinkai 珍海 (1091–1152).

Kitamuroin rekidai keifūsshi 北室院歴代系譜寫, *Kongōbuji shoinke sekihushū*. ZSZ 34. fasc. 10.

Kongōchō daikyōō kyōsho 金剛頂大教王經疏. T. 2223. Ennin.

Kongōchōgyō kaidai 金剛頂經開題. T. 2221. Kūkai.

Kongōchō mujōshū dendōroku zokuhen 金剛頂無上正宗傳燈廣錄續編. ZSZ 33.

Kongōkai daihō taijuki 金剛界大法對受記. T. 2391. Annen.

Kongōkai jōchiki 金剛界浄地記. T. 2386. Ennin.

Kōsō gōjō Shōchiin Dōhan den 高僧行狀正智院道範傳, *Kii zokufudōki*, ZSZ 39. Fasc. 10.

Kōya ōjōden 高野往生傳. ZJZ 6.

Kōyasan gobanshū ichimi keijō 高野山五番衆一味契狀. *Hōkanshū* 寶簡集 1.441 (*Dainihon komonjo* 大日本古文書, *Iewake daiichi* 家わけ第一, Kōyasan monjo 高野山文書).

Kōya shunjū hennen shūroku 高野春秋編年輯錄. DNBZ 131.

Kurodani Shōnin gotōroku 黒谷上人語燈録. T. 2611. Hōnen 法然 (1133–1212).

Kyōgyōshinshō 教行信證. T. 2646. Shinran 親鸞 (1173–1262).

Lidaisanbao ji 歴代三寶紀 (J. *Rekidaisanbō ki*). T. 2034. Fei Changfang 費長房 (late sixth century; J. Hi Chōbō).

Liuduji jing 六度經 (J. *Rokudo kyō*). T. 152. Kang Senghui 康僧會 (d. 280; J. Kō Sōe).

Liumentuoluonijing 六門陀羅尼經 (Skt. *Śaṇmukhī-dhāraṇī*, J. *Rokumondaranikyō*). T. 1360. Xuanzang.

Lushanji 廬山記 (J. *Rōsanki*). T. 2095. Chen Shunyu 陳舜俞 (d. 1075; J. Chin Junyu).

Manshushilipusa zhouzangzhong yizi zhouwangjing 曼殊師利菩薩咒藏中一字咒王經 (J. *Manjushiribosatsu juzōchū ichijijuōkyō*). T. 1182. Yijing.

Miaofa lianhua jing 妙法蓮華經 (Skt. *Saddharma-puṇḍarīka-sūtra*, J. *Myōhō renge kyō*). T. 262. Kumārajīva.

Miaofa lianhua jing wenju 妙法蓮華經文句 (J. *Myōhō rengekyō mongu*). T. 1718. Tiantai Zhiyi 天台智顗 (538–597; J. Tendai Chigi).

Modengjiajing 摩登伽經 (Skt. *Mātaṅgī-sūtra*, J. *Matogakyō*). T. 1300. Zhu Luyan and Zhi Qian.

Mohezhiguan 摩訶止観 (J. *Makashikan*). T. 1911. Tiantai Zhiyi.

Mulimantuoluo zhoujing 牟梨曼陀羅呪經 (J. *Murimandara jukyō*). T. 1007. 1 fasc.

Muryōju nyorai sakuhō shidai 無量壽如來供養作法次代. KDZ 2:495–521. Attributed to Kūkai.

Nanhai jigui neifa zhuan 南海寄歸内法傳 (J. *Nankai kiki naihō den*). T. 2125. Yijing.

Nanzan chūin shingon hihōshoso denpu 南山中院眞言祕法諸祖傳譜. ZSZ 32.

Nihon ōjō gokuraku ki 日本往生極樂記. NKBT 7. Yoshishige Yasutane 慶滋保胤 (933–1002).

Nyūshingonmon nyūnyojitsukenkōenhokke ryakugi 入眞言門入如實見講演法華略儀. T. 2192. Enchin.

Ōjōjūin 往生拾因. T. 2683. Eikan/Yōkan 永觀 (1033–1111).

Ōjō kōshiki 往生講式. T. 2725. Eikan.

Ōjōyōshū 往生要集. T. 2682. Genshin 源信 (942–1017).

Pubianguangming qingjing chicheng ruyibaoyin xinwunenbsheng damingwang dasuiqiu tuoluonijing 普遍光明清淨熾盛如意寶印心無能勝大明王大隨求陀羅尼經 (J. *Fuhenkōmyō shōjō shijō nyoishō inshin munōshō daimyōō daizuigu daranikyō*). T. 1153. Amoghavajra.

Pusadichi jing 菩薩地持經 (J. *Bosatsu jijikyō*). T. 1581. Jingying Huiyuan.

Putichang suoshuo yizi dinglun wangjing 菩提場所說一字頂輪王經 (Skt. *Ekāksara-cakravartin*, J. *Bodai jōsho setsu ichiji chōrin ōkyō*). T. 950. Amoghavajra.

Qianshou qianyan Guanshiyin Pusa dabeixin tuoluoni 千手千眼觀世音菩薩大悲心陀羅尼 (J. *Senju sengen kanseon bosatsu daihishin darani*). T. 1064. Amoghavajra.

Qianshou qianyan Guanshiyin Pusa guangdayuan manwuai dabeishin tuoluonijing 千手千眼觀世音菩薩廣大圓滿無礙大悲心陀羅尼經 (J. *Senju sengen kanzeon bosatsu kōdaienman muge daihishin darani kyō*). T. 1060. Bhagavaddharma 伽梵達摩 (seventh century; Ch. Qiefandamo, J. Gabondaruma).

Qianshou qianyan Guanshiyin Pusa laotuoluonishen jing 千手千眼觀世音菩薩姥陀羅尼身經 (J. *Senju sengen kanseon bosatsu modarani shinkyō*). T. 1058. Bodhiruci.

Qianshou qianyan Guanshiyin Pusa zhibing heyao jing 千手千眼觀世音菩薩治病合藥經 (J. *Senju sengen kanseon bosatsu jibyō gōyaku kyō*). T. 1059. Bhagavaddharma.

Qianyanqianbi Guanshiyin Pusa tuoluoni shenzhoujing 千眼千臂觀世音菩薩陀羅尼神呪經 (J. *Sengensenbi kanzeonbosatsu darani shinju kyō*). T. 1057. Zhitong.

Qianzhuan tuoluoni Guanshiyan pusa zhou 千轉陀羅尼觀世音菩薩呪 (Skt. *Sahasrāvartā-dhāraṇī*, J. *Senten darani kanzeonbosatsu ju*). T. 1035. Zhitong.

Qing Guanshiyin Pusa xiaofuhai tuoluoni zhoujing 請觀世音菩薩消伏毒害陀羅尼呪經 (J. *Shōkanzeon bosatsu shōbukudokugai daranikyō*). T. 1043. *Nandi 難提 (early fifth century; Ch. Nanti, J. Nandai).

Qingjing Guanshiyin puxian tuoluonijing 清淨觀世音普賢陀羅尼經 (J. *Shōkanzeon bosatsu shōbukudokugai daranikyō*). T. 1038. Zhitong.

Renwang huguo banruoboluomi jing 仁王護國般若波羅蜜多經 (J. *Ninnō gogoku hannya haramita kyō*). T. 246. Amoghavajra.

Ruilingye jing 蕤呬耶經 (J. *Suikiya kyō*). T. 897. Amoghavajra.

Rulai fangbian shanqiao zhoujing 如來方便善巧呪經 (J. *Nyorai hōben engyō jukyō*). T. 1334. Jñānagupta.

Rulengqie jing 入楞伽經 (Skt. *Laṅkāvatāra-sūtra*, J. *Nyūrōgakyō*). T. 672. With Śikṣānanda and Mitraśānta 彌陀山 (Ch. Mitoushan, J. Midasan).

Ruyibaozhu zhuanlun mimixianshenchengfo jinglun zhouwangjing 如意寶珠轉輪祕密現身成佛金輪呪王經 (J. *Nyoihōshu tenrin himitsu genshin jōbutsu kinrin shuōkyō*). T. 961. Amoghavajra.

Ruyilun tuoluoni jing 如意輪陀羅尼經 (Skt. *Cakravarticintāmaṇi*, J. *Nyoirin daranikyō*). T. 1080. Bodhiruci.

Sanjūjū sasshi 三十帖册子. Printed editions available in Taishō, Ryūkoku, Ōtani, and Kōyasan University archives. Kūkai.

Sanzhong xidi podiyuzhuanyezhang chusanjie mimituoluonifa 三種悉地破地獄轉業障出三界祕密陀羅尼法 (J. *Sanju shijji hajigoku tengosshō shussangai himitsu daranihō*). T. 905. Śūbhakarasiṃha.

Sarvatathāgata-tattvasaṃgrahaṃ nāma mahāyāna-sūtra. See *Jin'gangding yujia zhong luechu niansong jing, Jin'gangding yiqierulai zhenshishe dacheng xianzheng dajiaowangjing, Yiqie rulai zhenshishe dasheng xianzheng sanmei dajiaowang jing.*

Seiryūji ōshō rinjū kengyō 青龍寺和尙臨終觀行. Zentsūji 善通寺 archive, http://base1.nijl.ac.jp/iview/Frame.jsp?DB_ID=G0003917KTM&C_CODE=XSE1-21704.

Senchaku hongan nenbutsu shū 選擇本願念佛集. T. 2608. Hōnen.

Shakumakaenron ketsugihanan eshakushō 釋摩訶衍論決疑破難會釋抄. T. 2286. Saisen.

Shakumakaenron ryūgi bunryakushaku 釋摩訶衍論立義分略釋. T. 2287. Saisen.

Shelifu tuoluonijing 舍利弗陀羅尼經 (Skt. *Anatamukhasādhāka-dhāraṇī*, J. *Sharihotsu daranikyō*). T. 1016. 1 fasc. Attributed to Saṃghavarman 僧伽婆羅 (b. 460; Ch. Sengqiepoluo, J. Sōgyabara).

Shengman jing 勝鬘經 (Skt. *Śrīmālādevī-sūtra*, J. *Shōman gyō*). T. 353.

Shenheyehelifu daweinuwang lichen dashen yangongyang niansong yigui fapin 聖賀野紇哩縛大威怒王立成大神驗供養念誦儀軌法品 (J. *Shōgayakiriba daiinuōryūjō daijinken kuyō nenju gikihōbon*). T. 1072A. Amoghavajra.

Shidi jinglun 十地經論 (Skt. *Daśabhūmikasūtra-śāstra*, J. *Juji kyō ron*). T. 1522. Compiled by Vasubandhu 世親 (fifth century; Ch. Shiqin, J. Seshin). Translated by Bodhiruci.

Shimoheyanlun 釋摩訶衍論 (J. *Shakumakaenron*). T. 1668. Attributed to Nāgārjuna.

Shingonshū kyōjigi 眞言宗教時義. T. 2396. Annen.

Shingonshū sokushinjōbutsu gishō 眞言宗即身成佛義章. T. 2511. Kakuban.

Shixiang boreboluomi 實相般若波羅蜜經 (Skt. *Adhyardhaśatikā prajñāpāramitā-sūtra*, J. *Jissō hannyaharamitsu kyō*). T. 240. Bodhiruci.

Shiyimian Guanshiyin shenzhou jing 十一面觀世音神咒經 (Skt. *Ekādaśamukha-dhāraṇī*, J. *Jūichimen kanzeon shinju kyō*). T. 1070. Yaśogupta 耶舍崛多 (late sixth century; Ch. Yeshejueduo, J. Yashakutta).

Shiyimian Guanzizai pusa xinmiyan niansong yiguijing 十一面觀自在菩薩心密言念誦儀軌經 (Skt. *Ekādaśamukha-dhāraṇī*, J. *Jūichimen kanjizaibosatsu shinmitsugon nenju gikikyō*). T. 1069. Amoghavajra.

Shiyimian shenzhouxinjing 十一面神呪心經 (J. *Bussetsu Jūichimen kanzeon shinjukyō*). T. 1071. Xuanzang.

Shoajari shingon mikkyō burui sōroku 諸阿闍梨眞言密教部類總録. T. 2176. Annen.

Shōchiin ruiyō senshi meibo 正智院累葉先師名簿. In *Kongōbuji shoinke sekihushū*, ZSZ 34.

Shōjijissōgi 聲字實相義. T. 2429. Kūkai.

Shōmangyō gisho 勝鬘經義疏. T. 2185. Shōtoku Taishi 聖德太子 (574–622).

Shoshū shōshoroku 諸宗章疎録. DNBZ 95.

Shoulengyan sanmei jing 首楞嚴三昧經. T. 642.15.629. Zhi Qian (Skt. *Śūraṃgama-samādhi-sūtra*, J. *Shuryōgon sanmai kyō*).

Shūi Kurodani Shōnin gotōroku 拾遺黒谷上人語燈録. T. 2612. Hōnen.

Sokushin jōbutsu gi 卽身成佛義. T. 2428. Kūkai.

Soshijji gyarakyō ryakusho 蘇悉地羯羅經略疏. T. 2227. Ennin.

Soshitsuji myōshindai 妙心大. T. 2387. Ennin.

Soshitsuji taijuki 蘇悉地對受記. T. 2392.75.200. Annen.

Supohu tongzi qingwen jing 蘇婆呼童子請經 (J. *Sobakodōjishōmon gyō*). T. 895. Śubhakarasiṃha.

Suxidijieluo gongyangfa 蘇悉地羯羅供養法 (J. *Soshitsuji kyarakuyōbō*). T. 894. Śubhakarasiṃha.

Suxidijieluo jing 蘇悉地羯囉經 (J. *Soshitsuji kyarakyō*). T. 893. Śubhakarasiṃha.

Taizōkai daihō taijuki 胎藏界大法對受記. T. 2390. Annen.

Taizōkai kyōshinki 胎蔵界虛心記. T. 2385. Ennin.

Taizō kongō bodaishingi ryaku mondō shō 胎藏金剛菩提心義略問答鈔. T. 2397. Annen.

Taizō nyūzōnyūri shō 胎藏入理鈔. T. 2534. Raiyū 賴瑜 (1226–1304).

Tōji chōja honin 東寺長者補任, ZGRJ 2.

Tuoluoni ji jing 陀羅尼集經 (Skt. *Dhāraṇīsaṃgraha-sūtra*, J. *Darani jikkyō*). T. 901. Atikuta 阿地瞿多 (seventh century; Ch. Adijuduo, J. Achikuta).

Unjigi 吽字義. T. 2430. Kūkai.

Vajraśekhara-sūtra 金剛頂經. See *Jin'gangding yujia zhong luechu niansong jing, Jin'gangding yiqierulai zhenshishe dacheng xianzheng dajiaowangjing, Yiqie rulai zhenshishe dasheng xianzheng sanmei dajiaowang jing.*

Weimojing xuanshu 維摩經玄疏 (J. *Yuimakyō gensho*). T. 1777. Tiantai Zhiyi.

Weimo yiji 維摩義記. T. 1776. Jingying Huiyuan.

Wenshushilipusa genben dajiaowang jing jinchiniaowang pin 文殊師利菩薩根本大教王經金翅鳥王品 (J. *Monjushiribosatsu konpon daikyōō kyō konjichōō bon*). T. 1276, variant text of T. 1191. Amoghavajra.

Wuda xukongzangpusa suji dashenyan mimi shijing 五大虛空藏菩薩速疾大神驗祕密式經 (J. *Godai kokūzōbosatsu sokushitsu daijinken himitsushiki kyō*). T. 1149. Vajrabodhi.

Wufoding sanmei tuoluoni jing 五佛頂三昧陀羅尼經 (J. *Gobutsu sanmai darani kyō*). T. 952. Bodhiruci.

Wugoujing guangda tuoluonijing 無垢淨光陀羅尼經 (Skt. *Raśmivimalaviśuddhaprabhā-dhāraṇī*, J. *Mukujōkō daidaranikyō*). T. 1024. Mitraśānta.

Wuliangmen pomo tuoluonijing 無量門破魔陀羅尼經 (Skt. *Anantamukha-dhāraṇī*, J. *Muryōmon hama daranikyō*). T. 1014. Guṇabharman 功德直 (fifth century; Ch. Gongdezhi, J. Kudokujiki) and Xuanchang 玄暢 (416–484; J. Genchō).

Wuliang rulai guanxing gongyang yigui 無量壽如來觀行供養儀軌 (J. *Muryōju nyorai kengyō kuyō giki*). T. 930. Amoghavajra.

Xukongzangpusa wenqifo tuoluonizhoujing 虛空藏菩薩諸問七佛陀羅尼呪經 (J. *Kokūzōbosatsu shomon shichibutsu daranikyō*). T. 1333.

Yahō meitokuden 野峯名德傳. DNBZ 106.

Yanggwŏn muryangsu-kyŏng chong'yo 兩卷無量壽經宗要 (Ch. *Liangjuan wuliang-shou jing zongyao*, J. *Ryōkan Muryōju kyōshūyō*). T. 1747. Wŏnhyo 元曉 (617–686; Ch. Yuanxiao, J. Gangyō).

Yaoshirulai guanxing yigui fa 藥師如來觀行儀軌法 (J. *Yakushi nyorai kengyō giki hō*). T. 923. Vajrabodhi.

Yiqie rulai zhenshishe dasheng xianzheng sanmei dajiaowang jing 一切如來眞實攝大乘現證三昧大教王經 (Skt. *Sarvatathāgata-tattvasaṃgrahaṃ nāma mahāyāna-sūtra, Vajraśekhara-sūtra*; J. *Issai nyorai shinjisshō daijō genshō zanmai daikyōō kyō*). T. 822. Dānapāla.

Yizi qite foding jing 一字奇特佛頂經 (J. *Ichiji kitoku bucchōkyō*). T. 953. Amoghavajra.

Yokawa Shuryōgon-in nijūgo sanmai kishō 橫川首楞嚴院二十五三昧起請. T. 2724. Genshin.

Yokawa Shuryōgon-in nijūgo sanmai shiki 橫川首楞嚴院二十五三昧式. T. 2723. Genshin.

Yuimagyō gisho 維摩經義疏. T. 2186. Shōtoku Taishi 聖德太子 (574–622).

Yujia jiyao yankoushishi qijiao anantuo zhuyou 瑜伽集要焰口施食起教阿難陀諸由 (J. *Yuga shūyō enkusejikikyō ananda enyu*). T. 1319. Amoghavajra.

Yujia jiyao yankoushishiyi 瑜伽集要焰口施食儀 (J. *Yuga shūyō enkusejiki gi*). T. 1320.

Yujia shidi lun 瑜伽師地論 (Skt. *Yogācāra-bhūmi*, J. *Yuga shiji ron*). T. 1579. Xuanzang.

Za ahan jing 雑阿含経 (Skt. *Saṃyuktāgama*, J. *Zō agon gyō*). T. 99. Guṇabhadra.

Zengyi ahan jing 増一阿含経 (Skt. *Ekottarāgama*, J. *Zōichi agon kyō*). T. 125. Gautama Saṃghadeva 瞿曇僧伽提婆 (fourth century; Ch. Jutan Sengqietipo, J. Gudon Sōgyadaiba).

Zhufoxintuoluoni jing 諸佛心陀羅尼經 (J. *Shobutsu shindarani kyō*). T. 918. Xuanzang.

Zoku henjōhokki shōryōshū hoketsu shō 続遍照発揮性霊集補闕抄. TKDZ 8:127–211. Saisen.

Zoku senchaku mongi yōshō 續選擇文義要鈔. Jōhen.

Zoku senchaku mongi yōshō 続選択文義要鈔. Tokyo: Kokusho kankōkai, 1984.

Zuisheng foding tuoluoni jingchuyezhang zhoujing 最勝佛頂陀羅尼淨除業障呪經 (J. *Saishō bucchō darani jōjo gosshō shukyō*). T. 970. Divākara.

Zunshengfoding xiuyu jiafa yigui 尊勝佛頂脩瑜伽法儀軌 (J. *Sonshō bucchō shūyuga hōgiki*). T. 973. Śubhakarasiṃha.

Secondary Sources

Abbott, Terry. "The Chinese Version of the *Hevajra Tantra*." *Transactions of the International Conference of Orientalists in Japan* 23 (1978): 99–103.

Abé, Ryūichi 阿部龍一. "Bridging Ritual and Text: Kakuban's Writing on Meditative Practice." In *Kōgyō Daishi Kakuban kenkyū* 興教大師覚鑁研究, edited by Kōgyō Daishi Kenkyū Ronshū Henshū Iinkai 興教大師研究論集編集委員会, pp. 1076–1073. Tokyo: Shunjūsha, 1992.

———. "From Kūkai to Kakuban: A Study of Shingon Buddhist Dharma Transmission." PhD diss., Columbia University, 1991.

———. "Gorinkujimyō himitusyaku" 五輪九字明秘密釈. In *Nihon no Bukkyō: Tēma Nihon Bukkyō no bunken gaido* 日本の仏教: テーマ 日本仏教の文献ガイド, edited by Nihon Bukkyō Kenkyūkai 日本仏教研究会, pp. 80–83. Kyoto: Hōzōkan, 2001.

———. "Mikkyō girei to kenmitsu bukkyō: Myōe Kōben no nyūmetsu girei wo megutte" 密教儀礼と顕密仏教: 明恵房高弁の入滅儀礼をめぐって. In *Chūsei Bukkyō no tenkai to sono kiban* 中世仏教の展開とその基盤, edited by Masaharu Imai 今井雅晴, pp. 38–57. Tokyo: Daizō shuppan, 2002.

———. "Nara ki no mikkyō no saikentō—kyūseiki no tenkai o fumaete" 奈良期の密教の再検討-九世紀の展開をふまえて. In *Nara Bukkyō to zaichi shakai* 奈良仏

教と在地社会, edited by Nemoto Seiji 根本誠二 and Samueru C. Mōsu 根本誠二, サムエルC·モース (Samuel Morse), pp. 105–153. Tokyo: Iwata shoin, 2004.

——. *The Weaving of Mantra: Kūkai and the Construction of Esoteric Buddhist Discourse.* New York: Columbia University Press, 1999.

——. "Word." In *Critical Terms for the Study of Buddhism,* edited by Donald S. Lopez Jr., pp. 291–310. Chicago: University of Chicago Press, 2005.

Abe Yasurō 阿部泰郎. *Chūsei Kōyasan engi no kenkyū* 中世高野山縁起の研究. Nara: Gangōji bunkasai kenkyūjo, 1982.

——. "Shukaku hosshinnō to inseiki no bukkyō bunka" 守覚法親王と院政期の仏教文化." In Hayami Tasuku, *Inseiki no bukkyō,* pp. 118–142.

Abe Yasurō, and Yamasaki Makoto 山崎誠, eds. *Shukaku hosshinnō to Ninnaji goryū no bunkenteki kenkyū, ronbunhen* 守覚法親王と仁和寺御流の文献学的研究, 論文編. 2 vols. Tokyo: Benseisha, 1998.

Adolphson, Mikael S. *The Gates of Power: Monks, Courtiers, and Warriors in Premodern Japan.* Honolulu: University of Hawai'i Press, 2000.

Amino, Yoshihiko. *Rethinking Japanese History.* Ann Arbor: Center for Japanese Studies, University of Michigan, 2012.

Amstutz, Galen. *Interpreting Amida: History and Orientalism in the Study of Pure Land Buddhism.* Albany: State University of New York Press, 1997.

——. "The Politics of Pure Land Buddhism in India." *Numen* 45, no. 1 (1998): 69–96.

Amstutz, Galen, and Mark L. Blum, eds. "Varieties of Pure Land Experience." *Japanese Journal of Religious Studies* 33, no. 2 (2006).

Asai Jōkai 浅井成海. "Jikaku daishi Ennin no Jōdokyō" 慈覚大師円仁の浄土教. *Ryūkoku Daigaku ronshū* 龍谷大学論集 455 (2000): 1–25.

Aung, S. Z., and C. A. F. Rhys Davids. *Points of Controversy: Kathāvatthu.* London: Pali Text Society, 1915.

Barau, Dwijendralal. "Buddha-khetta in the Apadana." *B.C. Law Volume* 2 (1946): 183–190.

Basham, A. L. "Tantrism and the Decline of Buddhism in India." In *The Buddhist Tradition in India, China and Japan,* edited by William Theodore DeBary, pp. 110–124. New York: Modern Library, 1969.

Bauer, Mikael. "The Power of Ritual: An Integrated History of Medieval Kōfukuji." PhD diss., Harvard University, 2011.

Baxandallan, Michael. *Patterns of Intention: On the Historical Explanation of Pictures.* New Haven, CT: Yale University Press, 1985.

Bechert, Heinz. "Buddha-Field and Transfer of Merit in a Theravāda Source." *Indo-Iranian Journal* 35 (1992): 95–108.

Beghi, Clemente. "The Dissemination of Esoteric Scriptures in Eighth Century Japan." In Orzech, Sørensen, and Payne, *Esoteric Buddhism and the Tantras in East Asia,* pp. 661–682.

Berger, Patricia. "Preserving the Nation: The Political Uses of Tantric Art in China." In *Latter Days of the Law: Images of Chinese Buddhism, 850–1850,* edited by Marsha Weidner, pp. 89–93. Honolulu: Spencer Museum of Art, University of Kansas, in association with University of Hawai'i Press, 1994.

Bhattacharyya, Benoytosh. *The Indian Buddhist Iconography: Mainly Based on the Sādhanamālā and other Cognate Tāntric Texts of Rituals.* 1924. Reprint, New Delhi: Asian Educational Services, 1993.

———. *An Introduction to Buddhist Esotericism.* 1980. Reprint, Delhi: Motilal Banarsidass, 2009.

Bielefeldt, Carl. "Filling the Zen-shū: Notes on the 'Jisshū yōdō ki.'" *Cahiers d'Extrême-Asie* 7 (1993–1994): 221–248.

———. "Kokan Shiren and the Sectarian Uses of History." In *The Origins of Japan's Medieval World: Courtiers, Clerics, Warriors, and Peasants in the Fourteenth Century,* edited by Jeffrey P. Mass, pp. 295–317. Palo Alto, CA: Stanford University Press, 1997.

Blum, Mark. *The Origins and Development of Pure Land Buddhism: A Study and Translation of Gyōnen's Jōdo Hōmon Genrushō.* New York: Oxford University Press, 2002.

Bodiford, William M. "Emptiness and Dust: Zen Dharma Transmission Rituals." In *Tantra in Practice,* edited by David Gordon White, pp. 299–307. Princeton, NJ: Princeton University Press, 2000.

———. *Sōtō Zen in Medieval Japan.* Honolulu: University of Hawai'i Press, 1993.

———. "When Secrecy Ends: The Tokugawa Reformation of Tendai Buddhism and Its Implications." In Scheid and Teeuwen, *Culture of Secrecy in Japanese Religion,* pp. 309–330.

———. "Zen and Esoteric Buddhism." In Orzech, Sørensen, and Payne, *Esoteric Buddhism and the Tantras in East Asia,* pp. 924–935.

Bogel, Cynthea J. *With a Single Glance: Buddhist Icons and Early Mikkyō Vision.* Seattle: University of Washington Press, 2009.

Buijnsters, Marc. "Jichihan and the Restoration and Innovation of Buddhist Practice." *Japanese Journal of Religious Studies* 26, no. 1–2 (1999): 39–82.

Burnouf, Eugene. *Introduction to the History of Indian Buddhism.* Translated by Katia Buffetrille and Donald S. Lopez Jr. Chicago: University of Chicago Press, 2010.

Callahan, Christopher. "Kakunyo and the Making of Shinran and Jōdo Shinshū." PhD diss., Harvard University, 2011.

Campany, Robert F. “On the Very Idea of Religions (in the Modern West and in Early Medieval China).” *History of Religions* 42 (2003): 287–319.

Carr, Kevin G. *Plotting the Prince: Shōtoku Cults and the Mapping of Medieval Japanese Buddhism.* Honolulu: University of Hawai‘i Press, 2012.

Chandler, David. “Paul Mus (1902–1969): A Biographical Sketch.” *Journal of Vietnamese Studies* 4, no. 1 (2009): 149–191.

Chandra, Lokesh. *The Esoteric Iconography of Japanese Mandalas.* Satapitaka Series 92. New Delhi: International Academy of Indian Culture, 1971.

Chang, C. *A Treasury of Mahāyāna Sūtras: Selections from the Mahāratnakūta Sūtra.* University Park: Pennsylvania State University Press, 1983.

Chen, Jinhua. “The Construction of Early Tendai Esoteric Buddhism: The Japanese Provenance of Saichō’s Transmission Documents and Three Esoteric Buddhist Apocrypha Attributed to Śubhākarasiṁha.” *Journal of the International Association of Buddhist Studies* 21 (1998): 21–76.

——. *Crossfire: Shingon-Tendai Strife as Seen in Two Twelfth-Century Polemics, with Special References to Their Background in Tang China.* Studia Philologica Buddhica Monograph Series 25. Tokyo: International Institute for Buddhist Studies, 2010.

——. “The Formation of Early Tendai Esoteric Buddhism in Japan: A Study of Three Japanese Esoteric Apocrypha.” PhD diss., McMaster University, Hamilton, Ontario, 1997.

——. *Legend and Legitimation: The Formation of Tendai Esoteric Buddhism in Japan.* Mélanges chinois et bouddhiques 30. Leuven, Belgium: Peeters, 2009.

——. *Making and Remaking History: A Study of Tiantai Sectarian Historiography.* Tokyo: International Institute for Buddhist Studies, 1999.

Ch’en, Kenneth. *Buddhism in China: A Historical Survey.* Princeton, NJ: Princeton University Press, 1964.

Chiba, Jōryu. “Orthodoxy and Heterodoxy in Early Modern Shinshū: *Kakushi Nembutsu* and *Kakure Nembutsu*.” In *The Pure Land Tradition: History and Development*, edited by James Foard, Michael Solomon, and Richard K. Payne, pp. 463–496. 1996. Reprint, Berkeley: University of California Press, 2006.

Chiba Tadashi 千葉正. “Dōhan sen Teiōshō ni okeru shukuzensetsu, chūsei Nihon Bukkyō ni okeru shukuzen setsu no tenkai” 道範撰『貞応抄』における宿善説-中世日本仏教における宿善説の展開. *Indogaku Bukkyōgaku kenkyū* 60, no. 2 (2012): 609–614.

Chou, Yi-liang. “Tantrism in China.” *Harvard Journal of Asiatic Studies* 8 (1945): 241–332. Reprinted (without appendices) in Payne, *Tantric Buddhism in East Asia*, pp. 33–60.

Cleary, Thomas, trans. *The Flower Ornament Scripture: A Translation of the Avataṃsaka Sūtra.* 1984. Reprint, Boston: Shambhala, 1986.

Como, Michael. *Shōtoku: Ethnicity, Ritual and Violence in the Japanese Buddhist Tradition.* Oxford: Oxford University Press, 2008.

———. *Weaving and Binding: Immigrant Gods and Female Immortals in Ancient Japan.* Honolulu: University of Hawai'i Press, 2009.

Conlan, Thomas. *From Sovereign to Symbol: An Age of Ritual Determinism in Fourteenth-Century Japan.* Oxford: Oxford University Press, 2011.

Conway, Michael. "A Transformative Expression: The Role of the Name of Amituo Buddha in Daochuo's Soteriology." Paper presented at the 16th Biennial Conference of the International Association of Shin Buddhist Studies, University of British Columbia, Vancouver, May 31–June 2, 2013.

Cook, Francis H. *Hua-yen Buddhism: The Jewel Net of Indra.* University Park: University of Pennsylvania Press, 1977.

Copp, Paul F. *The Body Incantatory: Spells and the Ritual Imagination in Medieval Chinese Buddhism.* New York: Columbia University Press, 2014.

———. "*Dhāraṇī* Scriptures." In Orzech, Sørensen, and Payne, *Esoteric Buddhism and the Tantras in East Asia,* pp. 176–180.

———. "Notes on the Term *'Dhāraṇī'* in Medieval Chinese Buddhist Thought." *Bulletin of the School of Oriental and African Studies* 71 (2008): 493–508.

———. "Voice, Dust, Shadow, Stone: The Makings of Spells in Medieval Chinese Buddhism." PhD diss., Princeton University, 2005.

Corless, Roger J. "T'an-luan: The First Systematizer of Pure Land Buddhism." In *The Pure Land Tradition: History and Development,* edited by James Foard, Michael Solomon, and Richard K. Payne, pp. 107–137. Berkeley: University of California, 1996.

———. "T'an-luan's Commentary on the Pure Land Discourse: An Annotated Translation and Soteriological Analysis of the Wang-sheng-lun chu (T. 1819)." PhD diss., University of Wisconsin, 1973.

———. "T'an-luan: Taoist Sage and Buddhist Bodhisattva." In *Buddhist and Taoist Practice in Medieval Chinese Society,* edited by David W. Chappell, pp. 36–48. Honolulu: University of Hawai'i Press, 1987.

Cuevas, Bryan J., and Jacqueline I. Stone, eds. *The Buddhist Dead: Practices, Discourses, Representations.* Honolulu: University of Hawai'i Press, 2007.

Daigoji Bunkazai Kenkyūjo 醍醐寺文化財研究所, ed. *Daigoji shinyōroku* 醍醐寺新要録. 2 vols. Kyoto: Hōzōkan, 1991.

Dalton, Jacob. "A Crisis of Doxography: How Tibetans Organized Tantra during the 8th–12th Centuries." *Journal of the International Association for Buddhist Studies* 28 (2005): 115–181.

Davidson, Ronald M. *Indian Esoteric Buddhism: A Social History of the Tantric Movement.* New York: Columbia University Press, 2002.

——. "The Problem of Secrecy in Indian Tantric Buddhism." In Scheid and Teeuwen, *Culture of Secrecy in Japanese Religion*, pp. 60–77.

——. "Some Observations on the Usṇīsa Abhiṣeka Rites in Atikūṭa's *Dhāraṇīsaṃgraha*." In *Transformations and Transfer of Tantra: Tantrism in Asia and Beyond*, edited by István Keul, pp. 77–98. Berlin: Walter de Gruyter, 2012.

——. "Studies in Dhāraṇī Literature I: Revisiting the Meaning of the Term *Dhāraṇī*." *Journal of Indian Philosophy* 37 (2009): 97–147.

DeCaroli, Robert. *Haunting the Buddha: Indian Popular Religions and the Formation of Buddhism*. Oxford: Oxford University Press, 2004.

de la Vallée Poussin, Louis. *Bouddhisme: Études et Matériaux*. London: Luzac, 1989.

——. *Bouddhisme: Opinions sur l'histoire de la dogmatique*. Paris: Gabriel Beauchesne et Cie., 1908.

——. "Cosmology and Cosmogony (Buddhist)." Vol. 2 of *Encyclopedia of Religion and Ethics*, edited by James Hastings, pp. 129–138. Edinburgh: T. & T. Clark, 1908–1926.

——. "Tāntrism (Buddhist)." Vol. 12 of *Encyclopedia of Religion and Ethics*, edited by James Hastings, pp. 193–197. Edinburgh: T. & T. Clark, 1908–1926.

Demiéville, Paul. "Butsudo." In *Hōbōgirin, troisie'me fascicule*. Tokyo: Maison franco-japonaise, 1937.

Dobbins, James C. "Envisioning Kamakura Buddhism." In Payne, *Re-visioning "Kamakura" Buddhism*, pp. 28–38.

——. *Jōdo Shinshū: Shin Buddhism in Medieval Japan*. Honolulu: University of Hawai'i Press, 2002.

——. *Letters of the Nun Eshinni: Images of Pure Land Buddhism in Medieval Japan*. Honolulu: University of Hawai'i Press, 2004.

——, ed. Special Issue, *Kuroda Toshio and his Scholarship: Japanese Journal of Religious Studies* 23, no. 3/4 (1996).

Dolce, Lucia. "Criticism and Appropriation: Ambiguities in Nichiren's Attitude towards Esoteric Buddhism." *Japanese Journal of Religious Studies* 26 (1999): 349–382.

——. "Esoteric Patterns in Nichiren's Thought." PhD diss., Leiden University, Netherlands, 2002.

——. "Godai'in Annen." In Orzech, Sørensen, and Payne, *Esoteric Buddhism and the Tantras in East Asia*, pp. 768–776.

——. "Reconsidering the Taxonomy of the 'Esoteric': Taimitsu Hermeneutical and Ritual Practices." In Scheid and Teeuwen, *Culture of Secrecy in Japanese Religion*, pp. 130–171.

——. "Taimitsu: The Esoteric Buddhism of the Tendai School." In Orzech, Sørensen, and Payne, *Esoteric Buddhism and the Tantras in East Asia*, pp. 744–767.

———. "Taimitsu Rituals in Medieval Japan: Sectarian Competition and the Dynamics of Tantric Performance." In *Transformations and Transfer of Tantra in Asia and Beyond,* edited by István Keul, pp. 329–364. Berlin: Walter de Gruyter, 2012.

Dolce, Lucia, and Shinya Mano. "Yōsai and Esoteric Buddhism." In Orzech, Sørensen, and Payne, *Esoteric Buddhism and the Tantras in East Asia,* pp. 827–834.

Dreitlein, Thomas Eijō. "Amoghavajra's Amitāyus Ritual Manual." In *Pure Lands in Asian Texts and Contexts: An Anthology,* edited by Georgios T. Halkias and Richard K. Payne, pp. 242–243. Honolulu: University of Hawai'i Press, 2019.

———. "An Annotated Translation of Kūkai's *Secret Key to the Heart Sūtra. Kōyasan Daigaku mikkyō bunka kenkyūsho kiyō* 高野山大学密教文化研究所紀要 24 (2011): 1–41.

Dreitlein, Thomas Eijō, and Takagi Shingen. *Kūkai on the Philosophy of Language.* Tokyo: Keiyō University, 2010.

Drummond, Donald. "Negotiating Influence: The Pilgrimage Diary of Monastic Imperial Prince Kakuhō." PhD diss., Graduate Theological Union, Berkeley, CA, 2007.

Dutt, Nalinaksha. *Gilgit Manuscripts.* Vol. 1. Srinagar: Calcutta Oriental Press, 1939.

Eracle, Jean. *La doctrine Bouddhique de la terre pure.* Paris, Dervy-Livres, 1973.

Faure, Bernard. "Japanese Tantra, the Tachikawa-ryū, and Ryōbu Shintō." In *Tantra in Practice,* edited by David Gordon White, pp. 543–556. Princeton, NJ: Princeton University Press, 2000.

———. *The Rhetoric of Immediacy: A Cultural Critique of Chan/Zen Buddhism.* Princeton, NJ: Princeton University Press, 1991.

———. *Visions of Power: Imagining Medieval Japanese Buddhism.* Translated by Phyllis Brooks. Princeton, NJ: Princeton University Press, 1996.

Foard, James H. "In Search of a Lost Reformation: A Reconsideration of Kamakura Buddhism." *Japanese Journal of Religious Studies* 7, no. 4 (1980): 261–291.

Ford, James L. "Buddhist Ceremonials (kōshiki) and the Ideological Discourse of Established Buddhism in Early Medieval Japan." In *Discourse and Ideology in Medieval Japanese Buddhism,* edited by Richard K. Payne and Taigen Daniel Leighton, pp. 97–125. New York: RoutledgeCurzon, 2006.

———. "Competing with Amida: A Study and Translation of Jōkei's Miroku kōshiki." *Monumenta Nipponica* 60, no. 1 (2005): 43–79.

———. "Exploring the Esoteric in Nara Buddhism." In Orzech, Sørensen, and Payne, *Esoteric Buddhism and the Tantras in East Asia,* pp. 776–793.

———. *Jōkei and Buddhist Devotion in Early Medieval Japan.* Oxford: Oxford University Press, 2006.

——. “Jōkei and Kannon: Defending Buddhist Pluralism in Medieval Japan.” *Eastern Buddhist* 39, no. 1 (2008): 11–28.

Foulk, T. Griffith. “The Ch’an *Tsung* in Medieval China: School, Lineage, or What?” *Pacific World,* n.s., 8 (1992): 18–31.

——. “Myth, Ritual, and Monastic Practice in Sung Ch’an Buddhism.” In *Religion and Society in T’ang and Sung China,* pp. 147–208. Honolulu: University of Hawai‘i Press, 1993.

Fujii Masako 藤井雅子. *Chūse Daigoji to shingon mikkyō* 中世醍醐寺と真言密教. Tokyo: Bensei shuppan 勉誠出版, 2008.

Fujita, Kotatsu 藤田宏達. “An Aspect of the Buddhas, Found in the Early Buddhist Scriptures, with Reference to the Present-Other Worlds Buddhas.” *Indogaku Bukkyōgaku Kenkyū* 6, no. 2 (1958): 375–384.

——. *Genshi Jōdo shisō no kenkyū* 原始浄土思想の研究. Tokyo: Iwanami shoten, 1970.

——. “Pure Land Buddhism in India.” In *The Pure Land Tradition: History and Development,* edited by James Foard, Michael Solomon, and Richard K. Payne, pp. 1–42. 1996. Reprint, Berkeley: University of California Press, 2006.

Fukushima Kaneharu 福島金治. “Ninnaji go-ryū no Kamakura denpa: Kamakura Sasame Yuishin’in to sono yakuwari” 仁和寺御流の鎌倉伝播ー鎌倉佐々目遺身院とその役割. In *Shukaku hosshinnō to Ninnaji goryū no bunkenteki kenkyū, ronbunhen* 守覚法親王と仁和寺御流の文献学的研究, edited by Abe Yasurō 阿部泰郎 and Yamazaki Makoto 媒体情報, pp. 455–502. Tokyo: Benseisha, 1998.

Fussman, G. “La place des Sukhāvatī-vyūha dans le bouddhisme indien.” *Journal Asiatique,* 1999, 523–586.

Gardiner, David L. “The Consecration of the Monastic Compound at Mount Kōya by Kūkai.” In *Tantra in Practice,* edited by David Gordon White, pp. 119–130. Princeton, NJ: Princeton University Press, 2000.

——. “Maṇḍala, Maṇḍala on the Wall: Variations of Usage in the Shingon School.” *Journal of the International Association of Buddhist Studies* 19 (1996): 245–279.

Gernet, Jacques. *Buddhism in Chinese Society: An Economic History from the Fifth to the Tenth Centuries.* Translated by Franciscus Verellen. New York: Columbia University Press, 1995.

Gethin, Rupert. “Cosmology and Meditation: From the Aggañña-Sutta to the Mahāyāna.” *History of Religions* 36, no. 3 (1997): 183–217.

——. “Mythology as Meditation: From the Mahāsudassana Sutta to the Sukhāvatīvyūha Sūtra.” *Journal of Pali Text Society,* 2006, 63–112.

Giebel, Rolf W. “The *Chin-kang-ting ching yü-ch’ieh shih-pa-hui chih-kuei:* An Annotated Translation.” *Naritasan Bukkyō kenkyūjo kiyō* 成田山仏教研究所紀要 18 (1995): 107–201.

——, trans. *Kukai Texts: On the Differences between the Exoteric and Esoteric Teachings, the Meaning of Becoming a Buddha in This Very Body, the Meanings of Sound, Sign, and Reality, the Meanings of the Word Hūṃ, and the Precious Key to the Secret Treasury*. In *Shingon Texts*, pp. 13–204. Berkeley, CA: Numata Center for Buddhist Translation and Research, 2004.

——. "Notes on Some *Dhāraṇī-sūtras* in Chinese Translation." In *Higashi Ajia Bukkyō—sono seiritsu to tenkai: Kimura Kiyotaka Hakushi Kanreki kinen ronshū* 東アジア仏教—その成立と展開: 木村清孝博士還暦記念論集, edited by Kimura Kiyotaka Hakushi Kanreki Kinenkai 木村清孝博士還暦記念会, pp. 762(27)–743(46). Tokyo: Shunjūsha, 2002.

——, trans. *Two Esoteric Sutras: The Adamantine Pinnacle Sutra/the Susiddhikara Sutra*. Berkeley, CA: Numata Center for Buddhist Translation and Research, 2001.

——, trans. *The Vairocanābhisaṃbodhi Sutra*. Berkeley, CA: Numata Center for Buddhist Translation and Research, 2005.

Gimello, Robert M., Frederic Girard, and Imre Hamar, eds. *Avatamsaka Buddhism in East Asia: Huayan, Kegon, Flower Ornament Buddhism: Origins and Adaptation of a Visual Culture*. Wiesbaden: Harrassowitz Verlag, 2012.

Girard, Frederic. *The Stanza of the Bell in the Wind: Zen and Nenbutsu in the Early Kamakura Period*. Tokyo: International Institute for Buddhist Studies, 2007.

Goble, Geoffrey C. "Chinese Esoteric Buddhism: Amoghavajra and the Tang Ruling Elite." PhD diss., Stanford University, 2012.

——. *Chinese Esoteric Buddhism: Amoghavajra, the Ruling Elite, and the Emergence of a Tradition*. New York: Columbia University Press, 2019.

Gómez, Luis O. *The Land of Bliss: The Paradise of the Buddha of Measureless Light*. Honolulu: University of Hawai'i Press, 1996.

——. "Measuring the Immeasurable: Reflections on Unreasonable Reasoning." In Makransky and Jackson, *Buddhist Theology*, pp. 367–385.

Gonda, Jan. "Introduction: Some Critical Remarks Apropos of Substratum Theories." In *Change and Continuity in Indian Religion*, pp. 7–37. The Hague: Mouton, 1965.

Goodwin, Janet. *Alms and Vagabonds: Buddhist Temples and Popular Pilgrimage in Medieval Japan*. Honolulu: University of Hawai'i Press, 1994.

Gorai Shigeru 五来重. *Kōya hijiri* 高野聖. 1975. Reprint, Tokyo: Kadokawa bunko 角川文庫, 2011.

——, ed. *Kōyasan to Shingon mikkyō no kenkyū, Sangaku shūkyo shi kenkyū sōsho* 高野山と真言密教の研究, 山岳宗教史研究叢書. Tokyo: Meicho shuppan, 1976.

Goudriaan, Teun. "Part One: Introduction, History and Philosophy." Vol. 2.4.2 of *Hindu Tantrism: Handbuch der Orientalistik*, edited by Sanjukta Gupta, Dirk Jan Hoens, and Teun Goudriaan, pp. 7–93. Leiden: Brill, 1979.

Grapard, Allan. "*Keiranshūyōshū:* A Different Perspective on Mt. Hiei in the Medieval Period." In Payne, *Re-visioning "Kamakura" Buddhism,* pp. 55–69.

——. *The Protocol of the Gods: A Study of the Kasuga Cult in Japanese History.* Berkeley: University of California Press, 1992.

Gregory, Peter N., ed. *Traditions of Meditation in Chinese Buddhism.* Studies in East Asian Buddhism 4. Honolulu: University of Hawai'i Press, 1986.

Groner, Paul. *Ryōgen and Mount Hiei: Japanese Tendai in the Tenth Century.* Honolulu: University of Hawai'i Press, 2002.

——. *Saichō: The Establishment of the Japanese Tendai School.* Berkeley: University of California Press, 1984. Reprint, Honolulu: University of Hawa'i Press, 2000.

——. "Shortening the Path: Early Tendai Interpretations of the Realization of Buddhahood with This Very Body (*sokushin jōbutsu*)." In *Paths to Liberation: The Mārga and Its Transformations in Buddhist Thought,* edited by Robert E. Buswell Jr. and Robert M. Gimello, pp. 439–473. Honolulu: University of Hawai'i Press, 1992.

——. "Training through Debates in Medieval Tendain and Seizan-ha Temples." *Japanese Journal of Religious Studies* 38, no. 2 (2011): 233–261.

Guenther, Herbert V. *The Tantric View of Life.* Berkeley, CA: Shambhala, 1972.

Gyatso, Janet. "An Avalokiteśvara Sādhana." In Lopez, *Religions of Tibet in Practice,* pp. 266–270.

——. "Commemoration and Identification in Buddhānusmṛti." In *In the Mirror of Memory: Reflections on Mindfulness and Remembrance in Indian and Tibetan Buddhism,* edited by Janet Gyatso, pp. 215–238. Albany: State University of New York Press, 1992.

Hakeda, Yoshito S. *Kūkai: Major Works. Translated with an Account of His Life and a Study of His Thought.* New York: Columbia University Press, 1972.

Halkias, Georgios. *Luminous Bliss: A Religious History of Pure Land Literature in Tibet: With an Annotated English Translation and Critical Analysis of the Orgyan-glin Gold Manuscript of the Short Sukhāvatīvyūha-sūtra.* Honolulu: University of Hawai'i Press, 2013.

Hamar, Imre, ed. *Reflecting Mirrors: Perspectives on Huayan Buddhism.* Wiesbaden: Harrassowitz, 2007.

Hanawa Hokinoichi 塙保己一, ed. *Gunsho ruijū* 群書類従 (GR). Tokyo: Keizai zasshisha, 1898–1902.

Harrison, Paul. "Buddhānusmṛti in the Pratyutpanna-buddha-saṃmukhāvastita-samādhi-sūtra." *Journal of Indian Philosophy* 6 (1978): 35–57.

——, trans. *The Pratyutpanna Samādhi Sutra.* Berkeley, CA: Numata Center for Buddhist Translation and Research, 1998.

———. *The Samādhi of Direct Encounter with the Buddhas of the Present: An Annotated English Translation of the Tibetan Version of the Pratyutpanna-Buddha-Saṃmukhāvasthita-Samādhi-Sūtra with Several Appendices Relating to the History of the Text.* Tokyo: International Institute for Buddhist Studies, 1990.

Hasegawa Takeshi 長谷川岳史. "Fukūyaku kyōten no busshinkan" 不空訳経典の仏身観. *Ryūkoku Daigaku ronshū* 龍谷大学論集 453 (1999): 24–40.

———. "Mikkyō ni okeru gochi shisō no seiritsu ni kansuru kenkyū" 密教における五智思想の成立に関する研究. No. 1. *Ryūkoku Daigaku daigakuen Bukkyō kenkyūshitsu nenpō* 龍谷大学大学院仏教学研究室年報 6 (1993): 34–58.

Hashimoto Hatsuko 橋本初子. *Chūsei Tōji to Kōbōdaishi shinkō* 中世東寺と弘法大師信仰. Kyoto: Shibunkaku shigaku sōsho 思文閣史学叢書, 1990.

Hasuzawa Jojun 蓮沢浄淳. "Kakkai sonshi no monka" 覚海尊師の門下. *Mikkyō bunka* 密教研究 10 (1922): 151–166, 167–228.

Hayami Tasuku 速水侑. *Heian kizoku shakai to bukkyō* 平安貴族社会と仏教. Tokyo: Yoshikawa kōbunkan, 1975.

———. *Inseiki no bukkyō* 院政期の仏教. Tokyo: Yoshikawa kōbunkan, 1998.

———. *Jōdo shinkō ron* 浄土信仰論. Tokyo: Yūzankaku shuppan, 1978.

———. *Jujutsu shūkyō no sekai* 呪術宗教の世界. 1987. Reprint, Tokyo: Hanawa shinsho, 2007.

———. *Jujutsu shūkyō no sekai: Mikkyō no shuhō no rekishi* 呪術宗教の世界: 密教の修法の歴史. Tokyo: Hanawa shobō, 1987.

———. *Kannon shinkō* 観音信仰. Tokyo: Kōsenshō, 1981.

———. *Miroku shinkō—mō hitotsu jōdo shinkō* 弥勒信仰—もう一つの浄土信仰. Tokyo: Hyōronsha 評論社, 1971.

———. *Nara-Heian bukkyō no tenkai* 奈良, 平安仏教の展開. Tokyo: Yoshikawa kōbunkan, 2006.

Hayao Kawai, and Mark Unno. *The Buddhist Priest Myōe: A Life of Dreams.* Venice, CA: Lapis Press, 1992.

Himitsu nenbutsu shō kenkyūkai 秘密念仏抄研究会. "Dōhan cho 'Himitsu nenbutsu shō' no kenkyū—honbun kōtei to kaki kudashi, gochū" 道範著『秘密念仏抄』の研究—本文校訂と書き下し・語註. *Buzan gakuhō* 豊山学報 39 (1996): 105–130.

Hinonishi, Shinjo. "The Hōgō (Treasure Name) of Kōbō Daishi and the Development of Beliefs Associated with It." Translated by William Londo. *Japanese Religions* 27 (2002): 5–18.

Hinonishi Shinjō 日野西真定. "Kōbō daishi no hōgō no rekishi to sono shūkyō teki imi" 弘法大師の宝号の歴史とその宗教的意味. *Indogaku bukkyōgaku kenkyū* 印度学仏教学研究 90 (1997): 142–146.

———, ed. *Kōbō Daishi shinkō* 弘法大師信仰. Tokyo: Yūzankaku, 1988.

——. "Kōyasan no jōdoshinkō" 高野山の浄土信仰. *Indogaku bukkyōgaku kenkyū* 印度学仏教学研究 70 (1987): 227–230.

——. "Sangaku reiba ni matsurareru kami to hotoke: Toku ni Kōyasan no baai" 山岳霊場に祀られる神と仏: 特に高野山の場合. In *Sei naru Mono no Katachi to Ba* 聖なるものの形と場, edited by Yoritomi Motohiro 頼富本宏, pp. 470–489. Kyoto: Hōzōkan, 2004.

Hirakawa, Akira. *A History of Indian Buddhism: From Śākyamuni to Early Mahāyāna.* Translated and edited by Paul Groner. Honolulu: University of Hawai'i Press, 1990.

Hodge, Stephen. "Considerations on the Dating and Geographical Origins of the *Mahāvairocanābhisaṃbodhi-sūtra.*" Vol. 3 of *The Buddhist Forum*, edited by Tadeusz Skorupski and Ulrich Pagels, pp. 57–83. London: School of Oriental and African Studies, University of London, 1994.

——. *The Mahā-vairocanā-abhisambodhi Tantra with Buddhagugya's Commentary.* London: RoutledgeCurzon, 2003.

Horiuchi Noriyuki 堀内規之. *Saisen kyōgaku no kenkyū: Inseiki shingonmikkyō no shomondai* 済暹教学の研究: 院政期真言密教の諸問題. Tokyo: Nonburu, 2009.

Huntington, John C. "Note on a Chinese Text Demonstrating the Earliness of Tantra." *Journal of the International Association of Buddhist Studies* 10, no. 2 (1987): 88–98.

Huntington, Susan L. "Early Buddhist Art and the Theory of Aniconism." *Art Journal* 49 (1990): 401–408.

Hur, Namlin. *Death and Social Order in Tokugawa Japan: Buddhism, Anti-Christianity, and the Danka System.* Cambridge, MA: Harvard University Press, 2007.

Hurvitz, Leon. *Chih-I* 智顗 *(538–597): An Introduction to the Life and Ideas of a Chinese Buddhist Monk.* Bruxelles: I'Institut Belge des Hautes Études Chinoises, 1962.

——. *Scripture of the Lotus Blossom of the Fine Dharma.* New York: Columbia University Press, 2009.

Hyōtani Kazuko 俵谷和子. *Kōyasan shinkō to kenmon shinshi: Kōbō daishi nyūjō densetsu wo chūshin ni* 高野山信仰と権門貴紳: 弘法大師入定伝説を中心に. Tokyo: Iwata shoin, 2010.

Ichikawa Hiroshi 市川浩史. "Jōdo" 浄土. In *Nihon Bukkyō no kenkyūhō* 日本仏教の研究法歴史と展望, edited by Nihon Bukkyō kenkyūkai 日本仏教研究会 et al., pp. 154–167. Kyoto: Hōzōkan 法藏館, 2000.

Igarashi Takayuki 五十嵐隆幸. *Seizan Jōdokyō no kiban to tenkai* 西山浄土教の基盤と展開. Kyoto: Shibunkaku, 2010.

Inagaki, Hisao 稲垣久雄. *The Anantamukhanirhāra-Dhāraṇī Sūtra and Jñānagarbha's Commentary: A Study and the Tibetan Text.* Kyoto: Nagata bunshodo, 1987.

——. “The Esoteric Meaning of ‘Amida.’” In *Kōgyō daishi Kakuban kenkyū* 興教大師覺鑁研究, edited by Kōgyō Daishi Kenkyū Ronshū Henshū Iinkai 興教大師研究論集編集委員会, pp. 1104–1095. Tokyo: Shujūsha, 1992.

——. “Kūkai’s ‘Principle of Attaining Buddhahood with the Present Body.’” In Payne, *Tantric Buddhism in East Asia*, pp. 99–118.

——. *The Three Pure Land Sutras: A Study and Translation from Chinese.* Kyoto: Nagata bunshōdo, 1995.

Inamoto Taishō 稲本 泰生. “Narachō komikkyō no zenshi ni kan suru kakusho—chūgoku bushūki zengō no jōkyō wo chūshin ni” 奈良朝古密教の前史に関する覚書 一中国武周期前後の状況を中心に. In Nara Kokuritsu Hakubutsukan, *Komikkyō,* pp. 139–144.

Inatani Sukenobu 稲谷祐宣. “Nara jidai mikkyō kyōten to Kūkai” 奈良時代の密教経典と空海. *Mikkyō bunka* 密教文化 73 (1965): 52–59.

Ingram, Paul O. “Faith as Knowledge in the Teaching of Shinran Shonin and Martin Luther.” *Buddhist-Christian Studies* 8 (1988): 23–35.

Inoue Mitsusada 井上光貞. “Inseiki ni okeru Kōyasan no Jōdokyō” 院政期における高野山の浄土教. Vol. 7 of *Nihon Mikkyō* 日本密教, *Mikkyō taikei* 密教体系, edited by Miyasaka Yūshō 宮坂有勝, pp. 167–216. Kyoto: Hōzōkan 法蔵館, 1995.

——. *Nihon jōdokyō seiritsushi no kenkyū* 日本淨土教成立史の研究. Tokyo: Yamakawa shuppansha, 1956.

Ishida Mitsuyuki 石田充之. “Mikkyōkei Jōdo ganshōsha Jōhen sōzu no Jōdokyō tachiba” 密教系浄土願生者静遍僧都の浄土教的立場. *Ryūkoku Daigaku ronshū* 龍谷大学論集 336 (1949): 36–62.

Ishii Kōsei 石井公成. *Kegon shisō no kenkyū* 華厳思想の研究. Tokyo: Shunjūsha, 1996.

Ito Shigeki 伊藤茂樹. “Jōhen no shōgai ni tsuite” 静遍の生涯について. *Jōdokyō kenkyū* 浄土宗学研究 34 (2008): 93–94 (R).

——. “Jōhen no shūkyō katsudō” 静遍の宗教活動. *Indogaku Bukkyōgaku kenkyū* 印度学仏教学研究 117 (2009): 55–59 (R).

Iyanaga, Nobumi 彌永信美. “Secrecy, Sex and Apocrypha: Remarks on Some Paradoxical Phenomena.” In Scheid and Teeuwen, *Culture of Secrecy in Japanese Religion,* pp. 204–228.

——. “Tachikawa-ryū.” In Orzech, Sørensen, and Payne, *Esoteric Buddhism and the Tantras in East Asia,* pp. 803–814.

——. “Tachikawa-ryū to Shinjō *Juhō-yōjin shū* wo megutte” 立川流と心定『受法用心集』をめぐって. *Nihon bukkyō Sōgō Kenkyū* 日本仏教綜合研究 2 (2003): 13–31.

Jaffe, Richard. *Neither Monk nor Layman: Clerical Marriage in Modern Japanese Buddhism.* Princeton, NJ: Princeton University Press, 2001.

Jones, Charles B. *Chinese Pure Land Buddhism: Understanding a Tradition of Practice.* Honolulu: University of Hawai'i Press, 2019.

Jones, John James. *The Mahāvastu-Avadāna.* Vols. 1–3. London: Luzac, 1949.

Josephson, Jason Ananda. *The Invention of Religion in Japan.* Chicago: University of Chicago Press, 2012.

——. "Taming Demons: The Anti-superstition Campaign and the Invention of Religion in Japan (1853–1920)." PhD diss., Stanford University, 2006.

Kagiwada Seiko 鍵和田聖子. "Tōmitsu to Taimitsu no sōgo eikyō kara mita juyō to kensan no tenkai" 東密と台密の相互影響から見た受容と研鑽の展開. PhD diss., Ryūkoku University, 2014.

Kakehashi Nobuaki 梯信暁. *Jōdokyō shisōshi: Indo, Chūgoku, Chōsen, Nihon* 浄土教思想史:インド・中国・朝鮮・日本. Kyoto: Hōzōkan, 2012.

——. *Nara, Heianki jōdokyō tenkairon* 奈良・平安期浄土教展開論. Kyoto: Hōzōkan, 2008.

Kamai Shūchū 亀井宗忠. "Mikkyō shoka to ōjō shisō" 密教諸家と往生思想. *Buzan gakuhō* 豊山学報 2 (1954): 78–89.

Kamata Shigeo 鎌田茂雄. *Chugōku bukkyu shi* 中國佛教史. 6 vols. Tokyo: Tokyo Daigaku shuppankai, 1982–1999.

Kameyama Takahiko 亀山隆彦. "Chūsei Shingonshū ni okeru myōsoku shisō no tenkai—Shūkotsushō wo chūshin ni" 中世真言宗における命息思想の展開—『宗骨抄』を中心に. *Indogaku Bukkyōgaku kenkyū* 印度学仏教学研究 59 (2011): 651–654.

Kamikawa Michio 上川通夫. *Nihon chūsei Bukkyō to Higashi Ajia sekai* 日本中世仏教と東アジア世界. Tokyo: Hanawa shobō, 2012.

Kanayama Maboku 金山穆韶. "Chōkaishō (Dōhan ajari ki)" 聴海抄 (道範阿闍梨記). *Mikkyō kenkyū* 密教研究 10 (1922): 167–228.

——. "Chōkai shō ni tsuite" 聽海抄に就. *Mikkyō kenkyū* 密教研究 10 (1922): 229–231.

Kanda, Fusae C. "The Development of Amida Raigō Painting: Style, Concept, and Landscape." PhD diss., Yale University, 2002.

Kaneoka Shūyū 金岡秀友, ed. *Toganoo korekushon kenmitsu tenseki monjoshūsei* 栂尾コレク ション顕密典籍文書集成 5 (*Kyōsōhen* 教相篇 5). Tokyo: Heika shuppansha, 1981.

Kapstein, Matthew T., ed. *The Presence of Light: Divine Radiance and Religious Experience.* Chicago: University of Chicago Press, 2004.

——. "Pure Land Buddhism in Tibet? From Sukhāvatī to the Field of Great Bliss." In Payne and Tanaka, *Approaching the Land of Bliss,* pp. 16–52.

——. *The Tibetan Assimilation of Buddhism: Conversion, Contestation, and Memory.* Oxford: Oxford University Press, 2000.

Kasahara, Kazuo 笠原一男. "Akunin ōjō shisō no keihu" 悪人往生思想の系譜. *Nihon ni okeru kokka to shūkyō* 日本における国家と宗教, 1978, 117–132.

——, ed. *A History of Japanese Religion.* Translated by Paul McCarthy and Gaynor Sekimori. Tokyo: Kosei, 2001.

Katsuhisa Toshinori 勝又俊教. *Kōbō Daishi no shisō to sono genryū* 弘法大師の思想とその源流. Tokyo: Sankibō busshorin, 1981.

——. *Mikkyō no nihonteki tenkai* 密教の日本的展開. Tokyo: Shunjūsha, 1970.

——. "Nara jidai no mikkyō" 奈良時代の密. In *Mikkyō no rekishi* 密教の歴史, edited by Miyasaka Yūshō et al., pp. 168–183. Kōza mikkyō 2. Tokyo: Shunjūsha, 1977.

Katsuura Noriko 勝浦令子. "Higashi Ajia no 'Mukujōkō daidaranikyō' juyō to hyakumantō" 東アジアの『無垢浄光大陀羅尼経』受容と百万塔. In Hayami Tasuku, *Nara-Heian Bukkyō no tenkai,* pp. 2–31.

Kawai, Hayao, and Mark Unno. *The Buddhist Priest Myōe: A Life of Dreams.* Venice: Lapis Press, 1992.

Kawamura Teruo 川村晃生. "Saigyō no Shikoku gekō ichi daishi iseki junrei kagun ni tsuite" 西行の四国下向一大師遺跡巡礼歌群について. *Mita kokubun* 三田國文 1 (1983): 1–4.

Keyworth, George A. "The Esotericization of Chinese Buddhist Practice." In Orzech, Sørensen, and Payne, *Esoteric Buddhism and the Tantras in East Asia,* pp. 516–519.

Kieschnick, John. *The Eminent Monk: Buddhist Ideals in Medieval Chinese Hagiography.* Honolulu: University of Hawai'i Press, 1997.

——. *The Impact of Buddhism on Chinese Material Culture.* Princeton, NJ: Princeton University Press, 2003.

Kimbrough, R. Keller. "Reading the Miraculous Powers of Japanese Poetry: Spells, Truth Acts, and a Medieval Buddhist Poetics of the Supernatural." *Japanese Journal of Religious Studies* 32, no. 1 (2005): 1–33.

——. "Tourists in Paradise: Writing the Pure Land in Medieval Japanese Fiction." *Japanese Journal of Religious Studies* 33, no. 2 (2006): 269–296.

Kitagawa Masahiro 北川真寛. "*Keiran shūyōshū* niokeru jōdo shisō" 『渓嵐拾葉集』における浄土思想. *Mikkyō bunka* 密教文化 207 (2001): 1–32.

Kiuchi Gyōō 木内堯央. *Tendai mikkyō no keisei: Nihon Tendai shisōshi kenkyū* 天台密教の形成：日本天台思想史研究. Tokyo: Keisuisha, 1984.

Klautau, Orion. "Kindai Bukkyō to Shinshū no mondai" 近代仏教と真宗の問題. *Nihon shisōshi gakkai* 日本思想史学会 43 (2011): 35–43.

Klein, Christof. "Hermits and Ascetics in Ancient Japan: The Concept of Hijiri Reconsidered." *Japanese Religions* 22, no. 2 (1997): 1–46.

Kloetzli, Randy. *Buddhist Cosmology: From Single World System to Pure Land.* Delhi: Motilal Banarsidass, 1983.

Kobayashi Naoki 小林直樹. "Muju to Kongōōin sōzu Jitsugen" 無住と金剛王院僧正実賢. *Bungakushi kenkyū* 文学史研究 49 (2009): 55–64.

Köck, Stefan. "The Dissemination of the Tachikawa-ryū and the Problem of Orthodox and Heretic Teaching in Shingon Buddhism." *Indo tetsugaku Bukkyōgaku Kenkyū* インド哲学仏教学研究 7 (2000): 69–83.

Kōda Yūun 甲田宥吽. "Chūin-ryū no jaryū wo tsutaeta hitobito" 中院流の邪流を伝えた人々. *Mikkyōbunka* 密教文化 135 (1981): 19–37.

——. "Dōhan ajari no jagi sōden ni tsuite" 道範阿闍梨の邪義相伝について. *Mikkyō-gaku kaihō* 密教学会報 19, no. 20 (1981): 36–47 (L).

——. "Keika wajō igo no mikkyō sōtachi" 惠果和尚以後の密教僧たち. *Mikkyō bunka kenkyūjo kiyō* 密教文化研究所紀要 15 (2002): 29–62.

Kōyasan Daigaku Sensho Kankōkai 高野山大学選書刊行会. *Kōyasan no Dentō to mirai* 高野山の伝統と未来. Kōyasan Daigaku sensho 高野山大学選書 4. Tokyo: Shōgakkan, 2006.

——, ed. *Kōyasan to Mikkyō bunka* 高野山と密教文化. Kōyasan Daigaku sensho 高野山大学選書 1. Tokyo: Shōgakkan, 2006.

——. *Shingon Mikkyō no arata na tenkai* 真言密教の新たな展開. Kōyasan Daigaku sensho 高野山大学選書 2. Tokyo: Shōgakkan, 2006.

Kōyasan Reibōkan 高野山霊宝館. *Kōya Shōchi'in no rekishi to bijutsu* 高野正智院の歴史と美術. Wakayama: Kōyasan Reibōkan, 1998.

Kroll, Paul W. *Dharma Bell and Dhāraṇī Pillar.* Kyoto: Italian School of East Asian Studies, 2001.

Kumada Junshō 熊田順正. "Azuma kuni no genshi Shinshū kyōdan e no himitsu *nenbutsu* shisō no eikyō ni tsuite" 東国の原始真宗教団への秘密念仏思想の影響について. *Ryūkoku kyōgaku* 竜谷教学, 2004, 9–25.

——. "Jōhen Jōdokyō ni mieru shichi hachi kushiki setsu ni tsuite kōsatsu" 静遍浄土教に見える七八九識説についての考察. *Bukkyōgaku* 仏教学 48 (2006): 69–92.

——. "Jōhen kyōgaku no tokuisei ni tsuite—shoshi o hihan wo tooshite" 静遍教学の特異性について—諸師の批判を通して. *Tōyōgaku kenkyū* 東洋学研究, 2008, 97–121.

——. "Jōhen 'Zoku sentaku mongi yōshō' ni okeru Amida no busshin butsudo-kan ni tsuite" 静遍『続選択文義要鈔』における阿弥陀仏の仏身仏土観について. *Indogaku Bukkyōgaku kenkyū* 印度学仏教学研究 106 (2005): 86–89.

——. "Tōkoku no genshi Shinshū kyōdan e no himitsu nenbutsu shisō no eikyō ni tsuite" 東国の原始真宗教団への秘密 念仏思想の影響について. *Ryūkoku kyōgaku* 竜谷教学, 2004, 9–25.

Kuroda Toshio 黒田俊雄. "The Development of the Kenmitsu System as Japan's Medieval Orthodoxy." *Japanese Journal of Religious Studies* 23 (1996): 233–269.

——. "The Discourse on the 'Land of *Kami*' (*shinkoku*) in Medieval Japan." Special issue, *The Legacy of Kuroda Toshio: Japanese Journal of Religious Studies* 23 (1996): 353–385.

——. *Kenmitsu taisei ron* 顕密体制論. Kyoto: Hōzōkan, 1994.

——. *Nihon chūsei no kokka to shūkyō* 日本中世の国家と宗教. 1975. Reprint, Tokyo: Iwanami shōten, 2007.

——. *Nihon chūsei shakai to shūkyō* 日本中世社会と宗教. Tokyo: Iwanami shōten, 1990.

Kushida Ryōkō 櫛田良洪. "Himitsu *nenbutsu* shisō no bokkō" 秘密念仏思想の勃興. *Taishō Daigaku kenkyū kiyō tsūgō* 大正大学研究紀要 通号 48 (1963): 43–80.

——. *Kakuban no kenkyū* 覚鑁の研究. Tokyo: Yoshikawa kōbunkan, 1975.

——. *Kūkai no kenkyū* 空海の研究. Tokyo: Sankibō busshorin, 1981.

——. *Shingon mikkyō seiritsu katei no kenkyū* 真言密教成立過程の研究. Tokyo: Sankibō busshorin, 1964.

——. *Zoku Shingon mikkyō seiritsu katei no kenkyū* 続真言密教成立過程の研究. Tokyo: Sankibō busshorin, 1979.

Lamotte, Étienne. *L'enseignement de Vimalakīrti.* Bibliotheque du muséon 51. Louvain: Publications universitaires, 1962.

Lehman, F. K. "On the Vocabulary and Semantics of 'Field' in Theravāda Buddhist Society." *Contributions to Asian Studies* 16 (1981): 101–111.

Lehnert, Martin. "Myth and Secrecy in Tang-Period Tantric Buddhism." In Scheid and Teeuwen, *Culture of Secrecy in Japanese Religion,* pp. 78–104.

Lindsay, Ethan. "Pilgrimage to the Sacred Traces of Kōyasan: Place and Devotion in Late Heian Japan." PhD diss., Princeton University, 2012.

Linrothe, Robert, and Henrik H. Sørensen, eds. *Embodying Wisdom: Art, Text and Interpretation in the History of Esoteric Buddhism.* Copenhagen: Seminar for Buddhist Studies, 2001.

Londo, William. "The Other Mountain: The Mt. Kōya Temple Complex in the Heian Era." PhD diss., University of Michigan, 2004.

Lopez, Donald S. Jr., ed. *Buddhism and Science: A Guide for the Perplexed.* Chicago: University of Chicago Press, 2008.

——. "Burnouf and the Birth of Buddhist Studies." *Eastern Buddhist* 43, no. 1–2 (2012): 25–34.

——. *Curators of the Buddha: The Study of Buddhism under Colonialism.* Chicago: University of Chicago Press, 1995.

——. *Elaborations on Emptiness: Uses of the Heart Sūtra.* Princeton, NJ: Princeton University Press, 1996.

——. *From Stone to Flesh: A Short History of the Buddha.* Chicago: University of Chicago Press, 2013.

——. "Introduction to the Translation." In Burnouf, *Introduction to the History of Indian Buddhism,* pp. 1–28.

——. "'Lamaism' and the Disappearance of Tibet." *Comparative Studies in Society and History* 38, no. 1 (1996): 3–25.

——. *The Lotus Sutra: A Biography.* Princeton, NJ: Princeton University Press, 2016.

——. "Mindfulness of Death." In Lopez, *Religions of Tibet in Practice,* pp. 421–442.

——, ed. *Religions of Tibet in Practice.* Princeton, NJ: Princeton University Press, 1997.

Lü Jianfu 吕建福. *Zhongguo mijiao shi* 中国密教史. Beijing: Zhongguo shehui kexue chubanshe, 1995.

Lye, Hun Y. "Feeding Ghosts: A Study of the *Yuqie Yankou* Rite." PhD diss., University of Virginia, 2003.

——. "Song Tiantai Ghost-Feeding Rituals." In Orzech, Sørensen, and Payne, *Esoteric Buddhism and the Tantras in East Asia,* pp. 520–524.

Mack, Karen J. "Function and Context of Fudō Imagery from the Ninth to Fourteenth Century in Japan." PhD diss., University of Kansas, 2006.

——. "The Phenomenon of Invoking Fudō for Pure Land Rebirth in Image and Text." *Japanese Journal of Religious Studies* 33, no. 2 (2006): 297–317.

Makransky, John J., and Roger R. Jackson, eds. *Buddhist Theology: Critical Reflections by Contemporary Buddhist Scholars.* London: RoutledgeCurzon, 2000.

Manabe Shunshō 真鍋俊照. *Jakyō Tachikawa-ryū* 邪教·立川流. Tokyo: Chikuma shobō, 2002.

Mass, Jeffrey P. *Yoritomo and the Founding of the First Bakufu: The Origins of Dual Government in Japan.* Palo Alto, CA: Stanford University Press, 1999.

Masuzawa, Tomoko. *The Invention of World Religions, or How European Universalism Was Preserved in the Language of Pluralism.* Chicago: University of Chicago Press, 2005.

Matsumoto Bunzaburō 松本文三郎. "Tōbatsu bishamon kō" 兜跋毘沙門攷. *Tōhō gakuhō* 東方学報 10 (1939): 12–21.

Matsunaga, Daigan, and Alicia Matsunaga. *Foundation of Japanese Buddhism:* Vol. 1, *The Aristocratic Age.* Los Angeles: Buddhist Books International, 1974.

Matsunaga Yūkei 松長有慶 et al., eds. *Koyasan: Sono rekishi to bunka* 高野山: その歴史と文化. Kyoto: Hōzōkan, 1984.

——. *Mikkyō no rekishi* 密教の歴史. Kyoto: Heirakuji shoten, 1969.

Matsuo, Kenji 松尾剛次. *A History of Japanese Buddhism.* Dorset, UK: Global Oriental, 2007.

——. *Shinpan Kamakura shin Bukkyō no seiritsu: Nyūmon girei to soshi shinwa* 新版鎌倉新仏教の成立: 入門儀礼と祖師神話. Tokyo: Yoshikawa kōbunkan 吉川弘文館, 1998.

——. "What Is Kamakura New Buddhism? Official Monks and Reclusive Monks." *Japanese Journal of Religious Studies* 24, no. 1–2 (1997): 179–189.

Matsuzaki Keisui 松崎惠水. *Heian mikkyō no kenkyū: Kōgyō Daishi Kakuban wo chūshin toshite* 平安密教の研究: 興教大師覚鑁を中心として. Tokyo: Yoshikawa kōbunkan 吉川弘文館, 2002.

——. "Kakuban to Jōhen no Jōdo ōjō shisō" 覚鑁と静遍の浄土往生思想. *Buzan gakuhō* 豊山学報 53 (2010): 1–18.

McBride, Richard D. II. "Dhāraṇī and Spells in Medieval Sinitic Buddhism." *Journal of the International Association of Buddhist Studies* 28 (2005): 85–114.

——. *Domesticating the Dharma: Buddhist Cults and the Hwaŏm Synthesis in Silla Korea.* Honolulu: University of Hawai'i Press, 2008.

——. "Is There Really 'Esoteric' Buddhism?" *Journal of the International Association of Buddhist Studies* 27 (2004): 329–356.

——. "The Mysteries of Body, Speech, and Mind: The Three Esoterica (*sanmi*) in Medieval Sinitic Buddhism." *Journal of the International Association of Buddhist Studies* 29 (2006): 305–355.

——. "Popular Esoteric Deities and the Spread of their Cults." In Orzech, Sørensen, and Payne, *Esoteric Buddhism and the Tantras in East Asia,* pp. 215–219.

McCagney, Nancy. *Nāgārjuna and the Philosophy of Openness.* Oxford: Rowman & Littlefield, 1997.

McMahan, David. "Transpositions of Metaphor and Imagery in the Gandavyuha and Tantric Buddhist Practice." *Pacific World* 3, no. 6 (2004): 181–194.

McMullen, Matthew D. "The Development of Esoteric Buddhist Scholasticism in Early Medieval Japan." PhD diss., University of California, Berkeley, 2016.

——. "Raiyu and Shingi Shingon Sectarian History." MA thesis, University of Hawai'i at Manoa, 2008.

McMullin, Neil. "Historical and Historiographical Issues in the Study of Premodern Japanese Religions." *Japanese Journal of Religious Studies* 16, no. 1 (1989): 3–40.

——. "The Sanmon-Jimon Schism in the Tendai School of Buddhism: A Preliminary Analysis." *Journal of the International Association of Buddhist Studies* 7 (1984): 83–105.

McRae, John. "Chinese Buddhism." In *Encyclopedia of Religion,* edited by Lindsay Jones et al., pp. 1235–1241, s.v. "Buddhism, Schools of." Detroit: Macmillan, 2005.

——. *The Northern School and the Formation of Early Ch'an Buddhism.* Honolulu: University of Hawai'i Press, 1986.

Meeks, Lori. *Hokkeji and the Reemergence of Female Monastic Orders in Premodern Japan.* Honolulu: University of Hawa'i Press, 2010.

Michibata Ryōshū 道端良秀. "Donran to Dōkyō to no kankei" 曇鸞と道教との關係. *Tōyō bunka ronshū* 東洋文化論集 (1969): 1001–1020.

Mikkyō Bunka Kenkyūjo Seikyō Chōsa Han 密教文化研究所聖教調査班, ed. "Kōyasan shinnōin seikyō monjo chōsa gaiyō ichifu, shiryō kaishō, 'Dōhan nikka rinjū higi'" 高野山親王院聖教文書調査概要—付、資料紹介『道範日課臨終秘儀』. *Kōyasan Daigaku mikkyō bunka kenkyūjo kiyō* 高野山大学密教文化研究所紀要 16 (2003): 79–92.

Misaki Ryōshū 三崎良周. "Junmitsu to zōmitsu ni tsuite" 純密と雑密について. *Indogaku bukkyōgaku kenkyū* 印度學佛教學研究 15 (1967): 535–540.

——. "Nara jidai no mikkyō ni okeru shomondai" 奈良時代の密教における諸問題. *Nanto bukkyō* 南都仏教 22 (1968): 55–73.

——. *Taimitsu no kenkyū* 台密の研究. Tokyo: Sōbunsha, 1988.

——. *Taimitsu no riron to jissen* 台密の理論と実践. Tokyo: Sōbunsha, 1994.

Mitra, Rajendralala. *The Sanskrit Buddhist Literature of Nepal.* 1888. Reprint, New Delhi: Cosmo, 1981.

Miyagi Yōichiro 宮城洋一郎. "Nara jidai mikkyō no ichi keitai" 奈良時代密教の一形態. *Mikkyōgaku kenkyū* 密教学研究 18 (1986): 75–91.

Miyake, Hitoshi 宮家準. *The Mandala of the Mountain: Shugendo and Folk Religion.* Translated and edited by Gaynor Sekimori. Tokyo: Keiō University Press, 2005.

——. *Shugendo: Essays on the Structure of Japanese Folk Religion.* Ann Arbor: Center for Japanese Studies, University of Michigan Press, 2001.

Miyasaka Yūshō 宮坂 宥勝. "Mikkyō kanahōgo no shiryō (ichi)" 密教仮名法語の資料 (一). *Mikkyō bunka* 密教文化 41, no. 42 (1958): 23–42.

Mizuhara Gyōei 水原尭栄. "Chu'inryū seikyō no daijōsha Shingen daitoku ni tsuite" 中院流聖教の大成者真源大徳に就て. *Mikkyō Kenkyū* 密教研究 7 (1922): 45–68.

Mochizuki Shinkō 望月信亨. *Bukkyō daijiten* 佛教大辭典. 10 vols. 1909–1936. Reprint, Tokyo: Sekai shōten kankō kyōkai, 1974.

Moerman, Max. *Localizing Paradise: Kumano Pilgrimage and the Religious Landscape of Premodern Japan.* Cambridge, MA: Harvard University Press, 2005.

Mori Shigeki 森重樹, ed. *Toganō korekushon kenmitsu tenseki monjo shūsei* 栂尾コレクション顕密典籍文書集成. 12 vols. Tokyo: Hirakawa shuppansha, 1981.

Morita Kaneyoshi 森田兼吉. "Nankai ruroki kō" 南海流浪記考. *Nihon bungaku ronkyū* 日本文学論究 39 (1979): 32–39.

Morita Ryūsen 森田竜僊. “Mikkyō no jōdo shisō” 密教の浄土思想. *Mikkyō kenkyū* 密教研究6 (1921): 15–45.

Moriyama Shōshin 守山聖真. *Shingonshū nenpyō* 真言宗年表. Tokyo: Kokusho kankōkai, 1973.

——. *Tachikawa jakyō to sono shakaiteki haikei no kenkyū* 立川邪教とその社会的背景の研究. Tokyo: Rokuya-en 鹿野苑, 1965.

Morrell, Robert. *Early Kamakura Buddhism: A Minority Report.* Berkeley, CA: Asian Humanities Press, 1987.

——. *Sand and Pebbles (Shasekishu): The Tales of Muju Ichien, a Voice for Pluralism in Kamakura Buddhism.* Albany: State University of New York Press, 1985.

——. “Shingon’s Kakukai on the Immanence of the Pure Land.” *Japanese Journal of Religious Studies* 11, no. 2–3 (1984): 195–220.

Motoyama Kōju 元山公寿. “Himitsu nenbutsu ni tsuite” 秘密念仏について. *Gendai mikkyō* 現代密教 11, no. 12 (1999): 35–48.

Muller, Charles, ed. *Digital Dictionary of Buddhism.* Updated December 31, 2021. http://buddhism-dict.net/ddb.

Muller, Wilhelm K. “Shingon-Mysticism: Śubhākarasiṁha and I-hsing’s Commentary to the Mahāvairocana-sūtra, Chapter One, an Annotated Translation.” PhD diss., University of California, Los Angeles, 1976.

Murakami Hiroko 村上弘子. *Kōyasan shinkō no seiritsu to tenkai* 高野山信仰の成立と展開. Tokyo: Yūzankaku, 2009.

Murti, T. R. V. *Central Philosophy of Buddhism: A Study of Mādhyamika System.* Rev. ed. London: Allen and Unwin, 1960.

Mus, Paul. *Barabuḍur: Sketch of a History of Buddhism Based on Archaeological Criticism of the Texts.* Translated by Alexander W. Macdonald. New Delhi: Indira Gandhi National Centre for the Arts: Sterling, 1998.

Nagasaki, Ken 長崎健. “Nankai rurōki” 南海流浪記. *Kokubungaku kaishaku to kanshō* 国文学解釈と観賞 54, no. 12 (1989): 82–86.

Naitō Hide 内藤湖南. “Komikkyōten gaisetsu” 古密教展概説. In Nara Kokuritsu Hakubutsukan, *Komikkyō,* pp. 130–144.

Nakamikado Keikyō 中御門敬教. “Muryōju nyorai kengyō kuyō giki” 無量寿如来観行供養儀軌. In *Jōdokyōtenseki mokuroku* 浄土教典籍目録, pp. 27–28. Kyoto: Bukkyō Daigaku sōgō kenkyūjo 仏教大学総合研究所, 2011.

Nakamura, Hajime. *Indian Buddhism: A Survey with Bibliographical Notes.* Delhi: Motilal Banarsidass, 1987.

Nakamura Honnen 中村本然 (Masafumi Nakamura 中村正文). “Dōhan ki ‘Bodaishin ron dangi ki’ ni tsuite’” 道範記『菩提心論談義記』について. In *Mandara no shosō to bunka: Yoritomi Motohiro hakase kanreki kinen ronbunshū* マンダラの諸相と文化: 頼富本宏博士還暦記念論文集, edited by Yoritomi

Motohiro hakushi kanshiki kinen ronbunshū kankōka 頼富本宏博士還暦記念論文集刊行会, pp. 395–430. Kyoto: Hōzōkan 法藏館, 2005.

——. "Dōhan ki 'Shoshintongaku shō' ni tsuite" 道範記『初心頓覚鈔』について. In *Mikkyō to shobunka no kōryū: Yamasaki Taikō kyōju koki kinen ronbunshū* 密教と諸文化の交流: 山崎泰広教授古稀記念論文集, edited by Yamasaki Taikō kyōju koki kinen ronbunshū kankōkai 山崎泰広教授古稀記念論文集刊行会, pp. 151–184. Kyoto: Bunkōdo, 1998.

——. "Dōhan no Jōdo kan" 道範の浄土観. *Kōyasan Daigaku ronsō* 高野山大学論叢 29 (1994): 149–202.

——. *Dōhan no seibotsunen nitsuite* 道範の生没年について. *Kōyasan Daigaku Mikkyō bunka kenkyūjo* 高野山大学密教文化研究所 (blog). December 15, 2011. Accessed May 17, 2012. http://www.koyasanu.ac.jp/mikkyobunka/blog/diary.cgi?field=9.

——. "Dōhan sen 'Kongōchō kyō kaidai kanchū' ni tsuite" 道範撰 『金剛頂経開題勘註』 について. *Mikkyō bunka kenkyūjo kiyō* 密教文化研究所紀要 21 (2008): 29–52.

——. "Jōhen sōzu no shinkō no ichi sokumen ni tsuite" 静遍僧都の信仰の一側面について. *Mikkyō gakkaihō* 密教学会報 31 (1992): 1–49.

——. "Kakuhon bō Dōhan no seibotsu nen ni tsuite" 覚本房道範の生没年について. *Sangaku shugen* 山岳修験 60 (2017): 121–136.

——. "Kenmitsu nikyōron tekagami shō ni tsuite, tokuni 'Shakumakaenron' kaishaku ni kansuru shomondai wo chūshin to shite" 『顕密二教論手鏡鈔』について特に『釈摩訶衍論』解釈に関する諸問題を中心として. In *Bukkyō kyōri shisō no kenkyū: Satō Ryūken hakushi koki kinen ronbunshū* 仏教教理思想の研究: 佐藤隆賢博士古稀記念論文集, edited by Satō Ryūken hakushi koki kinen ronbunshū kankōkai 佐藤隆賢博士古稀記念論文集刊行会, pp. 333–263 (R). Tokyo: Sankibō busshorin, 1998.

——. "Senjaku hongan nenbutsushū ni tokareru gogyaku jūzai ni tsuite" 『選択本願念仏集』に説かれる五逆重罪について. *Indogaku Bukkyōgaku kenkyū* 印度学仏教学研究 116 (2008): 129–136 (R).

——. "Shakumakaenron niokeru huni makaenhō ni tsuite—kenge to mike no chūshakusho no hikaku wo chūshin toshite" 『釈摩訶衍論』における不二摩訶衍法 不二摩訶衍法について一顕 家と密家の註釈疏の比較を中心として. *Mikkyōgaku kenkyū* 密教学研究 15 (1983): 129–144.

——. "Shingon kyōgaku ni okeru shōshikan" 真言教学における生死観. *Nihon Bukkyōgaku nenpō* 日本仏教学会年報 75 (2010): 169–184 (R).

——. *Shingon mikkyō ni okeru anjinron* 真言密教における安心論. Kōyasan, Japan: Kōyasan University, 2003.

——. "'Shōji jissō gi shō' (Dōhan ki) ni tokareru nyogi gensetsu ni tsuite—sono ichi, 'Shaku makaen ron' to Kūkai no chosaku ni miru nyogi gensetsu wo chūshin toshite—" 『声字実相義抄』(道範記) に説かれる如義言説について—その一、『釈摩訶衍論』と空海の著作にみる如義言説を中心として—. *Mikkyō bunka* 密教文化 203 (1999): 1–20.

——. "Zenrinji Jōhen no sōmokuhihō jōbutsu ni tsuite" 禅林寺静遍の草木非情成仏説について. *Nihon Bukkyōgakkai nenpō* 日本仏教学会年報 68 (2003): 281–304.

——. "Zenrinji Jōhen no teishōshita kyōgaku ni tsuite" 禅林寺静遍の提唱した教学について. Kōyasan Daigaku ronsō 高野山大学論叢 26 (1991): 73–97.

Nakano Satoshi 中野聡. *Nara jidai no Amida nyoraizō to jōdo shinkō* 奈良時代の阿弥陀如来像と浄土信仰. Tokyo: Bensei shuppan 勉誠出版, 2013.

Nara Hiromoto 奈良弘元. "Kōgyō daishi Kakuban izen no Kōyasan jōdokyō" 興教大師覚鑁以前の高野山浄土教. In *Kōgyō daishi Kakuban Kenkyū: Kōgyō daishi happyaku gojūen goonkikinen ronshū* 興教大師覚鑁研究: 興教大師八百五十年御遠忌記念論集, edited by Kōgyō Daishi Kenkyū Ronshū Henshū Iinkai 興教大師研究論集編集委員会, pp. 683–698. Tokyo: Shunjūsha, 1992.

——. *Shoki Eizan Jōdokyō no kenkyū* 初期叡山浄土教の研究. Tokyo: Shunjūsha, 2002.

——. "Shoki Kōyasan Jōdokyō ni tsuite" 初期高野山浄土教について. *Seshin kagaku* 精神科学 35 (1996): 35–52 (L).

Nara Kokuritsu Hakabutsukan 奈良国立博物館, ed. *Jōdo mandara—gokuraku jōdo to raigō no roman—* 浄土曼荼羅—極楽浄土と来迎のロマン—. Nara: Nara kokuritsu hakubutsukan, 1983.

——, ed. *Komikkyō: Nihon mikkyō no taidō* 古密教-日本密教の胎動. Nara: Nara kokuritsu hakubutsukan, 2005.

Nasu Kazuo 那須 一雄. "Hōnen to sono monka ni okeru 'senju' 'zasshu' rikai—tokuni Ryūkan, Shōkū, Jōhen ni tsuite" 法然とその門下における「専修・雑修」理解—特に隆寛・証空・静遍について. *Shinshū kenkyū* 眞宗研究 52 (2008): 42–62.

——. "Jōhen to Hōnen Jōdokyō" 静遍と法然浄土教. *Indogaku Bukkyōgaku kenkyū* 印度学仏教学研究 106 (2005): 80–85.

——. "Myōhen kyōgaku to Jōhen kyōgaku" 明遍教学と静遍教学. *Shūkyo kenkyū* 宗教研究 363 (2010): 359–360 (R).

Nattier, Jan. *A Few Good Men: The Bodhisattva Path according to the Inquiry of Ugra (Ugraparipṛcchā).* Honolulu: University of Hawai'i Press, 2003.

——. "The Names Amitābha/Amitāyus in Early Chinese Buddhist Translations." *Sokadaigaku Kokusai bukkyōgaku kōdō kenkyūjo nenpō* 創価大学国際仏教学高等研究所年報 10 (2006): 359–394.

——. "The Realm of Aksobhya: A Missing Piece in the History of Pure Land Buddhism." *Journal of the International Association of Buddhist Studies* 23 (2000): 71–102.

Needham, Rodney. "Polythetic Classification." *Man* 10, no. 3 (1975): 349–369.

Nemoto Seiji 根本誠二. *Nara Bukkyō to Mikkyō* 奈良仏教と密教. Tokyo: Koshi shoin 高志書院, 2011.

——. *Nara jidai no sōryo to shakai* 奈良時代の僧侶と社会. Tokyo: Yūzankaku 雄山閣, 1999.

Newman, John R. "The Outer Wheel of Time: Vajrayāna Buddhist Cosmology in the Kālacakra Tantra." PhD diss., University of Wisconsin, 1987.

Nicoloff, Philip L. *Sacred Kōyasan: A Pilgrimage to the Mountain Temple of Saint Kōbō Daishi and the Great Sun Buddha.* Albany: State University of New York Press, 2007.

Ninnaji Konbyōshi Kozōshi Kenkyūkai 仁和寺紺表紙小双紙研究会, ed. *Shukaku hosshinnō no girei sekai: Ninnajizō konbyōshi kozōshi no kenkyū* 守覚法親王の儀礼世界: 仁和寺蔵紺表紙小双紙の研究. 2 vols. Tokyo: Bensei shuppan 勉誠出版, 1995.

Nishi Yayoi 西弥生. *Chūsei mikkyō jiin to shuhō* 中世密教寺院と修法. Tokyo: Bensei shuppansha 勉誠出版, 2008.

Norman, Kenneth Roy. *Pali Literature: Including the Canonical Literature in Prakrit and Sanskrit of All the Hinayana Schools of Buddhism.* Vol. 7, pt. 2 of *A History of Indian Literature: Buddhist and Jaina Literature,* edited by Jan Gonda. Wiesbaden: O. Harrassowitz, 1983.

Ogiwara Unrai 荻原雲来, ed. *Kan'yaku taishō bonwa daijiten* 漢譯對照梵和大辭典. Tokyo: Kan'yaku taishō bonwa daijiten hensan kankōkai, 1940–1943.

Oishio Chihoro 追塩千尋. *Chūsei no nanto bukkyō* 中世の南都仏教. Tokyo: Yoshikawa kōbunkan, 1995.

Ōkubo Ryōshun 大久保良峻. "Godai'in Annen no kokudokan" 五大院安然の国土観. *Nihon Bukkyō gakukai nenpō* 日本仏教学会年報 58 (1993): 155–170.

——. *Taimitsu kyōgaku no kenkyū* 台密教学の研究. Kyoto: Hōzōkan, 2004.

——. *Tendai kyōgaku to hongaku shisō* 天台教学と本覚思想. Kyoto: Hōzōkan, 1998.

——. "Tendai mikkyō no kenmitsu setsu" 天台密教の顕密説. In *Buppō sō ronshū: Fukuhara Ryūzen sensei kofukinen ronshū* 佛法僧論集: 福原隆善先生古稀記念論集, pp. 227–244. Tokyo: Sankibō busshorin, 2013.

Ōmori Gijō 大森義成. *Jisshu Shingonshū no mikkyō to shugyō* 実修真言宗の密教と修行. Tokyo: Gakken, 2010.

Ōmura Seigai 大村西崖. *Mikkyō hattatsushi* 密教発達志. 5 vols. Tokyo: Bussho kankōkai Zuzōbu Kokusho kankōkai, 1918.

Ooms, Herman. *Imperial Politics and Symbolics in Ancient Japan: The Tenmu Dynasty, 650–800.* Honolulu: University of Hawai'i Press, 2009.

Orlando, Raffaello. "A Study of Chinese Documents Concerning the Life of the Tantric Buddhist Patriarch Amoghavajra (A.D. 705–774)." PhD diss., Princeton University, 1981.

Orzech, Charles D. "After Amoghavajra: Esoteric Buddhism in the Late Tang." In Orzech, Sørensen, and Payne, *Esoteric Buddhism and the Tantras in East Asia,* pp. 315–228.

——. "Cosmology in Action: Recursive Cosmology, Soteriology, and Authority in *Chen-yen* Buddhism with Special Reference to the Monk Pu-k'ung." PhD diss., University of Chicago, 1986.

——. "Esoteric Buddhism in the Tang: From Atikūṭa to Amoghavajra (651–780). In Orzech, Sørensen, and Payne, *Esoteric Buddhism and the Tantras in East Asia,* pp. 263–285.

——. "Esoteric Buddhism under the Song: An Overview." In Orzech, Sørensen, and Payne, *Esoteric Buddhism and the Tantras in East Asia,* pp. 421–430.

——. "The 'Great Teaching of Yoga': The Chinese Appropriation of the Tantras, and the Question of Esoteric Buddhism." *Journal of Chinese Religion* 34 (2006): 29–78.

——. "Introduction: Esoteric Buddhism and the Tantras in East Asia: Some Methodological Considerations." In Orzech, Sørensen, and Payne, *Esoteric Buddhism and the Tantras in East Asia,* pp. 3–6.

——. "The Legend of the Iron *Stūpa.*" In *Buddhism in Practice,* edited by Donald S. Lopez Jr., pp. 314–317. Princeton, NJ: Princeton University Press, 1995.

——. "Mandalas on the Move: Reflections from Chinese Esoteric Buddhism, circa 800 CE." *Journal of International Association of Buddhist Studies* 19 (1996): 209–244.

——. "On Esoteric Buddhism in China: A Working Definition." In Orzech, Sørensen, and Payne, *Esoteric Buddhism and the Tantras in East Asia,* pp. 155–175.

——. *Politics and Transcendent Wisdom: The Scripture for Humane Kings in the Creation of Chinese Buddhism.* Hermeneutics: Studies in the History of Religions. University Park: Pennsylvania State University Press, 1998.

——. "Saving the Burning-Mouth Hungry Ghost." In *Religions of China in Practice,* edited by Donald S. Lopez Jr., pp. 278–283. Princeton, NJ: Princeton University Press, 1996.

——. "Seeing Chen-yen Buddhism: Traditional Scholarship and the Vajrayāna in China." *History of Religions* 29 (1989): 87–114.

——. "A Tang Esoteric Manual for Rebirth in the Pure Land." In *Path of No Path: Contemporary Studies in Pure Land Buddhism Honoring Roger Corless,* edited by Richard K. Payne, pp. 31–55. Berkeley, CA: Institute of Buddhist Studies and Numata Center for Buddhist Translation and Research, 2009.

——. "Translation of *Tantras* and Other Esoteric Buddhist Scriptures." In Orzech, Sørensen, and Payne, *Esoteric Buddhism and the Tantras in East Asia,* pp. 439–450.

——. "The Trouble with *Tantra* in China: Reflections on Method and History." In *Religion and Society: Transformations and Transfer of Tantra in Asia and Beyond,* edited by István Keul, pp. 303–328. Hawthorne, NY: Walter de Gruyter, 2012.

Orzech, Charles D., Richard K. Payne, and Henrik H. Sørensen. "Introduction: Esoteric Buddhism and the *Tantras* in East Asia: Some Methodological Considerations." In Orzech, Sørensen, and Payne, *Esoteric Buddhism and the Tantras in East Asia,* pp. 3–18.

Osabe Kazuo 長部和雄. *Tōdai mikkyōshi zakkō* 唐代密教史雑考. Kobe: Kōbe Shōka Daigaku gakujutsu kenkyūkai, 1971.

Ōshika Shinō 大鹿眞央. "Chūsei Tōmitsu kyōgaku ni okeru sankōdan kaishaku: Dōhan ni okeru daisankōdan kaishaku wo chūshin ni" 中世東密教学における三劫段解釈: 道範における第三劫段解釈を中心に. *Indogaku Bukkyōgaku kenkyū* 印度學佛教學研究 60, no. 1 (2011): 115–118.

——. "Chūsei Tōmitsu kyōgaku ni okeru shohōmyōdō no hensen: Daihachi jushin to no kankei wo chūshin ni" 中世東密教学における初法明道の変遷: 第八住心との関係を中心に, *Indogaku Bukkyōgaku kenkyū* 印度學佛教學研究 61, no. 1 (2012): 40–43.

——. "Chūsei Tōmitsu kyōgaku ni okeru shukuzen kaishaku no tenkai: Dōhan no shukuzen kaishaku wo chūshin ni" 中世東密教学における宿善解釈の展開: 道範の宿善解釈を中心に. *Chizan gakuhō* 智山學報 63 (2014): 131–149.

——. "Chūsei Tōmitsu kyōgaku ni okeru Yugikyō kaishaku no tenkai" 中世東密教学における『瑜祇経』解釈の展開. *Indogaku Bukkyōgaku kenkyū* 印度學佛教學研究 63, no. 1 (2014): 92–96.

——. "Tōmitsu ni okeru shochisokugyokusetsu no tenkai" 東密における初地卽極説の展開. *Tōyō no shisō to shūkyō* 東洋の思想と宗教29 (2012): 71–89.

Osto, Douglas. "Proto-tantric Elements in the Gandhavyuha-sūtra*." *Journal of Religious History* 33, no. 2 (2009): 165–177.

Ōtsuka Nobuo 大塚伸夫. "Fukūkensaku jinpen shingon kyō no jumon: Tayōna jumonkeitai ga mirareru kyōten" 不空羂索神変真言経の呪文: 多様な呪文形態が見られる経典. In Hisao Takahashi et al., *Shoki mikkyō,* pp. 121–133.

——. *Indo shoki mikkyō seiritsu katei no kenkyū* インド初期密教成立過程の研究. Tokyo: Shunjusha, 2013.

——. "Shoki mikkyō no zentaizō: Shoki mikkyō no hōga kara tenkai, kakuritsu he" 初期密教経典の全体像: 初期密教の萌芽から展開・確立へ. In Hisao Takahashi et al., *Shoki mikkyō,* pp. 5–21.

Ōtsuka Norihiro 大塚紀弘. *Chūsei zenritsu bukkyōron* 中世禅律仏教論. Tokyo: Yamakawa shuppansha, 2009.

——. "Chūsei 'zenritsu' Bukkyō to 'zenkyōritsu' jūshūkan" 中世「禅律」仏教と「禅教律」十宗観. *Shigaku zasshi* 史学雑誌 112, no. 9 (2003): 1477–1512.

Ōyama Kōjun 大山 公淳. "Dōhan daitoku no 'Kōya hiji'" 道範大徳の『高野秘事』. *Mikkyō bunka* 11 (1923): 116–135, 136–154.

Park, Jin Y. *Buddhism and Postmodernity: Zen, Huayan, and the Possibility of Buddhist Postmodern Ethics.* Lanham, MD: Lexington Books, 2008.

Pas, Julian. *Visions of Sukhāvatī, Shan-Tao's Commentary on the Kuan Wu-Liang-Shou-Fo Ching.* Albany: State University of New York Press, 1995.

Patrul Rinpoche. *The Words of My Perfect Teacher.* Translated by the Padmakara Translation Group. 2nd ed. Boston: Shambhala, 1998.

Payne, Richard K. "*Ajikan:* Ritual and Meditation in the Shingon Tradition." In Payne, *Re-visioning "Kamakura" Buddhism,* pp. 219–248.

——. "Aparamitāyus: '*Tantra*' *and* 'Pure Land' in Late Medieval Indian Buddhism?" *Pacific World,* 3rd. ser., 9 (2007): 273–308.

——. "The Cult of Arya Aparamitayus: Proto-Pure Land Buddhism in the Context of Indian Mahayana." *Pure Land* 13, no. 14 (1997): 19–36.

——. "The Fourfold Training in Japanese Esoteric Buddhism." In Orzech, Sørensen, and Payne, *Esoteric Buddhism and the Tantras in East Asia,* pp. 1024–1028.

——. "From Vedic India to Buddhist Japan: Continuities and Discontinuities in Esoteric Ritual." In Orzech, Sørensen, and Payne, *Esoteric Buddhism and the Tantras in East Asia,* pp. 1040–1054.

——. "Hiding in Plain Sight: The Invisibility of the Shingon Mission to the United States." In *Buddhist Missionaries in the Era of Globalization,* edited by Linda Learman, pp. 101–122. Honolulu: University of Hawai'i Press, 2005.

——. "Introduction." In Payne, *Tantric Buddhism in East Asia,* pp. 1–31.

——. *Language Conducive to Awakening: Categories of Language Use in East Asian Buddhism, with Particular Attention to the Vajrayāna Tradition.* Buddhismus-Studien 2. Düsseldorf: Hauses der Japanischen Kulter, 1998.

——, ed. *Re-visioning "Kamakura" Buddhism.* Honolulu: University of Hawai'i Press, 1998.

——. "Ritual Syntax and Cognitive Theory." *Pacific World,* 3rd ser., 6 (2004): 195–227.

——. "The Shingon *Ajikan:* Diagrammatic Analysis of Ritual Syntax." *Religion* 29 (1999): 215–229.

——. "Shingon Services for the Dead." In Tanabe, *Religions of Japan in Practice,* pp. 159–165.

——. "The Shingon Subordinating Fire Offering for Amitābha: 'Amida Kei Ai Goma.'" *Pacific World,* 3rd ser., 8 (2006): 191–236.

——, ed. *Tantric Buddhism in East Asia.* Somerville, MA: Wisdom, 2006.

——. *The Tantric Ritual of Japan: Feeding the Gods—the Shingon Fire Ritual.* Śata-Pitaka Series no. 365. New Delhi: International Academy of Indian Culture and Aditya Prakashan, 1991.

——. "Tongues of Flame: Homologies in the Tantric *Homa.*" In *The Roots of Tantra,* edited by Katherine Anne Harper and Robert L. Brown, pp. 193–212. New York: State University of New York Press, 2002.

Payne, Richard K., and Kenneth Tanaka, eds. *Approaching the Land of Bliss: Religious Praxis in the Cult of Amitābha.* Honolulu: University of Hawai'i Press, 2004.

Piggot, Joan R. *The Emergence of Japanese Kingship.* Palo Alto, CA: Stanford University Press, 1997.

Pinte, Klaus L. R. A. "Mui-sanzō Zen'yō/Wu-wei san-ts'ang Ch'an-yao 無畏三藏禅要: Een Vajrayāna-tekst (T. vol. XVIII, nr. 917, pp. 942b–946a)." Master's thesis, Ghent University, 2004.

Porcu, Elisabetta. *Pure Land Buddhism in Modern Japanese Culture.* Leiden: E. J. Brill, 2008.

Proffitt, Aaron P. "Dōhan no himitsu nenbutsu shisō: Kenmitsu bunka to Mikkyō Jōdokyō" 道範の秘密念仏思想: 顕密文化と密教浄土教. *Journal of World Buddhist Cul*tures 1 (2018): 117–138.

——. "Dōhan's Compendium on the Secret Nenbutsu: Fascicle One." In *Pure Lands in Asian Texts and Contexts: An Anthology,* edited by Georgios T. Halkias and Richard K. Payne, pp. 269–315. Honolulu: University of Hawai'i Press, 2019.

——. "Mysteries of Speech and Breath: Dōhan's (1179–1252) Himitsu nenbutsu shō 秘密念仏抄 and Esoteric Pure Land Buddhism." PhD diss., University of Michigan, 2015.

——. "Nenbutsu Mandala Visualization in Dōhan's *Himitsu nenbutsu shō:* An Investigation into Medieval Japanese Vajrayāna Pure Land." *Pacific World,* 3rd ser., 15 (2013): 153–170.

——. "Nenbutsu Orthodoxies in Medieval Japan." *Japanese Journal of Religious Studies* 47, no. 1 (2020): 135–160.

——. "Taking the Vajrayāna to Sukhāvatī: Reflections on the Study of Esoteric Pure Land Buddhism." In *Methods in Buddhist Studies: Essays in Honor of Richard Payne,* edited by Scott A. Mitchell and Natalie E. F. Quli, pp. 54–64. New York: Bloomsbury Academic, 2019.

Pruden, Leo M., and Paul L. Swanson, trans. *The Essentials of the Eight Traditions/The Candle of the Latter Dharma.* Berkeley, CA: Numata Center for Buddhist Translation and Research, 1994.

——, trans. *The Essentials of the Vinaya Tradition/The Collected Teachings of the Tendai Lotus School.* Berkeley, CA: Numata Center for Buddhist Translation and Research, 1995.

Quinter, David. "Creating Bodhisattvas: Eison, Hinin, and the 'Living Mañjuśrī.'" *Monumenta Nipponica* 62 (2007): 437–458.

———. "The Shingon Ritsu School and the Mañjuśri Cult in the Kamakura Period: From Eison to Monkan." PhD diss., Stanford University, 2006.

Rambelli, Fabio. *Buddhist Materiality: A Cultural History of Objects in Japanese Buddhism.* Palo Alto, CA: Stanford University Press, 2007.

———. "In Search of the Buddha's Intention, Raiyu and the Worlds of Medieval Shingon Learned Monks." In *Shingi Shingon kyōgaku no kenkyū: Raiyu sōjō shichihyakunen goenki kinen ronshū* 新義真言教学の研究: 頼瑜僧正七百年御遠忌記念論集, edited by Sanpa Gōdō Kinen Ronshū Henshū Iinkai 三派合同記念論集編集委員会, pp. 35–64. Tokyo: Daizō shuppan 大蔵出版, 2002.

———. "Tantric Buddhism and Chinese Thought in East Asia." In *Tantra in Practice,* edited by David Gordon White, pp. 361–380. Princeton, NJ: Princeton University Press, 2000.

———. "True Words, Silence, and the Adamantine Dance: On Japanese Mikkyō and the Formation of the Shingon Discourse." *Japanese Journal of Religious Studies* 21, no. 4 (1994): 373–405.

———. *Vegetal Buddhas: Ideological Effects of Japanese Buddhist Doctrines on the Salvation of Inanimate Beings.* Kyoto: Scuola Italian di Studi sull' Asia Orientale, 2001.

Rasmussen, William Brian. "An Annotated Transcription and Translation of the Gilgit Manuscript of the Ajitasena-vyākaraṇa-nirdeśana-mahāyāna-sūtra." Master's thesis, University of Texas, 1995.

Rawlinson, Andrew. "The Position of the *Aṣṭasashasrikạ̄ Prajñāpāramitā* in the Development of Early Mahāyāna." In *Prajñāpāramitā and Related Systems: Studies in Honour of Edward Conze,* edited by Lewis Lancaster, pp. 3–34. Berkeley: University of California Press, 1977.

Ray, Reginald A. *Buddhist Saints in India: A Study in Buddhist Values and Orientations.* New York: Oxford University Press, 1999.

Reader, Ian, and George J. Tanabe Jr. *Practically Religious: Worldly Benefits and the Common Religion of Japan.* Honolulu: University of Hawai'i Press, 1998.

Reider, Noriko T. "Animating Objects: *Tsukumogami ki* and the Medieval Illustration of Shingon Truth." *Japanese Journal of Religious Studies* 36, no. 2 (2009): 231–257.

Reischauer, Edwin O., trans. *Ennin's Diary: The Record of a Pilgrimage to China in Search of the Law.* New York: Ronald Press, 1955.

———. *Ennin's Travels in T'ang China.* New York: Ronald Press, 1955.

Reis-Habito, Maria. "The Amoghapāśa Kalparāja Sūtra: A Historical and Analytical Study." *Studies in Central and East Asian Religions* 11 (1999): 39–67.

——. "The Great Compassion Dhāraṇī." In *The Esoteric Buddhist Tradition: Selected Papers from the 1989 SBS Conference,* edited by Henrik H. Sørensen, pp. 31–49. Copenhagen: University of Copenhagen, 1994.

——. "The Repentance Ritual of the Thousand-Armed Guanyin." *Studies in Central and East Asian Religions* 4 (1991): 42–51.

Rhodes, Robert F. "The Beginnings of Pure Land Buddhism in Japan: From Its Introduction through the Nara Period." *Japanese Religions* 31, no. 1 (2006): 1–22.

Rhys Davids, T. W., and William B. Stede, eds. *The Pali Texts Society's Pali-English Dictionary.* 1925. Reprint, London: Luzac, 1966.

Rosenfield, John M. *Portraits of Chōgen: The Transformation of Buddhist Art in Early Medieval Japan.* Leiden: Brill, 2011.

Rowell, Teresina. "The Background and Early Use of the Buddha-kṣetra Concept. Chapter IV, with Appendices and Bibliography. (Concluded)." *Eastern Buddhist* 7 (1936–1939): 132–176.

——. "The Background and Early Use of the Buddha-kṣetra Concept. Chapters Two and Three." *Eastern Buddhist* 6, no. 4 (1932–1935): 379–431.

——. "The Background and Early Use of the Buddha-kṣetra Concept. Introduction and Chapter One." *Eastern Buddhist* 6, no. 3 (1932–1935): 199–246.

Ruegg, David. "Aspects of the Study of the (Earlier) Indian Mahāyāna." *Journal of the International Association of Buddhist Studies* 27, no. 1 (2004): 3–62.

Ruppert, Brian D. "Constructing Histories, Thinking Ritual Gatherings, and Rereading: 'Native' Religion. A Review of Recent Books Published in Japanese on Premodern Japanese Religion (Part Two)." *Japanese Journal of Religious Studies* 40, no. 2 (2013): 355–375.

——. "Dharma Prince Shukaku and the Esoteric Buddhist Culture of Sacred Works (Shōgyō) in Medieval Japan." In Orzech, Sørensen, and Payne, *Esoteric Buddhism and the Tantras in East Asia,* pp. 794–802.

——. *Jewel in the Ashes: Buddha Relics and Power in Early Medieval Japan.* Cambridge, MA: Harvard University Asia Center, 2000.

——. "Pearl in the Shrine." *Japanese Journal of Religious Studies* 29 (2002): 2–11.

Sakade Yoshinobu 坂出祥伸. "Shoki mikkyō to Dōkyō tono kōshō" 初期密教と道教との交渉. In Tachikawa Musashi and Yoritomi Motohiro, *Chūgoku mikkyō,* pp. 153–172.

Sakai Shiro 酒井紫朗. "Kōbō Daishi no *Chūjukankyōshi* ni tsuite" 弘法大師の中寿感興詩並序について. *Mikkyō bunka* 密教文化 147 (1984): 13–25.

Sakauchi Tatsuo 坂内龍雄. *Shingon darani* 眞言陀羅尼. Tokyo: Hirakawa shuppansha, 1981.

Sakuma Ruriko 佐久間留理子. "Henge Kannon kyōten" 変化観音経典. In Hisao Takahashi et al., *Shoki mikkyō,* pp. 77–89.

Samuel, Geoffrey. *The Origins of Yoga and Tantra: Indic Religions to the Thirteenth Century.* Cambridge: Cambridge University Press, 2008.

Sanford, James H. "The Abominable Tachikawa Skull Ritual." *Monumenta Nipponica* 46 (1991): 1–20.

——. "Amida's Secret Life: Kakuban's Amida hishaku." In Payne and Tanaka, *Approaching the Land of Bliss,* pp. 120–138.

——. "Breath of Life: The Esoteric Nembutsu." In Payne, *Tantric Buddhism in East Asia,* pp. 161–190.

——. "Wind, Waters, Stūpas, Mandalas: Fetal Buddhahood in Shingon." *Japanese Journal of Religious Studies* 24 (1997): 1–38.

Sango, Asuka. "Buddhist Debate and the Production and Transmission of 'Shōgyō' in Medieval Japan." *Japanese Journal of Religious Studies* 39, no. 2 (2012): 241–273.

——. "Making Debate Hell: Knowledge and Power in Japanese Buddhist Ritual." *History of Religions* 50, no. 3 (2011): 283–314.

Sasaki Daiju 佐々木大樹. "San darani" 三陀羅尼. In Hisao Takahashi et al., *Shoki mikkyō,* pp. 166–177.

Sasaki Kaoru 佐々木馨. *Chusei bukkyō to Kamakura bakufu* 中世仏教と鎌倉幕府. Tokyo: Yoshikawa kōbunsha, 1997.

——. *Chūsei kokka no shūkyō kōzō: Taisei bukkyō to taiseigai bukkyō no sōkoku* 中世国家の宗教構造—体制仏教と体制外仏教の相剋. Tokyo: Yoshikawa kōbunkan, 1988.

Saso, Michael. *Homa Rites and Mandala Meditation in Tendai Buddhism.* New Delhi: Motilal Banarsidass, 1991.

——. "*Kuden:* The Oral Hermeneutics of Tendai Tantric Buddhism." *Japanese Journal of Religious Studies* 14 (1987): 235–246.

——. *Tantric Art and Meditation: The Tendai Tradition.* Honolulu: University of Hawai'i Press, 1990.

Satō Hiroo 佐藤弘夫. *Kamakura Bukkyō* 鎌倉仏教. Tokyo: Daisan Bunmeisha, 1994.

——. *Kami, hotoke, ōken no chūsei* 神·仏·王権の中世. Kyoto: Hōzōkan, 1998.

Satō Mona 佐藤もな. "Chūsei Shingonshū ni okeru jōdo shisō kaishaku: Dōhan *Himitsu nenbutsu shō* o megutte" 中世真言宗における浄土思想解釈—道範『秘密念仏抄』をめぐって. *Indo tetsugaku bukkyōgaku kenkyū* インド哲学仏教学研究 9 (2002): 80–92.

——. "Dōhan cho Himitsu nenbutsu shō inyō bunken shutten chūki" 道範著『秘密念仏抄』引用文献出典注記. *Bukkyō bunka kenkyū ronshū* 仏教文化研究論集 4 (2000): 130–141 (L).

——. "Dōhan cho *Jōō shō* ni kansuru ichikōsatsu tōji kanchiin shozōhon wo chūshin toshite" 道範著『貞応抄』に関する一考察—東寺観智院所蔵本を中

心として. *Indogaku Bukkyōgaku kenkyū* 印度学仏教学研究 102, no. 51–2 (2003): 655–657.

——. "Dōhan ni kan suru kisoteki kenkyū—denki shiryō wo chūshin toshite" 道範に関する基礎的研究—伝記史料を中心として. *Bukkyō bunka kenkyū ronshū* 仏教文化研究論集 7 (2003): 85–95 (L).

——. "Dōhan no himitsu nenbutsu shisō—myōgokan wo chūshin toshite" 道範の秘密念仏思想-名号観を中心として. *Indogaku bukkyōgaku kenkyū* 印度学仏教学研究 98, no. 49–2 (2001): 108–110.

——. "Dōhan no kyōshugi ni tsuite" 道範の教主義について. *Nihon Bukkyō sōgō kenkyū* 日本仏教綜合研究 5 (2006): 67–78 (R).

——. "Jippan Byōchū shūgyō ki no shinshutsu shahon nitsuite" 実範『病中修行記』の新出写本について. *Indogaku Bukkyōgaku kenkyū* 印度学仏教学研究 114, no. 56–2 (2008): 5–9 (R).

——. "Shingon kyōgaku niokeru jōdo kan, Dōhan no baai" 真言教学における浄土観—道範の場合. *Shūkyō kenkyū* 宗教研究 331, no. 75–4 (2002): 214–215.

Satō Tetsuei 佐藤哲英. *Eizan Jōdokyō no kenkyū* 叡山浄土教の研究. 2 vols. Kyoto: Hyakkaen, 1979.

Saunders, E. Dale. *Mudrā: A Study of Symbolic Gestures in Japanese Buddhist Sculpture.* Princeton, NJ: Princeton University Press, 1960.

Sawada Mizuho 澤田瑞穂. *Chūgoku no juhō* 中国の呪法. Tokyo: Hirakawa shuppansha, 1984.

Scheid, Bernhard, and Mark Teeuwen, eds. *The Culture of Secrecy in Japanese Religion.* London: Routledge, 2006.

Schopen, Gregory. *Bones, Stones, and Buddhist Monks: Collected Papers on the Archaeology, Epigraphy and Texts of Monastic Buddhism in India.* Honolulu: University of Hawai'i Press, 1997.

——. *Buddhist Monks and Business Matters: Still More Papers on Monastic Buddhism in India.* Honolulu: University of Hawai'i Press, 2004.

——. *Figments and Fragments of Mahāyāna Buddhism in India: More Collected Papers.* Honolulu: University of Hawai'i Press, 2005.

——. "Kuṣān Image of Amitābha and the Character of the Early Mahāyāna in India." In *Figments and Fragments of Mahāyāna Buddhism in India,* pp. 247–277.

——. "The Mahāyāna and the Middle Period in Indian Buddhism: Through a Chinese Looking-Glass." In *Figments and Fragments of Mahāyāna Buddhism in India,* pp. 3–25.

——. "On Sending the Monks Back to Their Books: Cult and Conservation in Early Mahāyāna Buddhism." In *Figments and Fragments of Mahāyāna Buddhism in India,* pp. 108–153.

——. "Sukhāvatī as a Generalized Religious Goal in Sanskrit Mahāyāna Sūtra Literature." In *Figments and Fragments of Mahāyāna Buddhism in India,* pp. 154–189.

Sharf, Robert H. "Appendix: On Esoteric Buddhism in China." In *Coming to Terms with Chinese Buddhism: A Reading of the Treasure Store Treatise,* pp. 263–278. Honolulu: University of Hawai'i Press, 2002.

——. *Coming to Terms with Chinese Buddhism: A Reading of the Treasure Store Treatise.* Honolulu: University of Hawai'i Press, 2002.

——. "On Pure Land Buddhism and Ch'an/Pure Land Syncretism in Medieval China." *T'oung Pao* 33, no. 4–5 (2002): 282–331.

——. "Thinking Through Shingon Ritual." *Journal of the International Association of Buddhist Studies* 26, no. 1 (2003): 51–96.

——. "Visualization and Mandala in Shingon Buddhism." In Sharf and Sharf, *Living Images,* pp. 151–197.

Sharf, Robert H., and Elizabeth Horton Sharf, eds. *Living Images: Japanese Buddhist Icons in Context.* Palo Alto, CA: Stanford University Press, 2001.

Shimizutani Kyōjun 清水谷恭順. *Tendai mikkyō no seiritsu ni kansuru kenkyū* 天台密教の成立に關する研究. Tokyo: Bun'ichi shuppansha, 1972.

Shinohara, Koichi. *Spells, Images and Maṇḍalas: Tracing the Evolution of Esoteric Buddhist Rituals.* New York: Columbia University Press, 2014.

Shirai Yūko 白井優子. *Inseiki Kōyasan to Kūkai nyūjō densetsu* 院政期高野山と空海入定伝説. Tokyo: Dōseisha, 2002.

——. *Kūkai densetsu no keisei to Kōyasan: Nyūjō densetsu no keisei to Kōyasan nōkotsu no hassei* 空海伝説の形成と高野山 ： 入定伝説の形成と高野山納骨の発生. Tokyo: Dōseisha, 1986.

Shishiō Enshin 獅子王圓信. "Taitō ryōmitsu no kyōhanshijō ni okeru ronsō" 台東両密の教判史上における論争. *Mikkyō kenkyū* 密教研究 39 (1930): 1–43.

Shizuka Haruki 静春樹. "Kongōjō to Indo Bukkyōshi" 金剛乗とインド仏教史. *Mikkyō kenkyū* 密教文化 216 (2006): 5–35.

Shizuka Jien 静慈圓, ed. *Kōbō daishi Kūkai to tōdai Mikkyō: Kōbō daishi nittō sennihyakunen kinen ronbunshū* 弘法大師空海と唐代密教、弘法大師入唐千二百年記念論文集. Tokyo: Hōzōkan, 2005.

Silk, Jonathan A. "The Virtues of Amitābha: A Tibetan Poem from Dunhuang." *Ryūkoku Daigaku Bukkyō Bunka kenkyūjo kiyō* 龍谷大學佛教文化研究所紀要 32 (1993): 1–109.

——. "What, If Anything, Is Mahāyāna Buddhism? Problems of Definitions and Classifications." *Numen* 49, no. 4 (2002): 355–405.

Sinnet, A. P. *Esoteric Buddhism.* Boston: Houghton Mifflin, 1884.

Skilling, Peter. "Mahāyāna and Bodhisattva: An Essay Towards Historical Understanding." In *Phothisatawa barami kap sangkom thais nai sahatsawat mai,* edited by P. Limpanusorn, pp. 139–156. Bangkok: Thammasat University Press, 2004.

———. "Theravada in History." *Pacific World Journal* 3, no. 11 (2009): 61–93.

Skilling, Peter, Jason A. Carbine, Claudio Cicuzza, and Santi Pakdeekham, eds. *How Theravada Is Theravada? Exploring Buddhist Identities.* Chiang Mai, Thailand: Silkworm Books, 2012.

Skorupski, Tadeusz. "Funeral Rites for Rebirth in the Sukhāvatī Abode." *Buddhist Forum* 6 (2001): 137–172.

———. "A Tibetan Prayer for Rebirth in the Sukhāvatī." *Pure Land* 12 (1995): 205–253.

Smith, Jonathan Z. *Relating Religion: Essays in the Study of Religion.* Chicago: University of Chicago Press, 2004.

———. "The Unknown God: Myth in History." In *Imagining Religion: From Babylon to Jonestown,* pp. 66–89. Chicago: University of Chicago Press, 1988.

Snellgrove, David L. *The Hevajra Tantra: A Critical Study.* 2 vols. New York: Oxford University Press, 1959.

———. *Indo-Tibetan Buddhism: Indian Buddhists and Their Tibetan Successors.* London: Serindia, 1987.

Snodgrass, Adrian. *The Matrix and Diamond World Mandalas in Shingon Buddhism.* Śata-Pitaka Series 354–355. New Delhi: International Academy of Indian Culture and Aditya Prakashan, 1988.

Snodgrass, Judith. *Presenting Japanese Buddhism to the West: Orientalism, Occidentalism, and the Columbian Exposition.* Chapel Hill: University of North Carolina Press, 2003.

Sofū Sen'yōkai 祖風宣揚會, ed. *Kōbō Daishi zenshū* 弘法大師全集. 8 vols. Tokyo: Yoshikawa kōbunkan, 1910.

Sørensen, Henrik H. "Esoteric Buddhism (Milgyo) in Korea." In *The Esoteric Buddhist Tradition,* edited by Henrik H. Sørensen, pp. 73–96. Copenhagen: Seminar for Buddhist Studies, 1994.

———. "Esoteric Buddhism under the Koryŏ in the Light of the Greater East Asian Tradition." *International Journal of Buddhist Thought and Culture* 7 (2006): 55–94.

———. "On Esoteric Buddhism in China: A Working Definition." In Orzech, Sørensen, and Payne, *Esoteric Buddhism and the Tantras in East Asia,* pp. 155–175.

———, ed. *Religions in Traditional Korea.* Copenhagen: Seminar for Buddhist Studies, 1995.

Staal, Fritz J., ed. *Agni: The Vedic Ritual of the Fire Altar.* 2 vols. Berkeley, CA: Asian Humanities Press, 1983.

——. "The Meaninglessness of Ritual." *Numen* 26, no. 1 (1979): 1–22.

——. *Rules without Meaning: Ritual, Mantras, and the Human Sciences.* New York: Peter Lang, 1989.

Stevenson, Daniel B. "Feeding Hungry Ghosts." In *Buddhist Scriptures,* edited by Donald S. Lopez Jr., pp. 416–422. New York: Penguin Books, 2004.

——. "The Four Kinds of Samādhi in Early T'ien-t'ai Buddhism." In Gregory, *Traditions of Meditation in Chinese Buddhism,* pp. 45–98.

——. "Protocols of Power: Tz'u-yün Tsun-shih (964–1032) and Tien-t'ai Lay Buddhist Ritual in the Sung." In *Buddhism in the Sung,* edited by Peter N. Gregory and Daniel A. Getz Jr., pp. 340–408. Honolulu: University of Hawai'i Press, 1999.

Stone, Jacqueline I. "By the Power of One's Last Nenbutsu: Deathbed Practices in Early Medieval Japan." In Payne and Tanaka, *Approaching the Land of Bliss,* pp. 77–119.

——. "The Contemplation of Suchness." In Tanabe, *Religions of Japan in Practice,* pp. 199–209.

——. "Death." In *Critical Terms for the Study of Buddhism,* edited by Donald S. Lopez Jr., pp. 56–76. Chicago: University of Chicago Press, 2005.

——. "Deathbed Practices in Medieval Japan: Developments after *Ōjō yōshū.*" *Indogaku Bukkyōgaku kenkyū* 印度学仏教学研究 50, no. 1 (2001): 528–524 (L).

——. "The Dying Breath: Deathbed Rites and Death Pollution in Early Medieval Japan." In *Heroes and Saints: The Moment of Death in Cross-Cultural Perspectives,* edited by Phyllis Granoff and Koichi Shinohara, pp. 173–264. Cambridge: Cambridge University Press, 2007.

——. "Just Open Your Mouth and Say 'A': A-Syllable Practice for the Time of Death in Early Medieval Japan." *Pacific World* 8 (2006): 167–189.

——. "Medieval Tendai *Hongaku* Thought and the New Kamakura Buddhism." *Japanese Journal of Religious Studies* 22, no. 1–2 (1995): 17–48.

——. *Original Enlightenment and the Transformation of Medieval Japan.* Honolulu: University of Hawai'i Press, 1999.

——. *Right Thoughts at the Last Moment: Buddhism and Deathbed Practices in Early Medieval Japan.* Honolulu: University of Hawai'i Press, 2016.

——. "The Secret Art of Dying: Esoteric Deathbed Practices in Heian Japan." In Cuevas and Stone, *Buddhist Dead,* pp. 134–174.

——. "With the Help of 'Good Friends.'" In *Death and Afterlife in Japanese Buddhism,* edited by Jaqueline I. Stone and Mariko Namba Walter, pp. 61–101. Honolulu: University of Hawai'i Press, 2008.

Stoneman, Jack. "Why Did Saigyō Become a Monk? An Archaeology of the Reception of Saigyō's 'Shukke.'" *Japanese Language and literature* 44 (2010): 69–118.

Strand, Kendra. "Aesthetics of Space: Representations of Travel in Medieval Japan." PhD diss., University of Michigan, 2015.

Strickmann, Michel. *Chinese Magical Medicine.* Edited by Bernard Faure. Asian Religions and Cultures. Palo Alto, CA: Stanford University Press, 2002.

——. "The *Consecration Sūtra:* A Buddhist Book of Spells." In *Chinese Buddhist Apocrypha,* edited by Robert E. Buswell Jr., pp. 75–118. Honolulu: University of Hawai'i Press, 1990.

——. "Homa in East Asia." In Staal, *Agni: The Vedic Ritual of the Fire Altar,* 2:418–455.

——. "India in the Chinese Looking-Glass." In *The Silk Route and the Diamond Path: Esoteric Buddhist Art on the Trans-Himalayan Trade Routes,* edited by D. Klimberg-Salter, pp. 52–63. Los Angeles: University of California, Los Angeles, Art Council, 1982.

——. *Mantras et Mandarins: Le bouddhisme tantrique en Chine.* Bibliothéque des sciences humaines. Paris: Éditions Gallimard, 1996.

——. "A Seal of the Law: A Ritual Implement and the Origins of Printing." *Asia Major,* 3rd ser., 6 (1993): 1–83.

Strong, John S. "'Gandhakuṭī': The Perfumed Chamber of the Buddha." *History of Religions* 16, no. 4 (1977): 390–406.

Sueki Fumihiko 末木文美士. "Amida santai-setsu o megutte" 阿弥陀三諦説をめぐって. *Indogaku Bukkyōgaku kenkyū* 印度学仏教学研究 28, no. 1 (1979): 216–222.

——. "Annen: The Philosopher Who Japanized Buddhism." *Acta Asiatica* 66 (1994): 69–86.

——. *Heian shoki bukkyō shisō no kenkyū: Annen no shisō keisei chūshin ni tsuite* 平安初期仏教思想の研究. Tokyo: Shunjūsha, 1995.

——. *Kamakura Bukkyō keiseiron: Shisōshi no tachiba kara* 鎌倉仏教形成論: 思想史の立場から. Tokyo: Hōzōkan, 1998.

——. *Kamakura Bukkyō tenkairon* 鎌倉仏教展開論. Tōkyō: Transview, 2008.

——. *Nihon Bukkyō shi: Shisōshi to shite no apurōchi* 日本仏教史：思想史としてのアプローチ. Tokyo: Shinchōsha, 1992.

——. *Nihon Bukkyō shisōshi ronkō* 日本仏教思想史論考. Tokyo: Daizōs shuppan, 1993.

——. *Nihon shūkyō shi* 日本宗教史. Tokyo: Iwanami shoten, 2006.

——. "A Reexamination of the *Kenmitsu Taisei* Theory." *Japanese Journal of Religious Studies* 23, no. 3–4 (1996): 449–466.

Suzuki Gakujutsu Zaidan 鈴木学術財団, ed. *Nihon daizōkyō* 日本大藏經. Rev. ed. 100 vols. Tokyo: Suzuki Gakujutsu Zaidan, 1973–1978.

Swanson, Paul. *Clear Serenity, Quiet Insight: T'ien-t'ai Chih-i's* Mo-ho chih-kuan. Honolulu: University of Hawai'i Press, 2018.

———. "Dandala, Dhāraṇī, and Denarii: A T'ien-t'ai Perspective on *The Great Vaipulya Dhāraṇī Sūtra.*" *Buddhist Literature* 2 (2000): 197–233.

———. *Foundations of T'ien-t'ai Philosophy: The Flowering of the Two Truths Theory in Chinese Buddhism.* Berkeley, CA: Asian Humanities Press, 1989.

Swearer, Donald K. *Becoming the Buddha: The Ritual of Image Consecration in Thailand.* Princeton, NJ: Princeton University Press, 2004.

Tachikawa Musashi 立川武蔵, and Yoritomi, Motohiro 頼富本宏, eds. *Chibetto Mikkyō* チベット密教. 1999. Reprint, Tokyo: Shunjūsha, 2005.

———. *Chūgoku Mikkyō* 中国密教. 1999. Reprint, Tokyo: Shunjūsha, 2005.

———. *Indo Mikkyō* インド密教. 1999. Reprint, Tokyo: Shunjūsha, 2005.

———. *Nihon Mikkyō* 日本密教. 2000. Reprint, Tokyo: Shunjūsha, 2005.

Taira Masayuki 平雅行. "Kamakura chūki ni okeru Kamakura Shingon-ha no sōryo—Ryōyu, Kōhō, Jitsugen" 鎌倉中期における鎌倉真言派の僧侶—良瑜・光宝・実賢. *Machikaneyama ronsō* 待兼山論叢 43 (2009): 1–27.

———. "Kuroda Toshio and the *Kenmitsu Taisei* Theory." *Japanese Journal of Religious Studies* 23 (1996): 427–448.

———. *Nihon chūsei no shakai to Bukkyō* 日本中世の社会と仏教. Tokyo: Hanawa shobō 塙書房, 1992.

Takeuchi Kōzen 武内 孝善. "Dōhan cho, 'Himitsu nenbutsu shō,' honbun kōtei (ichi)" 「道範著『秘密念仏抄』本文校訂(一)」. *Kōyasan Daigaku ronsō* 高野山大学論叢 20 (1985): 13–71.

Takubo Shūyo 田久保周誉. *Shingon Daranizō no kaisetsu* 真言陀羅尼蔵の解説. Kotei zoho saihan. Tokyo: Kanoen, 1967.

Takuya, Hino. "Creating Heresy: (Mis)representation, Fabrication, and the Tachikawa-ryu." PhD diss., Columbia University, 2012.

Tanabe, George, J. "Kōyasan in the Countryside: The Rise of Shingon in the Kamakura Period." In Payne, *Re-visioning "Kamakura" Buddhism*, pp. 43–54.

———. *Myōe the Dreamkeeper: Fantasy and Knowledge in the Early Kamakura Period.* Cambridge, MA: Harvard University Press, 1992.

———, ed. *Religions of Japan in Practice.* Princeton, NJ: Princeton University Press, 1999.

Tanaka Hisao 田中久夫. "Dōhan no 'Shoshin tonkaku shō' ni tsuite" 道範の「初心頓覚鈔」について. *Nihonrekishi* 日本歴史 172 (1962): 87–89.

———. *Kamakura Bukkyō* 鎌倉仏教. Tokyo: Kyōiku sha, 1980. Reprint, Tokyo: Kōdansha gakujutsu bunko, 2009.

Tanaka Kenji 田中健二. "Komonjo kaitoku kōza, Kamakura jidai no ryūjin no nikki, 'Nankai rurōki' ni miru Sanuki no Sugata" 古文書解読講座 鎌倉時代の流人の日記「南海流浪記」に見る讃岐の姿. *Kagawa kenritsu monjokan kiyō* 香川県立文書館紀要 15 (2011): 1–13.

Tanaka, Kenneth K. *The Dawn of Chinese Pure Land Buddhist Doctrine: Chin-ying Hui-yuan's Commentary on the Visualization Sūtra.* Albany: State University of New York Press, 1990.

Teeuwen, Mark. "The Kami in Esoteric Buddhist Thought and Practice." In *Shinto in History,* edited by John Breen and Mark Teeuwen, pp. 95–116. Richmond, UK: Curzon Press, 2000.

———. "Knowing vs. Owning a Secret: Secrecy in Medieval Japan, as Seen through the *Sokui kanjō* Enthronement Unction." In Scheid and Teeuwen, *Culture of Secrecy in Japanese Religion,* pp. 172–203.

Teeuwen, Mark, and Fabio Rambelli, eds. *Buddhas and Kami in Japan: Honji Suijaku as a Combinatory Paradigm.* London: RoutledgeCurzon, 2003.

Tendai shūten hensanjo 天台宗典編纂所, ed. *Zoku tendaishū zensho* 続天台宗全書. 10 vols. Tokyo: Shunjūsha, 1987.

———. *Zoku tendai zenshō* 続天台宗全書. 15 vols. Tokyo: Shunjūsha, 1993.

ten Grotenhuis, Elizabeth. *Japanese Mandalas: Representations of Sacred Geography.* Honolulu: University of Hawai'i Press, 1999.

Tinsley, Elizabeth. "Indirect Transmission in Shingon Buddhism: Notes on the Henmyoin Oracle." *Eastern Buddhist* 45, no. 1–2 (2016): 77–111.

———. "Jūsan seiki Kōyasan no den Dōhan cho 'Henmyō-in daishi myōjin go takusen ki' no kōzō to seisaku katei ni tsuite 13" 世紀高野山の伝道範著『遍明院大師明神御託宣記』の構造と制作過程について. *Indogaku bukkyōgaku kenkyū* 印度学仏教学研究 53, no. 3 (2010): 1284–1287.

———. "Notes on the Authorship and Dating of the 13th Century Henmyōin Daishi Myōjin Go Takusen Ki (Attributed to Dōhan)." *Indogaku bukkyōgaku* 印度学仏教学 58 (2010): 168–171.

Toganoo Shōun 栂尾祥雲. *Himitsu bukkyō shi* 秘密佛教史. Kōyasan: Kōyasan Daigaku shuppanbu, 1933.

———. *Nihon Mikkyō gakudōshi* 日本密教学道史. Kōyasan: Kōyasan Daigaku shuppanbu, 1942.

Toki, Hōrin (a.k.a Doki Hōryū). "History of Buddhism and Its Sects in Japan." In *Neely's History of the Parliament of Religions,* edited by W. R. Houghton, pp. 222–226. Chicago: F. Tennyson Neely, 1894.

Tōkyō Daigaku Shiryō Hensanjo 東京大學史料編纂所, ed. *Daigoji monjo* 醍醐寺文書. 15 vols. Tokyo: Tōkyō Daigaku shiryō hensanjo, 1955.

Tomabechi Seiichi 苫米地誠一. "Guhari shoku Amidazō wo megutte" 紅頗梨色阿弥陀像をめぐって. *Chizan gakuhō* 智山学報 44 (1995): 53–79.

——. *Heianki shingonmikkyō no kenkyū: Heianki no shingonmikkyō to mikkyōjōdokyō* 平安期真言密教の研究: 平安期の真言教学と密教浄土教. Vol. 2. Tokyo: Nonburu sha, 2008.

——. "Nara jidai no mikkyō kyōten" 奈良時代の密教経典. In Hisao Takahashi et al., *Shoki mikkyō*, pp. 293–308.

Tsuchiya Megumi 土谷恵. "Chusei shoki no Ninnajji omuro" 中世初期の仁和寺御室. *Nihon rekikishi* 日本歴史 451 (1985): 46–63.

Tweed, Thomas. *The American Encounter with Buddhism, 1844–1912: Victorian Culture and the Limits of Dissent.* 1992. Reprint, Bloomington: Indiana University Press, 2000.

Ueda Shinjō 上田進城. "Hairyū no Ajari Dōhan" 配流の阿闍梨道範. *Misshū gakuhō* 密 宗学報 161 (1912): 617–642.

Ueshima Susumu 上島享. "Inseiki bukkyō no rekishiteki ichi—nihon bukkyō no keisei" 院政期仏教の歴史的位置-日本仏教の形成. *Bukkyō shigaku kenkyū* 仏教私学研究 43 (2001): 94–103.

Ujitani Yūken 宇治谷祐顯. "Hikekyō no Amidabutsu honjō setsuwa" 悲華経のアミダ佛本生説話考. *Indogaku bukkyōgaku kenkyū* 印度學佛教學研究 33, no. 1 (1968): 74–80.

Unno, Mark T. "As Appropriate: Myōe Kōben and the Problem of the Vinaya in Early Kamakura Buddhism." PhD diss., Stanford University, 1994.

——. "Recommending Faith in the Sand of the Mantra of Light." In Payne, *Revisioning "Kamakura" Buddhism*, pp. 167–218.

——. *Shingon Refractions: Myōe and the Mantra of Light.* Boston: Wisdom, 2004.

Urban, Hugh B. *Tantra: Sex, Secrecy, Politics, and Power in the Study of Religion.* Berkeley: University of California Press, 2003.

van den Broucke, Pol K. "Dōhan's Letter on the Visualization of Syllable A." *Shingi Shingon kyōgaku no kenkyū* 新義真言教学の研究 10 (2002): 65–87.

van der Veere, Hendrick. *Kakuban Shōnin: The Life and Thought of Kōgyō Daishi.* Tokyo: Nombre, 1998.

——. *A Study into the Thought of Kōgyō Daishi Kakuban with a Translation of His "Gorin kuji myō himitsushaku."* Leiden: Hotei, 2000.

van Gulik, Robert H. *Hayagrīva: The Mantrayānic Aspect of the Horse-Cult in China and Japan.* Leiden: Brill, 1935.

——. *Siddham: An Essay on the History of Sanskrit Studies in China and Japan.* New Delhi: Sharada Rani, 1980.

Wada Shūjō 和多秀乗. "Jūnen gokuraku iōshū ni tsuite" 十念極楽易往集について. *Indogaku Bukkyōgaku kenkyū* 印度学仏教学研究 63 (1983): 1–10.

——. *Kōyasan shinkō no keisei to tenkai* 高野山信仰の形成と展開. Kyoto: Hōzōkan, 1997.

Wada Ujō 和多昭夫. "Kōyasan ni okeru Kamakura Bukkyō" 高野山における鎌倉仏教. *Nihon Bukkyō gakkai nenpō* 日本仏教学会年報 34 (1969): 79–96.

Waddell, Laurence A. *The Buddhism of Tibet, or Lamaism: With Its Mystic Cults, Symbolism and Mythology, and in Its Relation to Indian Buddhism.* 1895. Reprint, London: W. H. Allen, 1972.

Walters, Johnathan S. "Mahāyāna Theravāda and the Origins of the Mahāvihāra." *Sri Lanka Journal of the Humanities* 23, no. 1–2 (1997): 100–119.

Warder, A. K. *Indian Buddhism.* 1970. Reprint, Delhi: Motilal Banarsidass, 2008.

Wayman, Alex. *Introduction to the Buddhist Tantric Systems.* 1978. Reprint, Delhi: Motilal Bandarsidass, 1998.

———. *Yoga of the Guhyasamājatantra, the Arcane Lore of Forty Verses, a Buddhist Tantra Commentary.* Delhi: Motilal Banarsidass, 1977.

Wedemeyer, Christian K. *Making Sense of Tantric Buddhism: History, Semiology, and Transgression in the Indian Traditions.* New York: Columbia University Press, 2012.

———. "Tropes, Typologies, and Turnarounds: A Brief Genealogy of the Historiography of Tantric Buddhism." *History of Religions* 40, no. 3 (2001): 223–259.

Weinstein, Stanley. "The Beginning of Esoteric Buddhism in Japan: The Neglected Tendai Tradition." *Journal of Asian Studies* 34 (1974): 177–191.

———. *Buddhism under the T'ang.* Cambridge: Cambridge University Press, 1987.

———. "The *Kanjin Kakumushō.*" PhD diss., Harvard University, 1965.

Wheelock, Wade T. "Buddhism: Schools of." In *Encyclopedia of Religion,* 2nd ed., edited by Mircea Eliade, pp. 482–487. New York: Macmillan, 1987.

———. "The Mantra in Vedic and Tantric Ritual." In *Mantra,* edited by Harvey P. Alper, pp. 96–122. Albany: State University of New York Press, 1989.

———. "The Problem of Ritual Language: From Information to Situation." *Journal of the American Academy of Religion* 50 (1982): 49–71.

Willemen, Charles. *The Chinese Hevajratantra: The Scriptural Text of the Ritual of the Great King of the Teaching, the Adamantine One, with Great Compassion and Knowledge of the Void.* Belgium: Uitgeverij Peeters, 1983.

———. "Tripitaka Shan-wu-wei's Name: A Chinese Translation from Prākrit." *T'oung Pao,* 2nd ser., 67 (1981): 362–365.

Williams, Duncan R. *The Other Side of Zen: A Social History of Sōtō Zen Buddhism in Tokugawa Japan.* Princeton, NJ: Princeton University Press, 2005.

Williams, Paul. *Mahāyāna Buddhism: The Doctrinal Foundations.* London: Routledge, 2008.

Winfield, Pamela. "Curing with Kaji: Healing and Empowerment in Japan." *Japanese Journal of Religious Studies* 32 (2005): 107–130.

——. *Icons and Iconoclasm in Japanese Buddhism: Kūkai and Dōgen on the Art of Enlightenment.* Oxford: Oxford University Press, 2013.

Wong, Dorothy C. "The Case of Amoghapāśa." *Journal of Inner Asian Art and Archaeology* 2 (2007): 151–158.

——. "Early Transmission of Esoteric Images from China to Japan in the Seventh and Eighth Centuries." *Huaxue* 9 (2008): 1696–1719.

——. "The Huayan/Kegon/Hwaŏm Paintings in East Asia." In Hamar, *Reflecting Mirrors,* pp. 349–396.

Wong, Dorothy, with Eric M. Field, eds. *Hōryūji Reconsidered.* Newcastle, UK: Cambridge Scholars', 2008.

Wright, Arthur F. "Fo-t'u-teng: A Biography." *Harvard Journal of Asiatic Studies* 11 (1948): 321–371.

Xing, Guang. *The Concept of the Buddha: Its Evolution from Early Buddhism to the Trikaya Theory.* London: RoutledgeCurzon, 2004.

Yamabe, Nobuyoshi. "The Sutra on the Ocean-Like Samādhi of the Visualization of the Buddha: The Interfusion of the Chinese and Indian Cultures in Central Asia as Reflected in a Fifth Century Apocryphal Sūtra." PhD diss., Yale University, 1999.

Yamada Shōzen 山田昭全. *Saigyō no waka to Bukkyō* 西行の和歌と仏教. Tokyo: Meiji shoin, 1987.

Yamaguchi Shikyo 山口史恭. "Dōhan cho Himitsu nenbutsu shō no hihan taishō ni tsuite" 道範著『秘密念仏鈔』の批判対象について. *Buzankyōgaku taikaikiyō* 豊山教学大会紀要 30 (2002): 81–122.

Yamakage Kazuo 山陰加春夫. "Chūsei Kōya kyōdan soshiki shōkō" 中世高野山教団組織小考. *Kōyasan Daigaku ronsō* 高野山大学論叢 19 (1984): 1–21.

Yamamoto Nobuyoshi 山本信吉. "Kōyasan Shōchi'in shozō Ajari Dōhan jihitsubon (nishu)" 高野山正智院所蔵阿闍梨道範自筆本(二種). Vol. 2 of *Kodai chūsei shiryō kenkyū* 古代中世史料学研究, edited by Minagawa Kanichi 皆川完一, pp. 342–375. Tokyo: Yoshikawa kōbunkan, 1998.

——, ed. *Shōchiin monjo* 正智院文書. Tokyo: Yoshikawa kōbunkan, 2004.

Yamanaka Takahiro 山中嵩裕. "Kōyasan niokeru nenbutsu shinkō to sono tenkai—nenbutsu sanmai kara risshu sanmai e" 高野山における念仏信仰とその展開ー念仏三昧から理趣三昧へ. *Mikkyō gakkai hō*密教学会報, 2013, 13–28.

Yan Yaozhong 严耀中. *Hanzhuan Mijiao* 汉传密教. Shanghai: Xuelin chubanshe, 2006.

Yoritomi Motohiro 頼富本宏. *Chūgoku mikkyō no kenkyū* 中国密教の研究. Tokyo: Daitō shuppansha, 1979.

——. "Chūgoku mikkyō no nagare" 中国密教の流れ. In Tachikawa Musashi and Yoritomi Motohiro, *Chūgoku mikkyō,* pp. 15–39.

——. "Chūgoku mikkyō no shisōteki tokushitsu" 中国密教の思想的特質. In Tachikawa Musashi and Yoritomi Motohiro, *Chūgoku mikkyō,* pp. 113–140.

——. "Nihon mikkyō no seiritsu to tenkai" 日本密教の成立と展開. In Tachikawa Musashi and Motohiro Yoritomi, *Nihon mikkyō,* pp. 23–73.

Yoshida, Kazuhiko. "Religion in the Classical Period." In *Nanzan Guide to Japanese Religions,* edited by Paul L. Swanson and Clark Chilson, pp. 144–162. Honolulu: University of Hawai'i Press, 2006.

Yu, Jimmy. "Revisiting the Notion of *Zong:* Contextualizing the Dharma Drum Lineage of Modern Chan Buddhism." *Chung-Hwa Buddhist Journal* 26 (2013): 113–151.

Zhiru. *The Making of a Savior Bodhisattva: Dizang in Medieval China.* Honolulu: University of Hawai'i Press, 2007.

Zürcher, Erik. *The Buddhist Conquest of China: The Spread and Adaptation of Buddhism in Early Medieval China.* 1959. Reprint, Leiden: Brill, 2007.

Index

About the Author

Aaron P. Proffitt received his PhD in Buddhist studies from the University of Michigan and is an associate professor of Japanese studies at the University at Albany-SUNY. His research focuses on the diversity of Pure Land Buddhism in premodern Japan and East Asia.

Made in the USA
Coppell, TX
30 July 2025

52524941R00273